The

MARK JOHNSON

The Aesthetics of Meaning and Thought

THE BODILY ROOTS OF PHILOSOPHY,
SCIENCE, MORALITY, AND ART

The University of Chicago Press   Chicago & London

The University of Chicago Press, Chicago 60637
The University of Chicago Press, Ltd., London
© 2018 by The University of Chicago
All rights reserved. No part of this book may be used or reproduced in any manner whatsoever without written permission, except in the case of brief quotations in critical articles and reviews. For more information, contact the University of Chicago Press, 1427 E. 60th St., Chicago, IL 60637.
Published 2018
Printed in the United States of America

27 26 25 24 23 22 21 20 19 18   1 2 3 4 5

ISBN-13: 978-0-226-53880-8 (cloth)
ISBN-13: 978-0-226-53894-5 (paper)
ISBN-13: 978-0-226-53913-3 (e-book)
DOI: https://doi.org/10.7208/chicago/9780226539133.001.0001

Library of Congress Cataloging-in-Publication Data

Names: Johnson, Mark, 1949– author.
Title: The aesthetics of meaning and thought : the bodily roots of philosophy, science, morality, and art / Mark Johnson.
Description: Chicago ; London : The University of Chicago Press, 2018. | Includes bibliographical references and index.
Identifiers: LCCN 2017024330 | ISBN 9780226538808 (cloth : alk. paper) | ISBN 9780226538945 (pbk. : alk. paper) | ISBN 9780226539133 (e-book)
Subjects: LCSH: Aesthetics. | Meaning (Philosophy) | Experience. | Pragmatism. | Philosophy and cognitive science. | Ethics.
Classification: LCC BH39 .J63 2018 | DDC 111/.85—dc23
LC record available at https://lccn.loc.gov/20170243304

♾ This paper meets the requirements of ANSI/NISO Z39.48-1992 (Permanence of Paper).

For Ted Cohen (in Memoriam),
who helped me see the arts as fundamental expressions of our
need for meaning; and for Tom Alexander, who taught me to
worship at the altar of pragmatist aesthetics of experience

CONTENTS

Introduction: The Aesthetics of Embodied Life *1*

PART I: *Philosophy and Science* 27

1. Pragmatism, Cognitive Science, and the Embodied Mind *31*
2. Philosophy's Debt to Metaphor *58*
3. Experiencing Language: What's Missing in Linguistic Pragmatism? *80*
4. Keeping the Pragmatism in Neuropragmatism *96*
5. Metaphor-Based Values in Scientific Models *115*

PART II: *Morality and Law* 135

6. Cognitive Science and Morality *139*
7. Moral Imagination *159*
8. Mind, Metaphor, Law *176*

PART III: *Art and the Aesthetics of Life* 199

9. Identity, Bodily Meaning, and Art *203*
10. Dewey's Big Idea for Aesthetics *224*
11. The Embodied Meaning of Architecture *242*
12. What Becomes of Philosophy, Morality, and Art? *259*

Acknowledgments 263
Notes 265
References 269
Index 281

INTRODUCTION

The Aesthetics of Embodied Life

The Need for an Aesthetics of Human Meaning and Understanding

We human beings are animals—highly complex, inescapably embodied, intrinsically social, and sometimes even intelligent, animals—who live, move, and have our being via our ongoing relations with our environments. As such, we have a deep visceral, emotional, and qualitative relation to our world. As a result of our embodied nature, meaning comes to us via patterns, images, concepts, qualities, emotions, and feelings that constitute the basis of our experience, thought, and language. This visceral engagement with meaning, I will argue, is the proper purview of aesthetics. Consequently, aesthetic dimensions shape the very core of our human being.

Unfortunately, much traditional aesthetic theory has overlooked many of these deeply embodied aesthetic processes. It is typically assumed that experience can be divided up into distinct kinds (moral, political, economic, religious, aesthetic, etc.), with each kind separate from the others and having its own unique character. Having fragmented experience into these types, aesthetic theory then focuses narrowly on the conditions of possibility for, and the cognitive status of, these so-called "aesthetic experiences" and the "aesthetic judgments" allegedly appropriate to "aesthetic objects." The fields that came to be known as aesthetics and the philosophy of art in the twentieth century consequently end up limited mostly to definitions of art, theories of beauty, attempts to explain "aesthetic" judgment, and accounts of how aesthetic experience differs from other forms of experience. Once the "aesthetic" gets compartmentalized and reduced to a unique feeling-based type of experience, its pervasive operations in all the goings-on of our daily lives come to be almost completely overlooked.

Following John Dewey ([1934] 1987), I contend that we need to transcend this overly narrow, fragmenting, and reductionist view in order to recognize that aesthetics is not merely a matter of constructing theories of something called aesthetic experience, but instead extends broadly to encompass all the processes by which we enact meaning through perception, bodily movement, feeling, and imagination. In other words, *all meaningful experience is aesthetic experience.*

In this book, I therefore construct an argument for expanding the scope of aesthetics to recognize the central role of body-based meaning in how we understand, reason, and communicate. The arts are thus regarded as instances of particularly deep and rich enactments of meaning, and so they give us profound insight into our general processes of meaning-making that underlie our conceptual systems and our cultural institutions and practices. Humans are *homo aestheticus*—creatures of the flesh, who live, think, and act by virtue of the aesthetic dimensions of experience and understanding.

From this embodied cognition perspective, it becomes possible to see the aesthetic aspects of experience as giving rise to mind, meaning, and thought. The view of meaning that emerges highlights the body-based, affective, and imaginative dimensions of our interactions with our environments as they shape the ways we make sense of, and reason about, our world. Once we develop what might be called an "aesthetics of meaning and understanding," we then have the resources necessary to explore how meaning actually works in a broad range of arts and expressive and communicative practices (e.g., painting, sculpture, architecture, music, dance, theatrical performance, spontaneous gesture, and rituals). What emerges is a view of humans as aesthetic, meaning-making creatures who draw on their deepest sensory, motor, and affective processes to make sense of, and orient themselves in, their world (Alexander 2013). Such an exploration of embodied cognition should give renewed and deepened meaning to the profound metaphor of the "art of living."

It follows from an aesthetics of embodied cognition approach that our highest creative achievements of thought are matters of aesthetic understanding. If this is so, then all our conceptual systems and forms of symbolic interaction are rooted in body-based meaning structures, such as images, bodily schemas, emotions, feelings, and metaphors (Lakoff and Johnson 1999; M. Johnson 2007, 2017). Consequently, the essays collected in this volume illustrate and explain what it means to say that meaning and thought are embodied aesthetic processes, and they then explore some of the ways these deep dimensions of meaning operate in philosophy, science, morality, law, and the various arts. In short, I argue for the pivotal role of aesthetic components in human meaning-making and understanding.

However, in order to make this case, we must first retrieve aesthetics from the philosophical dustbin into which it was discarded, especially as a result of Enlightenment views about the subjective character of aesthetic experience. My brief and selective analysis of that devaluing and narrowing of aesthetic dimensions of experience then opens the way for a recovery of aesthetics, but now understood from the perspective of an embodied cognition view of mind, thought, and language. However, since an embodied view challenges some deeply entrenched notions of mind and reason, we first need to understand the cluster of problematic assumptions that have led to the marginalization of the body and aesthetics in Western intellectual traditions.

The Folk Theory of Disembodied Mind and Reason

The mistaken idea that aesthetic considerations are mostly irrelevant to how we conceptualize and reason is based on a deeply rooted but profoundly mistaken conception of disembodied mind and reason. This model constitutes what is known as a folk theory: a cluster of related assumptions that underlie cultural ideas, values, institutions, and practices. For the most part, these assumptions are taken to be matters of common sense, and thus acquire an aura of self-evident truth. Simply stated, the folk theory I will be criticizing asserts that (1) humans are unique by virtue of their rational capacities; (2) reason is radically separate from emotion and feeling; (3) art and aesthetic experience are feeling based, and hence subjective; and therefore, (4) aesthetics has nothing significant to do with reason. Here is a more detailed and nuanced statement of the view:

THE FOLK THEORY OF DISEMBODIED MIND AND THOUGHT
1. *Humans are the quintessentially rational animals.* Humans are unique among the animals in possessing a rational capacity (including language) that transcends, and is independent of, any of our bodily processes.
2. *There are discrete types of experience.* It is assumed that all human experience comes to us separated into discrete functional types. For example, there are alleged to be perceptual, imaginative, moral, political, eco-

nomic, religious, aesthetic, and technological kinds of experiences, each with its own unique character and correlative forms of judgment.
3. *Mind consists of different faculties.* The "mind" is an integrated collection of independent faculties or powers, each geared toward performing different functions. A typical list of faculties would include sensation, feeling, understanding, reason, imagination, and will, at the very least. Since the Enlightenment, it has been popular to assume that each distinct type of experience could be explained as the product of a specific unique relation of one or more of the faculties. For example, aesthetic judgments were thought to be feeling based, whereas theoretical judgments in the sciences are the product of our capacity to receive sense impressions (sensation), to form concepts (understanding), and to draw inferences based on those concepts (reason).
4. *Thought is conceptual and propositional.* From the perspective of Enlightenment faculty psychology, thought involves the combining of concepts (as products of understanding) into propositional judgments (with a subject-predicate structure). Either the constituent concepts arise from perceptual experience, or else they are some form of innate formal representation. Thinking, within the context of knowledge production, then reduces to intellectual manipulations of concepts and propositions. Thought (or cognition) is thus viewed as operating via language-like propositional structures, and reason is our capacity to trace out relations among various propositions (according to logical principles). The only role for the body is to supply the perceptual content of some of our concepts and to serve as the medium of action in the world.
5. *Thinking and feeling are fundamentally different.* Thinking is a cognitive, conceptual, propositional process, whose structure is given by the innate characteristics of human understanding and reason. Feeling is a noncognitive, bodily sensation process. Consequently, thinking is not a feeling process, although it might occasionally give rise to feelings.
6. *Feelings are subjective and noncognitive.* Feeling states are bodily perturbations that have no "cognitive" or conceptual dimension (beyond the fact that we have concepts to name some of our feelings). As such, they play no role in our acquisition of conceptual knowledge. Feelings are always relativized to the embodied creature who is experiencing that feeling, as a subjective state.
7. *Concepts are literal and classically defined.* The concepts with which we reason and gain knowledge of our world have to be "literal"; that is, defined by necessary and sufficient conditions that are capable of map-

ping onto mind-independent objects, events, properties, and relations. Otherwise, we could never achieve objective knowledge of our world.
8. *Reason is disembodied.* The faculty of reason is our power to discern abstract relations between concepts and the propositions they make up. Reason is a universal human capacity for formal and logical operations, and in that sense it is considered transcendent of our bodily makeup.
9. *Aesthetics is subjective and relative.* Aesthetics, regarded as pertaining to felt sensations and to feeling-based appraisals of artistic and natural beauty, cannot be a matter of cognitive judgment or knowledge. Aesthetic judgment is thus a matter of "taste," not the result of cognitive or conceptual structures. Consequently, aesthetic judgments yield no knowledge.

This cluster of related views treats thought as relatively disembodied, in the sense that the structures of understanding and reasoning are formal operations supposedly untethered by body-based feelings and emotions. This "folk theory of disembodied mind and thought" received its most elaborate and rigorous articulation in Enlightenment philosophy, but it has remained dominant down to the present day, especially in ever-popular computational models of mind, which treat mental operations as algorithmic formal manipulations of meaningless symbols that allegedly constitute a language of thought (see Lakoff and Johnson 1999 for an account and critique of this view).

The Marginalization of Aesthetics

The folk theory of disembodied mind and thought tends to go hand in hand with a correlative folk theory according to which aesthetic dimensions of experience are taken to be wholly subjective and therefore completely separate from our knowledge producing faculty. This relegation of aesthetics to the philosophical hinterlands has been especially prominent since the emergence in the Enlightenment of a conception of philosophy-as-theory-of-knowledge. If, following Immanuel Kant ([1781] 1968, [1785] 1993, [1790] 1987), you conceive the job of philosophy to be explaining how various types of judgments are possible—especially those that are cognitive and generate knowledge—you will be tempted to downplay anything that is not believed to contribute to a theory of knowledge. You will tend to assume that our primary acts, as rational creatures, are the making and justifying of knowledge claims.

Kant is one of the most famous proponents of such a view, which privileges cognitive over aesthetic forms of judgment. Kant defined the task of what he called his "critical philosophy" to be providing an explanation of the nature, conditions of possibility, and limits of various types of judgments. Kant and many other Enlightenment philosophers were obsessed with questions about how knowledge is possible and capable of verification in experience. Richard Rorty (1979) correctly accused Kant of having "epistemologized philosophy" through his exclusive focus on the cognitive conditions for the possibility of certain types of knowledge-producing judgments. Whatever was not "cognitive" was regarded as more or less irrelevant to the mind's primary job of thinking, reasoning, and acquiring knowledge. The result was the relegation of aesthetic experience and judgment to noncognitive, subjective status, as set forth in

THE FOLK THEORY OF AESTHETICS AS SUBJECTIVE

1. *Feelings are bodily; concepts are mental.* Emotions and feelings are states of perturbation of our body. Thought, as conceptual, is based on understanding and reason, which are shared universal capacities of mind.
2. *Feelings are subjective.* Since feelings and emotions are bodily states, they are relative to the person who experiences them. Only I can experience my feelings and you yours. Feelings are thus subjective states; they cannot be the basis for shared (objective) understanding and knowledge.
3. *Cognitive judgments are conceptual; aesthetic judgments are based on feelings.* Cognitive judgments are operations on concepts (and propositions), which are mental structures. Aesthetic judgments are based on feelings (as body states). The former give rise to knowledge and thought, while the latter give rise to feeling responses of pleasure or displeasure.
4. *Aesthetic dimensions are merely subjective.* Aesthetic experience and judgment, as feeling based, are subjective and therefore fundamentally different in kind from acts of knowing and reasoning. Consequently, aesthetic aspects of experience are irrelevant when it comes to matters of knowledge production. Even if, as Kant ([1790] 1987) insisted, aesthetic reflective judgments of taste lay claim to universal validity, they do not constitute acts of knowing, because they are not based on determinate concepts.

If you assume the relatively disembodied view of mind sketched earlier—especially as it has developed since its heyday in the Enlightenment—you will deny any role for feelings in understanding and reasoning. If you mistakenly assume that aesthetics focuses exclusively on noncognitive bodily feeling states, and if you think that all knowledge is conceptual and propositional, then you will not find any place for feelings and emotions in our cognitive judgments. You will regard aesthetics as being about what happens when understanding and reasoning go on holiday and leave the mind to the fanciful hijinks of imagination and feeling, unfettered by rational constraints.

I want to probe a bit more deeply into the justification for banishing aesthetics to the nether reaches of human experience and cognition, as unfit for the lofty tasks of understanding and knowing. If, as I will be arguing, aesthetics is fundamentally about how we are able to have meaningful experience, then one might wonder why this has not seemed evident to philosophers throughout most of Western history. Why is it that people tend to think of aesthetics as exclusively concerned with art and so-called aesthetic experience, both of which they consider to be subjective matters of taste?

I am suggesting that the answer to this question can be found in the view of mind, meaning, and thought that solidified in Europe during the eighteenth century, when the philosophical field of aesthetics first emerged. To recapitulate: (1) Human mind was thought to consist of a set of independent faculties or powers (e.g., sensation, feeling, emotion, imagination, understanding, reason, will) that, in various combinations, give rise to the specific kinds of judgments we make. (2) Aesthetic judgments are based primarily on the faculties of perception, feeling, and imagination, whereas knowledge judgments are based on conceptual capacities and reason. (3) Feelings are private, noncognitive bodily states. (4) As noncognitive, feelings were not seen as contributing either to meaning, to understanding, or to reasoning. (5) Because philosophy had come to be narrowly defined as primarily an epistemological project concerned with the nature, possibility, and limits of human knowledge, there was no serious place within philosophy for any aesthetics, other than as an analysis of types of human feeling states and judgments.

The view I have just summarized found eloquent and exquisitely detailed articulation in eighteenth-century philosophy of art. Our modern use of the term *aesthetics* is typically traced to Alexander Baumgarten's *Aesthetica* (1750–58), where he defines aesthetics as an inquiry into the nature of taste—our sense of beauty—which he regarded as a matter of bodily feeling, rather than an activity of the intellect or reason. Immanuel Kant ([1790] 1987, 203) appropriated a similar notion of aesthetics, in his *Critique of Judgment*, where he defined an aesthetic judgment as feeling based, and therefore subjective. Since no conception of aesthetics has been more influential in shaping our contemporary views, it is helpful to sketch the outline of Kant's approach in order to see how it led to a marginalization and subjectivizing of aesthetics. With the faculty psychology described above in hand, Kant defined the "problem" of aesthetic judgments (especially judgments of beauty and sublimity in nature and art) as how judgments based on feelings can, nevertheless, claim universal validity.

Kant developed his treatment of aesthetic judgment within a broader project of explaining how certain types of mental judgments are possible. In his *Critique of Pure Reason* (1781), Kant focuses chiefly on the conditions of possibility of theoretical judgments in the natural sciences (especially in the form of universal causal laws of nature). He argues that theoretical judgments of a causally deterministic nature can be objective and universally shareable (i.e., communicable), precisely because they are based on universal concepts (such as the notion of causation).

Having supposedly established the basis for the universality and objectivity of scientific judgments, Kant next turns to the status of moral judgments, which presuppose the notion of freedom underlying ethical choice. In his *Critique of Practical Reason* (1787) he tries to explain the universal validity and unconditional bindingness of moral principles, as also resting on concepts, but this time on concepts derived from pure practical (rather than theoretical) reason alone.

In the first part of his *Critique of Judgment* (1790), he asks how a third type of judgment—a judgment of taste concerning the beautiful in nature and art—is possible. The problem is that judgments of taste appear to be grounded on *feelings*, whereas Kant typically requires that the universal validity of a judgment be grounded on a shared *concept*. So, it would seem that such noncognitive, feeling-based aesthetic judgments of this sort could never lay claim to universal validity. And yet, he strenuously affirms, they *do* make just such a claim! He insists that when we say that something is beautiful, we "demand" the agreement of others with our judgment, even though we lack any universal concept to ground such an agreement. So, how is it possible for a judgment to be at once aesthetic (feeling based and nonconceptual) and universally valid?

When Kant began his Third Critique with the claim that "a judgment of taste is not a cognitive judgment and so is not a logical judgment but an aesthetic one, by which we mean a judgment whose determining basis *cannot be other* than *subjective*" ([1790] 1987, 203; italics in the original), the fateful die was cast. Aesthetics came to be narrowly defined as an inquiry into the nature, possibility, and limits of judgments of taste (i.e., judgments of beauty in nature and art) and also of judgments of sublimity, both of which were held to be based on subjective feelings, even though they somehow supposedly lay claim to universal validity. Because Kant took feelings—as subjective—to be relative to the individual bodies experiencing those feelings, he could not use feelings to ground the alleged universal validity of the judgment of taste. Kant infamously tried to resolve this deep tension by arguing that aesthetic judgments of taste were not in fact *grounded on, or caused by*, feelings, but instead were based on a harmonious interplay of imagination and understanding that constitutes an unforced orderliness in our experience of certain objects and events (Kant [1790] 1987, sec. 9). The feelings involved in aesthetic experience and judgment are thus taken to be secondary effects; that is, they are not the *ground* or *cause* of the judgment of taste, but merely our felt consciousness (as effect) of the harmony of the interplay of the cognitive faculties (i.e., imagination and understanding) that is the basis for the judgment.[1]

Another highly influential aspect of Kant's philosophy of art is his formalism. What is it in our perception of an object that grounds our feeling of its beauty? The answer, he claims, must be its *formal* properties, since the *matter or content* of the object is merely empirical and therefore incapable of supporting a truly universal judgment (M. Johnson 1979). The underlying assumption is that whereas the material content of a perceptual judgment cannot guarantee universal validity, we all can nevertheless experience the formal features of an object in the same way, since space and time are the pure forms of sensuous intuition shared by all humans. The point to emphasize here is that the pure judgment of taste focuses only on the formal characteristics of an object and ignores any direct relation to the empirical and practical affairs of daily life. As we will see below, we find here the basis for a disengagement of art from our lived mundane experiences in the world that will prove fateful, in a problematic way, for subsequent aesthetic theory.

There is no need here to dwell on the intricacies and mental gymnastics of Kant's ingenious account. Kant never relinquished his conviction that only shared concepts could ground the universal validity of a judgment, and that is why he ends up performing a philosophical sleight of hand by conjuring up what he calls an "indeterminate concept" to ground the judgment of taste. However, this attempt to intellectualize judgments of taste cannot save them from subjectivity.[2] Kant's rigid faculty psychology and his unbridgeable dichotomies between feeling and thought, concept and percept, emotion and reason, imagination and knowledge made it impossible for him to salvage any significant role for aesthetics in the cultivation of a meaningful and moral human life, even though he devoted significant parts of the *Critique of Judgment* to arguing precisely this claim.[3]

My point here is not to enter into debate about the proper interpretation of Kant's aesthetic theory. Rather, I simply want to observe that Kant's legacy in the philosophy of art and aesthetic judgment is what Hans-Georg Gadamer calls "the subjectivisation of aesthetics in the Kantian critique" (1975, 39); for, after Kant, the problem of aesthetic judgment comes to be framed as how a judgment that is "merely subjective"—as based on feelings—can lay claim to universal validity.

Another fateful effect of Kant's account of aesthetic judgments of taste is the view that in order to experience the merely formal features on which the universality of the aesthetic judgment is based, one must abstract from any practical interest in the objects being experienced. Kant's phrase is a "disinterested satisfaction" in the object, by which he means that we care only for its form (and the harmony that generates in our minds) and not for any desire for, or practical interest in, the object. Although Kant is not entirely to blame for this, one unfortunate legacy of his insistence on disinterestedness has been the mistaken idea that a full and pure appreciation of natural or artistic beauty requires us to suspend any practical life engagement we might normally have with the object, so that we can focus exclusively on the interplay of the formal features that make possible a universally valid judgment of taste.[4] Kant, of course, does not say that we cannot also have a practical interest in the object of our aesthetic appreciation, but only that we must never allow any relation of the object to our interests, life emotions, or vital ends to be the basis of a pure judgment of taste. And he insists that only a "pure," disinterested judgment can support the claim of universal validity.

Unfortunately, many subsequent philosophers of art have latched on to the doctrine of disinterested judgment and what they call the "aesthetic attitude" as the key to a proper experience of an artwork. The basic idea is that only if we disengage from our practical involvement in the affairs of daily living are we then able to experience the beauty of nature or of an art object in its purity, universality, and transcendence. This is a historically consequential move, insofar as it puts aesthetic experience supposedly above and beyond the practical concerns of everyday life. From here it is but a short step to Oscar Wilde's quip that the value of art lies precisely in its having nothing to do with ordinary, day-to-day life.[5]

Kant's idea of disinterested satisfaction was taken to an absurd extreme in the art theory of Clive Bell, who ridiculously pontificates: "For, to appreciate a work of art we need bring with us nothing from life, no knowledge of its ideas and affairs, no familiarity with its emotions. Art transports us from the world of man's activities to a world of aesthetic exaltation. For a moment we are shut off from human interests; we are lifted above the stream of life" (Bell [1914] 1958, 27). Here we have art completely severed from any connection to the practical affairs of living, existing eternally in a realm that utterly transcends our contingent historical situatedness in the world. The wealthy and privileged patron, transported to the transcendent realm of significant form, need take no notice of the messiness and uncertainty of daily life. I cannot help but observe the irony that Bell was penning this vision of transcendent perfection and release from the affairs of human existence—as if art were an otherworldly reality that could take us beyond the cares of our lives—on the very eve of Britain's catastrophic plunge into the hell of the Great War. It is hard not to think of Bell as whistling in the dark. The juxtaposition of Bell's supernatural realm of timeless beauty (or "significant form") with the ugly tragedy of modern warfare that was about to be unleashed on the world could not be more stark. Nor could such an otherworldly and transcendent conception of art be more disengaged from the meaning of our daily lives. I daresay that the value of art for World War I poets like Siegfried Sassoon and Wilfred Owen, who experienced the unimaginable slaughter and terrors of trench warfare, lay not in escaping to some otherworldly realm, but consisted in the beauty of the love, sacrifice, courage, and caring they saw realized in the midst of the horrors that engulfed them.

Neither can we excuse Edward Bullough, who, just two years earlier (1912), advised us of the necessity of disengaging from life, if we hope to achieve an objective regard for an aesthetic object. Bullough's "aesthetic outlook" requires "putting the phenomenon, so to speak, out of gear with our practical, actual self; by allowing it to stand outside the context of our personal needs and ends—in short, by looking at it 'objectively,' as it has often been called" (Ridley and Neill 1995, 298–99). Here again we have the belief in a pure, shiny, exalted aesthetic object that could supposedly only be accessed by putting aside and rising above our daily existence.

I confess that I cannot but wonder: *Who* is experiencing the aesthetic object and grasping its meaning, once we have put the phenomenon "out of gear with our practical, actual self"? I, for one, would like my "actual self" to grasp the significance and meaning of the phenomenon, not my nonactual self! *How could an artwork have any meaning if it is disconnected from our selfhood and our visceral embeddedness in the world?* George Dickie (1974) long ago made mincemeat of aesthetic-attitude theories of art, so maybe there is no point in beating this dead horse any further. But we have not yet freed ourselves from the oppressive yoke of a view that makes art irrelevant to daily life, by extracting it from the visceral meaning of our mundane affairs of living and then projecting it into some allegedly eternal realm of timeless aesthetic ecstasy. As Tolstoy ([1896] 1960) argued so vehemently, art and aesthetics have too often become parlor games for those wealthy enough to afford museums, concerts, and performances, who then tout the eternal excellence of their preferred artistic achievements while recognizing no concrete connections to daily existence and the lives of ordinary folks.

Although there are no doubt exceptions to this denigration of the aesthetic, it mostly held sway from Kant's day up through the glory days of early and midtwentieth-century analytic philosophy. In describing the stranglehold that aesthetic attitude thinking has exercised over art theory, I am not overlooking the nineteenth-century romantic valorization of art as the key to the recovery of our lost or alienated souls. The romantic poets, novelists, composers, and painters had a deep sense of art as connecting us back up, in a quasi-religious way, with a healing nature from which industrialized modern society had alienated us. For them, *art matters for our daily lives* in the most profound way. Indeed, this romantic conviction that art reveals the meaning of our existence anticipates the view I am developing here.

However, this romantic movement too often assumed the cluster of defining dichotomies (e.g., mind/body, cognition/emotion, thinking/feeling, knowledge/imagination) that was the source of the problem and simply elevated the second (or bottom) half of each dichotomy above the first (or top) half, without substantially overcoming this fundamental metaphysical dualism. In other words, there was a tendency to celebrate passion and feeling over against reason, without recognizing that reason is itself intimately connected with desire. Despite this tendency to overemphasize feeling and desire, the romantics rightly saw the arts as fundamental necessities of a life that was meaningful and well lived.

Unfortunately, these romantic tendencies did not survive the onslaught of modernism at the dawn of the twentieth century. Much of what was good in romanticism came to be replaced with modernist sympathies closer to the Enlightenment perspective so well articulated by Kant. One need only thumb through anthologies of twentieth-century aesthetics to see the return to Kantian-influenced perspectives, with topics like aesthetic experience, the aesthetic attitude, aesthetic judgment, the definition of art, and the cognitive status of various arts, with passing mention of the institutional social context of art thrown in for good measure.

As evidence for this derogation of aesthetics, one need only peruse the writings of the most illustrious analytic philosophers of the last century to see how consistently they have ignored or disparaged aesthetics. You will search in vain for a serious treatment of aesthetics in the works of Gottlob Frege, Rudolf Carnap, Bertrand Russell, Carl Hempel, J. L. Austin, Willard Van Orman Quine, Donald Davidson, John Searle, Ernest Nagel, Hilary Putnam, and a host of less prominent figures in the Anglo American philosophical tradition. Even Wittgenstein's scattered remarks on art and aesthetics have not brought aesthetics to center stage. Among well-known analytic philosophers, only Nelson Goodman took aesthetics seriously, and then only within a nominalist theory of signs and language. I daresay that one can read through Goodman's *Languages of Art* or his *Ways of Worldmaking* with nary a serious encounter with the body, embodied meaning, or meaningful feeling. In so-called "analytic" philosophical circles, it has never been considered a shortcoming for a philosopher to have nothing significant to say about either art or aesthetics. Moreover, those analytically trained philosophers who did make forays into aesthetics tended to approach the subject strictly within the confines set out by Hume, Kant, and Hegel, and occasionally Aristotle. It is not surprising, then, that when the subject known as aesthetics and the philosophy of art was consolidated as a distinct philosophical field in the 1960s in the United States and England, it was dominated mostly by analytically trained philosophers interested in questions about the nature of the *concept* art: whether art was even definable, whether or not judgments of taste could claim universality, and whether art had anything to do with morality. A quick glance through the section headings in any anthology of aesthetics reveals the relative absence, until quite recently, of any recognition of aesthetics as relevant to what it means to be human, how we make and experience meaning, and how we ought to live.

In the face of this cultural marginalization of aesthetics, John Dewey wrote *Art as Experience* (1934) in part to counteract what he perceived to be the disengagement of art from life, especially the removal of art into museums, where artworks supposedly become eternal objects of pure aesthetic appreciation. According to the view he was challenging, the art museum becomes a temple where we are urged to put aside our worldly cares and engage some transcendent beauty, significance, or truth. Dewey was rightly reacting to the tendency to overlook the pervasiveness of art in all aspects of everyday life—a tendency reinforced by the view that artworks transport us above the affairs of day-to-day existence.

Following Dewey, I am arguing for an aesthetics of our bodily, worldly existence. Such a view places art squarely within everyday life and treats the aesthetic as pertaining to all the experiential components of human meaning, not merely to art and so-called "aesthetic" objects. I shall, therefore, henceforth assume that an artwork, or any object or event, is valuable and meaningful only as it affects me as I am, in this world I inhabit. Once we begin to focus on how we are so affected, we then come to realize the central role of aesthetic dimensions in all aspects of our lives.

Aesthetic Dimensions of Embodied Living Creatures

To say that human beings are complex bodily and social animals is to say that the locus of all our experience, meaning, thought, valuing, communicating, and action is an ongoing series of organism-environment interactions. Dewey ([1925] 1981) preferred the hyphenated term "body-mind" to capture the intimate and intricate interaction of the corporeal, interpersonal, and cultural dimensions of our selfhood. Body and mind are not separate realities, but rather aspects or dimensions of a process of organism-environment interaction, in which organism and environment are interrelated, interdependent, and interdefined. Consequently, meaning arises in the processes of organism-environment interaction that mutually define ourselves and our world. The meaning of any object, person, or event is what it affords us and points to by way of some experience we have or might have—either past, present, or future (possible) experience. For example, the meaning of the cup I see before me is actually a complex of actualized and possible experiences, including the visual perspectives I can have about it, the ways I can grasp it and use it to drink, the social contexts in which it plays a role, all the past experiences I've had with this and other cups, and a host of future interactions I might have with it as projected possible meanings.

This account of meaning is known as a "simulation semantics" (Barsalou 1999; Feldman 2006; Bergen 2012), according to which having a meaningful concept or thought of an object or event involves running a cognitive simulation of a range of possible experiences afforded you by that object or the scene enacted in the event. For example, our concept of a cup is not some abstract, intellectualized Platonic form of cuphood, but rather involves the activation of functional neuronal clusters for the perceptual images we have of cups and for motor programs for interacting with a cup (reaching for it, touching it, grasping it, raising it to one's lips, drinking from it). It also includes all the feelings and emotional responses associated with cups and their role in our lives, plus any cultural significance cups might have within a particular societal context. The cup exists for me as a horizon of actual and possible "affordances" (to use J. J. Gibson's favored term) that arise from the ways my body-mind can engage that object or event.

Aesthetics as a field of inquiry is therefore an investigation into everything that makes these experiential affordances possible and gives them whatever meaning they have for us. Consequently, we can explore how meaning emerges for us by examining the images, action schemas, radially structured concepts, conceptual metaphors, metonymies, feelings, and emotions that are afforded us by our world. These meaningful affordances will depend equally, and interdependently, on both the nature of our bodies and on the structure of the environments (both physical and cultural) that we inhabit. I will call this inquiry into the visceral sources of meaning "the aesthetics of human meaning and understanding."

Qualitative Aspects of Experience

Let us begin this aesthetic inquiry where Dewey ([1930] 1988, [1934] 1987) began, with the qualitative character of experience that has traditionally been the concern of aesthetics. Dewey said it best: "The world in which we immediately live, that in which we strive, succeed, and are defeated is preeminently a qualitative world. What we act for, suffer, and enjoy are things in their qualitative determinations" (Dewey [1930] 1988, 243). The central role of qualities in our lives should seem obvious, but that has not kept philosophers from mostly ignoring the workings of those qualities in our day-to-day experience, other than to mark them by concepts such as *red*, *sweet*, and *juicy*. Qualities, however, are not concepts. They are modes of interaction by which an organism discriminates significant aspects of its self and its world. When I earlier spoke of objects as "affording" possibilities for meaningful engagement, I was thinking of that engagement primarily in qualitative terms. Human organisms inhabit their world most immediately through their perception of qualities, often at a level beneath conscious awareness. We are in and of the world via qualitative determinations, "before we know it," by which I mean, before we relate to it as knowers.

One of the things we value most in the arts is their heightened capacity to present the qualitative aspects of experience—qualitative dimensions that we find it extremely difficult to capture in words and concepts. Matthew Arnold's "Dover Beach," for example, does not just *describe* or *represent* the qualities of a situation (namely, a situation in which two lovers are gazing forlornly through the night darkness out over the straits of Dover toward the French coast). Rather, the poem *presents* and *enacts* those qualitative dimensions of their experience by means of images, patterns, and rhythms of the work. When Arnold writes:

Listen! You hear the grating roar
Of pebbles which the waves draw back, and fling,
At their return, up the high strand,
Begin, and cease, and then again begin,
With tremulous cadence slow, and bring
The eternal note of sadness in.

the power of the lines comes not merely from any conceptual description, but rather through auditory images that present the qualitative experience of the "grating roar" of the pebbles, and the tremulous cadence of the waves advancing and retreating on the dark beach. Meanwhile, the syntax of the lines directly enacts the back and forth motion of the pebbles in the waves. The felt rhythm of the waves comes from our parsing of the motion realized by each succeeding phrase of the lines: "draw back, and fling / At their return, up the high strand, / Begin, and cease, and then again begin." Each temporal unit of these lines between the commas and line breaks presents an event of the back-and-forth motion that you feel, see, and hear as the waves move in and out upon the beach. In other words, our understanding of the poem operates partly through our sensory and motor simulation of the events presented therein.

If you doubt that we live for qualities, then you are out of touch with yourself and your world, for qualities provide the most primordial meaning available to us prior to, and underlying, any conceptual abstraction or conscious reflection we might engage in. Qualities are meaningful in the most immediate way possible for creatures like us. The red flesh around a wound tells us in one case of infection, and in another of the process of healing. The blue sky peeking through the clouds signals the passing of the storm. The desiccated green of the leaves reminds us that it is late summer and the rains have not come. The warm sun on our face on a cool day signals our being at home in the moment. The tartness of the raspberry on our tongue is very heaven, but a different heaven than the feel of your lover's flesh against your skin.

One of Dewey's most important and yet most elusive ideas about qualities is his claim that every experiential situation we find ourselves in is demarcated by a pervasive unifying quality that gives it its distinct identity and meaning. Although *every* situation has its distinctive unifying quality, Dewey appropriately illustrates this notion with the exemplary case of artworks, because in art the possibilities for meaning are intensified, enhanced, and expanded. In a work of art, Dewey says, "its quality is not a property which it possesses in addition to its other properties. It is something which externally demarcates it from other paintings, and which internally pervades, colors, tones, and weights every detail and every relation of the work of art. The same thing is true of the 'quality' of a person or of historic events" (Dewey [1930] 1988, 245). The important thing about the meaning of a pervasive unifying quality of any life situation, person, or work of art is that it is felt before it is known. The qualitative unity is what gives rise to any later abstractive distinctions we can note within our experience. Any attempt to conceptualize that unity will necessarily select out some particular quality or qualities and thereby miss the unity of the whole qualitatively demarcated situation. Dewey explains, "The situation cannot present itself as an element in a proposition any more than a universe of discourse can appear as a member of discourse within that universe" ([1930] 1988, 247).

Within a qualitatively unified situation, particular objects, with their qualities and relations, stand forth as focal points within a horizon of possible meanings. The "affordances" of any object, person, or event are the standing forth of certain possibilities for meaningful engagement with and within an encompassing situation. The meaning of the event, person, or thing is a cluster of affordances, including possible perceptions, concepts, feeling responses, and modes of interaction that the thing provides for creatures with bodies and cognitive capacities like we have. To offer an illustrative example, let us return to Arnold's "Dover Beach." The successive stanzas present and enact a complex meaningful situation, a situation that we abstractly describe as two lovers at a window at night gazing across the English Channel toward the French coast, in a way that occasions a somber and profound meditation on life's tumult, fragility, and uncertainty, in the face of which our only hope is our steadfast love and care for one another. The entire developing poem creates an organically unified situation in which this insight emerges and is experienced in all its anxiety and poignancy. That felt qualitative unity is not re-presented by the poem; rather, it is *enacted in* and *realized through* the continuous process of the unfolding of the poem. It is not an insight had apart from the poem, which could then be expressed by the lines. Rather, the unique qualitative unity exists only in and through the poem as a whole.

Image-Schematic Patterns of Meaning

Another important aesthetic dimension of meaning stems from the patterns of interaction with our environment that emerge from the makeup, situatedness, and purposive activity of our bodies. Relative to fleas and whales, we are middle-sized creatures whose perceptual and motor capacities allow us to see, touch, taste, smell, and hear certain other objects. We exist in a gravitational field that constrains the patterns of our bodily movement. We have evolved to stand erect, rather than moving on all fours, and we have an opposable thumb that lets us grasp and manipulate certain objects. Our visual system permits us to perceive only certain wavelengths of light and to have good depth perception only over a limited range of distances. Our auditory system records only a specific range of sound frequencies. In other words, out of our bodily interaction with our environmental affordances, we take the meaning of things and events in certain specified ways, according to specific interactional patterns. George Lakoff (1987) and I (M. Johnson 1987) have called these recurring patterns of interaction "image schemas." For example, given our bodily makeup, the contours of our physical environment, and our subjection to gravity, *verticality* is a fundamental meaning structure for creatures like us. Hence, *up* and *down* are used to mark all sorts of significant relations, from simple physical orientations ("He *went up* the hill") to abstract metaphorical relations ("She *climbed* the ladder of success," "Prices *rose* overnight," and "He *went up* the chain of command to get authority to act"). *Up* and *down* have intuitive meaning and value for us because we inhabit our world partly through verticality relations.

Another basic image schema is scalar intensity. We have evolved to experience degrees of intensity of any sensation or quality. Lights get brighter and dimmer, sounds get louder and softer, surfaces go from rougher to smoother, temperatures change from hotter to colder. Change of degree (or scalar intensity) is so basic to our perceptual makeup that every language has syntactic and semantic ways of signaling these basic image-schematic types of change.

Image schemas like these are pre-reflectively meaningful to us because they mark basic qualitative determinations of our day-to-day experience and they constitute recurring patterns of experiential change, given the nature of our bodies and environments. Besides verticality and scalar intensity, creatures built like us find immediately meaningful such schemas as center/periphery, near/far, in/out, front/back, right/left, balance/imbalance, containment, source-path-goal movement, iteration, straight/

curved, locomotion, and so forth. Because these meaningful structures are so important in our lives, and so connected to our physical being, languages and symbol systems around the world typically have found ways to indicate these primordial image-schematic meaning structures.

Importantly, image schemas have their own corporeal logic (M. Johnson 1987, 2017; Lakoff and Johnson 1999). If, for instance, a ball is in a box (container *A*), the box is in a basket (container *B*), and the basket is in a closet (container *C*), then the ball is in the closet. This is a spatial logic (here a logic of transitive containment), learned by infants prior to any language acquisition. The corporeal image-schematic relation of successive containment is known in formal logic as the principle of transitivity (i.e., if *A* is in *B*, *B* is in *C*, and *C* is in *D*, then *A* is in *D*). For the most part, humans learn this image-schematic logic without any need of conscious reflection. It is a logic meaningful to us, insofar as it indicates the possibilities and direction of a developing, unfolding experience. Image-schematic inferences guide our reasoning, both nonconscious and conscious.

Image schemas are basic structures of meaning that play a crucial role in every form of human symbolic interaction and communication. As already indicated, they are pervasive in natural languages across the world, operating in both our linguistic expressions concerning our spatial and bodily experience (e.g., "the balloon *went straight up*"), but equally in metaphorical structuring of our abstract concepts (e.g., "Car prices *shot up*," "The crime rate *rose* 20 percent"). They abound in spontaneous gesture (McNeill 1992) and American Sign Language (Taub 2001). Architecture vastly employs image-schematic patterns, such as containment, motion along a path, links, verticality, front/back, near/far, center/periphery (M. Johnson 2002; Robinson and Pallasmaa 2015). Dance is a symphony of bodily movements and gestures capable of exemplifying every expressive pattern of human motion (Sheets-Johnstone 1999), and this carries over directly into theater performance (McConachie 2003, 2015). Our musical experience and cognition are built partly on image-schematic patterns (M. Johnson and Larson 2003; Zbikowski 2002). The visual arts utilize the felt qualities—and the body logic—of image schemas and concrete images (Arnheim 1969; M. Johnson 2007).

Emotions and Meaning

Image schemas are not merely skeletal patterns of bodily perception, orientation, and motion. They are also intimately connected to values, emotions, and feelings. What could be more immediately meaningful to us than our visceral emotional engagement with our world? An experience that we mark out as particularly meaningful is bound to be emotionally charged. And yet, strangely, the field known as philosophy of language that emerged in the first half of the twentieth century in Europe and America found it necessary to exclude emotion from any serious treatment of linguistic meaning. The strategy for this dismissal is exemplified in Richards and Ogden's (1923) distinction between descriptive (cognitive and truth-conditional) statements and emotive (noncognitive) expressions. They gave as an example of symbolic or descriptive use of language "The height of the Eiffel Tower is 900 feet," and their examples of emotive use were "Hurrah!", "Poetry is a spirit," and "Man is a worm" (Richards and Ogden 1923, 149). Logical empiricists tended to distinguish what they called "cognitive" functions of language, such as using sentences with propositional content to describe states of affairs or to make truth claims, from what they liked to call "emotive" uses of language to express emotions or psychological attitudes.

Given their primary concern with cognitive meaning, they used this mistaken, overly rigid cognitive/emotive dichotomy as a basis for conveniently ignoring any serious discussion of the central role of emotion in conceptualization and reasoning. This neglect of the affective dimensions of thought has persisted unabated down to the present day in analytic philosophy of mind and language.

Today, however, cognitive neuroscience is rapidly dispelling the myth that cognition and reasoning can operate without the involvement of emotions and feelings. On the contrary, it is becoming evident that emotions lie at the heart of our ability to grasp the meaning of any situation in which we find ourselves. Emotions emerged evolutionarily in certain animal species as a way of nonconsciously and automatically monitoring an organism's ongoing relation with its environment and then instituting bodily changes to serve and protect the organism's interests in survival and well-being. In the words of cognitive neuroscientist Antonio Damasio, "Emotions provide a natural means for the brain and mind to evaluate the environment within and around the organism, and respond accordingly and adaptively" (2003, 54).

Damasio (1994) argues that the fundamental condition for life within an organism is the development of a permeable boundary within which a certain systemic equilibrium can be maintained. If that equilibrium is significantly disrupted, no organism can long continue to function properly, or even to survive. In response to a disrupted equilibrium, either the organism will seek return to a previously established homeostatic set point, or it may create a new dynamic equilibrium. Damasio treats both of these conditions as homeostasis, but some scientists use the term *allostasis* for the latter condition, in order to emphasize the dynamic character of a newly established balanced state within the organism (Schulkin 2011).

Emotions arose evolutionarily as one of the processes for monitoring and preserving the integrity, health, and well-being of the animal. They are mostly automatic bodily responses to stimuli that indicate changes in an animal's body state as a result of its changing interactions with its environment. They are a primary means by which an animal tries to re-establish the essential equilibrium of its internal milieu that it needs to continue functioning. In order to survive and flourish, animals need to instinctively avoid situations that could be threatening or harmful, and they need to seek situations that enhance their well-being. For the most part, negative emotions evolved to help an organism avoid unhealthy, dysfunctional, or harmful bodily states, by turning the organism away from the object or activity that is causing the harmful state. Fear reactions, for example, are complex neural and chemical bodily responses to perceived threats within one's environment. Positive emotions, in contrast, tend to move us toward the realization of bodily states conducive to our survival and well-being.[6]

Because emotions play the central role in the maintenance of an animal's integrity and well-being, it is hard to imagine anything more important for monitoring how things are going for the organism, and, therefore, it is hard to imagine anything more directly meaningful to us than our emotional experience. I have argued that, insofar as emotions allow us to "take the measure" of our current situation and make important responsive changes, they are meaningful to us at the deepest level of our existence (M. Johnson 2007). Emotional response patterns are, literally, changes in our body state in response to previous changes in our body state caused by our interactions with our environment, and they usually precede any reflective thinking or conceptualization. In that sense, they might be called "noncognitive" (as not conceptual and not propositional); but they are nevertheless at the heart of our cognitive processes, taken in the broadest sense, as concerned with all the ways we experience, make, and transform meaning. The central role of emotions in meaning is so obvious to ordinary people that it is puzzling to them to learn that analytic philosophers, until quite recently, have tended to dismiss emotion from their accounts of meaning and knowledge. This is a sad testament to the power of certain entrenched prejudices (such as that philosophy is primarily about the analysis and justification of knowledge claims) that lead us to ignore even the most important phenomena, such as emotions, qualities, and other the aesthetic dimensions of meaning.

Damasio (1994, 1999) distinguishes between emotional response patterns and feelings of an emotion. The former operate mostly automatically and nonconsciously, but sometimes we are able to become conscious of our emotional state; that is, we feel it. Damasio explains that feelings

> are first and foremost about the body, that they offer us the cognition of our visceral and musculoskeletal *state* as it becomes affected by preorganized mechanisms and by the cognitive structures we have developed under their influence. Feelings let us mind the body, attentively, as during an emotional state, or faintly, as during a background state. . . . Feelings offer us a glimpse of what goes on in our flesh, as a momentary image of that flesh is juxtaposed to the images of other objects and situations; in so doing, feelings modify our comprehensive notion of those other objects and situations. (1994, 159)

When we feel changes in our bodily state, we become conscious of their ebb and flow, and of the felt qualities of their various dimensions or components. In other words, felt emotions have aesthetic characteristics. As felt, they have a qualitative dimension, and therefore they are subject to changes in quality, intensity, pace (speed), and directedness. Think of that awful feeling of increasing anxiety—the adrenaline rush, the flushing, the tension of one's entire body, the churning in the gut—that comes in moments where we feel unsure of ourselves, overwhelmed by circumstances, or anxious about possible failure. That fear is a palpable, bodily, visceral meaning.

The arts can allow us to experience the aesthetic dimensions of emotions in an intensified and nuanced manner that is often richer or more refined than what we feel in our day-to-day living. Consider, for example, at least two ways in which the following short poem enacts a certain emotional state.

Quo Vadis
Sometimes I choose a cloud and let it
cross the sky floating me away.
Or a bird unravels its song and carries me
as it flies deeper and deeper into the woods.
Is there a way to be gone and still
belong? Travel that takes you home?
Is that life?—to stand by a river and go.
William Stafford, *The Way It Is: New & Selected Poems*, 1998

The first dimension of emotional engagement stems from the way each focal image in the poem evokes a particular quality of an emotional state.

There is a very specific floating feeling that accompanies our visual imaging of a cloud drifting silently across a bright sky. We feel light, airy, uplifted, floating. There is a sense of peace, attunement, and harmony. Our imagination of that scene carries us away, buoyed by that cloud. Then, the sweet, precise song of some bird gives rise to that same quality of gentle floating and graceful movement as we follow that sound further into the woods.

A second form of emotional resonance comes from the contour of our passing emotion—the flow and rhythm of the emotion as it develops. The two opening images carry us away, moving us to a different place and a different mood and emotional state.[7] Sometimes we are carried away to places alien, lonely, or frightening; but sometimes we are carried "home," back to a sense of belonging, safety, attunement, and nurturant care. Stafford wonders whether the secret of life is to find a way to let yourself be carried away, but with the faith that your journey will bring you "home." We must learn, he urges us, to "stand by a river and go"—to be present to our changing situation—and to go wherever it might take us. This second kind of emotional response is therefore the feeling of how we move from one mood or emotional state to another, and there is a distinctive rhythm and flow to such movement.

Art thus presents or enacts the very patterning of our waxing and waning feelings as they change in quality, force, directedness, or manner of movement. Music famously accomplishes this latter task, because musical experience is a form of metaphorical motion (M. Johnson and Larson 2003). Dance, too, involves gestural movements that engage the expressive capacities of the animate body through which our emotions are manifest (Sheets-Johnstone 1999). Put music and dance together in a musical, and you have a powerful visceral enactment of the complex and nuanced emotional dimensions of meaning. Consider, for example, the first few stanzas of "Singin' in the Rain," from the 1952 film of that name. Don Lockwood (Gene Kelly) kisses Kathy Selden (Debbie Reynolds) goodnight on her doorstep and turns around into the rain with a big smile on his face. He shoos away the idling car waiting for him in front of her apartment and begins to stroll merrily down the street, singing, "Doo dloo doo doo doo / doo dloo doo doo doo / doo dloo doo doo doo." The rhythm of this merry doo-dloo-doo-doo-ing fairly skips along as he glides and saunters down the street. His gait is open, free, graceful, and flowing, without hint of trouble or tension. Angry, frightened, or tense people do not "doo-dloo-doo-doo." Don pauses, his face uplifted toward the rain, shrugs his shoulders, and closes his umbrella, embracing the rain pouring down on his grinning countenance. He turns to walk again, and begins, "I'm si-i-ing-in' in the rain / Just si-i-ing-in' in the rain / What a glo-o-o-ri-ous fee-ee-lin' / I'm ha-a-a-ppy again!" The "I'm" (of "I'm si-i-ing-in' in the rain") is a low D, from which he climbs up to a middle E for the "si-i-ing" of "si-i-ing-in'in the rain." The arch up from "I'm" to "si-i-ing" is a felt rush of positive emotional tension—a surging up of sheer joy—mirrored in his floating walk, his upturned face, and his open posture. The melodic contour rises and falls as he saunters. When he gets to "What a glo-o-o-ri-ous fee-ee-lin'," he slides upward from "glo-o-o" (low D) to the "ri" (middle G), up to the "ous" (middle A), and even higher up to "fee-eel" (middle C), followed by a flowing drop down to "in'" (middle A). The effect is the felt swelling of positive feeling gushing up and dropping down slightly as it pours out. Analyzing the melodic contour in terms of tones strikes us as almost ridiculous, because that fact is, we just immediately feel the expansive, floating joy when we hear Kelly sing and watch him dance.

Most of this is so obvious that it may seem almost trivial to note it, but the felt contour of the musical motion is a concrete enactment of a familiar pattern of feeling we all know and desire. Notice that, even when Kelly is singing, "Let the stormy clouds chase / Everyone from the place / Come on with the rain"—words that might suggest the ominous or gloomy—the accompanying melody continually counteracts this gloomy possibility with its indefatigably cheery felt qualities that are immediately confirmed in the next line: "I've a smii-i-ile on my face!" This line is delivered at the very moment Don pauses, opens his arms wide, turns his face upward toward the rain, and smiles a smile big enough to swallow the storm—an iconic image that captures the entire qualitative character of the event. No description of this song and dance number can capture what is obvious to everybody, and which we struggle to express in words. If you know this piece, it will now be making a continuous encore performance in your auditory imagination, and you probably cannot help but be affected by its infectious positive feelings.

The Aesthetics of Embodied Meaning

I have been arguing that we should see aesthetics as not just a theoretical exploration of the nature of art, or of some allegedly distinct type of experience that we dub "aesthetic," but rather as pertaining to all the processes by which any aspect of our experience can be meaningful. I call this the "aesthetics of embodied meaning" (or the "aesthetics of embodied life"), and I have explained it here mostly in terms of images, image schemas, qualities (both pervasive unifying qualities and particular qualities of objects or scenes), emotions, and feelings, because these dimensions are too often overlooked in standard accounts of meaning, value, thought, and language. Aesthetics is about the ways embodied social creatures like us experience meaning, and these ways of meaning-making emerge from the nature of our bodies, the way our brains work in those bodies, our social interactions with other people, and the structure of the environments with which we are in continual visceral interaction. On this view, art is not a particular and unique type of activity (as opposed to, say, science, technology, morality, politics, or religion), but rather is a bringing to fulfillment of the possibilities for meaning that have their roots in everyday experience. Dewey captured this sense of any consummatory experience as art: "The doings and sufferings that form experience are, in the degree in which experience is intelligent or charged with meanings, a union of the precarious, novel, irregular with the settled, assured and uniform—a union which also defines the artistic and the esthetic" (Dewey [1925] 1981, 269). The arts are therefore exemplary modes of meaning-making, because they give us intensified, nuanced, and complex realizations of the processes of meaning in everyday life (Dewey [1934] 1987; Shusterman 2000, 2008; M. Johnson 2007; Alexander 2013).

The view I am presenting was first put forth eighty years ago by John Dewey in *Art as Experience* (1934), where he says, "I have tried to show in these chapters that the esthetic is no intruder in experience from without, whether by way of idle luxury or transcendent ideality, but that it is the clarified and intensified development of traits that belong to every normally complete experience" ([1934] 1987, 52–53). In art, we encounter the qualitative elements and processes of human meaning-making in ways that show us fuller possibilities for significance and growth. "Art," says Dewey, "in its form, unites the very same relation of doing and undergoing, outgoing and incoming energy, that makes an experience to be an experience. Because of elimination of all that does not contribute to mutual organization of the factors of both action and reception into one another, and because of selection of just the aspects and traits that contribute to their interpenetration of each other, the product is a work of esthetic art" (ibid., 54). We care about the arts and find them important, on the occasions we do, not merely because they entertain us, but more importantly because they enact worlds—or at least modes of experience—that show us the breadth and depth of possibilities for human meaning. Most important, the arts do this using the elements and processes of meaningful experience that constitute our everyday perceptions, judgments, and actions, but they organize these materials into wholes that explore new possibilities for meaning (Shusterman 2000).

Unsophisticated and overly simplistic imitation theories of art mistakenly place the value of an artwork in its ability to represent something other than itself, such as some aspect of a supposedly external, mind-independent reality. This imitation-as-copying account of mimesis evokes the obvious question of why anyone would want such an imitation, if they could get the "real" thing (object, event, experience). Once we realize that works of art do not *re*-present objects, events, meaning, knowledge, or experience, but instead that they *present and enact* possibilities for meaning and value in an exemplary manner, only then will we understand the significance of art, and of experience-as-art. Those who speak of an "aesthetic attitude" as a disengaged, disinterested, abstractive withdrawal from the affairs of everyday life, in search of some fixed, eternal artistic essence, are actually making it impossible for art to mean something for our lives. Though I would rather discard the term as misleading and dangerous, the only proper sense of "aesthetic attitude" is sensitivity to the forms, images, patterns, qualities, emotions, and feelings that constitute the stuff of meaningful experience. Only when we are attentive to, appropriately critical toward, and creatively engaged with these aesthetic dimensions of embodied life are we able to be "at home" in our world—connected to our environment and to the people around us in constructive, meaningful, and moral ways (Shusterman 2000; Alexander 2013).

The remaining chapters in this volume are explorations of the aesthetics of human understanding. They reveal how aesthetic dimensions lie at the very heart of our conceptual systems and are therefore manifest across the broad range of human symbolic activities. These visceral meaning structures and processes shape our science, philosophy, morality, and art—as well as every other aspect of experience and value. Appreciating that fact requires us to reconsider some of our most deeply entrenched views about ourselves and our world. The guiding theme unifying these chapters is Dewey's claim that "the characteristic human need is for possession and appreciation of the meaning of things" (Dewey [1925] 1981, 272), and that "the issue involved in experience as art in its pregnant sense and in art as processes and materials of nature continued by direction into achieved and enjoyed meanings, sums up in itself all the issues which have been previously considered" (ibid., 269).

PART I

Philosophy and Science

There is a long, deeply entrenched tradition in the West in which philosophy is regarded as the ultimate exercise of reason to address the most general and fundamental human questions about the nature of reality, knowledge, truth, morality, and values. Reason is held to be universal and pure—the uniquely defining capacity of all humans, operating according to a transcendent logic and free from the entanglements of bodily passions. From this perspective philosophy's theoretical focus is not to provide objective experimental knowledge of nature (that task is left to the sciences); instead, it uses reason to analyze the nature, possibility, and limits of various knowledge practices, types of judgment, and value systems. In the practical sphere, philosophy supposedly examines the source of our moral values and principles, whether in pure practical reason or in certain moral sentiments shared by all humans. On this view, then, philosophy allows us to understand how knowledge of the natural world and the imperatives of human morality is possible.

This popular and long-standing conception of philosophy and science, as the most eminent expressions of a universal understanding and reason, has been challenged from a number of philosophical and scientific perspectives over the past half century. Within philosophy—from traditions as diverse as analytic philosophy, phenomenology, hermeneutics, pragmatism, feminism, and postmodernism—a critical onslaught has arisen, mostly from considerations of the nature and limits of knowledge practices. During the same period, within the cognitive sciences (e.g., biology, anthropology, psychology, sociology, linguistics, neuroscience, and computer science), the critique came in the form of accounts of the ways our bodies, brains, environments, and cultures give rise to conceptualization and reasoning, thereby providing a naturalistic explanation of mind. In short, significant parts of our traditional conception of philosophy and science as the ultimate rational endeavors, freed from the encumbrances of the body and supplying objective absolute knowledge, have been discredited by research on the bodily basis of mind, thought, knowledge, and values that is emerging from the recent cooperation of philosophy with the cognitive sciences (Varela, Thompson, and Rosch 1991; Lakoff and Johnson 1999; Gibbs 2006; M. Johnson 2017).

An important basis for rethinking the nature of philosophy and science has been recent work on meaning, thought, and language that has dismantled the illusion of philosophy as the ultimate rational manifestation of pure reason. The research to which I am referring comes primarily from linguistics, psychology, and neuroscience, situated within an empirically responsible philosophical framework. It reveals that concepts do not work the way most people assume they do. Instead of there being literal concepts defined by necessary and sufficient conditions, our concepts tend to have a rich internal structure that lacks any single univocal core and is rooted in our bodies, brains, and social interactions (Lakoff 1987; Lakoff and Johnson 1999; Gibbs 2006). The empirical research shows that our abstract concepts are defined by multiple, often inconsistent metaphors, resulting in a complex radial structure of our concepts and categories, with central category members connected to noncentral members by various principles of extension (e.g., propositional, image schematic, metonymic, and metaphorical (Lakoff and Johnson 1980; Lakoff 1987; Kövecses 2010; Dancygier and Sweetser 2014). Contrary to what most people think, reason is not pure and disembodied, but instead emerges from our bodily perception, action, feeling, and values (M. Johnson 2017). As a consequence of the embodiment of mind and thought, there can be no God's-eye, omniscient perspective in any field of theoretical endeavor or practical engagement. We are situated, fallible, finite creatures.

In the chapters of part 1, I am thus interested in how we should conceive of philosophy and the sciences, once we take embodied cognition seriously. The introductory chapter ("The Aesthetics of Embodied Life") has given an overview of some of the most significant work on the bodily aesthetic roots of meaning, cognition, and reasoning. Chapter 1 ("Pragmatism, Cognitive Science, and the Embodied Mind") shows how this view of cognition as embodied and aesthetic makes it possible for pragmatist philosophy and embodied cognitive science to mutually critique, enrich, and expand each other through ongoing dialogue.

A growing body of empirical research on mind, thought, and language reveals that both our philosophical perspectives and our various scientific theories are built on systems of metaphors. These metaphors are grounded in aspects of our bodily perception, action, and feeling. Consequently, our understanding and reasoning about abstract notions is fatefully shaped by powerful metaphors, inextricably tied up with the aesthetic dimensions of our bodily experience. Chapter 2 ("Philosophy's Debt to Metaphor") gives examples of the ways in which philosophies are elaborations of particular sets of systematic conceptual metaphors that guide how we individuate, identify, and explain phenomena within particular philosophical systems. The metaphorical character of philosophy is not a problem to be overcome by some transcendental move; rather, the metaphors give us the only intelligent ways we have available for making sense of and reasoning about our experience. (Chapter 5 gives a similar account of how metaphors undergird our scientific theories and are inextricably tied to selected values.)

Chapters 3 and 4 argue that just as we have to choose our philosophical orientation carefully, in an empirically responsible way, so also we need to select the appropriate version of cognitive science that we draw on. I have argued elsewhere (M. Johnson 2007, 2014) that pragmatism provides the most comprehensive and insightful framework for understanding the implications of embodied cognitive science. However, chapter 3 ("Experiencing Language: What's Missing in Linguistic Pragmatism?") shows that all pragmatisms are not the same, and that what has come to be known as "analytic" or "linguistic" pragmatism tends to focus exclusively on language and thereby overlooks the crucial role of the body and of experience in the constitution of mind, meaning, and thought. At best, therefore, the newly emerging analytic pragmatism can offer only a considerably impoverished view of what philosophy can and should do in our lives. A more adequate theory would come from a classical pragmatist emphasis on *experience* (and not just language) as the starting and ending point of philosophical reflection. Such a view emphasizes the pervasive aesthetic dimensions of experience, showing how they shape what and how we understand, reason, and evaluate.

Turning then to the science side, chapter 4 ("Keeping the Pragmatism in Neuropragmatism") argues that just as pragmatisms vary, so also do various conceptions of cognitive science. Each conception, with its attendant methods, has intrinsic limitations as to what it focuses on and what its resources are for explaining the selected phenomena. Consequently, not just any conception of cognitive science will do. Moreover, no cognitive science and no conception of neuroscience is able to provide a comprehensive and fully adequate approach to mind all by itself. That is why we need multiple methods of scientific inquiry and a philosophical framework that both recognizes the assumptions and limitations of a given science and also explores the broader implications of bodies of scientific research. To get an adequate theory of mind, thought, language, and action, we need to keep up a dialogue between pragmatism and cognitive science that is both appropriately critical of the limitations of various sciences and that also generates and sustains an ongoing co-evolution of science and philosophy.

Philosophy, then, is not what most have thought it is, and neither is science. They are both endeavors of inquiry grounded in systematic metaphors, which are in turn grounded in our embodied and culturally embedded experience. Working together, they can give rise to an empirically responsible philosophy that grows in tandem and co-evolves with the developing sciences of mind.

CHAPTER I

Pragmatism, Cognitive Science, and the Embodied Mind

The approach to the view of mind, meaning, thought, and language that I develop in this book draws on cognitive science research over the past three decades, placed within a perspective on experience, nature, cognition, and values that I find most comprehensively and powerfully articulated in the pragmatist philosophy of William James and John Dewey. I begin, therefore, with an account of why I find pragmatism to be the most compelling philosophical framework within which to explore the bodily sources of meaning, understanding, and reasoning. There are similar insights on these important topics in the phenomenological investigations of Edmund Husserl, Martin Heidegger, and Maurice Merleau-Ponty, but in my own philosophical education I have felt the deepest resonances with James and Dewey, who paid considerable attention to the best science of their day as they addressed key problems about mind and thought.

Pragmatism and cognitive science have long had a rocky relationship, but recently it has improved dramatically. Early on, they were like two characters in the standard plotline of so many romantic comedies, who start off intensely disliking each other, noticing each other's faults and disagreeable traits. Eventually, however, fate brings them together, the sparks begin to fly, and they realize that they had a deep connection all along, though they were both blind to it. The early days of their relationship were fraught with suspicion, misunderstanding, and even hostility. The cognitive scientists ignored pragmatist philosophy, and the pragmatists either ignored or actively criticized the sciences of mind as they understood them. The chief reason for this was that, in its early adolescent stages of development, cognitive science was grounded on assumptions that were mostly incompatible with classical pragmatism. The situation was made even worse by the fact that many pragmatist philosophers accused the cognitive sciences of scientism, fearing that scientific theories of mind were bound to be overly reductionist in spirit and would fail to plumb the depths of mind, thought, and language. Consequently, until recently there has been very little recognition—from either party—of the great potential for a mutually beneficial working relationship between pragmatists and cognitive scientists. Or, to put it in today's somewhat pathetic romantic vernacular, it has only been in the last few years that the two have been able to "hook up."

Such a suspicion of cognitive science among pragmatists is ironic, given that Charles Sanders Peirce, William James, and John Dewey each championed the integration and co-evolution of philosophy and the sciences. These classical pragmatists made extensive use of the best available biological and cognitive science of their day in developing their views of mind, knowledge, and value. If they were alive today, I have no doubt that they would appreciate the importance of cognitive science research for the philosophy of mind and language, and they would see the importance of a pragmatist framework within which to understand the contributions of the sciences of mind. I propose to explore some of the shared ideas and perspectives that underlie the promise for a creative relationship between pragmatism and contemporary cognitive science.

Two Different Conceptions of Cognitive Science

So, what was it that kept the future partners feuding for so long? Why couldn't pragmatists and cognitive scientists get along together? The key to the answer is that earlier incarnations of cognitive science—which George Lakoff and I (1999) have dubbed "first-generation cognitive science"—rested on a somewhat disembodied conception of mind that was completely at odds with the embodied and action-oriented pragmatist understanding of mind, thought, and language. First-generation cognitive science was a blending of analytic philosophy of mind, information-processing psychology, generative linguistics, model theory, computer science, and artificial intelligence research. Its orientation was functionalist in the narrow sense that it took mental thought processes to be formal algorithmic operations on abstract meaningless symbols that could supposedly be run on any of a number of suitable hardwares (machines) or wetwares (biological organisms). Many functionalists are materialists who do not think "mind" and "body" are two separate ontological realities, but their view can still be labeled "disembodied," insofar as they think that an account of mental operations does not depend on the particular makeup of the body or other material that instantiates the functional program they call mind (Fodor 1975). Consequently, they do not think that the very structures of our thought and reasoning are determined by the nature of our bodies and brains—at least, not in any deep way. Furthermore, most functionalists assume that sentence-like propositions are the core of meaning and thought, and so they employ formal logic, propositional attitude theory, and speech act theory to represent the range of possible mental states and operations.

It is no surprise, therefore, that many pragmatists tended to dismiss first-generation cognitive science as being reductionist and disembodied in character, while cognitive scientists of this persuasion returned the insult by either ignoring or rejecting what they perceived to be just one more speculative and scientifically unsupported philosophical worldview unconnected to their empirical research. In my romantic comedy analogy, we would say that, in their mutual ignorance, arrogance, and disdain, the two partners were all too ready to point out each other's manifold faults, while remaining blind to their own faults and unappreciative of each other's respective virtues.

Fortunately, by the mid-1970s, the plot took an unexpected turn. One of the characters began to grow and change. Cognitive science underwent a makeover of substantial proportions. This new "second-generation," or "embodied," cognitive science was naturalistic, antidualist, emergentist, nonreductionist, and aware of the need for multilevel explanatory frameworks—just like pragmatism! A number of scientific research programs began to discover the importance of the body in the constitution of mind and thought. For example, research in cognitive psychology was revealing how human conceptual systems depend both on the nature of our bodies and brains, and also on the nature of our environments (Lakoff 1987; Varela, Thompson, and Rosch 1991; Barsalou 1999). The new orientation known as cognitive linguistics began to explore how meaning is grounded in our sensory, motor, and affective processes and how most of our abstract concepts are metaphorical (Lakoff and Johnson 1999; Gibbs 2006; Feldman 2006). Cognitive neuroscience began to provide at least somewhat psychologically realistic neurocomputational models of embodied cognitive operations, including cross-domain neural connections whereby sensory-motor processes are recruited for so-called "higher" cognitive functions (Feldman 2006; Lakoff and Narayanan, forthcoming).

But the growth and change was not just one-sided. Some pragmatist philosophers have grown over the last decade to appreciate the need to base our accounts of mind, thought, and language on the best empirical scientific work available (Solymosi and Shook 2014; Schulkin 2012). Although most of the people doing the scientific research and modeling today are still largely ignorant of pragmatist philosophy, the convergences between second-generation cognitive science and pragmatism are quite striking.

In this chapter I want to briefly explore some of the more important shared perspectives that speak to the possibility of a rich and very constructive ongoing collaboration between embodied cognitive science and pragmatist philosophy.

Areas of Convergence between Second-Generation Cognitive Sciences and Classical Pragmatism

Naturalistic, Multilevel Methods for the Study of Mind

By a naturalistic perspective on mind, I mean the view that what we commonly call "mental" phenomena, as well as all cultural phenomena, are part of nature. Naturalistic approaches typically share a materialist ontology, and so they deny the existence of supernatural and transcendent entities, agencies, and causes. Consequently, the empirical methods of inquiry utilized by the natural and social sciences are deemed appropriate and necessary for the study of all aspects of human cognition and symbolic interaction.

However, all naturalisms are not the same. There are differences concerning which methods of explanation are believed to be able to provide an adequately rich account of mind, thought, and language. For example, *strong reductionist naturalism* claims that in a suitably mature science of mind (which does not yet exist) *all* the relevant phenomena will be explained using only assumptions and methods employed in a single discipline, such as biochemistry or, perhaps ultimately, physics. Eventually, so the story goes, all our "higher-level" functions and processes (consciousness, perception, thinking, reasoning, willing, etc.) will be reduced to events and causes of the sort investigated in the physical sciences.

There is an alternative, less reductionist, conception of naturalism according to which a fully satisfactory theory will ultimately employ multiple levels of explanation, where each form of explanation is appropriate for a particular emergent level of functional organization within a creature in ongoing interaction with its environments. This second version might be called a *pluralistic naturalism*. For example, William Bechtel (2008) observes that since mechanisms consist of parts working together to produce whole functional units, reduction to the operations of the parts will be a key element for explaining the behavior of those wholes. However, these various functional wholes are sometimes part of larger, more extensive systems, and therefore each of those wholes will be caught up in broader causal patterns of interaction that may not be operative at the lower level of the individual parts. Consequently, although there will be some inter- and intralevel reduction possible, an adequate explanation of complex cognitive and affective phenomena will involve multiple levels of organization and will require different explanatory models and methods to capture the fullness of the phenomena being explained. Bechtel summarizes:

> A final feature of mechanistic explanation that should be noted is that, insofar as it emphasizes the contributions made by parts of a mechanism to its operation, a mechanistic analysis is, in an important sense, reductionist. However, insofar as it also recognizes the importance of the organization in which the parts are embedded and the context in which the whole mechanism is functioning, it not only sanctions looking to lower levels but also upward to higher levels. . . . Thus, far from sanctioning only a focus downward on the components, a mechanistic perspective as well requires an account of engagements with other systems at the same level and, potentially, of the constraints imposed by being incorporated into a higher-level mechanism. In fact, therefore the mechanistic perspective is inherently multilevel. (2008, 21–22)

Bechtel's focus is primarily on the nature and operations of mechanistic models, and the methods he countenances are mostly those of various sciences (e.g., physics, chemistry, molecular biology, dynamical systems theory, etc.). Pragmatists would insist that the natural sciences are not the *only* appropriate methods of inquiry, because other critical and interpretive methods may also prove necessary to explain the full range of cognitive phenomena at different levels of organization and complex interaction. Consequently, we would expect some methods to be appropriate at the cellular level, others required for an adequate explanation of the autonomic nervous system, others fitting for the whole-body organization of its various subsystems, and still other methods necessary for a complete explanation of social and cultural phenomena.

This broader pluralistic conception of naturalism is shared by many cognitive scientists and nearly all pragmatists. It is naturalistic in the sense that it understands humans to be complex, highly evolved, embodied dynamical systems in ongoing interaction with their environments. It is pluralistic insofar as it sees increased complexity of organism-environment interactions as giving rise to emergent qualities and functions, and thus requiring multiple explanatory models that are appropriate for each of the emerging levels of organization.

The Primacy of Continuous Organism-Environment Interactions

The view I am developing here is fundamentally dependent on the idea that the locus of all experience, meaning, thought, communication, value, and action is the ongoing interaction between an organism and its environment. *You can only think what your brain, body, and environment (physical and cultural) allow you to think. You can only mean and communicate what your brain, body, and environment (with its physical and cultural aspects) allow you to mean and communicate. You can only know what your brain, body, and environment allow you to know.* Consequently, any view that assumes a fundamental ontological dualism that locates the mind, thought, meaning, or value as merely *within the subject* and places "the world" (or any subset thereof) as *outside* the mind is already misguided from the start.

It is very tempting to regard mind as consisting of a set of pre-given capacities whose structures and formal operations are not determined by the environment in which they operate. According to this view, the environment might supply the content, but not the structures, of cognitive operations. In *The Principles of Psychology* (1890), William James presciently warned against this temptation as follows:

> Mental facts cannot be properly studied apart from the physical environment of which they take cognizance. The great fault of the older rational psychology was to set up the soul as an absolute spiritual being with certain faculties of its own by which the several activities of remembering, imagining, reasoning, willing, etc. were explained, almost without reference to the peculiarities of the world with which these activities deal. But the richer insight of modern days perceives that our inner faculties are *adapted* in advance to the features of the world in which we dwell, adapted, I mean, so as to secure our safety and prosperity in its midst. (1900, 3)

Those scientists and philosophers who began to realize that organisms are clusters of interrelated habits of perception, movement, feeling, and action soon also saw that *habits incorporate aspects of our environments.* This means that habits are not just structures or dispositions internal to organisms, but instead stretch out into the world and incorporate dimensions of our environments. Dewey regarded this fact as the key to developing a genuinely nondualistic philosophy. He observed that habits are internal and external all at once: "Habits are arts. They involve skill of sensory and motor organs, cunning or craft, and objective materials. They assimilate objective energies and eventuate in command of environment" (Dewey [1922] 1988, 15–16). He illustrated this fundamental ontological fact (i.e., that habits embody and project into aspects of their environment) by observing that

> habits are like functions in many respects, and especially in requiring the cooperation of organism and environment. Breathing is an affair of air as truly as of the lungs; digesting an affair of food as truly as of tissues of stomach. Seeing involves light just as certainly as it does the eye and optic nerve. Walking implicates the ground as well as the legs.... Natural operations like breathing and digesting, acquired ones like speech and honesty, are functions of the surroundings as truly as of a person. They are things done *by* the environment by means of organic structures or acquired dispositions. (Dewey [1922] 1988, 15)

The primacy of ongoing organism-environment interactions means that all the discriminations we make within our experience are just that—namely, recurring patterns of that interactive process that we notice and respond to, given our particular bodily capacities, needs, values, and social relations. The vast majority of these "noticings" are not conscious acts; rather, they are the result of what our brains and bodies, through nonconscious neural processes, allow us to experience and to focus on, given our physical makeup and our interests at the present moment. Dewey ([1925] 1981, [1938] 1991) emphasized that our conscious reflective processes of thought depend on, and are rooted in, these mostly nonconscious selections of qualities, patterns, and relations that organize experience. There is no inner homunculus or executive center doing the selecting, either at the nonconscious or conscious levels of processing. We are simply tuned up—through the evolutionary history of our species, and through our individual development—to attend only to certain kinds of affordances in our environment.

We also need to be careful not to regard the products of selective attention as representing everything that is significant in any given situation. Dewey thought that this problem of selective attention was such a major temptation that it he called it the "philosopher's fallacy": the error of taking the products of our preferred mode of inquiry (based on our interests and values) and then assuming that these constitute all of what matters in any situation (Dewey [1925] 1981). The fact that we cannot help but select parts or aspects of a particular situation (relative to our needs, perceptual makeup, and motor capacities) does not sanction the conclusion that only those selected dimensions are important for a full account of an experience. A good example of this is the way many philosophers assume that experience is a cognitive affair directed toward knowledge acquisition, and then proceed to ignore all the other dimensions of experience—especially qualitative and affective dimensions, which they regard as "noncognitive"—as if they were not important.

It is also important to remember that as long as a creature lives, the organism-environment transactions that make it what it is are *always in process*. Mind is not a fixed thing or static structure. As psychologist and neuroscientist Don Tucker has argued, "The mind's organization emerges through a developmental process of controlling neural activity, beginning in the womb and continuing throughout life" (Tucker 2017, chap. 5). Learning is not just a matter of adding new content to a fixed, prestructured mind; rather, cognition and learning *change the brain itself*, by changing neuronal connections and firing thresholds. Tucker summarizes his key insight: "Cognition is neural development, continued in the present moment. The neural connections that are formed in the process of forming a concept are then the scaffolding for further brain development that allows mental activity" (ibid.).

The Rich, Irreducibly Complex Character of Experience

So far, I have suggested that the ontological and epistemic starting point for an analysis of mind, thought, language, and value must always be the totality of the situation of the ongoing organism-in-interaction-with-its-environment. Any analysis or explanation that starts with anything less than this entire arc and process of organism-environment coupling leads to a narrowing and distorting of experience, in a way that is bound to leave out important factors. Obviously, we cannot articulate the entire environing situation, because understanding and thought are, by their very nature, selective. Any particular method of inquiry will therefore be partial and perspectival. It will circumscribe only what it takes to be the relevant phenomena within a situation, and it will focus only on those qualities, relations, and events that it deems significant for its purposes. This limited, perspectival character is not some catastrophic human failing, but merely a fact about the intrinsic limitations of human understanding.

The selective and perspectival nature of experience and inquiry reminds us of the need for multiple modes of inquiry and explanation, since no single method could even begin to encompass the richness and complexity of any situation. The best we can hope for is to find converging evidence arising from multiple methods. Pragmatist views of inquiry, meaning, reason, knowledge, and truth can be extremely helpful, insofar as (1) they reveal the basic limiting assumptions of particular methodologies and technologies of experiment and inquiry, (2) they provide a broader pluralistic framework for evaluating the insights gleaned from multiple modes of inquiry and explanation, and (3) they help us to integrate converging evidence from the various cognitive sciences to generate as comprehensive and multivalent a perspective as possible.

James and Dewey were especially insistent in warning that both common sense and philosophy suffer from the mistaken view that experience consists in our "inner" feeling of how we are affected by our world. Dewey in particular observed that focusing on only the "how" of experience—how we feel ourselves being impacted by our perception of our surroundings—leads to a subjectivizing of experience that has been especially prominent since the Enlightenment. This exclusive focus on experience as an "inner" perceiving and processing of mental representations creates an ontological and epistemic gap between the inner (the mental) and the outer (the physical), with no way to connect the two. Consequently, what "mind" knows, on this subjectivist view, is only its own inner ideas or representations, and we are then left with the skeptical problem of how we could ever be sure that our inner representations somehow correspond to objects and events in the outer world.

James and Dewey saw that such a skepticism is unnecessary and misleading, once we understand the unity of the organism-environment reciprocity. They struck at the heart of any dualism of inner/outer, subject/object, and mind/body by observing that our world comes to us as what James called a "much-at-once-ness"—an integrated, complex, multidimensional whole—from which we later select (mostly unconsciously) objects, properties, and relations on which we focus our attention and thinking (James [1911] 1979). James and Dewey repeatedly emphasized that, if philosophy is going to be grounded in our concrete situation in a way that makes it possible to reconstruct the world for the better, then we have to start with a nonreductive, suitably rich and complex account of experience. Experience, they argued, is neither inner nor outer, but both at once; and it far exceeds, in its richness, any particular theoretical account of it. In Dewey's words: "Experience is *of* as well as *in* nature. It is not experience which is experienced, but nature—stones, plants, animals, diseases, health, temperature, electricity, and so on. Things interacting in certain ways *are* experience; they are what is experienced. Linked in certain other ways with another natural object—the human organism—they are *how* things are experienced as well. Experience thus reaches down into nature; it has depth. It also has breadth and to an indefinitely elastic extent. It stretches. That stretch constitutes inference" ([1925] 1981, 12–13). Humans are not merely spectators of a shadow-play of inner representations. We are not locked up within an inner space of "mind" or "consciousness." Rather, *we are in and of the world,* always active within it in an ongoing process through which, by virtue of our continual coupling activities with aspects of our environment, we are at least partially in touch with our world and not wholly alienated from it. Inner/outer, mind/world, and subject/object are thus abstractions from the unified flow of experience.

One important implication of the James/Dewey nondualistic view of experience is that it is not correct to say that the mind is merely the brain, since experience encompasses the entire arc of organism-environment engagement, which is an enactive process (Varela, Thompson, and Rosch 1991). Sometimes neuroscientists are criticized (and rightly so) for claiming that all experience and thought takes place *within* the brain. What they should say, according to a pragmatist nondualist ontology and according to good cognitive science, is that thought takes place via structures and processes operating at many levels: in neurons, in a cortex, in a brain, in chemicals in the blood, in an active body, in bodily interactions with one's surroundings, in social interactions, within cultural institutions, and thus in a multidimensional environment. In other words, any satisfactory account of cognition will have to include the whole creative process of organism-environment engagement.

That said, there is still some very limited truth to the slogan that the mind is the brain. That truth is this: everything that we call experience, thought, conceptualization, feeling, valuing, and acting has to be enacted through neural and chemical activity within the brain-in-a-body-in-a-world. The brain needs a body and a world in order to survive and function, but without neural activity, none of the processes in the list of "mental" operations just mentioned can occur. Most neuroscientists realize that the mind is not just the brain (even though there is no mind without a brain), but since they spend their entire lives struggling to understand how brains work, it is understandable that they are prone to regard the brain as the locus of the action of cognition. When they are suitably reflective, however, they of course know that there is no mind, thought, valuing, feeling, or acting without a brain-in-a-body-in-an-environment, with each dimension being absolutely indispensable. Even if there could someday, via new technologies, be a brain in a vat, there could never be a mind in a vat, because "mind" requires processes of shared meaning arising from our engagement with our surroundings—surroundings that cannot be contained within any vat (Putnam 1981). It follows from this that we should mostly avoid locutions such as "Fear happens in the amygdala (and other organs)," or "Planning and inference take place in the prefrontal cortical areas," because the fear, planning, and inference, involve the person's ongoing engagement with their environment, and so they are not merely brain episodes.

A Nondualistic, Nonrepresentational Theory of Mind

Once we recognize the primacy of organism-environment interactions and the depth and breadth of experience, then all ontological dualisms are out. Distinctions like inner/outer, mind/body, subject/object—and even organism/environment—are not ontological primitives marking out different kinds of being, but rather dimensions of the continuous processes of experience that we happen to focus on as important in our inquiries, for one reason or another. Discarding such dualisms (i.e., denying them status as ontological absolutes) requires us to concomitantly discard the representational theory of mind, by which I mean the view that thinking is conceiving and operating on inner mental representations, or symbols, that are somehow supposed to be connectable to an objective world outside the mind. As mentioned earlier, such a view holds that minds know their "ideas," "concepts," or "representations," which supposedly are attributes of the mental. Thinking is taken to be inner episodes of quasi-perception of mental entities (ideas/images/concepts) whereby we discern conceptual relations and draw inferences. In other words, mental representations are supposed to mediate between the inner (mental) processes and the outer world, thereby making knowledge of our world possible.

The classical pragmatists saw that what we call "inner" and "outer" are simply selected aspects of the processes of organism-environment interactions. They saw (what was later confirmed by cognitive neuroscience) that there is no mind-homunculus that processes mysterious inner representations. Consequently, there is no need for a synthesizing transcendent ego that supposedly unifies and judges our discrete inner sensations, ideas, or thoughts, because there are no "inner" representations in the first place. Since "inner" and "outer" are not two separate and distinct metaphysical realities, there is no need for a third thing—an inner representation—to mediate between the assumed two types or dimensions of reality.

Of course, neuroscientists are in the business of identifying patterns of neural connection and activation associated with cognitive and affective processes, and they are prone to call these "representations." These patterns of neural connectivity are, indeed, "in" the brain. However, these are not representations in the traditional sense of being objects in some inner *mental* realm, because there is no such realm and no homunculus or executive center in the brain that could experience these representations, note their relations, or see how they map onto some aspect(s) of the world. Instead, there are just patterns, qualities, and structures of organism-environment couplings—realized neurally and chemically in our bodies—that shape our experience, both nonconscious and conscious. There is the much-at-once-ness of experience (James [1911] 1979), within which there are discriminative selections that direct the organism's engagement with its world. All this discrimination and discernment is realized through activated functional clusters of neurons and chemical processes, but none of this requires the existence of some inner interpreter whose job it is to "read" the meaning of the patterns and strengths of neural connections.

Some will protest by observing that even the best neuroscientists routinely employ the language of "representations" in their accounts of cognitive, conative, and affective phenomena. And so they do. Such talk is especially common in accounts of neural "maps" (e.g., Edelman 1992; Damasio 1999; Feldman 2006). What is meant by a "map" is a spatial relation of neurons or clusters of neurons in cortical sheets that preserves the corresponding topological relations of objects, events, and qualities in our experience of our environment as it interacts with our sensory systems. For example, there are auditory neural maps in which what we experience as "adjacent" pitch tones (A to B, or B to C, etc.) are "represented" in the spatial relation of neurons in the auditory cortex (above the ears). Thus, neurons activated when we hear middle A are located in auditory cortex next to those activated in hearing the pitch middle B, and those for middle C are located next to those for B.

However, this use of the term "representations" does *not* support the traditional representational theory of mind, because it does not say that hearing adjacent notes or pitches consists in some inner locus of awareness (often referred to as ego, mind, consciousness) interpreting aspects of particular neural maps as adjacent pitches. We do not perceive our neural maps! Instead, we perceive the *pitches*—partly because of the nature of our auditory environment (ambient sound waves), partly because of the structure of our inner ear, and partly because of neural maps in the activated neuronal clusters in our auditory cortex. The firings of those adjacent neuronal assemblies in some temporal sequence *just is* our hearing of the successive pitches middle A, B, C. We are not possessed of some mysterious inner ego that *interprets* the meaning of alleged inner auditory representations (maps) that have been given rise to by environmental cues. Consequently, there is no third thing—the mental representation—needed to mediate between self and world.

Notice that, on this view, humans were never separated, either ontologically or epistemically, from their world, because "mind," consciousness, meaning, thought, feeling, and inference are all just emergent phenomena and functions based on the structures and activities of the organism as it engages the organized energies of its environment.

Concepts Are Embodied, and They Go Beyond Their Neural Dimensions

If there are no ghostly inner entities (representations) to serve as the content of our thoughts, then what *is* there to serve as the stuff of conceptualization and reasoning? One might ask, "Where, and what, *are* these ideas or concepts that nearly all philosophers seem to regard as the objects and content of our thoughts?" The answer to this question that one finds in both pragmatist accounts of mind and recent cognitive neuroscience is that what we call "concepts" are motivated selections of qualities and structures from the much-at-once-ness of experience that are realized through activated patterns of neural connectivity and chemical processes in the body. Concepts are not abstract entities that could possibly be contained in some mental arena or psychic processing plant. If they are not located *in* something called "the mind," then what are they *in*? Perhaps one might say that concepts are in the brain, in the body, and in the world, all at once. However, these metaphors of containment simply reinforce the very inner/outer dualism we are trying to overcome. It would probably be less misleading if we said that the whole inner/outer dichotomy is simply not appropriate for explaining how we feel, conceptualize, reason, value, and act. Instead, we should say that concepts are realized via functionally bound clusters of neurons that are connected and coactivated as part of our embodied interactions with aspects of our environment.

One way to explore the nature of what we call "concepts" is to ask what it means to have a concept of, say, a chair. Most people assume what George Lakoff (1987) called the "classical objectivist theory of categories." The objectivist theory claims that a concept like *chair* is defined by a unique set of properties (e.g., piece of furniture, made to be sat on, capable of supporting a human body, typically having four legs) that make that object a chair (as opposed to, say, a sofa, bench, or table). However, as Lakoff has pointed out in considerable detail, there is ample cognitive science research showing that human brains do not, for the most part, work the way the classical theory claims. Instead, having a concept of a chair amounts to possessing the ability to simulate neurally certain specific kinds of experiences associated with chairs.

According to what has come to be known as the "simulation theory of meaning" (Feldman 2006; Bergen 2012), our understanding of a concept of some particular object or event consists in our ability to simulate a series of perceptions, body movements, feelings, emotions, and appraisals that are involved in our bodily and social engagement with those particular kinds of objects we call chairs. Benjamin Bergen (2012) has surveyed a large number of experimental studies showing how, as we hear or read certain words and sentences describing objects, persons, actions, events, and scenes, there is in our brain a partial activation of the clusters of functionally integrated neuronal assemblies that are involved when we actually see, touch, and interact with that object or person within a scene or an event. What is activated is only a portion of the neuronal clusters involved in actual perception and action. For example, in thinking of chairs, a subset of the neural connections that would be involved in seeing various kinds of chairs would be activated, such as simulating possible views and perspectives I might have as I walk around different chairs. There would also be an activation of selected parts of our motor and premotor cortex that are involved in our actually sitting on, lifting, and moving chairs. So, part of the meaning of "chair" would be the range of visual, tactile, olfactory, auditory, and motor interactions we have, or might possibly have, with chairs. Besides sensory and motor simulation, there would also be some activation of the sorts of feelings and emotions associated with our experience of chairs. Finally, there would be a simulation of possible social and cultural settings, practices, and events in which chairs play an important role in our lives. Our repeated experiences with various chairs would lead us to develop cognitive prototypes for central members of the category "chair" (Rosch 1975), so that certain kinds of possible simulated interactions with chairs would be more likely to occur in certain cultural settings. Consequently, whenever I see a chair, imagine a chair, or read or hear "chair," there would be complex simulative activity in my brain and body of these sensory, motor, affective, and cultural dimensions (Feldman 2006; Bergen 2012).

An Embodied View of Meaning

The simulation theory of meaning attempts to give an account of how meaning emerges for organisms that are embedded and acting in the world. It thus provides a radical alternative to disembodied views that claim that an account of the operations of mind can be given without any serious inclusion of how our bodies and brains work to generate, constrain, and open up meaning in and through our ongoing engagement with our environments. For the pragmatist, who denies mind/body dualism, therefore, the central problem about meaning is to explain how organisms with our types of bodies and brains could have evolved systems capable of performing the full range of cognitive processes, from the ability to experience objects, qualities, and events all the way up to our most creative achievements of thought and communication.

The view of meaning that is emerging from recent second-generation cognitive science research is roughly pragmatist: the meaning of any particular thing, event, or symbol is what it points to by way of experiences—experiences past, present, and future. The meaning of a given term is not some ghostly inner conceptual entity, but is instead realized as a set of activations of related and interconnected functionally organized neuronal clusters that are associated with that term (where the term has come to be associated with an object, person, quality, relation, event, etc.). As Charles Sanders Peirce argued in his celebrated theory of semiotics, meaning is a tripartite relation between a sign, an aspect of a situation picked out by that sign, and a living organism to and for which that sign has meaning. In Dewey's terms, a sign has meaning insofar as it calls up for that subject some past, present, or future (possible) experiences. Consequently, signs do not have meaning *in themselves*, as if a sentence could stand in an objective relation to some mind-independent state of affairs in the world. Rather, a sign is meaningful for a subject engaged in ongoing interaction with its surroundings, both physical and cultural.

As a result of this organism-sign-referent connectedness, the meaning of anything is shaped (1) by the nature of the perceiver/conceiver (i.e., one's brain and body); (2) by one's cultural embeddedness in systems of meaning, valuation, and action; and (3) by how the relevant environment is structured. Besides implicating some structured environment, meaning thus depends on the bodily makeup of the organism for whom things and events are meaningful, as well as their interpersonal relations. This is the reality behind my earlier claim that "you can only think what your brain, body, and environment (physical and cultural) allow you to think."

One may substitute for the word *think* in this sentence any of a number of terms, such as *understand, grasp the meaning of, perceive, conceive, feel, act, know, value*, and so on.

Examples will help to illustrate some of the bodily sources of meaning. In *Philosophy in the Flesh* (1999), Lakoff and I surveyed some of the ways our bodily makeup and our environments give rise to our spatial relations concepts. Spatial relations like front/back, near/far, right/left, up/down, center/periphery, in/out, and over/under are based on the patterns that emerge from the ways our particular types of bodies interact with their surroundings. For example, *up* and *down* are important concepts to us, because we are bodily creatures who can sometimes stand erect in a gravitational field in which we experience things going up and coming back down. There is no *up* and *down* intrinsically in the nature of the cosmos. Rather, *up* and *down* are defined relative to our embodied being, orientation, and movement in the world. Cultures the world over project body-part relations onto objects and scenes, such as when we speak of the *foot* of a bed, a mountain, or a sheet of paper. Clocks have *faces* and *hands*, but no *feet*. Rivers have *arms* and *head*waters. Our body and its generic relations to aspects of its environment provide images, schemas, and models for understanding not just our physical surroundings and spatial relations, but even relations between abstract metaphorical entities (as in, "Prices have *skyrocketed* since the drought," "The department *head* ran the faculty meeting," and "She showed us the *face* of things to come").

Our spatial relations concepts and body-part projections are based on meaning structures like UP/DOWN (i.e., VERTICALITY), which Lakoff and I (Lakoff 1987; M. Johnson 1987; Lakoff and Johnson 1999) have named "image schemas." Given the ways human bodies are typically (but not universally) put together, we are likely to be able to discriminate a large number of recurring patterns of organism-environment interaction that are intrinsically meaningful to us. Consider, for example, how people who have use of their legs routinely move around in their environment. There is a recurrent pattern to these acts of locomotion: A mover (person or animal) moves certain body parts (e.g., legs, torso, arms) using certain physiologically constrained gaits (such as walking, skipping, or running), with varying speeds (e.g., slow, medium, fast), and exerting varying levels of energy (e.g., trudging along versus scampering). There thus emerges what we might call a body-based LOCOMOTION schema, consisting of the following structural elements that can be realized via different parameterizations: mover (e.g., animal or person), gait (e.g., walk, run, skip, hop), speed (slow, medium, fast), effort (on a scale of exertion), and body part (e.g., leg, hand, foot, knee) (Dodge and Lakoff 2005). Different acts of locomotion can be characterized by inserting the relevant values of the parameters of the schema, such as varying the speed parameter from slow (= walk) to fast (= run). The neural systems governing such parameters of action have been fairly well mapped out, such as how the different gaits of a cat or a horse are generated.

In a similar fashion, a large number of body-based image schemas arising in perception and action have been identified and analyzed as operating in conceptual systems of cultures around the world, such as CONTAINER, SOURCE-PATH-GOAL, OBJECT, ACTION, VERTICALITY, BALANCE, COMPULSIVE FORCE, ITERATION, STRAIGHT, CENTER/PERIPHERY, LOCOMOTION, ATTRACTION, BLOCKAGE, and many more (see Hampe 2005 and Lakoff and Narayanan, forthcoming, for an extensive list). The embodied meaning hypothesis entails that all languages around the world will make use of many of the available image schemas to express meaning relations, though not always the same exact set. There is ample evidence that languages vary regarding which image schemas they use and how they are specifically elaborated, but the appropriation of such image schemas in conceptualization and reasoning appears to be a universal phenomenon. As Ellen Dodge and George Lakoff conclude: "We have seen that there is great cross-linguistic diversity in spatial-relations terms and their use of schematic structure. Languages differ as to the basic spatial distinctions they make, the combinations of distinctions they 'package' together in their spatial-relations terms, and the grammatical class membership of these spatial terms. . . . However, we have also seen that these spatial-relations terms can instead be analyzed as complex combinations of more primitive image-schematic structures" (2005, 67). One simple example of this combination of image-schematic structures is the semantics of the English word *into*. In English, *into* is understood via a blending of a CONTAINER schema (with a boundary, exterior, and interior) and a SOURCE-PATH-GOAL schema (with a source point, path, and destination). The source of the SOURCE-PATH-GOAL schema is mapped onto the exterior of the CONTAINER schema, and the goal onto the interior, with the path of motion running from outside the bounded area to the interior. Thus, the meaning of *into* involves motion starting from outside a container, crossing its boundary, and ending within the bounded area (as in "Aunt May sauntered *into* the parlor").

One might acknowledge the bodily basis of our concrete concepts (concepts for physical objects, events, and actions), but still wonder whether the embodied meaning hypothesis is capable of explaining abstract concepts, such as love, mind, knowledge, freedom, democracy, and thought.

An important part of the answer to this question is conceptual metaphor theory (Lakoff and Johnson 1980, 1999; Kövecses 2010; Dancygier and Sweetser 2014), which has supplied more than thirty years of research into the ways our abstract concepts are defined by vast systems of metaphors, in which we recruit the meaning and inference patterns from a body-based or social domain of experience in order to understand and reason about an abstract, or nonconcrete, domain of experience. To cite just one example, consider the meaning of the sentence "The presidential candidate came out of the closet." The use of "out of" activates a body-based CONTAINER schema, plus a SOURCE-PATH-GOAL schema, as we just saw with the semantics of "into," only this time the source maps onto the interior of the bounded region and the goal onto the exterior. The literal interpretation of this sentence has the candidate physically located initially in his or her closet and then exiting that enclosure along a path from the interior to the exterior. But in the metaphorical interpretation, the closet is a metaphorical container that "hides" the knowledge of the candidate's sexual orientation. The interior is metaphorically a space of the unknown, private, and inaccessible, whereas the exterior space is metaphorically the known, public, and accessible (Lindner 1981). Consequently, the candidate's coming "out of the closet" is understood as a revelation (a making public) of his or her sexual orientation. There exists a large and rapidly growing literature on the operation of large-scale conceptual metaphors in different cultures, practices, behaviors, and forms of communication (Lakoff and Johnson 1980; Gibbs 2008; Kövecses 2010; Dancygier and Sweetser 2014).

Image schemas, spatial relations, conceptual metaphors, and other types of body-based meaning are not linguistic per se; instead, they are conceptual, and they develop and operate in prelinguistic children and in meaningful activities that extend far beyond or beneath language in adult life. This shows that meaning is not just linguistic in nature, since there are many forms of meaning-making that do not depend on language. Embodied meaning processes like these lie at the heart of various, mostly nonlinguistic forms of expression and communication, such as painting, sculpture, visual advertising, film, music, dance, architecture, spontaneous gesture, ritual acts, and performance. In film, for example, in addition to spoken dialogue, there are all sorts of ways meanings are communicated through juxtaposition of images, temporal flow of action, sound effects, music, lighting, camera angle, and so forth (Tikka 2008). In other words, embodied meaning reaches deep into our visceral connection with everything that surrounds us and makes up the stuff of our lives, and it is not dependent on language, but rather underlies language and makes it possible.

Feeling and Emotion in Meaning and Thought

The classical pragmatists knew well that feeling and emotion are an essential part of our capacity to experience meaning, to understand, to conceptualize, to reason, and to value something. However, when pragmatism was eclipsed in professional philosophy by so-called analytic philosophy, this core insight was neglected and even denied. Analytic philosophy's exclusive focus on concepts, propositions, and inferences reinstated the thought/feeling and cognition/emotion dichotomies that have plagued philosophy throughout most of its history. Fortunately, with the emergence of second-generation cognitive science, research on the role of emotions in thought processes has recovered many of the lost insights from earlier pragmatist accounts of meaning and thought.

In his *Principles of Psychology* (1890), William James famously employed the term "thought-feeling" to emphasize the presence of feeling in all our thought processes. He even extended this to the claim that logical relations are *felt* just as much as they are thought. We feel, he boldly asserted, the direction, tendency, and connection of our patterns of thinking: "If there be such things as feelings at all, *then so surely as relations between objects exist in rerum natura, so surely, and more surely, do feelings exist to which these relations are known.* There is not a conjunction or a preposition, and hardly an adverbial phrase, syntactic form, or inflection of voice, in human speech, that does not express some shading or other of relations which we at some moment actually feel to exist between the larger objects of our thought" (James [1890] 1950, 1:238; italics in the original). James also argued that every thought of a particular object or event is surrounded by a "halo" or "fringe" of felt tendencies and connections that make up the field of meaning relations for that particular concept and that provide the basis for inferences.

Dewey went even further than James in claiming that our very capacity to think and reason intelligently depends on our felt sense of the entire situation in which our thinking emerges: "The selective determination and relation of objects in thought is controlled by a pervasive and internally integrating quality, so that failure to acknowledge the situation leaves, in the end, the logical force of objects and their relations inexplicable" ([1930] 1988, 246). His point was that the felt qualitative unity of a given situation is what gives us a sense of which relations and connections are relevant for our thought. Without this grounding in the felt sense of a situation, our thoughts would float free from our embodied engagement with our world. Within a relatively coherent and unified situation, our ability to "make sense" of any object, act, or event requires us to grasp—at a felt level—what is going on:

> This state of things in which qualitatively different feelings are not just had but are significant of objective differences, is mind. Feelings are no longer just felt. They have and they make *sense,* record and prophesy.
>
> That is to say, difference in qualities (feelings) of acts when employed as indications of acts performed and to be performed and as signs of their consequences, *mean* something. And they mean it directly. . . . Feelings make sense. (Dewey [1925] 1981, 198)

This classical pragmatist emphasis on the crucial role of feelings and emotions in meaning and thought was discarded and even ridiculed in the last three-quarters of the twentieth century during which analytic philosophy rose to prominence. Fortunately, recent cognitive science research on thought processes has helped us rediscover the importance of emotions and feelings in what and how we think (Tucker 2017). For example, Antonio Damasio (1994, 1999, 2003, 2010) has shown the indispensability of emotions for intelligent social reasoning. He distinguishes between emotional response patterns and feelings of emotions. Emotional response patterns are mostly automatic processes of bodily response generated by the body's monitoring of how its states are being affected by changes in its environment, thus leading to actions geared toward either maintaining or reestablishing a homeostasis, or dynamic equilibrium, within the body. Emotional response patterns evolved, generally, to keep the organism functioning relatively well as it confronts changes in its surroundings. Feelings arise on those occasions when we become aware of the ongoing changes in our body state, as we engage our environment and make adjustments to it to reestablish our internal equilibrium. In short, we *feel* our bodies being affected by our perception of, and action in, our world. Damasio concludes, "Emotions are complex, largely automated programs of *actions* concocted by evolution. . . . Feelings of emotion, on the other hand, are composite *perceptions* of what happens in our body and mind when we are emoting" (2010, 109). Following James, Dewey, and Damasio, I (M. Johnson 2007) have argued that emotions are central to meaning, insofar as they constitute the body's response to its continuous assessment and evaluation of "how things are going" for it. What could be more meaningful to you than your ability to take the measure, meaning, and import of the affordances provided by your environment? Feelings allow us to do this.

The Aesthetic Dimensions of Meaning

As soon as we begin to appreciate the embodied character of meaning and thought, it becomes clear that when we focus on meaning as constituted by patterns, images, qualities, relations, feelings, and emotions, we are dealing with what has traditionally been the subject matter of aesthetic theory. Unfortunately, as I argued in the introduction, aesthetics has long been denigrated as dealing only with subjective aspects of experience and judgment, and therefore as not worthy of a place in theories of objective meaning, thinking, knowing, and valuing. Following Dewey's ([1925] 1981, [1934] 1987, [1938] 1991) lead, in *The Meaning of the Body: Aesthetics of Human Understanding* (M. Johnson 2007), I argued that any adequate theory of meaning will have to focus on those qualitative and affective dimensions of experience that have usually been regarded as operative mostly in our experience, appreciation, and creation of various arts, but are now recognized as lying at the heart of all our meaning-making.

An account of meaning that recognizes the central role of aesthetic dimensions is precisely what is required if we hope to explain how we make and experience meaning in a broad range of arts and human nonlinguistic (or more-than-linguistic) practices. We have to abandon the mistaken idea that meaning is solely, or even mostly, a linguistic phenomenon. Instead, linguistic meaning has to be seen as a development and refinement of embodied meaning processes that emerge from our visceral connections with our world. This broader and richer conception of meaning allows us to overcome two pervasive mistaken prejudices of Western cultures: (1) that only words and sentences have meaning proper, and therefore that (2) since many of the arts (e.g., painting, architecture, music, dance) are not intrinsically linguistic in character, we cannot really talk about meaning in the arts that goes beyond the linguistic.

In sharp contrast, once you see that meaning is about how objects, events, and qualities provide meaningful affordances for us, you find nonlinguistic meaning everywhere and you can then begin to understand how and why the arts can be so meaningful to us (Shusterman 2000; M. Johnson 2007; McConachie 2015). Aesthetic theories that assume that only language has meaning tend to end up trying to reduce our experience of the arts to language-like structures, and they consequently miss most of what is really going on in art. In contrast, when you start with the aesthetics of embodied meaning, you have the resources to explain a wide range of more-than-linguistic meaningful experiences in spontaneous gesture, painting, sculpture, architecture, dance, the theater arts, film, and ritual practice. Even better, you then have the resources to give a more experientially nuanced account of linguistic meaning that reveals its grounding in aspects of our sensory, motor, and affective experiences.

Experience Is Not Just Linguistic

Just as you have to pick your cognitive science (namely, second-generation cognitive science), if you hope to get an adequate embodied account of experience, mind, concepts, thought, values, and virtually everything else, likewise, you have to pick your pragmatism carefully. Not all pragmatism is the same. As we will see in considerable detail in chapter 3, there has recently emerged a movement known as linguistic (or analytic) pragmatism, which owes its origins mostly to the influential work of Richard Rorty, an analytically trained philosopher who came to see some common themes in traditions as apparently disparate as analytic philosophy, pragmatist philosophy, and European philosophy (Rorty 1979, 1982). Rorty *liked* Dewey's critique of all forms of dualism and his dismantling of any form of foundationalism concerning knowledge, truth, or values. What Rorty *didn't* like was Dewey's insistence that philosophy must arise from, reconstruct, and then return to "experience," in the sense I have articulated above (Rorty 1982). Rorty accused Dewey of trying to use the notion of experience to achieve some sort of epistemic grounding—a place where philosophy might root—of the very sort Dewey had taken such pains to deconstruct throughout his career. Consequently, Rorty argued that what Dewey proposed as an "empirical metaphysics" was just another foundationalist metaphysics (Rorty 1982). According to Rorty, since any metaphysics is by definition foundationalist, there is no good metaphysics, and philosophy should confine itself to critique of ontological, epistemological, moral, and political foundationalism, rather than try to articulate a rich notion of experience as the basis for philosophical reflection.

Rorty's rejection of metaphysics rested on his claim that everything we can experience, think, know, and communicate is shaped by our language (or what he called our "vocabularies"), so that our only legitimate analytic focus should be on language practices, since we have no unmediated access to some world that supposedly lies beyond language.

Students of Rorty, such as Robert Brandom (2011), have subsequently developed this position into an extensive corpus of writings on how to understand the conditions for justified assertions and reason giving in making claims about knowledge and values. This work has plenty of insights about speech act and argument conditions, but you will not find any account of either the depth and qualitative richness of experience or the central role of embodiment in the experience, making, and communication of meaning. Not surprisingly, since the body is basically ignored, you will not find any adequate treatment of the importance of the embodied aesthetic dimensions of experience, because they are deemed to be irrelevant to our knowledge justification practices.

As soon as you put the modifying adjective *linguistic* or *analytic* in front of the term *pragmatism*, the deed is done. Analytic pragmatism is what you get when you keep the founding assumptions of analytic philosophy of mind and language and simply add the pragmatist insight that speaking and communicating are social *actions*, and so subject to social and institutional constraints. In like fashion, when you add the modifier *linguistic* to *pragmatism*, you are left with meaning being confined to language, which leaves out both the prelinguistic embodiment of meaning and also the role of qualities, feelings, and emotions in unifying and defining the character of a situation.

What this means is that, once pragmatism is eviscerated and narrowed into analytic/linguistic pragmatism, most of the common ground and possibilities for mutual development between embodied cognitive science and classical pragmatism are lost. Take away the embodiment of mind, meaning, and thought, and you are right back in first-generation cognitive science, with its view of meaning as propositional and constrained only by speech act, logical, and epistemic rules. You have a view of meaning, thought, language, and values divorced from the embodied aesthetic dimensions of experience. What we need, therefore, is an embodied cognitive science in dialogue with an experientially based pragmatism, if we hope to construct an adequate theory of mind, thought, and communication.

Meaning and the Seven E's

In those cognitive science and philosophy of mind orientations that appreciate the pragmatist insight about the primacy of ongoing organism-environment interaction, it has become quite popular over the past decade to speak of "the 4 E's" to indicate that cognition is *embodied, embedded, enactive*, and *extended*. To the traditional 4 E's, I am thus urging the addition of a fifth E, *emotional*; a 6th E, *evolutionary*; and a seventh, *exaptative*. The seven E's are a convenient way to summarize some of the key tenets of the perspective on mind, meaning, thought, and language that are shared by classical pragmatism and embodied cognitive science, as follows: (1) Our capacities for meaning-making, understanding, and reasoning are *evolved structures* that emerged over our ongoing evolutionary history through the appropriation of prior capacities for perceiving, doing, and feeling. (2) This appropriation of earlier structures and capacities that are repurposed for "higher-order" functions, such as abstract conceptualization and reasoning, is in evolutionary theory known as *exaptation*. (3) Both as our species evolves and in each individual's cognitive development, consciousness, mind, meaning, thought, and value are grounded in our *embodied* engagement with our world, and they are emergent phenomena arising from the increasing functional complexity of the organism. (4) These phenomena exist only because mind is, through our embodiment, *embedded* within our surroundings that offer affordances for our perceptions and actions. (5) The term *enactive* captures the way our ongoing transactions with aspects of our environment reconfigure experience. Meaning and value are enacted in the very process by which the organism engages its environment. (6) *Extended* mind recognizes the many ways we off-load cognitive processes, resources, and products onto structures in our environment. In fact, it recognizes that there is no mind or thinking that doesn't appropriate and depend on its surroundings outside our skins, so to speak. (7) Finally, the *emotional* dimensions of consciousness, meaning, and mind mark the felt, qualitative dimensions of our enactive coupling with, and remaking of, parts of our surroundings.

Embedded, Extended Meaning Requires Embodied Meaning

Recently, a lively in-house debate has arisen within what I am calling the 7E (previously 4E) community about whether there is a fundamental and irresolvable tension between the embodied and extended aspects of mind (Clark 2012). If aspects of meaning, thought, and mind can actually be deposited into the world beyond the organism, then it would appear that mind must go beyond its embodied dimensions. If mind, consciousness, and thought can (at least in part) be lodged "out there," then they cannot be only phenomena "in here" (i.e., within the embodied mind). This is an interesting and potentially fruitful debate that can help us sharpen our understanding of what it means to ground everything on organism-environment interactions. Here I want only to note that since meaning requires a sign, its referent (i.e., the experiences it indicates), and an embodied person to whom the sign is meaningful, it is not correct to assert that any of the objects, patterns, or actions that make up the world of extended mind outside and beyond our skins could have meaning in themselves. *Nothing in the "extended" world has any intrinsic meaning in itself, because in order to have a meaning relation, there must be someone for or to whom that object, relation, quality, or event is meaningful.* Meaning has to be enacted in the brain and body of a more or less functioning organism that possesses certain specific capacities (Tucker 2017). What we call "pens," "clouds," and "quarks" do not *mean* anything *in themselves*; instead, creatures like us experience them as meaningful patterns in our environment; because of our bodily makeup; because of the affordances provided us by our environment relative to our needs, values, and interests; and because of shared meaning and language.

In short, there is no extended mind or extended meaning without embodied mind and meaning. This crucially important point is easily overlooked by some extended-mind theorists, because when they talk about how elements, procedures, and products of mental operations are off-loaded onto the environment, they have already *assumed* that those off-loaded structures are meaningful, forgetting most of what was required to make them meaningful in the first place (namely, an at least partially functioning brain, in an at least partially functioning body, operating within an environment that is physical, interpersonal, and cultural). Those who speak of externalized aspects of mind, consciousness, and meaning as *entirely* "out there" in the "external" world, independent of people, are falling into the same error as those objectivists who think that sentences could have meaning merely by standing in relation to some external state of affairs, completely independent of the being for whom the sentence is meaningful.

I am thus urging the view that an adequate account of mind and thought will have to involve *all* the seven E's, with the acknowledgment that none of them alone adequately captures what goes into meaning, experience, and action.

It's Values All the Way Down

If everything starts from organism-environment interaction, then we begin, from the get-go, with values, insofar as to be an organism is to have certain needs that must be satisfied for its continued existence and flourishing. To live is to have values, which means that, as active organisms, we are preferentially directed toward specific states of affairs in the course of our interactions with our surroundings. As Damasio (2010) has pointed out, the continued existence of any organism requires a permeable boundary within which the conditions of life are maintained, and this requires the maintenance of homeostasis within the organism. If this homeostatic dynamic equilibrium is substantially disrupted, the organism will fail and eventually die. The very conditions of life thus give rise to what Damasio calls an ur-value: "For whole organism, then, the primitive of value is *the physiological state of living tissue within a survivable, homeostatic range*" (2010, 49; italics in the original).

The point here is that contemporary science has confirmed Dewey's pragmatist claim that values are part of nature, so we need not posit any special transcendent source of values to explain our biological, social, and moral values. Damasio goes so far as to hypothesize that even our highest moral values are grounded in the biological imperatives of our lives: "My hypothesis is that objects and processes we confront in our daily lives acquire their assigned value by reference to this primitive of naturally selected organism value. The values that humans attribute to objects and activities would bear some relation, no matter how indirect or remote, to the two following conditions: first, the general maintenance of living tissue within the homeostatic range suitable to its current context; second, the particular regulation required for the process to operate within the sector of the homeostatic range associated with well-being relative to the current context" (2010, 49).

Since people are not just biological organisms, they will have a number of other values that go beyond their need for sustaining the conditions of life. I (M. Johnson 2014) have argued that besides values arising from our biological makeup, there would also be values tied to our intimate interpersonal relations with other people (e.g., our need for nurturance, affection, care), values emerging from our role as members of larger social groups (e.g., our sense of justice, rights, and group responsibilities), and values pertinent to our quest for meaningful and fulfilled lives.

All these values are natural, which is to say that they arise for us given the kinds of bodily, interpersonal, and cultural beings we are. There is therefore no need to justify values as coming from some absolute or transcendent source. It is simply an experimental issue of determining what kinds of activities we value (both nonconsciously and consciously), what helps us live harmoniously with others, and what tends to give our lives meaning and a sense of purpose.

Toward a Consummated Union of Pragmatism and Cognitive Science

The previous list presents just some of the areas of overlap between classical pragmatism and recent cognitive science that suggest potentially productive avenues of dialogue and ongoing engagement between the two orientations. I have argued that the cognitive science of the embodied mind gives us considerable evidence to support many of the defining assumptions of the classical pragmatism of Peirce, James, and Dewey, though not of linguistic or analytic pragmatism.

So, I am hoping that the romance between pragmatism and cognitive science will grow in depth and meaning. In spite of the fact that they appear to have gotten off on the wrong foot in their early days of courtship, they now appear to have fallen for each other. Let us hope we have the pleasure of soon getting to know their lovely offspring. The ideas and theories arising from the intercourse of these two perspectives will grow like young babies who have learned to walk and are now discovering the wonders of human language and other forms of creative communication. May the union of classical pragmatism and second-generation cognitive science grow and prosper, just like it always does in our favorite romantic comedies.

CHAPTER 2

Philosophy's Debt to Metaphor

Throughout most of the twentieth century, the hegemonic orientation that came to be known as analytic philosophy conceived the core task of philosophy to be the rigorous analysis of a widely recognized set of key concepts that have defined the philosophical enterprise since the rise of pre-Socratic philosophy in the sixth and fifth centuries BCE. Among these allegedly core concepts were: *thing, Being, cause, force, reality, mind, perception, feeling, concept, thought, imagination, understanding, knowledge, truth, reason, logic, event, action, person, will, freedom, good, justice, rights, responsibility, value,* and *political state*.

Since the emergence of cognitive linguistics in the late 1970s, extensive cross-cultural research has amassed a large body of evidence indicating that virtually all our abstract concepts, of the sort just mentioned, are not literal, but are rather defined by multiple metaphors. The consequences of this for philosophy are startling, as I will argue. We therefore need to understand what this means for our conception of the nature, purpose, and conduct of philosophical reflection, which must be reconstructed in light of these new discoveries about mind, thought, and language.

What's at Issue in the Question of Metaphor?

Philosophy's debt to metaphor is profound and immeasurable. Without metaphor there would be no philosophy. However, philosophy's debt is no greater, nor less, than that of any other significant human intellectual field or discipline, insofar as all their fundamental concepts are metaphorically defined. Philosophers must use the same conceptual resources possessed by any human being, so the potential for any philosophy to make sense of a person's life depends directly on the fact that all of us are metaphorical animals; that is, that our abstract conceptualization and reasoning are shaped by metaphor.

What I have just claimed is not now, nor has it ever been, widely accepted by philosophers. In fact, for most of our philosophical history, the idea that metaphor lies at the heart of human conceptualization and reasoning has been rejected.[1] One could even make a crude but very telling distinction between two types of philosophy: objectivist-literalist philosophies that see metaphor as a dispensable linguistic appurtenance and those that see philosophies as creative elaborations of basic conceptual metaphors.

The history of Western philosophy is, for the most part, one long development of the objectivist dismissal of metaphor, punctuated by rare bold declarations of the pervasiveness of metaphor in thought, of which Nietzsche is the most famous proponent (M. Johnson 1981, introduction). Where a philosopher stands on this key issue can be determined by their answer to one question: Are our abstract concepts defined by metaphor, or not? Once the question is formulated in this manner, it is easy to see the profound philosophical implications at issue. For instance, if our most fundamental abstract concepts—such as those for causation, events, will, thought, reason, knowledge, mind, justice, and rights—are irreducibly metaphorical, then philosophical analysis must involve the analysis, criticism, and elaboration of the metaphorical concepts out of which philosophies are made. If, on the other hand, you believe that our most important philosophical concepts are, in the final analysis, literal, then you will regard metaphor as cognitively insignificant, and you will relegate it to what you disparagingly regard as some distant corner of philosophy, typically the unfairly maligned field of aesthetics.

Anyone who thinks that there is really nothing very important at stake here should consider the following. There are a number of perennial philosophical questions that arise over and over again throughout history any time you reflect on the nature of human experience. These are questions such as: What is mind, and how does it work? What does it mean to be a person? Is there such a thing as human will, and is it free? What is the nature of reality? What can I know, and how can I go about gaining that knowledge? What things or states are "good" and should therefore be pursued? Are certain actions morally required of us? Does God exist (and what difference would it make)? Is there any meaning to human existence, or is life absurd? *Both the framing of these questions and the kinds of answers we give to them depend on metaphor. You cannot address any of these questions without engaging metaphor.* Consequently, an adequate philosophy must include an extensive inquiry into the workings of metaphor and how it shapes our most important philosophical ideas.

Philosophical Concepts Are Metaphorical

From a practical standpoint, it is obviously not possible to make an exhaustive survey showing that *all* our philosophical concepts are defined by conceptual metaphors. Instead, I will examine one key representative concept—causation—to indicate its metaphorical constitution, and I will point to research suggesting that we use metaphors to define *all* our abstract concepts, and thus all our philosophical concepts.

I have selected causation as the exemplary metaphorically defined concept because it is hard to imagine a metaphysical concept that is more fundamental. It lies at the heart of all the sciences, is pervasive in our folk theories of the world, and is a philosophical lynchpin of virtually every ontology. When the first substantial metaphor analysis of our causal concepts emerged within cognitive linguistics over three decades ago, it became clear that the implications of this research were stunning in the way they challenged the traditional view of causation. In my own analytic philosophical training, most of the books and articles I read assumed science to be a superior form of knowledge, partly because of its ability to give causal explanations of events. In one philosophical treatise after another, I was struck by how philosophers referred to "causes" as if they were objective individual forces operating in the world and as if there existed basically one kind of natural causation (as revealed in expressions such as "X caused Y" and "The cause of Y is X"). Each "event" (as effect) was supposedly the result of a distinct individual "cause." In an attempt to explain human actions, many philosophers also spoke of "agent causality," in order to carve out a space for human "willing," which supposedly involved reason and deliberation. However, in the so-called physical world of material things, natural causes ruled the day. So, there seemed to be at least one central type of cause (i.e., natural), but not more than two types (adding agent causation to physical causation), and both conceptions were thought to be literal, not metaphorical. Causes were alleged to be discrete literal forces in the world.

This picture, as we will see, turns out to be mistaken, and badly so. It is a mistake that has disastrous consequences. To see why this is so, let's begin with an analysis of one of our most often used concepts of causation—that of causation as the operation of a physical force. Once detailed analyses were performed on the semantics of our causal terms, the metaphorical nature of this concept became quite evident. In cognitive linguistics the study of causal concepts emerged from the study of how people conceptualize events in general. The first important conceptual metaphor system for events involved an understanding of change of state as (metaphorical) motion from one location to another, according to the following general mapping:[2]

The LOCATION EVENT-STRUCTURE Metaphor

Source domain (motion in space)		*Target domain (event)*
Locations In Space	→	States
Movements From One Location To Another	→	Change Of State
Physical Forces	→	Causes
Forced Movement	→	Causation
Self-Propelled Movements	→	Actions
Destinations	→	Purposes
Paths To Destinations	→	Means To Ends
Impediments To Motion	→	Difficulties

The above diagram is useful in indicating the directionality of the mappings that constitute the metaphorical concept; that is, the direction of the mapping moves from the source domain of physical motion to the target domain of general event structure (i.e., not just physical motion events, but all kinds of events). In discussing the submappings that make up the metaphor (such as the mapping from spatial locations to states, using an arrow to indicate the direction of the mapping, from source domain to target domain) it is often more clear if we represent the submappings linguistically (as in STATES ARE (SPATIAL) LOCATIONS, and so I will hereafter often use this alternative form for stating the submappings of a metaphor.

The LOCATION EVENT-STRUCTURE metaphor comprises a vast complex system of several submappings, each of which is what Grady (1997) calls a "primary" metaphor. In English, the semantics of our terms for events is given by the detailed structure of the mappings. Each submapping supports a large number of expressions whose dependence on metaphor goes largely unnoticed in our ordinary discourse. For example, the submapping CHANGE OF STATE IS MOVEMENT underlies expressions such as "The water *went from* hot *to* cold," "The system is *moving toward* homeostasis," and "The pizza is *somewhere between* warm and cold." CAUSATION IS FORCED MOVEMENT is evident in "The fire *brought* the soup *to* a boil," "His treachery *pushed* the king *over the edge*," "The candidate's speech *threw* the crowd into a frenzy."

Notice how these submappings code various dimensions of what linguists call "aspect" and "manner," which concerns the means, manner, and temporal aspects of an action. For instance, we say "the stove *brought* the water to a boil" but not "the stove *threw* the water to a boil," and for a very good reason. In the source domain of physical forces and motions, to "bring" something to someone is to apply continuous force to an object to move it from one location to another. When metaphorically extended to causation in general, the semantics of *bring* thus entails continuous application of force to bring about change of state. Thus, *bringing* water to a boil entails the constant heating of the water until it boils (i.e., until it arrives at the metaphorical boiling state-location). *Throwing* a physical object, by contrast, involves an initial application of strong force with the object continuing to move to a new location, even after the force is no longer applied. Thus *threw*, according to the submapping, is not appropriate for the case of boiling water (which requires continuous causation), though it is just the right term for "Babe Ruth's home-run *threw* the crowd into a frenzy."

Now, how could a literalist philosopher have any adequate account of the semantics of *throw*, as revealed in this case of Ruth's home run? Will she say that there is a purely literal way to express the type of causation involved here? But there isn't. If we say, "Babe Ruth's home run *caused* the crowd to get emotionally excited," we lose the key semantic details expressed by *threw*. "Caused to get excited" does *not* capture the *manner* of the causation, which is rapid initial force followed by an extended trajectory after the initial event.

The crucial moral of this example is that the precise details of the semantics of basic causation terms are determined only by the submappings of the metaphors. The inferences we make about causal situations come from the metaphorical structure of our causation concepts. If, for example, you hear that the fire *brought* the water to a boil, you can infer that the heat from the fire was continuously applied to the pot of water being boiled. If you hear that the election of a president *threw* the whole country into turmoil, you can infer that there was a dramatic precipitating action (the election) that had strong, catastrophic effects on the nation. *You cannot grasp the meaning of the causal terms, nor can you do appropriate causal reasoning— without the metaphors.*

Moreover, the case of causation is even more complicated than it at first appears, because there turn out to be many different metaphorical conceptions of types of causation. Analyses to date reveal upward of twenty distinct metaphors that express twenty kinds of causation (Lakoff and Johnson 1999). A brief survey of just a few of these additional metaphors is highly instructive. It shatters the illusion of core literal (univocal) concepts of causation and of any objectivist philosophy that pretends to be founded on such concepts.

Consider, for instance, a second major metaphor system for certain types of causation: one that conceives of change of state or having an attribute (or property) as the acquisition of a possession.

The Object Event-Structure Metaphor

Attributes Are Possessions
Change Of State Is Movement Of Possession
Causation Is Transfer Of Possession
Purposes Are Desired Objects

The submapping Causation Is Transfer Of Possession is evident in expressions such as "Professor Johnson's lecture on causation *gave* me a headache, but the aspirin *took it away*," "Mary *gave* her cold *to* Janice," and "Janice *caught* Mary's cold." Moreover, even our common philosophical notion of a "property" is based on this metaphorical mapping. What does it mean for an object to "possess" a property? Property is something owned by a person, so when we say that some object *has or possesses a property*, we are saying that the property is bound to the object in a way that specifies a certain state the object is in. To have the property *blue* is to be blue in color. When something *loses* that property, it no longer manifests the features appropriate to that property. Additionally, there are many other submappings within this particular causation metaphor that specify various ways of acquiring a desired object, which equates metaphorically with acquiring a certain property or attribute and thus achieving a purpose. For example, there is the submapping Achieving A Purpose Is Getting Food, as in "I'm *hungry* for advancement," "All the best jobs were *gobbled up* early on," and "It was a *mouth-watering* opportunity." Each of the various ways we acquire food, such as hunting, fishing, and agriculture/gathering, show up in the language of our purposeful action, as in

TRYING TO ACHIEVE A PURPOSE IS HUNTING
Examples: "I'm still job *hunting.*" "She is *aiming* for rapid advancement in the firm." "Larry *bagged* a promotion." "That idea *won't hunt.*"

TRYING TO ACHIEVE A PURPOSE IS FISHING
Examples: "Ann *landed* a big promotion." "Before that, she *had a line out* for a new job." "My boss is always *fishing* for compliments." "Every night he's out *trolling* for a date."

TRYING TO ACHIEVE A PURPOSE IS AGRICULTURAL ACTIVITY
Examples: "Every worker should *reap the fruits* of his or her labor." "That promotion is *ripe for the picking.*" "Harry's been *cultivating* several job prospects."

TRYING TO ACHIEVE A PURPOSE IS GATHERING
Examples: "On the marketing project they were satisfied with *picking the low-hanging fruit.*" "She *garnered* the support of her coworkers." "They were *foraging for* even *the smallest* market *share.*"

Metaphorically based expressions like these are not just colloquialisms, used loosely in ordinary talk. Once again, the submappings of the metaphor specify the precise details of the semantics of causation and determine what types of inferences we will make. Some people harbor the illusion that good science would merely avoid such expressions in causal explanations. But, as it turns out, there is *no way* to avoid the use of one or another basic causal metaphor in science, and scientists reason on the basis of the entailments of the submappings of these metaphors.

In the social sciences, for example, there are a number of quite specific metaphors that can be used for the types of causal explanation appropriate for the science of those fields. One especially common case is the CAUSATION IS MOTION ALONG A PATH metaphor.

THE CAUSATION IS MOTION ALONG A PATH METAPHOR
Actions Are Self-Propelled Motions
An Actor Is A Traveler
States Are Locations
A Natural Course Of Action Is A Lone Path
Natural Causation Is Being On The Path
Results In Is Leading To
A Resulting Final State Is The End Of The Path

Examples: "Pot smoking *leads to* drug addiction." "As a nation, we're *careening* wildly *down* the *road to destruction.*" "That *path* will get you nowhere, man." "You're *heading for* catastrophe."

The CAUSATION IS MOTION ALONG A PATH metaphor plays a key role in certain types of causal explanation for human actions. It utilizes our common knowledge about motion through space to some destination: if you start down a certain path, you will naturally end up where that path leads you, unless something intervenes to retard or block your progress. Metaphorically, then, if you start down a certain "path" of action, it will typically lead you to a certain destination (end), unless something intervenes to retard or block your metaphorical movement. This argument is used by those who believe that certain actions or behaviors will necessitate a certain specific outcome in the ordinary course of events (as in the 1950s song lyric from "Hot Rod Lincoln": "I'll tell you son, you're gonna drive me to drinkin' / If you don't stop drivin' that hot rod Lincoln"). In politics the CAUSATION IS MOTION ALONG A PATH metaphor can be even more decisive. One often hears the argument that a certain third-world country is "on the road to democracy (read, capitalism)," so that, if we (the United States) will just eliminate any potential obstacles (i.e., we intervene politically, economically, militarily, or covertly), then that country will naturally and inevitably continue along the path to the desired end state (namely, *democracy-cum-capitalism!*). Millions of dollars and sometimes even the lives of citizens are sacrificed to supposedly insure the smooth unrestricted motion of some metaphorical entity (a country, an economy, or a political institution) along a metaphorical causal path to a metaphorically defined destination.

Another important metaphor in political and economic debate is the CAUSATION IS PLATE TECTONICS metaphor for social/political/economic change, which is appropriated from the geology of plate tectonics. According to the logic of the metaphor, continual, long-term application of "pressure" to a system, institution, or state will eventually result in a rapid, massive causal consequence. The rapid, surprising disintegration of the Soviet Union is supposed by some to be a classic example of this process. It is assumed that a number of economic, societal, and political forces operating over many decades eventually resulted in a massive rupture between the old and new regimes. Another manifestation of this conception is frequently brought to bear in our relations with "Third World" countries. Often, when large sustained infusions of funds or manpower do not appear to be producing the desired change in a government or economy (usually both), the CAUSATION IS PLATE TECTONICS metaphor is frequently invoked to argue for the continued commitment of resources by the US Congress, on the assumption that we need just a little bit more pressure to produce an eventual massive transformation.

The analysis of the full range of metaphors could be continued along similar lines. In *Philosophy in the Flesh* (1999), George Lakoff and I summarized the mappings and entailments of nearly twenty different causal metaphors, showing how several of them are employed within various sciences. A number of key philosophical points emerge from these analyses.

1. An adequate conceptual analysis (in this case, of causation concepts) must provide generalizations that explain the precise details of the semantics of the terms and must explain the inferences we make concerning those concepts. The details of the semantics and inference structure of each causal concept are provided by the submappings that jointly constitute the metaphor.
2. Nearly all the basic causation concepts we studied are metaphorical.
3. There appears to be what we called a "literal skeleton" shared by all causation concepts—namely, that a cause is a determining factor in a situation. However, this bare skeleton is far too underspecified to generate any serious causal reasoning in the sciences. It is the metaphors that give rise to the relevant conceptual structure and that constrain the appropriate causal inferences.
4. Several of the main causation metaphors are mutually inconsistent. In other words, there are significant metaphors that have incompatible ontologies. For example, in the LOCATION EVENT-STRUCTURE metaphor, STATES ARE (STATIONARY) LOCATIONS, and the object or agent changes by moving to a particular (metaphorical) state-location. In contrast, in the OBJECT EVENT-STRUCTURE metaphor, a state is an object that moves, rather than being a stationary location. Consequently, these two metaphors cannot be reduced to a consistent literal concept, because they involve different ontologies regarding states.
5. Causation is thus a massive radial category (Lakoff 1987). At the center of the category is the closest thing to a literal conception—something like the application of physical force to an object that results in a change in its state or location. One example of this is what we call "billiard-ball causation." Other less prototypical kinds of causation are metaphorically defined.

If we take stock of the argument so far, the results are devastating for any literalist/objectivist philosophy. At least with respect to causation, there is no single literal concept of *cause*, nor are there even two or three basic literal concepts. There is no set of necessary and sufficient conditions that define all causal concepts. Instead, there are fifteen or more metaphorical concepts used by ordinary people, scientists, and philosophers in their reasoning about causation. This conclusion does not undermine science at all. It only reminds us that different scientific approaches rely on different metaphorical concepts and frames, concepts that can be more or less appropriate in different situations and that dictate what counts as evidence and argument within a given science. What these analyses *do* undermine are objectivist philosophies that accept a classical theory of literal meaning, a classical objectivist metaphysics, and a classical correspondence theory of truth.

Moreover, it appears that what is true of our causal concepts holds for all our most important abstract philosophical concepts. The current evidence for this is inductive, but it is very impressive. Scores of studies have now shown the metaphorical constitution of basic concepts in the sciences (Magnani and Nersessian 2002), law (Bjerre 1999; Winter 2001), mathematics (Lakoff and Núñez 2000), ethics (Fesmire 2003; M. Johnson 1993, 2014), medicine (Wright 2002), politics (Lakoff 1996), psychology (Gibbs 1994, 2008; Fernandez-Duque and Johnson 1999, 2002), music (M. Johnson and Larson 2003; Cox 1999, 2016), theater/performance (McConachie 2015), religion (Sanders 2016), and many other fields. In light of this metaphorical constitution of our abstract concepts, we need to rethink what we are about as philosophers. There does not now exist (and probably never will exist) an exhaustive metaphorical analysis of the full range of philosophical concepts and arguments. That would be a daunting, unending task. However, a surprisingly large number of philosophical concepts have already been subjected to conceptual metaphor analysis over the past two decades. A partial list of some of the more prominent concepts for which we have at least a preliminary metaphorical analysis follows on the next page.

The number of key concepts analyzed so far, and the depth of those analyses, strongly supports the prospect that our abstract concepts are defined by conceptual metaphor and metonymy. If this is so, then philosophical analysis is primarily metaphor analysis—working out the logic and inferential structure of the metaphors that ground our basic philosophical understanding of experience. Philosophical theories, like all theoretical constructions, are elaborations of conceptual metaphors. In a very strong sense, philosophy *is* metaphor, and the critical dimension of philosophy requires a critical reflection on the fundamental metaphors of a particular philosophy.

A Partial List of Some Metaphorically Defined Concepts

Event	Knowledge	Happiness
Cause	Attention	Society
Action	Communication	Democracy
State	Self	Love
Property	Person	Marriage
Purpose	Will	Being
Mind	Moral rule	Number
Thought	Rights	Set
Concepts	Justice	Infinity
Reason	Duty	Addition (subtraction, multiplication, etc.)
		The Cartesian plane (and a host of other mathematical
Emotions	Good	concepts)

Metaphor and Contemporary Philosophy of Language

The reality of conceptual metaphor and its central role in abstract conceptualization and reasoning calls into question large parts of traditional Western views of meaning and truth, and it also challenges most of contemporary philosophy of language. If our abstract concepts are metaphorically structured, then the classic objectivist-literalist view must be false. According to objectivist metaphysics and theory of knowledge, the world consists of objects, properties, and relations that exist in themselves, independent of human mind, conceptual systems, and agency. Meaning is a matter of how our concepts map onto or pick out aspects of this mind-independent objective reality. Literal concepts are the direct connection between what we think (or what's in our mind) and how the world is, and this connection (sometimes called "intentionality" or "reference") is the basis for the possibility of truth, which is taken to be a correspondence relation between propositions and states of affairs in the world. There cannot be any significant role for metaphor in this objectivist and literalist picture of mind and world, since the cognitive content of any metaphor would supposedly be ultimately reducible to some set of literal concepts or propositions, thereby rendering the metaphor replaceable by proper literal discourse.

Quite obviously, if conceptual metaphor is irreducible to literal concepts and essential for abstract thought, then the classic objectivist-literalist picture cannot be correct. Conceptual metaphor is a structure of human understanding, and the source domains of the metaphors come from our bodily, sensory-motor, and social experience, which becomes the basis for abstract conceptualization and reasoning. From this perspective, truth is a matter of how our body-based understanding of a sentence fits, or fails to fit, our body-based understanding of a situation. And when we are thinking with abstract concepts, that understanding involves conceptual metaphor. There is a form of "correspondence" here—a fitting of our understanding of a statement and our understanding of a situation. But this is not the classic correspondence of literal propositions to objective, mind-independent states of affairs in the world. Instead, the correspondence is mediated by embodied understanding of both the sentence and the situation (Lakoff and Johnson 1999; M. Johnson 2017, chap. 8).

In spite of the growing body of empirical research on conceptual metaphor that has emerged over the past three decades, contemporary analytic philosophy of language has refused to recognize the existence of conceptual metaphor. This is not surprising, considering that to do so would undermine certain fundamental assumptions of traditional analytic philosophy. I want to briefly examine two of the most popular contemporary views of metaphor within analytic philosophy—that of John Searle and the view shared by Donald Davidson and Richard Rorty—in order to show why they cannot accept the reality of conceptual metaphor and how they are done in by its existence.

Searle (1979) approaches metaphor from a speech-act perspective, and he regards the activity of speaking a language as a highly conventionalized rule-governed form of behavior. Searle is also a literalist. He believes that the possibility of truth claims and a robust realism requires that all meaning be reducible to literal concepts and propositions that can, in the last analysis, correspond to states of affairs in the world. Various types of illocutionary speech acts would, according to Searle's account, be rule-governed functions on these basic propositional contents. So, the problem of metaphor within Searle's philosophy of language is to state the rules by which the literal sentence meaning ("S is P") used for a metaphorical utterance can come to be interpreted by a hearer as a different literal utterance meaning ("S is R") (Searle 1979). According to Searle's view, the hearer must recognize that the speaker cannot be intending to convey the literal meaning of her utterance, must then calculate the alternate meanings the speaker might possibly be intending, and must finally determine which is the most appropriate literal meaning in the present context.

The problem with this literalist/objectivist version of the speech-act approach is simply that it cannot explain how metaphors actually work. Searle correctly sees that most metaphors are *not* based on an underlying set of literal similarities that might explain how P (in "S is P") calls up R (in "S is R") when we hear the metaphorical utterance. But Searle has no alternative specification of the rules for cases that cannot be based on similarities. He must surely recognize that his final attempt to formulate a rule for certain types of metaphors *is no explanation at all!* "Things which are P are not R, nor are they like R things, nor are they believed to be R; nonetheless it is a fact about our sensibility, whether culturally or naturally determined, that we just do perceive a connection" (Searle 1979, 108). Saying that it just "is a fact about our sensibility" that we do make certain connections does not explain anything. When a literalist is forced to admit that certain metaphors are not based on any literal similarities between the source and target domains, then his literalism leaves him without resources to explain where the meaning comes from or how it is possible.

Conceptual metaphor theory solves this problem by rejecting literalism and by recognizing the pervasive structuring of our abstract concepts by metaphor. On this view, metaphors are based on experiential correlations, and not on similarities. Joseph Grady (1997) has analyzed the experiential grounding of a large number of what he calls "primary metaphors" that are sometimes combined into larger metaphor systems. Consider, for example, the primary metaphor AFFECTION IS WARMTH. Grady hypothesizes that this metaphor is based not on similarities between warmth and affection, but rather on our experience, from infancy, of being held affectionately and feeling warmth. Multiple experiences of this sort in childhood would involve a neuronal coactivation of brain areas tied to the experience of bodily warmth and those tied to the subjective experience of affection and nurturance. This coactivation (realized through neural connections between two different functional neuronal clusters, and no doubt also involving chemical changes leading to emotional responses) later becomes the basis for a primary metaphor, AFFECTION IS WARMTH. One of Searle's well-known arguments against the similarity theory of metaphor is that there are no relevant literal similarities between a person named Sally and a block of ice that could explain the meaning of the metaphorical expression "Sally is a block of ice." Quite so, for this expression is not based on similarities. Rather, it is an instance of the primary metaphor AFFECTION IS WARMTH, and so it is based on experiential correlations (of affection and warmth), rather than on similarities. If anything, any similarities that might be perceived are a result of the experienced correlation that grounds the metaphor. However, Searle cannot accept this alternative theory, because his literalism does not permit him to recognize that metaphorical source-to-target mappings could be equally as basic to our thought as are literal concepts. Searle's theory is constrained by his traditional objectivist views of meaning, knowledge, and truth.

Another extremely popular view of metaphor is Donald Davidson's deflationary rejection of metaphorical meaning. In his 1978 article "What Metaphors Mean," Davidson provocatively answers that they do not *mean* anything at all; or at least nothing beyond the ordinary literal meaning of the utterance. In short, Davidson simply denies that metaphor is a semantic phenomenon, and he thus denies that metaphor has anything to do with making truth claims: "We must give up the idea that a metaphor carries a message, that it has a content or meaning (except, of course, its literal meaning)" (1978, 45). Metaphor is only a pragmatic effect achieved by using a certain literal utterance to induce the hearer to notice something. Davidson says that a metaphorical utterance uses its literal meaning to "intimate" or "suggest" some nonpropositional insight: "Seeing as is not seeing that. Metaphor makes us see one thing as another by making some literal statement that inspires or prompts the insight" (ibid., 47).

Richard Rorty was the flamboyant spokesman for Davidson's non-semantic (sometimes called "pragmatic") theory of metaphor. Seizing on Davidson's claim that metaphor is not about some nonliteral propositional content or meaning, Rorty describes metaphors as linguistic flares that catch and redirect the hearer's attention: "Tossing a metaphor into a conversation is like suddenly breaking off the conversation long enough to make a face, or pulling a photograph out of your pocket and displaying it, or pointing at a feature of the surroundings, or slapping your interlocutor's face, or kissing him. Tossing a metaphor into a text is like using italics, or illustrations, or odd punctuation or formats. All these are ways of producing effects on your interlocutor or your reader, but not ways of conveying a message" (1989, 18).

This view of metaphor as a nonsemantic use of language for certain attention-getting purposes has an important implication that Rorty is quick to note. The distinction between the "literal" and the "metaphorical" is seen, not as one "between two sorts of meaning, nor a distinction between two sorts of interpretation, but as a distinction between familiar and unfamiliar uses of noises and marks" (Rorty 1989, 17). According to Rorty, these "unfamiliar" marks and noises *somehow* get us searching for new vocabularies in which they are no longer unfamiliar, *but he has no account whatever of how this process is supposed to work.*

The considerable popularity of both Searle's and the Davidson-Rorty view is easily understandable within the framework of analytic philosophy of language. As different as their two views may appear to be on the surface, they both share a set of grounding assumptions about meaning and truth that are foundational for analytic philosophy. In particular, they agree that (1) meaning is conceptual and propositional in nature, (2) meaning is truth-conditional, and (3) only literal concepts can be the bearers of meaning. Searle thinks that metaphors can have a semantic content of sorts, but he is at a loss as to how to explain that possibility, since he sees that they are not based on literal similarities and do not seem to be literal propositions. Davidson and Rorty think that metaphors have no semantic content, are not propositional, and so cannot be bearers of truth in any deep or interesting way.

Both theories are badly mistaken. Both theories ignore the growing body of empirical research on conceptual metaphor as a basic operation of abstract thinking. It should come as no surprise that neither Searle nor Davidson pays any serious attention to the work of cognitive linguists on the semantics of natural languages. If they had, they would have acknowledged the pervasive role of conceptual metaphor in abstract conceptualization and reasoning. How could Searle, or especially Davidson, explain our previous analysis of the semantics and inference structure of our metaphors for causation? Their literalist views have no resources whatever to explain the polysemy and inference generalizations that are explained in cognitive linguistics by the source-to-target mappings. Rorty sees quite clearly that his view has nothing whatsoever to say about the meaning and motivation for basic metaphors in science and philosophy: "For all we know, or should care, Aristotle's metaphorical use of *ousia*, Saint Paul's metaphorical use of *agapē*, and Newton's metaphorical use of *gravitas*, were the results of cosmic rays scrambling the fine structure of some crucial neurons in their respective brains. Or, more plausibly, they were the result of some odd episodes in infancy—some obsessional kinks left in these brains by idiosyncratic traumata. It hardly matters how the trick was done. The results were marvelous" (1989, 17).

This is extremely clever, and beautifully expressed, but it is quite wrongheaded. For it *does* matter "how the trick was done." It does matter where these metaphors come from—that is, why we have the ones we do, how they are grounded experientially, and how they shape our thought. Moreover, there are (at least partial) answers to such questions, answers provided by conceptual metaphor theory, that challenge some of the basic assumptions of contemporary analytic philosophy of language.

Rorty is probably right that we aren't going to explain precisely why Saint Paul came up with the metaphor for love that he did. But that does not mean that his metaphor was an inexplicable miracle, or a chance occurrence! Our inability to predict what novel metaphors will emerge does not entail that metaphors just happen, in an unmotivated and irrational irruption. On the contrary, there is a great deal that we can say about what Saint Paul's metaphor means, how it is experientially grounded, how it connects up with the other conceptual metaphors for love that were common in his time (and in ours), and about how his metaphor extends or creatively blends aspects of these other metaphors. Conceptual metaphor theory can explain how this new metaphor could possibly make any sense to people, through its emergence in our embodied understanding, and how they could draw inferences about its implications for how they should live their lives. Within cognitive linguistics there already exist extensive analyses of the mappings for the key metaphors for love in our culture (Lakoff and Johnson 1980; Kövecses 1988, 2000). Nor did the Aristotelian conception of *ousia* spring fully armed from the head of Aristotle. Lakoff and I (1999) have traced some of the main steps in the development of the metaphorical understanding of Being that begins with the pre-Socratic philosophers, blossoms in Plato, and is transformed in Aristotle. The idea of Being is a construction from various folk theories and conceptual metaphors concerning the nature of categories and entities in the world. Aristotle's ousia is a remarkable achievement, but it is not a miracle springing up from nowhere.

If, like Davidson and Rorty, you don't see that metaphor is a semantic phenomenon, then it should come as no surprise that, like them, you will regard metaphor merely as a nonrational rupture in a conceptual system (or, to use Rorty's favorite term again, a "vocabulary") that inexplicably gives rise to a new way of talking. If you miss the experiential grounding of primary metaphors, you will, like Rorty, think that metaphor change is relatively arbitrary and not experientially and rationally motivated. Moreover, you will not recognize the crucial role of metaphor in shaping and constraining inference in ordinary mundane thinking, scientific research, and philosophical theorizing. In other words, Davidson and Rorty are literalists. Because they are oblivious to the pervasive workings of conceptual metaphor in shaping our conceptual systems, they cannot see that or how metaphor lies at the heart of human understanding and reasoning.

Philosophy as Metaphor

Virtually all our abstract concepts appear to be structured by multiple, typically inconsistent conceptual metaphors. If this is true, then philosophical theories are not systems of foundational literal truths about reality, but rather elaborations of particular complex intertwining sets of metaphors that support inferences and forms of reasoning. Humanizing and embodying philosophy in this manner does not devalue it in any way. On the contrary, metaphor analysis reveals why we have the philosophies we do, explains why and how they can make sense to us, and traces out their implications for our lives.

In *Philosophy in the Flesh* (1999), Lakoff and I analyzed several philosophical orientations to reveal their underlying metaphors. That analysis included pre-Socratic metaphysics, Platonic versus Aristotelian doctrines of Being, Cartesian views of mind and thought, and some of the founding assumptions of analytic philosophy of mind and language. To provide just one representative example of how a metaphorical analysis of this kind might proceed, I want to consider Jerry Fodor's "language of thought" metaphor for mind, since it has been so influential in recent philosophy of mind. Fodor wants to defend what he regards as a scientifically sophisticated version of the widespread folk theory that to have a mind is to have mental states (e.g., beliefs, wants, fears, hopes) that purport to be "about" aspects of our world. Thinking, as he sees it, must consist of chains of inner mental states that are somehow connected to each other (i.e., one thought leads to another) and that are also somehow connected to aspects of our experience (i.e., things in the world "cause" us to have these specific mental representations that we have). There are thus two major parts to Fodor's theory: (1) how the mental states are related, and (2) how those mental states are connected to the world (or how they are caused).

The first part of his theory consists of the claim that these mental states form a "language of thought": "A train of thoughts ... is a causal sequence of tokenings of mental representations which express propositions that are the objects of the thoughts" (Fodor 1987, 17). The language of thought is purely computational: "Mental states are relations between organisms and internal representations, and causally interrelated mental states succeed one another according to computational principles which apply formally to the representations. This is the sense in which internal representations provide the domains for such data processes as inform the mental life. It is, in short, of the essence of cognitive theories that they seek to interpret physical (causal) transformations as transformations of information, with the effect of exhibiting the rationality of mental processes" (Fodor 1975, 198).

Fodor's "language of thought" (sometimes called "mentalese") consists of symbols that in themselves are completely meaningless, but that can supposedly be given meaning by the ways in which they are caused or "tokened" by certain events in the world. The mental representations in this language of thought are precisely like the arbitrary, meaningless symbols in computer programs. Within a computational program, operations are performed entirely on the formal (syntactic) features of the symbols, and Fodor believes that such features can "mimic" what we think of as semantic relations between our various mental representations: "Within certain famous limits, the semantic relation that holds between two symbols when the proposition expressed by the one is entailed by the proposition expressed by the other can be mimicked by syntactic relations in virtue of which one of the symbols is derivable from the other" (1987, 19).

The second key part of Fodor's theory concerns the causal grounding of the internal representations. His claim is that these symbols are mental *representations* by virtue of the way they are caused by aspects of the world. Fodor summarizes this aspect of his theory: "I want a naturalized theory of meaning: a theory that articulates, in nonsemantic and nonintentional terms, sufficient conditions for one bit of the world to be about (to express, represent, or be true of) another bit" (Fodor 1987, 98).

Fodor and his followers believe that the language of thought hypothesis expresses literal truths about the nature of mind—namely, that the mind is a computational functional program, that thinking is governed by syntactic rules, and that the symbols of mentalese are given meaning through their relation to aspects of our experience that cause them to be realized in our minds. There exists a large body of empirical research in the cognitive sciences that shows why this view of mind cannot be correct, but that is not my focus here. Rather, my point is to show that Fodor's entire model is composed of a series of interwoven complex metaphors that give rise to specific entailments about the nature of mind and the operations of thought.

Fodor's key claim that all human thinking has the form of a language is an idea (and a false one) deeply rooted in both our ordinary and philosophical ways of thinking. Because we so often express our thoughts in language, we are easily seduced into believing that human thinking has the form of a language. In other words, we presuppose the THOUGHT IS A LANGUAGE metaphor.

The THOUGHT IS A LANGUAGE Metaphor
- Thinking Is Linguistic Activity (Speaking/Writing)
- Ideas Are Made Of Words
- Complex Ideas (Thoughts) Are Sentences
- Communicating A Sequence Of Thoughts Is Spelling
- Memorization Is Writing

Our ordinary ways of thinking about the operations of mind and thought draw massively on our conception of written and spoken language. The idea that thoughts are linguistic forms written in the mind is the basis for expressions such as "Let me make a *mental note* of that," "She's an *open book* to me—I can *read* her every thought," "The public *misread* the president's intentions," and "Do you think I'm some kind of mind *reader*?" Spoken language also provides a rich source domain for our conception of thinking as hearing, as in "She doesn't *listen to* her conscience," "I *hear* what you're saying," "I can barely *hear* myself think," and "That *sounds* like a good idea." The THOUGHT IS A LANGUAGE metaphor covers all types of intellectual activity, as in "Liberals and conservatives *don't speak the same language*," "He can't *translate* his good ideas into practice," "What is the *vocabulary* of basic philosophical ideas?" and "I wouldn't *read too much* into what he's saying." Notice also that, according to this mapping, careful step-by-step thinking is conceived as careful spelling, as when we say, "Our theory of embodied meaning is *spelled out* in chapter 3," "Do I have to *spell it out* for you?" and "He always *follows the letter* of the law."

Fodor's LANGUAGE OF THOUGHT metaphor makes intuitive sense to many people precisely because most of us assume that a purely formal language can be meaningful in the same way that a natural language is meaningful. That is, we assume the FORMAL LANGUAGE IS A NATURAL LANGUAGE metaphor.

The FORMAL LANGUAGE IS A NATURAL LANGUAGE Metaphor

Abstract Formal Symbols Are Written Signs
A Formal Language Is A Natural Language
Well-formed Symbol Sequences Are Sentences
Principles For Combining Formal Symbols Are Syntactic Rules

Fodor correctly understands that a truly computational theory of mind requires that the language of thought be a formal language (akin to a computer language), and that a formal language cannot be modeled on a natural language. A "formal" language is an artificial language that, unlike natural languages, consists entirely of arbitrary meaningless symbols, each of which has specific formal (syntactic) features that play a role in formal operations specified for the language.

The key problem with this metaphor is that actual formal languages do not and cannot possess the key features that make it possible for natural languages to be meaningful (such as intonation contours and other sound-based phenomena). Consequently, if MIND IS A COMPUTATIONAL PROGRAM (i.e., the MIND IS A COMPUTER metaphor), then Fodor's "language of thought" will not, in itself, be meaningful in any way. As a result, Fodor must officially reject the FORMAL LANGUAGE IS A NATURAL LANGUAGE metaphor. But then he is left with the problem of how an intrinsically meaningless language of thought can somehow acquire meaning.

Fodor's answer, as noted above, is that "tokenings" of particular mental symbols must become "representations" by being "caused" by objects and events that we experience. In other words, the "inner" mental symbols must be causally connected to things outside the mind. In *Psychosemantics* (1987), Fodor tries to develop a causal theory of how at least some of the symbols in mentalese can become meaningful; that is, how the symbols can come to be related to things "outside" the mind. He then tries to give an account of how the other symbols—the ones not directly grounded causally—can acquire meaning through their relation to symbols that are causally grounded. Although I cannot argue this here, Fodor is ultimately unable to explain how there is a determinate connection between being in a certain situation and having certain specific symbols tokened in the mind's language of thought. He cannot establish such relations for the reasons that Quine (1960) so famously articulated—namely, the "input" is always subject to multiple interpretations under different contextual conditions, so there is seldom or never a one-to-one correspondence between a mental symbol (or even a word) and an aspect of the "world." In other words, there is an inescapable referential indeterminacy for any given sign.

Philosophy's Debt to Metaphor

My interest here is not to evaluate the adequacy of Fodor's theory of mind and language. It is, rather, to show that Fodor's theory is based on a set of intertwined conceptual metaphors that operate (mostly unconsciously) in our culture. It is no criticism of a philosophical or scientific theory to show the underlying metaphors on which it rests. On the contrary, it is the metaphors that make it possible for the theories to make sense of our experience. *All* theories are based on metaphors, because all our abstract concepts are metaphorically defined. Understanding the constitutive metaphors allows you to grasp the logic and entailments of the theory. Thus, we will discover various common metaphors underpinning our philosophical theories, ranging from the pre-Socratics' notions of Being and *physis*, to ideas about God in medieval theology, to Cartesian doctrines of mind, and up to twenty-first-century neurocomputational theories of cognition (Lakoff and Johnson 1999; Lakoff and Narayanan, forthcoming).

It would be impractical to try to survey the metaphorical foundations of all our philosophical theories. But it is a task that can and should be undertaken if we want to understand the inner workings of any particular theory in philosophy or science. This task will always include a metaphorical analysis of concepts such as cause, Being, reality, and event, but also of all aspects of mind and thought themselves, such as the grounding metaphors for concepts, reason, mind, thought, knowledge, logical relations, and values that lie at the heart of a specific theory. Even the theories of metaphor themselves must be analyzed. The theory of conceptual metaphor, for example, employs metaphors of "mapping" and "projection" to conceptualize the nature of metaphor itself. Such a conception could never be absolute—could never tell the whole story or cover all the relevant semantic phenomena—and so we must always be self-reflectively aware of our own metaphorical assumptions and their limitations.

I have argued that the single biggest reason that most traditional and contemporary philosophy cannot recognize the pervasive, theory-constituting role of metaphor in philosophy is the failure of philosophers to acknowledge the existence of deep systematic conceptual metaphor. They cannot recognize it, because to do so would require a fairly substantial revision of some of the founding assumptions of their philosophies. It would require them to abandon some of their favorite metaphorical conceptions in favor of other metaphors. If you acknowledge conceptual metaphor, then you have to give up literalism. If you give up literalism, you must abandon objectivist theories of knowledge. If you reject objectivist metaphysics and epistemology, you must abandon the classical correspondence theory of truth. Eventually, you will have to rethink even your most basic conception of what cognition consists in.

The hold on us of objectivist and literalist views is so strong that we are sorely tempted to go to great lengths to salvage our traditional theories of mind, thought, and language. Searle ultimately falls back on a form of literalism. Davidson retains his literalism by denying that metaphors have meaning beyond their literal sense. Rorty doesn't appear to be a literalist, since he sees that metaphors are terribly important in the history of philosophy, but he has no theoretical resources to explain the phenomena as anything more than contingent, irrational, inexplicable random events.

In sharp contrast, once you understand how conceptual metaphors lie at the heart of our abstract conceptualization and reasoning, you acquire a new set of tools for analyzing, explaining, and criticizing philosophical theories. Philosophies are built out of conceptual metaphors. We need not be slaves operating blindly under the harsh influence of our metaphors. We can learn what our founding metaphors are and how they work. We can learn the entailments and limitations of those metaphors. We can analyze the metaphors underlying other cultures and philosophical systems, too. Our ability to do this type of analysis is, admittedly, always itself shaped by metaphorical conceptions of which we are hardly ever aware. However, we *can* become aware of those metaphors, we can subject them to critical evaluation, and we can creatively elaborate them in developing new philosophies to help us deal with the problems that confront us in our daily lives.

CHAPTER 3

Experiencing Language: What's Missing in Linguistic Pragmatism?

Pragmatism is a growing, vital philosophical tradition, and one of its recent growth spurts has been the emergence of what has come to be known as "linguistic pragmatism" or "analytic pragmatism." This new brand of pragmatism is "linguistic" because it takes language to be the most distinctive capacity marking off humans from other sentient species; because it regards meaning as a linguistic phenomenon; and because it argues that there is nothing beyond language that might ultimately ground any particular truth claim emerging from any discipline or practice. Linguistic pragmatism is what you get when you start with analytic philosophy's founding assumption that language is our access to any meaning we are capable of experiencing and then supplement this with the pragmatist insight that meaning is a mode of action tied to values and forms of communicative interaction. If it is our language that supplies us with all the conceptual distinctions we can make, then one might be led to conclude, as linguistic pragmatists do, that philosophy's focus should be on the conditions that make linguistic assertion and performance possible as a communal activity.

This assumption about the primacy of language has generated a lively debate within pragmatist circles concerning the insistence in earlier "classical" pragmatist thinkers like James and Dewey that philosophy ought to emerge from, and return to, *experience*, and not just to language. The controversy about whether experience or language is the alpha and omega of philosophical reflection has also coincidentally turned into a contest over who can properly claim to be a pragmatist philosopher, as in "Will the real pragmatist please stand up?"

Now, to state the obvious, any strong contrast between *experience* and *language* is just one more big dichotomy! But aren't pragmatists supposedly known for eschewing dualisms that lead to rigid hypostatizations and thereby fail to capture the continuity, richness, and complexity of experience? How ironic, then, that self-proclaimed pragmatists would find themselves defending their preferred side of a basic experience/language dichotomy.

I am going to argue, in effect, that any experience/language dualism is profoundly misleading, because language itself is part of experience and operates only as experienced in specific contexts of action. *I will argue that there is no such thing as "language" in itself—no language without our experience of language, and no language experience without an enactment of meaning that involves more than just linguistic structures.* Consequently, we cannot pretend to escape the depths and complexities of experience by focusing only on language and linguistic practices of validation and justification, for there are no such practices that are not themselves experiences embedded within a context of perceiving, meaning-making, appraisal, and acting that is not itself all or only a matter of language. It is a mistake to set language over against experience, for all linguistic practices are forms of experience. In short, I will argue that there are three things missing in linguistic pragmatism: (1) a sufficiently nuanced account of language (as it is actually experienced), (2) an adequate understanding of meaning (including its nonlinguistic dimensions), and (3) a sufficiently rich notion of experience (that goes beyond linguistic events). It turns out that this issue is not just a minor in-house skirmish over who gets to be the "true" pragmatist. Rather, it is a matter of what philosophy ought to be and to do, if it hopes to make any significant positive difference in our lives.

Linguistic (Analytic) Pragmatism

One source of the experience-versus-language debate is Richard Rorty's contrast between the "good Dewey" and the "bad Dewey" (Rorty 1982). Rorty's good Dewey is the antifoundationalist, antidualistic philosopher who unmasked our inveterate but fruitless desire for certain and timeless truths, with their correlative modes of knowing. This is the Dewey who showed us the oversimplifications and confusions we are led to when we assume that our dualisms capture essential structures of some mind-independent reality that supposedly grounds all our claims to knowledge and truth. The bad Dewey, from Rorty's perspective, is the person who, having demolished foundationalist epistemology and jettisoned dualistic metaphysical thinking, lost the courage of his convictions when he claimed that we could ground our understanding and knowledge in something called "experience," which could be explored within an "empirical metaphysics" that focuses on the "generic traits of existence" (Dewey [1925] 1981). Rorty's bad Dewey, in other words, thinks we can still have a nonfoundationalist, "empirical" metaphysics of experience. Rorty regards the term *empirical metaphysics* as an oxymoron, because he thinks that metaphysics is an intrinsically foundational enterprise, and, as such, ought to be abandoned in the face of numerous antifoundationalist arguments arising in multiple philosophical traditions.

What came to be known as Rorty's (and, later, Putnam's) "neopragmatism" paved the way for a small number of subsequently influential philosophers who might be called either "new pragmatists," "analytic pragmatists," or "linguistic pragmatists." This new linguistic orientation is well represented in books such as Cheryl Misak's *New Pragmatists* (2007), Alan Malachowski's *The New Pragmatism* (2010), Robert Brandom's *Perspectives on Pragmatism* (2011), and Robert Talisse and Scott Aiken's *The Pragmatism Reader* (2011). The basic idea of linguistic or analytic pragmatism, which I will examine in more detail below, is that (1) the human mind is characterized by its capacity for reasoned judgments concerning various assertions and knowledge claims; (2) this entire process is dependent on language (via conceptual and propositional structures that are linguistic); and (3) our standards of assertion and our claims to reasonableness are constrained by conditions of social interaction within communities of inquirers and actors. In short, the mind's distinctive capacity for certain kinds of cognitive operations depends on our linguistic capacities and the communities of inquirers within which we find ourselves. Linguistic pragmatists hold that one cannot pretend to justify knowledge or truth claims by reference to some allegedly non- or prelinguistic "experience" that supposedly provides the ultimate constraints on what counts as meaning and knowledge. Experience, on this view, is either already a linguistic construct, or else it has no standing in selecting out which concepts, truth claims, and modes of knowing are sanctioned by communities of inquirers. Alan Malachowski sums up this suspicion of "experience" as follows: "New Pragmatism has not bound itself by the sorts of commitments that were always going to hold classic pragmatism back. Of these, empiricism, with the accent on experience, is the principal factor. New Pragmatists are able to discard much philosophical baggage by shifting its focus to language" (2010, 31).

In *Consequences of Pragmatism* (1982), Rorty praises Dewey for replacing the notion of language as a medium for representing an independent reality with the notion of language as tool for coordinating human behaviors. Rorty cautions us not to regard this tool analogy as implying that language is somehow separable from its users and their world:

> But we must be careful *not* to phrase this analogy so as to suggest that one can separate the tool, Language, from its users and inquire as to its "adequacy" to achieve our purposes. The latter suggestion presupposes that there is some way of breaking out of language in order to compare it with something else. But there is no way to think about either the world or our purposes except by using our language. One can use language to criticize and enlarge itself, as one can exercise one's body to develop and strengthen and enlarge it, but one cannot see language-as-a-whole in relation to something else to which it applies, or for which it is a means to an end. (1982, xix)

The key claim here is that, when it comes to matters of meaning, understanding, and knowing, there is nothing beneath or beyond language against which our linguistic articulations might be measured or evaluated. Rorty does not make the ridiculous claim that there is nothing beyond language, but only that our practices of communicating, assessing truth-claims, and coordinating action are linguistically structured, through and through. In short, "attempts to get back behind language to something which 'grounds' it, or which it 'expresses,' or to which it might hope to be 'adequate,' have not worked. The ubiquity of language is a matter of language moving into the vacancies left by the failure of all the various candidates for the position of 'natural starting-points' of thought, starting-points which are prior to and independent of the way some culture speaks or spoke" (Rorty 1982, xx).

More recently, Robert Brandom has expanded and articulated this linguistic perspective with a vengeance. In a series of impressive books, Brandom has given a very insightful and interesting account of the historical development of various pragmatist claims and commitments. He does justice to the pragmatist emphasis on activities of meaning-making as forms of engaged practice. However, after having surveyed a range of classic pragmatist themes, Brandom expresses his own preference for one specific linguistic version of what he calls "fundamental pragmatism," by which he means "the idea that one should understand knowing *that* as a kind of knowing *how* (to put it in Rylean terms). That is, believing *that* things are thus-and-so is to be understood in terms of practical abilities to *do* something" (Brandom 2011, 9). Brandom's way of phrasing the analytic pragmatist reconceptualization of knowing is to say that what he calls "discursive intentionality" (which many have regarded as the distinguishing human capacity) is actually a form of "practical" activity: "Practical intentionality is the kind of attunement to their environment that intelligent nonlinguistic animals display—the way they can practically take or treat things as prey or predator, food, sexual partner or rival and cope with them accordingly. Discursive intentionality is using concepts in judgment and intentional action, being able explicitly to take things to be thus-and-so, to entertain and evaluate propositions, formulate rules and principles. The fundamental pragmatist aspiration is to be able to exhibit discursive intentionality as a distinctive kind of practical intentionality" (Brandom 2011, 10). So far, so good, you might say, in that pragmatism sees thinking and communicating as types of practice and sees that our highest forms of discursive reasoning are grounded in our practical engagements with others in our shared social communities. Notice, however, that we have already slipped almost imperceptibly into an extremely narrow conception of experience that limits it to matters of belief, judgment, appraisal, and reason giving (albeit, conceived as modes of action). The experience that Brandom's pragmatist philosopher is interested in consists of experiences of assertion, reasoning, justification, and appraisal. This bias is evident in Brandom's description of experience as primarily about rational inquiry and justification. As he says, "The pragmatists' conception of *experience* is recognizably a naturalized version of the rational process of critically winnowing and actively extrapolating commitments" (ibid., 8). Everything is carried on linguistically, with no reference to any other aspect of experience.

It should not be surprising, therefore, when Brandom embraces the idea that analysis of language is the key to explaining conceptual structure. He describes the "linguistic turn" as "putting language at the center of philosophical concerns and understanding philosophical problems to begin with in terms of the language one uses in formulating them" (Brandom 2011, 22). He espouses what he calls "lingualism," which is a "commitment to understanding *conceptual* capacities (discursiveness in general) in terms of *linguistic* capacities" (ibid.). What we have here is an analytic philosophical perspective enriched with a pragmatist attention to action. Note, however, that the "actions" are principally linguistic acts.

Now, one might not find anything amiss in these statements, insofar as language gives us one way to explore aspects of our conceptualization and reasoning. Indeed, this is one of the key insights and motivations of analytic philosophy, which has taught us much about the nature of our conceptual systems. *The problems arise, however, from the exclusive focus on linguistic practices, which leads the linguistic pragmatist to ignore the importance of vast expanses of human experience and meaning-making.* Language is not the *only* window into our meaning and concepts, for there are many other forms of symbolic interaction that reveal our meaning, conceptual patterns, and modes of inference, including spontaneous gestures, music, painting, dance, theatrical performance, architecture, and ritual practices. Moreover, it does not necessarily follow from the importance of language as a lens for studying concepts that all our experience is linguistically structured and demarcated (a point to which I will return later).

Let us summarize the version of linguistic or analytic pragmatism operating here. *Thinking* is a doing, and it is a doing through language, under the guidance of shared norms for asserting and justifying claims within a particular community. *Experience* is understood predominately as forms of assertion and reason-giving in language according to norms of communal interaction. As Brandom says, "Pragmatists who have made the linguistic turn take it that the most important feature of the natural history of creatures like us is that we have *come into language:* come to engage in distinctively linguistic abilities" (2011, 26).

David Macarthur and Huw Price have espoused a similar lingualism when they write that "pragmatism begins with questions about the functions and genealogy of certain *linguistic* items—emphasizing that unless we stipulate otherwise, we're always assuming that these items may be mental, as well as strictly linguistic (in the ordinary sense)" (Macarthur and Price 2007, 95). A critic of this strong lingualism might be inclined to say that although pragmatism might possibly *begin* with analysis of linguistic expressions, it does not follow that its inquiries must *end* with language. In other words, the critic would argue that there is more to experience, and more to meaning, than what is presentable through language. However, Macarthur and Price are clear about the exclusively linguistic focus they are proposing, for they insist that "a pragmatist about causation asks not about the role of causation itself in human life, but about the role and genealogy of the notion, terms, or concept 'causation'" (Macarthur and Price 2007, 94). They go on to diagram their view as Pragmatism = Linguistic Priority *without* Representationalism (ibid., 97).

There are other versions of linguistic pragmatism, but I shall use Brandom's highly detailed and well-argued version as my stalking horse. I want to ask, first, how and why did we get to a place where "experience" gets cashed out primarily as "linguistic experience"? I am reminded of the old, tired joke about the drunk who is stumbling around looking for his car keys under a streetlight. A passerby inquires why he is searching there when the drunk's car is parked down the street. The intoxicated fellow replies that the light is better here, under the streetlight. Well, maybe that's the way it is with language and experience, too—language is alleged to be the light by which we understand anything, and so we conclude that what is discovered through language is all there is—or at least, all that matters. In other words, in the light of language, all experience seems to be linguistic, once it is assumed that we can only mark distinctions and see the patterns that our language provides us. And this view is reinforced by the fact that we can only *talk* about experience using language.

Meaning beyond and beneath Language

The experience-versus-language debate has come to take a predictable form. The experientialists observe that experience is not just a product of linguistic structures, concepts, and knowledge, but instead extends far beyond our ways of knowing and our linguistic tools for identifying and analyzing our conceptual structures. The linguist responds by observing that only language, which allows us to mark off relevant meaning structures, gives us access to our conceptual systems. Therefore, they insist, our capacity to think in the ways we do is contingent on our linguistic abilities, and the linguist goes on to assert that language is not a medium for expressing some nonlinguistic reality (i.e., experience), but is a way of coordinating human activities through speech acts.

I cast my fate with the experientialists—not to set language over against experience, but to see language as *one* form of experience, while at the same time insisting that there is much more to meaningful experience than language. While the linguistic pragmatists do capture important dimensions of Dewey's view, they leave out a crucial part of the story of experience, meaning, and thought. I will argue that their conception of language is too shallow, because it focuses only on linguistic elements (words, sentences, speech acts, and communicative norms for reason-giving). I take issue with the mistaken idea that whatever meaning there is must be expressible—in principle, at least—by some language (as linguists understand the nature of language). In other words, I challenge the idea that all thought is linguaform—linguistically expressible as a set of concepts, propositions, and their relations. Although our capacity for linguistic expression may well be a distinctly human ability that allows us to engage in all sorts of marvelous abstract thinking and communication, it does not follow that "whatever can be meant can be said" (Searle 1969, 19). Therefore, I need to show at least two things: (1) that if language is limited only to linguistic signs (words, sentences, etc.) and speech-act conditions, then there are important meaning-making processes besides linguistic ones; and

(2) there is no language without our experience of language, so that any alleged contrast of "language" *versus* "experience" can really only amount to a distinction between linguistic experience and other kinds of experience.

I begin my argument, then, with how our resources of meaning-making far exceed linguistic resources that are based only on words and their combinations. Let's start with a simple example of how meaningful experience exceeds language. When I was in high school, after a football or basketball game, I used to bring my girlfriend to my house, and sometimes we would dance together. I would put a Nat King Cole record album on my father's turntable, turn out most of the lights, and we would move slowly around the room, pressed steamily together under the sway of Cole's rich, deep, mellow voice. Now, there was plenty of highly charged meaningful action going on there, and there were several norms in play, but virtually none of them had anything to do with language proper. The ways we held each other, where my hand rested on her back, how she let her head rest on my shoulder, the fragrance of her hair, how we moved around the room as the old wooden floor creaked under our feet, how we hesitated briefly each time one song ended and we waited awkwardly for the next song to begin, hearing only the scratching and popping sound of the well-played record as it spun on the turntable. It was all meaningful, and there were shared intentions and interests and values permeating our experience, and *most of that was not dependent on language.*

The issue here is whether all meaning is linguistic (i.e., dependent on language), or whether linguistic meaning is rooted in a vast prelinguistic (and nonlinguistic) play of meaning structures. In my own work (M. Johnson 2007, 2017) I have devoted a good deal of effort to exploring these nonlinguistic, body-based aspects of meaning, but I know all too well that most contemporary analytic philosophers emphatically reject this view. The lingualist will insist that language gives us our only access to the depths of meaning, so that whatever cannot be expressed linguistically cannot properly count as meaning. They demand that the experientialist tell them what the dimensions of meaning are within a particular situation, and they then play their trump card by noting that the experientialist inescapably resorts to language in order to try to describe the hidden depths of meaning.

There are two ways one can respond to the linguistic or analytic pragmatist's exclusive focus on the linguistic. The first is to argue that there is far more to meaningful experience than can be captured in written and spoken language. The second tack is to argue that "language" is far richer and more encompassing than mere spoken and written words and sentences. Language in this broader sense includes any forms of symbolic interaction by which meaning is enacted, experienced, and communicated, including activities such a spontaneous gesture, dancing, theatrical performance, painting, vocal and instrumental music, architecture, and ritual practices. In the end, both of these arguments converge on the same claim: namely, that meaning exceeds, in its marvelous breadth and depth, our verbal capacities. Let us consider both strategies in turn.

First, let us address the idea of meaning beyond language. Is what I have just described in the dancing scenario really meaning? Well, it all depends on what one means by "meaning," of course. It is difficult to avoid the sneaking suspicion that there is no "fact of the matter" about what meaning is, so one is left stipulating a definition and then using that to construct arguments about the role of language in meaning-making. The linguists stipulate that there is no meaning that is not linguistic, whereas the experientialists contest this claim by observing many forms of non- or prelinguistic meaning-making.

I have elsewhere (M. Johnson 2007, 2017) argued that the meaning of any thing, sign, action, or event is the experiences that it in some way calls up or enacts for us. Those discriminated significant experiences can be past, present, or future (i.e., possibilities for actions or events that might occur). For instance, our experience of a blue, cloudless sky can mean many things, as it calls up past experiences with blue skies, our present experience of the sky, or projected future experiences that might occur subsequently. It might mean that it is not raining (present experience) and will not soon rain (future experience). It will therefore mean that I don't need to take my rain jacket with me when I go fishing. It might mean that fishing will slow down, because the fish will hunker down in deep waters to avoid the sunlight. It might mean that I might want to put on an extra layer of sunblock for the next few hours.

The linguist will object that I'm misusing the notion of meaning, because meanings of words, phrases, and sentences must be *conventionalized* to be shared and public, and this publicity and communicability are made possible only by a common language, in which terms can by convention come to stand for certain objects and events. They insist that the kinds of experience I'm referring to do not have meaning in the *proper* sense of that term, which must be restricted, they say, to something only sentences (or parts of sentences) can have.

My response to this challenge is to argue that there is meaning wherever and whenever some thing or event can stand, for a person or group of persons, as a sign of some experience.[1] Natural languages are perhaps our most remarkable tools for conventionalizing and stabilizing these sign relations, but they are not the sole means for shared meaning. Objects, qualities, and events can serve the signification function by employing various perceptual, motor, and affective processes, some of which are not language dependent. Moreover, who can give a linguistic or speech-act rule for including *it is not now raining* in the meaning of "The sky is blue," but not including *the fish will hunker down and seek the shade*? The fact is that the experience of the blue sky means a host of possible experiences, and there is no absolute way to separate out some of them as part of the meaning while definitively excluding other experiences that are connected with a blue sky. If meaning is about implications for experience, then why are these other connected experiences not part of the meaning?

Dewey gives mixed signals on the issue of whether we need language to have meaning. Sometimes he appears to suggest that we only experience genuine meaning where there is language, consisting of linguistic signs standing in multiple relations to one another and capable of indicating various experiences. In chapter 5 of *Experience and Nature* he argues that we achieve "mind" when we learn to interact and communicate with others in a communal way through language, and he repeatedly asserts that it is language that makes shared meaning possible.

However, in that same book, Dewey offers examples of pre-reflective and prelinguistic dimensions of experience that have meaning insofar as they recall experiences past and present, direct us to future consequences, guide our expectations, and influence our cooperative interactions. As such, these nonlinguistic dimensions seem to be primary bearers of meaning:

> This state of things in which qualitatively different feelings are not just had but are significant of objective differences, is mind. Feelings are no longer just felt. They have and they make *sense*; record and prophesy.
>
> That is to say, difference in qualities (feelings) of acts when employed as indications of acts performed and to be performed and as signs of their consequences, *mean* something. And they mean it directly; the meaning is had as their own character. . . . Without language, the qualities or organic action that are feelings are pains, pleasures, odors, colors, noises, tones, only potentially and proleptically. With language, they are discriminated and identified. . . . When named, they enable identification and discrimination of things to take place as means in a further course of inclusive interaction. (Dewey [1925] 1981, 198)

Here is Dewey giving something to the experientialists and something to the lingualists, both at the same time. As the *experientialist* would have it,

Dewey recognizes that whenever we can discriminate qualitative differences as a way of indicating possibilities for experience, we can then go beyond merely feeling a quality and grasp its sense and meaning for us. There are ways of marking differences in qualitative experience that are not strictly language dependent. On the other hand, Dewey gives to the *lingualists* the idea that language is our primary and most expansive means for marking differences, for understanding things, and for constructing meaning.

The key point here is that it is not just linguistic signs that can have meaning. There are many diverse types of things and events that are meaningful insofar as they function as vehicles of possible consequences in experience.

> The qualities of situations in which organisms and surrounding conditions interact, when discriminated, make sense. Sense is distinct from feeling, for it has a recognized reference; it is the qualitative characteristic of something, not just a submerged unidentified quality or tone. Sense is also different from signification. The latter involves use of a quality as a sign or index of something else, as when the red of a light signifies danger, and the need of bringing a moving locomotive to a stop. The sense of the thing, on the other hand, is an immediate and immanent meaning; it is meaning which is itself felt or directly had. (Dewey [1925] 1981, 200)

So, somewhat in line with Dewey, I am saying that our capacity to experience and make meaning—to make sense of things—does indeed require use of some thing, event, or quality as an indication of some past, present, or future experience(s). "Making sense" is not just having a feeling about a situation, but instead involves marking significant patterns, tendencies, and consequences of some aspect of an experience. To say that a situation "makes sense" is to say that we are relatively *at home* in that situation and can operate within it. Our linguistic signs are not our only resources for sense making. There are meaningful patterns in spontaneous gesture, music, painting, sculpture, architecture, dance, and ritual practices, and all of these allow us to grasp the meaning of a situation. I see no good reason to deny that these nonlinguistic processes of experience are part of human meaning-making.

What I have just called "nonlinguistic processes of meaning-making," Dewey sometimes included as part of *language*, because he uses that term in a very broad way that far exceeds the use of words alone. This expansion of the scope of language was quite explicit by the time Dewey published *Logic: The Theory of Inquiry* (1938), where "language" includes *anything* that could stand in a sign relation to something else: "Language is taken in its widest sense, a sense wider than oral and written speech. It includes the latter. But it includes also not only gestures but rites, ceremonies, monuments and the products of industrial and fine arts. A tool or machine, for example, is not simply a simple or complex physical object having its own physical properties and effects, but is also a mode of language. For it *says* something, to those who understand it, about operations of use and their consequences" ([1938] 1991, 51–52).

This broad use of the term *language* is the second possible strategy for answering the linguistic pragmatist. The first strategy was to posit meaning—and thus meaningful experience—that is significant and normative, even though it is not dependent on language. Meaning in this sense reaches down deep into our ways of inhabiting and making sense of our world. It involves feelings, emotions, images, and qualities. When it gets expressed through language, it may achieve depth and scope of meaning that is not otherwise possible without language. But there is pre- or nonlinguistic meaning there nonetheless, and sometimes it is a fullness of meaning that cannot be grasped by any linguistic structure.

The second strategy is simply to include all these embodied meaning-making processes under the category of language processes, broadly construed. This amounts to Dewey's wide and expansive sense of language.

I prefer the first strategy, chiefly because most people think of language as constructed out of words and sentences, and so they have a hard time expanding that term to encompass the full range of meaning processes to include nonlinguistic elements. Linguistic pragmatists tend to adopt this traditional narrower notion of language, and therefore showing the existence of meaning that exceeds language (in this sense) is an appropriate counterargument to their lingualist view.

The Experience of Language

So far, I have been arguing that our forms of meaning-making are not necessarily or exclusively bound to a capacity for spoken or written language. It might well be a condition of meaning that a thing, quality, or event must be able to stand as a sign of some experience or aspect of an experience, but the range of things that can realize such a sign relation is clearly not limited to language. Consequently, the linguistic pragmatist idea that philosophy need only focus on matters concerning our uses, via language, of certain concepts, propositions, or speech-act conditions, is both false and misleading.

Beyond this argument about the nature of meaning, there is another deep issue that needs to be considered. The linguistic pragmatist argues that we cannot resort to "experience" as a ground for the possibility of language, because we can never step outside language to grasp some essential feature(s) of a particular experience. Recall Rorty's well-known words with which I introduced the notion of linguistic pragmatism: "But there is no way to think about either the world or our purposes except by using our language. One can use language to criticize and enlarge itself, as one can exercise one's body to develop and strengthen and enlarge it, but one cannot see language-as-a-whole in relation to something else to which it applies, or for which it is a means to an end" (Rorty 1982, xix).

Can you "think" about the world without *language*? Once again, it depends on what you mean by "think" and what you mean by "language." Can you, without language, have experience that is meaningful, that makes sense to you, that generates inferences, and that leads to further experience? I have argued that you can, and not just on rare occasions (through, say, poetry and art), but much of the time in our lives when we grasp the meaning of what is happening in ways that do not rely on words (M. Johnson 2007).

Can you make truth claims (and other speech acts) without language (and the attendant notions of concepts and propositions)? Well, J. L. Austin showed that you most certainly can, even if most of our speech acts do require language. He showed just some of the many ways of making assertions without saying anything, such as the rolling of one's eyes to express disbelief of what another has just claimed, or the shaking of one's head from side to side, or the extending of one's arm with palm upright and facing the interlocutor, in order to indicate refusal of a proposition. These are all meaningful signs, even though none are linguistic.

Linguistic pragmatists tend to endorse Rorty's infamous claim that we cannot depend on any notion of the nature of experience as a way of validating a particular philosophical view, for experience is always linguistically mediated from the get-go. My response to this is to acknowledge Rorty's insight that no account of experience can serve the role of some allegedly ultimate ground of meaning, knowledge, or value. Rorty was right to dismiss objectivist metaphysical projects that pretend to ground our philosophies and sciences in some absolute description of the character of experience. Saying that we can experience meaning and think without language does not deny Rorty's reasonable claim that all our sense-making is perspectival and that our systems of signs are not windows on absolute reality.

However, Rorty's rejection of foundational metaphysics is perfectly compatible with the idea that philosophy cannot avoid reference to experience, *since linguistic activity is itself an experience*. We cannot set up language as an autonomous object or system completely independent of some person's and group's experience of language. There is no use of language, for any purpose, mundane or philosophical, that does not involve our *experience* of language. Rorty was probably right that we cannot contrast language-as-a-whole with some nonlinguistic experience, but he failed to appreciate that language is a dimension or aspect of experience—one way experience plays out.

Sometimes this claim strikes me as obvious, but at other times it appears to me to be a very subtle point, so let me explore it a bit further. My key point is that language has to be enacted, realized, undergone, and experienced in order to be meaningful and useful. Words, phrases, and sentences do not have meaning *in themselves!* They have meaning *for someone who has developed linguistic capacities and is currently enacting meanings within some language community*. Words have meanings for us just because, and insofar as, our hearing or reading of those words within an experiential context activates in our body and brain certain patterns of neural connectivity, plus the release of hormones and other chemicals within the body that affect our bodily states.

The strongest support I know for this claim comes from recent empirical research from the perspective of what is known as the "simulation theory of meaning" (or simulation semantics). The basic idea of simulation semantics is that processing language is not an intellectual grasping of fixed and stable conceptual entities, but rather involves a neural simulation that activates the sensory, motor, and affective structures that would actually be activated in the scene being described. Cognitive scientist Benjamin Bergen describes the simulation view as follows: "The idea is that you make meaning by creating experiences for yourself that—if you're successful—reflect the experiences that the speaker, or in this case the writer, intended to describe. Meaning, according to the embodied simulation hypothesis, isn't just abstract mental symbols; it's a creative process, in which people construct virtual experiences—embodied simulations—in their mind's eye" (2012, 16).

You experience and make meaning by enacting experiences that use the same brain regions for perception, feeling, and action that would be used if you were actually engaged in the situation being described. For example, your concept of a *cup* is not some transcendent Fregean *sense*—some allegedly abstract quasi-entity grasped by something called the mind. Rather, your concept *cup* is constructively enacted in a given context in terms of the types of perceptions (visual, tactile, auditory, etc.) you might have with cups, the motor processes involved in picking up, holding, moving, and drinking from cups, and the emotional dimensions of various situations in which cups are used in different practical and social settings.

Simulation semantics, as a new approach, has so far focused mostly on how we process language, but it can easily be extended to many other forms of (nonlinguistic) meaning-making. We enact—simulate—not just when we hear or read words, but also when we hear music or view painting, sculpture, architecture, dance, visual scenes, and ritual practices. *There is no meaning without an experience of meaning unfolding in time.*

For our purposes, the upshot of this is that you cannot have meaning through language without simulated experience (which, note well, is still experience), and the experiences themselves are not linguistic through and through, since they involve the whole relevant physically and culturally embodied situation or context in which you are operating. One important consequence of this is that you cannot use *language* as a contrast term to *experience*, in any way that pretends to deny experience a crucial role in our acts of thinking, meaning-making, communicating, problem solving, and creativity. The mistaken idea that we can replace our experience of something with our language for talking about that experience is a nonstarter from the perspective of human cognition. What I am objecting to is the tendency of linguistic pragmatists either to cash out experience in linguistic terms, or else to reject any serious reference to experience as transcending language through deeply embodied dimensions of meaning-making.

The view I have developed here can be summarized as follows: Linguistic or analytic pragmatism takes language in way too narrow a sense that cannot capture the multitude of ways humans make and experience meaning. If, following Dewey, they were to expand their conception of language to include all forms of symbolic interaction and meaning-making (e.g., art, music, dance, gesture, sculpture, ritual), then they would need a vastly enriched theory of meaning that cannot be modeled on the views of language they have so far provided. They would need to think of meaning—and, in turn, language—in a far richer and deeper way than they can countenance. However, should they attempt such an expanded view of meaning, they will then have to acknowledge that meaning (and language) involve an embodied, enacted, embedded *experience* of meaning. Therefore, they cannot continue to insist that we should eschew any significant account of experience.

Dewey devoted a large part of his mature career to writing influential books on experience, nature, logic, art, and morality that argue for his view that everything we perceive, think, feel, and do is a matter of experience, and furthermore, that all this activity takes place within an experiential context that cannot itself be made entirely explicit through linguistic descriptions. This is not the place to lay out again Dewey's notion of the pervasive qualitative unity of a given situation as the basis for all meaning, relevance, and thought (Dewey [1930] 1988; M. Johnson 2007; Pappas 2016). It must suffice to say that the world we inhabit, and in relation to which we suffer, strive, value, and act—our world as meaningful—is a world of qualitative experience, and not just a world of linguistic experience.

One implication of this is that you cannot claim, as linguistic pragmatists do, that pragmatism begins with our language, because beginning with language is already beginning with an experience of language, in which dimensions of that experience are integral to, but not constituted by, language (i.e., linguistic structures). So, when Brandom tells us that linguistic pragmatism begins and ends with language, and when Macarthur and Price tell us that pragmatism is concerned not with the experience of *X* but with our language about *X*, they are wrong. Philosophy, I want to protest, ought to emerge from and reconstruct our experience. Language is *one* part of this working, reconstructive practice, but only one part. Language itself is built from and on other nonlinguistic practices, norms, and processes of meaning. When you're dancing with your lover, words tend to get in the way of the meaning transpiring between the two of you. Your preferred philosophy will use words, of course, to talk about that experience, but that doesn't turn dancing into talking.

CHAPTER FOUR

Keeping the Pragmatism in Neuropragmatism

Whenever I hear the term *neuropragmatism*, I am reminded of J. L. Austin's opening words in his famous article "Performative Utterances," where he says, "You are more than entitled not to know what the word 'performative' means. It is a new word and an ugly word, and perhaps it does not mean anything very much" (1970, 233). Likewise, you are more than entitled not to know what *neuropragmatism* means. It is, indeed, a *new* word, and it is perhaps an *ugly* word, but I daresay that it is not an inconsequential word. Therefore, the first question to ask is what the term *might* mean? The second question is why neuroscience needs pragmatism. The third and most important question is, why we ought to care about neuropragmatism?

I shall argue that although we have good reasons for thinking that cognitive neuroscience has a great deal to offer toward a psychologically sophisticated view of mind, experience, thought, and language, this promise will best be realized when the neuroscience is embedded in a pragmatist philosophical framework. What pragmatist philosophy has to offer is the broader philosophical context necessary for understanding the grounding assumptions of cognitive neuroscience, its fundamental limitations, and its implications for our lives. In short, to riff on Kant's famous quip: pragmatism without neuroscience is (partially) empty, but neuroscience without pragmatism is (partially) blind.

My insistence on "keeping the pragmatism in neuropragmatism" is a warning against the temptation to think that the work of neurophilosophy—or at least its important work—is done by the neuroscience alone, thereby denying any serious role for philosophical reflection. This would be a big mistake. Therefore, I shall be arguing that cognitive neuroscience needs a more comprehensive philosophical framework of the sort developed in the pragmatist tradition.

What Is Neuropragmatism?

As Tibor Solymosi has suggested, "neuropragmatism" is what you get when you plug "pragmatism" into the "philosophy" slot of neurophilosophy (Solymosi 2011, 348). As far as I am aware, the first person to use the term *neurophilosophy* was Patricia Churchland, who argued for a constructive dialogue between the emerging empirical discoveries of the biological and neurosciences on the one hand, and philosophy and other disciplines that have traditionally carried the burden of explaining "mind" on the other. Churchland described her project as follows: "The sustaining conviction . . . is that top-down strategies (as characteristic of philosophy, cognitive psychology, and artificial intelligence research) and bottom-up strategies (as characteristic of the neurosciences) for solving the mysteries of mind-brain function should not be pursued in icy isolation from one another. What is envisaged instead is a rich interanimation between the two, which can be expected to provoke a fruitful co-evolution of theories, models, and methods, where each informs, corrects, and inspires the other" (Patricia Churchland 1986, 3). "Interanimation" and "co-evolution" are the right kinds of terms to capture the complex nonreductive relation among various theories, models, and modes of explanation that are needed to understand human cognition. Churchland's enthusiasm for this relatively new perspective stems primarily from her sense that recent advancements in brain imagining and the cognitive sciences have given us shiny new tools for exploring how we perceive, feel, experience meaning, conceptualize, value, communicate, and act in the world. The insights that come from the neurosciences are both critical and constructive—*critical* insofar as they reveal the inadequacies of certain philosophical ideas, methods, and theories; and *constructive* insofar as they suggest new ways of explaining various phenomena of human experience and cognition. Scientists are developing substantial bodies of solid research that give us empirically responsible ways to explore the operations of "mind," and their various methods can either critique, replace, or supplement the typical armchair theorizing that plagues so much contemporary philosophy. Notice that in none of this does the neuroscience claim to make the philosophical dimension unnecessary. On the contrary, the philosophical framework is essential for understanding the limits, implications, and uses of the neuroscience.

Proponents of neuropragmatism claim that many of the insights that recommend pragmatism as a general philosophical orientation are supported by well-established results of empirical research in the neurosciences. In other words, pragmatist philosophy is much more compatible with our best current neuroscience than are many philosophical methods that set themselves over against the sciences and claim critical and reflective supremacy over empirical disciplines. In other places I have praised the contributions of *both* the cognitive sciences and neurosciences, because neuroscience is obviously not the whole of cognitive science; but here I shall restrict my focus to the contribution of the neurosciences alone, leaving out other cognitive science research that would be necessary to tell a more comprehensive and nuanced story.[1]

Key Shared Themes of Pragmatism and Neuroscience

What follows is a brief list of some of the key insights of what is loosely known as "pragmatist" philosophy that are strongly supported by some of the more robust findings of recent neuroscience.

Organism-Environment Transaction as the Locus of Activity

Dewey argued throughout his mature works that the locus of all experience, meaning, thought, and action is a living organism in ongoing interaction with environments that are complex and multidimensional, including at least physical, interpersonal, and cultural dimensions (Dewey [1925] 1981). He repeatedly criticized the dualistic errors of placing all the cognitive, epistemic, or ontological weight on either the organism (with its "inner" functions) or the environment (regarded as wholly independent of the organism). In *Art as Experience* (1934) Dewey expressed the intimate organism-environment transaction as follows: "The first great consideration is that life goes on in an environment; not merely *in* but because of it, through interaction with it. No creature lives merely under its skin; its subcutaneous organs are means of connection with what lies beyond its bodily frame, and to which, in order to live, it must adjust itself, by accommodation and defense but also by conquest.... The career and destiny of a living being are bound up with its interchanges with its environment" ([1934] 1987, 13).

Neuroscientist Antonio Damasio observes that the very continuation of life requires an organism to maintain a permeable boundary within which some measure of systemic equilibrium is possible: "Life is carried out inside a boundary that defines a body. Life and the life urge exist inside a boundary, the selectively permeable wall that separates the internal environment from the external environment." (1999, 137). The key word here is "permeable," because life cannot be sustained without an ongoing exchange between the internal and external environments. Damasio's claim is that the life of an organism requires what Walter B. Cannon called "homeostasis": "The coordinated physiological reactions which maintain most of the steady states of the body . . . and which are so peculiar to the living organism" (Cannon 1932, quoted in Damasio 1999). Jay Schulkin has recently proposed the term "allosatsis" (*allo*, "change"; *stasis*, "stable, same") to emphasize that the equilibrium required for life need not be merely a return to some preset stable state, but rather often involves the dynamic generation of new set points for equilibrium as the organism engages new aspects of its environment (2011, 5). Damasio (in conversation) has stated that his view of homeostasis includes the dynamic equilibrium that Schulkin distinguishes as allostasis.

It is a commonplace of the biological sciences today that any organism exists only in and through its ongoing engagement with its surroundings, in a continuous give-and-take of activity and receptivity. No environment, no organism. Moreover, boundaries between organisms and environments, however real, must be somewhat permeable for the organism to sustain life. *Inner* and *outer* are thus just convenient names for salient aspects of the unified processes of certain types of living beings as they engage their surroundings, but they do not mark intrinsic ontological distinctions, and they cannot be defined independently of each other. The cluster of views that have come to be known as "externalism" emphasize the way organism processes are "off-loaded" onto "external" environmental entities and structures, and also how aspects of the environment are incorporated by the organism (Clark and Chalmers 1998).

Because some neuroscientists assume such an inner/outer split, they have been justly criticized for treating what goes on *in* the brain as though it were somehow independent of the environing conditions that make cognition possible. One problematic result is a tendency to speak as if different types of cognition occur strictly *within* specified brain regions. This is the error of attributing some activity, relation, or property to a particular part, when the proper locus should be the whole multilevel and multidimensional organism as it is situated within its environments. M. R. Bennett and P. M. S. Hacker (2003) are therefore rightly critical of familiar tendencies in the neurosciences to attribute various cognitive capacities and activities to selected parts of the brain, when it is actually the whole organism (typically a *person*) that has the capacities and performs the action, and not just their brain parts. One should add to this that it is not just the whole person, but the person engaging their environments (both physical and cultural), who thinks, performs the action, executes a particular function, or has an experience. Bennett and Hacker cite scores of passages from neuroscientists who slip into the error of attributing complex enactments to specific brain regions, as when one claims something like "the amygdala experiences fear" or "vision occurs in the various regions of the visual cortex."

The error here is just one of mistaking the part for the whole. It is also the error of conceiving the environing conditions of specific kinds of cognitive activity as externalities not intrinsically part of the cognition. That said, it certainly does *not* follow that neuroscience is intrinsically reductive in that unwanted sense. For example, Bennett and Hacker attribute to Antonio Damasio the view that "emotions [are] essentially ensembles of somatic changes caused by thoughts [mental images]" (Bennett and Hacker 2003, 213). Although Damasio (1994, 1999, 2003, 2010) does hold a view of this sort, he takes great pains to show that emotions require and manifest ongoing relations with environments (both "external" and "internal" environments). Only a willful misreading of Damasio could overlook his constant insistence that emotions are the way in which certain advanced complex organisms take the measure of their interactions with their environment, and this involves monitoring changes in body states resulting from the organism's transactions with its surroundings, followed by adjustments to the internal milieu to regain some measure of dynamic equilibrium in the organism. Indeed, Damasio's theory of emotions depends upon the existence of what he calls an "emotionally competent stimulus" (Damasio 2003, 53), which is some aspect of the organism or environment that evokes changes in the body states of the organism and requires subsequent adjustments within the body to restore some measure of homeostasis. Emotions are therefore not locked up within organisms or minds; instead, they implicate the world inhabited by the organism. It was for this reason that Dewey famously insisted that the locus of an emotion is not an isolated subject or experiencing organism, but instead the entire "situation" in which the organism lives and moves ([1930] 1988, 248).

However much neuroscientists occasionally lapse into mistakenly speaking as if specific types of cognitive operations are performed by specific brain regions, the vast majority of them realize that *the mind is* not *the brain*, and that cognition implicates the environment just as much as it does the makeup of the organism.

The Continuity of Experience

There are at least two important and related notions of continuity central to pragmatist accounts of experience. The first has to do with the integrity and unity of experience, so that any distinctions we might mark within a particular situation are merely selected aspects of a unified, continuous process of organism-environment interactions. One of the distinctive contributions of the pragmatism of William James and John Dewey is their careful attention to the actual character of any given experience. They argued that unless we begin with an adequate sense of the breadth, depth, and nuanced richness of experience, our philosophical theories will lose any relevance and transformative potential for our lives. Dewey called this encompassing world of experience a "situation": "What is designated by the word 'situation' is *not* a single object or event or set of objects and events. For we never experience nor form judgments about objects and events in isolation, but only in connection with a contextual whole. This latter is what is called a 'situation'" ([1938] 1991, 72). Both James and Dewey repeatedly argued that philosophy and psychology far too often begin with some part of a situation, such as an object, event, structure, or quality—or, even worse, some reduction of experience to an alleged set of discrete sensations—then proceed to focus only on the selected feature and thereby to ignore everything else that matters in that situation. A classic example of this impoverishment of experience is the reducing of experience to discrete sense inputs that supposedly somehow become associated in the mind. We do not experience atomistic sense impressions, but rather trees, people, mountains, tables, and sunsets. Another example is treating experience as if it consists only, or primarily, of "objects of knowledge" known through various types of mental judgment, as if all our experience were reducible to acts of knowing.

In his extraordinary two-volume *Principles of Psychology* (1890), James gave a remarkable phenomenological description of experience as a continuous "flow" or "stream" of thought-feelings, out of which we subsequently identify objects and events, based on our values, interests, and purposes: "Consciousness, then, does not appear to itself chopped up in bits. Such words as 'chain' or 'train' do not describe it fitly as it presents itself in the first instance. It is nothing jointed; it flows. A 'river' or a 'stream' are the metaphors by which it is most naturally described. *In talking of it hereafter, let us call it the stream of thought, of consciousness, or of subjective life*" ([1890] 1950, 1:239).

Dewey is famous—or some would say infamous—for stressing the idea that every complete experience involves a situation unified by what he called a "pervasive quality": "The pervasively qualitative is not only that which binds all constituents into a whole but it is also unique; it constitutes in each situation an *individual* situation, indivisible and unduplicable. Distinctions and relations are instituted *within* a situation; *they* are recurrent and repeatable in different situations" ([1938] 1991, 74). Dewey's point here is that (1) the integrity of a given situation depends on the unique pervasive unifying quality that marks it out from the stream of thought as *this experience here and now*, and (2) experience is thus meaningful and constituted for us not merely as *known* (which is a reductive and selective take on an experience), but rather as felt and encountered in all its cognitive, affective, and evaluative dimensions. Consequently, one important sense of the continuity of experience is the refusal to allow the fragmentation of any integral experience into discrete sensations, feelings, objects, actions, or events, without recognizing the operative power of the whole situation of which they are a part. Obviously, we can and do make such discriminations for various purposes, but we should never pretend that these selective processes constitute the fullness of an integrated, continuous experience. Rather, they are merely useful abstractions from what James called the much-at-once-ness of experience—selections we make because of our bodily capacities, our habits of perception and conception, or our interests and values. In sum, the first notion of continuity is the unity and coherence of an experience, in which the distinctions we notice are not absolute and independent characteristics, but rather selections made from the continuous flow of experience.

A second important notion of continuity that is central to most pragmatist philosophy is the idea that in our explanations of any human actions, behaviors, or capacities, we treat them as emergent from "lower-level" animal capacities and activities. Dewey regarded this methodological imperative as so important that he christened it the "principle of continuity": "The primary postulate of a naturalistic theory of logic is continuity of the lower (less complex) and the higher (more complex) activities and forms. The idea of continuity is not self-explanatory. But its meaning excludes complete rupture on one side and mere repetition of identities on the other; it precludes reduction of the 'higher' to the 'lower' just as it precludes complete breaks and gaps" ([1938] 1991, 31).

The principle of continuity appears to be a fundamental postulate of most contemporary neuroscience, insofar as "higher" cognitive operations are explained via the emergence of functional abilities, processes, and states on the basis of increasing complexity of "lower" systems. Our higher capacities (e.g., planning, drawing inferences, critically appraising values) recruit lower sensory, motor, and affective capacities. What is denied in all naturalistic approaches is the sudden appearance on the scene of new metaphysical entities, forces, or activities as a way of explaining higher cognitive phenomena. As neuroscientist and psychologist Don Tucker explains,

> Primary process cognition is driven by the visceral controls at the core of the brain, and secondary process cognition [our more conscious cognitive operations] must fit the somatic constraints of the sensory and motor interface with the world. This is an interpretation that fits all mammalian brains, and yet it must produce the most complex abstractions of the human mind. Complex psychological functions must arise from bodily structures. There is no other source for them. . . . There are no brain parts for abstract faculties of the mind—faculties such as volition, insight, or even conceptualization—that are separate from the brain parts that evolved to mediate between visceral and somatic processes. (Tucker 2007, 218)

The term used in evolutionary theory for this continuous emergent process is *exaptation*—the appropriation of earlier developing structures for subsequent new (and later developing) functions. The continuity of higher and lower capacities and operations involves the recruitment of "lower" (sensory and motor) structures and processes to carry out "higher-level" cognitive functions, such as conceptualization and reasoning. Consequently, there is no need to posit new externally imposed causes, forces, or powers to explain higher-level mental operations.

Antidualism

As conceived in both pragmatist philosophy and cognitive neuroscience, one of the most significant implications of the continuity of experience and of close attention to the intertwining of organism and environment is a rejection of ontological and epistemic dualism. Neuroscience provides abundant evidence that our preferred dualisms are not intrinsic to experience, but are rather after-the-fact selections we make, for various purposes, from the ongoing flow of our experience. To cite the most obvious case, there can be no "mind" without a living brain in a living body. We speak of the "mental" versus the "physical," yet there is no mental process or experience that does not require bodily and brain processes in a living, functional sentient creature. Damasio says that "the apparatus of rationality, traditionally assumed to be *neo*cortical, does not seem to work without that of biological regulation, traditionally presumed to be *sub*cortical.

Nature appears to have built the apparatus of rationality not just on top of the apparatus of biological regulation, but also *from* it and *with* it" (1999, 128). Although Damasio focuses here on rationality, one might extend this basic antidualism more broadly to encompass the traditional mind/body, mental/physical split. In other words, our capacities for what we call conceptualization and reasoning recruit structures and processes evolved for processing various bodily perceptual and motor activities (Lakoff and Narayanan, forthcoming). Reason (and thus more broadly, mind) is not separable from our other bodily capacities and operations, and this undercuts any strict separation of supposed cognitive faculties according to a dualistic metaphysics of mind.

This assertion of the nondualistic embodiment of mind is not an a priori truth, nor is it capable of any formal proof. Rather, it is a fundamental methodological assumption of naturalism without which neuroscience cannot get off the ground. It is, in other words, a working hypothesis and a methodological promissory note that neural (and other bodily) correlates will eventually be found for any so-called "mental" operations of perception, conceptualization, reasoning, and willing. It is a hypothesis that recognizes our various projected ontological and epistemic dualisms for what they are: not absolute, pre-given metaphysical realities, but convenient markers of dimensions of situations that we find it useful to notice, in our attempts to explain certain aspects of our experience.

There are dualistic neuroscientists (such as Francis Crick), but cognitive neuroscience is, for the most part, predicated on continuity and the emergence of "higher" functions from "lower" ones via increasing complexity of organism-environment organization. In short, take virtually any received dualism—mind/body, subject/object, reason/emotion, knowledge/imagination, thought/feeling—and you can find extensive empirical evidence undermining the postulation of that dualism and suggesting that we use these dualistic terms, at best, only to mark aspects or dimensions of dynamic processes of experience that we find it methodologically useful to identify. I am not suggesting the draconian reconstructive project of attempting to give up all dichotomies and refrain from using terms like *mental/physical*, *mind/body*, *reason/emotion*, and so forth. That would be impossible and unnecessary. Rather, we simply need to take great care to avoid treating our commonplace selections of various dichotomous aspects of our experience as if they constituted absolute ontological characteristics of particular sentient beings.

I trust that it is hardly necessary to recapitulate any of the numerous arguments against epistemic and ontological dualisms that populate virtually all Dewey's major works and that have their counterparts in William James. Suffice it to say that Dewey spent hundreds of pages across several books showing how and why certain classic yet historically contingent dualisms arose in our language and conceptual systems. He then showed why hardening those dualities into absolute ontological or epistemic divisions leads us to dramatically mis-describe our experience and thereby to ruin our entire philosophical analysis by reading intellectual distinctions back onto our primary lived experience in a way that distorts its significance and causes us to ignore the complexity and richness of what is going on in our lives (Dewey [1925] 1981).

The Intertwining of Reason and Emotion

One of our most deeply rooted and troubling dichotomies that underlies so many traditional philosophical systems is the alleged split between our "higher" faculty of reasoning and our "lower" (bodily) capacity for feeling and emotion. On this view, reason is taken to exist independently of feelings and to function properly only by rising above the influence of the emotions.

The denial of any rigid reason/emotion or thought/feeling dichotomy has been a staple of pragmatist psychology, epistemology, and ontology. Even as early as the late nineteenth century, James (in "The Stream of Thought," vol. 1, chap. 9, of his *Principles of Psychology*) had notoriously argued for a "feeling of thinking," and he often used the hyphenated term "thought-feeling" to remind us that every thought has its corresponding feeling tone. James claimed that reasoning involves the "transitive" movement from one thought to another, and he argued that there would always be a felt sense of the urgency, direction, and connection within the movement from one thought to another:

> If there be such things as feelings at all, *then so surely as relations between objects exist in rerum natura, so surely, and more surely, do feelings exist to which those relations are known.* There is not a conjunction or preposition, and hardly an adverbial phrase, syntactic form, or inflection of voice, in human speech, that does not express some shading or other of relation which we at some moment actually feel to exist between the larger objects of our thought.... We ought to say a feeling of *and*, a feeling of *if*, a feeling of *but*, and a feeling of *by*, quite as readily as we say a feeling of blue or a feeling of cold. ([1890] 1950, 1:245; italics in the original)

In this Jamesian framework, patterns of thought are metaphorical motions along paths to various metaphorical destinations.[2] Thought *moves* (metaphorically) from one thought-location to another, and we *feel* the *tendency* and *direction* of any particular movement of thought.

James's focus was primarily on the feeling dimensions of thought (thinking). Damasio (1994, 2003, 2010) adds to this a focus on the role of emotions in certain types of reasoning. He is known for demolishing this reason/emotion dualism not in James's way, but by stressing the fact that reason relies on emotion. What he shows, using neuroimaging and lesion studies in clinical settings, is the necessity of an intact emotional system for proper social and practical reasoning:

> I propose that human reason depends on several brain systems, working in concert across many levels of neuronal organization, rather than on a single brain center. Both "high-level" and "low-level" brain centers, from the prefrontal cortices to the hypothalamus and brain stem, cooperate in the making of reason. The lower levels of the neural edifice of reason are the same ones that regulate the processing of emotions and feelings, along with the body functions necessary for an organism's survival. In turn, these lower levels maintain direct and mutual relationships with virtually every bodily organ, thus placing the body directly within the chain of operations that generate the highest reaches of reasoning, decision making, and, by extension, social behavior and creativity. (Damasio 1999, xiii)

James and Dewey stand out among the classical American pragmatists for their recognition of the intertwining of thought, quality, feeling, and emotion. What contemporary neuroscience brings to the discussion is the neuroimagining technology that allows us to move beyond the self-reflective phenomenology of our experience that was the hallmark of earlier pragmatist inquiry. We are now in a position to begin to see *that* and *how* parts of the brain (and hormonal systems) responsible for emotional response patterns and our occasional feeling of those states are coactivated with, and partially constitute, our patterns of reasoning.

Nonreductionism That Involves Multiple Levels of Explanation

One of the classic objections to any reliance on neuroscience in constructing a theory of mind, thought, and value is the fear that all science is intrinsically reductionist in its methods and cannot therefore engage the depth and richness of the phenomena to be explained. However, Robert McCauley (2007) has argued that wholesale intertheoretic reductions—that is, a reduction in which one theory is replaced by another from a different science—are extremely rare. Actual scientific practice typically recognizes the need for multiple levels of explanation coming from different scientific perspectives. The pragmatist response to this anxiety about reductionism is also to note that if there is genuine emergence of new levels of organizational complexity as we evolve and grow, then there may be forms of explanation emergent at a particular level of functional organization that are not necessary or appropriate for "lower" levels of functional explanation. Different levels of structure and activity (for example, processes at the cellular level, processes of the autonomic nervous system, operations of organ systems, and complex interactions among subgroups within a society) are each likely to require different methods of inquiry whose key concepts are not reducible to those of a different level. William Bechtel argues that although mechanistic explanations in the sciences are inherently reductive, it does not follow from this that we can always reduce "higher" levels of organization to "lower" ones: "A final feature of mechanistic explanation . . . is that, insofar as it emphasizes the contributions made by parts of a mechanism to its operation, a mechanistic analysis is, in an important sense, reductionistic. However, insofar as it also recognizes the importance of the organization in which the parts are embedded and the context in which the whole mechanism is functioning, it not only sanctions looking to lower levels but also upward to higher levels" (2008, 21). Bechtel insightfully observes that the entrenched fear of reductionism stems partly from the mistaken view that all explanations in the sciences fit the deductive-nomological model, in which every particular phenomenon is regarded as an instance of a causal law of some sort. However, deduction from so-called universal covering laws plays only a very small part in any of the cognitive sciences, where mechanistic models of what makes a certain cognitive activity possible are the norm.

Since, as just noted, mechanistic explanations are not just about the component parts of a mechanism (hence, reductionistic), but also about the organization of the parts into a functioning whole operating within a typically complex and multidimensional environment, there is always a need for multiple levels of explanation, each with their own terms and modes of explanation: "Mechanistic reduction only proposes to explain the response of an entity to the causal factors impinging on it in terms of its lower-level constituents. It does not try to explain the causal factors impinging on the mechanism. Understanding these requires inquiry focused on the mechanism as a whole, and often on yet higher-level systems in which the mechanism is embedded. Independence stems from the fact that inquiry at each level provides information additional to that which can be secured at other levels, and generally does so using different tools of inquiry" (Bechtel 2008, 157).

The typical need for multiple levels of explanation in accounting for all things human is one basis for the recognition that the mind is not the brain. Good neuroscience does not claim that we can explain all the phenomena of mind by the firing of neurons in connected or coactivated clusters (even though there can be no mental activity without that). It recognizes, instead, that experience is a process of organism-environment interaction, and that our environments are at once physical, interpersonal, social, and cultural. Over decades and even centuries, we have developed a plurality of methods for inquiring into the various ways in which aspects of our bodily makeup and our complex environments shape our experience, thought, action, and communicative interactions. This methodological pluralism is a good and necessary thing, since we need multiple methods of inquiry that carve up the phenomena differently, indicate the complexity of underlying mechanisms, and operate at different explanatory levels in order to construct a suitably rich account of any cognitive process, action, or event.

Why Neuropragmatism Needs Pragmatism

As the previous highly selective list of insights shared by neuroscience and pragmatist philosophy suggests, cognitive neuroscience has a great deal to contribute to a pragmatist naturalized approach that values empirical research relevant to our understanding of concepts, meaning, thought, feeling, knowledge, values, action, communication, problem articulation, methods of inquiry, and so forth. Some of the discoveries and advances of cognitive neuroscience are so stunning, and are coming so quickly, that it is easy to be seduced into the mistaken view that if we were just to let neuroscience research run its course for the next fifty years, we would be well on the way to a complete explanation of mind, thought, language, and nearly everything human. This, however, would be a serious mistake, because *neuropragmatism is not just neuroscience on steroids—neuropragmatism is the recruitment of neuroscience in the service of a pragmatist reconstruction of philosophical and cultural frameworks, based on a rich, expansive, and nondualistic conception of experience.*

There are three main reasons we cannot simply replace philosophy with neuroscience—three reasons there is an important role for pragmatist philosophy: (1) Most scientific disciplines typically do not have sufficient critical insight into their own founding values, goals, and methods of investigation. Pragmatism can supply an appropriate critical perspective from which to appreciate the limitations and merits of different bodies of scientific research. (2) No single scientific perspective can accommodate all the levels of explanation necessary to account for the multidimensionality and complexity of the human organism in its physical and cultural settings. Pragmatist philosophy can explain why these multiple levels of organization exist, and it gives us a way to see how the various levels interact and fit together. It thereby helps us understand why we need multiple nonreducible levels of explanation, and what those levels are. (3) Pragmatism gives us a way to explore the implications of the cognitive sciences for our understanding of ourselves and our world.

Let us consider in greater detail each of these three reasons for adopting a pragmatist philosophical orientation toward cognitive neuroscience.

The first reason is that a pragmatist perspective gives us a way to analyze and criticize the methods and values underlying particular bodies of scientific research, whereas the sciences are seldom sufficiently aware of (or sufficiently critical toward) their own limitations. One of the principal results of the past fifty years of philosophy of science is an appreciation of the partial, perspectival, and value-laden nature of any scientific methodology. *Every* method must make assumptions about (1) how the relevant phenomena are to be individuated and described, (2) what counts as pertinent data in testing a theory, and (3) what constitutes an acceptable form of explanation of the phenomena we are studying. It is not self-evident either how scientists should individuate the phenomena, or how they should determine which ones are important enough to be the objects of their inquiry. *What* we choose to focus on, and *how* we characterize what is significant within that focus, is relative to a large number of values and interests that scientists are seldom fully aware of, so that they often lack an appropriate critical stance on their own projects. Contrary to a centuries-old commonplace of metaphysical realism, the world does not come to us prestamped with the basic categories of phenomena specified in some mind-independent, objective fashion (Putnam 1981). Rather, what we take the phenomena to be—how we circumscribe and understand them—depends on our values, interests, technologies, theoretical framework, and practical situation in the world (Kuhn 1962). The methods we employ emerge in response to various historical circumstances that include cultural values, existing technologies, and institutional constraints on the conduct of science, to name but a few of the influencing factors.

Failure to appreciate the selective and value-dependent nature of our methods of inquiry is so pervasive and problematic that William James called it the "psychologist's fallacy": "The great snare of the psychologist is the *confusion of his own standpoint with that of the mental fact* about which he is making his report" ([1890] 1950, 1:196; italics in the original). In other words, the psychologist, philosopher, or scientist comes to regard the basic conceptual distinctions that they have found useful in constructing their theories as actually constituting the experience of ordinary people—or at least as constituting what matters most in experience. The psychologist or philosopher reads their own theoretical (reflective, abstractive, selective) distinctions back onto the experience under examination, and then assumes that it is just *those and only those* selected elements that matter in peoples' experience, thought, and action. To cite one representative case of this type of error, recall how Enlightenment philosophers often assumed that experience had to consist of unorganized, disconnected perceptual "givens" in the form of discrete atomistic sensations, which the mind must then unify and organize, through imagination, into meaningful perceptions of objects that are then knowable through concepts. In *Philosophy and the Mirror of Nature* (1979), Richard Rorty reminds us that our world does not come to us as a series of atomistic sensations lacking any organization or unity. We do not experience individual tones, color blotches, isolated tactile features, and the like, that have to be combined by imagination and thought under concepts we bring to our experience. Instead, we experience objects, persons, and events, and only then do we begin to mark distinctions within our experience and pick out relevant qualities that are salient for us, given our bodily makeup, interests, and values.

Dewey had his own list of common fallacies that lead us to impoverished accounts of experience. One of the worst is the still-rampant error of regarding *all* experience as if it were fundamentally a mode of knowing. We then focus only on those aspects of cognitive processing that seem to give rise to knowledge claims. Everything else—feelings, emotions, qualities, aesthetic elements, and values—go by the wayside. The result is a narrowing and disfiguring of experience, which leads us to ignore all the other forms of meaning-making, experienced values, and action that make up our world. This intellectualist mistake is explained by Dewey: "By 'intellectualism' as an indictment is meant the theory that all experience is a mode of knowing, and that all subject-matter, all nature, is, in principle, to be reduced and transformed till it is defined in terms identical with the characteristics presented by refined objects of science as such. The assumption of 'intellectualism' goes contrary to the facts of what is primarily experienced. For things are objects to be treated, used, acted upon and with, enjoyed and endured, even before they are things to be known. They are things *had* before they are things cognized" (Dewey [1925] 1981, 21).

One of the central claims of classical pragmatism is that experience is far more deep, rich, and multivalent than can be captured by any single form of inquiry. Consequently, pragmatist accounts of experience help us discern what is left out of any single mode of inquiry, and they reveal the complex layers of organization that cannot be explored through any one method. Pragmatism can thus uncover, and submit to critical reflection, any set of knowledge practices, in the service of a broader and deeper characterization of experience.

The psychologist's fallacy is not just the characteristic sin of cognitive psychologists and philosophers. It is rampant in the sciences, too. For example, what George Lakoff and I (1999) have called "first-generation cognitive science" was and continues to be fraught with tendencies to read back onto experience theoretical assumptions implicit in various models, methods, and conceptions of explanation taken for granted in early artificial intelligence, generative linguistics, information-processing psychology, analytic philosophy, and logic. Thus, what was known as "information-processing psychology" assumed something like a faculty psychology (with distinct cognitive operations performed by distinct faculties, sometimes thought to be modular processing systems of the brain), brought to bear on raw perceptual inputs, that were supposedly manipulated and "processed" by internal mechanisms, to produce outputs such as behaviors like speech or bodily movement. This information-processing model got combined with a functionalist theory of mind popular in early artificial intelligence research, which conceived the "mind" as basically a computational program operating on meaningless symbols according to rigidly defined and automated processing rules. Mind was the software; the brain was the hardware (or wetware).

After initially championing just such a functionalist view of mind, Hilary Putnam, having discovered his pragmatist leanings, later had the courage and flexibility to mount a radical critique of functionalist theory of mind and thought. Even without using emerging neuroscience research, Putnam was able to raise deep concerns about the adequacy of such information-processing models by showing how they leave out the crucial role of the body interacting with its environment in how we make meaning (Putnam 1981).[3] Only later did the emergence of sophisticated neuroimaging technologies make it possible to show how perceptual and motor capacities are crucial in carrying out many of our "higher" cognitive functions associated with understanding, reasoning, and communicating

(Feldman 2006; Tucker 2007; Damasio 2010; Bergen 2012). This research has led to a major criticism of disembodied views of cognition, to be replaced by an embodied cognition model.

The serious oversimplifications and selective abstractions to which neuroscience, and sciences in general, are prone are certainly understandable in light of the extreme difficulty of getting any reliable, reproducible results from experiments. Without idealizations and partial models, there would be no growth of science. But our appreciation of how hard the experimental science is to carry off successfully should not blind us to the limitations of specific models, research technologies, and theoretical frameworks. The scientific work, in other words, simply cannot stand on its own, for it cannot criticize its own limiting assumptions and still go about getting its experimental work accomplished. Something more is needed beyond the science itself—a broader, more encompassing philosophical reflection on how the many different bodies of research, with their many different assumptions and methods, can fit together in a more comprehensive picture.

This leads us directly to the second major reason we need a philosophical orientation that is pluralistic regarding methods of inquiry and levels of explanation. Since any given scientific approach will typically focus on but one level of explanation, we will always need a broader reflective take on how the various levels of explanation—corresponding to different levels of complexity in organism-environment interaction—are related to one another and require different explanatory models. In a few cases, there might be a relation of reduction from a "higher" to a "lower" level, but, as we saw above, this will be rare in the sciences of mind (Bechtel 2008). More often, we will need to examine how the multiple methodological perspectives might possibly fit together to form a partial picture of the complexity of human experience, thought, and behavior.

Although I do not have space to argue this here, pragmatism is committed to ontological, epistemic, and value pluralism (James [1890] 1950; Dewey [1925] 1981; Alexander 2013; Fesmire 2015). The extensive writings of James and Dewey, in particular, recognize that emergent functions within experience give rise to the need for multiple levels of explanation. The more complex systems become as they grow and establish more extensive connections and relations with other organisms and aspects of their surroundings, the more we need additional modes of explanation, if we hope to characterize the multiple levels of connectivity and mutual influence that we find in "higher" organisms and their societies. A pluralistic approach of this sort is the only one capable of even beginning to discern what is operative at various levels of organization.

This brings us to the third reason for bringing a pragmatist perspective to bear on cognitive neuroscience. We need to understand what the science means for our lives—for how we understand who we are, for how we relate to our world, and how we engage with other people and other animals. In other words, we need not just knowledge, but the wisdom to utilize available knowledge in the service of enduring and liberating values.

There are a small number of distinguished philosophically minded cognitive neuroscientists who manifest a disposition to explore the broader philosophical implications of their science. In this group I would include neuroscientists and cognitive scientists such as Antonio Damasio, Gerald Edelman, Vittorio Gallese, George Lakoff, Srini Narayanan, Jay Schulkin, Giulio Tononi, and Don Tucker, to name but a few. There are also a number of philosophers of mind, language, and science who have at least some familiarity with, and a favorable attitude toward, a pragmatist philosophical framework. This group would include philosophers like William Casebeer, Patricia Churchland, Paul Churchland, Owen Flanagan, Shaun Gallagher, James Garrison, Larry Hickman, Alva Noë, John Shook, Tibor Solymosi, Paul Thagard, Evan Thompson, and, I would hope, myself. Not all these philosophers explicitly espouse a pragmatist orientation, nor do they all cite the work of major pragmatists, but I see in much of their work significant parallels with pragmatist views of experience, mind, meaning, thought, reason, and value, and they all pay close attention to the sciences of mind.

One of the most important contributions to science from pragmatist thought has been its steadfast insistence on the fullest articulation of the breadth, depth, and multidimensionality of the experience that is the subject of our inquiries. Most of the errors of philosophy are due to failures to respect experience as we actually encounter and live it, rather than through the selective lens of our preferred theory. Dewey nicely sums up the two prongs of this emphasis on the fullness of experience and how it matters for our lives:

> Reference to the primacy and ultimacy of the material of ordinary experience protects us, in the first place, from creating artificial problems which deflect the energy and attention of philosophers from the real problems that arise out of actual subject-matter. In the second place, it provides a check or test for the conclusions of philosophic inquiry; it is a constant reminder that we must replace them, as secondary reflective products, in the experience out of which they arose. . . . In the third place, in seeing how they thus function in further experience, the philosophical results themselves acquire empirical value; they are what they contribute to the common experience of

man, instead of being curiosities to be deposited, with appropriate labels, in a metaphysical museum. ([1925] 1981, 18–19)

In short, we need what Lakoff and I (1999) have called an "empirically responsible" philosophy, that is, a philosophy that, in Patricia Churchland's (1986) word, "co-evolves" with the work of the various sciences.

In closing, I want to return to our somewhat ugly neologism *neuropragmatism*. What are the prospects for its future? Pretty bright, on the whole, and that for two reasons. First, nothing is about to stop the ever-increasing tsunami of cognitive neuroscience as it sweeps across the contemporary scientific, philosophical, and commonsense cultural landscape. There is too much excellent and highly transformative research being done to ever doubt that cognitive neuroscience is now (and will remain into the distant future) *the* principal mode of insight into mind, thought, language, and values. Second, since the sciences themselves will always need critical analysis of their assumptions, exploration of their relations to other disciplines, and reflection on their significance for human existence, there will always be a pressing need for an empirically responsible, pragmatically oriented philosophy. "Neuropragmatism" is as good a name as any for this blended approach for inquiring into the human condition. Its mantra, once again: pragmatism without neuroscience is (partially) empty; neuroscience without pragmatism is (partially) blind.

CHAPTER 5

Metaphor-Based Values in Scientific Models

In chapter 2 I developed the hypothesis that philosophies are rigorous elaborations of systematic conceptual metaphors. According to conceptual metaphor theory, virtually *all* our abstract concepts are metaphorical, and therefore the same should be true for our scientific concepts. Most scientific research is model based. There is a rapidly growing body of evidence that scientific models are largely metaphorical (Magnani and Nersessian 2002; Brown 2003). Moreover, these model-defining metaphors give rise to crucial values that determine the nature and course of scientific research. I propose to give substance and credibility to these claims by focusing on one interesting field of contemporary metaphor-based science: the cognitive psychology of attention. An examination of the three most important contemporary theories of attention shows how and why the metaphors are indispensable. The first half of the present chapter draws extensively from published work I have done with psychologist Diego Fernandez-Duque on the three major attention metaphors that shape research in cognitive psychology and cognitive neuroscience (Fernandez-Duque and Johnson 1999, 2002). In the second half I examine how the various metaphors specify some of the values embedded within different research programs for studying attention. I conclude with a speculation about the possible grounding of scientific values in our organic, embodied experience.

The ATTENTION IS A SPOTLIGHT Metaphor

We all think we know what attention is. It's whatever is involved in our "paying attention" to something, right? But precisely what's going on when we "pay attention"? As we'll see, even attention researchers cannot agree on which mental phenomena are properly cases of "attending to something." Even less do they agree about how to explain the phenomena. In fact, depending on which particular metaphorical model of attention researchers are assuming, the alleged phenomena of "attention" get individuated in quite different ways. It is not the case that we start with agreed-on phenomena of attention and then develop alternative explanations of them. Instead, which specific metaphorical model we adopt determines what we'll count as attention, how we'll go about studying it, and what we'll recognize as relevant evidence.

In order to flesh out these claims, let us begin with what is probably the oldest and most used metaphor in the scientific study of attention: the conception of an internal mental "spotlight" that shines on particular perceptual contents or mental representations. What we are attending to is whatever is "illuminated" at the present moment of consciousness. Scientists have argued that "attention may be compared to a beam of light in which the central brilliant part represents the focus surrounded by a less intense fringe. Only the items located in the focus of attention are distinctly perceived whereas we are less aware of the objects located in the fringe of attention" (Hernández-Peón, cited in Wachtel 1967, 418). The ATTENTION IS A SPOTLIGHT metaphor consists of the following conceptual mapping:

The ATTENTION IS A SPOTLIGHT Metaphor

Source Domain (Spotlight)	Target Domain (Attention)
Spotlight	→ Orienting System (mechanism of attention)
Light	→ Attention
Agent Who Controls The Spotlight	→ Executive System
Agent Who Sees	→ Awareness System
Seeing	→ Attending
Potential Field Of Vision	→ Representational Space
Area Illuminated By The Spotlight	→ Attended Representations

The conceptual metaphor here is the entire mapping from the entities in the source domain (visual perception and devices of illumination) to constructed entities in the target-domain (attention). The source-to-target mapping allows researchers to use their knowledge of the source domain to construct a parallel knowledge of the target domain. For example, on the basis of how a spotlight works, researchers may reason that attentional "*scanning* . . . is a measure of how much the *beam* moves around the *field*, while the *focusing* . . . refers in some way to the *width* of the *beam*" (Wachtel 1967, 418; italics mine). Such inferences come from the way we use our knowledge of the source-domain structure ([a] through [f], below) to construct a parallel knowledge of the target domain of attention ([a'] through [f'], below), as follows:

Source-Domain Knowledge

(a) There is a perceptual field with (b) objects in it. (c) The spotlight (d) shines light over parts of the field, (e) making it easier to see specific objects. When the spotlight illuminates a target object, (f) the target object is seen by the observer.

Target-Domain Knowledge

(a') There is a mental field with (b') unconscious ideas in it. (c') The attentional system (d') directs attention over the brain areas (or mental field), (e') making representations accessible by our awareness system. When the attentional system focuses on some target idea, (f') that target idea is acquired by the awareness system, and it becomes conscious (taken, with modifications, from Fernandez-Duque and Johnson 1999, 93–94).

This metaphor-based knowledge about attention is not merely a folk model. Rather, this metaphorical model has become the basis of a substantial body of empirical research within cognitive psychology (Cave and Bichot 1999; Fernandez-Duque and Johnson 1999). In recent years, the internal structure and logic of the ATTENTION IS A SPOTLIGHT metaphor has also influenced research in cognitive neuroscience. Consider the following examples (from Fernandez-Duque and Johnson 2002), in which scientists explored the "physiological correlates of the 'spotlight' of visual attention" (Brefczynski and DeYoe 1999) by measuring hemodynamic and/or electrophysiological response in areas of the visual cortex:

1. Several areas of the visual cortex can create retinotopic maps of perceptual scenes. This means that objects close or adjacent to one another

in the world activate brain areas close or adjacent to one another in the visual cortex. If attention "shines light" over sensory areas, then cueing attention to more central areas of the visual field should activate brain regions that map central locations, whereas cueing attention to a peripheral part of the visual field should increase blood flow in peripheral areas that map that part of the visual field. There is some evidence for this prediction coming from research designed to test these metaphorical entailments (Brefczynski and DeYoe 1999).

2. Since a spotlight moves in analog fashion, the target domain inference is that attention moves in an analog fashion. Therefore, the electrophysiological enhancement associated with the processing of attended stimuli should also move in an analog fashion—a prediction that has been tested and confirmed in the laboratory (Woodman and Luck 1999).

3. Since it takes time for a spotlight to move from one location to another, the delay between the onset of a cue and the enhancement of the electrophysiological response at the cued location has been taken to be a measure of how long it takes the attentional spotlight to move to the cued location (Müller, Teder-Sälejärvi, and Hillyard 1998).

4. In the source domain, the spotlight is a different entity from whatever it shines on and from the agent who controls it. In the target domain, therefore, one expects to find something like an independent executive system that controls attention and is separate from both the orienting system and from the sensory areas that are attended to. This concept of the executive system as defined by the ATTENTION IS A SPOTLIGHT metaphor led researchers to discover a network of cortical areas that participate in attentional control, moving attention from one location to another. Whether a stimulus is displayed at the attended location has no impact on the activation of these controlling areas. In other words, the perceptual systems that benefit from the attentional modulation appear to be separate from the neural system that controls the attentional spotlight and from the spotlight itself (Hopfinger, Buonocore, and Mangun 2000, Corbetta et al. 2000; Martinez et al. 1999).

What these four examples of attention research show is precisely how the highly articulated internal structure of the source domain of the ATTENTION IS A SPOTLIGHT metaphor generates entailments that shape our understanding of the target domain and gives rise to the ways we experimentally investigate and reason about attention. The entities in the source domain (such as a spotlight and an independent operator who directs the spotlight) have specific characteristics (e.g., the beam has a particular width at a given moment and moves in an analog fashion from one illuminated location to another) that structure scientists' conceptualization of the phenomena of attention. A different metaphor, with different source-domain entities and knowledge, would obviously give rise to a substantially different conception of attention and a different research program for studying it. As an example of this, let us consider a second major metaphor system in which attention is conceptualized as a valuable limited resource that is allocated for various cognitive tasks.

The ATTENTION IS A LIMITED RESOURCE Metaphor

One of the chief competitors to the ATTENTION IS A SPOTLIGHT metaphor is the metaphor ATTENTION IS A LIMITED RESOURCE, which can be allocated by a general-purpose central processor in a graded fashion for the performance of different tasks. Pashler succinctly characterizes the folk model built upon this metaphor:

> Folk psychology postulates a kind of substance or process (attention) that can be devoted (paid) to stimuli or withheld from them. Whether or not attention is allocated to a stimulus is usually thought to depend on a voluntary act of will; in the metaphysics of folk psychology, this ultimately depends on the choice made by the self. . . . The available quantity of attention is assumed to be finite, and this finiteness is supposed to account for capacity limitations; this means having less attention available to pay to other things. Attention, according to folk psychology, can be devoted not only to stimuli, but also to activities, tasks, and behaviors (as in "pay attention to your driving"). Allocating more attention to a given task enhances performance. (1998, 2–3)

Scientific versions of Resource models are most eloquently described in Kahneman's influential book *Attention and Effort* (1973) and have been further developed by several researchers, such as Norman and Bobrow (1975), Navon and Gopher (1979), and Hasher and Zacks (1979). Limited-resource models are used to explain many psychological phenomena, such as dual-task interference (Christie and Klein 1996), automaticity (Norman and Bobrow 1975; Schneider and Shiffrin 1977), priming (Posner and Tudela 1997), and mental rotation (Carpenter et al. 1999).

The internal logic of the ATTENTION IS A LIMITED RESOURCE metaphor is made evident by the following mapping, in which cognitive operations are conceptualized as distributions of physical resources that are used up in various tasks:

The ATTENTION IS A LIMITED RESOURCE Metaphor

Source domain (resources)		Target domain (attention)
Valuable Resource	→	Attention (Capacity/Arousal)
Quantity Of Resource	→	Amount Of Available Attention
Allocation Of Resource	→	Allocation Of Attention To Tasks
Budget	→	Task Strategy For Allocating Attention
Controller Of The Resource	→	Executive System

The ATTENTION IS A LIMITED RESOURCE metaphor drives research strategies by generating questions that come from our experience of using *physical* resources to carry out various tasks. The logic of the source domain thus gives rise to a corresponding set of questions about the nature and use of attentional resources, such as: What is the nature of such limited resources? How should they be quantified? Do those resources play a causal role, and if so, who or what controls their allocation? Answers to such questions can be developed only within a larger theoretical framework that includes models of the mind, which are irreducibly metaphorical (Fernandez-Duque and Johnson 1999). Our beliefs about what attention *is*, and our understanding of how it works, make sense only in the context of those metaphorical models. Attention is not literally a limited substance (like water, soil, or gasoline) that can be quantified and parceled out. Neither is there a homunculus whose job it is to monitor this putative "scarce" and "valuable" resource. Yet the ATTENTION IS A LIMITED RESOURCE metaphor postulates an executive system that allocates attentional resources to various tasks on the basis of its monitoring of inputs from other systems.

In other words, it is the inferences generated by the individual submappings of the ATTENTION IS A LIMITED RESOURCE metaphor that permit researchers to design and carry out attention experiments. This can be seen quite clearly in the way our basic knowledge of the source domain carries over into our understanding of attentional phenomena. For instance, in the source domain there is

(a) a *limited commodity* (e.g., some substance or object, or its surrogate, money), that is
(b) controlled by someone who allocates it where he deems it most necessary, and

(c) does so in a flexible way, applying resources to different goals in graded fashion.
(d) The amount of resource needed varies for each task or product, and
(e) affects its quality.

When basic source domain knowledge like this is then applied to our conceptualization of the target domain, we get a series of corresponding knowledge claims (or entailments) about attention. Therefore, each piece of shared knowledge about the source domain ([a] through [e], above) correlates with a piece of knowledge about aspects of the target domain ([a'] through [e'], below), and this shows up in scientific research, as can be seen in the following quotations from the research literature:

(a') "Attention has been used to refer to . . . all aspects of cognition having to do with *limited resources* or capacity" (Shiffrin 1988, 739; italics mine).
(b') Such attentional resources are *controlled by an executive system*, or general-purpose central processor, at the very top of the decision-making tree, that distributes the attentional resources: "[Attention] means a laborious process, whereby processing resources are *voluntarily allocated* to a particular task or activity at the expense of other tasks and activities" (Umiltà 1988, 175; italics mine).
(c') "The *allocation* of attention is a matter of *degree*. . . . Attention is . . . *controllable*. It can be *allocated* to facilitate the processing of selected perceptual units or the execution of selected units of performance" (Kahneman 1973, 201; italics mine).
(d') "The *amount* of attention or effort exerted at any time *depends* primarily *on the demands* of current activities" (ibid.; italics mine).
(e') Finally, the amount of attention given to some percept *affects its information processing*; that is, attention "causes" modulation in the product of information processing.

The concept of limited mental resources has also been extended to neural systems: "Just as *physical energy* systems require resources, so do neural energy systems. It is the consumption of different types of resources that may be indexed by various metabolically based neuroimaging methods, including fMRI. Specifically, greater task demand translates into greater resource demand" (Carpenter et al. 1999, 20–21; italics mine).

The ATTENTION IS A LIMITED RESOURCE metaphor has influenced theory and guided many research agendas. For example, the models predict that as the system becomes overloaded, performance is expected to degrade in a smooth fashion (Norman and Bobrow 1975). When a task requires more resources than are available, decreased performance should be expected: "Once the capacity limit is exceeded, selection of the information to be processed will be required" (Lavie 1995, 452). Task interference would be expected to be nonspecific, because all cognitive processes tap into the same unitary resource. Even if the tasks do not share any mechanisms of perception or response, interference will occur whenever the system's capacity is overloaded.

The previous analysis shows how the understanding provided by the ATTENTION IS A LIMITED RESOURCE metaphor permits researchers to identify the phenomena, set research strategies, and test specific hypotheses about attention. It is the entailments of the metaphor that give rise to the knowledge we construct. This can be seen, for example, if we contrast the entailments of the ATTENTION IS A SPOTLIGHT metaphor with those of the ATTENTION IS A LIMITED RESOURCE metaphor, which reveals why each is apt in certain contexts and for certain purposes.

The ATTENTION IS A LIMITED RESOURCE metaphor works well for modeling the graded allocation of attention to different tasks. In contrast, the ATTENTION IS A SPOTLIGHT metaphor has difficulty explaining this dimension of attention, since a spotlight does not allow the person who controls it to split the beam or to reduce its intensity so that the light can be saved to illuminate another location at another time. On the other hand, as we have seen, the ATTENTION IS A SPOTLIGHT metaphor works well for explaining spatial orienting and attention, whereas the basic ATTENTION IS A LIMITED RESOURCE metaphor does not account for the phenomena of spatial attention.

The entailments of the ATTENTION IS A LIMITED RESOURCE metaphor are specific enough to generate predictions that can be tested experimentally. For example, "effortful" tasks sometimes do not interfere with one another (perfect-time sharing) (Navon 1984), and there are cases where increasing the difficulty of one task is not followed by a cost in the performance of the secondary task (difficulty insensitivity). Moreover, sometimes changes in the modality of one of the tasks affect performance of the other task, even in the absence of difficulty changes (structural alteration effect) (Wickens 1984). These experimental results challenged the initial ATTENTION IS A LIMITED RESOURCE metaphor and led to a replacement of the original single-capacity model by a multiple-resource model (Navon and Gopher 1979; Wickens 1984; Pashler 1998), which proposes that interference between two tasks occurs only when the same reservoir of limited resources is accessed, but not otherwise.

The versions of the ATTENTION IS A SPOTLIGHT and ATTENTION IS A LIMITED RESOURCE metaphors analyzed above are what theorists call "causal" models, because they treat attention as somehow being efficacious in affecting our cognitive performances—that is, causing changes in perception and other cognitive activities. Cognitive psychologists using these "causal" models thus regard "attention" as a term that refers to a selective process by which attended information is processed more efficiently than nonattended information. The chief problem for both theories is to explain what system allocates the precious attentional resource. What does the selecting of one stimulus over another? Both the ATTENTION IS A SPOTLIGHT and ATTENTION IS A LIMITED RESOURCE metaphors (in the versions described) require some kind of executive system.

Causal theories can be contrasted with "effect" theories, which deny the existence of any central causal mechanism of attention. Whereas causal theories claim that attention "modulates" perception, effect theories conceptualize attention as an effect—a by-product—of the normal operation of various sensory and cognitive systems (James [1890] 1950; Johnston and Dark 1986). For example, representations that rise to a certain level of activation are given temporary priority in the functioning of the organism, but there is no central system that monitors this competition.

The principal metaphor underlying "effect" theories is the ATTENTION IS RESOURCE COMPETITION metaphor in which there is *no* central mechanism to determine who or what "wins" the competition; that is, there is no central system determining which stimuli will be attended to.

The ATTENTION IS RESOURCE COMPETITION Metaphor

To avoid seemingly insoluble homunculus problems that confront "cause" theories, many researchers, spurred by recent developments in cognitive neuroscience, have adopted "effect" theories that treat attention as a by-product of information processing among multiple systems: "Attention is not a high-speed mental spotlight that scans each item in the visual field. Rather, attention is an emergent property of slow, competitive interactions that work in parallel across the visual field" (Desimone and Duncan 1995, 217). In such models, there is *no executive system* required. Instead, perceptual objects are seen as vying for limited attentional resources, that is, they compete for activation in areas of perceptual processing: "Objects in the visual field *compete* for processing in several cortical areas" (Rees, Frackowiak, and Frith 1997, 835).

Competition models are typically based on the following metaphorical mapping:

The Attention Is Resource Competition Metaphor

Source domain (resources)		*Target domain (attention)*
Competing Individuals	→	Stimuli
Valuable Resource (e.g., food)	→	Mental Resources / Neuronal Receptive Fields
Goal: Securing Limited Resources Necessary For Survival	→	Goal: Securing Resources For Mental Processing And Aware Perception
Competition for Resources	→	Competition For Neuronal Activation
Survival Of The Individual	→	Activation Above A Specified Threshold

In this mapping, perceptual inputs are conceived as competing for limited attentional resources. Stimuli that are not strong enough are eliminated, while strong stimuli succeed in gathering enough processing resources so that we become "conscious" of them. The competitive process gives rise to awareness, which is stable but also evolves (as in James's "stream of consciousness"). In this model, awareness is not a natural kind. It is only a collection of inputs that succeed in rising above a certain *awareness threshold*. Attention and awareness are not supramodal systems, but rather emergent processes of brain activity.

Dennett and Kinsbourne's (1992) multiple-draft model of consciousness (an effect model) provides a good illustration of the relation between awareness and attention in the context of Attention Is A Limited Resource metaphors. In that model, a conscious representation is not a mental entity viewed within some internal Cartesian theater; it is a representation that becomes activated above a criterion level, by virtue of which it acquires a certain property (i.e., the property of being something of which we are consciously aware). Hence, "neuronal activation" is a *valuable resource*, since consciousness can only be achieved by gathering a certain amount of activation. Inputs *compete for* this *valuable* and *limited* "activation" *resource*.

Just as we saw earlier with the Attention Is A Spotlight metaphor, the entailments generated by the metaphor mapping give rise to specific predictions, experimental programs, and theoretical explanations. In each case, it is the logic of the source domain that determines our conceptualization of workings of attention and defines the relevant research programs. One good example of this is the literature on binocular rivalry. When different images are presented to the two eyes, perception alternates such that each image is visible for a few seconds at a time. This "binocular rivalry" phenomenon is usually understood as a competition between neuronal responses, so that at a given time one representation is dominant and the other is suppressed. Current views of binocular rivalry argue that "the neural representation of the two stimuli *compete* for visual awareness" (Logothetis, Leopold, and Sheinberg 1996, 621; italics mine). Binocular rivalry is a process in which "each region of the retinal image in one eye seems to fight with the corresponding region in the other eye" (Wolfe 1996, 588).

A second area where ATTENTION IS RESOURCE COMPETITION models also provide an alternative interpretation of many findings is the neuropsychology of attention. When attention is cued to a location and the target is situated somewhere else, patients with right parietal lesions and hemispatial neglect respond very slowly. SPOTLIGHT models explain this pattern of results as a deficit in disengaging attention and "moving" it to the new location. In contrast, competition models argue for an attentional bias, that is brought about by competitive weights that favor stimuli represented in the undamaged areas over stimuli represented in the lesioned areas. Brain areas that code visual stimuli play a double role: they process perceptual, visuospatial, and oculomotor information, but they also weight attention toward the stimulus location. Lesions in areas that code for visuospatial information, such as the parietal cortex, would lead both to an information-processing deficit and to attention imbalance. However, those areas do not constitute a specialized attentional system.

Other experimental support comes from the directional theory of attention, which argues that *rival* hemispheres have opposing orienting vectors that compete with each other (Kinsbourne 1977). Lesions to one hemisphere lead to an imbalance in the opposite hemisphere. Thus, presenting a "competing stimulus" to the unaffected side exaggerates the bias, leading to an "extinction" of the stimulus represented by the impaired side. Due to the lack of competition from the lesioned hemisphere, perception in the unaffected side is better than normal (Làdavas, Petronio, and Umiltà 1990).

Once again, the message is clear: our very conception of attentional phenomena depends directly on which metaphor we are using. The submappings of a particular metaphor provide the details of the explanation of the relevant phenomena. The metaphors are the instruments of scientific reasoning and experiment design.

Metaphor-Based Values in Science

The analysis given so far supports my claim that scientific research on attention is inescapably shaped by metaphor-based models. I have argued that each of the three principal models of attention is metaphorical and that the nature and structure of the source domain for each metaphor determines how researchers working with that particular model will conceptualize and explain the phenomena. There is a rapidly growing body of evidence suggesting that metaphor plays a central role in *all* science, not just in specific fields like the cognitive psychology of attention. Of course, one could never *prove* that every scientific model one could imagine must necessarily be metaphorical. The best strategy is to stand ready to investigate the workings of the key metaphors in any case of scientific research that might be brought before us. The more we do this, the more inclined we will be to give up the illusion of metaphor-free science.

An analysis of the mappings that constitute the metaphors in a given theory provides considerable insight into another controversial issue—namely, the role of values in science. Implicit throughout the previous metaphor analyses is the idea that the particular mappings give specific content to, and make it possible for us to apply, the values that guide scientific research.

Talk concerning the normative dimension of science routinely calls to mind a classic list of values recognized by most scientists as crucial to the growth and success of their science:

1. *Generalization.* Scientific explanations are expected to be framed as generalizations over data or phenomena. That generalization is a value becomes evident when it is contrasted with the demand in some disciplines today for highly particular "thick" descriptions of phenomena, instead of seeking causal laws and other generalizations.
2. *Comprehensiveness.* Empirical science sets a high value on generalizations that cover and unify the widest possible set of phenomena. All other things being equal, the generalization with a broader scope of applicability is typically preferred as giving more powerful and productive explanations.

3. *Empirical testability.* Even though philosophers of science have argued for decades about such notoriously problematic notions as confirmation, these arguments exist only against a background of shared agreement that scientific hypotheses must be subject to experimental test and empirical evaluation.
4. *Relevance.* Every science makes value judgments about what counts as a phenomenon, and this determines what the theory must explain and what is taken as appropriate evidence.
5. *Importance.* Even within the range of relevant phenomena, some phenomena are regarded as more important than others. Failure to explain fully the prototypical members of a category will be more damaging to a theory than a failure to explain nonprototypical or marginal cases.
6. *Simplicity.* Other things being equal (which they seldom are), the simplest explanation is typically preferred.
7. *Elegance.* Elegance is always the most elusive and, therefore, the last-mentioned value of good explanation. It is relegated to an "aesthetic" category and then promptly ignored; yet one often hears scientists admiring the elegance of a certain theory.

This list is meant only to be indicative of typical values involved in science. It is neither exhaustive nor absolute, since there are other possible values in science (e.g., quantification, mathematical representation), some of which may, in certain cases, conflict with—and perhaps even override—one or more of the values on this list.

My interest in this list is to point out that these values, as stated, are usually too abstract to be useful in the actual practice of science. They get their meaning, power to constrain explanations, and applicability via the metaphors that define specific scientific models. I want to consider a few simple examples of this value-specifying role of the metaphors that shape science.

The adequacy of a given explanation is relative to the theory's determination of which phenomena are *relevant* (i.e., require explanation) and what form an explanation must take (i.e., what the relevant parameters are). So, for example, a model of attention that incorporates the ATTENTION IS A LIMITED RESOURCE metaphor will place a high explanatory value on *quantification*. The ATTENTION IS A LIMITED RESOURCE metaphor defines attention as a valuable quantifiable substance or resource that can be allocated differentially to multiple cognitive tasks. It favors explanations that make it possible to measure the amount of attentional resource used for a given task. It also gives high priority (that is, *importance*) to explaining how these resources are allocated.

By contrast, theories based on the ATTENTION IS A SPOTLIGHT metaphor do quite poorly on this allocation issue, since the ontology of this metaphor lacks an appropriate concept of the "amount" of attentional light that can be directed to a particular cognitive task. In classic ATTENTION IS A SPOTLIGHT models, the spotlight has homogeneous intensity and fixed size. Moreover, attentional light is not a quantifiable substance that can be divided up and differentially allocated to multiple tasks. So, experimental evidence suggesting that attentional fields are heterogeneous (Downing and Pinker 1985) led to a revised model that posits a peak of attention at the center of the focal area, shading off in a graded continuous fashion as the field extends outward from the focus (LaBerge 1995). This ATTENTION HAS A GRADIENT metaphor (Fernandez-Duque and Johnson 1999) is an attempt to satisfy the value of quantificational description of attention phenomena. In contrast, in the original ATTENTION IS A SPOTLIGHT models, quantification was taken to be relatively unimportant, whereas phenomena connected with our ability to move and reorient the attentional spotlight were given primary importance.

Another crucial issue—one that is tied closely to the value of *empirical testability*—is which entities or agencies are required for a satisfactory account. Causal theories (including the ATTENTION IS A SPOTLIGHT metaphor and some versions of the ATTENTION IS A LIMITED RESOURCE metaphor) require some system or entity/agent that directs, controls, or allocates attention. ATTENTION IS A SPOTLIGHT theories handle this by postulating an executive system (the controller of the attentional spotlight), while many ATTENTION IS A LIMITED RESOURCE theories require some type of homunculus that decides how the resource will be used.

ATTENTION IS RESOURCE COMPETITION theories, in contrast, place a high value on the fact that no control system is required to account for attentional phenomena, since everything is supposed to work "from the bottom up." The ATTENTION IS RESOURCE COMPETITION metaphor thus emphasizes the ontological *simplicity* of its account, which posits neither an attentional substance nor an executive mechanism for its allocation and control. In this way, the values of *relevance* and *importance* are also given significance, since the metaphors tell us what range of phenomena we must account for and which phenomena within that range are most characteristic of attention (and consequently most *important*).

Empirical testability requires a determination of what adequate experimental confirmation (or experimental support) amounts to. We saw earlier that the internal logic of the ATTENTION IS A SPOTLIGHT metaphor has no place for features of the object in determining what gets attended to—the "spotlight" shines on a location and illuminates everything within that location, so it does not differentially affect features of what is illuminated. Experiments revealing that features of objects play a role in attentional affects are thus regarded as challenging ATTENTION IS A SPOTLIGHT theories.

The fact that the source domain of a particular metaphor determines the "ontology" of the target domain, and thereby determines what counts as relevant phenomena, *is a value judgment*. One's preferred metaphor tells you what to take as important. It tells you what the relevant phenomena are. It tells you what to look for in an explanation. We too easily forget, if we ever knew, that deciding what constitutes "the phenomena to be explained" is never a value-neutral endeavor. For example, ATTENTION IS A LIMITED RESOURCE models treat attention as a substance-like commodity. Attention is a "real" resource that can be "allocated" to this or that particular task. Having substantial existence is a positive value in "cause" theories, whereas attention does not even "exist" according to effect theories based on ATTENTION IS RESOURCE COMPETITION metaphors. Causal theories thus regard themselves as superior, insofar as they purport to explain attention as a causally efficacious force or process; while effect theories claim superiority for precisely the opposite reason—namely, that they do not require the postulation of attention as a force or substantial reality. How we evaluate the importance of something alleged to have substantial reality is thus dependent on which metaphor of attention we have appropriated and which values it incorporates.

Similarly, in ATTENTION IS A SPOTLIGHT theories, the spotlight mechanism has a reality different from the light it sheds, different from the field where the light is shed (presumably sensory areas of the brain), and different from the controlling agent (presumably some executive system). In fact, much of the current debate in the brain imaging of attention revolves around the evaluative judgment of whether attention should be described as having a "source" (spotlight), a "substance" (light), and a "target" (field) that is illuminated. Once again, this stands in radical opposition to ATTENTION IS A COMPETITION theories that are taken by their proponents to be superior precisely for the opposite reason—that they assign attention an epiphenomenal status rather than the status of a real entity, substance, or force.

The principal point I am trying to make with these admittedly sketchy examples is that each metaphor will carry its own distinctive matrix of values that guide the research that flows from the metaphor. The metaphors do not necessarily generate the generic values that have been alleged to underlie the sciences. That is, we might think that generalization, comprehensiveness, empirical testability, relevance, importance, and simplicity are general theoretical values shared by all creatures with cognitive systems like ours. But *what the metaphors do is to give meaning, specificity, and force to those values. In other words, these generic values do not actually mean anything concrete and do not have specific implications for scientific research until they are given substance and application by the metaphors that organize our scientific models.* For example, consider: What could "comprehensiveness of explanation" in the abstract mean? Nothing more than an empty ideal that we should try to cover the widest range of phenomena. But this ideal becomes a workable concept once we have metaphorical models that circumscribe the range of relevant phenomena that need to be explained. This was my earlier point when I observed that we don't know what "attention" is, independent of some particular metaphorically structured model of it. Once a metaphorical model tells us what phenomena count as instances of attention, only then is it possible to know what a more versus a less comprehensive account would be. Only then would we know what data are relevant for testing a particular hypothesis or model.

Where Do Scientific Values Come From?

I have tried to provide some evidence that the metaphors tell us what the values are and give content and constraining force to the basic values that underlie particular sciences. I want to close with a brief speculation about the source of these values. My research (M. Johnson 1987, 2007, 2017; Lakoff and Johnson 1999) on the bodily grounding of meaning and on the way structures of our sensory-motor processes shape our conceptualization and reasoning suggests the hypothesis that our deepest scientific values come out of our organic interactions with our environment. In other words, our values result from the nature of our bodies, our brains, the environments we inhabit, and our ways of interacting with those environments (Damasio 1999, 2003, 2010). Such values are not, therefore, a priori givens that are intrinsic to some supposedly absolute, transcendent structure of scientific reasoning.

John Dewey ([1925] 1981, [1938] 1991) argued that the values that most people believe to be intrinsic to science and to shape the logic of scientific thinking are actually the result of patterns of inquiry rooted in our biological makeup that have proved useful for our functioning within our environments over our evolutionary history. We tend to distill from our methods of everyday problem solving certain inference patterns, habits of inquiry, and methodological assumptions that have made it possible for us to deal (more or less successfully) with certain types of problems that we have historically encountered, given our embodiment and the kinds of environments we inhabit. As a species, through exaptation, we have recruited the meaning, logic, and inference patterns embedded in our sensory, motor, and affective experiences in order to perform "higher-level" modes of conceptualization and reasoning.

There is nothing absolute about these modes and methods of inquiry and their embedded values, nothing that guarantees that they should stand as timeless standards of thought and action. Rather, they are what have so far proved reliable for our purposes in certain contexts of problem solving. Most assuredly, situations might well change in ways that would make these methods less than satisfactory and would require us to rethink our science in light of changing conditions. The failure to retain such a critical flexibility could conceivably undermine the success of a given theoretical perspective.

Dewey would thus observe that our most cherished scientific methods, our most taken-for-granted epistemological values, and our most productive metaphors for doing science are historically conditioned products of human problem solving. They emerge, in other words, from our embodied practices and situations. They grow out of the very patterns of activity by which embodied organisms monitor and negotiate their environment so as to deal with problems that arise. Dewey puts this boldly when he connects physical problem solving with abstract inquiry: "The term 'naturalistic' has many meanings. As it is here employed, it means, on the one side, that there is no breach of continuity between operations of inquiry and biological and physical operations. 'Continuity,' on the other side, means that rational operations *grow out of* organic activities, without being identical with that from which they emerge" ([1938] 1991, 26). These "organic activities" of which Dewey speaks are an organism's attempts to survive and function successfully within the environments it inhabits. Dewey saw inquiry as an activity (an intellectual process) by which an organism seeks to resolve a problematic situation—an indeterminate state of affairs in which the organism's fluid functioning is blocked or disrupted—into a determinate situation in which the organism can pursue its ends and grow. Inquiry at this bodily level thus involves actual changes in the organism-environment interaction. Inquiry alters the situation that gives rise to it and results in a different state of affairs than existed before the inquiry was initiated. Successful inquiries are those that lead to growth and fluid functioning.

Once you have Dewey's embodied, situated notion of inquiry, you see scientific inquiry as continuous with our embodied day-to-day problem solving. Science may differ from commonsense problem solving in the ways it employs language, symbol systems, and sophisticated tools to aid in its search for solutions, but it shows the same patterns of inquiry that characterize our organic, bodily functioning, namely, need-demand (or search) -satisfaction (1925, ch. 7). Values of inquiry thus emerge out of our bodily engagement with our world.

Consider, for example, the value of comprehensiveness of scope in science. I suggest that such a value comes out of the fact that an organism has the best chance of growing and flourishing the more conditions of its environment that it can interact fluidly with, incorporate as part of its activities, and unify relative to its needs and purposes. Thus, the more comprehensive a hypothesis is, the more possibilities for action and growth it presents to us. That is why we value breadth of scope in an explanatory hypothesis. However, this certainly does not mean that comprehensiveness will always be an absolute value. There are other possible bases in organic activity that might recommend, say, narrow focus, depth of focus, or attention to a single, exclusive function, as a means for an organism's survival. That is why it is possible to have cases of competing values within a particular science, or even within a particular theory. The bodily grounding of values is no guarantee that those values will be mutually consistent or compatible with one another.

To cite another example, consider the value of simplicity. Other things being equal, an organism might tend to seek, most of the time, the least expenditure of energy necessary to accomplish its purposes. Simplicity is a positive value just insofar as it leads to efficient functioning and ease of action. It is no surprise that such a value would be carried up into even our most abstract theoretical inquiries, since they are no less geared to the solving of problems and to successful interaction with our world. However, simplicity is not an absolute value, by any means. One can imagine situations in which complexity would be preferred, because of the way it might enhance growth of meaning and possibilities for action. Once again, the fact that our values emerge from our embodied experience does not guarantee that they are either absolute or fixed for all situations.

The value of empirical adequacy comes out of this account almost as a given, since, at the level of sensory-motor experience, what we strive for is fluid functioning *within our actual empirical situation*. In other words, we have to be in touch with our world. We have to take experiential conditions into account in planning our actions, lest we risk making our inquiries and problem solving irrelevant to, and out of gear with, our day-to-day existence.

The Importance of Metaphors for Science

These abbreviated speculations about the possible bodily grounding of scientific values are offered only to suggest a direction for future inquiry into a naturalistic theory of scientific models and their values. The bodily basis of such values goes hand in hand with the bodily grounding of the metaphors that shape our thinking and our inquiry. I have suggested that the values operative in scientific investigations come out of the bodily source domains within the metaphors that guide the scientific inquiry. An adequate account would obviously also have to examine the importance of historical and cultural factors that determine which values have held sway at different times, and why (Dewey [1925] 1981; Longino 1996).

My principal focus has been on the way metaphors allow scientists to circumscribe the relevant phenomena, to define research strategies, to decide what will test their hypotheses, and to evaluate their explanatory progress. The metaphorical mappings are what allow us to carry over knowledge, inferences, and values within the source domain to knowledge, inferences, and values in the target domain. The corporeal, spatial logic of the source domain is the basis for our reasoning about the target domain. It thereby establishes the values operative in the target domain and gives them specificity, definition, and force.

This central role of metaphor in science should strike us as unremarkable once we see that *all* our abstract concepts are defined by one or more (often mutually inconsistent) metaphors (Lakoff and Johnson 1999). Science, unsurprisingly and necessarily, draws on the same conceptual and cognitive resources of our ordinary commonsense understanding and reasoning; but science operates with highly refined symbolic representations and subjects its performance to rigorous standards that are not as strictly maintained in commonsense evaluation. It often uses tools and technologies not readily available to the ordinary person. Nevertheless, there is no rupture of continuity between everyday and advanced scientific inquiry.

Only a literalist about meaning and an objectivist about knowledge will find this claim about the centrality of metaphor disturbing. And well they should, since it undermines their pretension to absolute knowledge and disembodied meaning and thought. On the contrary, the inescapable working of metaphor in all science is not a lamentable shortcoming, as though it were a sign of an immature science. Rather, the metaphors are what make possible the great achievements of science, because they set research programs, structure scientific inferences, and give concreteness and explanatory force to our deepest scientific values.

PART 2

Morality and Law

Morality and law are human creations. They may have their sources in animal habits and behaviors, but they do not achieve their full human depth and richness until they cross over that blurry, shifting line that distinguishes us from other animal species, wherever and however that line gets drawn at any point in history. The old theological idea that Almighty God created us in His image—a little lower than the angels and a little higher than the beasts—ought to be discarded, but it can be repurposed to the insight that on the one hand, we are not possessed of God-like understanding or reason, but on the other, we represent a level of organized life above (though intimately related to) that of dogs, cats, dolphins, and elephants, however dear those creatures may be to us.

Throughout much of Western history, the dominant view has held that it is our rationality that places us above other animals (who are allegedly determined entirely by their embodiment), while it is our embodiment that places us lower than the gods (or any purely rational creatures). Our rationality is thought to be tainted by our bodily passions and desires, but not so much that we cannot sometimes aspire to act on principles and from motives of an idealized pure reason. In that expression of reason, so the story goes, lies our particular glory in the animal kingdom.

It would be nice if we had absolute, certain, eternal knowledge of our world. We do not, because our world is forever changing and our perspective is limited and partial. It would be nice if we had absolute, certain, eternal knowledge of how we should live as moral creatures. We do not, because the very nature of our situated, embodied engagement with our world and other people gives rise to a plurality of values and ways of ordering our lives. We are not, to quote Dewey, "little gods" possessed of pure reason ([1925] 1981, 324).

What we are is embodied creatures whose understanding and values emerge from our ongoing transactions with our physical, interpersonal, and cultural environments. That makes our morality perspectival, fallible, and subject to change over time. An appreciation of our nature as embodied finite creatures is the premise on which this claim about the limitations of our moral understanding is based.

The history of philosophy is not lacking in challenges to the rationalistic account of morality, most notably coming from those who see our emotions and sentiments (rather than pure practical reason) as the ground of our moral appraisal and choice. Over the last half century, the sciences of mind have developed this criticism and attempted to explore in far greater detail how actual human moral reasoning and choice operate. The result has been a naturalistic conception of morality as grounded in our body-based and culturally influenced understanding, reasoning, and emotional response.

The three chapters in this section are partial and selective attempts to explore the implications of our embodied mind, thought, and values for our understanding of moral thinking and choice. Chapter 6 ("Cognitive Science and Morality") indicates some of the ways in which cognitive science research is relevant to moral philosophy, not just in the negative, critical way of challenging selected assumptions of various moral theories, but also by adding to our constructive understanding of human values and better and worse moral cognition. Chapter 7 ("Moral Imagination") explores what morality becomes when it gives up the illusion of disembodied thought and embraces the central role of imagination in our capacity for moral deliberation. It argues that the grounding of our moral cognition in bodily and culturally shaped experience supports an understanding of moral deliberation as what John Dewey called the imaginative "dramatic rehearsal" of possibilities for enhanced and expanded meaning. It thus makes a case for seeing imagination as key to our ability to frame moral ideals and to expand and deepen our grasp of the meaning and significance of a morally problematic situation. In a similar vein, chapter 8 ("Mind, Metaphor, Law") suggests that our legal concepts and reasoning are, just like morality, shaped by deep conceptual metaphors rooted in our body-based and culturally influenced values. Law, too, is shaped by metaphor and built on concepts that are open ended, flexible, and historically contingent.

Morality and law, then, are human creations, just like philosophy and science. They are not the result of moral or legal directives issued from above, via some allegedly transcendent source of norms and values. Rather, they both grow from the biological and cultural matrices that define our embeddedness in the world. The result is a human morality, rooted deeply in our visceral engagement with our world (both physical and cultural) and relying on imaginative insight as the way to make things better. The morality and law that emerge from our finite experience are neither absolute nor certain, but they give us the only reliable guidance we can have for how we ought to live, what we ought to value, and how we can dwell together with others.

CHAPTER 6

Cognitive Science and Morality

Every moral tradition and every moral theory necessarily presupposes some specific view of how the mind works and of what a person is. The cognitive sciences constitute our principal source of knowledge about human psychology and sociality. Consequently, the cognitive sciences are absolutely crucial to moral philosophy. They are crucial in two basic ways. First, any plausible moral system must be based on reasonable assumptions about the nature of concepts, reasoning, the self, and moral psychology (Flanagan 1991). Second, the more we know about such important issues as the role of emotions and feelings in moral deliberation, the nature of moral development, and the most realistic conceptions of human well-being, the more informed we will be in our moral thinking. Empirical investigations into mind thus provide a way to examine the link between the "is" of mental functioning (e.g., how concepts are structured, the nature of moral appraisal, the role of emotion in reasoning) and the "ought" of morality— that is, the normative claims of our ethical systems.

As an example of the critical function of cognitive science for ethics, consider its implications for two of our most prominent philosophical theories of morality: utilitarianism and Kantianism. In its classical form, utilitarianism is the view that the morally correct action for a given situation is that action that would maximize the good, or well-being, that is realizable in that situation for the largest number of people affected by that action. Utilitarianism thus requires highly determinate concepts of "the good" (including concepts of self-interest and happiness), as well as a capacity to calculate rationally the probabilities for which actions are most likely to realize these ends or values that we deem good. However, empirical research on human conceptualization and reasoning shows that most of our concepts of well-being are relatively indeterminate and culturally variable (Prinz 2007), and that people are quite poor at performing the kinds of interest and welfare calculations required by classical utilitarianism, to such an extent that the theory becomes psychologically unrealistic (Kahneman 2011; Haidt 2012). In other words, cognitive science research calls into question some of the fundamental assumptions of utilitarianism.

Kantianism holds that morality is a system of absolute, universally binding moral laws that come from a universal reason (i.e., pure practical reason) and that can be applied to concrete cases to give us moral guidance. Kantianism thus requires the existence of a universal reason and of moral principles that contain clearly defined literal concepts applicable to the kinds of situations we encounter in our lives. But there is ample experimental evidence to suggest, first, that human reason is not transcendent, since it is inextricably bound up with our embodiment and emotions (Damasio 1994; Tucker 2007; M. Johnson 2007); and second, that our moral concepts are not literal but rather metaphorical in nature (M. Johnson 1993, 2014; Lakoff and Johnson 1999; Kövecses 2010). In this way, empirical results about cognition place major constraints on what an adequate, psychologically realistic moral theory would look like.

It is a shocking fact, therefore, that until quite recently mainstream moral philosophy of the last two centuries has largely denied any significant role for empirical research on mind, thought, and values. Cognitive science is typically dismissed as being irrelevant on the basis of the mistaken assumption that there exists a rigid dichotomy between facts and values, *is* and *ought*. The irrelevance-of-cognitive-science argument takes the following form: The cognitive sciences deal with empirical facts, seeking to describe and explain natural phenomena of mind, such as why people think and behave as they do. It is then asserted that such facts about human thinking and behavior cannot give rise to normative claims about how people ought to think and behave. Those norms have to come from some autonomous source. Therefore, cognitive science has little or no bearing on moral philosophy.

Fortunately, over the past two or three decades there has been a significant change of perspective. Extensive experimental research in moral psychology and cognitive neuroscience has led to a growing awareness: that cognitive science research should be an essential part of our moral understanding and theorizing, insofar as it provides crucial knowledge of how people conceptualize, reason, and make moral judgments. Knowledge of this sort is the key to intelligent moral deliberation.

The Philosophical Prejudice against Cognitive Science

The hostility of moral philosophy toward cognitive science rests primarily on the notorious is/ought dichotomy—the erroneous view that facts and values are radically distinct and independent of each other. David Hume argued famously that he could see no justification for moral philosophers slipping imperceptibly from talk about what *is* (about facts concerning human behavior and valuing) to talk about *what ought to be* (normative moral judgments) (Hume [1739–40] 2000, bk. 3, pt. 1). Hume held a naturalistic perspective on the moral sentiments, and so he presumably would have welcomed cognitive science research on emotions and feelings. However, generations of philosophers have focused only on Hume's puzzlement over how it is that people could possibly move from factual statements to moral appraisals and imperatives, and they conclude that no moral (normative) constraint can be derived from factual statements.

Kant reinforced this purported split between descriptive empirical knowledge and normative moral judgments by claiming that the universality and necessity of absolute moral laws could never stem from merely empirical scientific generalizations, but must come instead from the normative capacity of pure reason to issue universally binding moral principles. He concludes that "not only are moral laws together with their principles essentially different from every kind of practical cognition in which there is anything empirical, but all moral philosophy rests entirely on its pure part. When applied to man, it does not in the least borrow from acquaintance with him (anthropology) but gives a priori laws to him as a rational being" (Kant [1785] 1993, 389).

This vehement denial of the relevance of empirical study for moral guidance was reinforced in a most fateful way at the beginning of the twentieth century by G. E. Moore's *Principia Ethica* (1903), which had a profound problematic influence on the direction taken by moral theory for many decades to follow. Moore asserted that the fundamental moral concept *good* denotes a simple, unanalyzable, nonnatural property of certain experiences or states of affairs. Moore never really explained what the nature of a nonnatural property was. He simply contrasted it with the "natural" properties—properties perceivable and measurable—that were the objects of study of the empirical sciences. He then proceeded to give examples of what he regarded as nonnatural properties, but without explanation or serious argument. Moore concluded that what he saw as the fundamental question of moral philosophy, the question of what "good" is, could never be answered by reference to empirical scientific investigations of natural properties. He then went on to coin the term "naturalistic fallacy" for what he regarded as the mistake of attempting to define the concept *good* in terms of natural properties (or *any* properties, for that matter). The only role that Moore allowed for empirical inquiry in ethics was to supply causal knowledge of which actions were most likely to realize certain ends or states of affairs that were deemed to be good.

Moore influenced generations of subsequent moral theorists who have simply assumed a radical split between moral psychology (as an empirical, descriptive discipline) and moral philosophy (as rational analysis and normative prescription). They see no possible link between the *is* of moral psychology and the *ought* of moral philosophy.

Areas Where Cognitive Science Bears on Ethics

From the perspective of the cognitive sciences, then, the most fundamental challenge is to show that the alleged is/ought split is mistaken by showing how research in cognitive science is important for our moral understanding and judgment. We must examine the ways in which cognitive science both constrains and enriches our moral understanding. Every moral theory must necessarily make assumptions about conceptual structure, reasoning, the self, emotions, values, and the nature and limits of human understanding. It is the business of cognitive science to investigate just such issues, and in this way, our empirical knowledge of the mind is directly relevant to moral philosophy.

The idea that empirically based inquiry is not a servant to moral philosophy, but is in fact the core of ethics, was set forth cogently by John Dewey in *Human Nature and Conduct* (1922), and by Dewey and James Hayden Tufts in *Ethics* (1932). In the former, Dewey argues that ethics is "ineradicably empirical, not theological nor metaphysical nor mathematical. Since it directly concerns human nature, everything that can be known of the human mind and body in physiology, medicine, anthropology, and psychology is pertinent to moral inquiry" (Dewey [1922] 1988, 204).

Dewey's argument that moral philosophy must incorporate the best empirical research on mind was mostly ignored by Anglo American analytic moral theory throughout much of the twentieth century. Only in the last two or three decades have a number of empirically minded philosophers begun to take seriously the importance of cognitive science for moral theory (Flanagan 1991; Paul Churchland 1996; Hinde 2002; Kitcher 2011; Patricia Churchland 2012; M. Johnson 2014). Most notably, Owen Flanagan (1991) has argued that a minimal psychological criterion of any adequate moral theory is that it be compatible with our most stable and reliable knowledge of human psychology. He formulates this requirement as a "Principle of Minimal Psychological Realism (PMPR): Make sure when constructing a moral theory or projecting a moral ideal that the character, decision processing, and behavior prescribed are possible, or are perceived to be possible, for creatures like us" (Flanagan 1991, 32). To know what's possible for creatures like us, we need good science.

However innocuous this principle might seem to most people, it has radical implications for the relation of cognitive science to moral theory. It entails that normative moral theory ought to be constrained by what the cognitive sciences are discovering about the mind and human psychology. It means that the normative dimension of moral thinking is not independent of the facts of moral psychology.

The chief challenge for a more naturalistic view of ethics is to survey the kinds of empirical research that are relevant to moral theory and to show how these results ought to influence our moral evaluations. As I will discuss below, cognitive science has important insights for a positive account of values and moral guidance. However, for the most part, results from the cognitive sciences presently available function primarily to set basic constraints on the nature of a psychologically and cognitively realistic moral theory. These fundamental requirements for a tenable moral theory come from empirical research on the following major areas:

Concepts and Rules

There is a dominant moral law tradition in the West that encompasses stoicism, most of Judeo-Christian morality, Enlightenment rationalist ethics, and several contemporary moral theories, according to which morality is regarded as a system of universal moral laws or rules, discernible by human reason and directly applicable to the kinds of concrete moral situations that people encounter in their lives (M. Johnson 1993, 2014). Different traditions see these moral rules as having different sources—either coming from God (as in Judaism and Christianity), coming from a universal human reason (as in Kantianism), or as being socially constructed (as in Rawls's theory of justice)—but all seeing morality as based on moral laws or principles.

Cognitive science research on the nature of conceptualization and reasoning bears directly on the psychological plausibility of moral law theories. For example, moral law theories typically require a set of universal, absolute, strict rules that specify morally correct behavior for the kinds of ethical situations we are likely to encounter (Donagan 1977; M. Johnson 1993). To avoid relativism, these rules must apply for all times and cultures. Each rule must have a fixed, clear, literal meaning that is directly interpretable by ordinary people so that they can decide how to act in a specific situation. Otherwise, there would be no proper or correct application of a given rule.

In *Women, Fire, and Dangerous Things* George Lakoff (1987) surveys a massive body of cognitive research showing that virtually none of our more abstract human concepts have this clear, literal, univocal internal structure. It is difficult to find an abstract natural (as opposed to artificial) concept that is literal, defined by necessary and sufficient conditions, and uniform in structure. On the contrary, many concepts are "fuzzy," in the sense that they have shaded boundaries and a graded internal structure. More important, most concepts are not defined by a unique set of properties shared by every member of the category. Instead, our categories exhibit "prototype effects," where one category member will be more prototypical and representative—a more central member of the category—than other members. This constitutes what Lakoff (1987) calls a "radial category structure," in which central category members are connected to noncentral members by principles of extension that are either image based, propositional, metaphorical, or metonymic. Consequently, most members of a category will not share a core set of defining features with other category members. Paul Churchland (1996) has explored some of the ways that our moral judgments are grounded in experientially developed moral prototypes, such as prototypical cases of lying or cases of unfairness in distribution of goods, services, or opportunities. He observes that children early on learn these moral prototypes, such as when a child protests that he didn't get as big a cookie as his sister, or when his sister complains that he got more time riding the bicycle or playing a video game than she did.

It is typical for people to conceptualize and reason by means of prototypes and their imagistic, propositional, metaphorical, and metonymic extensions rather than by lists of essential features that are supposed to define a category. For example, I (M. Johnson 2014) have analyzed the concept of *moral personhood* to show that it is a radially structured category lacking any core set of essential features common to all and only members of the category. In the case of our concept of *moral personhood*, the set of beings to whom moral personality has been attributed has varied widely over the past several centuries and across different cultures, relative to historical developments and cultural beliefs and values. For centuries in Western culture the central member of the category *person* was taken to be a white, adult (and typically heterosexual, and often Christian) male. Non-"white" men, women, children, and animals were either not granted full personhood, or they were marginally included. Over the past century, women, nonwhites, and children (but only to a certain extent) have been allowed into the category in some cultures not because it was finally realized that they had been *persons* all along, but because changing historical conditions and cultural institutions led us to *remake* the category of personhood. The point is that the radial category of *personhood* is always a work in progress, changing its structure over time, relative to emerging historical developments and changing cultural values. There is no essential, literal, univocal concept of personhood valid at all times and in all places. This transformation continues today, as changing cultural conditions give rise to arguments for attributing personhood to corporations, certain machines (e.g., computers with artificial intelligence programs), some nonhuman animals, and even ecosystems.

Another important outcome of cognitive research that undermines moral law theories is the discovery that most of our abstract concepts are defined by sets of metaphors (Lakoff and Johnson 1980, 1999), some of which are typically inconsistent with one another. I (M. Johnson 1993, 2014) and Lakoff (1996) have analyzed a number of moral concepts, such as *rights, justice, revenge, well-being*, and *will*, to reveal underlying conceptual metaphors that jointly define our entire moral orientation—metaphors such as MORALITY IS HEALTH, MORAL STRENGTH IS PHYSICAL STRENGTH, MORAL BOUNDARIES ARE PHYSICAL BOUNDARIES, MORAL BEHAVIOR IS NURTURANCE, GOOD IS LIGHT/BAD IS DARK, MORAL CHARACTER IS UPRIGHTNESS, and MORAL CHARACTER IS PURITY. If our fundamental moral concepts are defined by *multiple* and possibly inconsistent conceptual metaphors, then the literalist picture of moral thinking (in which concepts are supposed to map directly and univocally onto situations) cannot be correct.

Reasoning

This large body of research on conceptual structure thus wreaks havoc with any traditional moral law theory, since it shows that morality is not principally a matter of learning and following univocal, literal rules. Because our moral concepts are structured by prototypes, metaphors, metonymies, and other imaginative devices, the moral reasoning we do with such concepts is almost never strictly deductive. Only in the most trivial cases—those where the specific situation is simple and routine enough to fit some prototype within a moral category—can we simply subsume a particular case under a general ethical principle. Even then, contextual differences may make simple subsumption problematic. When we face real moral problems, those will be cases where our received habits, values, and principles are not adequate to the emerging complexity of our situation, so that we must explore possible metaphorical and metonymic extensions from prototypical cases to nonprototypical cases. This does not mean that there is no place for moral principles; rather, the principles we do have should be understood as based on past experience of factors we have found to be important in our moral deliberations, and defined via prototypes, models, and metaphors. The mistake is to regard those principles as strict pre-given rules, rather than as summaries of the collective wisdom of a group regarding certain kinds of recurring moral situations encountered in the past (M. Johnson 2014).

The way we reason about a situation depends on the way we *frame* it (Fillmore 1985; Lakoff 1996). Consider, for instance, the abortion debate. How is it to be framed as a moral issue? Typically, it is framed as a matter of rights—the rights of the fetus (as a person) versus the rights of the mother (as a person)—and within this context the debate focuses almost exclusively on whose rights should take precedence. However, the abortion issue does not come with the label "rights" stamped on it. Framed instead as a question of social welfare, the debate would center around whether communal well-being is enhanced or diminished by the practice of abortion under certain specific constraints. Or, within the framework of political liberation, abortion might be regarded as justified only in situations where it is a means to realizing human freedom of oppressed communities.

Moreover, within various framings of the abortion issue, there is the further problem of deciding what counts as a "person," since the debate has typically centered on restrictions about how *persons* are to be treated. As I have just noted above, the concept *person* is what W. B. Gallie (1956) called an "essentially contested concept," one that may have an underspecified core that is not contested, but that can be extended in any number of highly controversial and contested ways. There is no absolute or frame-neutral stance from which to define or extend such terms; rather, social, historical, religious, philosophical, and political factors will give rise to potentially incommensurable framings of these concepts (Lakoff 2006).

In sum, this sort of complexity and frame dependence for our concepts and reasoning makes a traditional moral law account impossible. Moral law theories must presuppose precisely what cannot be taken for granted; namely, that our moral concepts are literal, internally homogeneous, and uncontested in any fundamental sense. Such cognitive science results thus undermine any form of moral fundamentalism—the view that humans have access to univocal universal moral principles and absolute values.

Another important source of converging empirical evidence concerning framing comes from psychological studies of the heuristics and models people use in making probability determinations under conditions of risk. Much contemporary moral theory rests on a classic economic conception of rationality, according to which people are seen as being incentive driven by what they perceive as their self-interest and as basing their decisions, using logical reasoning, on all available information—including the impact that current choices will have on future choices. Both classical utilitarianism (which determines the moral correctness of an action by how well it contributes to the overall well-being of all affected people) and egoism (which requires the calculation of self-interest) have tended to assume some form of economic rationality.

A host of studies growing out of the work of Daniel Kahneman and Amos Tversky (Tversky and Kahneman 1974; Kahneman 2011) suggest that a strict economic conception of rationality is not psychologically and cognitively realistic. People typically do not, and probably cannot, make good probabilistic judgments of the sort required by an economic conception of rationality. The way a decision under risk is framed makes a big difference in what people will decide is in their best interest in a particular situation. For example, people tend to be risk averse when deciding about possible gains and risk seeking when considering possible losses. The "endowment effect" makes people reluctant to risk assets that belong to their endowment, even when objective probabilities might suggest that possible substantial gains are likely to result from accepting a certain amount of risk. The extreme difficulty of making good probability judgments calls into question any simple economic model of rationality.

Critics of the Kahneman-Tversky studies have tried to defend the economic conception of rationality by arguing that the studies are flawed and that people are not really so bad at probabilistic reasoning. Still, no one disputes the fact that people do employ a range of frames and heuristics for reasoning. Our reasoning is not, therefore, neutral in frame or context; and this challenges both the absolutistic pretensions of classical moral law views and also the classical model of economic rationality. Simply put, the rational calculations of either self-interest or communal well-being, if not humanly impossible, are certainly extremely difficult to perform, and they often require information either that we cannot obtain or that is highly complex. This calls into question any theory that requires a fairly precise calculation of goods or benefits as the basis for correct moral reasoning. To make matters even worse, achieving most of our moral goals (and thereby realizing certain goods) often requires complex cooperative activity among many people over long periods of time. However, we have little or no control over others' participation or lack of it, so how can we figure their participation into our deliberations? The idea that individuals can accurately and realistically calculate what is in their own or others' best interest appears to be an illusion, not to mention the impossibility of calculating what will produce the greatest communal good.

Emotion and Moral Deliberation

Most contemporary moral theory—as well as most of the Western moral tradition—assumes a fundamental ontological and epistemological gap between reason and emotion. This is true even of moral theories centered on emotions and sentiments, since they emphasize the importance of emotions in moral appraisal and judgment, and they tend to deny any serious role for reasoning. Based on this alleged dichotomy, philosophers typically argue that morality stems either from reason alone or from feeling alone. In the first camp, Kant was the most notorious champion of "pure" practical reason, rejecting feeling as an inappropriate basis for moral judgment, since he thought that feeling was subjective, individual, and therefore incapable of supporting absolutely binding universal moral laws (which Kant took to be the ground of our moral obligation). In the second camp, Hume argued that moral judgments are based, not on reason, but on moral sentiments of approval and disapproval of certain acts. He saw reason as a calculating faculty that issues judgments about matters of fact and relations of ideas, whereas the passions and sentiments alone move us to action: "Since morals, therefore, are meant to have an influence on the actions and affections, it follows, that they cannot be deriv'd from reason. . . . Morals excite passions, and produce or prevent actions. Reason of itself is utterly impotent in this particular. The rules of morality, therefore, are not conclusions of reason" (Hume [1739–40] 2000, bk. 3, pt. 1, sec. 1, p. 457). Following Hume, twentieth-century emotivists, such as A. J. Ayer and C. L. Stevenson, claim that moral judgments are not cognitive or truth-conditional, but rather expressions of emotion or attitude intended to influence action.

However much they appear to differ, both the champions of reason and the champions of emotion alike share the same mistaken assumptions that reason is radically separate from emotion and that moral judgment can only be based on one side of this split, to the total exclusion of the other. Both of these assumptions are false. Neither side in the debate has paid sufficient attention to research on effect and reason, which is why so many moral theories cannot provide an adequate account, either of moral motivation or of the role of emotions and feelings in moral deliberation.

The recent interest in so-called "dual-process" theories of moral appraisal and judgment tends to reinforce the reason-versus-passion split, rather than dissolving it. The basic claim is that there are two tracks of moral appraisal: (1) an intuitive track that is automatic, fast, nonconscious, and unreflective; and (2) a rational track that consists mostly in after-the-fact justifications and rationalizations of what the intuitive track has already decided and done (Hauser 2006; Haidt 2012). The intuitive track tends to be regarded as doing most of the work of moral appraisal, whereas the rational track is relegated primarily to making up likely stories to justify our intuitive judgments.

Fortunately, there has recently been a surge of interest in exploring the interrelatedness of emotional and rational dimensions of thought. Some of the most significant research on the role of emotion in reasoning is Antonio Damasio's (1994, 2003) investigation of brain damage that affects reasoning, including social reasoning and moral deliberation. Damasio argues that "certain aspects of the process of emotion and feeling are indispensable for rationality" (1994, xiii). Especially in practical and social reasoning, reason cannot do its job independent of complex emotional processes that are connected to body monitoring systems involved in our survival and well-being. Emotions situate us in our world and move us toward the realization of certain values. This does not mean that morality is not rational, but rather that our practical and moral reasoning are always oriented and guided by affective states. Thus, moral deliberation is neither purely rational nor purely a matter of feeling or emotion alone. Instead, reason can act only in concert with our emotions.

John Dewey saw that reason should be viewed neither as a power wholly separate from, nor in competition with, emotion and feeling. In moral deliberation we are faced with a plurality of competing and conflicting desires or perceived goods, and "rational" deliberation consists in reducing the conflict as much as possible, with the hope of harmonizing (to the extent that we are able) these multiple desires:

> But reasonableness is in fact a quality of an effective relationship among desires rather than a thing opposed to desire. It signifies the order, perspective, proportion which is achieved, during deliberation, out of a diversity of earlier incompatible preferences. Choice is reasonable when it induces us to act reasonably; that is, with regard to the claims of each of the competing habits and impulses. (Dewey [1922] 1988, 135)

Another striking result of Damasio's research is that there is no such thing as a "pure" reason wholly independent of human embodiment and feeling. Bodily processes and experiences establish the patterns of our reasoning: "Our most refined thoughts and best actions, our greatest joys and deepest sorrows, use the body as a yardstick" (Damasio 1994, xvi). We are just beginning to understand the profoundly important role of embodiment in human moral understanding (Lakoff 1996; M. Johnson 2014), but the evidence indicates that the traditional conception of will and reason as disembodied, pure, and radically free is bankrupt (Flanagan 2002; Eagleman 2011).

Empathy and Self-Formation

Empirical studies suggest that from a cognitive and developmental point of view, empathetic feelings are the principal basis for our ability to care about other people, and so they are essential to morality (Goldman 1993). Moreover, the self is an interpersonal self, existing in relation to others and by virtue of its ability to have empathetic, nuturant feelings for others. Stern (1985) presents a broad range of studies of infant development showing that although there obviously are innate capacities, the infant's sense of self emerges only through interpersonal interactions in which the child becomes cognitively and affectively attuned to parents and siblings. This "affect attunement" is a communicative, interactive, embodied process in which parent and child respond reciprocally to each other's moods, feelings, and attention, typically at a level beneath conscious awareness. In such an ongoing process of mutual coordination, parent and infant tend to match or loosely imitate each other's behavior, but often in different sensory modes, such as when a baby succeeds in grabbing a toy and lets out an exuberant "Aaaaah!," followed by the mother's scrunching up her shoulders and shimmying her upper body for a period approximating the duration of the "Aaaaah!"

Stern sees affect attunement as a precondition for true empathy, which involves additional cognitive processes, such as abstracting empathetic knowledge from the experience of emotional resonance, and thereby understanding how another person feels and experiences a situation. In a series of studies over many years, Martin Hoffman (1993, 2000) has assembled a massive case for the central role of empathy in any account of moral experience. He shows how empathy develops from birth, examines its crucial role as a moral motive, and studies sex differences and the contribution of sex-role socialization in empathy-based morality. Hoffman's results suggest five major ways in which empathy lies at the heart of moral motivation and judgment: (1) Early on, children who witness the distress of another person come to respond empathetically with feelings more appropriate to the person in distress than to themselves. (2) This empathetic distress scheme is readily extended to people who are not present and to imagined sufferings, because we have the imaginative capacity to represent to ourselves the experience of others. (3) Empathetic affects are largely congruent with forms of caring and also with various forms of justice. In this way, our moral principles may be activated by basic empathy. (4) Because "cool" affective states can become "hot" cognitions, even abstract moral principles can acquire a motive force via the heating up of the empathetic component of the principle. (5) Empathy plays a crucial role in moral judgment, such as when it supports moral impartiality.

This picture of the interpersonal self and of the crucial role of empathy and other emotions undercuts the traditional Enlightenment view of moral agents as autonomous, atomistic, rational egos with moral personality formed prior to their actions and social relations. Cognitive research supports the communitarian critiques set forth in works such as Alasdair MacIntyre's *After Virtue* (1981) and Michael Sandel's *Liberalism and the Limits of Justice* (1982), which argue that contemporary versions of Enlightenment rationalism, such as Rawls's *A Theory of Justice* (1971) and Nozick's *Anarchy, State, and Utopia* (1974) assume a mistaken view of moral agents as existing prior to, and independent of, their actions and social interactions. The archetypal Kantian conception of the self as a radically free rational ego capable of deliberating and willing in accordance with pure practical reason is an illusion. We exist in and through others, and our moral concern depends on our ability to empathize with others. Cognitive studies of empathy and emotion thus promise to shed light on some of the most vexing problems of moral theory, such as how moral principles can have any motive force, why we care about the well-being of others, how impartiality is experientially grounded, and why there is no radical split between reason and emotion.

Moral Development

Every moral theory presupposes some theory of moral development. Until quite recently, Kantians and other moral law theorists took great comfort from knowing that two major studies of moral development, Jean Piaget's *The Moral Judgment of the Child* (1932) and Lawrence Kohlberg's *Essays on Moral Development* (1981), seemed to support their generally Kantian view of the structure of adult moral understanding. Kohlberg's view in particular recognized Kantian autonomy as the pinnacle of moral development. Kohlberg's six stages of possible moral development ranged from children following rules laid down by external parental authority (first stage), through intermediate stages of social constraint, and aiming toward autonomous guidance by universal ethical principles (highest, final stage).

Over the last two decades, the model of mature morality as autonomous rule following in accordance with universal rational principles has come under severe criticism from further studies of cognitive development. Flanagan (1991) summarizes five major areas in which research has challenged the model of discrete, homogeneous stages through which children may pass on their way to moral maturity. The main objections include evidence against the existence of holistic, unified general-purpose stages and also evidence that people seldom rise beyond a mixed blend of stages ⅔ and ¾. Much has also been made of the problem of drawing any psychologically realistic claims from standard tests, especially those (like Kohlberg's) based on verbal reports about hypothetical situations, administered to boys but not girls. Carol Gilligan (1982) expanded her survey to include girls, and she got a very different, more pluralistic and care-oriented picture of moral responsibility. Moreover, when one begins to unpack some of the guiding assumptions built into the tests—such as that morality is a system of rules for behavior—it appears that many studies are begging key questions about the scope and nature of morality. For example, the assumption that "later" stages are "higher" stages automatically excludes the real possibility that mature moral understanding would integrate a number of different considerations and forms of judgment, instead of focusing on one privileged "highest" mode of thought.

What cognitive science discovers about moral development places substantial constraints on the structure of a psychologically realistic moral theory. If, for instance, cross-cultural studies (such as Richard Shweder's *Thinking through Cultures* [1991]), reveal wide cultural differences concerning moral ideals and patterns of moral development, then claims either about absolute, universal values or universal moral rules become highly questionable (Prinz 2007).

Another important aspect of moral development concerns the role of the family as a basis for moral understanding and growth. The analysis in Lakoff 1996 and Lakoff and Johnson 1999 of the relation of morality and politics reveals the central role of family morality as a basis both for a person's general moral values and also for their political orientation. Lakoff contrasts "strict-father morality" (a morality that prizes authority, discipline, moral strength, and order) with "nurturant-parent morality" (emphasizing empathy, care, nurturance, and compassion). Lakoff then argues that developmental studies in the area known as attachment theory uncover severe problems with strict-father morality. For example, strict-father morality prides itself on producing self-reliant, disciplined, and autonomous moral agents. However, in fact, studies show that it tends to produce people who lack self-confidence and cannot make decisions for themselves, are unable to criticize authority, and do not manifest great moral strength. In short, studies of moral development can sometimes lead directly to fundamental critiques of moral frameworks and can establish the range of psychologically plausible moral systems.

Gender

Especially since the Enlightenment, moral agency has typically been characterized by mainstream philosophers as gender neutral, based on an allegedly universal rationality or else on a universal capacity for moral sentiments, both of which are supposedly shared by all free and equal rational beings. Feminist philosophers have lately subjected this myth to scathing critique, pointing out the many ways that assumptions based on traditional gender typing are built into the structure of the dominant universalist view. They argue that what is presented as a universal view of moral reason and virtues is, in fact, based on masculinist assumptions that exclude women and often members of "nonwhite" cultures. Only in the last thirty years has empirical research on gender differences been brought to bear on this important issue. As mentioned above, Gilligan (1982) challenged the Kohlberg studies (which were based on a small number of young males) and opened the way for a more thorough and self-critical investigation of possible gender differences in moral understanding. While she distinguishes a morality of rights and justice from a morality of care and responsibility, she is careful not to draw this distinction strictly along gender lines. She suggests, however, that girls are—and boys are not—typically socialized into the culture of care, thereby often learning very different ways than boys to handle moral conflicts.

The main questions are, does this gender-differentiated model really stand up under scrutiny, and if there are such differences, are they based on genetic differences or on socialization? The evidence does not appear to be available yet to fully decide such issues. Flanagan (1991) offers an extensive survey of recent work on the issue of gender and moral orientation. He looks at studies of virtually every aspect of this question, from whether women score lower than men on Kohlberg-type tests (answer: no statistically significant differences), to whether there are only two basic gestalts (justice and care) for moral orientation (answer: no), and to whether the justice and care gestalts appear to split neatly along gender lines (answer: no). Flanagan concludes that, although such gender studies have been important in greatly enriching our moral understanding and in revealing underlying assumptions and values, there is simply not yet sufficient experimental evidence to draw strong conclusions about the role of gender in morality: "Moral personality is, in the end, too variegated and multipurpose to be analyzable in terms of a simple two-orientation scheme—even blended together" (ibid., 233).

Bridging the Is/Ought Gap

The alleged fact/value split rests on the assumption that there must be an independent source of norms (moral and otherwise), since no descriptive statements generate or justify normative claims. On this view, our moral values must issue from some transcendent normative source to impose imperative obligations on us as rational creatures. More than ninety years ago, John Dewey pointed out that morality is not a matter of justifying values and principles by reference to some innate value-generating capacity. Rather, it is a matter of problem solving, through which we try to make the world better. We have more values than we can shake a stick at, and we have plenty of excellent explanations of why people have these values (Hinde 2002; Flanagan 2007; Damasio 2003) I (M. Johnson 2014), for instance, have grouped these norms into four tiers: (1) values emerging from our needs as biological organisms (e.g., food, air, water, shelter protection from bodily harm), (2) values grounded in our intimate interpersonal relations (e.g., care, empathy, love), (3) values emerging in larger social communities (e.g., rights, duties, justice, civic-mindedness), and (4) values tied to our human desire for meaningful lives (e.g., actualization of our higher capacities, meaningful work, caring interpersonal relations). There is nothing special or exhaustive about this taxonomy. It is meant only to show that we are always immersed in a sea of values, and that we have more explanations than we need for why these various values matter for us.

Dewey ([1922] 1988) saw that our greatest moral problems stem, therefore, not from ignorance of values and their sources, but rather from the fact that we often encounter conflicting and incommensurable values, and we are not sure how to resolve the tensions among them. We come into any situation armed with a host of values that determine what we experience, care about, think, and do. Thus what we most need is not an alleged inner faculty of conscience that generates our values and moral principles; instead, we need *conscientiousness*—the ability to utilize our intelligence to determine how best, in a given situation, to balance out competing desires and values, both within ourselves and between us and others. Moral reasoning is not about discovering allegedly absolute values and applying them to our situation. It is more about composing situations in which multiple values are at work in some measure of harmony, so that we realize as much well-being as is possible in our current situation (Dewey [1922] 1988; Fesmire 2003; Kitcher 2011).

Dewey ([1939] 1981) explains the role of what he called "valuation" (i.e., critical reflection on our values to determine which ones lead toward genuine and longer-lasting flourishing within a given context) with an analogy to the health sciences. Medical science is a fundamental life-sustaining practice that has existed as such for millennia. It has a long history of developing practices and methods about how best to realize the goods internal to the practice, such as avoiding disease, sustaining bodily functions, repairing injuries to the body, and enhancing the quality of life. Although there are serious differences of opinion about what methods and techniques are optimal, many values, outcomes, and methods are widely recognized as part of excellence in that practice (MacIntyre [1981] 1984). However, even the ultimate goals and ends of medical science can be called into question by emerging unanticipated conditions (Wright 2002). Such issues are not settled by recourse to pure reason or absolute norms, because some of those norms are precisely what are being questioned. Instead, they are worked out in an ongoing fashion in various cultures and in response to emerging conditions. Dewey concludes:

> While there is no a priori standard of health with which the actual state of human beings can be compared so as to determine whether they are well or ill, or in what respect they are ill, there have developed, out of past experience, certain criteria which are operatively applicable in new cases as they arise. Ends-in-view are appraised or valued as *good* or *bad* on the ground of their serviceability in the direction of behavior dealing with states of affairs found to be objectionable because of some lack or conflict in them ([1939] 1981, 233).

Dewey is here proposing his account of inquiry in the health sciences as a model for the process of moral inquiry in general. We investigate the history of cultural values and practices to see how those values arose, and in response to what conditions they appeared appropriate. Empirical research then plays a key role in determining both how best to realize a preferred state and which values are most appropriate in our present situation.

The key to overcoming the fact/value dichotomy is to recognize that, in every situation in which we find ourselves, we always *start* with values that have emerged from previous human experiences, and therefore the normative is already pervasive in our lives. We are awash in values. For example, the simple fact that, as bodily organisms, we need certain goods if we are to survive, already directs us toward trying to realize certain (valuable) states of affairs that are conducive to life. The simple fact that we depend inescapably on others for our well-being already directs us to values of empathy, interpersonal bonding, and care.

Owen Flanagan and Robert Williams (2010) point out that, indeed, we do not *derive* norms from factual statements about the world or humans (that is, we don't derive *ought* from *is*). Instead, because we are normatively directed from the beginning of our lives, we have to assess the importance and consequences of the various values present in each morally problematic situation we encounter. Our inferences about what ought to be done are not typically deductive reasonings, but rather hypotheses that are either inductive (based on what has apparently worked well in the past) or abductive (inferences to the best explanation among the alternatives available). Moral decision making is a form of problem solving, and Flanagan and Williams observe that in various practices, accomplished problem solvers make use of the best information available and often discuss the validity of competing goods, ends, or values that might underlie their entire practice: "'Oughts' are not (normally) derived or deduced. But 'oughts' do not sit out in thin air in such a way that only the ghost-whisperers can explain. 'Oughts' are reasoned to in a holistic network that operates over both propositions about facts and propositions about antecedently settled values and 'oughts,' all of which are open to conversational challenges" (2010, 444).

If this is a correct view of moral reasoning, then the cognitive sciences are just one part of the empirical knowledge we bring to bear in any moral reasoning that is intelligent, suitably self-critical, and open to revision.

Why Cognitive Science Matters to Morality

The above areas mark out substantial domains of empirical research in the cognitive sciences that should directly constrain the form and content of any humanly realizable morality. Quite obviously, the joint constraints established by research in these areas leave open a wide range of possible moral orientations—a plurality of conceptions of moral growth and well-being. There is no psychologically realistic way to avoid such pluralism. Nor would it be advisable to do so even if we could, since it is the very existence of multiple conceptions of human well-being and modes of living that make us aware of the limits of our own moral views and that also open up possibilities for moral growth and improvement.

Those who think that empirical research is irrelevant to moral theory often argue that empirical theories change over time, so that today's popular theory of cognition, selfhood, or values may be tomorrow's whipping boy as new empirical studies raise questions and criticisms. But this is no argument against the relevance of cognitive science for morality, because morality, as Dewey said, is experimental—it is a massive ongoing communal experiment in resolving the issues of human living and flourishing that confront us every day. A morality that cannot be revised as new results about mind become known is a dead morality, incapable of meeting the kinds of change that are part of human existence.

Owen Flanagan has articulated just the sort of de-transcendentalized, empirically grounded, experiential, and experimental morality that I am suggesting here:

> Morals consists of habits of heart, mind, and behavior. Morality is "normative" in the following sense: It consists of the extraction of "good" or "excellent" practices from common practices. Ethics consists of wisdom based

on historical experience about how best to arrange our affairs, and how to develop our nobler potential, as this too is judged on the basis of historical experience. Moral habits, wisdom, and skills consist largely of "know-how" that allows for smooth interpersonal relations, as well as for personal growth and fulfillment. Ethical reasoning is a variety of practical reasoning designed to help us negotiate practical life, both intrapersonal and interpersonal, as it occurs in the ecological niche we occupy. (2007, 126)

The cognitive sciences will not generally tell us how to act in particular situations. They provide moral guidance because they contribute to our moral understanding—our understanding of human nature, of the workings of the mind, of how we make sense of and reason about moral issues, of where our values come from, and of what our world is like and how it works. Their normative significance comes from what they reveal about what it means to be human and about what is required for intelligent, critical, and constructive moral judgment and action. Their significance comes from the way they present to us psychologically realistic conceptions of human, and more-than-human, well-being and flourishing.

CHAPTER 7

Moral Imagination

For hundreds of years in mainstream Western philosophy it has been a commonplace to regard "moral imagination" as an oxymoron. The terms *moral* and *imagination* are often thought to be incompatible by those who conceive of morality as a system of *rational* moral principles and who regard imagination as a free play of images and ideas unconstrained by reason. The result of this mistaken bifurcation between reason and imagination is that imagination is not seen as having any constitutive role in determining what is right and wrong, lest we risk arbitrariness, idiosyncrasy, subjectivism, and rampant relativism.

This widespread misconception that imagination is unsuited to the lofty office of moral appraisal has led (for most of history and with only rare, though very important, exceptions) to a profound neglect of moral imagination by philosophers and psychologists. Over the past three decades, however, an increasing number of philosophers have begun to use the term unapologetically to name a crucial process of imaginative moral deliberation by which we are able to explore how experience would play out under the influence of various values and commitments. From this perspective, moral imagination is regarded as the chief means we have for reducing moral indeterminacy, resolving conflicts among competing ends, and addressing clashes of values. In short, imagination is viewed as *constitutive* of our moral reasoning and not merely subservient to the alleged application of preestablished, rationally derived moral principles.

Imagination as a Key Component of Moral Sentiments Theory

The widespread neglect of imagination is mostly the result of rationalistic theories of moral cognition that arose at the end of the eighteenth century, most notably Kant's theory of pure practical reason. This rationalism was partly a reaction against the moral sentiments theory, which held that moral judgments are based shared feelings or sentiments, rather than on rationally derived moral laws. The moral sentiments theory recognized a significant role for imagination in moral deliberation. Francis Hutcheson, David Hume, and Adam Smith famously argued that moral judgments are not acts of reason, but are instead based on the shared human sentiments of approbation and disapprobation that we feel as we contemplate various actions and states of character. In his *Treatise of Human Nature* (1739–40) and *An Enquiry Concerning the Principles of Morals* (1751), Hume argued that only emotions and passions can move us to action, and therefore any morally effective motive must be based on our capacity to experience moral sentiments and on the general sympathy most people have for the well-being of others. The sympathy we feel toward others requires a capacity to imagine how it feels to be in their situation.

A more elaborate and nuanced account of moral imagination was developed by Adam Smith in *The Theory of Moral Sentiments* (1790). Like Hume, Smith begins with the claim that no matter how selfish and egocentric humans may be, they are also born with a natural disposition to care for the welfare of others. We judge an action right, or a character trait virtuous, to the degree that we feel a sentiment of approval when we perform that action or exercise that disposition in ourselves.

But how are we able to participate in the way others feel, think, and act? Smith's answer is that we can imagine how they are feeling in a given situation: "As we have no immediate experience of what other men feel, we can form no idea of the manner in which they are affected, but by conceiving what we ourselves should feel in the like situation. . . . By the imagination we place ourselves in his situation, we conceive ourselves enduring all the same torments, we enter as it were into his body, and become in some measure the same person with him" (Smith 1790, part 1, sec., 1, chap. 1). This empathetic capacity is "the source of fellow-feeling for the misery of others," and "it is by changing places in fancy with the sufferer, that we come either to conceive or to be affected by what he feels" (ibid.). The goal of our moral self-cultivation should therefore be to nurture our sympathetic feelings and to expand our capacity for imaginative grasp of other people's experience and situation. Smith concludes that "there may be some correspondence of sentiments between the spectator and the person principally concerned, the spectator must, first of all, endeavour, as much as he can, to put himself in the situation of the other, and to bring home to himself every little circumstance of distress which can possibly occur to the sufferer. He must adopt the whole case of his companion with all the minutest incidents; and strive to render as perfect as possible, that imaginary change of situation upon which his sympathy is founded" (Smith 1790, part 1, sec., 1, chap. 4). As we will see below, Smith's subtle and sensitive understanding of the nature of, and need for, an imaginative grasp of other people's experience is very much in line with late-twentieth- and early twenty-first-century treatments of moral imagination. He even recognizes the importance of our capacity to mirror the feelings and bodily states of others that neuroscientists over two centuries later will attribute to our mirror-neuron systems.

Unfortunately, the heyday of moral sentiment theories was brief. Their eclipse by Kantian rationalist moral philosophy led to a profound neglect of moral imagination for the next hundred and twenty years.

The Marginalization of Imagination in Moral Philosophy

It is not too much of an oversimplification to assert that Kant's celebrated attack on moral feeling led to the subsequent dismissal of imagination as a source of moral insight and appraisal. This suspicion of imagination stemmed primarily from the hegemony of what I (M. Johnson 1993) have called the moral law folk theory, which can be summarized as follows:

1. Humans are distinguished from brute animals by their capacity to reason and to act under the guidance of universally binding rational principles.
2. Moral principles are rules that categorically determine which actions are morally acceptable, which are morally impermissible, and which are obligatory.
3. Acting morally requires (a) determining rationally which principle applies to a present situation, and (b) having the willpower to act on that principle in order to "do what is right."
4. To avoid moral relativism, moral laws or commands must be defined in terms of determinate literal concepts capable of fitting the concrete situations we find ourselves in.

There are two popular versions of the moral law folk theory. Theological versions posit absolute moral commandments issued by God (or gods), while rationalist versions regard ethical guidance and constraint as products of universal human reason. Both versions agree in denying imagination any constitutive role in moral judgment, on the grounds that imagination and reason are fundamentally different and nonoverlapping cognitive faculties. In the rationalist camp, Kant famously argued that moral laws must be universally and necessarily binding on all rational creatures, and he insisted that such universality and necessity could only be the product of a "pure" practical reason, independent of any reliance on experience or empirical considerations. Kant summarizes: "It is clear from the foregoing that all moral concepts have their seat and origin completely a priori in reason. . . . In this purity of their origin lies their very worthiness to serve us as supreme practical principles; and to the extent that something empirical is added to them, just so much is taken away from their genuine influence and from the absolute worth of the corresponding actions" ([1785] 1983, 411).

By "empirical" here, Kant meant anything grounded in human experience, including anything tied to our bodily and affective selves. Although Kant did not think of our rational and bodily natures as two different substances, there is, nevertheless, a lingering dualism in his metaphysics, insofar as he regarded reason as an activity of the transcendent self or ego (as noumenal), in contrast with imagination, which he thought of as tied to our bodily (hence, phenomenal) nature. On this view, moral judgment requires a rational act of seeing how a concrete case falls under a specific moral imperative. Kant saw that this process of bringing a particular case under a universal rule cannot itself be governed by rules, for that would lead to an infinite regress of rules for correctly applying rules. However, he steadfastly insists that the moral judgment cannot be based on imagination: "Thus the moral law has no other cognitive faculty to mediate its application to objects of nature than the understanding (not the imagination)" (Kant 1787, 69). In his *Lectures on Ethics* he therefore warns against subordinating rational authority to the seductive power of imagination: "If he surrenders authority over himself, his imagination has free play; he cannot discipline himself, but his imagination carries him away by the laws of association; he yields willingly to his senses, and, unable to curb them, he becomes their toy" (Kant [1775–80] 1963, 140).

It is this Kantian logic that most fatefully and erroneously regards moral imagination as an oxymoron—a dissonant yoking together of two allegedly incompatible ideas; namely, morality as a system of rationally derived moral laws and moral deliberation as a process of imaginative projection. Kant's influence on subsequent moral philosophy was so profound that (with perhaps the exception of philosophers such as Nietzsche, James, and Dewey) the idea that imagination might play a central role in moral appraisal and judgment is almost unheard of in mainstream Western philosophy until the late twentieth century. Delaying until later an account of Dewey's seminal contribution to the view that moral imagination is the crux of our ethical problem solving, let us briefly consider how imagination has slowly gained a foothold in accounts of moral cognition over the past three or four decades.

The Movement toward a More Constitutive View of Imagination in Moral Cognition

In the latter half of the twentieth century, the term *imagination* begins to appear ever more frequently in discussions of ethical reasoning. One finds a number of views that promisingly acknowledge a place for imagination in our moral life. Unfortunately, most of them remain unwilling to allow imagination a fully constitutive role as performing the principal work of moral thinking. Too often, they gesture toward imagination without providing any detailed account of its operations. For example, in *Freedom and Reason* (1963), R. M. Hare acknowledges that in order to correctly apply his rationally derived universalizability principle to a concrete situation, we must be able to imagine that situation from various perspectives to see how it would affect others. However, Hare insists that imagination does not generate our moral obligations; it only helps us see what is required concretely in a particular situation of moral judgment. This function is carried out more by artists than philosophers, because "to cause people to exercise their imaginations is above all the task of the artist—especially the novelist and the dramatist" (Hare 1963, 181). It is through literary fictions, he suggests, that we often cultivate a sympathetic imagination that helps us understand the situation of others and empathize with them. Nevertheless, the normative dimension of the universalizability principle is alleged to come from reason alone.

Steven Fesmire (2003) surveys other philosophers who find a limited role for moral imagination but still insist that reason alone is the source of moral principles and guidance for our lives. He cites as an example Oliver Williams (1997), who—although he treats imagination as part of

Aristotelian practical wisdom—argues that the moral constraint must issue from independently defined standards of right action. Williams claims that "while moral images and the stories they compose shape reason 'to see rightly,' they do not replace reason.... The stories and images of the Christian community help one to discover God's will but, in principle, human insight and reasoning can discover this same will in the form of moral obligations" (Williams 1997, 5). Patricia Werhane (1999) also recognizes the indispensability of moral imagination for exploring different possible framings of a moral situation or problem. She illustrates this process by investigating the crucial role of imagination—or lack thereof—in certain landmark business ethics cases. Unfortunately, she nevertheless ends up stressing the necessity of rational constraints on the workings of imagination: "Moral imagination enables one to assess one's situation, to evaluate present and new possibilities, and to create decisions that are not parochially embedded in a restricted context or confined by a certain point of view.... However, one should not confuse moral imagination with practical moral reasoning.... Imagination alone can create fantasies that, too, become dominating and falsifying narratives" (Werhane 1999, 13). What both Williams and Werhane stress is that without proper guidance from moral reason, imagination is liable to lead us astray. Consequently, imagination can never be constitutive of moral deliberation.

John Kekes's *The Enlargement of Life: Moral Imagination at Work* (2006) at first appears to grant imagination a very substantial role in our moral understanding, but he soon qualifies this by insisting on the necessity of rational moral constraint. In a view that seems to echo some of John Dewey's key ideas (although without any serious acknowledgement of Dewey), Kekes says, "Moral imagination, self-transformation, and reflective self-evaluation together enlarge life by enlarging its possibilities and overcoming obstacles to their realization.... Moral imagination is one chief means by which this reflective self-evaluation proceeds. Its moral component is concerned with living a good life, understood as combining responsibility and fulfillment" (2006, xiv). Kekes describes three kinds of imaginative process that he regards as crucial to human ethical behavior and fulfillment. *Corrective imagination* is a backward-looking act through which we attempt to grasp the full range of possibilities that might have been available in a past situation, but which we may have overlooked at the time. *Exploratory imagination* then permits us to investigate the range of morally appropriate actions currently available to us as we struggle with a moral problem. This capacity allows us to engage complex cognitive, emotional, and volitional processes relevant to living moral lives. *Disciplined imagination* mediates between corrective imagination's discovery of what about ourselves and the situation needs to be corrected or reconstructed on the one hand, and on the other, exploratory imagination's survey of the moral options available to an individual. This promising assessment of the importance of imagination is, however, limited by Kekes's refusal to grant imagination a fully constitutive role. Clinging to an outdated faculty psychology, Kekes ultimately concludes that imagination must always be subject to the constraints of moral reason. This insistence on rational constraint is evident when Kekes criticizes Martha Nussbaum's (1990, chap. 4–5) celebration of the novelist's creative imagination as key to our moral enlightenment. Kekes responds that "the idea that living a good life is like creating a work of art, that moral imagination is a species of creative imagination in which the artist's work in the medium of their own lives, is pernicious because it leads to the rejection of moral limits" (2006, 113). In the final analysis, then, Kekes does not trust imagination to do the work of moral thinking.

There is a pattern emerging in these views, in which initial enthusiasm for moral imagination comes to be tempered by a deep concern that, left unchecked by reason, imagination might lead to an uncontrolled moral relativism. In light of centuries of neglect of imagination, these and other theories do at least recognize some role for imagination in moral deliberation, and so they are definitely steps forward in moving beyond a strictly principle-governed perspective. Nonetheless, they never fully extricate themselves from the mainstream view that all or most moral constraint, as well as the definition of right action, must come from some cognitive faculty or source besides imagination. In short, the key issue is whether imagination is to be granted a *constitutive* role in moral appraisal, or whether it remains but a subsidiary function that only helps us grasp how our ultimate moral laws and values apply in a concrete situation.

In *The Many Faces of Realism* (1987), Hilary Putnam argues that moral theories are not—as many of their progenitors conceive them—issuances of some universal reason that supposedly specifies absolute constraints. Instead, every moral perspective or theory presupposes and articulates some particular *moral image of the world*:

> A moral image, in the sense in which I am using the term, is not a declaration that this or that is a virtue, or that this or that is what one ought to do; it is rather a picture of how our virtues and ideals hang together with one another and of what they have to do with the position we are in. It may be as vague as the notions of "sisterhood and brotherhood"; indeed, millions of human beings have found in those metaphors moral images that could organize their moral lives. (Putnam 1987, 51–52)

This embrace of a complex imaginative framework as our horizon of moral values and practices is tantalizing insofar as it suggests that moral appraisal is more about imagining how the world might be made better, than it is about applying unconditionally and eternally valid principles to a particular situation. Putnam's pluralistic moral vision is also admirable, insofar as he recognizes our need to blend a number of inherited moral images—such as liberty, equality, and brotherhood and sisterhood—into a more or less coherent view of character, right action, and flourishing. In other words, we need imaginative pictures of how our world might look under the influence of complex virtues, principles, and values. Unfortunately, Putnam has not given any detailed account of what this alleged process of constructing a moral image involves, nor has he explained how it is supposed to work in our lives.

At first glance, Richard Rorty (1989) appears to advance beyond Putnam when he embraces the idea that moral sensitivity requires us to be able to imagine the lives of others, and that narrative fictions are one of the primary vehicles for such a process of empathetic imagination. In appreciating the power of narratives to develop our moral perceptiveness and empathy, Rorty joins a chorus of those who see imaginative engagement with fictional stories as a primary means of our moral self-cultivation (Gardner 1978; Ricoeur 1984; Eldridge 1989; Nussbaum 1990; Gregory 2009). But the question that has to be answered is how moral imagination works in such experiences. Here Rorty has little to offer, because his account of language gives him no resources for explaining growth and expansion of meaning and value.

The limitations of Rorty's view stem from his insistence that we should replace talk of "experience" with talk about "vocabularies." "Experience," he famously argues, is a problematic term that too often gets illegitimately utilized in an attempt to ground or justify our moral values. But Rorty observes that there is no way to describe anything beyond or beneath vocabularies against which they can be assessed, for we can only describe something in language (that is, using some vocabulary). Consequently, "attempts to get back behind language to something which 'grounds' it, or which it 'expresses,' or to which it might hope to be 'adequate,' have not worked" (Rorty 1982, xx). Rorty concludes from this that having a moral perspective is equivalent to adopting a particular moral vocabulary.

And what defines a given "vocabulary"? Rorty's answer is that vocabularies are fields of interrelated words that set up systems of literal meanings and truth claims. He sees change from one vocabulary to another as effected by the creation of a novel metaphorical framework that later comes to be regarded as a new system of literalities. However, Rorty does not think that metaphors themselves are meaningful; rather, they are just pragmatic tools for moving us from one moral vocabulary to another. Following Donald Davidson, Rorty asserts that metaphors are not semantic phenomena: "One should not think of metaphorical expressions as having meaning distinct from their literal ones. To have a meaning is to have a place in a language game. Metaphors, by definition, do not. . . . In his view, tossing a metaphor into a conversation is like suddenly breaking off the conversation long enough to make a face, or pulling a photograph out of your pocket and displaying it, or pointing at a feature of the surroundings, or slapping your interlocutor's face, or kissing him" (1989, 17–18). According to this nonsemantic conception of metaphor, changes from one moral vocabulary to another (such as a change from a utilitarian to a Christian, Kantian, or existentialist vocabulary) do not occur through rational analysis and argument, but rather through the imaginative capacity of a "strong poet" to come up with a new metaphorically structured moral vocabulary to replace an entrenched one.

What Rorty gets right is that our moral systems are, indeed, structured by systematic metaphors (M. Johnson 1993, 2014; Lakoff and Johnson 1999; Lakoff 1996, 2006) and that novel metaphorical frames can play a crucial role in the transformation of our moral perspective. However, Rorty's impoverished conception of meaning provides him with no resources for explaining how imagination supposedly operates in this process of change. A particular metaphor, on his view, is merely an irrational rupture in the fabric of one moral vocabulary that opens the way to a new metaphorical vocabulary, which will gradually come to be taken as a system of literal truths.

Since he thinks metaphors are not semantic, Rorty ignores any serious linguistic or cognitive science research on semantic change or on the workings of imagination and simply asserts that somehow a new moral vocabulary, complete and total, springs up to replace the reigning moral vocabulary. He famously describes this process as blind, contingent, and mechanical: "Think of novelty as the sort of thing which happens when, for example, a cosmic ray scrambles the atoms in a DNA molecule, thus sending things off in the direction of the orchids or the anthropoids. . . . Analogously, for all we know, or should care, Aristotle's metaphorical use of *ousia*, Saint Paul's metaphorical use of *gape*, and Newton's metaphorical use of *gravitas*, were the results of cosmic rays scrambling the fine structure of some crucial neurons in their respective brains. . . . It hardly matters how the trick was done. The results were marvelous" (Rorty 1989, 17).

Contrary to Rorty's claim that it does not really matters how metaphors work, I would argue that it matters a great deal, because our ability to explain how moral imagination actually works makes all the difference regarding our ability to determine whether moral imagination is *constitutive* of our moral understanding, rather than merely an act of irrational rupture leading to vocabulary change. It makes all the difference whether it is possible to speak of "better" and "worse" moral deliberation.

Consequently, when it comes to normative ethical claims, Rorty thinks that arguments are of little or no practical value; he instead praises the role of literary narratives in helping us appreciate the experience and suffering of others. This is an important insight, but it is not self-explanatory or self-justifying. Rorty correctly observes that people of a liberal persuasion, for example, tend to value the metaphor of brotherhood and sisterhood, and they consequently set a high value on avoidance of cruelty as crucial for the improvement of the human condition. They are therefore attracted to fictional narratives that help them imaginatively empathize with others, see others as like themselves, and therefore act to minimize others' suffering and treat them with respect. There is little point in trying to argue the merits of kindness over cruelty with someone under the sway of a different metaphorical moral vocabulary than the one you espouse. Rorty explains: "In my utopia, human solidarity would be seen not as a fact to be recognized by clearing away 'prejudice' or burrowing down to previously hidden depths but, rather, as a goal to be achieved. It is to be achieved not by inquiry but by imagination, the imaginative ability to see strange people as fellow sufferers" (1989, xvi). Rorty is right about the power of empathetic imagination to help us enlarge the circle of people and animals that deserve our respect and care. He sees that imaginative fictions can enact a narrative understanding of other peoples' lives, struggles, and hopes, and can often engender empathy for their plight.

Nevertheless, because Rorty eschews reference to any experience beyond or beneath language (and vocabularies), and because he regards metaphors as nonsemantic, he has nothing significant to say about moral imagination, other than merely to assert that new metaphors help us imagine new ways of feeling and acting toward others. Rorty sees that fictional narratives can show us ideals of what we might become; however, beyond noting this fact, he has no explanation of how this process works, since, from his perspective, all that remains is just the supplanting of one "metaphoric" by another, blindly and irrationally.

To say something useful and psychologically realistic about moral imagination, we have to understand how things are meaningful to us and how we are able to imagine how various attitudes and values would play out in our lives. For an account of that sort, we are better served by turning away from Rorty's linguistic pragmatism toward John Dewey's experiential pragmatism (see chap. 3 for this distinction), which gives a central role to moral imagination.

Dewey's Conception of Moral Imagination

I regard Dewey's nuanced and detailed account of the role of imagination in moral inquiry and deliberation as the model around which we can eventually construct a workable view of moral imagination. Dewey articulated incisive criticisms of the traditional moral law view of moral cognition, as well as other popular moral philosophies, and he proposed a radical alternative picture of moral reasoning as imaginative deliberative problem solving. From this perspective moral imagination is *constitutive of*, and not just supplementary to, moral reasoning.

Dewey argued that what I have called the "moral law" theory (or any theory that claims to have identified absolute principles, values, or ends) is a misguided attempt to freeze conceptions of right and wrong for all time, based on the erroneous assumption that we inhabit a closed and completed moral universe that operates under the constraint of absolute moral laws adequate for appraising any possible ethical situation. From a broadly evolutionary perspective, Dewey emphasized the reality of change and novelty in nature and human affairs. With respect to morality, this means that new moral problems are bound to arise from time to time, due to changing conditions. Human beings are mostly creatures of habits they have unthinkingly developed in response to regular features of their environment, and these habits more or less automatically and unconsciously determine their behaviors—not just their bodily movements, but all the way up to habits of thinking and valuing. Much of the time our habits may serve us reasonably well, but they can become dysfunctional in situations where novel conditions arise that were not anticipated when the habit was first formed. Then problems emerge when our taken-for-granted habits are not adequate for dealing with changing conditions of experience, such as when two or more agents espouse incompatible values or conceptions of the good, or when an individual experiences conflicting values or goals in his or her life. What we need most in such cases of moral conflict is not reversion to alleged absolute, pre-given principles, virtues, or concepts of goodness, because it is precisely these that may be called into question by novel conditions and events. Rather, what we need is an intelligent process of moral inquiry that helps us resolve conflicts, harmonize competing values, and expand possibilities for growth of meaning. For this reason, Dewey conceived of moral reasoning as a form of problem-solving inquiry by which we transform situations to resolve conflict, disharmony, and tension, typically without knowing in advance what our end or good is or ought to be.

It is within this context of ongoing problem solving that Dewey introduced his notion of imaginative reasoning. Recall that the reason we encounter a problematic situation in the first place is that our ordinary habits of thought, feeling, and action have ceased to deal adequately with the changed experiential conditions that we are encountering. What is needed in such cases is a nuanced understanding of the historical context in which our received moral values and practices arose, a deep appreciation of the sources and nature of our current moral problems, and an imaginative grasp of the possible ways experience might be transformed and carried forward for the better. Thomas Alexander has eloquently summarized Dewey's conception of imaginative intelligence in the service of moral betterment:

> We act in order to realize on a deeper, aesthetic level a sense of meaning and value in our very existence. Knowledge may play a crucial role in this, but in the last analysis, for Dewey, we are creatures seeking a kind of dynamic, embodied fulfillment that goes far beyond generating mere propositional attitudes and other abstractive cognitive needs. As active beings, we are in constant touch with the *possibilities* of our situations. Indeed, this is Dewey's definition of intelligence: to see the actual in light of the possible. This is also his definition of imagination. Imagination is rooted in organic embodiment of our existence and flowers in our highest consciously articulate moments. (2013, 194)

Moral imagination is thus not a distinct *faculty*; instead, it is the expansive dimension of intelligence at work in the ongoing remaking of experience. It is a *process* of experiential transformation and growth—the embodied, situated, aesthetically sensitive manner by which experience expands and gains enriched depth, breadth, and meaning. Alexander observes that "the role of imagination becomes pivotal, for it is a phase of activity—that phase in which possible activities are envisaged in relation to our own situations, thereby amplifying the meaning of the present and creating the context from which present values may be criticized, thus liberating the course of action in itself" (ibid.).

Dewey famously described this exploratory phase of the moral problem-solving process as a dramatic rehearsal of possibilities for developing various courses of action, in order to see which projected course best resolves the indeterminacy of our present situation:

> Deliberation is a dramatic rehearsal (in imagination) of various competing possible lines of action. It starts from the blocking of efficient overt action, due to that conflict of prior habit and newly released impulse to which reference has been made. Then each habit, each impulse, involved in the temporary suspense of overt action takes its turn in being tried out. Deliberation is an experiment in finding out what the various lines of possible action are really like. It is an experiment in making various combinations of selected elements of habits and impulses, to see what the resultant action would be like if it were entered upon. But the trial is in imagination, not in overt fact. ([1922] 1988, 132–33)

Moral imagination is our fundamental capacity to imagine how certain values and commitments are likely to play out in future experience, without actually performing those actions and having to deal with their lived consequences. The quality of our moral thinking therefore depends on (1) the depth and breadth of our knowledge of the physical and social worlds we inhabit, (2) our understanding of human motivation and cognitive/affective development, (3) our perceptiveness of which factors are most relevant in a particular situation, and (4) our ability to simulate the experiences and responses of other people with whom we are interacting. It is thus as much an affair of imagination as it is an appropriation of prior knowledge.

Moral Imagination as Simulation

This fourth dimension—simulating the experience and feelings of others—is particularly important. In order to imagine how various situations might play out based on different values, states of character, motivations, virtues, and principles, we also need a deep sense of how others might experience a situation. That is, we need empathy, which Frans de Waal defines as "the capacity to (a) be affected by and share the emotional state of another individual, (b) assess the reasons for the other's state, and (c) identify with the other, adopting his or her perspective. This definition extends beyond what exists in most animals, but the term 'empathy' applies even if only (a) is met" (2008, 281). In *Moral Imagination: Implications of Cog-*

nitive Science for Ethics (1993), I called this "empathetic imagination," which makes it possible for us to appreciate and take up the part of others: "Unless we can put ourselves in the place of another, unless we can enlarge our own perspective through an imaginative encounter with the experience of others, unless we can let our own values and ideals be called into question from various points of view, we cannot be morally sensitive" (M. Johnson 1993, 199). As Steven Fesmire says, "Taking the attitudes of others stirs us beyond numbness so we pause to sort through others' aspirations, interests, and worries as our own" (2003, 65). Empathetic imagination thus requires not just an ability to *intellectually conceive* how others see and think about their world, but also requires an ability to *feel* their moods and emotional responses to their situation. After decades and even centuries of neglect in moral philosophy and psychology, empathy has now come to be regarded in many circles as *the* basis of our ability to properly care for and nurture others, and to act morally toward them (Hoffman 2000; Gilligan 1982; Noddings 1984).

Moral imagination—both as our capacity to empathetically understand and feel with others and our ability to imagine how experience would play out under the shaping influence of various values and choices—, is thus dependent on our ability to simulate experiences. The new approach known as "simulation semantics" has begun to explore experimentally how people understand experiences, visual scenes, and linguistic expressions by simulating, in their own neural and bodily systems, the perceptual experiences, motor programs, and affective valences that are involved in someone having those experiences. According to this perspective, conceptualization and reasoning are experiential simulations. Lawrence Barsalou argues that "a concept is not a single abstracted representation for a category, but is instead a skill for constructing idiosyncratic representations tailored to the current needs of the situated action" (2003, 521). Problem solving and decision making are processes of "specializing a simulated plan in different ways to see which specialization produces the best outcome.... Skill results from compiling simulations for most of the plans in a domain through extensive experience" (Barsalou 1999, 605).

Another simulation semantics account is provided by Benjamin Bergen (2012), who surveys scores of experiments showing how our processing of sentences involves successive sensory-motor-affective simulations of the scenes being described. Although Bergen's experimental focus is primarily language processing, simulation processes are operative also when we *imagine* how situations might play out under various conditions, and they are thus not limited only to reading or hearing language describing scenes and events.

Research on the human "mirror neuron" system suggests that not only do some of the same sensory and motor neuronal groups fire when we perform certain actions as when we see another person performing those same actions, but they also fire when we *imagine* those actions happening (Decety and Grèzes 2006; Aziz-Zadeh et al. 2006). It thus appears that our mirror neuron system is an important basis for our ability to imaginatively explore various complex courses of action. It helps us put ourselves in the place of another—that is, to appreciate, to a certain limited extent, their experience of a situation or event and to feel how they feel.

It is worth noting that more than two centuries ago, Adam Smith had already emphasized the importance of embodied simulations in our ability to sympathize with others. Although he had no explanation of embodied mirroring activity, he gave several examples of it in various places in *The Theory of Moral Sentiments*; for instance: "When we see a stroke aimed and just ready to fall upon the leg or arm of another person, we naturally shrink and draw back our own leg or our own arm; and when it does fall, we feel it in some measure, and are hurt by it as well as the sufferer. The mob, when they are gazing at a dancer on the slack rope, naturally writhe and twist and balance their own bodies, as they see him do, and as they feel that they themselves must do if in his situation" (Smith 1790, bk. 1, pt. 1., sec. 1). Smith famously places this capacity to feel with and for others at the heart of our sympathetic moral understanding and appraisal.

I have summarized the key role of simulation in acts of moral imagination as follows: "*Moral deliberation is a process of cognitive-conative-affective simulation. Simulation allows us to try out, via imaginative projection, various courses of action that appear to be available in a given problematic situation, and the simulation also activates emotional responses to the projected situations*. These simulations thereby permit us to give voice to various impulses, interests, and values that may be in conflict or tension and then to experience (through feeling) the extent to which a given simulation reduces, or even eliminates, the tension" (M. Johnson 2014, 110, italics in the original). This passage emphasizes mostly our ability to imaginatively run through a possible situation without taking overt action, in order to explore how things would be under the influence of various perspectives and values. In addition, as mentioned above, the simulation process also allows us to experience something of the feelings and emotional responses of other people, both in the present problematic situation (i.e., how others see and feel about something) and also within those simulated scenarios (i.e., how others and ourselves might feel in the imagined conditions we are exploring).

The Scope of Moral Imagination

I have indicated above what it would mean to see moral imagination as not merely a handmaiden to the proper work of a morally practical reason, but instead as constituting our primary means for assessing a moral problem, projecting possible solutions, and experiencing how a situation would play out according to certain values. Taking moral imagination seriously requires us to grant it the broadest possible scope of operation in moral inquiry. Once we acknowledge that moral imagination does the primary work of moral deliberation, we will have already abandoned the fundamental tenet of the moral law folk theory, according to which we inhabit a closed and completed moral universe, in which principles of right—as well as conceptions of the good—are supposedly imposed on experience from some transcendent source. Instead, we will see moral deliberation as an imaginative problem-solving activity that depends on our perception of and sensitivity toward what matters in any given situation of moral conflict. It also requires an openness to move beyond and to reconstruct our present moral habits when the need arises.

The importance of moral imagination helps account for the large number of philosophers, literary theorists, and psychologists who argue that moral cultivation comes more properly from our engagement with historical and fictional narratives than from treatises of moral philosophy that seek to articulate either absolute moral principles, catalogues of the virtues, or ultimate conceptions of the good. It is the narrative depth, complexity, and existential validity of literary fictions that situates our moral perception and appraisal in contexts that are psychologically more valid than those we typically encounter in most moral philosophy. Reading fictional narratives can be morally transformative, insofar as we come to imaginatively inhabit the world and lives of characters that are both like and unlike ourselves and the people we encounter in our lives (Gardner 1978; Eldridge 1989; Nussbaum 1990; Gregory 2009).

Our involvement with morally significant narratives can change the way we understand situations, feel toward others, and see them as vulnerable creatures worthy of our care and respect. Taking moral imagination seriously therefore often requires us to abandon certain assumptions about morality that are deeply rooted in our moral traditions. We have to give up the idea that our moral categories and values are given to us from a completed and fixed moral universe. We therefore have to give up the idea that the right moral decision is given in advance, just waiting for us to discover it and apply it correctly to our present situation. We have to move beyond the view that morality is a system of rationally derived principles that conjointly define our moral responsibilities. We have to recognize that moral deliberation is a trying out, via imaginative projection, of ways our world might be. Moral imagination is our chief resource for enhancing the quality of life for ourselves, others, and our world in general. Thomas Alexander summarizes Dewey's revolutionary view of imaginative moral deliberation as follows:

> *Morality is concerned with the growth of meaning through action.* It aims for a continuous process of integration in which new values can be discovered. This process cannot be guided merely by duty, pleasure, freedom, the universalizability criterion, self-interest, or any other single end. A plurality of values, however incommensurate, must be integrated. The dynamic integration is character. To acquire sensitivity to the developmental meanings of events, which define the significance of the situations in which we find ourselves and the values they possess, is what I have called here "the moral imagination." A moral imagination requires experience, a body of developing habits, education, an ability to understand the way other people think and live, and the ideal of discovering through cooperative action solutions to conflicts. It is the ability to see the meanings at issue in a given situation. It is the moral imagination which thus continually strives to create those ideals that offer the possibility of directing situations toward ends that are most fulfilling. This is what it is to have a moral character. (2013, 199–200; italics in the original)

Moral imagination is thus not merely a single faculty for applying ethical principles to concrete situations. It is, rather, a person's way of being in and transforming his or her world by means of the ability to imagine how situations might develop toward greater harmony, cooperation, freedom, growth of meaning, and envisioning of moral ideals. As such, it is not a deductive process of bringing cases under rules or principles, but more like an artistic process for creatively remaking our world in search of enriched meaning and fulfillment for all concerned. It should be judged by a person's sensitivity, care, and wisdom in envisioning new ways of being in the world that harmonize competing values and open up new relations and possibilities for enhanced meaning and well-being.

CHAPTER 8

Mind, Metaphor, Law

Change, as John Dewey ([1925] 1981) observed, is a basic fact of human experience. We are temporal creatures, and the situations we find ourselves in—the situations that make up the fabric of our lives—are always evolving and developing. The omnipresence of change throughout all human experience thus creates a fundamental problem for law; namely, how law can preserve its integrity over time while managing to address the newly emerging circumstances that continually arise throughout our history. If, following one extreme, we think of law as fixed, static, and univocal in its content, then law runs the risk of losing its relevance to the new conditions and issues that face us from time to time. However, the opposite extreme—that law is completely malleable—is equally untenable, for that would make law nothing more than a tool of those in power. Our problem, therefore, is how law can be both stable and capable of growth.

I believe that part of the answer to this foundational question is beginning to emerge from recent research in the cognitive sciences. Human law is a many-splendored creation of the human mind; that is, of human understanding and reasoning. The primary business of the cognitive sciences is to study empirically how the mind works. Therefore, cognitive science ought to give us insight into the nature of legal concepts and legal reasoning (Bjerre 1999; Winter 2001).

Even though the "cognitive science of law" is a very recent development, its potential for transforming legal theory is substantial. However, most people do not believe that the cognitive sciences are theoretically rich enough, and sufficiently nonreductionist in character, to do justice to the depths of legal understanding. This prejudice is based, I suspect, on the fact that people tend only to know about what I call "first-generation" cognitive science, which grew out of work in the 1950s in computer science and artificial intelligence, and which assumed views of meaning and thought that came straight out of early information-processing psychology, analytic philosophy of mind and language, and generative linguistics. I have to admit that this type of cognitive theory has almost nothing to tell us about the nature of law, because it has turned out to tell us very little about how the mind actually works (Edelman 1992; Lakoff and Johnson 1999; Edelman and Tononi 2000; Damasio 2010).

The Need for a Cognitive Science of Law

Happily, things have changed dramatically over the past three decades, in light of the emergence of a second generation of cognitive science that has called into question virtually all the major assumptions of the first-generation paradigm. Instead of seeing the mind as a disembodied computational program, the newer research reveals that our conceptualization and reasoning are grounded in our bodily experience, shaped primarily by patterns of perception and action (Varela, Thompson, and Rosch 1991; Lakoff and Johnson 1999; Feldman 2006; Tucker 2007; Noë 2009; M. Johnson 2017). There is a logic of our bodily experience that is imaginatively appropriated in structuring our abstract concepts and our reasoning with them. Imaginative processes of this sort depend on the nature of our bodies, our brains, and the patterns of our interactions with our environment. Imagination—which is the soul of human thinking—is therefore constrained and orderly, even though it can be flexible and creative in response to novel situations.

This new cognitive science of the embodied mind is predicated on the assumption that there is no human conceptualization or reasoning without a functioning human brain, which operates a living human body that is continually engaging environments that are at once physical, social, cultural, economic, moral, legal, gendered, and racialized. Our embodiment shapes both what and how we experience, think, mean, imagine, reason, communicate, and do. This claim is a bold one, and it directly challenges our received folk wisdom that what we call "mind" and "body" are somehow two fundamentally different kinds of entities. From a philosophical point of view, one of the hardest tasks you'll ever face is coming to grips with the fact of your embodiment, because this fact requires a serious rethinking of the nature of mind, thought, and language. What makes this task so very difficult is the omnipresent idea of disembodied mind and thought that leaves its traces everywhere we turn, from claims about pure logical form, to pure concepts, to ideas of noncorporeal thought, to spectator views of knowledge, to correspondence theories of truth.

What is at stake here? Why should any of this matter? My answer is this:

1. A disembodied view of mind is often used to support a literalist and objectivist view of thought, concepts, and reason.
2. On the objectivist view, concepts and categories are believed to have strict, fixed boundaries defined by necessary and sufficient conditions. This is what George Lakoff calls the "classical theory" of categories, according to which any concept is allegedly defined by a unique necessary and sufficient set of features possessed by all objects or events that fall within that category (Lakoff 1987). The classical theory is mostly false, and it applies only to a few—mostly artificial—categories.
3. An objectivist-literalist paradigm supports a view of moral and legal reasoning as the application of literally defined objective concepts/categories to situations in an all-or-nothing fashion, according to fixed criteria.
4. This objectivist-literalist theory is based on an empirically false view of cognition, mind, and language. It presupposes a dangerously misguided view of what a person is and how the mind works.
5. As a result, empirical research on the nature of cognition should have important implications for our understanding of moral and legal concepts and reasoning.

Where Does Meaning Come From?

If you think, as I do, that there is no mind without a body—a body in continuous interaction with ever-changing environments—then you've got to explain how this bodily activity gives rise to all our glorious abstract thoughts and symbolic interactions. I want to give a sketch of my version of certain key parts of this massive story of embodied meaning and thought, and I then want to suggest how this new view bears on our understanding of legal reasoning.

Second-generation cognitive science has been developing a bold new theory of the bodily basis of meaning, imagination, and reason (Lakoff and Johnson 1999; Gibbs 2006; M. Johnson 2017). Here I can focus only on three of the most important aspects of human cognition that have potentially profound implications for law:

- Radially structured categories that manifest prototypicality effects
- Image schemas as a basis for embodied meaning and logical inference
- Conceptual metaphors, by which we appropriate embodied meaning for abstract conceptualization and reasoning

Radial Categories and Prototypicality Effects

The classical theory of categories—which is the default view held by nearly everyone in our culture—is that categories have a fixed, stable, objective structure, with each category defined by a unique set of features (Lakoff 1987). On this view, a concept like *dog* is believed to be defined by a set of features an object must possess to be *that* particular type of thing we call a dog. If some object has that particular set of properties, then it is a dog, and not otherwise. Notice that assuming this view of concepts leads us to a very specific view of moral and legal reasoning. If a principle, rule, or law consists of a set of classically structured moral concepts or categories, then that law would apply in a certain clear fashion solely to those situations where the defining conditions for the concepts were satisfied in our experience. If "thou shalt not murder," and if you know the necessary and sufficient conditions that define murder, then your only problem in evaluating a proposed course of action is to determine precisely whether it satisfies the conditions for an act of murder. If a certain act manifests the requisite properties to constitute it as murder, then it is morally (and typically legally) prohibited, period. This classical objectivist view of categories, if it were true, would make law a neat little process of strict rule application. How a legal concept might grow without completely redefining the concept, and how legal judgment might change in a rational, stable manner, could never be explained on this view. But at least a very conservative view of law would be upheld.

Contrary to the classical objectivist view, there is now a massive and steadily growing body of empirical evidence that large parts of human conceptualization and reasoning do not work in the way the classical theory requires (for surveys of this research, see Lakoff 1987 and Feldman 2006). What the evidence shows is that many of our most basic concepts—from those for simple objects like cups and beds, all the way to abstract concepts in morality, politics, science, religion, and law—have complicated internal radial structures and are often not definable by any set of necessary and sufficient conditions.

As an example of this, consider the phenomenon known as "prototypicality effects," that was made famous by the work of Eleanor Rosch and her colleagues (Rosch 1975). Rosch showed that, from a cognitive perspective, people often build their categories around prototypical (central) members, and they then understand less-prototypical members by virtue of their relations to the prototypes. Rosch found, for example, that in America, prototypical birds include robins and sparrows. They establish cognitive reference points for people's reasoning about birds. Less-prototypical birds—such as chickens, emus, ostriches, roadrunners, and penguins—are cognized as lying at varying distances from the center of the category according to various principles of extension (Lakoff 1987). The result is a complex internal structure to our categories. In some cases, there may even turn out to be no univocal set of classical defining features shared by all members of the category. Yet, we do manage to reason quite effectively by virtue of our complex understanding of our radial categories and how they apply to different situations.

To illustrate my point about this complex prototypicality structure of concepts, I want to tell a sad, sad story. Something awful happened in 2006. You know what I'm referring to, right? I'm talking about Pluto, which—I can hardly utter the words—is now *not* a planet! And I'm really upset with President George W. Bush for not standing up for Pluto back in those tumultuous days. Bush was someone who claimed to stand four-square behind the idea that our most important concepts are literal and are fixed in their essence—fixed by God, man, or nature. He stood for this principle, for example, when he insisted that marriage is a divinely blessed union between a man and a woman. He asserted that it has always been that way and that this is clearly a manifestation of the essential nature of marriage. But I ask you, where was our president when those planetary activists decided to ignore the obvious essence of planethood and brazenly declared Pluto kicked out of the planetary family? Well, he wasn't there to defend his conceptual objectivism and essentialism.

You thought Pluto was quite obviously a planet, right? Your whole astronomical education was based on this. And now what are we supposed to do with all those little solar system models we made with Styrofoam balls? Pluck Pluto right out of there, I suppose!

What happened to Pluto? The answer goes something like this: The concept of a planet has turned out to be radially structured, just like nearly all our other concepts. Moreover, it is defined relative to our historically situated values, interests, purposes, institutions, and philosophical views. The *fact* of what constitutes a planet turns out to depend quite substantially on the *values* certain people called astronomers hold dear, especially their view about which phenomena are most important. What we discover is that smart, highly educated people differ greatly about what those foundational values are or should be. Let me explain. There are scads of small bodies circling the sun. Why do we call some of them planets and others not? One reason is that they have a certain size. Marble-sized bits of astrodust don't count. We *could* decide that astrodust should count, but we appear to have good reasons for excluding it from consideration. In other words, astronomers have to decide just what importance size should play in defining the notion of a planet. For example, Pluto is apparently smaller than our moon, yet we have thought of it as a planet ever since its discovery, in 1930. When Mike Brown of the California Institute of Technology discovered 2003 UB^{313} (first dubbed "Xena" and then "Eris"), it looked like there was at least a tenth planet (Adler 2006). Now, Xena is bigger than Pluto. Oh, no! What are we to do? Should we keep adding planets of a certain size range as we find them? Where, and how, do we draw the line between too small and just right? Sometimes size *does* matter, but there is no absolute metric for deciding what the right size range is.

The next criterion that came into play for some (but not all) astronomers was whether or not the planet lies within the orbital plane of the other planets in our galaxy. It turns out, however, that Pluto's plane is slightly different than the plane shared by the other planets. Is that enough reason to boot it from the planetary family? Other astronomers propose other criteria, such as appropriate shape. This is actually a question about the formation of the planet—it has to be roughly spherical, which gives evidence that it was formed by a certain sequence of geological processes. So, two-hundred-mile-long slivers of rock do not count as planets. Some people even attribute metaphysical import to the spherical shape of planets, claiming that the sphere is the perfect shape in the great ontological scheme.

Okay, so maybe we can just say that planets are roughly sphere-shaped rocky objects that orbit the sun and not another body. However, it appears that this doesn't quite work for Pluto, because it has a moon that is almost half its size, and it is not really clear whether the moon circles Pluto or whether, like two squirrels running around a tree trunk, they circle each other. It gets worse. Some astronomers then decided that it would be useful to stipulate that a true planet has to dominate its own orbit in a way that it would clear out other objects in its orbit.

I trust that the point I am trying to make is clear enough by now. It is starting to look as though our old, once-faithful idea of planets as appropriately sized balls of rock orbiting the sun is neither a metaphysically necessary essence, nor merely an arbitrary choice. Instead, our concept of a planet is defined relative to the history of our astronomy, our metaphysical systems, our observational technology, and a host of other facts and values upon which the science of astronomy is based. Those values and theoretical commitments show themselves, I am suggesting, in the fact that to answer the question "Is Pluto a planet?" depends, at the very least, on which of two competing orientations you choose: (1) the planetary scientists who are interested mostly in the composition and geologic processes of the celestial bodies; or (2) the so-called dynamicists, who are more interested in a celestial body's mass, its orbit, and the way it clears out its orbital plane. There is no absolute fact of the matter about what a planet is. Any facts about planets are likely to depend on various values and theoretical commitments held by the people (certain privileged astronomers and astrophysicists) who get to decide the issue.

My point is that what we have just seen about the nature of planets reveals some very important insights about the nature of human conceptualization in general. Concepts can grow and change; but there are, nonetheless, various kinds of constraints on that growth. Accordingly, this is clearly not an arbitrary process, even though it is a value-dependent process. I get upset, therefore, when people complain that our nation is under the sway of a bunch of liberal legal activists. These activists are misrepresented as holding the view that the law means whatever judges say it means, as if there were no constraints on their legal judgments. And with what is the alleged activist-legislation-posing-as-judicial-judgments contrasted? The answer, apparently, is that legal concepts supposedly have a fixed, literal, objective meaning, and there is a universal logic underlying legal reasoning.

This extreme dichotomy between arbitrary constructivism and legal absolutism and objectivism is a false dichotomy. The original-intent doctrine, with its attendant notion of literal and objectively defined legal concepts, is incompatible with virtually any of the evidence I know of about how human conceptualization and reasoning work. It looks to me, instead, that most of our moral and legal concepts are more like the concept of a planet than they are anything like classical categories.[1] Concepts are ways we make distinctions and mark patterns. We do this for various purposes and relative to the developing situations in which we find ourselves. The proper application of concepts requires an imaginative grasp of how newly emerging conditions can be accommodated by the complex internal structure and plasticity of the concepts.

I am proposing that we should think of our ethical and legal concepts as, for the most part, having complex radial structures, manifesting prototypicality effects, and being somewhat malleable in the face of new, previously unanticipated conditions. There will typically be clear, relatively straightforward central instances of a moral or legal category, but much of the category will consist of a network of noncentral cases connected by various principles of extension. Take, for example, the category "harm." At its conceptual center (which we might call "core harm") are cases of direct physical injury to an organism, such that it suffers some bodily dysfunction, often accompanied by pain. However, there are many other types of harm. Via metaphorical extension, there are also cases of nonprototypical harm, such as emotional harm, psychological harm, social harm, economic harm, ethical harm, legal harm, and so on. There is no set of essence-defining features shared by all these types of harm. None of these is necessarily more experientially basic than any other, but from the viewpoint of how we cognize things, some are more central and prototypical than others. We orient the moral or legal category in terms of prototypical central members, such as core harm, surrounded by a web of less central members connected to the central members and to other noncentral members by various relations.

A good example of a metaphorical extension within this "harm" category is the relatively new notion of "moral injury" to military personnel. Over the last decade, it has become clear that their training for warfare and their horrific experiences in combat often run directly counter to their most deeply held ethical values and beliefs. For instance, soldiers have to be habituated to have no empathy for the enemy they must fight, even to the point of regarding them as subhuman. But empathy is a crucial condition for moral action, insofar as we need to feel and understand the experience of others and to care for their well-being. This is precisely what soldiers are trained *not* to do. We are now coming to understand the moral injury this training and subsequent war experience inflicts on many soldiers who are trying to reintegrate into civilian life. The injury to their moral center is profound, traumatic, and sometimes tragic. Moral injury or harm does not share a unique set of defining features with instances of prototypical physical harm, but it falls clearly in the "harm" category as a metaphorical extension from prototypical physical injury.

As Lakoff (1987) showed, radial categories are structured by four principles of extension from central category members: image structure, propositional structure, conceptual metaphor, and metonymy. These principles of extension allow for cognitive flexibility in the face of changing situations, even as they provide cognitive motivation and constraint for how we think creatively. By virtue of this internal flexibility, our moral and legal concepts can adapt to newly emerging, previously unanticipated moral or legal situations. This is how embodied, imaginative meaning and understanding can grow. This is how innovation is possible, and how it is constrained. So, we need to recall briefly the account in earlier chapters on the role of image schemas and metaphors in embodied meaning and in abstract conceptualization and reasoning.

Image Schemas and Logical Inference as a Basis for Embodied Meaning

In the introduction and chapter 1, I surveyed some of the image-schematic patterns that structure our meaningful interactions with our environment.[2] The main idea is that, given the makeup and development of our bodies and brains (both over evolutionary time periods and in individual ontogenesis), relative to the types of environments we inhabit, certain recurring experiential patterns will be intrinsically meaningful to us. For example, based on the nature of our visual processing organs (eye muscles, retina, rods and cones, optic nerve, processing areas in our visual cortex, etc.), our visual perception is organized so that we experience focal areas surrounded by a horizon of increasingly less focused areas in our visual field. In other words, there is a basic center/periphery organization of our visual field. The CENTER/PERIPHERY image-schematic pattern is not limited only to vision but shapes our auditory perception as well. Maurice Merleau-Ponty (1962) described this horizontal structure as a general pattern of human perception, in which our "world" spreads out from a center with an extensive horizon that fades off, at the edges, to a nonconscious background of perceptual possibilities that have not yet come into conscious awareness, but which nevertheless affect how we experience focal phenomena.

As observed in the introduction, there are scores of such meaningful image-schematic patterns that we acquire naturally through our unreflective daily engagement with our surroundings. We see objects go *up* and *down*, *rise* and *fall* in our visual field. We thereby automatically acquire an understanding of the VERTICALITY schema, and it serves as a basic bodily meaning structure in terms of which we experience and make sense of the up-and-downness of our world. By moving our bodies in space, we also acquire a basic LOCOMOTION schema, which has an internal structure defined by parameters (with specific parameter values) such as an agent that moves (animal, person), body part(s) moved (legs, torso, arms), the gait of the agent (walk, run, skip, hop), the speed of the motion (slow, medium, fast), and the effort exerted (skipping versus trudging) (Dodge and Lakoff 2005). To cite a third example, because internal and bodily balance are so crucial to our well-being, we develop an understanding of the meaning and significance of balance—what balance is, what happens when it is upset, how it can be recovered, and so on. We know in our bodies the very meaning of the BALANCE schema not as an abstract concept, but as a viscerally felt embodied meaning structure.

We learn such image schemas merely by living and acting within our surroundings, given the kinds of brains and bodies we have. No conscious attention or reflection is required. Creatures like us—that is, beings with bodies and brains like ours, and who dwell in environments like the ones we typically inhabit—are going to experience and make sense of the world via image-schematic patterns of this sort. This is meaning at the most bodily and visceral level for humans, and it is intimately intertwined with our biological and interpersonal values and the emotions and feelings that go along with those values. Balance, or lack thereof, is not merely a cognitively meaningful experience, but is also always generative of certain emotions and feelings. These feelings (such as the feeling of losing one's balance) are not optional additions to the BALANCE schema, but are instead central to it.

As discussed in the introduction, images schemas can also be combined to generate more complex meaning structures. The example I gave there was the meaning of *into* and *out of* in English, as being based on a blending of the CONTAINER and SOURCE-PATH-GOAL schemas. To get schemas for concepts like *in* and *out*, you must add structure that profiles various parts of the CONTAINER schema. The concept *in* profiles (highlights or activates) the interior of the CONTAINER schema, whereas the concept *out* profiles the exterior that surrounds the boundary. *In* and *out* also require identification of a figure/ground (or trajectory/landmark) structure relative to the CONTAINER schema. When we say, "Elvis has left the building," Elvis is the figure (rajectory) relative to the building, which is the ground (or landmark) (Talmy 2000). As Lakoff and Núñez (2002) have shown, the INTO schema is a composition of the IN schema and the To schema, whereas the OUT OF schema combines the OUT schema and the FROM schema.

INTO Schema

- *The IN schema*: consisting of a CONTAINER schema, with the interior profiled and taken as landmark

- *The To schema*: consisting of a SOURCE-PATH-GOAL schema, with the goal profiled and taken as landmark
- *Correspondences*: (interior; goal) and (exterior; source)

OUT OF Schema

- *The OUT schema*: consisting of a CONTAINER schema, with the exterior profiled and taken as landmark
- *The FROM schema*: consisting of a SOURCE-PATH-GOAL schema, with the source profiled and taken as landmark
- *Correspondence*: (interior; source) and (exterior; goal)

Image schemas are important not just as basic embodied meaning patterns, but also as shaping how we reason and draw inferences. They have what I (M. Johnson 1987, 2007, 2017) have called a "corporeal" or "spatial" logic. Consider, for example, the bodily logic of the VERTICALITY schema. We learn—just by being alive and encountering our world—the logic of vertical motion. If two equal projectiles are launched at the same time, traveling vertically upward, and if projectile A is moving faster than projectile B, then at any given time T, we can infer that projectile A will be higher than projectile B. However obvious or even trivial this might seem, it is nonetheless an example of how, through our bodily interactions with our surroundings, we gain inferential knowledge of our world. To give another example, from our recurring encounter with SOURCE-PATH-GOAL motions, we come to infer that if an object is moving along a path from starting point A to ending point E, then, at a given time T, if the object is at location C on the path, it will have already traversed all the intermediate points on the path from A to C. Such is the logic of our incarnate experience.

A full accounting of the image-schematic structure of our experience and understanding might extend to scores of structures. However, most of these would be complex combinations of a smaller number of more basic image schemas. In summary, there are four major points to keep in mind concerning the nature and activation of image schemas:

1. Image schemas characterize the recurring structure of much of our sensory-motor experience.
2. Image schemas are learned automatically through our bodily interactions with aspects of our environment, given the nature of our bodies and brains in relation to the possibilities for experience that are afforded

us within different environments. Image schemas are meaningful to us even when, as is typical, they operate beneath the level of conscious awareness. They are a basic part of embodied meaning.
3. Image schemas have highly determinate "spatial" or "bodily" logics that support and constrain inferences.
4. Image schemas are compositional, in that they combine and blend with one another, yielding even more complex embodied meaning and inference patterns.

To say that meaning is grounded in the body is to say that the meaning of our experience emerges pre-reflectively from sensory experience and patterns of our bodily orientation, perceptual interaction, movement, and feeling. Image schemas constitute much of the semantic and inferential structure of this embodied understanding. All of this is tied intimately to the nature of our bodies and to the nature of the environments we inhabit. The range of image schemas is thus wide, but it is highly constrained and motivated by how our bodies and brains are structured, and how those structures interact with aspects of our environment.

Applying this embodied meaning conception to our moral and legal concepts reveals that such concepts typically have their meaning grounded in basic human bodily experiences that become the source domains for the conceptual metaphors operative in our moral and legal reasoning. In short, our moral and legal concepts are defined by metaphors that are rooted in our sensory, motor, affective, and social experiences.

Conceptual Metaphors

The conceptual metaphor theory I have presented in earlier chapters argues that neural structures central to sensory and motor processing must be recruited to carry out the inferences that make up our abstract patterns of thinking. Structures of perceiving and doing must be exapted to serve as structures of thinking and knowing. Much recent work in this area has come from the relatively new field of cognitive neuroscience, in studies of the functional neural clusters and processes that make it possible for us to appropriate bodily meaning for abstract conceptualization and reasoning. I will not address this highly technical literature here (see Feldman 2006; Lakoff and Narayanan, forthcoming).

The basic account I have developed earlier in the book and in other works (Lakoff and Johnson 1980; M. Johnson 1987, 2007, 2017;) is that over the course of evolutionary history, our brains have developed so as to recruit structures of our perception, movement, and feeling to perform what we think of as abstract conceptualization and reasoning. It is not surprising that all our perceptual, spatial-relation, and body-movement concepts are intimately tied to our embodiment. But how can we move from embodied meanings tied to our sensory-motor experience all the way to abstract concepts like love, justice, mind, knowledge, and freedom? How can we move from embodied spatial logic and inferences all the way to abstract logical relations and inferences?

The answer is exaptation, the appropriation of sensory-motor structures that evolved for perception and movement to carry out conceptualization and reasoning. Conceptual metaphor works by mapping a source domain tied to our sensory, motor, and social interactions onto a target domain that we think of as abstract or nonphysical. Lakoff and I (1980) have argued that such conceptual metaphors are based on experienced correlations between the source and target domains. For example, consider our recurrent experience of increase in height correlating with increase in quantity, such as when we add objects to a pile and it *goes up*, or when we add more liquid to a container and the level *rises*. Based on such experiential correlations, we come to understand increase or decrease in quantity in terms of change of height, as in "The crime rate *fell* during the Obama administration," "The number of deaths from pneumonia *rose* last year," "Our taxes just *go higher and higher!*," "Gas prices *skyrocketed*."

To explain where our metaphors come from and why we have the ones we do within a given culture, Joseph Grady (1997) proposed a theory of "primary metaphors" that shows how more-complex systems of conceptual metaphors arise from and are built out of more primitive body-based metaphors. Grady's work drew on Christopher Johnson's (1997) study of metaphor acquisition in young children. Johnson hypothesized that young children go through a "conflation stage" in which certain subjective experiences and judgments are conflated with—and therefore are not differentiated from—certain sensory-motor experiences. An infant that is being held in its mother's arms, for instance, will experience simultaneously affection and warmth. During this conflation period the young child will automatically acquire a large number of associations between these two different domains of affection and warmth, since they are co-active domains. Neural connections between the areas of the brain involved in our experience of temperature and our feelings of affection will be established and strengthen through repeated coactivations of the two domains. Later, the child enters a "differentiation stage" in which it can conceptually distinguish the different domains, even though they remain coactivated and associated. These cross-domain associations are the basis of mappings that define a large number of primary metaphors, such as AFFECTION IS WARMTH. The AFFECTION IS WARMTH metaphor is grounded in experienced correlations between, for example, being held affectionately and feeling warm. Such correlations give rise to cross-domain mappings that underlie such expressions as "She received a *cool* reception from the committee," "He shot her an *icy* glare," "She's *warming* to me slowly," and "Relations *thawed* as the two ambassadors spent more time together."

Grady analyzed a large number of primary metaphors that result from basic cross-domain correlations in our shared bodily experience. What follows are a few representative examples of primary metaphors, along with their grounding and examples of linguistic manifestations of the underlying mapping.

INTIMACY IS CLOSENESS
Subjective judgment: Intimacy
Sensory-motor domain: Physical closeness
Experiential basis: Being physically close to people you are intimate with
Examples: "We've been *close* for years." "Now we seem to be *drifting apart.*"

BAD IS STINKY
Subjective judgment: Evaluation
Sensory-motor domain: Smell
Experiential basis: Being repelled by foul-smelling objects and pleased by good-smelling ones
Examples: "This whole affair *stinks!*" "Something *smells fishy* with this contract."

MORE IS UP
Subjective judgment: Quantity increase or decrease
Sensory-motor domain: Vertical orientation
Experiential basis: Observing the rise and fall of levels of piles and fluids as more is added or taken away
Examples: "Prices are *skyrocketing!*" "The number of crimes *rose precipitously* this year."

ORGANIZATION IS PHYSICAL STRUCTURE
Subjective judgment: Abstract form or relationships
Sensory-motor domain: Perceiving and manipulating physical objects
Experiential basis: Interacting with physical objects and recognizing their

functional correlation between observing part/whole structures of physical objects and forming cognitive representations of functional and logical relationships

Examples: "The *pieces* of his theory don't *fit* together." "I can't see how the premises are *connected to* the conclusion in your argument."

Purposes Are Destinations

Subjective judgment: Achieving a purpose
Sensory-motor domain: Reaching a destination
Experiential basis: Correlation of reaching a destination and thereby achieving a purpose
Examples: "You've finally *arrived*, baby." "She's got *a long way to go* to finish her graduate degree."

Knowing Is Seeing

Subjective judgment: Knowledge
Sensory-motor domain: Vision
Experiential basis: Gaining knowledge through visual perception
Examples: "I finally *see* the answer to our problem." "That's an *obscure* part of your theory."

The Johnson-Grady hypotheses together give us an account of how mostly unconscious correlations in our experience could be the basis for primary conceptual metaphors, which are then combined into complex metaphors. In *Philosophy in the Flesh* (1999), Lakoff and I provided some tentative evidence that we can translate *experiential correlation* into a neural account of the creation and neural binding of reentrant neural networks. In other words, the experienced correlations across different domains are realized neutrally via functional neuronal clusters connecting different cortical areas and involving a directional firing from one brain area to the other, establishing a neural network for each particular metaphor learned. Since then, structured (constrained) connectionist models have been developed for conceptual metaphors (Feldman 2006). Srini Narayanan and George Lakoff have constructed neural models that can "learn" certain types of metaphors and carry out metaphor-based reasoning (Narayanan 1997; Lakoff 2008; Lakoff and Narayanan, forthcoming).

Over the past two decades, Raymond Gibbs has carried out a number of major experiments to test for the existence of conceptual metaphors in our thinking and to probe the alleged bodily grounding of such metaphors. Gibbs's early work is powerfully summarized in his book *The Poetics of Mind* (1994); in a number of books and articles, he has continued to explore various experimental techniques to test selected hypotheses concerning conceptual metaphor (see Gibbs 2006). To cite just one representative example of this kind of research, Gibbs investigated the bodily and experiential basis of conceptual metaphors for desire that underlie expressions in English and Brazilian Portuguese (Gibbs 2003).[3] Consider the question of whether there exists a conceptual metaphor DESIRE IS HUNGER. How could we show this using psychological testing methods? In the following passage an American college student describes her romantic attraction to a boy she knew in high school: "Back in high school, I had this HUGE crush on this guy, James, who was a total hunk. He would flirt with me when we'd talk, but I didn't get a chance to know him very well, nevermind ever be alone with him. I was dying to get closer to him, and felt starved for his attention. I walked around for over five months feeling silly and empty because I wanted him so bad. I wanted to eat him alive! He was yummy!" (Gibbs 2003, 9).

Is this embodied way of talking about her desire as hunger merely a way of talking, or is it a conceptual metaphor grounded in her bodily experience of hunger? In other words, is DESIRE IS HUNGER a primary metaphor, or perhaps a metonymy? Or is it just a propositional name for a set of superficial linguistic expressions? An initial inspection of the language of desire in English and Brazilian Portuguese revealed that the concepts of hunger and thirst are used extensively in both languages to talk about a broad range of abstract desires. For instance, we can *hunger* or *thirst* for attention, promotion, righteousness, justice, power, revenge, or equality. But what evidence could there be that this is more than just talk—that it is conceptual and guides our reasoning?

What Gibbs and his colleagues did was first to determine how their American and Brazilian subjects understood hunger—or, one might say, what their cognitive model of hunger was. For example, both cultures associate hunger with *local symptoms* like a grumbling stomach, having one's mouth water (salivating), and a stomachache; with *general symptoms* like feeling discomfort, feeling weak, becoming dizzy; and *behavior symptoms* like feeling anxious and feeling out of balance. Now, if such symptoms are strongly associated with hunger, and if they thus form a shared cultural model of hunger that is intimately tied to our shared bodily experiences, then this conceptualization should show up in manifestations of the DESIRE IS HUNGER metaphor—assuming, of course, that there really is such a conceptual mapping for us.

One way in which this hypothesis was tested was to formulate a number of linguistic expressions in the two languages concerning lust, love, and other desires. Some of these were constructed using the knowledge of the idealized cognitive model of hunger that was elicited in the earlier study. The other expressions were made up of a range of symptoms judged in the first study to be only weakly associated with hunger or not associated at all. Expressions of the following sort were used: "My whole body aches for you," "I have a strong headache for knowledge," "My hands are itching for you," "My knees ache for information about my ancestry." Participants read such statements, either in English or Portuguese, and were asked to rate how acceptable each of these ways of talking would be in their culture. As one would expect, if there actually exists a DESIRE IS HUNGER metaphor, then subjects would rate the sentences with expressions tied to the local, general, and behavior symptoms of hunger much higher (as more appropriate) than those that conceptualized desire only with very weakly or nonassociated bodily experiences. Indeed, that is precisely what they found. Gibbs concludes that "the data demonstrate how knowing something about people's embodied experiences of hunger allows one to empirically predict which aspects of desire will, and will not, be thought of, and talked about, in terms of our complex embodied understandings of hunger. This evidence is generally consistent across two different languages and cultural communities. People use their embodied knowledge as the primary source of metaphorical meaning and understanding. In this way, the answer to the question 'where does metaphor come from?' is given by understanding how embodiment provides the foundation for more abstract concepts" (2003, 10).

The "prediction" of which Gibbs speaks here is an experimental prediction about what expressions will be properly motivated by our shared embodied knowledge of hunger. He is not claiming that we can predict which primary metaphors will exist; rather, we can explain how the conceptual metaphors we do find are grounded in bodily experience and motivated by it, and we can explain why we have the specific inferential structure in our conception of desire that we do.

What makes the theory of primary metaphor so potentially important is that it suggests answers to two crucial questions: (1) Why do we have the conceptual metaphors we do? And (2) How can the meaning of abstract concepts be grounded in our bodies and our sensory-motor experience? The answer to the first question is that we have certain primary metaphors because of the way our brains, bodies, and environments are structured. Because of the specific kinds of cross-domain neural connections that we acquire through our mundane, mostly nonconscious experience, we will naturally acquire a shared set of primary metaphors. The nature of our bodies and environments determines what precisely those metaphors will be. This explanation does not predict which metaphors will be activated for a particular person and thus show up in their symbolic interaction and expression; rather, it shows how the conceptual metaphors that we actually have in a given culture at a given time are motivated by, and make sense relative to, the kinds of cross-domain associations that are possible for creatures embodied like us.

The second crucial question that the theory of primary metaphor allows us to answer is how it might be possible for creatures embodied in the way we are to use their embodied meaning and inference patterns to develop abstract concepts and to reason with them. The key to all this imaginative activity is the coactivation of sensory-motor areas along with areas thought to be responsible for so-called "higher" cognitive functions. Sensory, motor, and affective processes are recruited for abstract conceptualization and reasoning. Primary metaphors are thus cross-domain mappings based on neural connections between sensory-motor maps and structures involved in judgment and reasoning about abstract domains. In other words, there is a directionality to the mapping—from the source domain to the target domain—and this is instantiated in the flow of activation from a sensory-motor area to a neural assembly responsible for what we regard as "higher" cognitive activity. Grady calls this second area a domain of "subjective judgment," but we really do not have a fully adequate account yet of how to describe these neural regions (Lakoff 2008). The key point is that the inferences are actually performed in the sensory, motor, and affective areas, and that these inferences are then carried over to the target domain via the cross-domain correlations that define the primary metaphor.

Once we have primary metaphors, we are off and running, so to speak. Through various types of blending and composition, we develop vast coherent systems of metaphorically defined concepts (Fauconnier and Turner 2002; Lakoff 2008). Detailed analyses have been performed of how metaphor shapes such basic concepts as events, states, causes, purposes, desire, thought, mind, reason, knowledge, values, morality, law, and politics (Lakoff 1996; Lakoff and Johnson 1999; Winter 2001; Lakoff and Núñez 2000; Kövecses 2010). As we saw above in chapters 2 and 5, many studies have been done to show that some of our most impressive intellectual achievements—in physics, biology, anthropology, sociology, mathematics, logic, philosophy, religion, and art—involve irreducible and indispensable conceptual metaphors. In other words, the key concepts in all these disciplines are defined by multiple (often inconsistent) metaphors, and we reason using the internal logic of those metaphors.

I cannot here survey the evidence for the pervasiveness of conceptual metaphor. However, there is a virtual cottage industry built around studying the role of conceptual metaphor in every area of human thought. Over the past thirty years, research has come up with at least nine types of empirical evidence for the existence of conceptual metaphor in all aspects of our symbolic expression—evidence such as polysemy generalizations, inferential generalizations, extensions to novel cases, sign language, gesture studies, psychological priming experiments, historical semantic change, discourse analysis, and cognitive neuroscience research (Gibbs 1994; Lakoff and Johnson 1999; Dancygier and Sweetser 2014).

The implications of the constitutive nature of conceptual metaphors are quite far reaching. We come to see that even our most abstract concepts and theories are webs of body-based metaphors. This discovery does not denigrate theory. On the contrary, it humanizes it and shows us why it is even possible for us to understand a theory and to use it to organize our inquiries into experience. Such analyses give us new cognitive tools for exploring the internal logic of our conceptual systems and theories, seeing how they are experientially grounded, and tracing out their insights and limitations. And most important, this approach gives us a way of understanding how embodied creatures like us can come to think what and how we do.

A Radial, Metaphorically Defined Category from Law

Steven Winter (2001) gave one of the first detailed treatments of the importance of conceptual metaphor in law. He showed how legal reasoning in certain landmark cases was based on the assumption of particular metaphors that supported the inferences made by the justices. Since then, conceptual metaphors in law have received increased attention. I want to bring together the various aspects of conceptual structure I have been discussing, by showing how they converge in the legal category of *property*. I want to hold up this example as representative of the nature of the vast majority of legal concepts, and of our abstract concepts in general. I had the good fortune to work with my colleague in the law school, Carl Bjerre, as he was preparing a law review article on intellectual property law (Bjerre 1999). What follows is a small part of what we found in our analysis of the radial category of *property*.

At the center of the category are prototypical instances of property, such as a house, hand tool, or land. It is such cognitive prototypes that are activated first for us when we read, hear, or think about the term *property*. These prototypical instances satisfy a common "idealized cognitive model" (Lakoff 1987), in which property (1) is a discrete physical object or spatial expanse that (2) persists through time, (3) is subject to exclusion from use by others, (4) is alienable, and (5) is useful (Bjerre 1999).

Extending out from the central prototypes are many noncentral members that do not possess all the features specified by the central idealized cognitive model. For example, water is, in mainstream American culture—though not in certain Native American cultures—conceived of as potential property, even though it is not a discrete object. The human body is often regarded as property, but we typically do not think of it as alienable or transferable. Garbage is apparently designated by the law as property, although it seems somewhat at odds with our notion of prototypical property, because it is not typically a discrete physical object and the notion of usefulness is suspect. Extending even further out from the center are other types of property that are not physical or material. The primary principle of extension for most of these cases is conceptual metaphor. For example, we speak of intellectual property, such as ideas we have that can be copyrighted, patented, and excluded from use by others. Intellectual property is only metaphorically an entity, and it is transferable only in a metaphorical sense to another for their use. Pensions, stocks, and bonds are also metaphorical property. We have an alleged right to utilize such abstract metaphorically defined entities for our own purposes under certain specifiable conditions. One's privacy is metaphorical property, just like one's own name, and they both can become the subject of litigation.

In addition to metaphorical principles of extension within the category, there are often metonymic principles coupled with the metaphors. For example, a share of stock stands metonymically for a share of the company, which is itself a metaphorical entity, and the company in turn stands metonymically for the company's assets. One's name is metaphorical property, but it is also metonymic for the person named.

One could continue this sort of analysis, but the key points are evident. The concept *property* is not a classical category defined by a set of necessary and sufficient conditions. Instead, the concept is a vast radially structured category with a small number of central members or prototypical cases surrounded at various distances by noncentral members, according to principles of extension such as conceptual metaphor and metonymy. Legal judgments in property law operate relative to this complex and potentially growing conceptual structure. Property is at least partially a metaphorically defined concept. You cannot do property law without metaphor! Finally, the historical contingency of such concepts results from the way that newly emerging conditions (events, technologies, institutions, practices) lead to the expansion and restructuring of the concept in an ongoing fashion. For instance, the notion of intellectual property makes little sense in a preliterate culture that lacks writing and the ability to record an individual's thoughts or ideas. However, once there are technologies for recording a person's ideas, and once a legal system of property has arisen, it then makes sense to extend the category to include intellectual property.

Despite what I have argued about the central role of metaphor in human abstract conceptualization, you may still be thinking that it is just a figure of speech, just an alternative way of talking, but not really very important—and certainly not constitutive of our moral and legal thinking. In response to this, I want to remind you of the critical importance of metaphorical framing for our lives. We humans understand things relative to frames and idealized cognitive models (Lakoff 1987, 1996; Lakoff and Narayanan, forthcoming). Much of ethical and legal reasoning is a matter of framing situations and problems relative to various cognitive models, within which image schemas, radial categories, and metaphors play a central role. Let me cite just two examples of this important phenomenon that exemplify the entire framing process.

I once received an email from Richard Koenigsberg, director of the Library of Social Sciences, in which he identified an overarching metaphor that the Nazis used to frame their Final Solution, that of the Jew as "disease within the body of the people."[4] Hitler apparently claimed that he was not one of those politicians who "doctored around on the circumference of the distress," and he insisted on the necessity of discovering and removing the "cause of the inflammation." Koenigsberg writes: "On February 22, 1942, when the Final Solution was in full swing, Hitler expounded his conviction that the discovery of the Jewish virus was one of the 'greatest revolutions that has taken place in the world.' The battle in which he was engaged, he said, was of the same sort as the 'battle waged by Pasteur and Koch.' Himmler stated that Germany had the 'moral right to destroy this people that wanted to destroy us. We do not want to be infected by the bacillus and to die.'"

Genocide could be justified by the need for drastic hygienic action. Hitler argued, "One must act radically. When one pulls out a tooth one does it with a single tug and the pain quickly goes away. The Jew must clear out of Europe."[5] Metaphorical framing is not a game. It can be a life-and-death matter.

Immediately after the September 11, 2001, attacks, many people thought of the events as constituting a "crime." That metaphorical framing carries with it its own specific logic. If there is a crime, then we send the police, there are laws, there are courts to pass judgments, and justice must be done. On the international level, this would involve international courts and law enforcement subject to the provisions of international laws, treaties, and agreements. Very quickly, however, the metaphor "the war on terrorism" took hold and this led to a very different set of entailments than those defined by the "crime" framework. If we are then engaged in war, alternative expectations, justifications, and actions are sanctioned by the metaphor that were not permitted under the "crime" metaphor. This let us justify the attacks in Afghanistan, and it was the basis for the Bush administration's decision to invade Iraq. Based on actions taken on such metaphors, thousands of people—including US and foreign soldiers, insurgents, and many thousands of completely innocent Iraqi citizens—have died. Many times that number have been injured or maimed, and they are now suffering horribly. The economic, social, and political harm is incalculable. Our image in the world has been dramatically altered. Our conception of appropriate moral and legal action has been torn asunder.

So, we must not think of metaphor, in the old way, as a mere figure of speech. It is a figure of life. It is a figure of thought. It is a figure of value. We live, love, fight, die, and enact law by metaphors.

PART 3

Art and the Aesthetics of Life

In what I shall call the Kingdom of Mainstream Western Philosophy, logic and epistemology reign supreme. Logic supposedly captures the essence of reason, and epistemology tells us what counts as knowledge and how it may be achieved. A little further down in the pecking order fall metaphysics (theory of being), philosophy of language (concerned with cognitive meaning and truth), and philosophy of science (an account of the nature and possibility of objective scientific knowledge and causal explanation). Below that, we move into the somewhat murky "value" realms of ethics and political theory, which study the sources of our moral and political values and legitimation procedures, and in some cases, claim to offer normative guidance for our lives. Finally, way down at the bottom of the status hierarchy, we find poor old aesthetics—another value field, but one that is allegedly not even capable of the more objective value judgments that are thought to operate in ethics and politics. Aesthetics, which is narrowly construed as theory of art and aesthetic experience, is basically taken to be about subjective judgments of taste and the imaginative (noncognitive) processes of art. Here we are, left to muck around in the subjective world of "mere" taste, about which, so the story goes, there can be no disputing. No wonder that aesthetics is mostly ignored as being of little scientific or philosophical importance.

Now, the principle of rank ordering in the Kingdom of Mainstream Western Philosophy rests on a hierarchy of cognitive content and value. "Real" knowledge is cognitive in the fullest sense, insofar as it involves concepts and propositions expressing verifiable truth claims ordered by a universal logic. The sciences are believed to be our best examples of this objective empirical knowledge, because they supply universal causal laws. However, even within the sciences there is a rank ordering, with the physical sciences (the "hard" sciences) at the top and the social sciences (the "soft" sciences)—where values enter in and definitive causal knowledge is rare—at the bottom. The further you descend into the realms of value, there may still be some cognitive content, and there may occasionally be objective knowledge judgments, but even the most confident believers in rational foundations of moral values recognize that moral philosophy cannot achieve the status of a science.

When you supposedly bottom-out in the lowest realm of the Kingdom of Philosophy—that of aesthetics—hardly anyone pretends that we are dealing with cognitive content or claims to knowledge. Consequently, if your hierarchical scale of philosophical importance gives ultimate priority to cognitive content and ideals of objective knowledge and truth, you are likely to dismiss aesthetics as hardly worthy of philosophical scrutiny. And that, I submit, is pretty much how most philosophers within the analytic tradition have tended to regard aesthetics and art theory for the previous hundred years! If you doubt this, just take a look at course offerings in philosophy departments across America and see how very few of them touch on anything related to art and aesthetics.

In radical contrast to this widespread disparagement of aesthetics, I am proposing that it is ultimately the aesthetic dimensions of experience that underlie and make possible philosophy and all other modes of thinking. Without aesthetics, there is no ethics, no politics, no science, no art, and no philosophy. Aesthetics deals with the basic constituents of human meaning, understanding, reasoning, and value, and so it lies at the heart of our ability to have meaningful experience and to think intelligently about it. Instead of being a light entertainment to which philosophers turn when they need rest from their arduous intellectual labors in "real" philosophy, aesthetics, as Dewey ([1925] 1981, [1934] 1987) claimed, is where philosophy must start and where it must end: in the depths of experience. In other words, in a complete reversal of the cognitive-importance hierarchy of Anglo American analytic philosophy, everything is seen as resting on aesthetics, properly understood in this broad and rich sense.

The chapters in this third part sketch what aesthetics becomes when it is recognized as dealing with our visceral engagement with our world and other people, and therefore as revealing how meaning and value arise in our daily experience. Earlier, in the introduction ("Aesthetics of Embodied Life"), I already indicated several of the key aesthetic dimensions of experience and thought—dimensions such as qualities, image schemas, emotions, feelings, and metaphors—and I showed briefly some of the ways those dimensions play a central role in our ability to have meaningful experience and to reason about it. In chapter 9 ("Identity, Bodily Meaning, and Art") I expand my account of embodied, aesthetic meaning structures and processes, especially as they enter into our experience of art in a way that shapes our self-understanding. Chapter 10 ("Dewey's Big Idea for Aesthetics") then goes straight to the heart of the idea that the aesthetics stone that was cast out of the Kingdom of Mainstream Western Philosophy shall become the cornerstone of our new Kingdom of Aesthetics, which explores the bodily basis of meaning, thought, and value. I focus especially on Dewey's argument for the importance of qualitative dimensions in providing a philosophically and existentially adequate account of mind, thought, and language. In chapter 11 ("The Embodied Meaning of Architecture"), I offer an illustration of how architecture, as representative of the importance of art for our lives, appropriates the embodied aesthetic structures and elements that make meaningful experience possible.

Aesthetics becomes the core of our philosophy of experience and of everything connected with experience, including meaning, concepts, understanding, reason, knowledge, action, communication, and values. I close, therefore, in chapter 12 ("What Becomes of Philosophy, Morality, and Art?), with a brief survey of how an aesthetics of the embodied mind requires us to rethink many of our received notions about the nature and purpose of science, philosophy, morality, law, and art. I explore what becomes of these important undertakings once we recognize that they are all projects of our aesthetic engagement with our world.

CHAPTER 9

Identity, Bodily Meaning, and Art

One of the more important themes emerging from the last century of philosophy and the past three decades of cognitive neuroscience is that the self that defines our personal identity is not a thing, but rather an ongoing experiential process. In American philosophy, William James and John Dewey were among the first to realize that the self is a cluster of habits of experiencing, valuing, thinking, and acting, so that what we call a person's character is nothing but what Dewey called an "interpenetration of habits" ([1922] 1988, 29) of a particular embodied creature acting within some physical and cultural environment. In this chapter, I will explore Dewey's contention that because the self is intrinsically embodied and connected to its environment, it can be dramatically influenced by art, which is a culmination of intensified, unified, and harmonized experience

I begin by observing that we have inherited a roughly Kantian view of experience as divided into distinct types. This assumption relegates aesthetic experience to one particular noncognitive type of feeling experience. Such a view provides no adequate way to explain how a person's identity might be tied to their experience of art, since it regards art as affecting only one dimension of a person's being. My claim is that Dewey rejected any partitioning of experience into discrete types, emphasizing that the self develops in and through its organic biological and cultural engagement with its environments. Dewey places art at the center of the development of the self, insofar as art is an exemplary form of experience that optimizes our sense of meaning.

The Self and Embodied Meaning

The greatest obstacle to a full appreciation of the power of art to shape a person's identity is any metaphysical partitioning of the self into different, and discrete, mental faculties. Within such a faculty psychology, if you think of the identity of the self as based principally on its rational capacities, and if you think of art as primarily affecting our perceptual and emotional systems, then you will never be able to explain fully all the ways art can be meaningful to us and how it can influence our self-understanding.

To see why this is the case, let us consider Immanuel Kant's treatment of art in relation to self-identity. I mention Kant because we today are inheritors of some of his most influential views about the nature of aesthetic judgment. In his *Critique of Pure Reason* (1781), Kant worked out his insight that the unity of the self exists in and through that self's synthesis of objects of experience. As Kant expressed it, "The original and necessary consciousness of the identity of the self is thus at the same time a consciousness of an equally necessary unity of the synthesis of all appearances according to concepts, that is, according to rules, which . . . determine an object for their intuition, that is, the concept of something wherein they are necessarily interconnected" ([1781] 1968, A108). To put it a bit more concisely and less abstrusely, the unity of the self is constituted in and through our experience of objects. Subjectivity and objectivity are thus two aspects of one and the same experiential process.

The self that Kant saw as emerging in the combining of perceptions into objects of experience was what he called "empirical" consciousness—our awareness of ourselves as we experience ourselves, which Kant regarded as our phenomenal self. Unfortunately, Kant's epistemological quest for pure (i.e., nonempirical) foundations for selfhood and knowledge led him to a more disembodied view of the self. Kant mistakenly assumed that perception is merely a passive receiving of sense impressions that are supposedly "given" in intuition as a "manifold," or many-ness of separate sensations. These sensations therefore have to be combined by imagination into a unified image over time, which then have to be organized into a cognized object through application of a concept that identifies the unified object. This might all be well and good, if the unifying and knowing self were just our empirical (phenomenal) consciousness. However, Kant claimed that the "I" that thinks or knows cannot be just one more physical object among other objects in the world; instead, it must be the very source of unifying activity that makes possible our experience of objects. In other words, for some set of perceptions to become part of my particular consciousness, they must previously have been organized into a coherent whole and cognized by a nonempirical source of unifying activity that is my "pure" (or noumenal) self.[1] This noumenal self is posited not as a self that we can experience, but rather on epistemic grounds as the pure unifying agency for all mental representations that I can call "mine." Unifying activity of this sort, therefore, cannot be known, but it can be thought. Though, as noted above, Kant recognized an "empirical consciousness" of our inner states (i.e., our phenomenal self), nevertheless he ultimately argued that our true self must be the active unifying noumenal subject that operates behind the scenes of our experience. This view of the self as pure agency meshed nicely with Kant's mostly Christian conception of the self as free, autonomous generator of action. Consequently, Kant was led to downplay the material, bodily, emotional aspects he attributed only to the "empirical self" in favor of claims about our "true" noumenal self as the unknowable and inexplicable originator of action in the world.

Under the pressure of this epistemically centered approach, by the time Kant got around to the self in relation to art and beauty, in his *Critique of Judgment* (1790), his overintellectualized conception of the self left him more or less unable to account for the power of natural and artistic beauty to affect the entire identity of a perceiver. For if one's true identity is tied to an alleged noumenal (nonempirical) self as a pure spontaneous activity, incapable of being manifested in perception, feeling, or emotion, then we are at a loss to explain how a sensuous, emotionally charged artwork or natural scene can shape that pure noumenal self.

The inability of Kant's great system to do justice to art and aesthetic experience can be tied to his erroneous psychology of distinct faculties (powers of judgment) and to his obsession with the epistemological project of explaining the nature of, conditions for, and limits to various kinds of mental judgments. The chief problem that so much twentieth- and twenty-first-century aesthetic theory inherited from Kant is his assumption that the key question of aesthetics is fundamentally epistemic (i.e., a question about cognitive status and universality), concerning the nature and possibility of aesthetic reflective *judgments* that claim universal validity. More specifically, Kant assumed that only a shared concept could support a universal judgment. But in Kant's system, judgments of "taste" (of the form "This *X* is beautiful"), as aesthetic, were noncognitive and subjective, based apparently on feelings rather than concepts. From this perspective, then, how could it be possible that a judgment of taste should claim universal validity?

As we saw in the introduction, Kant's notorious "solution" to the problem of the alleged universal validity of pure judgments of taste was to insist (in sec. 9 of his *Critique of Judgment*) that the feeling involved in a judgment of taste is not the *ground or cause* of the judgment of taste (and its claim to universality), but instead merely an *effect* of a prior cognitive state—a state in which a representation of some object or event puts imagination and understanding into a mutually enlivening, harmonious "free play." Kant says that the feeling is merely our way of being aware of the harmony of our cognitive faculties in experiencing some scene or object. In short, the feeling of pleasure or displeasure is not the basis (cause) of the judgment of taste, but only the mere "effect" of the pure judgment.

My concern here is not so much with the intricate and often obscure details of Kant's ingenious system, but rather with the consequences of Kant's turning of aesthetics into an exclusively epistemic project, coupled with his neglect of the body as a source of meaning and value. Kant's system has no resources to explain how the noumenal self (i.e., the self as nonempirical source of unity for our experience) that is supposedly the ground of theoretical and practical judgments alike is constituted or affected by our experience of beauty in nature and art. If you make knowledge entirely a matter of conceptually based determinate judgment and then regard beauty in nature and art as noncognitive, you can never get the two (i.e., knowledge and beauty) back together again. To preserve his view of the noncognitive character of art while also trying to recognize its effect on us, Kant famously said that art generates "aesthetical ideas," by which he meant an imaginatively rich play of thoughts to which no determinate concept can ever be adequate. So, in art, we sense a depth and richness of meaning that we cannot express conceptually. This is quite true, as I am arguing in this book—art presents and enacts meaning to which we cannot give adequate linguistic expression. The aesthetic dimensions of meaning reach deep into our visceral connection to our world. However, beyond describing this play of meaning, Kant's system and assumptions about the mind do not give him an adequate way to explain what is involved in such a process.

I am suggesting that Kant's metaphysical system gives us a self that exists as a unifying agency prior to any experience of art, and that a transcendental unity of this sort could not derive its identity in any way from experiences of art. My claim is that to find a view of the self capable of explaining the transformative power of art, we need to turn to someone like John Dewey, who—nearly a century and a half after the *Critique of Judgment*—rejected the faculty psychology that relegated the aesthetic to feeling alone. In *Experience and Nature* (1925), he provided a view of self-formation, growth of meaning, and the processes of art that were up to the task of making sense of the role of art experience in one's identity. What Dewey saw that Kant could not see was how important art is in the construction of human meaning by means of the basic aesthetic dimensions of ordinary experience.

Dewey's Naturalistic Alternative to Kant

One of the things that most sets Dewey apart from Kant is Dewey's focus on a nondualistic, multidimensional view of experience, mind, and language.[2] As Richard Rorty showed in *Philosophy and the Mirror of Nature* (1979) and *Consequences of Pragmatism* (1982), Kant's principal error was to regard philosophy primarily as epistemology—to define philosophy as the examination of the possibility, nature, and limits of various types of mental judgments, both those that generate knowledge and those that do not. Once philosophy is narrowed down to epistemology, experience gets reduced to an overly intellectual set of judgment types supposedly based on the alleged workings of discrete faculties of mind. In other words, experience becomes experience-as-cognized, ignoring all the crucial conative and affective dimensions of our lived existence.

For Dewey, by contrast, experience is what happens when an active complex organism engages its multidimensional environments. Experience is neither exclusively subjective nor objective, cognitive nor emotive, theoretical nor practical, mental nor physical. Instead, on Dewey's nonreductionist, process-oriented view, experience is all those dimensions interwoven—not as ontological or epistemological dichotomies, but as inseparable yet distinguishable threads of an ongoing process of organism-environment interactions or transactions. Experience thus includes both *what* is experienced as well as *how* it is experienced (Dewey [1925] 1981, chap. 1), and it encompasses every aspect of our bodily being in the world.

As we saw in chapter 1, according to Dewey's naturalistic orientation, the chief problem for an adequate theory of mind is to account for emerging levels of functional organization and qualities of experience, as the result of increasing complexity of organism-environment interactions. The main challenge is to provide such an explanation without bringing in forces, causes, or metaphysical entities alleged to stand outside experience itself (as Kant had done). In other words, as a philosophical naturalist, Dewey insisted on continuity among all levels and dimensions of experience. Naturalism, he claimed, "means, on one side, that there is no breach of continuity between operations of inquiry and biological operations and physical operations. 'Continuity,' on the other side, means that rational operations *grow out of* organic activities, without being identical with that from which they emerge" (Dewey [1938] 1991, 26; italics in the original).

It could almost be said that Dewey's entire reconstruction of philosophy is predicated on the retention of continuity among all aspects of any experience. This means, among other things, that meaning, conceptualization, reasoning, and valuing are all embodied processes of experience. In other words, you have to explain human conceptualization, reasoning, and valuing as growing out of, and being rooted in, organic bodily activities and biological functioning. Dewey argued that a full appreciation of the importance of continuity in all experience would solve many or most of our philosophical conundrums:

> The isolation of nature and experience from each other has rendered the undeniable connection of thought and effectiveness of knowledge and purposive action, with the body, an insoluble mystery. Restoration of continuity is shown to do away with the mind-body problem. It leaves us with an organism in which events have those qualities, usually called feelings, not realized in events that form inanimate things, and which, when living creatures communicate with one another so as to share in common, and hence universalized, objects, take on distinctively mental properties. The continuity of nature and experience is shown to resolve many problems that become only the more taxing when continuity is ignored. ([1925] 1981, 7–8)

Among the many philosophical problems that Dewey thought would be either solved (or more properly, *dissolved*) by continuity were the nature of the self and the power of art to transform the self. The key to dissolving all these problems is remembering that there are no fundamental, primary dualities in our experience. Rather, dualisms and other distinctions are selections and discriminations we mark in our experience for various purposes of grasping meaning, planning action, thinking, and acting. On such a view, meaning is embodied, the self is an embodied process of meaning-making, and art is often the most eminent realization of the possibilities of embodied meaning.

Embodied Meaning

Dewey saw that if you were going to articulate an adequate theory of art and aesthetics, it would have to be founded on a view of how embodied humans discover and make meaning. Obstacles to a theory of embodied meaning are as numerous and as deeply rooted in our day as they were in

Dewey's. Chief among those obstacles is a view of mind and language that treats meaning almost exclusively as conceptual and propositional.

The Conceptual/Propositional View of Meaning

The key tenets of this orientation can be summarized as follows:

Meaning is regarded solely as a property of language.
Concepts and propositions—along with the words we use to symbolize them—are what have meaning.
Therefore, if the arts have any meaning, it can only be via structures analogous to words, phrases, and sentences in a language.[3]

If you assume something like this conceptual/propositional notion of meaning, you will not be able to explain most of the meaning that operates in our experience of an artwork in virtually any medium, including even poetry and prose fiction. Your conception of aesthetics will be significantly impoverished, in two ways:

1. If you assume that meaning is essentially linguistic and tied to concepts and propositions, then anything in art that is not expressible conceptually and propositionally is ignored or dismissed as meaningless and cognitively insignificant.
2. This derogation of art is reinforced by the mistaken idea that most art is only about the evocation of feelings and emotions, which are regarded as merely subjective, noncognitive, and private.

The proper critical response to such a drastically limited conception of meaning and art is an embodied view of meaning; that is, a theory of how meaning emerges from qualities and patterns of bodily interaction with various aspects of our environment. My main hypotheses in this chapter are Dewey's views that meaning is embodied and that art employs the very same meaning-making materials and processes as are found in our ordinary day-to-day experiences of the meaning of objects, events, and persons.[4] Meaning reaches down into the depths of our ongoing bodily engagement with our environment, which is at once physical, interpersonal, social, and cultural. This meaning-making goes beyond the operations of language in important ways. If we want to understand how humans make and experience meaning, we should therefore pay special attention to the processes by which our arts enact basic ways for us to inhabit our world.

I should begin by saying again what I mean by "meaning." According to my pragmatist view, the meaning of any event, object, or symbol is relational—that is, its meaning is what it points to by way of past, present, or future (possible) experience. The meaning of any thing is what it affords by way of experience. Take, for example, a bottle. The meaning of a bottle might involve any number of experiences it has provided or might provide us. The bottle means the possibility of containing liquids, some of which I might drink to quench my thirst. It means that if I reach out to take hold of the bottle, I can pick it up with a certain specific grasping movement of my hand, and I can then manipulate it in certain ways, such as raising it to my lips for a drink. It means that, when half full of water, it will provide a certain anticipated weight in my hand. Perhaps there is a wine label on the bottle, and this provides a meaningful recollection of the evening I spent over that particular wine with someone I care about. Meaning emerges from the structures, qualities, and felt direction of our embodied experience. Meaning is first tied directly to sensory-motor-affective processes, which have both structure and emotional valence. What we call abstract concepts are typically metaphorical extensions of these sensory-motor meanings. Whenever I hear or read the word *bottle,* or even when I imagine a bottle, these and many more experiences are available to me as a horizon of meaning, out of which some specific meanings will be selected by the context of my hearing or reading the word, or imagining a bottle.[5]

Dewey's ([1925] 1981, [1934] 1987) pragmatist view is that art is experience in its eminent, most fulfilled, sense. Although much of our mundane experience is slack and undeveloped, never actually having any significance for our lives, there are moments and events in which some experiences coalesce and acquire meaning. Art realizes meaningful possibilities for experience with a depth, intensity, focus, and consummation that is seldom achieved in our day-to-day activities. In this sense, art shows us what experience can become when it achieves an exemplary presentation (enactment) of the possibilities of human meaning. It employs all the structures and processes of mundane human meaning-making, and it does this in an intensified and enriched manner, often without abstract conceptual and propositional content. Therefore, on Dewey's view, aesthetics is not just about art; rather, it concerns the structures, processes, qualities, and feelings that make any meaningful experience possible. It thus provides an ideal starting point for any adequate account of human experience and understanding.

In what follows, I propose a cursory survey of certain selected aspects of embodied meaning that are crucial to our capacity to make sense of virtually any experience. A partial list of these embodied dimensions includes the following:

- The felt sense of a word, phrase, or passage
- Qualities and the pervasive qualitative unity of a situation
- Emotions and feelings
- Embodied schemas and feeling contours

The Felt Sense of a Word, Phrase, or Passage

To give some preliminary idea of what it means to say that meaning is embodied and that meaning goes deeper than our conceptual and propositional structures, I want to consider briefly some of Eugene Gendlin's work on what he calls the "felt sense" that is intimately connected to the structural, conceptual, representational patterns of meaning that are typically thought to constitute the entirety of linguistic meaning. Gendlin asks us to reflect on how it is that a poet who is searching for the next word or the next line in his or her burgeoning poem knows that one candidate is better than others that offer themselves as ways to carry the meaning forward. Imagine that you were the anonymous early sixteenth-century poet of "O Western Wind," who was trying to find the final line to finish the now-famous quatrain. The poem begins:

O Western wind, when wilt though blow,
that the small rain down can rain.
Christ, that my love were in my arms,
. . . . ?

What comes next? How do you know which of the possible endings that might suggest themselves to your thought is the one you actually want—or rather, that works best in your poem-in-process? How about, "Christ, that my love were in my arms / and all of my fortunes gain." Terrible! And you know it's terrible because you feel that tension and rejection in your diaphragm, even as the words of the line are forming in your mind. Maybe "Christ, that my love were in my arms / and I should not die in vain." Better. Not bad, but not great, either. It still does not bring to fulfilment the meaning working in the previous line. The tension is still there.

Gendlin observes:

> The poet reads the written lines over and over, listens, and senses what these lines need (want, demand, imply, . . .). Now the poet's hand rotates in the air. The gesture says *that*. Many good lines offer themselves; they try to say, but

do not say—*that*. The blank is *more precise*. Although some are good lines, the poet rejects them.

That . . . seems to lack words, but no. It knows the language, since it understands—and rejects—these lines that came. So it is not pre-verbal; rather, it knows what must be said, and knows that these lines don't precisely say that. It knows like a gnawing knows what was forgotten, but it is new in the poet, and perhaps new in the history of the world. (1991, under "Introduction")

You keep on trying out alternatives until something changes—until you feel that release in your gut and your diaphragm. You keep going until the meaning seems to flow forward to a culmination. "Christ, that my love were in my arms / and I in my bed again." That's it! That is a fulfilling way to carry forward the meaning working in those lines. Maybe not the only possible ending to the quatrain, but a good one. Once again, you know what is better by the felt sense of the emerging line. The blank (the . . .) is satisfied. Gendlin explains:

This. . . . must be directly referred to (felt, experienced, sensed, had, . . .). Therefore, whatever term we use for such a blank, that term also needs our direct reference.

The blank brings something new. That function is not performed by the linguistic forms alone. Rather, it functions *between* two sets of linguistic forms. The blank is not just the already written lines, but rather the *felt sense* from re-reading them, and *that* performs a function needed to lead to the next lines. (1991, under "Introduction")

What Gendlin is bringing to our attention is how the meaning of the words is never accomplished only through the structural/conceptual/linguistic patterns we use. There is what William James ([1890] 1950) called a "fringe" or "halo" of meaning surrounding and supporting any word, phrase, or sentence. The "felt sense" testifies to the more-than-linguistic, more-than-conceptual dimensions of meaning-making. Gendlin's project has been to help us recover the neglected deep meanings that go beyond language and other symbol systems (see Levin 1997). He suggests that "we can develop a new mode of language and thinking which enters, and speaks from, what is *more than* conceptual patterns (distinctions, differences, comparisons, similarities, generalities, schemes, figures, categories, cognitions, cultural and social forms . . .), although these are always inseparably at work as well. For example, 'more than' is a pattern, but here it says more than the pattern." (Gendlin 1997, 3; italics in the original).

Qualities and the Pervasive Qualitative Unity of a Situation

Gendlin's notion of the felt dimensions of meaning calls to mind the crucial role of qualities in our meaningful experience of our world. Dewey regarded one of his greatest missions to be the recovery of the central role of the qualitative in all aspects of human experience, meaning, thought, and symbolic interaction. In his important but underappreciated essay "Qualitative Thought" (1930), Dewey begins by observing that what matters to us in life are qualities that we seek to realize or to avoid: "The world in which we immediately live, that in which we strive, succeed, and are defeated is preeminently a qualitative world" ([1930] 1988, 243. We humans live for the qualities that form our experiential realities. We learn, for instance, to discriminate and care about a vast array of "reds" that have special meaning for us: the red of a ripe tomato sitting on a small white plate, the red of a lover's luscious lips, the red of the sun setting on the Oregon coast, or the red of the blood that gushes from a wounded comrade. Our English word *red*, even with all the qualifying adjectives we can attach to it, is never fully adequate to the meaning of the reds we encounter in our lives. In the following short poem, we are called to a very special meaningful experience of felt qualities evoked and carried forward by the words, but certainly not fully comprehended by those words:

Level Light
Sometimes the light when evening fails
stains all haystacked country and hills,
runs the cornrows and clasps the barn
with that kind of color escaped from corn
that brings to autumn the winter word—
a level shaft that tells the world:

> *It is too late now for earlier ways;*
> *now there are only some other ways,*
> *and only one way to find them—fail.*

In one stride night then takes the hill.
                      William Stafford, *The Way It Is: New & Selected Poems*, 1998

The opening lines call up (and, we might even say, *enact*) an experience of a very specific color quality of autumn light. Have you experienced that golden-corn twilight of late autumn that stains the haystacks and clasps the barn as the sun is setting? It is a dying light that suggests the end of one sea-son and the coming on of winter. Perhaps insight comes to us in the fading of some unique quality of the corn-colored light with the felt approach of night moving toward you through the crisp chill of autumnal air—cold, dry, rich with the scent of decaying life. Through this light we come to understand how "other things" can come only upon the death and passage of what has been. It is a somber, anxious world that requires death before the emergence of new possibilities: "*now there are only some other ways, / and only one way to find them—fail.*"

One of Dewey's most important—yet least appreciated and most dismissed—claims is that all meaning and thought emerges first from what he called the "unifying qualitative whole of a situation." Here is how he formulated this insight: "An experience has a unity that gives it its name, *that* meal, that storm, that rupture of a friendship. The existence of this unity is constituted by a single *quality* that pervades the entire experience in spite of the variation of its constituent parts. This unity is neither emotional, practical, nor intellectual, for these terms name distinctions that reflection can make within it" (Dewey [1934] 1987, 37).

To grasp Dewey's seminal idea of the qualitative whole, let us reflect on the way a good work of art "grabs you" and pulls you into its world. As Paul Ricoeur (1984) was fond of saying, an artwork draws the perceiver into the "world of the work," where the perceiver can experience the possible ways of inhabiting that world. What "grabs you" is the pervasive unifying quality of the whole work, prior to most of the conceptual discrimination you might subsequently lavish on the work. Dewey has described this experience of being caught up by an artwork or a scene: "The total overwhelming impression comes first, perhaps in a seizure by a sudden glory of the landscape, or by the effect upon us of entrance into a cathedral when dim light, incense, stained glass and majestic proportions fuse in one indistinguishable whole. We say with truth that a painting strikes us. There is an impact that precedes all definite recognition of what it is about" ([1934] 1987, 50).

Dewey certainly acknowledged that when you encounter an artwork, you are not simply or only enraptured by its overall qualitative unity. Of course, you also quickly see lines, shapes, colors, objects, spaces, animals, people, and even events that might be depicted or referenced. However, these perceived patterns and objects are selections and discriminations within the total unifying background quality of the world you are engaging in the artwork. Yes, you "see" objects, but those objects stand forth from, and within, the felt qualitative unity of the whole scene.

Based on studies of the various neural architectures of the brain (e.g., right/left, front/back, core/shell), neuroscientist and psychologist Don Tucker has traced the path of a developing experience that begins with a feeling-rich synthetic whole that is subsequently differentiated in areas of the sensory cortices, which in turn feed back into our developing holistic grasp of the scene or situation we are encountering: "In early attempts to understand a novel situation, therefore, the first patterns to be formed may be holistic, visceral representations at the limbic network level. Reflecting the residuals of personal history, these representations take the form of . . . inherent expectancies for what should happen. Such visceral concepts are formed at the core of each hemisphere. . . . The result is a fast and abstract—if syncretic—comprehension of the novel situation that is organized within the linked network architecture of the right hemisphere" (2007, 236). It is just such a holistic, affect-laden take on a situation that leads us to feel that we have an "intuition" about that given situation. It (the situation) is threatening, joyful, welcoming, promising, intriguing, disruptive, calming, and so forth. The joyful situation is not just a subjective feeling *in us*; rather, it is the qualitative unity of the entire scene that defines its character and direction. Consequently, any distinctions or patterns or qualities we mark within the scene have their meaning only in relation to the defining qualitative unity from which they emerge.

Emotions and Feelings

Attention to the felt qualities of a situation leads us to the role of emotions in the meaning of an artwork. The field of emotion studies is a vast and rapidly growing venue of psychological, biological, anthropological, and neural research that has become immense. I have selected Antonio Damasio's celebrated theory of emotions for the briefest possible treatment, as it bears on the nature of meaning. The basic idea, I shall argue, is that emotions arise within the flow of our ongoing experience with our environment, and they are a primary way by which we assess the quality, meaning, and development of our experience. Therefore, emotions are a key part of how we gauge the meaning of what is happening to us.

In a series of four important books by Damasio (1994, 1999, 2003, 2010), he presents the following evolutionarily grounded account:

1. In order to survive and grow, an animal must continually monitor and take stock of changes in its current body state, so as to effect changes

within the body to maintain or restore the disrupted internal systemic homeostasis that is necessary for survival and effective functioning within the animal's environment.

2. Most of this regulatory activity takes place automatically and without conscious awareness. The result is an automated system of emotional response patterns that are based on the organism's assessment of how its body state is being affected by its engagement with its environment. Emotional response patterns are sometimes accompanied by our conscious feeling of our emotional responses, but these feelings are mostly an after-the-fact way the animal has of being aware of how things are going for it.

3. Emotions are thus a key part of the process by which our bodies monitor and assess their state and make adjustments to maintain a homeostasis within our internal milieu, the loss of which could be debilitating or even fatal.

4. The range of human feelings includes primordial feelings (i.e., the feeling of being alive in a body), background emotions (e.g., energy or malaise, edginess or calmness), primary emotions (e.g., fear, sadness, anger, joy), and social emotions (e.g., shame, honor, pride, jealousy).

5. Consequently, what Daniel Stern (1985) calls "feeling contours"—such as build-up of tension followed by release, hard-driving rhythms, felt speeding up and slowing down, experiences of floating, noticing an increase or decrease of the intensity of a quality—are one of the primary nonconceptual ways we become aware of the meaning and significance of our experience, as we evaluate "how things are going."

6. In this way, emotions and feelings lie at the heart of our ability to make sense of our world and to act intelligently within it, and feeling contours have an intrinsic body-based meaning for us.

7. Finally, in addition to emotions evoked by direct experiences, Damasio (1994, 1999, 2003, 2010) describes what he calls an "as-if body loop" by which we can experience emotional responses and have emotional feelings in relation to imagined scenes or events like dramatic plays, musical works, or paintings. The key idea here is that we don't necessarily require actual bodily experiences with an environment, since emotions and feelings can also be elicited by merely imagining some situation or scenario. In cases where you can become utterly terrified, erotically charged, or calmly invigorated in a movie theater, or while reading a novel or exploring a painting, it is this "as-if" loop that gives rise to the appropriate emotions. According to Damasio's theory of emotional experience, emotions and feelings are central to our ability to experience

the meaning of any situation, whether it be a "real-world" encounter with an enemy or an "as-if" encounter with an enemy in some artwork, whether it be the felt anxiety of a tense situation at one's workplace or the tense anxiety of one of Picasso's cubist paintings, whether it be the joyful exuberance of one's wedding day or the joyful exuberance of a Kandinsky painting.

To sum up: Emotions and their attendant feelings lie at the heart of our meaning-making. Nonlinguistic, as well as linguistic, dimensions of artworks evoke meaningful emotional patterns that are felt to be significant, even when we cannot express their meaning in words.

Embodied Schemas and Feeling Contours

The great psychologist of art Rudolf Arnheim has given us brilliant analyses of many of the bodily patterns and processes by which artworks can be meaningful to us (Arnheim 1954, 1969). Arnheim argues, like Dewey, that there is no grand metaphysical or epistemic gap between the processes of perception and feeling and those we think of as matters of conceptual and propositional reasoning. More than nearly fifty years ago, Arnheim used his gestalt psychology studies of perception to argue that perceiving and thinking are not radically distinct functions, but rather utilize the same types of cognitive operations:

> The cognitive operations called thinking are not the privilege of mental processes above and beyond perception but the essential ingredients of perception itself. I am referring to such operations as active exploration, selection, grasping of essentials, simplification, abstraction, analysis and synthesis, completion, correction, comparison, problem solving, as well as combining, separating, putting in context. These operations are not the prerogative of any one mental function; they are the manner in which the minds of both man and animal treat cognitive material at any level. There is no basic difference in this respect between what happens when a person looks at the world directly and when he sits with his eyes closed and "thinks." (1969, 13)

In *Art and Visual Perception* (1954), Arnheim takes pains to describe a large number of patterns and types of psychological processes by which human beings—with the bodies and brains they have evolved—are able to make some sense of what they perceive, interact with, and imagine. An adequate aesthetics would seek a more or less comprehensive taxonomy of these patterns and processes of human meaning-making. That would be a daunting task, but we have some exploratory forays into that vast little-known realm of meaning-making (Fauconnier and Turner 2002).

As I understand such an aesthetics of human meaning and understanding, it would explore not only the parallel operations involved in perceiving and thinking (as in Arnheim), but would also include the role of images, image schemas, conceptual metaphors and metonymies, semantic frames, qualities, feelings, and emotions as crucial to the ways we make and expand meanings. So far, I have only discussed three of these dimensions (i.e., qualities, feelings, emotions). I would like to end by saying a few words about embodied image schematic structures of meaning and some of the feeling contours that play a role in our engagement with the arts.

In 1987 George Lakoff and I (Lakoff 1987; M. Johnson 1987) coined the term "image schemas" to describe recurrent patterns or organism/environment interactions that are mostly automatic, nonconscious, and directly meaningful to creatures with bodies and brains like ours, as a result of our interactions with our shared environments. For example, given our upright stance within a gravitational field and our proprioceptive and kinesthetic senses, we humans have developed a sense of bodily balance as key to successful transactions with our world. We know what it feels like to be balanced and to lose our balance. We know the possible consequences of losing our balance and falling. As Arnheim (1954) has observed, we see objects in our surroundings as balanced, unbalanced, or teetering precariously between the two states. We thus acquire a felt sense of the meaning of balance. Were we to have radically different bodies, or were we to have radically different environments—such as existing outside a gravitational field—we might have either no sense of balance or a quite different sense than we currently possess. The BALANCE schema is thus a basic image-schematic meaning structure for beings embodied in the same ways we are and emdedded in the same general types of environments we routinely inhabit.

Another basic image schema is that of a RUSH, which consists of a rapid buildup of intensity in a qualitative dimension of some situation. Everyone knows the common feeling contour of a rush of fear, a rush of joy, a rapid increase of brightness of light or sound, or some drug-induced bodily rush. A rush is the result of an increase in the firing rate of certain neuronal functional clusters and the felt response to chemicals released into our bloodstream that affect our bodily response patterns.

Developmental psychologist Daniel Stern has named feeling patterns such as rushes, "vitality-affect contours." He notes that infants must experience their world through an extensive range of just such affect contours, which are felt rather than conceptualized. When we "grow up," we don't leave these basic meaning patterns behind. We continue to experience them, but we often incorporate them into our more abstract systems of meaning. Vitality affect contours are the patterns of flow and change of our felt experience: "These elusive qualities are better captured by dynamic, kinetic terms, such as 'surging,' 'fading away,' 'fleeting,' 'explosive,' 'crescendo,' 'decrescendo,' 'bursting,' 'drawn out,' and so on" (Stern 1985, 54).

Vitality affect contours are most evident in temporal arts, such as music and dance, in which there is some kind of actual or virtual movement. In dance, for instance, bodies actually move through space with leaps, twists, crouches, sweeps, loss and restoration of balance, and various explosions and curtailing of expressed energy. However, image-schematic affect contours are also present in events and art experiences where there is no literal movement in space, but only temporal "motion." Steve Larson and I (M. Johnson and Larson 2003), for example, have analyzed some of the chief metaphors by which we understand musical "motion" through musical "space," such as when we say, "The music *goes faster* here," "Here *comes* the recapitulation," "The soloist is waiting *to come in* seven measures *from here*," and "The melody takes a *leap* toward the end and then *slows down* until it *stops*."

Susanne Langer has argued that music was the quintessential art of virtual motion. She described music as the "tonal analogue of emotive life" (Langer 1953, 27) in which *patterns of feeling* are what are experienced most directly in music, and in art generally. Art is an expressive form, by which Langer meant "any perceptible or imaginable whole that exhibits its relationships of parts, or points, or even qualities or aspects within the whole, so that it may be taken to represent some other whole whose elements have analogous relations" (1957, 20).

Although Langer sometimes, as in the previous quotation, uses the word "represents," she saw that art does not primarily "*re*-present" or "*re*-create" some experience; on the contrary, art is a *presentation*, *enactment*, or *creation* of meaning through what she called "living form":

> "Living form" is the most indubitable product of all good art, be it painting, architecture, or pottery. Such a form is "living" in the same way that a border or a spiral is intrinsically "growing": that is, it *expresses* life—feeling, growth, movement, emotion, and everything that characterizes vital existence. This expression, moreover, is not symbolization in the usual sense of conventional or assigned meaning, but a presentation of a highly articulated form wherein the beholder recognizes, without conscious comparison and judgment but

rather by direct recognition, the forms of human feeling: emotions, moods, even sensations in their characteristic passage. (1953, 82)

If proof of the correctness of Langer's account is wanted, we need only consider what goes on "inside us" as we experience a piece of music that we find really "moving." We are drawn in and carried along by the music, not just in intellectual comprehension, but also through our whole animate bodily feeling of the affect contours enacted in the music. We are swallowed up in the music, moving and feeling in and through the music. Music can give us an experience, on steroids, of our vitality and of the felt contours of our emotional being. It is a short step from music to dance, in which our bodies act out the emotions and affect contours that define our lives and selfhood. The gestures of the dancing and singing body present the qualities, feelings, affect contours, emotions, images, and image schemas that are the flesh, bone, and blood of embodied meaning. In my book *The Meaning of the Body* (chap. 11) I have tried to do a bit of this type of embodied meaning analysis for a simple musical work like "Over the Rainbow," but there are much more profound and sophisticated treatments of embodied musical meaning by music theorists like Steve Larson (2012), Lawrence Zbikowski (2002), Hallgjerd Aksnes (1997), Janna Saslaw (1996), Michael Spitzer (2004), Juha Ojala (2009), Arnie Cox (1999, 2016), and many others. Once you appreciate the embodied sources of our experience of musical motion and space, every structure, pattern, or quality of bodily movement and expression can be appropriated for our experience of musical meaning. Music can *move* by changes in pitch, key, meter, rhythmic modulations, tone qualities, and temporal dynamics of all sorts.

It is more difficult to recognize some of these affect contours and movement patterns in supposedly nontemporal arts like painting and architecture, but Arnheim (1954) has famously shown how paintings can invite the experience of perceptual forces and movement of the eyes through the work. Consider, for example, Henri Matisse's beautiful cutout, *Acanthus*. Even if you were unaware of the title Matisse gave to this work, you would experience an eruption of organic forms emanating upward from the bottom, or perhaps from the bottom right corner. You *feel* an upsurge of life. You *feel* growth, expansion, and the coming-to-fruition of things in one consummatory moment. The colors sing and give you a joyful feeling of vitality and exuberance. Matisse invites you to inhabit his world of light, color, and life. Your identity in such a world would be quite different from your sense of self in the dark, somber, foreboding, desolate, tortured, memorializing landscape of an Anselm Kiefer painting.

Bodily Meaning and Self Identity in Art

I have been suggesting that works of art can provide the perceiver with possible ways of being in and inhabiting a world (of the work). Works of art are no less, nor no more, "real" than the events of our everyday practical reality. As Dewey argued in his early essay "The Postulate of Immediate Empiricism" (1905), "Things are what they are experienced to be" ([1922] 1988, 159). There is a real experience of an artwork—as developing a world that we can inhabit—just as there is a real experience of a computer keyboard, a loaf of bread, or a rainy day. These experiences are all equally real, insofar as they each afford us with different opportunities of meaningful engagement. Moreover, as Ted Cohen has argued, the feelings and emotions evoked by literary fictions are just as real as those we experience in our day-to-day existence: "It seems to me a natural extension from this fact about people that they take an interest in stories, to the intimately related fact that people's involvement in these stories includes genuine feelings" (2008, 38). There is meaning (and nutrition!) that you can get from a loaf of bread that is unavailable from an abstract painting, but likewise there is meaning available in that painting which none of these other experiences can precisely enact. Given that each of these is equally "real," the only question is, at this present moment, which of these opportunities for engagement best satisfies your needs, opens up possibilities for growth, and deepens and enriches meaning for you. Dewey's claim is that good works of art provide exemplary instances of just such a development, expansion, and liberation of meaning, and they thereby provide depths and intensities of meaning that are not routinely available in our ordinary day-to-day affairs.

Dewey's metaphysics gives us a way to get over the mistaken view that an artwork derives its significance and validity from fixed and complete experience that it allegedly *re*-presents. Overly simplistic imitative theories of art are a prime example of our tendency to think that a work of art gets whatever value it has by pointing to some independent, already complete experience. If that were the case, then artworks would have only derivative, second-rate value relative to their representational function. But just the opposite is the case. As Dewey ([1934] 1987) argued, art is a unique developing experience, not a static thing. As experience, it is neither merely objective (as nothing more than a re-presentation of a pre-given, finished object), nor merely subjective (as nothing more than an inner experience). It is instead an occasion for meaningful encounter with aspects of our world, in which both self and world are transformed. As experience, it reaches beyond the present, back into parts of what has come before to define a context, and forward into future possible experiences (and meanings) that are opened up by the artwork. Consequently, there is no eternal or fixed essence of any given artwork. "The artwork" is different at different moments and in different developing situations. The artwork exists in its enactment through a perceiver engaging a set of affordances for possible meanings—affordances presented via some organization of marks, colors, tones, words, movements, gestures, thoughts, feelings, and so on. It makes no sense to speak of the artwork "in itself," as though it were a completed object or event. Susanne Langer made this point well when she observed that artworks do not "re-present" feelings; rather, they *present* or *enact* felt situations: "But a work of art does not point us to a meaning beyond its own presence. What is expressed cannot be grasped apart from the sensuous or poetic form that expresses it. In a work of art we have the direct presentation of a feeling, not a sign that points to it" (1953, 133–34).

I would want to expand this claim beyond the presentation of feeling to embrace all the ways we make and discover meaning; but the basic idea—that the artwork is an enactment of meaning—is sound. The work of art is a *working* of art—a process of engagement between a human being and some aspects of her environment. However, the *artworking* occurs not just in some objective environment, nor exclusively in some inner experiential space, but in the developing organism-environment interaction, where the environments are at once physical, interpersonal, and cultural. The enactment of the artwork has meaning in the very same ways, and by the same neural and embodied means, as our "ordinary" experience is meaningful, but Dewey has suggested that what makes an artwork more significant than most affairs of everyday life is its capacity to enact meaning with a harmony, wholeness, intensity, or scope that is not routinely possible in our day-to-day affairs. The coffee cup on my desk can have plenty of meaning for me, but Matisse's rendering of a cup in a still life can reveal—through its imaginative exploration—aspects of significance that are not routinely afforded me by the cup that sits before me.

So, where does the issue of personal identity reside in this account of enacted meaning? My answer is that you are who you are in and through the meanings that are afforded you by your experience. Some of these aspects of your identity are profoundly bodily and physical, while others are interpersonal or cultural. You are the relatively stable habits of experiencing, thinking, valuing, feeling, and acting that interpenetrate in your life. You gain self-understanding not by allegedly pure acts of reason turning reflectively inward to discover some essence of your inmost being. Rather, you learn who you are by seeing the patterns and content of what you have experienced—what matters to you, what you find appealing, what you find repulsive, and what you have undergone and done. Often, you get this sense of your identity by what other people reveal to you about how you engage your world (physically, interpersonally, and culturally).

Therefore, although a work of art does not directly tell you "who you are," what it can do is open a world of possible experience—an encounter with ways of being in the world, in relation to which your identity develops. Matisse cutouts are just as much "affordances" of possible experience as are pork cutlets. Do you find your identity in pork cutlets? Well, you find that either you are a carnivore and a great lover of the pig, or else, perhaps as an orthodox Jew, you find pork cutlets repulsive (or at least, something off limits to your gustatory experience). Do you find yourself in Matisse cutouts? Well, perhaps you find that you are attracted to certain shapes and organic contours, and that you feel at home in the dynamic play of his lovely organic forms with their luscious color. Or maybe you learn that your aversion or lack of interest in the cutouts reminds you that you are more comfortable with the controlled yet dynamic rectilinearities and precision of a Mondrian world.

In any of these cases, it is crucial to remember that your identity is not locked up within you; it is not something wholly "subjective." It is the identity of you-in-your-world. The things you experience shape the matter and form of your self-understanding. The part of this that Kant got right was that you are what and who you are only in your world; that is, only in ongoing interaction with your situation in a shared world. What Kant got wrong was his postulating of a transcendent individual self working behind the scenes. There is no "you" beyond this embodied world-in-process. There is no fully fixed self, but only a self-in-process that is shaped by what it experiences and enacts.

I would end by observing, as Dewey did, that there is nothing "merely subjective" about this process of experience in which your self-identity is carried forward. The qualitative unities of an artwork as experienced—which are correlative with the qualitative unity of our selves—are "really there." They are not just idiosyncratic "feelings" in you. They are in and of your world, whether it is the world of soccer balls and automobiles, or the world of Mondrian geometries and Matisse organic harmonies.

CHAPTER 10

Dewey's Big Idea for Aesthetics

Dewey's Big Idea

Brothers and sisters, in the Gospel according to Matthew (21:42, English Standard Version), Jesus says: "Have you never read in the Scriptures: 'The stone which the builders rejected has become the cornerstone; this was the Lord's doing, and it is marvelous in our eyes'?" If I remember correctly from my undergraduate religious studies course, in Matthew's narrative, the stone that was cast out is Jesus, the Son of God, upon whom the new Kingdom of God will supposedly be founded. Now, in the story I'm about to tell, the stone that was cast out is aesthetics, and the new kingdom will be a philosophical orientation built on aesthetics. I shall call this view about the primacy of aesthetics the Gospel according to John (Dewey, that is), encapsulating it with: "The stone of aesthetics that was cast out shall become the foundation of our new kingdom—our new philosophy of experience" (Book of Dewey 0:0).[1]

When I was in graduate school in the 1970s, the common wisdom was that real (manly) philosophy was epistemology, logic, and analytic metaphysics, whereas aesthetics was for the mushy minded, the intellectual weaklings, the faint of heart. Aesthetics was what you did if you couldn't hack it in the world of serious philosophy. After all, the story went, aesthetic experience is a matter of feelings, feelings are subjective, and none of this can play any role in our cognition or knowledge of our world.

In response to this prejudice, Dewey had turned the traditional epistemological conception on its head, arguing that it should be aesthetics, above all else, that provides the proper basis for our account of human nature, human meaning, human knowing, and human value. Dewey's gospel calls for the outcast stone of aesthetics to become the cornerstone, the foundation of everything else.

Why has the aesthetics stone been cast out in Western culture? The chief reason is that aesthetics has been conceived far too narrowly as concerned with something called "aesthetic experience," which is then distinguished from other modes of experience and thought (e.g., theoretical, technical, and moral) that make up the fabric of our daily lives. This partitioning of experience into discrete types, each having its own distinctive characteristics, is one of our most problematic Enlightenment legacies. Assume that philosophy is primarily concerned with the nature and conditions of knowledge, relegate aesthetics to matters of "mere" feeling, denigrate the role of feeling in human cognition, and you can then conveniently marginalize aesthetics in philosophy and life. Once reduced to a single type of feeling-based process, aesthetic experience is taken to be subjective—a mere matter of taste. Kant surely was partly to blame for this, with his impressive systematic treatment of distinct types of cognitive and noncognitive judgments; but he is just one voice in a deafening chorus that denies aesthetic experience any significant role in cognition and knowledge.[2] Insofar as aesthetics is conceived as embracing only the sensuous, perceptual, imaginative, feeling, and emotional dimensions of experience, aesthetic experience is viewed as too subjective to serve as the basis for our shared experience, cognition, and knowledge of our world.

As a corrective to this drastically impoverished account of experience and thinking, Dewey argued that what we call "aesthetic" dimensions are not just characteristics of a single isolated type of experience, but rather provide the basis for our ability to grasp the meaning and significance of *any and every* developed experience. He therefore understood aesthetics in a broad sense, as involving form and structure, qualities that define a situation, our felt sense of the meaning of things, our rhythmic engagement with our surroundings, and our emotional transactions with other people and our world. This was Dewey's thick notion of the aesthetic dimensions of experience, spelled out in great works such as *Experience and Nature* (1925), *Art as Experience* (1934), and *Logic: The Theory of Inquiry* (1938). In short, aesthetics concerns everything that goes into our experience and creation of meaning, and the arts are recognized as exemplary cases of this pervasive process of meaning-making.

Dewey's philosophical orientation is thus shaped by his conviction that (1) *philosophy should begin and end with experience, taken in the richest, deepest sense*; (2) *aesthetic dimensions are what constitute the character of any fully developed and meaningful experience*; and (3) *attention to the qualitative aspects of experience is the key to an adequate understanding of human mind, thought, language, and value.* In other words, the test of a philosophy is its ability to deepen, expand, enrich, and liberate our experience, and this requires that we begin and end our philosophical inquiries in the qualitative depths of experience.

This emphasis on the qualitative provides the basis for what I am calling

Dewey's Big Idea for Aesthetics

Every relatively meaningful and fulfilled experience is individuated by a pervasive unifying quality.

I have highly intelligent philosophical colleagues who roll their eyes and shake their heads when they encounter Dewey's reference to the pervasive qualitative unity of a situation. Some of them no doubt regard such claims as proof positive of the mushiness and untenability of Dewey's view. They wonder who can make any sense of such a strange idea, and, even if you could give it any meaning, what possible difference would it make, either for how you live your life or how you do philosophy? Yet Dewey never ceased to regard what I am calling his "big idea for aesthetics" as the cornerstone of his philosophy. He insisted that pervasive qualities were the ground of all experience and thought. He argued that genuine thinking (including logic) must emerge from, and lead to, a qualitative unity (Dewey [1930] 1988; [1938] 1991). He charged philosophy with the task of rooting itself in, and then transforming when necessary, these qualitative unities of experience.

Something about Dewey's big idea resonates with me, and so I want to try to make sense of his claim, especially as it plays a fundamental role in his view of aesthetics and art. I want to explore this notion as the key to the possibility of an aesthetics of meaningful experience. I cannot here address its implications for thinking in general, for logic, for knowledge, or for moral deliberation, but Gregory Pappas (2016) has done a marvelous job of showing the crucial role of the qualitative in all these aspects of thinking and valuing. I hope at least to show why Dewey was correct in thinking that we should put aesthetics—with its emphasis on the qualitative—at the heart of our philosophical inquiries.

Our World Is Qualitative

Dewey's entire philosophical orientation is based on the fact that we dwell, perceive, think, feel, value, and act in and for a world of qualities: "The world in which we immediately live, that in which we strive, succeed, and are defeated is preeminently a qualitative world. What we act for, suffer, and enjoy are things in their qualitative determinations. The world forms the field of characteristic modes of thinking, characteristic in that thought is definitely regulated by qualitative considerations" ([1930] 1988, 243. Qualities are what we live for—the fresh, soft, translucent greens of leaves in early spring contrasted with the hardened, fatigued, dessicated greens in early fall; the supple flesh of a woman's bare shoulders against the unforgiving hardness of the oak chair on which she sits; the muscular, explosive grace of a basketball player pivoting for a fallaway jump shot; the angularity of work-worn hands holding the knife as it parts the semi-resisting skin of a ripe tomato. This is the stuff of our lives.

The late poet William Stafford captures the power of felt qualities to lead us to meaning:

Just Thinking
Got up on a cool morning. Leaned out a window.
No cloud, no wind, Air that flowers held
for awhile. Some dove somewhere.

Been on probation most of my life. And
the rest of my life been condemned. So these moments
count for a lot—peace, you know.

Let the bucket of memory down into the well,
bring it up. Cool, cool minutes. No one
stirring, no plans. Just being there.

This is what the whole thing is about.
William Stafford, *The Way It Is: New & Selected Poems* (1998)

Early morning. You can feel the cool, motionless air at your window. You lean out into a clear, still world. You breathe in the flower-held air. You feel it cool on your skin. A dove coos from somewhere. All is peaceful—both in the world outside your window and in your inner being, if only for these brief moments. Memories rise, like cool water drawn up from a deep well. The air, the water, the memories—all cool and refreshing. And while it lasts, *there you are, too,* present, just present, taking it in, feeling the morning and the world and peace. And that is the meaning of it all.

It is qualities like these for which we live. They are the very stuff of our meaningful experience. Dewey's claim about the primordial qualitativeness of our lives would seem almost trivial, were it not for the fact that it is hard to think of a philosophy that does justice to this insight.[3] Even in aesthetic theory, where one might expect qualities to be central, it is striking how few theories pay any serious attention to the phenomena Dewey has described. Undertake a quick historical survey of aesthetic theories and you will encounter factors such as mimesis, unity in variety, aesthetic ideas, significant form, expression of ideas, emotional communication, the role of social practices and institutions, and aesthetic judgment. But try to find a theory besides Dewey's that is grounded in the qualitative unity of an experience and you will discover that somehow, this whole notion has more or less escaped serious attention in most traditional and contemporary aesthetic theory.[4]

Experience, Situations, and Qualitative Unity

Behind Dewey's focus on the qualitative is his insistence that philosophy (and all thought) must begin and end in experience, if it hopes to have any significance for our lives. Dewey took experience to be a continual process of organism-environment interactions. Consequently, experience is neither exclusively an affair "of the mind" (the subjective having of sense perceptions, feelings, or emotions), nor exclusively "in the world" (the grasping of a mind-independent reality). He stated: "Experience is *of* as well as *in* nature. It is not experience which is experienced, but nature—stones, plants, animals, diseases, health, temperature, electricity, and so on. Things interacting in certain ways *are* experience; they are what is experienced. Linked in certain other ways with another natural object—the human organism—they are *how* things are experienced as well. Experience thus reaches down into nature; it has depth. It also has breadth and to an indefinitely elastic extent. It stretches. That stretch constitutes inference" (Dewey [1925] 1981, 12–13). Passing over Dewey's intriguing notion of experiential inference, let us focus on his key assertion that experience is an interactive process. What we call "mind" and "body," "subject" and "object" are, for Dewey, just abstractions of what is actually an ongoing, continuous flow of organism-environment transactions. The reality of qualitative dimensions of experience results from the fact that for creatures like us—who have evolved certain modes of perception, sentience, and consciousness—there is always *what* is experienced and also *how* things are experienced, and the *how* is present to us as felt qualities.

Much of the time, we engage our world routinely, habitually, and inattentively, unaware of how various qualities are shaping the meaning of our lives. In other words, what we colloquially call "experience" is typically slack, not clearly unified; and it is had without any significant sense of meaning. Much of the time there is no unified experience. We start something and are interrupted, never carrying the action to completion. We passively take in a flood of impressions that have no particular meaning and barely hold our attention. We settle into what Dewey called passive "undergoing" without any active doing that organizes the materials of our awareness into a meaningful whole. At other times, we have an excess of "doing," as we rush through life so harried and driven that we never take in the potential meaning of what we are about at that moment. There is no reflective appreciation of what our present, developing situation means. Things happen, but we do not recognize any consummatory meaning or significance. However, in contrast with inchoate experience of this sort, there are also moments of intensity and focused awareness, moments when our world stands forth as meaningful. We are energized, engaged, and at least somewhat aware of the significance of what is happening:

> Experience in the degree in which it *is* experience is heightened vitality. Instead of signifying being shut up within one's own private feelings and sensations, it signifies active and alert commerce with the world; at its height it signifies complete interpenetration of self and the world of objects and events. Instead of signifying surrender to caprice and disorder, it affords our sole demonstration of a stability that is not stagnation but is rhythmic and developing. Because experience is the fulfillment of an organism in its struggles and achievements in a world of things, it is art in germ. (Dewey [1934] 1987, 19)

When we are able to grasp the developing meaning of a situation, we speak, rightly, of *having an experience*. When, for example, we say to a fellow sports fan, "That was really an amazing game last night," we are recognizing that a dramatic sequence of related events came together for us in such a way as to be marked off as meaningful, in contrast with the more routine, unreflective, insignificant and relatively undeveloped goings-on in our daily affairs.

For Dewey, the primary unit of meaningful experience is what he called a *situation*, by which he meant "a complex existence that is held together in spite of its internal complexity by the fact that it is dominated and characterized throughout by a single quality" ([1930] 1988, 246). Few of us are in the habit of noting the "single quality" that pervades a situation. Although we often, and quite easily, select out salient qualities of a situation (as in, "That key lime pie was really tart!"), we are not accustomed to consciously noticing the qualitative unity of our whole situation. Yet it *is* there, underlying everything we experience, think, and do. For example, consider the difference you experience—feel in your guts—of listening to a lecture in which you are intensely captivated by the ideas being developed by the speaker, versus listening to a lecture that you are beginning to feel is overly simplistic, forced, or just plain misguided. These are two quite different experiences, with different qualitative unities that synthesize their parts into meaningful wholes. The intense "Aha!" of discovery that pervades the former experience contrasts sharply with the uneasy, frustrated, desultory character of the latter episode.

Each situation, of course, is always deeper, more extensive, and richer in meaning than you can grasp in any one act of understanding. Every act of understanding and thinking is a selective process that necessarily involves attention only to parts of the horizon of meaning that demarcates your present situation. The meaning that is working in a given situation is not just a matter of your focus on what is being said, for it expands to include the sound of the speaker's voice, his or her fluent gestures, the quality of light in the room, the smell of books lining the walls, and the communal energy or malaise of the audience as a whole.

Dewey explained his notion of a "pervasive unifying quality" of a situation as follows: "An experience has a unity that gives it its name, *that* meal, that storm, that rupture of a friendship. The existence of this unity is constituted by a single *quality* that pervades the entire experience in spite of the variation of its constituent parts. This unity is neither emotional, practical, nor intellectual, for these terms name distinctions that reflection can make within it" ([1934] 1987, 37; italics in the original).

In observing that the unity is "neither emotional, practical, nor intellectual," Dewey is avoiding any artificial partitioning or segmenting of experience. The unity is not exclusively and definitively any *one* of these types or dimensions of experience. Rather, it is all of these—and more—woven together. We have a tendency to focus on selected dimensions at the expense of others, and then we miss what unifies and demarcates the situation. For example, in narrowly defining an encountered problematic situation as a matter of *ethical* judgment, we thereby tend to overlook the *aesthetic, political, religious, economic, scientific* components that played—or should have played—such a crucial role in our deliberation and judgment (Dewey [1922] 1988).

Our tendency to regard the world as a concatenation of discrete qualities stems from the fact that we are creatures evolved to differentiate and discriminate. Within the qualitative unity of a situation, we immediately and automatically note distinguishing qualities, often overlooking the whole from which they emerge. Dewey described this selective prejudice as follows: "All thought in every subject begins with just such an unanalyzed whole. When the subject-matter is reasonably familiar, relevant distinctions speedily offer themselves, and sheer qualitativeness may not remain long enough to be readily recalled" ([1930] 1988, 249). One unfortunate result of this tendency to quickly and automatically discriminate particular qualities is that we then lose our sense of the pervasive unifying quality that defines our whole situation. Even if we can experience such a quality, we certainly cannot describe it, since any proffered description will involve discrimination of particular qualities of the experience, and so will lose the unifying character itself.

Undaunted, Dewey simply reminds us that as we attend more carefully to the various discriminated aspects of a situation, our attention itself is directed and controlled by the background out of which seemingly discrete properties arise: "Even at the outset, the total and massive quality has its uniqueness; even when vague and undefined, it is just that which it is and not anything else. If the perception continues, discrimination inevitably sets in. Attention must move, and, as it moves, parts, members, emerge from the background. And if attention moves in a unified direction instead of wandering, it is controlled by the pervading qualitative unity" ([1934] 1987, 192).

The heart of Dewey's big idea is that every situation comes to us first as a unified whole, prior to our carving it up through our selection of specific qualities for our attention—a process itself guided by the pervasive unifying quality. Imagine walking into a large gallery of a museum and seeing a painting on the far wall. You have never seen this particular painting before, but you immediately recognize it as a Picasso, a Van Gogh, or a Dufy. Its unifying quality is not its *Picasso-ness*, its *Van Gogh-ness*, or its *Dufy-ness*, although that is certainly part of what you are picking up on. Rather, there is a *pervasive unifying quality of* this *particular work you are now engaging*, which just happens to be, say, a Picasso. And the meaning of that particular work is realized, as a horizon of possibilities for meaning, in and through its qualitative unity: "The total overwhelming impression comes first, perhaps in a seizure by a sudden glory of the landscape, or by the effect upon us of entrance into a cathedral when dim light, incense, stained glass and majestic proportions fuse in one indistinguishable whole. We say with truth that a painting strikes us. There is an impact that precedes all definite recognition of what it is about" (Dewey [1934] 1987, 150).

Art and the Enactment of Meaning

When Dewey asserts that fulfilled experience is "art in germ," he is claiming that art is experience in its consummatory, eminent sense. Art reveals, through immediate presentation of qualities unified in a comprehensive whole, the meaning and significance of some aspect of our world, either as it was, is, or might be. At its best, art shows us the meaningful possibilities of our world. However quaintly romantic this might sound, it *is* the heart of Dewey's view. He is saying that art will matter to us just insofar as it enacts meaning in our lives, and that meaning is present in and through the qualitative unity of the work, not in any other way, or by any other means.

Dewey's central question here is *how* art realizes meaning. His answer is that art achieves meaning by enacting in us a heightened awareness of the "pervasive unifying quality" of a given situation. It does not *re*-present some meaning already formulated; rather, it *presents*, *enacts*, and *realizes* that meaning through its experienced particularity. If it were a mere re-presentation, then the meaning would already be accessible in some other way, outside and independent of the artwork. But it is not. We are attracted to and care about works of art not just because they can be entertaining and enjoyable, but more important, because they afford us possibilities for enriched and expanded meaning. They enact the meaning of what has been, is now, or might be experienced. Dewey's claim is compatible with Heidegger's view that an artwork presents us with a world and shows us how our "world worlds"; that is, how it unfolds before us as a horizon of meanings (Heidegger 1971). His claim is also similar to Paul Ricoeur's (1984) suggestion than an artwork shows us a world we might inhabit, dwell in, experience, take up, and carry forward in our lives.

Dewey sums up the crucial role of qualitative unity as follows: "The undefined pervasive quality of an experience is that which binds together all the defined elements, the objects of which we are focally aware, making them a whole. The best evidence that such is the case is our constant sense of things as belonging or not belonging, of relevancy, as sense which is immediate" ([1934] 1987, 194). Dewey goes so far as to say that we "intuit" this pervasive mood and significance of a work: "But the penetrating quality that runs through all the parts of a work of art and binds them into an individualized whole can only be emotionally 'intuited.' The different elements and specific qualities of a work of art blend and fuse in a way which physical things cannot emulate. This fusion is the felt presence of the same qualitative unity in all of them" (ibid., 192).

Through this qualitative unity, an artwork presents a world or situation of possible meaningful experience that you might inhabit. This is not limited only to representational scenes. The qualitative unity of the work can be manifest in a portrait, in abstract forms and relations in a nonrepresentational piece, or in a color-field painting, each of which is circumscribed and experienced as an individual qualitatively unified situation.

Consider, for example, the very different worlds enacted in the paintings of Piet Mondrian as compared with any of the late cutout works by Henri Matisse. These are abstract works, with little or no obvious representational content; they nonetheless draw us into two fundamentally different ways of inhabiting and experiencing the world. Mondrian's is a world of rectilinearity, right angles, squares, rectangles, and precise delineations. Matisse's cutouts are populated with organic forms that float joyfully and freely in harmonious relation and movement. Matisse's works enact organic growth through vibrant living colors and perceptually moving forms. Mondrian's works can be equally full of life and activity, as in his *Broadway Boogie Woogie*, but the colors are sharper, more intense, and more precisely contrasting. His is a palette of primary colors, whereas Matisse envelops us in rich, complex, and subtle hues that are often nonprimary. Both painters realize basic dimensions of our lived experience, but in quite different ways, resulting in dramatically different qualitative unities. Thus, the issue is not the *representation* of a world, but rather the *enactment* of a world (or a situation)—a way of being in the world that reveals possible meanings and expands our awareness. Dewey explains the sense of meaning presented via the qualitative unity:

> The resulting sense of totality is commemorative, expectant, insinuating, premonitory.
>
> There is no name to be given it. As it enlivens and animates, it is the spirit of the work of art. It is its reality, when we feel the work of art to be real on its own account and not as a realistic exhibition. ([1934] 1987, 193)

Robert Innis has captured the ways a viewer of an artwork experiences the unity of the work and simultaneously carries forward and transforms that unity through her exploratory perception: "Integral experience, in Dewey's sense of the term, obtains form through dynamic organization (1934, 62) in as much as the perceiver is caught up in and solicited by the emerging experiential whole. Even while experiencing the perceptual whole as an *outcome* over which it has no explicit control, the perceiver is *creating* its own experience through continuous participation (1934, 60)" (Innis 1994, 61).

Some Empirical Support from Cognitive Neuroscience

What I have been arguing so far is that Dewey's big idea for aesthetics is not wacky. On the contrary, his account is the best available explanation of the felt sense of meaning we get from works of art that capture our attention. Dewey's argument is mostly phenomenological, focusing our attention on our felt encounter with an artwork. However, beyond the phenomenological evidence, there is at least some additional supporting evidence emerging from recent empirical work in cognitive neuroscience. In *Mind from Body: Experience from Neural Structure* (2007), Don Tucker focuses on the evolved basic architecture of the brain as the key to the nature of our cognitive abilities, with special attention to the central role of feelings and emotions in all aspects of cognition. Tucker explores the cognitive processing that results from three fundamental architectural features of the human brain: front/back orientation, hemispheric bilateralism (right/left organization), and core/shell relationships. For my purposes, I shall focus only on the third (core/shell) of these three architectures.

Through evolutionary development, new functional layers of brain structure were added to those that were present in the brains of our animal ancestors. The addition of new "layers" required restructuring and "rewiring" of the earlier layers and functional structures, thereby establishing novel connections among shell and core functional assemblies. As a consequence, our brains currently have a core-shell architecture, with the "core" consisting mostly of limbic structures that are responsible for body monitoring, motivation, emotions, and feelings, whereas the "shell" consists of "higher" cortical layers that perform a host of both narrow and broad cognitive tasks, such as perception, body movement, action planning, and action control.[5]

The crucial point for our purposes is Tucker's claim that (1) structures in the core regions are massively interconnected, whereas (2) structures in the cortical shell regions are more sparsely interconnected, which means that there is more functional differentiation and modularity in brain areas in the cortical shell than in the densely interconnected and emotionally modulated limbic core. Tucker summarizes:

> *The greatest density of connectivity within a level is found at the limbic core.* There is then a progressive decrease in connectivity as you go out toward the primary sensory and motor modules. . . . In fact, the primary sensory and motor cortices can be accurately described as modules because each is an isolated island, connected with the diencephalic thalamus but with no other cortical areas

except the adjacent unimodal association cortex of that sensory modality of motor area.

The exception is that the primary motor cortex does have point-to-point connections with the primary somatosensory cortex. (2007, 81; italics in the original)

Tucker's account gives a plausible explanation of Dewey's claims about the experience of a qualitative unity that gives rise to our perception of the specific qualities and structures in an artwork. The limbic core, with its dense interconnections and strong emotional valences, would present us with a holistic, feeling-rich, emotionally nuanced grasp of a situation—Dewey's felt, pervasive unifying quality. The more modular and highly differentiated sensory and motor regions of the shell (cortical) structure would permit the discrimination and differentiation of objects, particular qualities, and relations within the artwork. Just as Dewey claimed, the meaning of a situation (here, an artwork) starts with an initial intuitive grasp of its significance and grows as we progressively discriminate more qualities and relations emerging out of the background of the pervasive unifying quality of the work.

The core/shell relationships are far more complex than I have so far suggested. Cognitive processing is ordinarily not just a unidirectional movement outward from core to shell, in which an experience runs its course and is done. Instead, through reentrant connections, what occurs at "higher," or more differentiated, levels can also influence what happens in the limbic areas, which then feed back up to shell regions, and this recurrent cyclic activity continues as our experience develops.

The core-to-shell movement of cognition helps explain why (and how) there can be pervasive qualities that give rise to acts of discrimination and conceptualization. Tucker summarizes the structural basis for this growing arc of experience that was described by Dewey as the movement from a holistic pervasive qualitative situation to conceptual meaning:

> At the core must be the most integrative concepts, formed through the fusion of many elements through the dense web of interconnection. This fusion of highly processed sensory and motor information . . . together with direct motivational influences from the hypothalamus, would create a *syncretic* form of experience. Meaning is rich, deep, with elements fused in a holistic matrix of information, a matrix charged with visceral significance. Emanating outward—from the core neuropsychological lattice—are the progressive articulations of neocortical networks. Finally, at the shell, we find the most differentiated networks. . . . The most differentiated networks of the hierarchy are the most constrained by the sensory data, forming close matches with the

environmental information that is in turn mirrored by the sense receptors. (Tucker 2007, 179)

Our experience of a pervasive qualitative unity of a situation is the product, not just of core/shell architecture, but also of differential processing in the right and left hemispheres. Tucker describes the holistic, viscerally rooted grasp of the right hemisphere in ongoing dialogue with the more modular left hemisphere: "We can see that this progression—from syncretic on the right toward differentiated on the left—is the same one that we have deduced from examining the core-to-shell progression of network organization within each hemisphere. At the visceral core, the fully distributed pattern of network organization leads to syncretic representations, within which all of the elements are fused in dynamic interaction" (2007, 235).

The chief value of Tucker's account, for our purposes, is his explanation of the way our more finely differentiated acts of experience and thought arise from our holistic, affect-rich grasp of the situations in which we find ourselves. Tucker claims that this pattern holds for *all* our experience, not just for art; but Dewey adds that it is art's intensive focus on presenting the qualitative unity of a situation that gives art its special role in our lives—the role of enacting consummatory meaning. Tucker's view gives at least one account that would show how Dewey's claims could be explained and justified from a biological and neural perspective.

What Are We to Do with Dewey's Big Idea?

In the middle of his essay "Performative Utterances," J. L. Austin pauses to reflect on how his analysis seems to be going: "So far we have been going firmly ahead, feeling the firm ground of prejudice glide away beneath our feet which is always rather exhilarating, but what next? You will be waiting for the bit when we bog down, the bit where we take it all back, and sure enough that's going to come but it will take time" (1970, 241). One might wonder whether we have reached just such a point of breakdown where all this wonderful talk about pervasive unifying qualities of situations and the role of art in realizing such qualities seem to come to nothing. So, either we have to beg off, or else we have explain how taking Dewey's big idea seriously should affect the way we do aesthetics.

The problem here is that, having observed the existence of pervasive qualitative unities, there doesn't seem to be anything more one can say about them and how they do their work. Everything we *say* will necessarily involve marking out distinct qualities or structures within a situation (here, the artwork, or some aspect of nature), and then we will be talking about those specific qualities or structures instead of the overall unifying quality. Are we thus constrained to silence when it comes to what we are claiming is one of Dewey's most important insights?

If Dewey is on the right track, then all our cognition, all our conceptualization, all our thinking, and all our valuing ought to be tied to the working of pervasive unifying qualities. It would follow from this that *all* reasoning, insofar as it has any relevance to life, must be grounded in qualitative unity of some situation or other. And Dewey in fact made just such a claim ([1930] 1988, [1938] 1991). The same conclusion should follow for our ethical deliberations—that they arise from and must return to some qualitative situation in the world (Dewey [1922] 1988). As mentioned earlier, Pappas (2016) has investigated these connections between the qualitative unity of a situation and the way we think, draw inferences, and make normative appraisals. My focus here is primarily on art, but a full treatment would have to explore the working of qualitative unities in both logical inference and moral reasoning. We need to show that Dewey's big idea makes a difference in how we think about art and the aesthetic dimensions of our everyday experience. Then, once we see art as an exemplary manifestation of meaning, we will see that all experience is aesthetic experience, and we will appreciate the need for an aesthetics of meaning-making. Here are some of the more important tenets of an aesthetics of human meaning, understanding, and art experience.

The first and most important point is that it is the pervasive qualitative unity of a situation that makes an experience what we would call "aesthetic." As Dewey puts it, "In as far as the development of an experience is *controlled* through reference to these immediately felt relations of order and fulfillment, that experience becomes dominantly esthetic in nature" ([1934] 1987, 50). Any experience, however vapid or undeveloped, will have whatever meaning it does by virtue of what we can call its "aesthetic" dimensions, such as qualities, structures, relations, feelings, and emotions. Dewey describes these only partially developed experiences as "inchoate," and he contrasts them with "consummated experiences" that we more properly call aesthetic, in order to mark out those cases where experience develops and acquires meaning and direction as it reaches a certain fulfillment marked by its unifying quality. Therefore, there can be no adequate account of the aesthetic dimensions of experience without reference to the notion of a qualitative unity of a situation.

The second major implication (which is perhaps just a variation on the first) is that the main significance of a work of art depends on its capacity to realize a distinctive unifying quality of some situation. In other words, the starting point, the central focus, for our experience of an artwork is its qualitative unity, because *that* is what defines it as the unique artwork it is. Everything we value in an artwork—its formal aspects, its expressive qualities, its sensuous textures, its "way of worldmaking" (as Goodman [1978] puts it)—depends on its qualitative unity.

This leads to a third major point, which is that any aesthetic theory or critical analysis that attends only to selected features of an artwork will necessarily fail to capture what is most important about the work. It is often observed that the problem with most traditional aesthetic theories is their selection of some particular aspect of an artwork, which then gets elevated to the status of *the* essential art-constituting or aesthetically valuable feature. This has given rise to our long history of successive theories that are one-dimensional: mimetic theories, expressivist theories, formalist theories, social institution theories, minimalist theories, and so on. The obvious moral is simply to treat each traditional theory as giving us insight into important dimensions of art, and then try to see how *all* the theories fit together, rather than taking any one of them as definitive.

The fourth major implication is that artworks are significant only insofar as they enact meaningful experience (grounded in the grasp of the qualitative unity) for some audience at a particular moment in history. An art object or event is an occasion for an experience. Indeed, an artwork *is* an experience that typically unites a perceiver, some made or found object, and an environing world. There is no ghostly metaphysical artwork complete in itself and encapsulating its eternal meaning. On the contrary, *the art exists only as enacted, realized, and experienced, and such experience extends over time, even though it is realized always at some specific point in time*. Consequently, there is no artwork-in-itself, existing eternally for all time. Any theory that posits the artwork as some ideal or autonomous object or quasi-object is bound to be one-sided, because it leaves the fullness and depth of experience out of the equation. Artworks are "ideal" insofar as they present an imaginative vision of possible meanings, but this does not amount to the illusory notion of an ideal that stands beyond time and temporal change, transcendent of our ordinary experience.

At the other extreme are theories that reduce the meaning and value of an artwork to nothing more than a single present experience within a perceiving subject. This denies the ongoing temporal nature of the art-as-experience. The mistake of subjectivist theories of taste is to forget that any artwork has meaning that reaches out toward the future and develops temporally as material, social, and cultural conditions change. *There is no single meaning* of an artwork, just as there is no single, autonomous artwork. The art is the working of some event of meaning-making as it contributes to the ongoing experience of various people. This is why there are so many different *Hamlet*s, so many different *West Side Story*s, so many different interpretations of *Moby Dick*. All those different meanings are equally real, because they are meanings experienced in the developing relation between some made object, particular perceivers, and the surrounding environment.

The fifth related point is that art is separated from science (to name just one other type of practice) not because of some absolute difference in kind, but as a matter of degree along a continuum. Science and art alike are modes of inquiry. They are both ways of exploring the meaning of our world. Dewey, like James, famously argued that even in scientific, mathematical, and logical thinking there is always a felt pervasive quality to the character of any developed thought process and situation about which we are thinking (Dewey [1930] 1988; [1938] 1991). However, science typically selects features or structures of experience and then seeks explanatory generalizations over a broad range of phenomena in terms of those abstracted dimensions, typically with an interest in causal and functional relations. Art selects, too, but art is primarily about the enactment of the pervasive unifying quality, as well as particular qualities, of a past, present, or future possible situation and less about the quest (as in science) for generalizations over abstract selected qualities or patterns within some domain of experience. What we call prototypical artworks focus on the immediate presentation or enactment of the felt situation and its qualities: "The doing or making is artistic when the perceived result is of such a nature that *its* qualities *as perceived* have controlled the question of production. The act of producing that is directed by intent to produce something that is enjoyed in the immediate experience of perceiving has qualities that a spontaneous or uncontrolled activity does not have. The artist embodies in himself the attitude of the perceiver while he works" (Dewey [1934] 1987, 48).

Sixth, we are thus brought back to our previous observation that what we call "art" is continuous with any fully developed ordinary experience, insofar as it gives rise to meaning and value. "Because experience is the fulfillment of an organism in its struggles and achievements in a world of things, it is art in germ" (Dewey [1934] 1987, 19), and "art is thus prefigured in the very processes of living" (ibid., 24). Contrary to the otherworldly yearnings of an aesthetician like Clive Bell, who insisted that art transports us to a world beyond all time, Dewey is right to see that art is an ongoing temporal experience of meaning, an experience typically orchestrated by an artist and/or performer for an audience that is always situated at some point in time, but whose experience of meaning can be reconfigured over time. Thus, any artwork can change over time and across cultures.

Dewey is not embarrassed to insist that art matters because it is meaningful. He would not have been impressed by postmodern denials of meaning. There are things, events, and experiences that entertain, delight, distract, or unsettle, and art can do all these things, but what makes art most important is its power to present or realize meaning. Notice that many postmodern obsessions—such as rupture, loss of meaning, paradox, negation, self-fragmentation, frustration, and anxiety—are just as much part of our experience as are our more constructive and creative engagements with our world. So, an artwork can enact disintegration and failure to find significance, just as much as it can enact life's fulfillment and experiences of meaning and value. However, *both of these ways of being are strands of meaningful experience*; that is, they are themselves experiences, and as such manifest some qualitative unity that has some meaning for our lives. Consequently, Dewey sticks with his view that art enacts possibilities for meaning and growth: "Art is the living and concrete proof that man is capable of restoring consciously, and thus on the plane of meaning, the union of sense, need, impulse and action characteristic of the live creature. The intervention of consciousness adds regulation, power of selection, and redisposition. . . . But its intervention also leads in time to the *idea* of art as a conscious idea—the greatest intellectual achievement in the history of humanity" ([1934] 1987, 25).

I want to close where I began, with the idea that what we call "the aesthetic" is not some special aspect, feature, or kind of experience, but rather the very stuff of any meaningful experience. One of the biggest errors we can make in aesthetic theory is the fetishizing of "the aesthetic," as if only certain very special kinds of experience are aesthetic. That road wrongly leads to the separation of art from life (as if ordinary living was not an aesthetic undertaking), and it robs us of the means to explain the power of artworks to matter to us and to change us. It is perfectly acceptable to speak, as Dewey sometimes does, of "aesthetic experience" when we are trying to observe that certain experiences are marked out as meaningful unities, while others (the "nonaesthetic" ones) are unconsummated, undeveloped, unfulfilled. But what is not acceptable is to treat "the aesthetic" as some quality or feature that descends—we know not why or wherefrom—upon a certain select set of experiences. That way leads to just another fragmentation of human experience and to the marginalization of aesthetics.

I do not think it an exaggeration to say that Dewey's entire philosophical orientation is founded on his insight that all experience, perception, understanding, imagining, thinking, valuing, and acting begins and ends in the aesthetic dimensions of human experience. Dewey was correct in observing that virtually all the errors and reductionist tendencies of philosophies can ultimately be traced to their impoverished conceptions of experience, and to their ignorance and dismissal of the significance of the aesthetic. Therefore, it is fitting to end, as we began, with our passage from the Gospel according to John (Dewey, that is): "The stone of aesthetics that was cast out shall become the foundation of our new kingdom—our new philosophy of experience" (Book of Dewey 0:0).

CHAPTER 11

The Embodied Meaning of Architecture

Human beings are creatures of the flesh who arrange spaces and physical structures fitted to their bodies. We live in and through our ongoing interactions with environments that are both physical and cultural. The structures we make are loosely adapted to the functions we perform. Some of these functions are necessary for our survival and flourishing, such as working, eating, having shelter, playing, and sleeping. However, we also order our environments to enhance meaning in our lives and to open up possibilities for deepened and enriched experience. In other words, although we are animals evolved for fitness, we are just as much animals with a deep desire for meaning as part of our attempts to grow and flourish (Flanagan 2007; Alexander 2013). Architecture is ideally located at the intersection of these two complementary aspects of our lives (i.e., fitness and flourishing), insofar as the ways we organize space and buildings address simultaneously our need for protection from the elements and our need for meaningful experience. I want to reflect on the nature of human meaning-making through architecture, as it bears on both of these fundamental human needs.

Embodied Human Meaning

Toward the beginning of *Art as Experience* (1934), John Dewey argues that the key to appreciating the central role of the aesthetic dimensions of *all* human experience is the recognition that everything important arises from the ongoing interactions of a living creature with its complex environment:

Life goes on in an environment; not merely *in* it but because of it, through interaction with it. No creature lives merely under its skin; its subcutaneous organs are means of connection with what lies beyond its bodily frame, and to which, in order to live, it must adjust itself, by accommodation and defense but also by conquest. At every moment, the living creature is exposed to dangers from its surroundings, and at every moment, it must draw upon something in its surroundings to satisfy its needs. The career and destiny of a living being are bound up with its interchanges with its environment, not externally but in the most intimate way. ([1934] 1987, 13)

We live and become what we are only in and through our engagements with the many aspects of our environment. All our perceptions, feelings, emotions, thoughts, valuings, and actions are thus consequent on our embodied transactions with our physical surroundings, our interpersonal relations, and our cultural institutions and practices. Our capacity to experience, make, and communicate (share) meaning not only is a result of the makeup of our brains and bodies, but depends equally on the ways the environment we inhabit is structured.

Before we can examine some of the ways architecture enacts meaning, we need to be clear again about what is meant by "meaning." To reiterate, this is a very serious and deep issue because several decades of work in linguistics and the philosophy of language within the "analytic" (Anglo American) philosophical tradition has reinforced the mistaken idea that all meaning is a matter of language, so that it is words and sentences alone that have meaning. It is also usually assumed that sentences are meaningful because they express concepts and propositions that map onto states of affairs in the world. In short, meaning is thought to be a matter of how words (and sentences) can be "about" the world, and it is thought to be conceptual, propositional, and truth-conditional in nature.

The first obvious thing to point out about this mainstream conception of meaning as linguistic is that such a view can have almost no significant application to our experience of architecture—or of any other art, for that matter. For the most part, architectural structures are not linguistic signs that could have meaning in the way that sentences, phrases, and words are thought to. I submit that such an impoverished view of meaning-as-linguistic gives us virtually no useful way of explaining either the meaning or power of architecture in our lives. Our inability to turn buildings into quasi-sentences and parts of buildings into quasi-phrases or quasi-words in order to show that and how they can be meaningful should make it evident that there is something fundamentally wrong, in the first place, with the view of meaning as entirely conceptual, propositional, and linguistic. In short, although one can probably find some very weak analogies between buildings and sentences, the dominant meaning-as-linguistic view turns out to be a profoundly inadequate way to understand the meaning of architecture, or any other art.[1]

Fortunately, we need not be encumbered by such an inadequate and impoverished theory of meaning. Cognitive science research over the past three decades has given us a dramatically richer view of the nature and sources of meaning. The general framework is one suggested nearly a century ago by John Dewey: "A thing is more significantly what it makes possible than what it immediately is. The very conception of cognitive meaning, intellectual significance, is that things in their immediacy are subordinated to what they portend and give evidence of. An intellectual sign denotes that a thing is not taken immediately but is referred to something that may come in consequence of it" ([1925] 1981, 105). *The meaning of any object, quality, event, or action is what it points to by way of some experience. Meaning is relational, and the meaning of a certain object would be the possible experiences it affords us—either now, in the past, or in the future (as possibilities).*

We can see this relational, experiential, enactive character of meaning in our understanding of physical objects and events. Psychologist Lawrence Barsalou coined the term "perceptual symbols" for the sensory-motor-affective structures by which we experience, understand, and think about physical objects in our environment. He argues that "cognition is inherently perceptual, sharing systems with perception at both the cognitive and neural levels" (Barsalou 1999, 577). The central idea is that to say we have a concept of some object is to say we can enact a series of sensory, motor, and affective experiences that would be associated with objects of that sort. Barsalou explains: "Perceptual symbols are modal and analogical. They are modal because they are represented in the same systems as the perceptual states that produced them. The neural systems that represent color in perception, for example, also represent the colors of objects in perceptual symbols, at least to a significant extent. On this view, a common representational system underlies perception and cognition, not independent systems. Because perceptual symbols are modal, they are also analogical. The structure of a perceptual symbol corresponds, at least somewhat, to the perceptual state that produced it" (ibid., 578).

For example, the meaning of a bowl is not just some abstract concept specifying a defining set of features that jointly constitute it as a bowl. Rather, the meaning of a bowl is all the experiences it can afford us. Some of those experiences will be present sensory-motor activations, such as the visual properties it presents; the way it feels in the hand as it's lifted; the smoothness of its ceramic, wooden, or plastic surface; or its capacity to hold soup, rice, guacamole, and the like. However, the meaning of the bowl is not just what it affords us by way of physical perception and motor interaction, because it also includes the social functions of various types of bowls, given our cultural values and practices surrounding our use of bowls and their significance, both in our daily lives, as well as on more formal and special occasions. Finally, in addition to this public, shared meaning, there will be each individual's own personal past experiences with bowls and perhaps with this very same bowl that now sits before you. Perhaps it is the painted bowl given to you by your students at the end of a philosophy of art course, and which has sat on your desk for the past thirty years, connecting you with those students, that class, and the experiences you shared with them.

In this account of embodied meaning, I have been appropriating J. J. Gibson's (1979) notion of perceptual "affordances." Gibson, like Dewey, saw that objects are and mean the possibilities for experience that they afford us. What any object affords is the result of the nature of our bodies and brains—our perceptual apparatus, our neural processes, our affective responses, our motor programs—*as they interactively engage patterns and structures of our environments*. So, for a human being with fingers, hands, and arms, a ceramic bowl affords pick-up-ability, whereas for an ant it might provide climb-up-ability. Properties, modes of interaction, and meanings are therefore relative to the character of the organism (live creature) and to the objective characteristics of its environments. The objects that populate our world greet us with their meaningful affordances as we engage them in activity. Such affordances define the spaces in which creatures like us can be "at home" in our world; that is, the affordances define the types of couplings and transformative operations we can experience with our environments.

An important component of the newer, second-generation cognitive science of meaning and thought is the utilization of neural imaging research. Each of the experiences related to bowls that I described in the previous paragraphs is correlated with activation of functional clusters of neurons, and often with the release of chemicals in the body. We now know from neural imaging studies that seeing a bowl not only is a *visual* experience, but also activates some of the neurons in the motor and premotor cortical areas of the brain that would be activated if we actually picked up the bowl, manipulated it, or ate from it (Gallese and Lakoff 2005). These so-called *canonical* neural clusters are what make our concepts multimodal, involving activation of various modes of perception and interaction connected with a particular object. There are also *mirror neuron* systems, so that when we see someone performing a specific action with some object, many of the same sensory and motor clusters are activated in our brains as if *we* were performing that action (Rizzolatti and Craighero 2004). Although this research began with monkeys, it has been extended to human cognition, and we now know that mirror-neuron effects are present even when we imagine performing an action, read about such an action, or hear someone describing the action (Gallese and Goldman 1998; Feldman 2006; Bergen 2012). This is embodied meaning in the most direct and intimate sense.

The conception of meaning that I have briefly sketched here has been substantially developed by a number of linguists, psychologists, neuroscientists, and philosophers over the past thirty years, especially within what are known as cognitive linguistics and the neural theory of thought (Lakoff and Narayanan, forthcoming). This orientation begins with organism-environment interactions and the mostly nonconscious selection by an organism of certain relations or qualities of the interaction that are taken as signs of other experiences. Barsalou (1999) argues that we should think of concepts as "simulators," because they simulate in our brains and bodies the kinds of experiences we might have with particular objects, events, or situations. A similar view has recently been expanded into what is known as simulation semantics. Benjamin Bergen, a cognitive scientist with a background in linguistics, describes the "embodied simulation hypothesis" as the view that "we understand language by simulating in our minds what it would be like to experience the things that the language describes" (2012, 13). We use the same systems for conceptualization, reasoning, and communication that we use in experiencing and manipulating the objects we conceptualize, reason about, and write and talk about. "The idea is that you make meaning by creating experiences for yourself that—if you're successful—reflect the experiences that the speaker, or in this case the writer, intended to describe. Meaning, according to the embodied simulation hypothesis, isn't just abstract mental symbols; it's a creative process, in which people construct virtual experiences—embodied simulations—in their brains" (ibid., 16).

Bergen's focus is primarily on the dynamic, constructive processes of meaning-making in language. However, I want to suggest that the enactive processes of meaning and thought he is describing are equally present in experiences of meaning that are not merely linguistic. Any form of symbolic interaction will manifest these same sensory-motor-affective simulations that are meaningful to humans, given their bodily makeup;

the types of environment they dwell in; and the cultural history, practices, and institutions they inhabit. The crux of this view is that meaning is not just some abstract, disembodied conceptual content, but rather involves the activation of sensory, motor, and affective processes that we associate with the thing or event that has meaning for us. My point is that the only way to explain the meaning and power of architectural affordances in our lives requires these multimodal, enactive, simulation processes of meaning-making.

The Qualitative Dimensions of Experience and Meaning

In addition to the previously sketched embodied simulation account of meaning, the second thing I want to bring to bear on our understanding of how architecture is meaningful is the central role of the qualitative aspects of experience. We dwell in a world of qualities—the fresh, earthy scent of a cool breeze coming in through the window on a spring morning, the sounds of children playing, the honking of horns in congested traffic accompanied by the smell of exhaust and the feeling of cars and trucks pressing in around us, and the refreshing shock of the cold mountain lake after a strenuous sweaty hike. We act to realize some qualities and avoid others. Our eros draws us to the eyes of our lover and to their scent, skin, breath, and lips—all of which are experienced qualitatively without any need for reflective thought. Our world is a realm of immediately felt qualities that have meaning for us even before and without language. This is not to deny that language and other forms of symbolic interaction can sometimes dramatically enrich our possibilities for meaning, but linguistic meaning is already itself parasitic on embodied, qualitative meaning.

Dewey argued at great length that although the sciences are important because of the way they selectively abstract out certain relations among objects and events, in order to discover new relations and to frame causal laws, it is precisely such abstractions that can lead us to ignore some of the important qualitative dimensions of our experience. Of particular concern in science is the tendency to focus on the quantitative dimensions at the expense of the qualitative. What is needed to reconnect our scientific understandings to our lived experience is recognition of the role of qualities in what and how things are meaningful to us.

As we have seen in previous chapters, one of Dewey's most radical ideas was that in addition to specific sensory qualities, every situation we encounter is unified and marked off by what he called its "pervasive unifying quality" (see chapter 10). To find yourself enmeshed in an experience is to feel the qualitative unity that gives meaning, identity, and direction to what is happening to you. Dewey's argument is that only within such a unified situation do we *then* experience individual objects, persons, and events, with their particular qualities and affordances. Humans, like all other animals, are selective creatures; that is, our survival and flourishing depends on our ongoing, mostly unconscious, selection of aspects of our environment for attention, interaction, and transformation.

So, *objects are events with meanings* that "stand out" within the context of a situation. An object is "some element in the complex whole that is defined in abstraction from the whole of which it is a distinction. The special point made is that the selective determination and relation of objects in thought is controlled by reference to a situation—to that which is constituted by a pervasive and internally integrating quality" (Dewey [1930] 1988, 246). Objects are clusters of affordances of possible interactions we have had, or might have. Objects stand out for us because they are significant for the kinds of creatures we are, with the kinds of perceptual and motor capacities we have, and the kinds of purposes and values we cherish: "Things, objects, are only focal points of a here and now in a whole that stretches out indefinitely. This is the qualitative 'background' which is defined and made definitely conscious in particular objects and specified properties and qualities" (Dewey [1934] 1987, 197).

The relevance for architecture of this conception of the qualitative unity of a situation or experience is that any encounter with an architectural structure begins with a felt qualitative sense of our whole situation, prior to any definite attention to component parts, relations, or qualities. Dewey's way of making a similar point (though one not explicitly directed at architecture) is to differentiate the *sense* of a situation from the *signifying* functions of various elements within that situation:

> The qualities of situations in which organisms and surrounding conditions interact, when discriminated, make sense. Sense is distinct from feeling, for it has a recognized reference; it is the qualitative characteristic of something, not just a submerged unidentified quality or tone. Sense is also different from signification. The latter involves use of a quality as a sign or index of something else. . . . The sense of a thing, on the other hand, is an immediate and immanent meaning, it is meaning which is itself felt or directly had. . . . The meaning of the *whole* situation as apprehended is sense. ([1925] 1981, 200)

So, the *sense* of a situation or experience is felt as a meaningful whole within which we then discriminate relevant objects, qualities, events, and persons that matter to us because they signify—point to—other objects, events, relations, and experiential consequences that are connected to our present situation. *My hypothesis is that architectural structures are experienced by humans as both sense giving and signifying. That is, architectural structures present us, first, with a way of situating ourselves in, or being "at home" in, and making sense of our world, and, second, they provide physical and cultural affordances that are meaningful for our survival and flourishing as meaning-seeking creatures.* Consequently, any encounter with an architectural structure begins with the overall sense of place (of being in a particular world), followed almost immediately by a growing grasp of the numerous meanings afforded by its various parts, light patterns, structural relations, contrasts, flow, rhythms, and other significant elements of meaning within the architectural work.

Bodily Structures of Meaning in Architecture

I am suggesting that we need an embodied view of mind and meaning to appreciate the significance of architecture. Any architectural theory based on a disembodied view will therefore be proportionately inadequate to the extent that it overlooks the embodiment of meaning. Examples of this shortcoming are certain types of computational modeling that disregard history and embodied consciousness. Alberto Pérez-Gómez observes that computational architectural models cannot incorporate the pre-reflective and embodied dimensions and qualities that ground human meaning: "These instrumental processes are necessarily dependent on mathematical models, and often become an empty exercise in formal acrobatics. Architects soon forget the importance of our verticality (our spatial engagement with the world that defines our humanity, including our capacity for thought), our historicity (we are, effectively, what we have been), and gravity (the 'real world' of bodily experience into which we are born, and that includes our sensuous bond to all that which is not human)" (2002, 36). Pérez-Gómez is criticizing misguided attempts to model our sense of space and place in a manner that presupposes the mistaken view that mind is disembodied and that human understanding can be decontextualized. If we forget our embodiment—including the fact of our being situated within a particular concretely experienced environment—we lose the very means for explaining the power and importance of architecture. Thus, Dalibor Vesely concludes that "to perceive, to move and to learn, in the human world is possible only due to a corporeal involvement. The disembodied nature of computer programs is the main reason for their inability to match human intelligence" (2002, 66).

What we need, then, is an understanding of "mind" as embodied and enactive relative to our experience and comprehension of architectural spaces. I am arguing that such an account needs to keep in mind two fundamental points: (1) the meaning of any object is grounded in the affordances for possible experiences related to that object, and (2) our account of these affordances must include the crucial role of the qualitative dimensions of any experience. I want to put some flesh on these skeletal claims by giving a few brief examples of some of the more important patterns of our embodied interactions that thereby gain considerable significance for our experience of architecture.[2] In *The Body in the Mind* (1987), *The Meaning of the Body* (2007), and *Embodied Mind, Meaning, and Reason* (2017), I described various *image-schematic* patterns of recurring structures of experiences that humans (and some other animals) encounter through their mostly unreflective bodily engagement with our environments. I argued that such image schemas are immediately significant for us through the affordances they provide for how we can meaningfully interact with our world. Body-based meaning structures of this sort have obvious relevance for the meanings of constructed environments. Here are a few of the more important image schemas, with some indication of their relevance for architecture.

Containment

Life plays out within boundaries. Our bodily organisms are defined by semipermeable boundaries into which we must incorporate energy and out of which we must expel waste. As Antonio Damasio argues, life goes on within the boundaries that define organisms, and "for whole organisms, then, the primitive of values is *the physiological state of living tissue within a survivable, homeostatic range*" (2010, 49). Whatever else we do, our bodies must maintain an appropriate dynamic equilibrium internally, in ongoing response to changing aspects of our environments. Otherwise, we become dysfunctional, and may even perish.

We thus learn the meanings of containment in the most intimate bodily way, first through our visceral sense of our bodies as containers, and then through our bodily manipulations of containers. Very early on, babies begin to learn the "spatial logic" of containment, as they play with nesting objects (cups, bowls, pans, boxes) and experience, through their bodily interactions, movements into and out of bounded spaces. They learn that if the small ball is placed in cup A, and cup A is nested within cup B, then the ball is "in" cup B. In formal logic, this is known as the transitivity relation (If A is in B, and B is in C, then A is in C); however, babies learn this logical relationship as a spatial or corporeal logic not reflectively, but in a bodily fashion through sensory-motor activities.

This kind of *ecological logic* lies at the heart of our experience of architecture, so that we learn the meaningful affordances of particular kinds of containment structures in relation to our bodily makeup, needs, desires, and ideals. Consider, for instance, the sheltering function of much architecture. Shelter requires a relative strength, stability, and at least some measure of impenetrability. We learn which materials are strong, which insulate, and which are available and cost effective, and we respond in certain ways emotionally to structures that we feel to be strong, solid, and well grounded. Typically, we also desire enclosed spaces that are not claustrophobic and oppressive. From infancy on, we climb in and out of boxes, baskets, cribs, closets, cars, and other containers. We find what it feels like to be confined within tight containers, as compared to roaming more freely in open spaces. We know how bad it can feel to be "boxed in." There is a way it feels to be constrained within in a relatively closed, dark, damp space (e.g., a cave), which is experientially quite different from flat, open sweeping expanses of the plains, or from standing high on some mountain with an elevated view of the world spread out below. Consequently, we come to desire shelters of a certain size, height, and configuration, depending on our physical makeup, purposes, available materials, and means to realize our building projects. Most of us do not feel at home in completely closed containers. We want access to light and air, so we want windows and doors that open us to exchanges with our surroundings. We want a certain—perhaps culturally variable—degree of privacy, but we also need ways to learn what is going on in the world beyond our door or gate. In other words, we want to be in and of the world when we think that serves our purposes, and we want shelter and privacy at other times.

Verticality (and Other Spatial Orientations)

Insofar as we are creatures embraced by gravity, what goes up must come down. This is something we have to learn as children, but no reflection is required for this, since we only have to observe how objects and people move in their environment. We therefore dwell at least partly in an up/down world. Because of gravity, the very accomplishment of rising up requires effort, power, control, and balance. One of the most significant human transitions from infancy to childhood is the emergence of an upright posture. We struggle to stand erect, and we learn that standing requires a firm base (ground) and an appropriate balance.

Our mundane encounters with the meanings of verticality give rise to distinctive architectural experiences. Contrast, for example, the experience in a Gothic cathedral of being carried upward with your gaze into an unknowable darkness beyond this world versus the Hopi focus on the kiva as the portal from which spirits enter our world out of the earth or ground. The Christian cathedral is meant to direct us upward toward a projected supernatural realm of perfect and complete Being, while the kiva locates us on the earth, from which life, including the universe, supposedly springs.

Balance

Maintaining balance is one of the key values of all living organisms. We must keep both internal balance (homeostasis or allostasis), and we strive for bodily balance as the basis for our capacity to remain upright, in control, and able to act effectively. Balance is first encountered by us as a bodily experience of our wobbly relation to our surroundings. Babies, after many trials over an extended period, come to tentatively master an upright posture. Eventually, they push forward and have to learn the balance of a walking motion. We are aware of the crucial role of balance in our lives mostly when we lose it, rather than when we unconsciously achieve and maintain it. We eventually learn to project the qualities of our felt experience of balance onto objects that populate our world. The Leaning Tower of Pisa makes some people feel vertiginous and others slightly uneasy. Some experience it as profoundly unbalanced and disturbing, while most enjoy it as a playful, if unintended, divergence from normal vertical stability. Likewise, Richard Serra's *Tilted Arc* made many people so uncomfortable that it was removed eight years after its installation in the Federal Plaza in Manhattan. Some complained that the sculpture partitioned the public space in a way that dramatically restricted public access and movement in the plaza; others felt threatened by the imposing 12-foot-high, 120-foot-long steel wall tilting precariously over them. For them, this did *not* create a happy public space where they could feel comfortable and free in their comings and goings.

One of Dewey's more controversial claims was that the feelings and emotions that Western cultures tend to attribute to the subjective inner states of persons ought actually to be recognized as defining the objective situation. Instead of saying merely, "*I* am fearful," we ought rather to say, "The situation is fearful" (Dewey [1934] 1987, chap. 3). Dewey saw that the proper locus of the affective quality of a situation (as created by the entire cycle of organism-environment interactions) is not just an internal, subjective response. Dewey would have said that it is not merely that a certain structure makes us feel unbalanced; rather, that building *is* unbalanced, relative to the normal relations in which physical objects, both inanimate and living, typically stand within our gravitational field.

Forces

Our world is a scene of ongoing forceful interactions of energy fields. From infancy, we are lifted, lowered, turned over, patted, stroked, squeezed, buffeted about, breathed on, constrained, contained, ministered to, fed, burped, wiped, rocked, comforted, kissed, talked to, and on and on through all the bodily events that make up our surroundings. In this intimate bodily way, we learn the types, consequences, and meanings of the various forces within our cosmos.

Physical structures shape the range of actions possible for us in our environment. You may enter here, but not there. You must walk up these steps, or down this stairway, to gain access. You may, or may not, open this door or window. You must move along this narrow corridor. You may or may not tarry here in this space. All these experiences of restricted-versus-free-access involve structured, forceful interactions. Even when we merely see a building, before ever entering it, we *feel* its affordances for how it will shape our forthcoming engagement with it.

Massive tilting objects tend to frighten us because we have learned that forces of nature and gravity tend to topple such tilting objects, unless they are very strong and firmly rooted. Large, heavy objects supported by thin legs seem unstable to us. The fall of a building is a powerful event that reaches deep down into our emotional experience of falling, disintegration, and the release of overwhelming forces. We are mesmerized by building implosions and demolitions, which we experience as almost sublime— all that energy released as all twenty stories crumble to the ground, sending out a shock wave of dust. We are overwhelmed by the catastrophic destabilization that occurs as massive forces are released and the structural integrity fails. The collapse of the World Trade Center towers bore tragic witness to this horrific experience.

Movement

A vast amount of the information we receive about the world comes as a result of our ability to move ourselves within our environment and to move our hands over surfaces. At a very deep level, we learn the contours of our world and the possible ways we can interact with it via movement. As Maxine Sheets-Johnstone has argued: "In the beginning, we are simply infused with movement—not merely with a *propensity* to move, but with the real thing. This primal animateness, this original kinetic spontaneity that infuses our being and defines our aliveness, is our point of departure for living in the world and making sense of it" (1999, 136). Even though much of the time we are not consciously aware of our bodily movements, we continually experience the qualities of different types of movement. We feel the rhythms of various movements—short, jerky hop-and-skip motions versus smooth, continuous flowing motions. We contrast, within our bodies, the felt difference of gradual accelerations and decelerations versus jolting starts and stops. Felt rhythms provide basic kinesthetic and temporal contours for our experience. Moving objects speed up and slow down, creep along, rush past, dance, stumble, drag by, and float.

By complex perceptual and cognitive processes, we eventually learn to experience what we might call perceptual motion in physically fixed or static visual arrangements. For example, a series of connected Romanesque arches carry our perception along in a smooth, recurring pattern of curving visual motion that is precise and tightly constrained, even as it generates a sense of movement. Contrast this with Frank Gehry's Fondation Louis Vitton, where much more irregular jutting forms thrust up from the ground and seem almost jumbled together, creating a markedly different experience of perceptual movement. The jarring angles of certain Kandinsky paintings have a very different felt quality of perceptual motion than one experiences as the eye moves over the curvilinear, organic forms of Winslow Homer country scene and which has a different sense of organic movement than a Hockney landscape. The playful, and sometimes incongruous angles and lines of various postmodern architectural designs present a very different overall unifying quality than the austere, machine-like regularities and rectilinearities of modernist glass-wall box buildings. Some will prefer Mies van der Rohe, others Art Moderne lines, others Gaudí's organic ecologies, and still others Frank Lloyd Wright's modernist sensibilities, because of the way each of these markedly different qualitative unities afford us dramatically different imaginative experiences for how we can engage and interact with those structures in a meaningful way.

What I have been suggesting via this brief reflection on image-schematic structures in architecture is that architecture can provide us with meaning in at least two different, but related, ways. First, every architectural structure will present us with a felt qualitative unity of the whole that in essence gives us a world (however small), and a certain way of inhabiting that world. Second, the building's particular affordances—based on its particular structures, forms, and qualities—provide the possibilities for meaningful engagement with the building or constructed space. We can talk about these meanings using language, but the meanings are not, as we have seen, for the most part linguistic in nature. Rather, they employ the meaning of our bodily interactions with our environments, and this exists prior to and beneath our linguistic resources.

At the level of the overall qualitative unity of the work, it can be said that each building or organized space gives us a world that we can inhabit—not just a physical world, but a social and cultural world with its defining values. With respect to narrative, Paul Ricoeur (1984) was fond of claiming that each narrative work (historical or fictional) offers us a "world of the work" into which we can project our inmost needs and desires for meaning and value. Going beyond narrative to include architecture, Heidegger claimed that the Greek temple enacts a world of the sixth-, fifth-, or fourth-century BCE Athenian: "The temple-work, standing there, opens up a world and at the same time sets this world back again on earth, which itself only thus emerges as native ground" (1971, 42). Although neither Ricoeur nor Heidegger used Dewey's language of the pervasive unifying quality of a situation or of an experience, Dewey's description of our felt encounter with a loosely or tightly ordered world applies to their examples. It is for this reason that we are prone to identify particular works as embodying historical and cultural experiences and values that capture certain salient characteristics of a specific time, place, and social reality.

From Fitness to Flourishing

In describing but a very few of the image-schematic patterns that are immediately meaningful to us via our embodiment, we have already moved across the boundary between fitness and flourishing.[3] We have made the transformation from what we value for the sake of our survival and fitness within our particular environments to what we value because we crave enriched and deepened meaning. This exposes the artificiality of the fitness/flourishing distinction, because both fitness and flourishing are about how things are meaningful and significant for the kinds of bodily and cultural creatures we are in relation to the physical and cultural aspects of our environment. In this way, we have slipped almost imperceptibly from architecture's functional usefulness for survival to its capacity to give us meaning and to present ideals for how our world might be transformed.

Architecture is thus one of our most human (and potentially humane) ways of relating to our environing world. What Dewey says about all art—that it is a form of human making in which possibilities for meaning are realized—is amply illustrated by architecture. Art takes materials (both physical and cultural) of our embodied and social experience and transforms them into new experiences that intensify, harmonize, and enrich meanings and possibilities for living and acting in the world. Contrary to many traditional theories that isolate "fine" art from the "practical" arts of ordinary life, Dewey recognized that art brings to consummation and fulfillment materials and aesthetic dimensions that permeate our everyday experiences. Dewey saw art not as disengaged from, or rising above, ordinary life, but rather as continuous with forms of meaning-making and problem solving that intelligent creatures utilize to improve the quality of their daily lives.

Architecture is a wonderful example of this meaning-making process. It grows out of our need for shelter and a more-or-less harmonious relation to our surroundings. It is a response to the human desire to feel ourselves at home in our surroundings. It responds to our primary problem of dwelling safely and happily in our world. It draws on our ability to fabricate structures and to transform the materials we find in nature. It is a form of problem solving that addresses equally our need for physical security and our need for meaning and aesthetic well-being (where aesthetics is about everything that goes into our capacity to have any sort of meaningful experience (see M. Johnson 2007)]. In short, architecture is an act of imaginative problem solving and meaning-making that resonates with the deepest levels of our connection to our environment. In the words of Juhani Pallasmaa, "architecture is a mode of existential and metaphysical philosophy through the means of space, matter, gravity, scale and light" (Pallasmaa 2002, 26–28). This captures what I have been saying about the embodied and existential way architecture explores the possible ontologies and ecologies of the human world, though without the use of linguistic propositions that are the darlings of linguistically articulated philosophical systems. Instead, architecture helps us enact what George Lakoff and I (Lakoff and Johnson 1999) have called a "philosophy in the flesh." Drawing on the work of the phenomenologist Maurice Merleau-Ponty, Pallasmaa emphasizes architecture's ability to realize various ways of being in, or inhabiting, our world in the most intimate, embodied, situated manner:

"The task of architecture is 'to make visible how the world touches us,' as Maurice Merleau-Ponty wrote of the painting of Paul Cézanne. . . . We live in the 'flesh of the world,' and architecture structures and articulates this existential flesh, giving it specific meanings. Architecture tames and domesticates the space and time of the flesh of the world for human habitation. Architecture frames human existence in specific ways and defines a basic horizon of understanding" (2002, 18).

The term "understanding" in this passage refers not to some conceptual or propositional belief structure, but rather to a certain specific way of inhabiting and being at home in one's world. I have described but a few of the modes of embodied meaning by which this existential sense giving plays out in our constructed spaces. My contribution to this discussion has been primarily the elaboration of a theory of embodied meaning adequate to the task of understanding how architecture enacts and transforms meaning, including the role of the qualitative dimensions of meaningful experience. I have emphasized that the meaning involved here is a more direct, embodied realization of sense, quality, and significance for our lives. I think Pallasmaa captures this characterization of meaning as embodied, qualitative, and affective when he says, "Architecture mediates and evokes existential feelings and sensations. The buildings of Michelangelo, for instance, represent an architecture of melancholy and sorrow. But his buildings are not symbols of melancholy, they actually mourn" (2002, 22). This is a prime example of what I am calling "the embodied meaning of architecture."

I want to close by reiterating my claim that buildings do not merely reveal our sense of our world and manifest our embodied ways of making sense of that world. If architecture had only this representative function, it might not do anything more than merely express some person's or society's dysfunctional, inharmonious, and highly problematic situation. Indeed, this is often what bad architecture does—it holds before us and habituates the impoverishment of our lives, social arrangements, and relations to our environment and to other people.

To state what most will consider obvious, architecture at its best goes beyond the mere expression of a world to creatively transform the conditions of our human habitation and interaction. This is its moral imperative: to make the world a better place in which to live. It carries out this task whenever it helps resolve problematic situations people find themselves in, and when it enriches the meaning and leads to the growth of our experiences. Because human meanings and values are plural and complex, there can be no single universal way to realize "the better" for human existence (M. Johnson 2014). Nevertheless, even as we must embrace a certain pluralistic set of architectural norms for growth and enrichment of meaning, this does not mean that we cannot, in a particular context, determine better and worse solutions to our need for meaningfully ordered spaces and buildings, as anyone knows who has ever lived in a crummy apartment.

CHAPTER 12

What Becomes of Philosophy, Morality, and Art?

To most philosophers trained in the analytic traditions of Anglo American philosophy of the past century, the idea that philosophy, science, morality, and law are based on deep conceptual metaphors and operate via aesthetic dimensions such as image schemas, qualities, emotions, and feelings will seem like a huge blow to the dignity and importance of philosophy. But not so! I have argued that none of the accounts of our highest intellectual and creative achievements provided above deprecate these noble undertakings. On the contrary, recognition of the aesthetic aspects of human meaning, thought, and values makes it possible for us to understand why these intelligent, creative activities are able to help us make sense of our world—why they can be both meaningful and valuable to us.

However, taking aesthetics seriously does require us to change some of our received views about these lofty endeavors. The most important change is that we can no longer regard these creative intellectual achievements as issuing from some transcendent source of meaning, concepts, inferences, or values. There is no pure reason, no transcendent ego, no disembodied mind. All the meaning we grasp, all the thinking we do, and all our values have to arise from the ongoing bodily, interpersonal, and cultural activities in which we engage on a daily basis. But we will be better off from this realization of our profoundly embodied and aesthetic nature, because we will recognize these undertakings of meaning and thought for the human situated realities they are, and for what they contribute to our ability to live meaningful, moral, and intelligent lives. We will realize that they represent our human efforts to use the resources of our bodily perception, action, and feeling in order to make sense of things and to give us direction in life.

So, what becomes of philosophy? Well, philosophy becomes the *human* quest for meaning and values in our lives—the means by which we can make sense of, criticize, and enrich our experience from a very broad and pluralistic perspective. Our philosophical understanding comes not from some impossible God's-eye transcendent viewpoint, but through our embodied, imaginative interaction with our world—a world that is at once material, interpersonal, and cultural. Dewey ([1925] 1981) called philosophy "a criticism of criticisms," by which he meant that philosophy provides us the tools for critically assessing our ideas, values, institutions, and practices in the service of helping us make the world better, rather than worse. None of this requires absolutes, or any eternal truths; but it does require us to understand how we make sense of things, how our physical and social worlds work, where our values come from, and how we can have meaningful and fulfilled lives. Empirically responsible, aesthetically grounded philosophy is certainly up to this task of helping us understand and critically evaluate our sense of the meaning of experience. In fact, it is our only scientifically supported alternative to inadequate absolutist and objectivist perspectives.

What becomes of morality? Well, morality becomes an embodied *human* morality, situated within the ongoing development of our species and our world. It does not require the commands and sanctions of a deity (or a diety surrogate like universal reason); nor does it need to issue from some allegedly transcendent source of norms. Instead, our moral values arise from our biological needs, our interpersonal relations, our membership in larger communities, and our desire for meaning (Hinde 2002; Kitcher 2011; M. Johnson 2014). Morality is not a grasping of ultimate moral laws of right conduct, but rather the use of human imagination, feeling, and intelligence to make the world better (Dewey [1922] 1988). It is about solving the moral problems we encounter in our lives the best we can right now, realizing that as future conditions change, new problems will arise, requiring new embodied, aesthetically shaped processes of inquiry and deliberation. It is about developing the art of living well and rightly.

What becomes of aesthetics? Well, aesthetics becomes the cornerstone of our new understanding of what it means to be *human*. It goes straight to the heart of our meaning-making, our ability to inquire intelligently, and our capacity to artfully compose situations. It reveals our status as *homo aestheticus*—lovers and makers of embodied meaning and values. Because aesthetics concerns the ways humans make meaning and enact values, it becomes the basis of an embodied, empirically responsible philosophical perspective. Without the aesthetic elements and processes of meaning-making, there could be no philosophy, no science, no morality, no law, and no art. The aesthetic dimensions of experience are what make possible our ability to make sense of, be at home in, and intelligently reconstruct our world.

What becomes of the arts? Well, the arts are valorized as exemplary enactments of the possibilities for human meaning, intelligence, and value in our world (Dewey [1934] 1987; Gadamer 1975). They show us how things might be, by enacting occasions of fulfillment, harmonization of competing values, and good (and bad) ways of being in the world. The arts help us intelligently manage the contingencies that arise in our lives (Nussbaum 1986), and they often show us what experience can become when the possibilities for meaning are deepened, enriched, expanded, and liberated.

The aesthetics of meaning and understanding is what replaces our quest for certainty and our illusion of absolute foundations of knowledge and value. In its fullest manifestation, it is a uniquely *human* endeavor. It is rooted in our animality, and therefore is partly shared with other animals. However, because this aesthetics of meaning-making develops within human language, arts, and cultural institutions and practices that open up new possibilities for meaning, thought, and value, it typically surpasses most of what other animal species are capable of.

So, to know ourselves and others, we need to delve ever deeper into our aesthetic processes of meaning, understanding, and valuing. To begin this expansion and deepening, there are plenty of appropriate resources to be gleaned from many long-standing philosophical and scientific traditions around the world. In my opinion, it was philosophers like Maurice Merleau-Ponty, William James, and John Dewey who got us started on this path toward an embodied, aesthetically shaped, transformative philosophy, and there are many recent developments in the cognitive sciences, phenomenology, neuroscience, pragmatism, hermeneutics, and several Asian traditions that can make significant contributions to this new approach. But a fully adequate, aesthetically based philosophy does not yet exist. It is up to us to create it, like a massive work of art that is only just beginning to emerge in the history of humankind.

ACKNOWLEDGMENTS

Once again, I find myself deeply indebted to Johanna Rosenbohm for her superb editing and expert guidance in preparing this book, which is now more elegant and eloquent than it would ever have been were I left to my own devices. I want also to express my gratitude for the detailed and careful work done by Sarah McLay in preparing the index.

All but one of the chapters in this book are based on articles and book chapters previously published elsewhere, and are included here by permission of the publishers of each.

The introduction incorporates, with some revisions and the substantial addition of new material, "The Aesthetics of Embodied Life," in *Aesthetics and the Embodied Mind: Beyond Art Theory and the Cartesian Mind-Body Dichotomy*, ed. A. Scarinzi (Dordrecht: Springer, 2015), 23–38.

Chapter 1 is a slightly revised and expanded version of "Pragmatism, Cognitive Science, and Embodied Mind," in *Pragmatism and Embodied Cognitive Science: From Bodily Intersubjectivity to Symbolic Articulation*, ed. Roman Madzia and Matthias Jung (Berlin: De Gruyer, 2016), 101–26.

Chapter 2 is a minor revision of "Philosophy's Debt to Metaphor," in *The Cambridge Handbook of Metaphor and Thought*, ed. Raymond Gibbs (Cambridge: Cambridge University Press, 2008), 39–52.

Chapter 3 is a minor revision of "Experiencing Language: What's Missing in Linguistic Pragmatism?" *European Journal of Pragmatism and American Philosophy* 6, no. 2 (2014): 14–27.

Chapter 4 is a minor revision of "Keeping the Pragmatism in Neuropragmatism," in *Neuroscience, Neurophilosophy, and Pragmatism: Brains at*

Work with the World, ed. Tibor Solymosi and John R. Shook (London: Palgrave Macmillan, 2014), 37–56.

Chapter 5 is a minor revision of "Metaphor-Based Values in Scientific Models," in *Model-Based Reasoning: Science, Technology, Values*, ed. Lorenzo Magnani and Nancy Nersessian (New York: Kluwer Academic/Plenum Publishers, 2002), 1–19.

Chapter 6 is a revision and expansion of "Ethics," in *A Companion to Cognitive Science*, ed. William Bechtel and George Graham (Oxford: Blackwell Publishers, 1998), 691–701.

Chapter 7 is a minor revision of "Moral Imagination," in *The Routledge Handbook of Philosophy of Imagination*, ed. Amy Kind (London: Routledge / Taylor & Francis, 2016), 355–67.

Chapter 8 incorporates, with substantial changes, "Mind, Metaphor, Law," *Mercer Law Review* 56, no. 3 (2007): 845–68.

Chapter 9 is a minor revision of "Identity, Bodily Meaning, and Art," in *Art and Identity: Essays on the Aesthetic Creation of Mind*, ed. Tone Roald and Johannes Lange (Amsterdam: Rodopi, 2013), 15–38.

Chapter 10 is a minor revision of "Dewey's Big Idea for Aesthetics," in *Rethinking Aesthetics: The Role of Body in Design*, ed. Ritu Bhatt (London: Routledge/Taylor & Francis, 2013), 36–50.

Chapter 11 is a minor revision of "The Embodied Meaning of Architecture," in *Mind in Architecture: Neuroscience, Embodiment, and the Future of Design*, ed. Sarah Robinson and Juhani Pallasmaa (Cambridge, MA: MIT Press, 2015), 33–50. Approximately one-third of that essay was based on an earlier article published as "Architecture and the Embodied Mind," *OASE* 58 (2002): 75–96, though with sometimes considerable changes made to the earlier text, and with substantial additions of new material.

NOTES

Chapter 1

1. In the key section nine of the *Critique of Judgment* Kant says, "This subjective universal communicability can be nothing but [that of] the mental state in which we are when imagination and understanding are in free play," and "this merely subjective (aesthetic) judging of the object, or of the presentation by which it is given, precedes the pleasure in the object and is the basis of this pleasure, [a pleasure] in the harmony of the cognitive powers" ([1790] 1987, 217–18).

2. Indeed, Kant insists that judgments of taste have a "universal subjective validity," in contrast to knowledge judgments, which have a "universal objective validity" that is based on shared concepts ([1790] 1987, 62).

3. See, especially, the infamous section 59 of the *Critique of Judgment*, which is entitled "On Beauty as the Symbol of Morality." There is no doubt that Kant is exploring in this enigmatic section some deep connections between our experience of beauty and the conditions necessary for morally practical judgments; however, he cannot overcome—though he strains mightily to do so—the fundamental gap he has assumed between cognitive and aesthetic judgments.

4. This obsession with aesthetic disinterestedness was taken to its logical absurdity in Clive Bell's ultraformalism in *Art* (1914), and also in Edward Bullough's (1912) infamous treatment of "psychical distance" as a model for the aesthetic attitude—the proper distanced stance for perceiving the aesthetic qualities of an object. The "myth of the aesthetic attitude" was demolished by George Dickie (1974), and much earlier by John Dewey ([1934] 1987).

5. Consider, for example, such well-known comments as "All art is quite useless" (preface to *The Picture of Dorian Gray*, 1891] and "All bad art comes from returning to Life and Nature, and elevating them into ideals" ("The Decay of Lying" in *Intentions and the Soul of Man*, 1891).

6. Positive emotions can, of course, sometimes come to be associated with pleasurable states (such as a drug-induced high) that are actually dysfunctional. However, this does

not challenge the hypothesis that positive and negative emotions arose over evolutionary history to help types of higher organisms survive, realize well-being, and avoid harm. That these pleasurable feelings can be activated by ultimately harmful substances and situations is simply a reality of contemporary global events, technologies, and practices.

7. As Lakoff and I (1999) have shown, via the STATES ARE LOCATIONS metaphor, we can understand change of state as a change of location (as in "I *fell into* a depression," "She *pushed* me *over the edge*," "I *went* from joy to anger *in a flash*"). In the poem, then, a change of location (i.e., "floating away" with the cloud and carried by the birdsong) enacts a change in your emotional state.

Chapter 2

1. In *Philosophical Perspectives on Metaphor* (1981), I have surveyed some of the more influential expressions in Western philosophy of the denial of a serious cognitive role for metaphor.

2. The analysis of causal concepts that follows, along with their role in shaping philosophy, is adapted, with minor changes, from Lakoff and Johnson 1999, chap. 11, which is an extensive survey of the several metaphors that define our multiple concepts of events and causes.

Chapter 3

1. Here I speak only of "persons," but I would be prepared to acknowledge that certain animals who are capable of communicative interactions might also experience and make meaning.

Chapter 4

1. George Lakoff and I (Lakoff and Johnson 1999) have surveyed some of the broader cognitive science research that supports an embodied cognition approach to mind, thought, and language. See also Feldman 2006 and Gibbs 2006 for summaries of some of the relevant empirical research.

2. An analysis of the basic metaphors for thinking—including a detailed treatment of the metaphor THINKING AS MOVING—can be found in Lakoff and Johnson 1999, chap. 12.

3. This criticism began as early as "Brains in a Vat" and other key essays in *Reason, Truth, and History* (Putnam 1981), which drew hardly at all from the sciences of the mind and focused at first mostly on thought experiments that traded on allegedly shared intuitions about various mental states and processes.

Chapter 8

1. I suspect that this has been observed before, but what does any notion of original intent tell us about how the law should view in vitro fertilization, genetic cloning, nuclear waste contamination, or any other newly emerging condition that the founders couldn't have possibly even imagined?

2. Selected parts of the following sections on image schemas and conceptual metaphor are taken from chapter 7 of my book *The Meaning of the Body: Aesthetics of Human*

Understanding (Chicago: University of Chicago Press, 2007). Also, several of these image schemas are explained more fully in *Embodied Mind, Meaning, and Reason* (2017), including their role in conceptual metaphor.

3. The following discussion of DESIRE IS HUNGER and of the questions raised by the primary metaphor theory also appears in *Embodied Mind, Meaning, and Reason* (M. Johnson 2017, 115–18).

4. Email from Richard Koenigsberg to the author, September 15, 2002.

5. Ibid.

Chapter 9

1. Kant sums up his account of the nonempirical self: "All the manifold of intuition has, therefore, a necessary relation to the 'I think' in the same subject in which this manifold is found. But this representation is an act of *spontaneity*; that is, it cannot be regarded as belonging to sensibility. I call it *pure apperception*, or, again, *original apperception*, because it is that self-consciousness which, while generating the representation "*I think*" (a representation which must be capable of accompanying all other representations, and which in all consciousness is one and the same), cannot itself be accompanied by any further representation" ([1781] 1968, B132). He later concludes that we can think, but never know, that pure self: "In the transcendental synthesis of the manifold of representations in general, and therefore in the synthetic original unity of apperception, I am conscious of myself, not as I appear to myself, nor as I am in myself, but only that I am. This *representation* is a *thought*, not an *intuition*" (Kant [1781] 1968, B157).

2. Kant was not, of course, a substance dualist, but his metaphysical system is founded on an extensive set of grounding dichotomies such as phenomena/noumena, cognition/feeling, concept/intuition, and so forth. The ultimate result of this is a self (as transcendent ego) that is fundamentally separate from any bodily perceptions or feelings, even though it actively organizes them on some occasions.

3. This objectivist theory of meaning is described in more detail and extensively critiqued in M. Johnson 1987 2007.

4. I owe this reading of Dewey to Thomas Alexander, who first set it out in his book *John Dewey's Theory of Art, Experience & Nature* (1987).

5. I am assuming some form of what has come to be called a "simulation" view of meaning, as set forth, for example, by Lawrence Barsalou in his article "Perceptual Symbol Systems" (1999) and Benjamin Bergen in *Louder Than Words: The New Science of How the Mind Makes Meaning* (2012).

Chapter 10

1. A version of this opening paragraph first appeared in "'The Stone That Was Cast Out Shall Become the Cornerstone': The Bodily Aesthetics of Human Meaning," *Journal of Visual Arts Practice* 6, no. 2 (2007): 89–103.

2. I do not wish to undervalue Kant's many profoundly insightful treatments of reflective judgment, imagination, and creativity. However, Kant's faculty psychology and his taxonomy of kinds of judgment led him to regard aesthetic judgments far too narrowly as noncognitive and as strictly feeling based.

3. A notable exception to this dismissal or overlooking of Dewey's insistence on the qualitative unity of a situation is Thomas Alexander's *John Dewey's Theory of Art, Experience & Nature: The Horizons of Feeling*, and his *Human Eros: Eco-ontology and the Aesthetics of Existence*. I was first introduced to Dewey's aesthetic theory in a seminar I sat in on that was taught by Alexander, so I owe my interest in and understanding of Dewey's account of the qualitative mostly to his sage tutelage. Most recently, Gregory Pappas (2016) has made a compelling argument for Dewey's notion of a pervasive unifying quality as the basis of all experience and thought.

4. As noted above, Thomas Alexander 1987 and 2013 are striking exceptions to this undervaluing of the qualitative. See also Innis 1994.

5. This is an oversimplification, since there are certain limbic functions that are realized in cortical architectures as well.

Chapter 11

1. In fact, the view of meaning as conceptual/propositional/linguistic turns out to be inadequate in explaining even how sentences have meaning for us (Lakoff and Johnson 1999; M. Johnson 2007).

2. I am painfully aware of the shortcomings of this present section. I trust it is clear that I am here only able to make somewhat sweeping gestures toward but a few of the many embodied structures of meaning that are relevant to all experience, and hence to all architecture.

3. I take the useful phrase "from fitness to flourishing" from Owen Flanagan (2007).

REFERENCES

Adler, Jerry. 2006. "Of Cosmic Proportions: Astronomers Decide Pluto Isn't a Real Planet Anymore." *Newsweek*, September 4.
Aksnes, Hallgjerd. 1997. "A Cognitive Approach to Musical Analysis: Metaphorical Projection in Music." In *Proceedings of the Third Triennial European Society for the Cognitive Science of Music Conference*, edited by Alf Gabrielsson. Uppsala, Sweden: Uppsala University, Department of Psychology, 551–56.
Alexander, Thomas. 1987. *John Dewey's Theory of Art, Experience & Nature: The Horizons of Feeling*. Albany: State University of New York Press.
———. 2013. *The Human Eros: Eco-ontology and the Aesthetics of Existence*. New York: Fordham University Press.
Arnheim, Rudolf. 1954. *Art and Visual Perception: A Psychology of the Creative Eye*. Berkeley: University of California Press.
———. 1969. *Visual Thinking*. Berkeley: University of California Press.
Austin, J. L. 1970. "Performative Utterances." In *Philosophical Papers*, edited by J. O. Urmson and G. J. Warnock, 233–52. Oxford: Oxford University Press.
Aziz-Zadeh, Lisa, S. M. Wilson, Giacomo Rizzolatti, and Marco Iacobini. 2006. "Congruent Embodied Representations for Visually Presented Actions and Linguistic Phrases Describing Actions." *Current Biology* 16 (18): 1818–23.
Barsalou, Lawrence. 1999. "Perceptual Symbol Systems." *Behavioral and Brain Sciences* 22:577–660.
———. 2003. "Situated Simulation in the Human Conceptual System." *Language and Cognitive Processes* 18 (5/6): 513–62.
Bechtel, W. 2008. *Mental Mechanisms: Philosophical Perspectives on Cognitive Neuroscience*. New York: Psychology Press.
Bell, Clive. (1914) 1958. *Art*. London: Chatto and Windus.
Bennett, M. R., and P. M. S. Hacker. 2003. *Philosophical Foundations of Neuroscience*. London: Blackwell Publishing.

Bergen, Benjamin. 2012. *Louder Than Words: The New Science of How the Mind Makes Meaning*. New York: Basic Books.

Bjerre, Carl. 1999. "Secured Transactions Inside Out: Negative Pledge Covenants, Property and Perfection." *Cornell Law Review* 84 (2): 305–93.

Brandom, Robert. 2011. *Perspectives on Pragmatism: Classical, Recent, and Contemporary*. Cambridge, MA: Harvard University Press.

Brefczynski, J. A., and E. A. DeYoe. 1999. "A Physiological Correlate of the 'Spotlight' of Visual Attention." *Nature Neuroscience* 2 (4): 370–74.

Brown, T. 2003. *Making Truth: Metaphor in Science*. Champaign, IL: University of Illinois Press.

Bullough, Edward. 1912. "Psychical Distance as a Factor in Art and an Aesthetic Principle." *British Journal of Psychology* 5:87–118.

Cannon, W. B. 1932. *The Wisdom of the Body*. New York: W. W. Norton.

Carpenter, P. A., M. A. Just, T. A. Keller, W. Eddy, and K. Thulborn. 1999. "Graded Functional Activation in the Visuospatial System with the Amount of Task Demand." *Journal of Cognitive Neuroscience* 11 (1): 9–24.

Cave, K. R., and N. P. Bichot. 1999. "Visuospatial Attention: Beyond a Spotlight Model." *Psychonomic Bulletin & Review* 6 (2): 204–23.

Christie, J., and R. M. Klein. 1996. "Assessing the Evidence for Vowel Pop-Out." *Journal of Experimental Psychology: Human Perception and Performance* 125 (2): 201–7.

Churchland, Patricia. 1986. *Neurophilosophy: Toward a Unified Science of the Mind-Brain*. Cambridge, MA: MIT Press.

———. 2012. *Braintrust: What Neuroscience Tells Us about Morality*. Princeton, NJ: Princeton University Press.

Churchland, Paul. 1995. *The Engine of Reason, the Seat of the Soul: A Philosophical Journey into the Brain*. Cambridge, MA: MIT Press.

———. 1996. "The Neural Representation of the Social World." In *Mind and Morals: Essays on Ethics and Cognitive Science*, edited by Larry May, Marilyn Friedman, and Andy Clark, 91–108. Cambridge, MA: MIT Press.

Clark, Andy. 2012. "Embodied, Embedded, and Extended Cognition." In *Cambridge Handbook of Cognitive Science*, edited by William Bechtel and George Graham, 275–91. Cambridge: Cambridge University Press

Clark, Andy, and David Chalmers. 1998. "The Extended Mind." *Analysis* 58 (1): 7–19.

Cohen, Ted. 2008. *Thinking of Others: On the Talent for Metaphor*. Princeton, NJ: Princeton University Press.

Corbetta, J. D., J. M. Kincade, J. M. Ollinger, M. P. McAvoy, and G. L. Shulman. 2000. "Voluntary Attention Is Dissociated from Target Detection in the Human Posterior Parietal Cortex." *Nature Neuroscience* 3 (3): 292–97.

Cox, Arnie. 1999. "The Metaphoric Logic of Musical Motion and Space." PhD diss., Department of Music, University of Oregon.

———. 2016. *Music and Embodied Cognition: Listening, Moving, Feeling, and Thinking*. Bloomington: Indiana University Press.

Damasio, Antonio. 1994. *Descartes' Error: Emotion, Reason, and the Human Brain*. New York: G. P. Putnam's Sons.

———. 1999. *The Feeling of What Happens: Body and Emotion in the Making of Consciousness*. New York: Harcourt Brace.

———. 2003. *Looking for Spinoza: Joy, Sorrow, and the Feeling Brain*. Orlando, FL: Harcourt.

———. 2010. *Self Comes to Mind: Constructing the Conscious Brain*. New York: Pantheon Books.

Dancygier, Barbara, and Eve Sweetser. 2014. *Figurative Language*. Cambridge: Cambridge University Press.

Davidson, Donald. 1978. "What Metaphors Mean." *Critical Inquiry* 5 (1): 31–47.

Decety, Jean, and Julie Grèzes. 2006. "The Power of Simulation: Imagining One's Own and Other's Behavior." *Brain Research* 1079 (1): 4–14.

Dennett, Daniel C., and M. Kinsbourne. 1992. "Time and the Observer: The Where and When of Consciousness in the Brain." *Behavioral and Brain Sciences* 15 (2): 183–247.

Desimone, R., and J. Duncan. 1995. "Neural Mechanisms of Selective Visual Attention." *Annual Review of Neuroscience* 18:193–222.

de Waal, Frans. "Putting the Altruism Back in Altruism: The Evolution of Empathy." *Annual Review of Psychology* 59: 279–300.

Dewey, John. (1922) 1988. *Human Nature and Conduct*. Vol. 14 of *John Dewey: The Middle Works, 1899–1924*. Edited by JoAnn Boydston. Carbondale: Southern Illinois University Press.

———. (1925) 1981. *Experience and Nature*. Vol. 1 of *The Later Works, 1925–1953*. Edited by Jo Ann Boydston. Carbondale: Southern Illinois University Press.

———. (1930) 1988. "Qualitative Thought." In *The Later Works, 1925–1953*, edited by Jo Ann Boydston, 5:243–62. Carbondale, IL: Southern Illinois University Press, 1988.

———. (1932) 1989. *Ethics*. With James Hayden Tufts. Vol. 7 of *The Later Works, 1925–1953*. Edited by Jo Ann Boydston. Carbondale: Southern Illinois University Press.

———. (1934) 1987. *Art as Experience*. Vol. 10 of *The Later Works, 1925–1953*. Edited by Jo Ann Boydston. Carbondale: Southern Illinois University Press.

———. (1938) 1991. *Logic: The Theory of Inquiry*. Vol. 12 of *The Later Works, 1925–1953*. Edited by Jo Ann Boydston. Carbondale, IL: Southern Illinois University Press.

———. (1939) 1981. *Theory of Valuation*. Vol. 13 of *The Later Works, 1925–1953*, edited by Jo Ann Boydston. Carbondale, IL: Southern Illinois University Press, 1991.

Dickie, George. 1974. *Art and the Aesthetic: An Institutional Analysis*. Ithaca, NY: Cornell University Press.

Dodge, E., and G. Lakoff. 2005. "Image Schemas: From Linguistic Analysis to Neural Grounding." In *From Perception to Meaning: Image Schemas in Cognitive Linguistics*, edited by Beate Hampe, 57–91. Berlin: Mouton de Gruyter.

Donagan, Alan. 1977. *The Theory of Morality*. Chicago: University of Chicago Press.

Downing, C. J., and Steven Pinker. 1985. "The Spatial Structure of Visual Attention." In *Attention and Performance*, edited by M. I. Posner and O. S. M. Marin, 171–88. Hillsdale, NJ: Lawrence Erlbaum Associates.

Eagleman, David. 2011. *Incognito: The Secret Lives of the Brain*. New York: Pantheon.

Edelman, Gerald. 1992. *Bright Air, Brilliant Fire: On the Matter of Mind*. New York: Basic Books.

Edelman, Gerald, and Giulio Tononi. 2000. *A Universe of Consciousness: How Matter Becomes Imagination*. New York: Basic Books.

Eldridge, Richard. 1989. *On Moral Personhood: Philosophy, Literature, Criticism, and Self-Understanding*. Chicago: University of Chicago Press.

Fauconnier, Gilles, and Mark Turner. 2002. *The Way We Think: Conceptual Blending and the Mind's Hidden Complexities*. New York: Basic Books.

Feldman, Jerome. 2006. *From Molecule to Metaphor: A Neural Theory of Language*. Cambridge, MA: MIT Press.

Fernandez-Duque, Diego, and Mark Johnson. 1999. "Attention Metaphors: How Metaphors Guide the Cognitive Psychology of Attention." *Cognitive Science* 23 (1): 83–116.

———. 2002. "Cause and Effect Theories of Attention: The Role of Conceptual Metaphor." *Review of General Psychology* 6 (2): 153–65.

Fesmire, Steven. 2003. *John Dewey and Moral Imagination: Pragmatism in Ethics*. Bloomington: Indiana University Press.

———. 2015. *Dewey*. New York: Routledge.

Fillmore, Charles. 1985. "Frames and the Semantics of Understanding." *Quaderni di Semantica* 6:222–53.

Flanagan, Owen. 1991. *Varieties of Moral Personality: Ethics and Psychological Realism*. Cambridge, MA: Harvard.

———. 2002. *The Problem of the Soul: Two Visions of Mind and How to Reconcile Them*. New York: Basic Books.

———. 2007. *The Really Hard Problem: Meaning in a Material World*. Cambridge, MA: MIT Press.

Flanagan, Owen, and Robert Williams. 2010. "What Does the Modularity of Morals Have to Do with Ethics? Four Moral Sprouts Plus or Minus a Few." *Topics in Cognitive Science* 2:430–53.

Fodor, Jerry. 1975. *The Language of Thought*. New York: Thomas Y. Crowell.

———. 1987. *Psychosemantics: The Problem of Meaning in the Philosophy of Mind*. Cambridge, MA: MIT Press.

Gadamer, Hans-Georg. 1975. *Truth and Method*. Translated by G. Barden and J. Cumming. New York: Crossroad.

Gallese, Vittorio, and Alvin Goldman. 1998. "Mirror Neurons and the Simulation Theory of Mind-Reading." *Trends in Cognitive Science* 2 (12) 493–501.

Gallese, Vittorio, and George Lakoff. 2005. "The Brain's Concepts: The Role of the Sensory-Motor System in Conceptual Knowledge." *Cognitive Neuropsychology* 22: 455–79.

Gallie, W. B. 1956. "Essentially Contested Concepts." *Proceedings of the Aristotelian Society* 56:167–98.

Gardner, John. 1978. "Moral Fiction," in *On Moral Fiction*, 105–26. New York: Basic Books.

Gendlin, Eugene. 1991. "Crossing and Dipping: Some Terms for Approaching the Interface between Natural Understanding and Logical Formulation." *Minds and Machines* 5 (4): 547–60. http://www.focusing.org/gendlin/docs/gol_2166.html.

———. 1997. "How Philosophy Cannot Appeal to Experience, and How It Can." In *Language beyond Postmodernism: Saying and Thinking in Gendlin's Philosophy*, edited by David Michael Levin, 3–41. Evanston, IL: Northwestern University Press.

Gibbs, Raymond. 1994. *The Poetics of Mind: Figurative Thought, Language, and Understanding*. Cambridge: Cambridge University Press.

———. 2003. "Embodied Experience and Linguistic Meaning." *Brain and Language* 84 (1): 1–15.

———. 2006. *Embodiment and Cognitive Science*. Cambridge: Cambridge University Press.

———. 2008. *The Cambridge Handbook of Metaphor and Thought*. Cambridge: Cambridge University Press.

Gibson, James J. 1979. *The Ecological Approach to Visual Perception*. Boston: Houghton Mifflin.

Gilligan, Carol. 1982. *In a Different Voice: Psychological Theory and Women's Development*. Cambridge, MA: Harvard University Press.

Goldman, Alvin. 1993. "Ethics and Cognitive Science." *Ethics* 103:337–60.

Goodman, Nelson. 1978. *Ways of Worldmaking*. Indianapolis: Hackett.

Grady, Joseph. 1997. "Foundations of Meaning: Primary Metaphors and Primary Scenes." PhD diss., Department of Linguistics, University of California, Berkeley.

Gregory, Marshall. 2009. *Shaped by Stories: The Ethical Power of Narratives*. Notre Dame, IN: University of Notre Dame Press.

Haidt, Jonathan. 2012. *The Righteous Mind: Why Good People Are Divided by Politics and Religion*. New York: Pantheon Books.

Hampe, Beate, ed., with Joseph Grady. 2005. *From Perception to Meaning: Image Schemas in Cognitive Linguistics*. Berlin: Mouton de Gruyter.

Hare, Richard M. 1963. *Freedom and Reason*. Oxford: Oxford University Press.

Hasher, L., and R. T. Zacks. 1979. "Automatic and Effortful Processes in Memory." *Journal of Experimental Psychology: General* 108 (3): 356–88.

Hauser, Marc. 2006. *Moral Minds: How Nature Designed Our Universal Sense of Right and Wrong*. New York: Harper Collins.

Heidegger, Martin. 1971. *The Origin of the Work of Art*. In *Poetry, Language, Thought*. Translated by Albert Hofstadter. New York: Harper & Row.

Hinde, Robert. 2002. *Why Good Is Good: The Sources of Morality*. Routledge.

Hoffman, Martin. 1993. "The Contribution of Empathy to Justice and Moral Judgment." *Readings in Philosophy and Cognitive Science*, edited by A. Goldman, 647–80. Cambridge, MA: MIT Press.

———. 2000. *Empathy and Moral Development: Implications for Caring and Justice*. Cambridge: Cambridge University Press.

Hopfinger, Joseph., M. H. Buonocore, and G. R. Mangun. 2000. "The Neural Mechanisms of Top-Down Attentional Control." *Nature Neuroscience* 3 (3): 284–91.

Hume, David. (1739–40) 2000. *A Treatise of Human Nature*. Oxford: Clarendon Press.

———. (1751) 1998. *An Enquiry Concerning the Principles of Morals*. Edited by Tom Beauchamp. Vol. 4 of the Clarendon Edition of the Works of David Hume. Oxford: Oxford University Press.

Innis, Robert. 1994. *Consciousness and the Play of Signs*. Bloomington: University of Indiana Press.

James, William. (1890) 1950. *The Principles of Psychology*. 2 vols. New York: Dover.

———. 1900. *Psychology*. American Science Series, Briefer Course. New York: Henry Holt.

———. (1911) 1979. "Percept and Concept." In *Some Problems of Philosophy*, 21–60. Cambridge, MA: Harvard University Press.

Johnson, Christopher. 1997. "Metaphor vs. Conflation in the Acquisition of Polysemy: The Case of SEE." In *Cultural, Typological and Psychological Issues in Cognitive Linguistics*, edited by M. K. Hiraga, C. Sinha, and S. Wilcox. Current Issues in Linguistic Theory, 152:155–70. Amsterdam: John Benjamins.

Johnson, Mark. 1979. "Kant's Unified Theory of Beauty." *Journal of Aesthetics and Art Criticism* 37 (2): 167–78.

———. 1981. "Metaphor in the Philosophical Tradition." In *Philosophical Perspectives on Metaphor*, edited by M. Johnson, 3–47. Minneapolis: University of Minnesota Press.

———. 1987. *The Body in the Mind: The Bodily Basis of Meaning, Imagination, and Reason*. Chicago: University of Chicago Press.

———. 1993. *Moral Imagination: Implications of Cognitive Science for Ethics*. Chicago: University of Chicago Press.

———. 2002. "Architecture and the Embodied Mind." *OASE* 58:75–96.

———. 2007. *The Meaning of the Body: Aesthetics of Human Understanding*. Chicago: University of Chicago Press.

———. 2014. *Morality for Humans: Ethical Understanding from the Perspective of Cognitive Science*. Chicago: University of Chicago Press.

———. 2017. *Embodied Mind, Meaning, and Reason: How Our Bodies Give Rise to Understanding*. Chicago: University of Chicago Press.

Johnson, Mark, and George Lakoff. 2002. "Why Cognitive Linguistics Requires Embodied Realism." *Cognitive Linguistics* 13 (3): 245–63.

Johnson, Mark, and Steve Larson. 2003. "Something in the Way She Moves: Metaphors of Musical Motion." *Metaphor and Symbol* 18 (2): 63–84.

Johnston, W. A., and V. I. Dark. 1986. "Selective Attention." *Annual Review of Psychology* 37:43–75.

Kahneman, Daniel. 1973. *Attention and Effort*. Englewood Cliffs, NJ: Prentice-Hall.

———. 2011. *Thinking, Fast and Slow*. New York: Farrar, Straus and Giroux.

Kant, Immanuel. (1775–80) 1963. *Lectures on Ethics*. Translated by Louis Infield. Indianapolis, IN: Hackett.

———. (1781) 1968. *Critique of Pure Reason*. Translated by Norman Kemp Smith. Reprint, New York: St. Martin's Press. Original edition, *Critik der reinen Vernunft*. Riga: Hartknoch, 1781.

———. (1785) 1993. *Grounding for the Metaphysics of Morals*. Translated by James Ellington. 3rd ed. Indianapolis, IN: Hackett.

———. (1790) 1987. *Critique of Judgment*. Translated by Werner Pluhar. Indianapolis, IN: Hackett.

Kekes, John. 2006. *The Enlargement of Life: Moral Imagination at Work*. Ithaca, NY: Cornell University Press.

Kinsbourne, Marcel. 1977. "Hemi-Neglect and Hemisphere Rivalry." *Advances in Neurology* 18:41–49.

Kitcher, Philip. 2011. *The Ethical Project*. Cambridge, MA: Harvard University Press.

Kohlberg, L. 1981. *The Philosophy of Moral Development: Moral Stages and the Idea of Justice*. Vol. 1 of *Essays on Moral Development*. San Francisco: Harper and Row.

Kövecses, Zoltán. 1988. *The Language of Love: The Semantics of Passion in Conversational English*. Lewisburg, PA: Bucknell University Press.

———. 2000. *Metaphor and Emotion: Language, Culture, and Body in Human Feeling*. Cambridge: Cambridge University Press.

———. 2010. *Metaphor*. Oxford: Oxford University Press.

Kuhn, Thomas S. 1962. *The Structure of Scientific Revolutions*. Chicago: Chicago University Press.

LaBerge, D. 1995. *Attentional Processing: The Brain's Art of Mindfulness*. Cambridge, MA: Harvard University Press.

Làdavas, E., A. Petronio, and C. Umilta. 1990. "The Deployment of Visual Attention in the Intact Field of Hemineglect Patients." *Cortex* 26:307–17.

Lakoff, George. 1987. *Women, Fire, and Dangerous Things: What Categories Reveal about the Mind*. Chicago: University of Chicago Press.

———. 1996. *Moral Politics: What Conservatives Know That Liberals Don't*. Chicago: University of Chicago Press.

———. 2001. "Metaphors of Terror," unpublished essay, September 16, 2001.

———. 2006. *Whose Freedom? The Battle over America's Most Important Idea*. New York: Farrar, Straus and Giroux.

———. 2008. "The Neural Theory of Metaphor." In *The Cambridge Handbook of Metaphor and Thought*, edited by Raymond Gibbs, 17–38. Cambridge: Cambridge University Press.

Lakoff, George, and Mark Johnson. 1980. *Metaphors We Live By*. Chicago: University of Chicago Press.

———. 1999. *Philosophy in the Flesh: The Embodied Mind and Its Challenge to Western Thought*. New York: Basic Books.

Lakoff, George, and Srini Narayanan. Forthcoming. "The Neural Mind: What You Need to Know about Thought and Language." Unpublished manuscript, last modified 2017. PDF.

Lakoff, George, and Rafael Núñez. 2000. *Where Mathematics Comes From: How the Embodied Mind Brings Mathematics into Being*. New York: Basic Books.

Langer, Susanne. 1953. *Feeling and Form*. New York: Charles Scribner's Sons.

———. 1957. *Problems of Art*. New York: Charles Scribner's Sons.

Larson, Steve. 2012. *Musical Forces: Motion, Metaphor, and Meaning in Music*. Bloomington: Indiana University Press.

Lavie, N. 1995. "Perceptual Load as a Necessary Condition for Selective Attention." *Journal of Experimental Psychology: Human Perception and Performance* 21 (3): 451–68.

Levin, David, ed. 1997. *Language Beyond Postmodernism: Saying and Thinking in Gendlin's Philosophy*. Evanston, IL: Northwestern University Press.

Lindner, Susan. 1981. "A Lexico-semantic Analysis of Verb-Particle Constructions with *Up* and *Out*." PhD diss., University of California, San Diego.

Logothetis, N. K., D. A. Leopold, and D. L. Sheinberg. 1996. "What Is Rivalling during Binocular Rivalry?" *Nature* 380:621–24.

Longino, H. 1996. "Cognitive and Non-cognitive Values in Science: Rethinking the Dichotomy." In *Feminism, Science, and the Philosophy of Science*, edited by L. H. Nelson and J. Nelson, 39–58. Dordrecht, The Netherlands: Kluwer Academic Publishers.

MacIntyre, A. (1981) 1984. *After Virtue*. 2nd ed. Notre Dame, IN: Notre Dame University Press.

Magnani, Lorenzo, and Nancy Nersessian, eds. 2002. *Model-Based Reasoning: Science, Technology, Values*. New York: Kluwer Academic/Plenum.

Malachowski, Alan. 2010. *The New Pragmatism*. Durham, Great Britain: Acumen Publishing Limited.

Martinez, A, L. Anllo-Vento, M. I. Sereno, L. R. Frank, R. B. Buxton, D. J. Dubowitz, E. C. Wong, H. Hinrichs, H. J. Heinze, and S. A. Hillyard. 1999. "Involvement of Striate and Extrastriate Visual Cortical Areas in Spatial Attention." *Nature Neuroscience* 2 (4): 364–69.

McCauley, Robert. 2007. "Reduction: Models of Cross-Scientific Relations and their Significance for the Psychology-Neuroscience Interface." In *Handbook of the Philosophy of Science: Philosophy of Psychology and Cognitive Science*, edited by Paul Thagard, 105–58. Amsterdam: Elsevier.

McConachie, Bruce. 2003. *American Theater in the Culture of the Cold War: Producing and Contesting Containment, 1947–1962*. Iowa City: University of Iowa Press.

———. 2015. *Evolution, Cognition, and Performance*. Cambridge: Cambridge University Press.

McNeill, David. 1992. *Hand and Mind: What Gestures Reveal about Thought*. Chicago: University of Chicago Press.

Merleau-Ponty, Maurice. 1962. *Phenomenology of Perception*. Translated by Colin Smith. London: Routledge.

Misak, Cheryl, ed. 2007. *New Pragmatists*. Oxford: Oxford University Press.

Müller, M. M., W. Teder-Sälejärvi, and S. A. Hillyard. 1998. "The Time Course of Cortical Facilitation during Cued Shifts of Spatial Attention." *Nature Neuroscience* 1 (7): 631–34.

Narayanan, Srini. 1997. "KARMA: Knowledge-based Action Representations for Metaphor and Aspect." PhD diss., Department of Computer Science, University of California, Berkeley.

Navon, D. 1984. "Attention Division or Attention Sharing." In *Attention and Performance*, edited by M. I. Posner and O. Marin, 133–46 Hillsdale, NJ: Lawrence Erlbaum Associates.

Navon, D., and D. Gopher. 1979. "On the Economy of the Human-Processing System." *Psychological Review* 86 (3): 214–55.

Noddings, Nel. 1984. *Caring: A Feminist Approach to Ethics and Moral Education*. Berkeley: University of California Press.

Noë, Alva. 2009. *Out of Our Heads: Why You Are Not Your Brain, and Other Lessons from the Biology of Consciousness*. New York: Hill and Wang.

Norman, Donald A., and D. G. Bobrow. 1975. "On Data-Limited and Resource-Limited Processes." *Cognitive Psychology* 7:44–64.

Nozick, Robert. 1974. *Anarchy, State, and Utopia*. New York: Basic Books.

Nussbaum, Martha. 1986. *The Fragility of Goodness: Luck and Ethics in Greek Tragedy and Philosophy*. Cambridge: Cambridge University Press.

———. 1990. *Love's Knowledge: Essays on Philosophy and Literature*. 1990. Oxford: Oxford University Press.

Ojala, Juha. 2009. *Space in Musical Semiosis: An Abductive Theory of the Musical Composition Process*. Helsinki: Hakapaino.

Pallasmaa, Juhani. 2002. "Lived Space, Embodied Experience and Sensory Thought." *OASE* 58:13–34.

Pappas, Gregory. 2016. "John Dewey's Radical Logic: The Function of the Qualitative in Thinking." *Transactions of the Charles S. Peirce Society* 52 (3): 435–68.

Pashler, H. 1998. *The Psychology of Attention*. Cambridge, MA: MIT Press.

Pérez-Gómez, A. 2002. "Phenomenology and Virtual Space: Alternative Tactics for Architectural Practice." *OASE* 58:35–58.

Piaget, J. 1932. *The Moral Judgment of the Child*. London: Kegan Paul, Trench, Trubner.

Posner, Michael, and P. Tudela. 1997. "Imaging Resources." *Biological Psychology* 45:95–107.

Prinz, Jesse. 2007. "Is Morality Innate?" In *The Evolution of Morality: Adaptations and Innateness*, edited by W. Sinnott-Armstrong, vol. 1 of *Moral Psychology*, 367–406. Cambridge, MA: MIT Press.

Putnam, Hilary. 1981. *Reason, Truth, and History*. Cambridge: Cambridge University Press.

———. 1987. "Equality and Our Moral Image of the World." In *The Many Faces of Realism*, 40–62. LaSalle, IL: Open Court.

Quine, W. V. O. 1960. *Word and Object*. Cambridge, MA: MIT Press.

Rawls, John. 1971. *A Theory of Justice*. Cambridge, MA: Harvard University Press.

Rees, G., R. Frackowiak, and C. Frith. 1997. "Two Modulatory Effects of Attention That Mediate Object Categorization in Human Cortex." *Science* 275:835–38.

Richards, Ivor A., and C. K. Ogden. 1923. *The Meaning of Meaning*. New York: Harcourt Brace.

Ricoeur, Paul. 1984. *Time and Narrative*, vol. 1. Translated by Kathleen McLaughlin and David Pellauer. Chicago: University of Chicago Press.

Ridley, A., and A. Neill. 1995. *The Philosophy of Art: Readings Ancient and Modern*. New York: McGraw-Hill.

Rizzolatti, G., and L. Craighero. 2004. "The Mirror-Neuron System." *Annual Review of Neuroscience* 27:169–92.

Robinson, S., and J. Pallasmaa. 2015. *Mind in Architecture: Neuroscience, Embodiment, and the Future of Design*. Cambridge, MA: MIT Press.

Rorty, Richard. 1979. *Philosophy and the Mirror of Nature*. Princeton, NJ: Princeton University Press.

———. 1982. *Consequences of Pragmatism*. Minneapolis: University of Minnesota Press.

———. 1989. *Contingency, Irony, and Solidarity*. Cambridge: Cambridge University Press.

Rosch, Eleanor. 1975. "Cognitive Reference Points." *Cognitive Psychology* 7:532–47.

Sandel, M. (1982) 1998. *Liberalism and the Limits of Justice*. 2nd ed. Cambridge: Cambridge University Press.

Sanders, J. 2016. *Theology in the Flesh: How Embodiment and Culture Shape the Way We Think about Truth, Morality, and God*. Minneapolis: Fortress Press.

Saslaw, Janna. 1996. "Forces, Containers, and Paths: The Role of Body-Derived Image Schemas in the Conceptualization of Music." *Journal of Music Theory* 40 (2): 217–42.

Schneider, W., and R. M. Shiffrin. 1977. "Controlled and Automatic Human Information Processing: 1; Detection, Search, and Attention." *Psychological Review* 84:1–66.

Schulkin, Jay. 2011. *Adaptation and Well-Being: Social Allostasis*. Cambridge: Cambridge University Press.

———. 2012. *Naturalism and Pragmatism*. New York: Palgrave Macmillan.
Searle, John. 1969. *Speech Acts*. Cambridge: Cambridge University Press.
———. 1979. "Metaphor." In *Expression and Meaning: Studies in the Theory of Speech Acts*, 76–116. Cambridge: Cambridge University Press.
Sheets-Johnstone, Maxine. 1999. *The Primacy of Movement*. Amsterdam: John Benjamins.
Shiffrin, R. M. 1988. "Orienting of Attention." In *Steven's Handbook of Experimental Psychology: Learning and Cognition*, edited by R. C. Atkinson, R. J. Herrnstein, G. Lindzey, and R. D. Luce, 739–811. New York: John Wiley & Sons.
Shusterman, Richard. 2000. *Pragmatist Aesthetics: Living Beauty, Rethinking Art*. Lantham, MD: Rowman & Littlefield.
———. 2008. *Body Consciousness: A Philosophy of Mindfulness and Somaesthetics*. New York: Cambridge University Press.
Shweder, Richard. 1991. *Thinking through Cultures: Expeditions in Cultural Psychology*. Cambridge, MA: Harvard University Press.
Smith, Adam. 1790. *The Theory of Moral Sentiments*.
Solymosi, Tibor. 2011. "Neuropragmatism, Old and New." *Phenomenology and the Cognitive Sciences* 10 (3): 347–68.
Solymosi, Tibor, and John R. Shook, eds. 2014. *Neuroscience, Neurophilosophy, and Pragmatism: Brains at Work with the World*. London: Palgrave Macmillan.
Spitzer, Michael. 2004. *Metaphor and Musical Thought*. Chicago: University of Chicago Press.
Stafford, William. 1998. *The Way It Is: New & Selected Poems by William Stafford*. St. Paul, MN: Graywolf Press, 1998.
Stern, Daniel. 1985. *The Interpersonal World of the Infant: A View from Psychoanalysis and Developmental Psychology*. New York: Basic Books.
Talisse, Robert, and Scott Aiken, eds. 2011. *The Pragmatism Reader: From Peirce through the Present*. Princeton, NJ: Princeton University Press.
Talmy, Leonard. 2000. *Toward a Cognitive Semantics*. 2 vols. Cambridge, MA: MIT Press.
Taub, Sarah. 2001. *Language from the Body: Iconicity and Metaphor in American Sign Language*. Cambridge: Cambridge University Press.
Tikka, Pia. 2008. *Enactive Cinema: Simulatorium Eisensteinense*. Jyvaskyla, Finland: University of Art and Design Helsinki.
Tolstoy, Leo. (1896) 1960. *What Is Art?* Translated by Almyer Maude. New York: MacMillan.
Tucker, Don. 2007. *Mind from Body: Experience from Neural Structure*. Oxford: Oxford University Press.
———. 2017. "Right Wing, Left Wing: The Dialectical Development of Identity." Unpublished manuscript, May.
Tversky, Amos, and Daniel Kahneman. 1974. "Judgment under Uncertainty: Heuristics and Biases." *Science* 185:1124–31.
Umiltà, C. 1988. "Orienting of Attention." In *Handbook of Neuropsychology*, edited by F. Boller and J. Grafman, 175–192. Amsterdam: Elsevier.
Varela, Francisco, Evan Thompson, and Eleanor Rosch. 1991. *The Embodied Mind: Cognitive Science and Human Experience*. Cambridge, MA: MIT Press.
Vesely, Dalibor. 2002. "Space, Simulation and Disembodiment in Contemporary Architecture." *OASE* 58:59–74.

Wachtel, P. L. 1967. "Conceptions of Broad and Narrow Attention." *Psychological Bulletin* 68 (6): 417–29.

Werhane, Patricia. 1999. *Moral Imagination and Management Decision-Making*. Oxford: Oxford University Press.

Wickens, R. C. 1984. "Processing Resources in Attention." In *Varieties of Attention*, edited by R. Parasuraman and D. R. Davies, 120–42 Orlando, FL: Academic Press.

Williams, O. 1997. *The Moral Imagination: How Literature and Films Can Stimulate Ethical Reflection in the Business World*. Notre Dame, IN: University of Notre Dame Press.

Winter, Steven L. 2001. *A Clearing in the Forest: Law, Life, and Mind*. Chicago: University of Chicago Press.

Wolfe, J. M. 1996. "Resolving Perceptual Ambiguity." *Nature* 380:587–88.

Woodman, G. F., and S. J. Luck. 1999. "Electrophysiological Measurement of Rapid Shifts of Attention during Visual Search." *Nature* 400:867–69.

Wright, Hollis G. 2007. *Means, Ends, and Medical Care*. Dordrecht: Springer.

Zbikowski, Lawrence. 2002. *Conceptualizing Music: Cognitive Structure, Theory, and Analysis*. Oxford: Oxford University Press.

INDEX

abstraction, 5, 10, 14, 16, 26, 40, 43, 102, 112, 127–28, 130, 151, 172, 239, 244, 247–48; of human mind, 93, 103; psychologist's fallacy, 110–11
action, 14–15, 25–26, 28–30, 36, 40, 48, 50, 54–55, 58, 60–65, 67, 80–81, 83–84, 87–89, 98, 100, 102, 108, 110, 131–33, 150, 160, 162, 170, 172, 173, 177, 197, 201, 205, 208, 229, 240, 243–44, 246, 256, 260; mental, 32, 44, 47, 54–55, 93, 234; moral, 60, 139, 142, 147–49, 151, 158, 160–62, 164–66, 170–71, 173, 175, 179, 183, 197; social, 45, 47, 53, 173, 175, 246
Adler, Jerry, 181
aesthetics, 1–15, 18, 22, 24–26, 28, 51, 59, 110, 127, 170, 199–201, 203–6, 208–10, 224–26, 228, 230, 234, 236–41, 256, 259–61, 265n1, 265n3, 265n4, 267n2 (chap. 10), 268n3 (chap. 10); "the aesthetic," 240; aesthetic dimensions of experience/meaning, 2–3, 5–6, 14, 18, 22, 26, 29, 51, 53, 200, 206–7, 225, 237, 241–42, 256, 259, 261; aesthetic theory, 1, 6, 9–12, 51, 205, 228, 238, 240; defined, 7–8, 25, 200, 210, 217, 260; of embodied meaning, 2, 3, 13, 24–25, 51, 201; Enlightenment, 3, 5–6, 8–10;

experience, 1–4, 6–7, 9, 12, 205, 225, 240; *homo aestheticus*, 2
affect, 2, 14, 24, 33, 35, 39, 42, 50, 52, 56, 70, 89, 93, 103, 121, 123, 129, 131, 148–51, 160, 162, 171–73, 184, 187–88, 193, 203–5, 210, 215–16, 218, 236, 244–47, 252, 257
affective contours. *See* feeling contours
affective dimension, 2, 20, 38, 44, 51, 102, 207
affordance, 15, 17–18, 37, 50–51, 54–55, 151–52, 222–23, 245, 247–51, 253, 255
agency, 68, 153, 205–6
Aiken, Scott, 82
Aksnes, Hallgjerd, 220
Alexander, Thomas, 170, 175, 177, 267n4 (chap. 9), 268n3 (chap. 10), 268n4
allostasis, 21, 99, 252. *See also* equilibrium; homeostasis
analytic philosophy, 12–13, 21, 27, 49, 50, 52, 58, 60, 69, 72, 80, 111, 200; Anglo American, 142, 200, 243, 259; of language, 20, 53, 69, 72, 74, 177, 243; of mind, 20, 32, 53, 74, 177; moral theory, 142; pragmatism, 29, 49, 52–53, 57, 80–82, 94; twentieth century, 12, 20, 50, 58, 142

antidualism, 33, 37, 40–41, 81, 103–4, 108, 207
antifoundationalism, 81–82
a priori, 104, 130, 141, 156, 162
architecture, 2, 48, 51, 85, 88, 90, 94, 201, 219–20, 242–44, 247–52, 254–58; computational architectural models, 249; embodied, 201, 242, 249, 256; as involving image schemas, 19, 250–51, 254
Aristotle, 13, 72–73, 167
Arnheim, Rudolf, 19, 217–18, 220
art: artworking, 222; as experience, 14–15, 25; living form, 219
artificial intelligence, 32, 97, 111, 145, 177
assertion, 52, 80, 82, 84–85, 92
atomism, 101, 110, 151
attachment theory, 153
attention, 67, 115–30, 132, 150, 231; attentional fields, 128; cause theories of, 123, 129; cognitive psychology of, 115, 126; directional theory of, 125; effect theories of, 123, 129; neuropsychology of, 125
Austin, J. L., 13, 92, 96, 236
Ayer, A. J., 148
Aziz-Zadeh, Lisa, 173

Barsalou, Lawrence, 14, 33, 172, 244, 246, 267n5 (chap. 9)
beauty, 1, 5, 7–11, 13, 205–6, 265n3
Bechtel, William, 35, 107, 108, 112
Being, 58, 73–74, 78, 252
Bell, Clive, 10–11, 239, 265n4
Bennett, M. R., 99–100
Bergen, Benjamin, 14, 44, 93, 112, 172, 246, 267n5 (chap. 9)
Bichot, N. P., 117
biology, 27, 32, 97, 99, 193, 215, 236; biochemistry, 34; biological imperative, 56; molecular, 35
Bjerre, Carl, 67, 176, 194–95
Bobrow, D. G., 119, 122
bodily perception, 4, 28–29, 47, 50, 102, 104, 172, 245, 260, 267n2 (chap. 9); bodily experience, 29, 36, 42, 48, 177, 187, 189, 191–92, 216, 246, 249–50, 252; bodily makeup, 5, 18, 33, 45–46, 55, 108, 110, 184, 246, 250; bodily source domains, 69, 133; body-based meaning, 2, 13, 22, 25, 28, 31, 36, 45–46, 48, 55, 87, 130, 178, 184–85, 187, 201, 203, 206, 216–17, 221, 249–50, 255, 259; cross-domain correlations/associations, 33, 189, 192, 193. *See also* embodiment
body, 2–7, 9, 12–15, 17–23, 27–30, 33, 35–37, 40–41, 43–48, 50, 53, 55–56, 58, 69–70, 83, 92–93, 98–100, 102–6, 111, 130–33, 135–36, 142, 149–50, 155–56, 160–62, 169, 172–73, 175, 177–78, 183–88, 190–95, 205, 207–9, 215–20, 222, 228, 234, 242–43, 245, 250–55
boundary, 47, 99, 144–45, 185, 250, 255; as fixed, 178; as permeable, 20, 55, 98, 99, 250
brain, human, 25, 28, 33, 36–38, 40–42, 44–45, 55, 70, 72, 93, 99–100, 103, 106, 111, 117–18, 124–25, 129–30, 149, 167, 177, 184–88, 190, 192, 215, 217–18, 234, 243, 245–46, 266n3; binocular rivalry, 125; brain-in-a-body-in-a-world, 40; core-shell brain architecture, 215, 234–36; cross-domain neural connections, 33, 189–90, 192–93; and mind, 20, 38, 40, 43, 45, 55, 97, 100, 103, 108, 117
Brandom, Robert, 52, 82–85, 95
Brefczynski, J. A., 117–18
Brown, Mike, 181
Brown, T., 115
Buonocore, M. H., 118

Cannon, Walter B., 99
Carpenter, P. A., 119, 121
Cartesianism, 68, 74, 78, 124; mind/body dualism, 12, 39, 41, 45, 104
Casebeer, William, 113
categories, 44, 66, 73, 91, 109, 127, 144–46, 161, 172, 174, 179–80, 183, 194–96, 212; classical theory of, 178–79, 182, 195; objectivist theory of, 43, 178–79; radial, 28, 66, 144–45, 179–80, 183, 195–96
causation, 8, 9, 21, 34–35, 58, 60, 62–63, 64–66, 67, 74–75, 77, 85, 100, 103, 107, 120, 123, 129, 206–7, 123, 129, 142, 199–200, 239, 247; laws of, 8, 107, 126, 200,

247; metaphorically defined, 59–67, 72, 78, 193, 266n2 (chap. 2); natural/physical causes, 34, 60–61, 74
Cave, K. R., 117
Chalmers, David, 99
Churchland, Patricia, 97, 113, 114, 143
Churchland, Paul, 113, 143–44
Clark, Andy, 54, 99
cognition, 4, 7, 12, 19–20, 22, 31, 34, 38, 40, 49, 78, 94, 97, 99–100, 103, 121, 136, 140–41, 151, 157, 160, 163, 169, 178, 212, 224, 225, 234–35, 237, 244, 246, 266n1 (chap. 4), 267n2 (chap. 9); embodied, 2–3, 28, 53, 103, 112; neurocomputational theories of, 33, 78
cognitive linguistics, 33, 58, 60–61, 72–73, 246
cognitive science, 28–31, 33, 39–40, 44, 50, 75, 97–98, 107, 136, 139–44, 147, 152, 157–58, 167, 176–77, 244, 261; cognitive neuroscience, 20, 33, 41, 43, 96–97, 103, 108–9, 113–15, 117, 123, 140, 187, 194, 203, 234, 261; of embodied mind, 28, 31, 52, 57, 177, 266n1 (chap. 4); first generation (disembodied), 32–33, 53, 111, 177; of law, 176–78; and philosophy, 28, 53, 96–97, 109, 114, 139–42, 261; and pragmatism, 30–32, 34, 39–40, 45, 49, 53, 56–57, 96, 103–4, 108–9, 113, 261; second generation (embodied), 29, 33–34, 45, 49, 52–53, 57, 177–78, 245, 261
Cohen, Ted, 221
communication, 2, 8, 14, 36, 45, 48, 52–53, 57, 67, 76, 83–84, 86, 88, 94, 97, 108, 111, 150, 177, 201, 208, 228, 246, 265n1; expression, 2, 17, 19–20, 23–24, 47–49, 61, 64, 75, 83, 85–87, 91, 105, 135, 149, 166–67, 172, 191–94, 206, 217, 219–20, 222, 228, 238, 243, 257; gesture, 2, 19, 48, 51, 85, 88, 90–91, 94, 163, 194, 211, 220, 230, 268n2; role of meaning in, 2, 19, 48, 53, 80, 88–89, 91, 94, 243, 266n1 (chap. 4); as spoken/linguistic dialogue, 48, 76, 83, 85–87, 91, 206, 243
computer science, 32, 117
concepts, 4–6, 8, 15, 17, 28, 43, 46, 49, 59–63, 66–68, 85–86, 91–92, 108, 110, 136, 139–40, 178–80, 182, 185, 193, 201, 204, 209–10, 243, 265n2, 266n2 (chap. 2); abstract, 19, 33, 43, 47–48, 58–60, 67–70, 74, 78, 115, 133, 144–45, 177, 188, 192–94; conceptual metaphors, 15, 29, 48, 59–61, 68–69, 72–74, 77–79, 115, 117, 136, 145, 179, 183, 187–88, 190–95, 218, 259, 266n2 (chap. 8); development of, 139, 146, 180, 182, 196; disembodied view of, 6, 41, 178; embodied, 43, 47, 52, 177, 187–88, 192–94; fuzzy, 144; idealized cognitive models, 196; legal, 136, 176, 178, 182, 184, 187, 194; moral, 139–40, 145–47, 161–62, 169, 179, 182; neural basis of, 43, 245; as simulators, 246
conceptual metaphors. *See* concepts; metaphor; metaphors, conceptual, examples of
consciousness, 9, 15–16, 19, 22, 34, 37, 40, 42–43, 54–56, 103, 116–17, 124, 170, 184–85, 187, 204, 216, 219, 228–29, 240, 248, 267n1 (chap. 9); embodied, 54, 170, 249; empirical, 204–5; multiple-draft model of, 124; stream of, 101, 124
contingency, 11, 79, 86, 105, 136, 167, 196, 261
continuity, 102–4, 131, 207–8; of experience, 81, 101–3, 207–8; principle of, 102
Corbetta, J. D., 118
corporeal. *See* body
Cox, Arnie, 67, 220
Craighero, L., 246
Crick, Francis, 104

Damasio, Antonio, 20–22, 42, 50, 55–56, 98–100, 103–4, 106, 112–13, 130, 140, 149–50, 154, 177, 215–16, 250
Dancygier, Barbara, 28, 48, 194
Dark, V. I., 123
Davidson, David, 13, 69, 71–73, 78, 167
Decety, Jean, 173
Dennett, Daniel, 124
Desimone, R., 123
development, 20, 37–38, 48, 51, 93, 103, 145, 150–53, 158, 169, 175–76, 184–85, 193, 203, 215, 218, 221–23, 229, 234–35,

Index

development (*continued*)
237, 239, 260–61; cognitive, 44, 54, 152, 171; conflation stage, 188; differentiation stage, 188; infant, 150–51; ontogenesis, 184

de Waal, Frans, 171

Dewey, John, 2, 13–17, 25–26, 31–32, 36–37, 39–40, 45, 49–52, 56–57, 80–82, 86, 89–91, 94–95, 98, 100–102, 105–6, 110–13, 130–33, 136, 142, 149–50, 154–57, 163–64, 169–71, 175–76, 200–201, 203, 206–10, 213–14, 217, 221–37, 239–42, 244–45, 247–48, 252, 255–56, 260–61, 265n4, 267n4 (chap. 9), 268n3 (chap. 10)

DeYoe, E. A., 117–18

dichotomy. *See* dualism

Dodge, Ellen, 47, 185

Downing, C. J., 128

dualism, 12, 36, 41, 52, 81, 103–6, 162, 208, 267n2 (chap. 9); arbitrary constructivism/legal objectivism, 182; art/life, 240; cognition/emotion, 12, 20, 49; dualistic metaphysics of mind, 104; dualistic neuroscience, 104; epistemological dichotomies, 105, 207; experience/language, 81; fact/value, 140, 156; inner/outer, 39, 41, 43; is/ought, 140–41; knowledge/imagination, 9, 12, 104; mental/physical, 104; mind/body, 12, 39, 41, 45, 104; mind/world, 40; ontological dichotomies, 105; reason/emotion, 9, 104–6, 148; subject/object, 39, 104; subject/world, 36; thought/feeling, 9, 12, 49, 104–5

Duncan, J., 123

dynamic systems theory, 35

Eagleman, David, 150

economics, 1, 65, 147–48, 177, 183, 197, 230

ecosystem. *See* environment

Edelman, Gerald, 42, 113, 177

egoism. *See* self-interest

embodied meaning, 13, 24, 47–48, 51, 54, 76, 91, 178–79, 184–85, 186–88, 193, 201, 204, 208, 210, 220, 222, 242, 245–46, 257, 260, 268n2

embodiment, 1–2, 4, 14, 25–26, 28, 30, 35, 46, 52–54, 69, 73, 93–94, 115, 131–32, 135–36, 140, 150, 170, 173, 177, 187–88, 191–94, 201, 203, 208, 210–11, 217, 220, 222–23, 246, 249, 255–57, 259–61; embodied dimension, 53–54, 94, 211, 249; embodied engagement, 43, 49, 54, 135, 243, 250, 260; and metaphor, 48, 69, 73, 76, 187–88, 191–93; and mind, 3, 28, 31, 53–55, 57, 104, 136, 177, 201, 249, 266n1 (chap. 4); and reason, 3, 177; and thought, 28, 53, 136, 177, 178, 192. *See also* body

emotions, 1–3, 5–7, 9–12, 14–15, 19–26, 44, 49–51, 53–54, 62, 68, 70, 91, 94, 100, 104–6, 110, 136, 139–42, 148–49, 151–52, 160, 164, 171–73, 183, 185, 201, 204–5, 209–11, 214–21, 225, 228, 230, 232, 234–35, 237, 243, 251–53, 259, 265n6, 266n7; background, 216; emotional response patterns, 21–22, 50, 106, 216–17; emotion studies, 50, 100, 106, 149, 151, 215–16, 232; primary, 216; social, 50, 106, 173, 225. *See also* body

empathy, 150–51, 153, 155–56, 160, 163, 166, 168, 172, 183; as basis of care, 150–51, 153, 155–56, 168, 172, 183; and mirror neurons, 161, 173

empiricism, 20, 52, 82, 221; empirical testability, 127–28, 130

enactment, 14, 16–17, 22–24, 40, 53–54, 88, 93–94, 168, 197, 213, 220–23, 233, 240, 244, 250, 255–56, 261, 266n7; of meaning, 2, 17, 23, 25–26, 54–55, 81, 88, 93–94, 206, 209–10, 219, 222, 232–33, 236, 238, 240, 243–44, 246–47, 257, 261

Enlightenment, 3–4, 6, 12, 39, 151, 153, 165, 225; Enlightenment philosophy, 5–6, 110; Enlightenment rationalist ethics, 143; Enlightenment rationality, 151

environment, 1, 15, 18, 21, 25–26, 28, 33, 36–38, 40–43, 45–46, 54–55, 84, 99–100, 107–8, 130–31, 169, 184, 193, 215–16, 218, 222, 236, 239, 242–44, 247–48, 250, 253, 255–57; bodily interactions with, 2, 18, 21, 40, 43, 45–46, 50, 55, 111, 130–31, 177–78, 184–87, 192–93, 203, 209,

216, 243, 245, 249–51, 255; cultural, 15, 45, 55, 100, 108, 136, 203, 222, 242, 255; ecosystem, 145; interpersonal, 55, 108, 136, 218, 222; organism-environment interaction, 14, 20, 34–42, 46, 53–55, 98–101, 103–4, 108, 112, 131–32, 207, 218, 222, 228, 242–43, 245–46, 253; physical, 15, 18, 36, 45, 55, 100, 108, 136, 203, 222, 242, 253, 255

epistemology, 6–7, 38–39, 43, 52, 78, 105, 112, 148, 199, 204, 206–7, 224; epistemic dualism, 98, 103–5; epistemic rules, 53; foundationalist, 81; objectivist theory of knowledge, 27–28, 68, 71, 78, 133; values, 131

equilibrium, 20, 98–99; dynamic, 21, 50, 56, 99, 100, 250; internal, 21, 50, 250. *See also* allostasis; homeostasis

essentialism, 180

ethics, 8, 67, 139, 142–44, 157, 162–64, 168–69, 182–83, 196, 199, 230; deliberation, 237; ethical principles, 146, 152, 175; Kantian, 139–40, 143, 151–52, 161–62, 167; moral cognition, , 136, 160, 163, 169; naturalistic view of, 143; utilitarianism, 139, 140, 147, 167; virtue, 153, 165–66, 169, 171, 174. *See also* morality

European philosophy, 52

evolution, 30, 32, 37, 50, 53–54, 97, 103, 131, 169, 184, 187, 215, 234, 265–66n6; exaptation, 53–54, 103, 131, 187–88

exaptation. *See under* evolution

executive system, 37, 42, 116, 118, 120–21, 123, 128–29

existentialism, 167, 256–57

experience, 1–4, 6, 9–10, 14, 19, 21–22, 25–26, 29–30, 38–42, 45, 49, 51, 54, 68, 80–82, 84, 88–89, 91, 93–94, 98, 100–101, 108, 110–13, 137, 146, 151, 159, 162, 166, 170–73, 176, 186, 190, 192, 199–201, 203–4, 207, 211, 214–15, 221, 223, 225, 229, 233, 235–42, 244–46, 251, 256, 261; affective, 39, 51, 70, 102, 131, 162, 188–89, 219, 236; as art in germ, 232; bodily, 19, 25, 29, 37, 40, 43, 46, 55, 69, 102–3, 108, 136, 150, 162, 172, 175, 177, 185–87, 189, 191–92, 207, 216, 243, 245, 249, 251; embodied, 24, 30, 52–53, 94, 115, 132, 179, 177, 188, 192, 201, 208, 210, 220, 222, 268n2; inner, 37, 39, 74, 77, 220–21; linguistic, 84–86, 87, 89, 92–95, 168; nondualistic conception of, 40, 81, 103–5, 108, 208; nonlinguistic, 81, 87, 90–91, 93, 95, 246; prelinguistic, 82, 89; qualitative, 15–18, 42, 51, 53, 90, 95, 102, 207, 213–14, 215–16, 223, 226–28, 230–33, 235–36, 238–40, 247–48, 250, 252, 254–55, 257, 268n3 (chap. 10); simulated, 14, 44, 93–94, 172–73

experientialism, 53, 86–89, 157, 169

externalism, 99

Fauconnier, Gilles, 193, 218

feeling, 1–9, 12–13, 15, 17, 19–20, 22–26, 28–29, 36, 39–40, 43–44, 49–51, 53–54, 58, 89–91, 93, 102, 104–6, 108, 110, 139, 141, 148–50, 160–61, 168, 170–71, 173, 185, 187–88, 191, 201, 203, 205–6, 208–11, 215–25, 228–29, 234–35, 237, 243, 248, 252, 257, 259–60, 265–66n6, 267n2 (chap. 9), 268n3 (chap. 10); of emotions, 22–23, 50, 216; primordial, 216; thought-feeling, 49, 101, 105–6

feeling contours, 24, 211, 216–18, 220; affective contours, 218–20

Feldman, Jerome, 14, 33, 42, 44, 112, 177, 179, 187, 190, 246, 266n1 (chap. 4)

feminist philosophy, 27, 153

Fernandez-Duque, Diego, 67, 115, 117, 120, 128

Fesmire, Steven, 67, 112, 155, 163, 172

Fillmore, Charles, 146

Flanagan, Owen, 113, 139, 143, 150, 154, 156–57, 242, 268n3 (chap. 11)

flourishing, 21, 55, 132, 155, 157–58, 166, 242, 248–49; fitness-flourishing distinction, 255, 268n3 (chap. 11)

Fodor, Jerry, 33, 74–77

folk theory, 3, 5–6, 60, 73–74; folk model, 117, 119; folk psychology, 119; folk wisdom, 177; moral law folk theory, 161–62, 174

foundationalism, 52; epistemological, 81; metaphysical, 52, 82, 93; political, 52

four E's. *See under* seven E's
Frackowiak, R., 124
freedom, 8, 47, 58–59, 146, 150–51, 175, 188, 205; liberty, 166
Frege, Gottlob, 13, 93
fringe, 49, 116, 212
Frith, C., 124
functionalism, 32–33; functionalist theory of mind, 111
functions, 3–4, 14, 20, 33–37, 42–44, 100, 103, 112, 123, 130, 131–32, 139, 155, 163, 165, 187, 190, 207–8, 212, 234, 242, 245, 248, 251, 256–57, 268n5; higher-order, 33–34, 54, 69–70, 102–3, 107, 111, 193

Gallagher, Shaun, 113
Gallese, Vittorio, 113, 245, 246
Gallie, Walter Bryce, 146
Gardner, John, 166, 174
Garrison, James, 113
gender, 153–54, 177
Gendlin, Eugene, 211–12
genealogy, 85
Gibbs, Raymond, 20, 28, 33, 48, 67, 178, 190–92, 194
Gibson, J. J., 15, 245
Gilligan, Carol, 152–53, 172
Goldman, Alvin, 150, 246, 272
Goodman, Nelson, 13, 238
Gopher, D., 119, 122
Grady, Joseph, 61, 70, 188–90, 193
Gregory, Marshall, 166, 174
Grézes, Julie, 173
growth, 25, 112, 126, 132, 153, 158, 176, 182, 219–20, 233, 240, 257; as meaning, 166, 170, 175, 207, 221, 240, 257–58; and morality, 157, 170, 175

habit, 36–37, 102, 135, 146, 150, 157–58, 169, 171, 175, 183, 222, 228–29, 257; as basis of thought, 169–70, 222, 257; Dewey's theory of, 203; external/ internal, 37; of inquiry, 131
Hacker, P. M. S., 99–100
Haidt, Jonathan, 140, 149
halo. *See* fringe
Hare, Richard M., 163

harm, 155, 183, 197, 265–66n6; moral, 183; psychological, 183; as radial category, 183
Hasher, L., 119
Hauser, Marc, 149
Heidegger, Martin, 31, 232, 255
hermeneutics, 27, 261
Hernández-Peón, Raúl, 116
Hickman, Larry, 113
Hillyard, S. A., 118
Hinde, Robert, 143, 154, 260
Hoffman, Martin, 151, 172
home, 16, 90, 223, 245, 249, 251, 256–57, 261
homeostasis, 20, 50, 55–56, 62, 99, 100, 216, 250, 252
homunculus, 37, 41, 42, 120, 128
Hopfinger, Joseph, 118
human: beings, continuities with nonhuman animals, 1, 20–21, 102, 135, 234, 248, 261; beings vs. nonhuman animals, 3, 80, 83–84, 161; body, 43, 46, 142, 150, 177, 195, 246 (*see also* body); brain (*see* brain, human); cognition, 7, 34, 94, 97, 178, 225, 246; *homo aestheticus*, 2; humanizing, 74; mind, 7, 68, 82, 103, 142, 226; nature, 142, 158; reason, 4, 73, 106, 136, 140, 143, 176–77, 179, 182, 200, 208; understanding, 4, 38, 69, 73, 142, 150, 162, 176, 196, 200, 210, 237, 249
Hume, David, 13, 141, 148, 160
Husserl, Edmond, 31
Hutcheson, Francis, 160

identity. *See* self
image schema, 18–19, 28, 47–48, 184–85, 197, 201, 218–20, 250, 254–55, 259; defined, 18, 46, 186–87; as embodied meaning, 47, 179, 184, 186, 218, 250; examples of (*see* image schemas, examples of); and reason, 19, 47, 186–87, 196
image schemas, examples of: balance, 18, 47, 185, 218–19, 252; containment, 18–19, 47, 48, 185–86, 250–51, 253; into, 185, 186; locomotion, 19, 46–47, 184; source-path-goal, 18, 47–48, 185, 186; verticality, 18–19, 46, 184, 186, 251–52

imagination, 2, 4, 7, 9, 12, 23–25, 58, 104, 110, 159, 162, 167, 171, 174, 177–78, 182, 184, 193, 256, 260, 265n1, 267n2 (chap. 10); corrective, 164–65; creative, 165; disciplined, 164; empathetic, 151, 160–61, 163, 166, 168, 172–73; exploratory, 164–65; imaginative dramatic rehearsal, 136, 171; imaginative projection, 163, 173, 175; moral, 174, 136, 137, 146, 159, 160–65, 166, 168–75; and simulation, 171. *See also* morality
imitation, 26, 150, 221; mimesis, 26, 228, 238
individual. *See* self
Innis, Robert, 233, 268n4
inquiry, 15, 30, 34–35, 37–39, 84, 90, 106–13, 130–33, 142, 156, 168–70, 174, 207, 239, 260; community of inquirers, 82; as growth and fluid functioning, 131–32; as resolution of problematic situations, 131, 170
intellectualism, 110
intellectual property, 194–96
intentionality, 68, 84; discursive, 83–84; practical, 84
interpersonal relations, 14, 45, 55–56, 98, 108, 136, 150–51, 155–56, 158, 185, 209, 222–23, 243, 259–60; shared meaning, 41, 55, 89, 245; social, 1, 25, 28, 37, 40, 44, 48, 56, 82, 84, 151, 155, 188, 257; socialization, 151, 154

James, William, 31–32, 36, 39–40, 42, 49–50, 57, 80, 101–2, 105, 106, 110, 112, 123–24, 163, 203, 212, 239, 261
Johnson, Christopher, 188
Johnson, Mark, 2, 9, 18, 19, 21, 23, 25, 28–29, 46, 50–51, 56, 59, 67, 69, 87–88, 92, 95, 130, 140, 143–46, 150, 154, 161, 167, 172–73, 177, 178, 186–87, 218–19, 256, 258, 260, 267n3 (chap. 9), 268n1
Johnston, W. A., 123
judgment, 1, 4–10, 12–13, 25, 27, 82, 84, 101, 127, 129, 147–49, 151, 188, 193, 199–200, 204–7, 219, 225, 228, 230, 265n2, 265n3, 267n2 (chap. 10); legal, 179, 182; moral, 8, 141–42, 144, 148–49, 151–52, 158, 160, 162–63, 230; subjective, 10, 51, 189–90, 199
justice, 56, 58–59, 68, 143, 145, 151, 154–55, 188, 191, 194, 197; equality, 166, 191; rights, 56, 58–59, 67, 145, 154–55
justification, 53, 81, 84–85, 141, 149, 154, 166, 197. *See also* epistemology

Kahneman, Daniel, 119, 121, 140, 147
Kant, Immanuel, 5–10, 12–13, 96, 139–41, 143, 148, 151–52, 160–63, 167, 203–7, 223, 225, 265n1, 265n2, 265n3, 267n1 (chap. 9), 267n2 (chap. 9), 267n2 (chap. 10)
Keke, John, 164–65
Kinsbourne, Marcel, 124–25
Kitcher, Philip, 143, 155, 260
knowledge, 4–6, 9, 12, 21, 26–28, 38–39, 41, 47, 52–53, 58–59, 67–68, 71, 78, 81–82, 86, 92, 104, 108, 110–11, 113, 117, 121, 133–35, 139, 141–42, 151, 157, 171, 178, 186, 188, 190, 193, 199–201, 204, 206–8, 224, 226, 261, 265n2; as construction, 117, 122; embodied, 170, 192; knowing how, 83; knowing that, 83; propositional, 7
Koenigsberg, Richard, 196
Kohlberg, Lawrence, 152–54
Kövecses, Zoltán, 28, 48, 73, 140, 193
Kuhn, Thomas, 109

LaBerge, David, 128
Làdavas, E., 125
Lakoff, George, 2, 5, 18–19, 28, 32–33, 43, 46–48, 63, 66–67, 69, 73–74, 78, 104, 111, 113–14, 130, 133, 140, 144–46, 150, 153, 167, 177–80, 183, 185, 187–88, 190, 193–96, 218, 245–46, 256, 266n7, 266n2 (chap. 2), 266n1 (chap. 4), 268n1
Langer, Susan, 219–20, 222
language, 1, 3–4, 13, 18–20, 25, 28–32, 34, 38, 42, 47–48, 51–53, 55, 58, 64, 69, 71, 74–78, 80–96, 105, 108, 114, 132, 166–68, 172, 177, 191–92, 194, 201, 207, 209, 212, 226, 243, 247, 261, 266n1 (chap. 4); artificial, 77; bodily basis of, 47, 48, 87, 93, 247, 255; as constructed, 91; embodied

language (*continued*)
  simulation hypothesis, 93, 173, 246–47; experience of, 80–81, 86–87, 91, 93–95, 177–78; formal, 76–77; language-as-a-whole, 92–93; natural, 19, 72, 76–77, 88; wide scope, 90–91, 94; written and spoken, 76, 78
Larson, Steve, 19, 23, 67, 219–20
Lavie, Nilli, 122
Leopold, David A., 125
Levin, David Michael, 212
Lindner, Susan, 48
lingualism, Brandom's theory of, 84–91
linguistics, 27–28, 243, 246; cognitive, 33, 58, 60–61, 72–73, 246; generative, 32, 111, 177
logic, 4–5, 8, 19, 27, 53, 58, 95, 102, 111, 131, 147, 162, 179, 182, 184, 193, 199–200, 224, 226, 237, 239; formal logic, 19, 33, 250; linguistic turn, 84–85, 268n1; logical relations, 49, 78, 190
Logothetis, Nikos K., 125
Luck, S. J., 118

Macarthur, David, 85, 95
MacIntyre, Alasdair, 151, 155
Magnani, Lorenzo, 67, 115
Malachowski, Alan, 82
Mangun, G. R., 118
maps, mapping, 42, 43, 47, 48, 61–64, 66, 73, 76, 78, 116–20, 124, 126, 133, 188–89, 191, 193, 243; neural, 42; source-to-target, 71–72
Martinez, A. L., 118
mathematics, 67–68, 127, 142, 193, 239, 249
McConachie, Bruce, 19, 51
meaning, 1–3, 5, 7, 9, 11–26, 28, 31, 33, 36, 39, 41, 43, 45–49, 51, 53–56, 60, 70–71, 81, 85–95, 97–98, 108, 110, 113, 127, 130–32, 136, 167, 170, 175, 177, 184–85, 200–201, 203–4, 206–11, 213–22, 225–40, 242–61, 268n2; body-based, 25, 28–29, 31, 45–46, 48, 55, 87, 93, 111, 130, 178, 184–85, 187, 201, 203, 206, 209, 216, 221, 243, 249–50, 255, 259; as conceptual and propositional, 33, 53, 71–72, 209, 211, 235, 243, 268n1; as creative process, 95, 246; disembodied view, 134, 247; embodied, 2, 13, 24, 45, 47–48, 51, 53–55, 76, 91, 93–94, 170, 178–79, 184–88, 201, 204, 208–11, 220, 242, 245–46, 249, 256–57, 260; as linguistic, 20, 48, 51–53, 80, 83, 87, 90, 92, 167, 209, 211, 243, 244, 246–47, 255; literal, 67, 69–71, 78, 133, 144, 182, 267n3 (chap. 9); meaning-making, 48, 51, 53, 83–84, 86–87, 90–92, 94, 110, 208–10, 212, 217–18, 225, 237, 239, 242, 246, 256, 260–61; naturalized theory of, 75; nonlinguistic, 81, 87–88, 90–92, 94–95, 247, 255; prelinguistic, 48, 53, 88–89, 91, 247; pre-reflective, 18, 89, 187, 249; as relational, 45, 210, 244; sense vs. signification, 90, 248; simulation theory, 14, 44–45, 93–94, 267n5 (chap. 9); tripartite structure of, 45; as truth-conditional, 72. *See also* embodied meaning
mentalese, 75, 77
Merleau-Ponty, Maurice, 31, 184, 256–57, 261
metaphor, 2, 15, 18–19, 23, 28–30, 33, 46, 58, 62, 66–68, 78, 107, 130, 144, 146, 168, 183–84, 190–97, 210, 218–19, 259, 266n1 (chap. 2); causal, 61–64, 66, 123, 266n2 (chap. 2); conceptual metaphors, examples of (*see* metaphors, conceptual, examples of); conceptual metaphor theory, 48, 60–70, 72–73, 77–79, 115, 136, 167, 179, 183, 187–88, 190–91, 194–95; cross-domain mapping structure, 189, 192–93; Davidson's theory of, 69, 71–73, 78; experiential correlations, 70, 188–90; inferential structures of, 68, 187, 192; metaphorical mapping, 61–64, 66, 73, 76, 78, 117, 119, 124, 133; metaphorical source-to-target-mappings, 61–63, 71, 117–18, 120–21, 124, 129, 133, 188; nonsemantic theory of, 71, 167–68; primary metaphor, 61, 70, 73, 188–90, 192–93; Rorty's theory of, 71–73, 78, 166–68; in science, 115, 126–31, 133–34, 259; Searle's theory of, 69–72, 78; similarity theory of, 70

metaphors, conceptual, examples of: affection is warmth, 70, 189; attention, 115–24, 127–30; causation, 61–67, 74–75, 120, 123, 128; containment, 43, 48; desire is hunger, 191–92, 266n3; formal language is a natural language, 76–77; language of thought, 5, 74–77; location event-structure, 61; mind is a computer, 77; morality, 140, 145, 165, 167–68; thought is a language, 74–76

metaphysics, 52, 119, 162, 199, 204, 206, 221, 256; analytic, 224; classical objectivist, 67–68, 78, 92; dualistic, 104; empiricist, 52, 82; foundationalist, 52, 82, 93; of mind, 104; pre-Socratic, 74; Rorty's critique of, 52, 82

mind, 4, 6–7, 12, 14–15, 20, 22, 28–29, 32, 34, 36, 38–41, 43, 47, 50, 53, 58–59, 68, 76, 78, 82, 89, 93, 96–97, 100–101, 103, 106, 108, 110, 120, 139–40, 142–43, 158, 176, 178, 206–9, 217, 226, 228, 246; Cartesian view of, 39, 41, 45, 74, 78, 104, 177; computational theory of, 5, 75–77, 111, 177; disembodied conception of, 3, 5, 32–33, 45, 178, 249, 259, 266n3; embodied conception of, 3, 14–15, 28, 31–33, 43, 52–55, 57, 103, 136, 177–78, 201, 249, 266n1 (chap. 4); extended, 54–55; metaphors for, 74–75, 77, 120; representational theory of, 39, 40–42; science of, 31–32, 34, 112–13, 136

mirror neurons, 246; as basis for empathy, 161, 173

Misak, Cheryl, 82

Moore, G. E., 141–42

morality, 1, 3–4, 13, 25–27, 95, 135–37, 139–40, 143, 145, 148–54, 157, 159, 169, 174, 179, 193, 201, 259–61; appraisal, 136, 139, 141, 148–49, 159, 161, 163, 165, 173–74; calculation, 139–40, 147–48; of care, 151, 154; deliberation, 136, 139, 141, 146, 148–50, 159–60, 163–65, 168–69, 171, 173–75, 226, 230, 237, 260; embodied, 136, 260; experimental, 140, 154, 157, 172; Judeo-Christian, 143; literalist accounts of, 145; moral fundamentalism, 147; moral imagination as basis of deliberation and reasoning, 136, 137, 146, 159, 160–65, 166, 168–75; moral injury, 183; moral psychology, 139–40, 142–43; moral self-cultivation, 160, 166, 164; moral sentiments theory, 27, 141, 148, 153, 160; naturalistic conception of, 136, 141–43, 207; nurturant-parent morality, 153; pluralism, 136, 149, 152, 157, 166, 175; strict-father-model, 153

moral law. *See* moral principle

moral law folk theory. *See* folk theory

moral principle, 8, 27, 140–41, 143–44, 146, 151–52, 154–55, 159, 161–63, 165, 171, 174–75, 179–80, 183, 195, 199; as moral law, 141, 143; not absolute, 146, 147, 152, 159, 166, 169

much-at-once-ness of experience, 39, 42–43, 102

Müller, M. M., 118

multimodality, 245, 247

Narayanan, Srini, 33, 47, 78, 104, 113, 187, 190, 196, 246

narrative, 164, 166, 168, 174, 255

naturalism, 28, 33–34, 75, 84, 102–4, 108, 131, 133, 136, 141, 143, 207; pluralist, 35; strong reductionist, 34

Navon, D., 119, 122

Nersessian, Nancy, 67, 115

neural maps, 42. *See also* brain, human

neurophilosophy, 96–97

neuropragmatism, 96, 98, 108, 114; defined, 97, 108

neuroscience, 28, 30, 98–100, 102–4, 106, 108, 112, 261; dualist, 104; neural connectivity, 33, 38, 42–44, 70, 93, 188, 192–93; and pragmatism, 96–98, 106, 108, 114

Newton, Isaac, 72, 167

Nietzsche, Friedrich, 59, 163

Noddings, Nell, 172

Noë, Alva, 113, 177

nonhuman animals, 21, 39, 84, 113, 135, 145, 161, 168, 171, 217, 228, 261; continuities with humans, 20–21, 102, 135, 234, 248, 261

Norman, Donald A., 119, 122
normativity, 91, 126, 139–43, 154, 156–58, 163, 168, 199, 237
norms. *See* values
noumenal, 162, 205–6, 267n2 (chap. 9)
Nozick, Robert, 151
Núñuz, Rafael, 67, 185, 193
Nussbaum, Martha, 165–66, 174, 261

objectivism, 43, 55, 59, 63, 66–69, 71, 78, 92, 133, 178–80, 182, 260, 267n3 (chap. 9)
Ojala, Juha, 220
ontology, 33–34, 37–38, 40–41, 52, 60, 66, 104–5, 128–29, 181, 256; dualism, 36, 41, 98–99, 103–5, 148; pluralism, 112
organism, 15, 20–21, 32, 36, 40–42, 45, 50, 54–56, 90, 98–100, 106, 109, 112, 123, 131–32, 154, 156, 183, 208, 228–29, 239, 245, 248, 250, 252, 265–66n6; coupling with environment, 38, 42; ontogenesis, 184; organism-environment interaction, 14, 20, 36–41, 43, 46, 53–55, 98–101, 103–4, 108, 112, 131–32, 207, 216, 218, 222, 228, 246, 253
organization, 25, 35–36, 38, 104, 106–7, 109–12, 184, 189, 222, 233–34, 236; functional, 34, 107, 207

Pallasmaa, Juhani, 19, 256–57
Pappas, Gregory, 95, 226, 237, 268n3 (chap. 10)
Pashler, H., 119, 122
Peirce, Charles, 32, 45, 57
perception, 2, 7, 9, 15, 17–19, 25, 28–29, 34, 36, 39, 44, 47, 50, 58, 93–94, 102, 104, 110, 117, 122–24, 174, 177, 184, 188, 190, 204–5, 217, 228, 231, 233–35, 241, 243–45, 254, 260, 267n2 (chap. 9); binocular rivalry, 125; perceptual affordance, 17, 54; perceptual symbols, 244
Pérez-Gómez, Alberto, 249
pervasive qualitative unity, Dewey's theory of, 16–17, 95, 102, 211, 213, 214, 226, 230–32, 235–37, 239, 247, 255, 268n3 (chap. 10)
pervasive unifying quality. *See* pervasive qualitative unity, Dewey's theory of
Petronio, A., 125

phenomenal, 162, 204–5
phenomenology, 27, 106, 261
philosopher's fallacy, 37
philosophy as metaphor, 29, 58, 60, 68, 74
philosophy of language, 20, 32, 68, 199; analytic, 53, 69, 72, 74, 177, 243
philosophy of mind, 32, 53; analytic, 20, 32, 53, 74, 177
Piaget, Jean, 152
Pinker, Steven, 128
Plato, 14, 73–74
pluralism, 35, 39, 108, 112, 152, 258, 260; epistemological, 112; moral, 152, 157, 166, 175; ontological, 112
politics, 25, 65, 67, 179, 193, 199–200; relation with morality, 153
Posner, Michael, 119
possibility, 8, 19, 25, 27, 68–69, 90, 132, 136, 157, 164, 170–71, 214, 242, 245; role in meaning, 15, 17, 25–26, 88, 90, 132, 136, 170, 175, 208, 210, 221, 231, 244, 247, 255–56, 261
postmodernism, 27, 240, 254
pragmatism, 27–29, 31–35, 39–40, 43, 45, 49, 52–53, 56, 71, 80–85, 95–98, 101–3, 105–9, 111–14, 167, 169, 210, 261; analytic, 29, 52–53, 57, 80–83, 87, 94; classical, 29, 31–32, 34, 40, 49–50, 53, 57, 82, 101, 111; and cognitive science, 30–32, 34, 39–40, 45, 49, 53, 56–57, 96, 103–4, 108–9, 113, 261; experientially based, 53, 169; linguistic, 29, 52, 57, 80–82, 84–86, 91–92, 94–95, 169; neopragmatism, 82; new, 82. *See also* neuropragmatism
Price, Huw, 85, 95
principle of minimal psychological realism, 143
principles. *See* moral principle
principles of extension, 28, 144, 180, 183, 195
Prinz, Jesse, 140, 153
property, 17, 63, 67, 99, 123–24, 141; properties, 5, 9, 17, 39, 43, 68, 91, 141, 144, 179, 208, 231, 244–45, 248
prototype, 66, 127, 179–80, 183, 194–95, 239; cognitive, 44, 180, 195; effects, 144, 179; moral, 144–46

psychology, 27–28, 32–33, 36, 38, 101, 105, 115, 125, 139–40, 142, 143, 147, 172, 174, 205, 215, 217–18, 235, 244, 246; cognitive, 33, 97, 117, 123; cognitive psychology of attention, 115, 126; developmental, 218; faculty, 4, 8–9, 111, 165, 204–6, 267n2 (chap. 10); Gestalt, 217; information-processing, 111, 177; moral, 139, 140, 142–43

purpose, 38, 56, 58, 61, 63–64, 67, 71, 83, 92–93, 101, 119, 121–22, 132, 152, 154, 180, 190, 193, 248, 251; purposive, 18, 208

Putnam, Hilary, 13, 41, 82, 109, 111, 165–66, 266n3

qualitative unity. *See* pervasive qualitative unity, Dewey's theory of

qualities, 1, 15–17, 19, 22, 24–26, 36–38, 42–43, 45, 51, 53, 89–91, 110, 201, 207–11, 213, 215, 218–20, 225–32, 235–39, 246–49, 252, 254–55, 259, 265n4; qualitative dimensions, 15–16, 22, 54, 201, 218, 228, 247, 250, 257. *See also* pervasive qualitative unity, Dewey's theory of

Quine, W. V. O., 13, 77

race, 177

radial category, 15, 28, 66, 144–45, 179–80, 182–83, 194–96

rationality, 3, 75, 84, 103–4, 135–36, 139, 141–43, 147–49, 151–54, 159–65, 167, 175, 179, 200, 204; discursive reasoning, 84, 209; disembodied view of, 28, 135, 162; economic model of, 147–48; embodied view of, 131

Rawls, John, 143, 151

realism, 33, 69, 109

reason, 2–9, 12, 19, 27–29, 31, 34, 36, 39, 43, 47, 49, 52, 58, 82, 84, 103–4, 135, 139–40, 142, 144, 146–47, 155–56, 160–62, 172, 176, 178, 180, 182, 187–88, 191, 193–94, 199, 217, 222, 225, 259–60; embodied, 28, 31, 33, 104, 111, 130–31, 133, 150, 177–79, 184, 208; ethical, 158, 164, 196; and imagination, 159, 162, 164, 170–71, 177; moral, 136, 141, 145–49, 153, 155, 157–58, 164–65, 169–70, 178–79; pure practical, 27, 136, 151, 160; role of emotion in, 12, 20, 49–50, 53, 105–6, 149, 152; role of metaphor in, 29, 48, 59, 63, 66–69, 72–74, 78–79, 144, 190, 194, 201

Rees, G., 124

reference, 45, 54, 56, 68, 77, 90, 180

reflection, 6, 16, 19, 21, 29, 37, 40, 52, 58, 68, 78, 80, 93, 96, 106, 110–12, 114, 205, 247, 251, 267n2 (chap. 10)

relativism, 144, 159; moral, 161, 165

religion, 1, 4, 25, 67, 146, 179, 193, 224, 230; God, 60, 78, 135, 142–43, 162, 164, 224; and morality, 135, 143, 162, 164

representationalism, 41–42, 85

responsibility, 56, 58, 97, 152, 154, 164, 175, 193; empirically responsible philosophy, 28–30, 114, 260–61

Ricoeur, Paul, 166, 214, 232, 255

Rizzolatti, G., 246

Rorty, Richard, 6, 52, 69, 71, 72–73, 78, 81–83, 92–93, 110, 166–69, 207

Rosch, Eleanor, 28, 33, 40, 44, 177, 179–80

Ryle, Gilbert, 83

Sandel, Michael, 151

Sanders, John, 67

Saslaw, Janna, 220

Schulkin, Jay, 21, 34, 99, 113

science. *See* cognitive science; evolution; neuroscience; psychology

scientific values, 115, 126–29, 130–32, 133–34

Searle, John, 13, 69–72, 78, 86

self, 11, 14–15, 43, 151, 157, 162, 203–8, 220–21, 223, 229, 267n1 (chap. 9), 267n2 (chap. 9); agent, 116, 118, 128, 129, 151, 153, 169, 184; autonomous, 151, 153, 205; character, 1, 145, 166, 175, 203, 245; embodied, 203, 208, 222; identity, 16, 203–7, 220, 222–23, 248; interpersonal, 150–51; moral personhood, 144, 151, 152, 160; as process, 203; self-in-progress, 223; self-transformation/cultivation, 160, 164

self-interest, 139, 147–48, 175; egocentrism, 160; egoism, 147 semiotics, 45; referent, 45, 54, 77; sign, 13, 45, 50, 54, 76–77, 88–92, 194, 222, 243–44, 248; symbol, 5, 19, 26, 41, 45, 75–77, 85, 94, 132–33, 178, 193–94, 209–10, 212, 246–47, 257

sensory-motor systems, 2, 33, 44, 52, 69, 93, 103, 130–32, 172, 186–90, 192–93, 210, 244, 246–47, 251

seven E's, 53–55; embedded, 53–54; embodied, 53–55; emotional, 53–54; enactive, 53–54; evolutionary, 53–54; exaptative, 53–54; extended, 53–55; the four E's, 53

Sheets-Johnstone, Maxine, 19, 23, 254

Sheinberg, David A., 125

Shiffrin, Robert M., 119, 121

Shook, John, 34, 113

Shusterman, Richard, 25–26, 51

Shweder, Robert, 153

simulations, 14, 16, 172, 247; cultural, 44; embodied, 93, 173, 246–47; and moral deliberations, 173; motor, 44

simulation semantics, 14, 93–94, 172, 246; embodied simulation hypothesis, 93, 246

situation, 15–17, 20–21, 23, 38–39, 49, 53, 90, 94–95, 100–102, 131–33, 146, 155–56, 160, 163–65, 169, 171–77, 182–83, 211, 213–16, 222–23, 225–26, 228–29, 236, 246, 248–49, 260; Dewey's definition of, 229–33, 235–39, 248, 252, 255; problematic, 131, 136, 170, 173, 257

skepticism, 39

Smith, Adam, 160–61, 173

Solymosi, Tibor, 34, 97, 113

source domain. *See* metaphor: cross-domain mapping structure

spatiality, 9, 19, 42, 46, 48, 61, 122, 125, 133, 186–88, 195, 249–51; spatial relations terms, 46–48, 188

speech-act theory, 33, 52–53, 69, 86, 89, 91–92; literalist/objectivist version of, 69

Spitzer, Michael, 220

Stafford, William, 23

states of affairs, 20, 45, 55, 68–69, 131–32, 141–42, 156, 171, 243

Stern, Daniel, 216, 218–19

Stevenson, C. L., 148

subjectivism, 10, 39, 159, 238

Sweetser, Eve, 28, 48, 194

sympathy, 163; Hume's theory of, 160; Smith's theory of, 160–61, 173. *See also* empathy

synthesis, 41, 204, 215, 217, 230, 267n1 (chap. 9)

Talisse, Robert, 82

Talmy, Leonard, 185

target domain. *See* metaphor: cross-domain mapping structure

Teder-Sälejävi, W., 118

Thagard, Paul, 113

Thompson, Evan, 28, 33, 40, 113, 177

thought, 1–6, 9, 14, 25, 28–34, 36–38, 40–41, 43, 45, 47, 49–55, 58–59, 67–68, 71–72, 74–78, 83, 86, 95–96, 98, 100–102, 104–6, 108, 110–14, 131, 134, 136, 140, 149–50, 152, 170, 177–78, 193–94, 196–97, 201, 205–6, 208, 213–14, 222, 225–28, 231, 236, 239, 243, 245–49, 259, 261, 266n1 (chap. 4), 266n3, 267n1 (chap. 9), 268n3 (chap. 10)

time, 9, 94, 125, 145, 148, 157, 169, 176, 184, 186, 195, 204, 238–40, 255, 257; past, present, future, 14, 45, 88–90, 116, 171, 210, 221–22, 238, 239, 244–45, 260; temporality, 62, 176, 219, 238, 240, 254; temporal processes, 16, 43, 48, 219–20

Tononi, Giulio, 113, 177

transaction, 38, 54, 98, 100, 136, 207, 218, 228, 243, 255; organism-environment interaction, 14, 20, 34–42, 46, 53–55, 98–101, 103–4, 108, 112, 131–32, 207, 218, 222, 228, 242–43, 245–46, 253

transcendent ego, 34, 41, 162, 223, 259, 267n2 (chap. 9). *See also* mind: disembodied conception of

truth, 3, 13, 20, 27, 39, 52, 58, 68–69, 71–72, 74–75, 80–83, 92, 199–200, 243; classical correspondence theory of, 67–68, 78, 178; embodied, 69; not absolute, 81, 260; pragmatist theory of, 39, 52, 80, 82–83, 166–67, 214

Tucker, Don, 38, 50, 55, 103, 112–13, 140, 177, 215, 234–36
Tudela, P., 119
Tufts, Hayden James, 142
Turner, Mark, 193, 218
Tversky, Amos, 147

Umiltá, Carlo, 121, 125
understanding, 1–7, 9, 15–16, 26–27, 29, 31, 38, 44, 46, 53, 58, 69, 73, 82–83, 111, 118, 120, 133, 135–36, 140, 142, 150, 152–54, 158, 162, 164, 168, 173, 176, 177, 180, 184, 186–87, 192, 200–201, 204, 206, 210, 218, 222–23, 230, 237, 241, 249, 257, 261, 265n1, 268n3 (chap. 10)

valuation, 45, 155, 189; role in moral deliberation, 164
values, 3, 19, 27–29, 31, 37, 47, 52–53, 55–56, 78, 80, 87, 101–3, 108–10, 115, 136–37, 140–43, 146–47, 149, 153–59, 166, 169–75, 180–82, 184, 193, 199–201, 248, 250, 252, 255, 257, 259–61; biological, 56, 137; cultural, 109, 136–37, 145, 156, 245; interpersonal, 156, 185; moral, 27, 56, 153–55, 165–66, 170, 183, 200; in science, 115, 126–31, 133–34; social, 56, 155; value pluralism, 112, 136, 175
Varela, Francisco, 28, 33, 40, 177

Vesely, Dalibor, 249
vitality-affect contours, 218–19
vocabularies, 52, 71, 166, 168

Wachtel, P. L., 116–17
Werhane, Patricia, 164
Wickens, R. C., 122
will, 7, 58–59, 67, 104, 119, 145, 150
Williams, Oliver, 163–64
Williams, Robert, 156
Winter, Stephen, 67, 176, 193–94
Wolfe, Jeremy A., 125
Woodman, G. F., 118
world, 1–2, 4–5, 9, 11, 14–16, 18, 20, 25–27, 36, 39–43, 45–46, 49–51, 54–55, 60, 68, 73–75, 77, 91, 95, 100–101, 109–10, 118, 132–33, 135–37, 149, 165–66, 172, 174–75, 184–86, 197, 199–201, 205–7, 209, 212–14, 216–18, 220–21, 223, 225–30, 232–33, 237–40, 243, 245, 247, 249–57, 259–61; cultural, 137, 223, 255, 260; of linguistic experience, 52, 83, 92, 95, 243; shared, 172, 174–75, 223, 256, 260; social, 171, 223, 255, 256, 260
Wright, Hollis, 67, 155, 254

Zacks, R. T., 119
Zbikowski, Lawrence, 19, 220

The Los...
A Spiritual ...

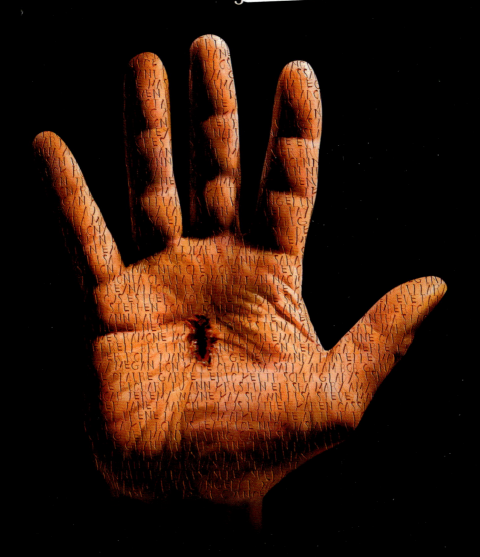

LOOKING FOR MORE THAN CONVENTIONAL CHRISTIANITY?
DISCOVER THE *NON-HOW TO* WAY THAT UNLOCKS GOD'S POWER.
A WORLD OF LOVE, BLESSINGS, AND FULFILLED DESTINY AWAITS!

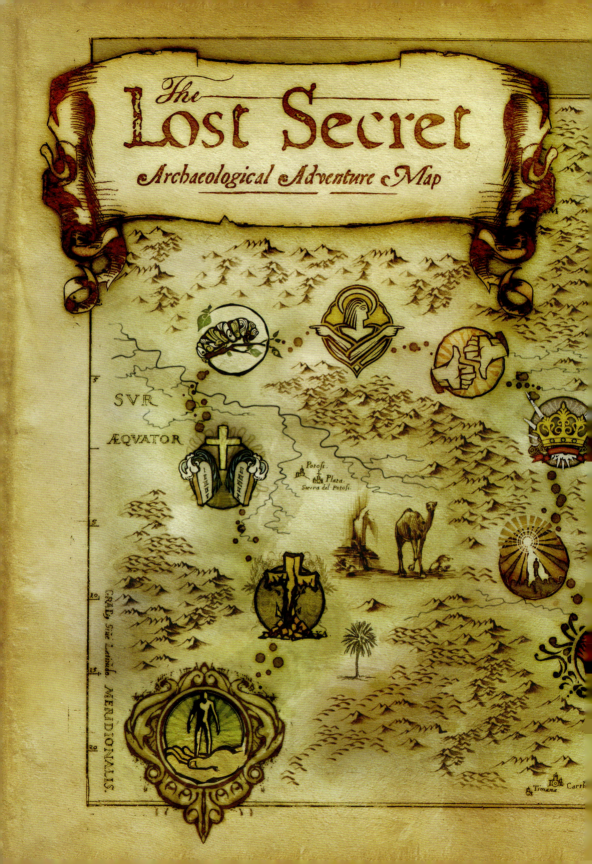

The Lost Secret
by Rick Suarez

Copyright © 2008 by Rick Suarez
All rights reserved for all words and images.

Published by
Fresh Start Ministries
P.O. Box 35217
Canton, Ohio 44735
www.lostsecret.org | info@lostsecret.org

This book or parts thereof may not be reproduced in any form, stored in a retrieval system, or transmitted in any form by any means—electronic, mechanical, photocopy, recording, or otherwise—without prior written permission of the publisher, except as provided by United States of America copyright law.

Unless otherwise noted, all Scripture quotations are taken from the New King James Version of the Bible. Copyright © 1982 by Thomas Nelson, Inc., publishers. Used by permission.

Scripture marked NIV are taken from the Holy Bible, New International Version. Copyright © 1973, 1978, 1984 by International Bible Society. Used by permission of Zondervan Bible Publishers. All rights reserved.

Scripture marked NASB are taken from the New American Standard Bible. Copyright © 1960, 1962, 1963, 1968, 1971, 1972, 1973, 1975, 1977, 1995 by The Lockman Foundation. Used by permission. All rights reserved.

Scripture marked Amplified are taken from The Amplified Bible, Expanded edition. Copyright © 1987 by The Zondervan Corporation and The Lockman Foundation. All rights reserved.

Scripture marked Phillips are taken from J.B. Phillips: The New Testament in Modern English. Copyright © 1958, 1960, 1972 by J.B. Phillips. Copyright © renewed 1986, 1988 by Vera M. Phillips. Permission by Macmillan Publishing Company.

References consulted:

Strong's Exhaustive Concordance of the Bible by James Strong, S.T.D., L.L.D. Copyright © 1979 by Thomas Nelson Inc., Publishers. All rights reserved.

The Merriam-Webster Dictionary. Copyright © 1998 by Merriam-Webster, Incorporated. All rights reserved.

Webster's New World Dictionary. Copyright © 2002 by Wiley Publishing, Inc. All rights reserved.

ISBN 978-0-615-19597-1

Printed in China

It's not just a book…it's a journey.

INTRODUCTION: Are you a Christian who loves God but has left church? Do you still go to church, maybe you're even a minister, but you know deep in your heart that something is missing? You may not be a born-again Christian, but are you searching for God and yet convinced conventional Christianity isn't where you're going to find Him? Finally, are you sincerely seeking God through one of the many religions around the world? No matter who you are, is the cry of your heart to God, "Where's the love and where's the power?" If so, *The Lost Secret* may be for you.

OUR GOD GIVEN BIRTHRIGHT: There are two things that every human being wants and needs—to be loved unconditionally and to have access to God's power to be blessed and have the ability to bless others. God gave this birthright to Adam and Eve in the Garden of Eden. They lived in this world of love with God and each other. And they were given power and dominion for rulership over the entire earth…but their fall caused them to lose it.

In 33 AD Jesus died on the cross and was raised from the dead in order to buy our birthright back. During the first century, believers lived in a wonderful two-dimensional world. They had supernatural love, joy, and peace even in the midst of their persecutions and trials. They also had access to God's power for victory over sin, Satan, and curses—to be blessed and fulfill their destiny to bless others with signs and wonders following. But then something happened, and their world was lost.

THE SECRET WAS LOST: During the second and third centuries, things began to slowly change with believers. And in 313 AD, the emperor Constantine legalized Christianity. This appeared to be a move that would help the church flourish, but instead, things took a turn for the worse. Once the church became organized, it began to take on many of the characteristics of worldly organizations. When this happened, the secret to God's love and power was lost. Since then, sincere Christians have gone through a lot of religious motions that have produced little love and supernatural power in the church. But now that the lost secret has been found, the time for change has come.

The Un-book: Many good books have been written on how to tap into God's love and power by giving people a formula, or a set of rules to follow. This book is not a how to formula. In fact, in that sense it could be called "the unbook." I don't have it all figured out, but I'm in the process of having my life transformed by the lost secret, and more and more I'm experiencing His love, joy, peace, and power.

In this unbook, I hope to open up a conversation among Christians and ministers who long for more than what conventional Christianity has to offer. I also believe people who have not accepted Jesus as Lord and Savior will be attracted to Him as they see Christianity in a different light.

I share my spiritual journey and some concepts and principles the Lord has shared with me. I also ask many questions for individuals to ask themselves and for groups to discuss together. The Lord is the one with the answers. My prayer is that He might use this book as part of a dynamic process in our lives as we seek to move beyond conventional Christianity into a world of love and power.

Join The Journey: Refer to the archaelogical adventure map in the front of the book and join the journey to this lost world. As you read each chapter, you will understand what each icon symbolizes, and in the end be able to decipher the riddle on the map. On your journey, you will find the secret that has been lost for 1,600 years and discover how to make it part of your life. We're about to get back everything that was lost!

Let the journey begin...

Rick Suarez

The Author's Journey
A Parable of Grace

CHAPTER 1

The Author's Journey
A Parable of Grace

Could an avowed atheist become a minister of the gospel of Jesus Christ crucified? Could the son of a blue-collar worker become a millionaire at the age of twenty-three? Could a multi-millionaire lose almost everything and yet, through such loss, gain the one thing he really needed? This is my journey, and as you read it, you will find out that yes, these things are possible.

I call my testimony a "parable of grace" because God's grace is really what it's all about. His lavish grace—and severe mercy—are the themes of my life. Like Greek theater, my makeup and actions have been so extreme at times that it may seem an exaggeration—just a story told to make a point. Well, it's not an exaggeration, and the point is that God is full of grace. At times my life has been as bad as it could get, and yet His grace and mercy were enough even then—especially then—to redeem me. I guarantee you, if Jesus never gave up on Rick Suarez, He'll never give up on you.

I was born and raised Catholic, the son of a blue-collar worker, in Canton, Ohio. In first grade, at St. Benedict's Catholic School, I felt a call on my life to be a priest. Now, I know every Catholic boy wants to be a priest, and every Catholic girl wants to be a nun, but this was the real deal. I loved God. Even at that young age, I heard His voice calling me into ministry.

There was a nun at St. Benedict's who was my teacher. Her name was Sister Mary Daniel, and one day she came into class and told us that her father was very ill and dying. I could see that she was very sad. My heart reached out to help her, and with childlike faith, I believed that God wanted to heal her father.

When we went to mass that day, I said five rosaries for her father. (Any good Catholic knows that is no small feat, especially for a little boy!) Back in class, I raised my hand. Sister Mary Daniel called on me, and I told her what I had done. She was so touched that she wept, and I wept with her.

I look back at that little boy—ornery, yes, like any little boy—but with such a soft heart. I remember the childlike faith I had, the trusting, open love for God and people. The innocence. I look back at that little boy and a part of me wants to turn back time, to rush back and save him, because as I look back, I can also see what is coming.

In front of that little boy lie two paths. The path of life, of God's grace and childlike faith and love, will soon be abandoned by him. He'll get no further than those first few steps he took in first grade. In second grade he turns from it onto the bright and shining path of the world's system of knowledge and works to achieve "success," but it will be a path of death. And after he turns down that road, it will be a hard road—and a long time until he sees the path of life again.

I'd been told by my parents that I was an accident; I wasn't planned. I felt very deeply rejected, and so in second grade—I know this sounds crazy for a seven-year-old—I made the decision that I was going to be successful. I was going to get good grades, and that was the way I'd gain love and acceptance. Just like in the Garden of Eden, knowledge and works came into my life that year—as a way to make God and people like me. A way to feel good about myself. And even though I didn't realize it as a second grader, I realize now that I chose being successful over remaining in the love of God as a little child. Now please understand, I'm not saying that

> I'M NOT SAYING THAT BEING EDUCATION-ORIENTED, HARD-WORKING, AND SUCCESSFUL IS A BAD THING, BUT HAVING YOUR SELF-WORTH ATTACHED TO IT IS.

A Life & Death Choice

GOD'S GRACE
CHILDLIKE FAITH & LOVE
1st Grade

KNOWLEDGE & WORKS
STRIVING FOR SUCCESS
2nd Grade

being education-oriented, hard-working, and successful is a bad thing, but having your self-worth attached to it is. Success does not make us sinners anymore than poverty makes us saints. The Lord doesn't look at our outward appearance, He looks at our hearts.

Throughout grade school I excelled in my grades. I still planned on becoming a priest, and so the summer before eighth grade I went to a pre-seminary entrance camp. While there I got the award for being the "best future seminarian." That fall a priest from the seminary called me and said, "Richard, it's time to get enrolled, you know. You're our number one guy, and you're going to be checking in here in September."

Instead of being excited, I flipped out! I don't know why, but I just freaked out. I lied and told him I couldn't enroll because my mom wouldn't let me. I did not go to seminary. Instead, I went to a Catholic high school from 1965 to 1969.

Those were times of great change, both in my personal life and in our country. The Vietnam War and upheaval in the United States set the tone for my early adulthood as an atheist.

First, I started asking questions about God and the church. In the beginning it was an honest search. I was a very truth-oriented guy, like I am today, very direct. I wanted to get to the bottom of some questions I had, and the brothers at my high school couldn't answer me. I started getting disillusioned with the church and God.

Second, I was a big patriot. As a youngster, I had read every World War II book in the world and wanted to join the military and become a fighter pilot. I believed in freedom, loved America, and loved what it stood for. However, with the Vietnam War I became disillusioned with my country too. I just started getting the sense that we were being sold out. I thought I was being sold a bill of goods by both my church and my country, and it's almost like I was a child who found out there was no Santa Claus. I felt betrayed and got extremely upset. I gradually came to the conclusion that my country wasn't worth anything; it was full of hypocrites and so was the church. I decided God didn't exist. So, by the time I graduated from high school and entered college, I was an atheist.

As an atheist I took on a very, very wild lifestyle. I was not a passive atheist. I was an atheist who wanted to go about and ruin everybody else's faith, like Saul in the Bible, who wanted to kill Christians. I would go around to anybody I knew who had faith and tell them how stupid they were to believe in God.

I had some very wild friends in the sixties and seventies. I'm not proud of it, but I must admit I did a lot of drugs. One time—and this has to be the epitome of stupidity, but it shows the far reaches of God's grace—some friends and I went to an amusement park. We had taken LSD, and we were tripping out. We got on a roller coaster, and I sat in the front seat. As the roller coaster was beginning to take off, I turned around and looked at everybody else on the ride. They could actually see my face. At the top of my lungs, I yelled, "There is no God! There is no God! If there is a God, I defy Him to strike me dead on this roller coaster ride!"

> I YELLED, "THERE IS NO GOD! THERE IS NO GOD! IF THERE IS A GOD, I DEFY HIM TO STRIKE ME DEAD ON THIS ROLLER COASTER RIDE!"

Those poor people turned white; their eyes were as big as fifty-cent pieces. I'm sure they were thinking, *How did we get on this ride with this nut,* and *We're all going to die!* It freaked everybody out.

When we reached the end of this wild roller-coaster ride, the other riders were all praying and making the signs of the cross. I looked back at them and defiantly said, "See, I told you, there is no God!"

That's just the way I was—a lunatic. A jerk. I lived a life of mocking God. In my room in college, I had a crucifix with the Beatle's "Sgt. Pepper's Lonely Hearts Club Band" poster behind it. I stuck a five-dollar bill between Jesus' legs, and a sign I made said "The Church of You Never Know When You're Going to Go." I was a brazen hellion of a kid who just mocked God. That was me in the wild sixties and seventies.

In 1970, when I was nineteen years old, I was at the University of Cincinnati. After four students were shot and killed by the National Guard during a Kent State war protest, they shut down all the state schools early. When I went home, my brother, brother-in-law, and I decided to go into business. We didn't have anything—our parents were blue-collar workers. Just like the classic American dream, we started in the basement of my brother's home. Our only money was wedding money from my brother-in-law, what we borrowed from my dad, and other loans my brother and I took out. Everything we tried failed. We tried thirteen different things, from a food delivery business to preprinted catalogs, and a pay-only-if-you-sell classified newspaper. You name it, we tried it, and nothing worked!

We were $100,000 in debt and about to go bankrupt when we hit on the idea of selling computerized horoscopes for three bucks. We had people send in their time and place of birth, and we used a huge IBM mainframe computer at our bank to create personal horoscopes. We talked an ad agency guy into extending us credit and ran a nationwide ad in August of 1973. It was a big winner. Here we were in this little ranch home—that's where the whole company was—and in just a few weeks, those ads pulled in $150,000 in cash sales. The mailbags came in full of money—forty-thousand envelopes full of cash and checks. We had money stacked two feet high on eight-foot Formica tables. That was more money than I had ever seen in my entire life. It was amazing.

> THE MAILBAGS CAME IN FULL OF MONEY—FORTY-THOUSAND ENVELOPES FULL OF CASH AND CHECKS. WE HAD MONEY STACKED TWO FEET HIGH ON EIGHT-FOOT FORMICA TABLES.

But there was a price to be paid for all of that success. In October 1973 my brother and I, who had always been close, split. My brother-in-law and I formed one company, and my brother formed another, separate company. Then my sister and brother-in-law got divorced. Our family was ripped apart. It was a terrible loss.

On the outside things looked good. Both businesses were wildly successful—each doing about 3.2 million dollars in sales the next year, so if we had stayed together, we would have gone from $150,000 a year in sales to $6.4 million in a single year. In those days that was huge, huge money. My company had eighty employees, and I was making three hundred thousand dollars a year in salary and bonuses. Based on my net worth, at the age of twenty-three I was a millionaire. By the world's standards, what could be more fulfilling?

But with all of that success, I still felt very empty. Through the years 1968-74, I'd suffered losses that could never be compensated for: my relationship with my brother, the deaths of my mother, my grandfather, and my godfather, and developing friction with my father. But empty or not, success to gain self-worth and love was still all I knew. It's interesting to me now, looking back, because considering the goof-ball I had been, it seems the Lord would have just let me go. Instead, my life took a different turn during that time, as the Lord with His grace and compassion began to draw me back to Him.

In the fall of 1975, I met my future wife Lu Ann. Her aunt wanted her to work at my company, so she invited me to a wedding to meet her, and I went. It was the old "love at first sight." As soon as I saw her, I said, "That's the girl I'm going to marry." And I meant it!

Very shortly thereafter we started dating, and a real weird thing happened to me. The only way I know how to describe it is that it was like becoming a born-again Christian without being born again. Her love inspired me. I told all of my friends I was finished doing drugs. I stopped chasing women, and I didn't hang around my old friends anymore. I just wanted to be with Lu Ann, and I wanted to get married. What's more, I wanted to do it right: no sex before marriage, no drugs, nothing impure.

My friends were surprised. Everyone was asking me, "What has happened to you?" And I remember telling them, "I don't know, but this is the happiest I've ever been in my entire life."

It was bizarre, considering there was no real spiritual transformation, but loving another human being—and being loved—lifted me onto a higher plane. I saw things differently. I wanted my life to be better, and I wanted to make her happy. I actually went back to the Catholic church and went to confession so I could get married in the Catholic church. I remember the priest asked me, "What do you have to confess?" And I said, "You wouldn't even want to know. All I can tell you is that I haven't killed anybody. I don't have time to tell you everything else."

Those years, from 1975 to 1978, were the happiest I could ever remember since I was a child. It was really an incredible miracle—a true outpouring of God's grace. But then my old friends decided to buy a house nearby, catty-corner from us, and I got back into the old life I had known. I started running around with my old friends, smoking pot again, and basically going down the drain. I put my wife through hell, and life wasn't happy anymore.

In the meantime my sister had remarried, and her new husband and she had become born-again Christians. They were planting seeds in our lives about accepting Jesus, and even though I thought they were crazy, I never said anything to put them down, because I loved them.

We had purchased a vacation home out in Jackson Hole, Wyoming. In February of 1979, I was still a pretty cocky guy. I went skiing with some friends, and we went "out of bounds." That's where you go up the tram, to the top of a 10,600 foot mountain, and then you don't come down the regular ski runs. Instead you go off the back of the mountain to ski out of bounds. Well, we took off and immediately got lost in the mountains, in the complete wilderness.

Any skier knows that if you lose a ski and have to sidestep up a mountain for a few yards, it's horribly hard work. When we got lost, we had to start sidestepping, with big heavy skis on, up the sides of mountains, and then when we got over one mountain, there would be another mountain, and then another and another. It was the hardest thing I ever did in my life. Here I was, this big successful millionaire, and my existence was reduced down to one thing. I would look down at my foot and say to myself, "If I can move my ski two feet, then that is a victory." And after I did that, I'd say it again and again and again, trying to make it to the top of the mountain. Each time I made it up one mountain, I thought that if there were another one on the other side, I would lay down and die because I couldn't make it up another one. It seemed like there always was another mountain to climb.

> While this was happening, there was an amazing occurrence deep in my spirit. It was like the rhythm of my heart was beating out, "Jesus, Jesus, Jesus."

While this was happening, there was an amazing occurrence deep in my spirit. It was like the rhythm of my heart was beating out, "Jesus, Jesus, Jesus." I could hear it in my spirit, but at the time I had no idea where it was coming from. "Jesus. Jesus. Jesus." Up through my body and out, over and over—"Jesus."

Five or six hours later, when to my surprise I was still alive and made it back to civilization, I went home, fell down on my knees beside the bed, and said, "Jesus, I thought I was going to die today, but You let me get back home. I'm accepting You as Lord and Savior of my life. I'm sorry for what I've been doing—the pot and all of the mess I've made—and I *promise* I will stop. I want to dedicate my life to You and follow through with my calling to be a minister." That was February of 1979, and that was my salvation experience.

Two weeks later it was St. Patrick's Day, and Lu Ann was pregnant with our first child. I was back at home, and I got high again. Along with that, I drank whiskey and went over to the neighbor's house. They had teenage girls. I wanted to show off, so I took them and their friend for a ride in my 911 Porsche. We were blasting the stereo, and ironically, I remember it was the Cars' song "Let the Good Times Roll" that was playing. I was going one-hundred-twenty miles per hour on a back road when I came to a curve and the car left the road. We were completely airborne. The car flipped end over end and landed on its side. The windshield wipers were going, the song was still playing, and miraculously no one was hurt. And I heard a voice—the closest thing ever to an audible voice of God in my life—and He said, *You broke your promise.*

I got out of the car, and my wife came and picked us up. As we examined the Porsche, a sensation came over me that something supernatural had happened. There were no trees anywhere in sight, and yet it looked as if we had hit two trees. There were two huge dents—one on each side of the rear of the car. All I can figure is that an angel grabbed hold of it in the air and set it down. I could have killed us all, but God, with His great grace and mercy, spared our lives. And He reminded me, *You broke your promise.*

> ALL I CAN FIGURE IS THAT AN ANGEL GRABBED HOLD OF IT IN THE AIR AND SET IT DOWN. I COULD HAVE KILLED US ALL, BUT GOD, WITH HIS GREAT GRACE AND MERCY, SPARED OUR LIVES.

After this near-death experience, I prayed again, and I said, "Okay, Lord. I am so sorry. You have spared my life again, and I'm really going to try to get this right now." For the first time in my life, I began to read the Bible. As I read the Gospel of Matthew and learned about Jesus, I wept for a week straight. I kept saying to myself, "I really like Jesus, everything about Him; I just never knew Him." Then the Lord spoke this to my heart: "Beware the yeast of the Pharisees." Little did I know that these two concepts, that *Jesus is the best* and *beware the yeast of the Pharisees*, would become the guardrails of my Christian walk.

Lu Ann got saved, too, and we started going to church and really walking with the Lord. As we grew and learned more about the Bible and Christianity, I began to really deal with the known sins in my life, like the drugs and cursing. I also realized that the horoscope business was not an appropriate place for a Christian businessman, but we had built up such a high standard of living that I didn't feel I could just drop out of it.

From 1979 to 1981, my plan was to develop other product lines and slowly phase out of the horoscope business. I just did not have the faith to get out without something else to replace it, so I tried to get into other products, like health and fitness. My idea was that as those new areas progressed, the horoscopes would fade out, but it didn't happen. Part of it was because I didn't want to lay people off—I had over 150 employees at the time—and part of it was that I didn't want to change my lifestyle or go bankrupt.

In 1982 I just said, "I can't handle it; I'm a hypocrite doing horoscopes." I knew this was wrong but I was afraid to stop selling them. I did not have the faith. I was ashamed, so I backslid. But just like for Jonah, when he tried to run from God, everything went wrong. I bought a stereo; it blew up. I had a boat down on the Ohio River; the engine blew up. We went back to the marina and put another motor in; it blew up. I had bought another car, an ice-green Porsche Turbo, and it stopped running whenever I drove it down the road. We'd tow it to the garage, and they'd say nothing was wrong. I'd take the car back out, and five minutes later the engine would stop.

Then I started getting sick. I went to a lot of doctors, but nobody could help me; in fact what they did only made things worse. I got back into smoking pot, and things got worse and worse and worse—I mean my life just shut down. It's as if God was saying, You can run, but you cannot hide.

So, being the brilliant guy that I was, after fifteen months of this, in the spring of 1983, I said, "Lord, that's it. I'm making a wholehearted commitment to you." And, this time, finally, I followed through on that commitment. I stopped smoking pot, after trying to quit fifteen times already. This time I really stopped, and my garbage collectors had some of the finest Hawaiian marijuana of anybody in the world, because I got rid of all of it. God gave me victory over it.

I stopped cussing, and I resolved to get out of the horoscopes and answer the call on my life to be a minister.

I thought I'd just kill two birds with one stone and sell the company so I could go into ministry. That way I wouldn't have to worry about money or my employees losing their jobs. But a funny thing happened when I put the company up for sale. For some reason, nobody wanted to buy it. And the Lord told me, *Rick, you birthed it. I don't want you to sell it because it will go on, and it is evil. I want you to kill it. You created it, and you have to be the one to end it.*

I said, "Okay." But I didn't know how. I started down the same path again with fitness, thinking that if I could get a winner with that, then I could just dissolve the horoscope business. And we did get a winner. The first fitness TV winner we did in 1985 was the Trim Track. It shot up like a rocket. But just as I was feeling comfortable that the Trim Track was my ticket out of horoscopes, the rocket came back down. There were no other winners on the horizon, and I lost faith. I started waffling again. It was scary.

Finally the Holy Spirit spoke to my heart. He showed me that my life had been like the parable of the sower. The first seed, which was stolen by the birds of the air, was when as a young person I lost my childlike faith and became an atheist. The second seed—the one that had no root and shriveled up and died—was when I met my wife and changed but then went right back into the old lifestyle. There was never any real change because I had not accepted Jesus as my Savior. The third part of the parable is that there's a plant, but it grows up and gets choked out by the cares and riches of this world. That's what kept happening to me after I was born again, because of the wealth horoscopes had generated for me.

Now, however, the Holy Spirit impressed on me that I had no more chances—there were no more parts to the parable—except to have a pure heart, which would represent good soil. It was either get out of the horoscope business and face possible bankruptcy or lose my own soul in hell. The Lord literally scared the daylights out of me. I knew He wasn't kidding, so I had to make a choice, possible bankruptcy or losing my soul.

So one day in February of 1986—seven years after I got saved—I finally sealed my wholehearted commitment to the Lord. My wife and I took our whole multi-million dollar horoscope business and stuffed it in a big trash can behind our company building. This was a business that had made us rich, and it could have made millions of dollars more in the future. We took all of the ads, all of the computer software, the mailing lists—everything to do with that business—and we poured gasoline on it and burned it. I knew that was the only way to kill it. I didn't trust myself not to go back, so I knew I had to totally destroy it.

After the big bonfire, Lu Ann and I went out to dinner. We expected to have a very spiritual time, to feel like a mighty man and woman of faith, and to celebrate. When the server set our appetizers in front of us, we looked at each other and said, "You know what? We're going to go bankrupt." We lost our appetites, our hearts were completely sick, and we went home.

An amazing thing happened next. There was an exercise product called the Stomach Streamliner sitting around in one of our warehouses. It was in our catalog, but nobody wanted to buy it. Then a TV scriptwriter came in and said, "Do you have any products you think may work on TV?"

When I told him about the Stomach Streamliner, he said, "I kind of like it. Would you give me a shot to write a two minute TV commercial for it?" I was desperate, so I said, "Sure."

He wrote a script, calling the product the "Gut-Buster." This was a play on the movie *Ghostbusters*, which had just come out. We tested it in August of 1986, and the Gut-Buster was one of the biggest mail order winners of all time. In six months we sold 2.2 million of them at $22.95, which brought in fifty million in sales. We actually made nine million dollars of profit in six months off of this one product, and it was as if God were saying, *I told you to get out of the horoscope business a long time ago.* But I had not had the faith to do it. Oh, me of little faith.

> IT WAS AS IF GOD WERE SAYING, I TOLD YOU TO GET OUT OF THE HOROSCOPE BUSINESS A LONG TIME AGO. BUT I HAD NOT HAD THE FAITH TO DO IT. OH, ME OF LITTLE FAITH.

After that we changed the name of the company to Fitness Quest. As Fitness Quest, we pioneered the industry of selling fitness products on television and then in retail stores. We had winner after winner: the Trim Track, Gut Buster, the E-Z Glider and Fit One cross country ski machines, the Abdominizer, and the Jane Fonda Step Aerobics system.

After taking that big leap of faith, burning the horoscopes, and sealing our wholehearted commitment to the Lord, Lu Ann and I were on-fire Christians. The Lord had blessed us, and we were committed to Him. The company was dedicated to the Lord; we had tracts in the lobby to witness to people; we opened up every day with prayer and had two Bible studies a week at work. We were giving thirty percent of our income into the kingdom, with plans to increase it to fifty, and were blessing a lot of people with bonuses and gifts.

Outwardly everything seemed perfect. The conventional Christian formula fit: the more we did for God, and learned about God, the better our lives got. The better we felt about ourselves. We were finally getting it right, we thought. Why had we waited so long?

A plus B equaled C, and Christianity made sense.

But then something happened in the spring of 1987. I guess you could say that's when my unconventional Christianity started. What I thought was going to happen didn't, and it all stemmed from a good intention.

I had a six-foot-four guy test the Gut Buster, and he couldn't go all the way back to do a full sit-up. So I said, "Gee, I want everybody to be able to use the Gut-Buster," and I lengthened the safety cord on it for people like him. It was a good intention, but it caused injury. Some people got hurt as they used it because the spring started breaking when it overextended with the longer safety cord. It would hit people and injure them. A very innocent mistake.

Unfortunately, this very innocent mistake got the attention of the Consumer Products Safety Commission and the Federal Trade Commission. I got into big legal trouble. This was no traffic ticket; it was the federal government, and it was a complete nightmare.

Looking back now, the years from 1987 to 1991 seem like a sort of twilight zone. On the one hand, we were making huge amounts of money. We went from twenty-five million a year to fifty million a year in sales, and then finally from 1990 to '91, the business went from fifty million to one hundred-thirteen million in sales in just one year. We were dedicated to the Lord—giving huge amounts of money to His kingdom as we felt directed.

But with the start of those legal problems in 1987, other things began to go downhill, even as the business grew. For one thing, I started getting sick. I had been a person with supernatural-like energy who never got sick. Then I got the flu—and kept getting it. That turned into Chronic Fatigue Syndrome, which means I was sick and had no energy. It was a disease that was caused by my pushing myself too hard, which resulted in a suppressed immune system. I was living on Coca-Cola, coffee, and aspirins. I still had a big company to run; still had legal problems because once the government gets on you, your problems last a long time; plus I had competitors who filed frivolous lawsuits. Conventional Christianity, the idea that I could put God in a box and A plus B would always equal C, was no longer making a lot of sense. Something was wrong with that picture.

> CONVENTIONAL CHRISTIANITY, THE IDEA THAT I COULD PUT GOD IN A BOX AND A PLUS B WOULD ALWAYS EQUAL C, WAS NO LONGER MAKING A LOT OF SENSE.

In the spring of 1992, I was on a trip, and the Holy Spirit spoke to my heart. I had all of these big plans for managing and expanding my business over the summer, and I felt Him say, *Rick, stop striving. You need to slow down, take the time to do things right, and spend more time with your family. If you don't, come October, when you move into your big mansion and open your 100,000-square-foot new addition to the company, you're going to be in big, big trouble.*

When I got back from the trip, I shared this with my board of directors and I asked for input. One of the thoughts shared at the board meeting was "We have to feed this monster. If we slow down, the business will be adversely affected." And, I made a very poor decision. I thought, "You know, the house is scheduled to be done in August; the new addition to the company is scheduled for completion in August, not October; maybe I didn't hear God right; I better not slow down." I chose to listen to a man instead of God and be influenced by fear instead of having faith.

Well, a not-so-funny thing happened after that. The house was not done in August; it was done in October. The 100,000 square-foot addition was not done in August either; it was done in October. And when October came up the company was in big trouble—just like the Holy Spirit had told me on my trip. I learned this, among other things: in human terms "big" means one thing, but when God says "big," you'd better understand that it means really *BIG*.

All of a sudden, the guy who had the Midas touch—I'd generated hundreds of millions of dollars in sales—could not make a dime. It was like the hand of God turned off a faucet. He told me, *You didn't obey Me, and I'm turning the faucet off. You can get the biggest monkey wrench, with the strongest men in the world to try to turn it back on, but it will not be back on until I say it is time.* And we could not make a dime. We went from doing 113 million in sales, with huge profits in 1991 to breaking even in 1992. We lost 10.8 million dollars in 1993 and were going bankrupt because I didn't obey the voice of the Lord. I listened to man instead of God, and operated out of fear instead of faith—and this time God turned off the faucet.

The year of 1993 was total despair. It was the darkest time of my entire life. For ten years I'd been a poster child for conventional Christianity. Even through trials I hadn't wavered in my commitment, but, in the summer of 1993 I hit a wall. I was sick as a dog, I had huge legal problems, and I was going bankrupt. You know in the Bible, when it talks about famine, plague and sword? I had all three curses at the same time. If I tried to take care of my health and rest, the legal and financial problems were not attended to, and vice-versa. I felt like I was doomed—like there was nothing I could do.

One day I sat down with Lu Ann and my assistant, who had been through everything with us, and I said, "I'm done with God. I don't want anything to do with Him anymore. That's it. I just wanted you to know."

They both acted like they were seeing a ghost. I'd been a spiritual leader for both of them, our company, and in our church—a rock during every storm—and they just couldn't believe their ears. Then a very weird thing happened. At that very moment when I thought I was giving up on God, He reached out to me. He gave me a vision of a canning jar on a shelf—that got my attention—and I said, "Lord, what is that?"

He then spoke to my heart and said, *Rick, that's your spiritual pride. You thought you were some big hotshot Christian, but you just said you were done with Me; you put Me on a shelf, because I didn't perform up to your expectations.*

I realized then, and am still coming to terms with the fact, that He is God. He is not a jar we can take on and off of some shelf. He is in charge—not us. I had begged the Lord to help me—to make my problems go away—and I was doing everything right according to conventional Christianity. But He still said no. Therefore I was ready to be done with Him. But He was not done with me. In His severe mercy, He allowed me to see that *A* plus *B* does not always equal *C*. He said, *Son, let me show you what your real problems are.*

In the fall of that year, the Lord showed me I needed spiritual surgery. (I will share this story in greater detail later in the book, but I will share a little bit of it here.) He wasn't willing just to put a Band-Aid over my problems. I asked Him to search me, and that's when He cut into my heart and showed me that I had drive gone mad. He showed me how I'd been striving to win approval in order to gain the love I desperately longed for. I'd been working so hard to heal my own wounds of rejection that I'd made a disease out of success—an idol. Through spiritual surgery, the Lord started to truly heal me. That's when I began to understand that I was not as big of a hotshot Christian as I thought, and an unconventional brand of Christianity began to take root. As with most physical surgeries, things got worse before they got better. The Lord had to take me to the cross.

We put everything we had—all of the money we'd made—into the company to try to save it. As a Christian I did not want to let it go bankrupt; regardless of my pride, it was against my convictions. However, nothing worked. We were totally broke. It finally got down to the point that if we didn't find a buyer for the company we were going to go bankrupt, and all of these employees whom we cared very, very much about were going to lose their jobs.

I sent my top people out to go find deals, and we ended up getting an offer from Time Warner. I won't go into all of the details, but for the readers who have gone through the pain of betrayal, I want you to know I've been there too. This process felt like a Judas experience. The Lord has healed the hurt of it, and taught me valuable things through it, but it was very difficult. I was forced against my wishes to sell the company out of a 360-145 bankruptcy—if I hadn't taken the deal, everyone would have lost their jobs.

So I took that deal. Almost everyone kept their jobs, the creditors were paid close to 100 percent and remained as vendors to the company—and I lost the company completely. We had to sell our mansion and most of our land; we lost about eighty-five percent of our net worth. I felt betrayed, violated, robbed—stripped of everything. It was all gone. The death of a dream.

After this great loss, the Lord shared something with me that really touched my heart. It was the beginning of a personal resurrection. He said, *All I ever wanted was you, not your performance, and I want you to want Me for Me, not what I can do for you.* Wow, He loves me for me, just the way I am, even if I'm not successful! What's more, the same need exists in *His* heart, to be loved just for Him, not how He can perform for me. This was an amazing and higher form of love—a love that can set a person free from fear and striving! I now understand, that apart from failure and great loss, I never would have found this love, a healing love that I had been seeking my whole life. And I then remembered the very first vision I had as a Christian. I was a little boy, and Jesus took me by the hand to lead me up a mountain road. That's the opening painting of this chapter, and that's what was happening to me; he was taking that little boy who had lost his way in second grade and bringing him to a better place. The journey would not be easy, but the destination of living in a world of love, joy, peace and power would be worth it.

> ALL I EVER WANTED WAS YOU, NOT YOUR PERFORMANCE, AND I WANT YOU TO WANT ME FOR ME, NOT WHAT I CAN DO FOR YOU.

Since that time, the message of Philippians 3:7-11 has become the theme of my life:

> *But what things were gain to me, these I have counted loss for Christ. Yet indeed I also count all things loss for the excellence of the knowledge of Christ Jesus my Lord, for whom I have suffered the loss of all things, and count them as rubbish, that I may gain Christ and be found in Him, not having my own righteousness, which is from the law, but that which is through faith in Christ, the righteousness which is from God by faith; that I may know Him and the power of His resurrection, and the fellowship of His sufferings, being conformed to His death, if, by any means, I may attain to the resurrection from the dead.*

My particular journey to the cross is not a path I would have ever chosen for myself, and I must admit that I didn't handle it well. Through the process I've had to face a lot of ugly things that were inside of me and ask for a lot of forgiveness. And, just as Paul goes on to say in verse thirteen and fourteen, I have not arrived. I am still reaching for the goal, still being transformed. I am still learning what it means to be loved by Him apart from my performance and to love Him back in the same way. Just me and God.

In the end, that is the prize. That is what I gained out of everything I lost: I gained more of Jesus than I ever had before—and in gaining Him I gained a much closer relationship with the Father. And I can honestly say that They are worth it! I'm going to share more of my story throughout the book—how God not only gives us love, joy, and peace *during* our trials, but also the power to change our circumstances to be blessed and be used by Him to bless others.

Here's a tip before we continue our spiritual journey. God created us all differently, and we are all at a different place in our walk with Him. He isn't asking you to be just like me or anyone else. Give God the leeway to take you on your spiritual journey the way He knows best.

My Personal One-on-One Encounter With The Lord

ALSO FOR HOME GROUP DISCUSSION

In what ways is my conventional Christianity not working in my life? Do I believe God may have something more—something better ahead in my journey with Him?

_____
_____

Is my identity and self-esteem attached to my personal success? What areas of my life can I now see that I am striving for success in order to gain love?

_____
_____

The Christian life is all about God's grace. Sometimes His grace comes softly, and other times it is severe—even painful. What are some ways He has demonstrated His grace in my life to this point?

_____
_____

Do I understand that in God's Kingdom, sometimes loss is God's love and it actually represents gain? What examples can I think of in my own life where loss has turned into gain?

_____
_____

REFLECTING ON THE ART

- What did the painting of the hand of Jesus mean to me?
- In what way does the painting that opens this chapter speak to me?
- Did the sketch have an impact on me? If so, how?

_____
_____

The Wisdom of the World Empties the Cross of Its Power

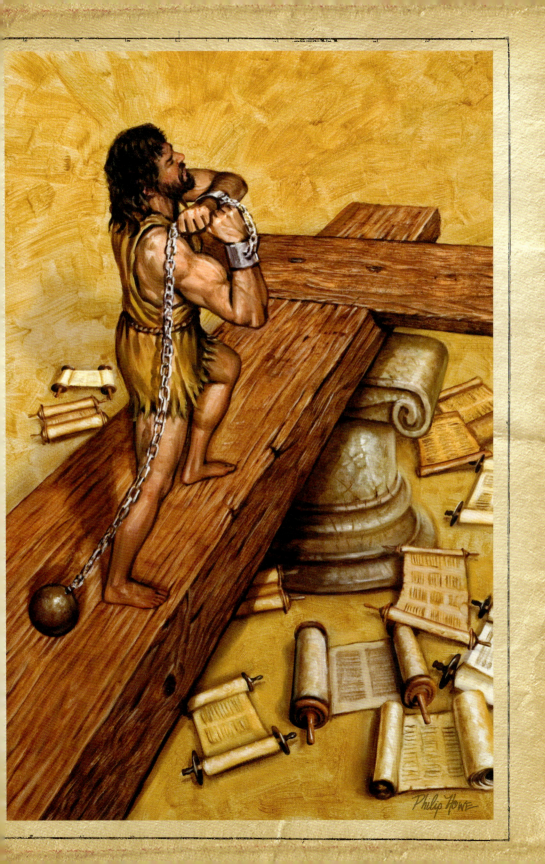

CHAPTER 2

The Wisdom of the World Empties the Cross of Its Power

It's the crime of the century. No, it's the greatest crime of all time! God Himself came down from heaven to die a horrible death to save all of mankind. Jesus' crucifixion and resurrection is the single most important thing for all believers. But somehow, the most important thing in Christianity is no longer the most important thing—it's been lost.

How? The message of the cross has been stolen.

It takes a very clever crook to pull off a heist of this magnitude. Let's continue our spiritual journey by taking on the role of a detective. We'll follow five clues and find out who stole *the message of the cross, which is the first part of the lost secret*. Then, let's find out why and how it was stolen to begin the process of getting God's power back. A world of love, blessings, and fulfilled destiny awaits!

Let's read a few key scriptures to get started. First Corinthians 1:18 (NIV) reads, "For the message of the cross is foolishness to those who are perishing, but to us who are being saved it is the power of God." Paul goes on to say that the "Jews demand miraculous signs and Greeks look for wisdom, but we preach Christ crucified: a stumbling block to Jews and foolishness to Gentiles, but to those whom God has called, both Jews and Greeks, Christ the power of God and the wisdom of God" (vss. 22-24). This verse adds "wisdom" to the description of the cross. And

notice Paul's words in verse 17: "For Christ did not send me to baptize, but to preach the gospel—not with words of human wisdom, lest the cross of Christ be emptied of its power."

If we look at the key words there, *wisdom* and *power*, we see that *Jesus Christ crucified is the wisdom and power of God*. But, the wisdom of the world empties the cross of its power. That's clue number one: the wisdom of the world.

The word empty in that scripture is actually a pretty powerful word. It means "to nullify, to void, and reduce to nothing." The wisdom of the world brings the cross to nothing, or reduces it to nothing.

What is the wisdom of the world? I was walking down the hallway in my daughter Elisha's high school one day and I saw a big sign that summed it up perfectly: *Knowledge is power.* Sounds good, doesn't it? The same message was on CNN the other day. One of their ads said, "In today's world, information is power."

Along those same lines, what age are we living in today? "The Technology Age." And what is technology? The dictionary definition is "applied scientific knowledge." Simply put, technology is knowledge that can do work. When the computer was invented, they took the simple binary system and figured out a way to have a computer apply that scientific knowledge and make it work for people. Technology is knowledge and works.

What the world seems to be saying is that if you have knowledge and work hard, you're going to get power, right? In the natural world it makes a lot of sense. Caring parents instruct their children, "Get a good education, work hard, and you'll do well." The idea is that if you learn something and take what you learn and apply it by hard work, things will go well with you. You'll have power over your own life.

In the natural world, this can be a good formula. Remember, being an education-oriented and hard-working successful person is not bad in itself, but when my self-worth and love come from the success that it brings, that is a bad thing. As we will soon learn, though, taking a principle that works in the world and bringing it into God's kingdom is very destructive.

> AS WE WILL SOON LEARN, TAKING A PRINCIPLE THAT WORKS IN THE WORLD AND BRINGING IT INTO GOD'S KINGDOM IS VERY DESTRUCTIVE.

The wisdom of the world is *knowledge and works*. It's so good that the thief himself uses it! And that's our *second clue*. Let's use that clue to find the next one.

In the Bible, what do the words *knowledge* and *works* describe? Romans 7:7 gives this explanation of the law: "What shall we say then? Is the law sin? Certainly not! On the contrary, I would not have known sin except through the law. For I would not have known covetousness unless the law had said, 'You shall not covet.'" What that verse is saying is that the only way we can understand sin is through the law. Without it we would have no knowledge of right or wrong. The law came to show us the difference.

Galatians 3:12 says another interesting thing about the law. It says, "Yet the law is not of faith, but 'the man who does them shall live by them.'"

Those two scriptures tell us that the law is the knowledge of right and wrong, good and evil, and it involves obeying the commands—doing what is right and not doing what is wrong. Our *third clue is the law, because it's about knowledge and works*. That sounds a lot like the wisdom of the world, doesn't it?

I know we always think of the law as a Judeo-Christian thing, but guess what? The whole world has embraced the concept of the law. Every township, every city, every state, every government has laws—we can go through the entire world without finding an exception. It's not just a Judeo-Christian thing. Everybody has a system of knowledge and works.

But how could the thief—an enemy of the cross and its power—be at work anywhere near God's sacred law? Think for a moment about the Old Covenant and what we know about the Israelites under the law. What was their number one problem? Time and time again we see the same pattern throughout the Old Testament: idolatry. God gave them His love to motivate them and His laws to protect them...but they turned away from these gifts and turned to idols instead. *Idolatry is the fourth clue.*

Throughout the Old Testament (see Deuteronomy 32:21; 1 Kings 16:13,26; 2 Kings 17:12 and 21:11,21) we see how idolatry proliferated under the Old Covenant. Like a great incubator or greenhouse, the law's system was the perfect environment for idols to spring up and grow. Why do you think that was true then? Do you see how it is still true today?

Idols are our own creations. They exist by the work of our minds and hands. Our knowledge plus our work produces idols. In an environment that values works, like the world under the Old Covenant—and like the world we live in today—idolatry is going to be a big problem, and that problem creates the perfect opportunity for the thief.

To find the thief, we need only go one step further. First Corinthians 10:19-21 says, "What am I saying then? That an idol is anything, or what is offered to idols is anything? Rather, that the things which the Gentiles sacrifice they sacrifice to demons and not to God, and I do not want you to have fellowship with demons. You cannot drink the cup of the Lord and the cup of demons; you cannot partake of the Lord's table and of the table of demons." This verse says demons are associated with idols.

Now we are right on the heels of the thief. In Matthew 12:24 (NIV), Satan is called "the *prince of demons.*" If demons are attached to idols, and Satan is the prince of demons, then it follows that *where we have demons, we can find Satan.*

As we connect a few more scriptures, we will find Satan's fingerprints all over the scene of the crime.

CLUE #1: THE WISDOM OF THE WORLD. In John 12:31 (NIV), Satan is called "the prince of this world."

CLUE #2: KNOWLEDGE AND WORKS. In 1 John 4:3, Satan is described as being "the spirit of the Antichrist." If we can be saved through knowledge and works, why do we need Jesus Christ crucified? We don't.

CLUE #3: THE LAW—OLD COVENANT. If the Old Covenant could have brought us into right relationship with God, why would we need a new one? We wouldn't. (See Hebrews 8:7-13.)

CLUE #4: IDOLATRY. First Corinthians 8:1 (NIV) states, "Knowledge puffs up, but love builds up." Under the law, our knowledge puffs up our pride, and instead of resting in the love of God, we build idols out of the work of our own hands. The cause of Satan's fall was pride. He literally wanted to be a god and to become an idol.

CLUE #5: DEMONS. First Corinthians 10:19-21 says that idols have demons attached to them, and where demons are, so is their prince.

Satan, the prince of demons, is the thief who stole the message of the cross.

Why would Satan want to steal the message of the cross from believers today? Remember 1 Corinthians 1:18: "For the message of the cross is foolishness to those who are perishing, but to us who are being saved it is the power of God." *It's all about power!* Now, this is fascinating to me. In Genesis 1:26 the Bible says that as God was creating the world, He said, "Let Us make man in Our image, according to Our likeness; let them have dominion over the fish of the sea, over the birds of the air, and over the cattle, over all the earth and *over every creeping thing that creeps on the earth*" (italics mine).

We know that nothing is in the Word by accident, right? "Creeping thing" is not in there by coincidence. It states that man had dominion

Satan is the Thief

5. Demons

4. Idols

3. Law—Old Covenant

2. Knowledge & Works

1. Wisdom Of World

over everything, including every creeping thing. Guess what the word *creeping* means in Hebrew? It means "to glide swiftly" and "a reptile or any other rapidly moving animal that creepeth."

What does that describe? A snake! In Genesis 3:1, it says, "The serpent [a reptile that glides swiftly and was represented by the devil] was more cunning than any beast of the field." Guess what? In God's original plan He created us to have dominion over Satan. He gave us dominion over this entire world, including Satan, and including all of his demons. That's our God-given birthright!

Why did Satan want man to go to the tree of the knowledge of good and evil in the Garden of Eden? To steal our birthright, which gave us power and dominion over him. He deceived Adam and Eve into thinking that knowledge would make them powerful, like God, but it really took away their power. It gave him power in their lives. That's the why of it.

But Jesus bought it all back for us on the cross. His final words before He died were "It is finished." In a very real sense, Jesus' last words were a death sentence for the enemy: "It is finished" meant, "Satan, you are finished!"

> IN A VERY REAL SENSE, JESUS' LAST WORDS WERE A DEATH SENTENCE FOR THE ENEMY: "IT IS FINISHED" MEANT, "SATAN, YOU ARE FINISHED!"

What a blow! Satan hates the cross. He hates the power it made available for believers and the power it wrested from him. *Satan will do anything he can to try to get that power back.*

We now know who stole the message of the cross and why he did it. If we are to get it back, however—to claim the birthright and power that is ours through the cross of Jesus—we have to figure out what Satan is doing, on a personal level, to lure believers away from the cross. How does he accomplish it?

The Great Deception:
You may have heard the old adage, "Give the devil his due." While we never want to give any glory to Satan or honor him in any way, he is still our enemy, and in this battle for power and victory it pays for us to know something about who we're fighting

against. In John 8:44 (NIV) Jesus provides insight into the character of our enemy. He states, "There is no truth in him. When he lies, he speaks his native language, for he is a liar and the father of lies."

I can't, but imagine I could speak German. If I learned German, and I don't care how much I practiced, if I went to Germany, the people there would still know I'm not a native German. Why is that? I'd have an accent. But if I was raised in Germany, and German was my native tongue, I wouldn't have an accent, right?

That's the way it is with Satan. When he lies, there is no accent. He's the greatest liar in the world. Lying is his native language, so we will never hear an accent when he lies to us. What's the devil's best lie? The ultimate deception for an on-fire Christian is a good intention. Second Corinthians 11:14 tells us that "Satan *disguises himself as an angel of light*" (NASB). One way he does this is to take something good and misapply it and then misdirect us. This is the only thing that will work with a sincere Christian.

> THE ULTIMATE DECEPTION FOR AN ON-FIRE CHRISTIAN IS A GOOD INTENTION.

Think back to the time right after you were first saved. Remember the joy? Remember the excitement? Like being in love, you just can't get enough of that special person—Jesus is your first love. In fact, if you make a wholehearted commitment to Him as Lord, there's only one thing that really appeals to you, one place Satan can attack. For the sincere Christian, the most beautiful, desirable thing is our own service to God. It's the ultimate scam.

We start doing—and striving—and laboring. Satan cheers us on. "This is something good!" He says, "This is pleasing God!" But he misapplies it in our lives, we then put it in a place of preeminence where it doesn't belong, and suddenly we are misdirected. We leave our first love at the cross and go back—back to the wisdom of the world, back to knowledge and works, back to the law. Pretty soon, instead of soaring like eagles, we're caught like a rat on a treadmill: working ourselves to death but powerless, going nowhere. It's a brilliant deception. He has used the wisdom of the world to empty the cross of its power—to nullify, void, and bring to nothing.

In closing, I would like to share how I found the first part of the lost secret, or better put, how it found me. In the fall of 2000, I was sitting in an Applebee's restaurant, having lunch with my friend Steve, when the power of God unexpectedly fell. In my spirit, the Lord asked me a question: "Where is Jesus Christ crucified in the church?" The question was followed by the analogy of scoring a prizefight. The judges at ringside keep track of every blow, and in the end, give a score for each fighter. What if, just in America, every sermon in every church, every TV and radio show, every book and teaching tape, and every conversation between Christians was scored for one year on how many times the cross was mentioned? The answer resounded in my heart like a deafening blow: The cross would lose. Jesus Christ and Him crucified gets a very small percentage of conventional Christianity's time.

> PRETTY SOON, INSTEAD OF SOARING LIKE EAGLES, WE'RE CAUGHT LIKE A RAT ON A TREADMILL: WORKING OURSELVES TO DEATH BUT POWERLESS, GOING NOWHERE.

Then I got a mental vision of God the Father and Jesus standing face to face, looking into each other's eyes. Their faces were full of sorrow. What They were saying was this: "Did We do this for nothing?" The impression was that after the horrible pain and agony They both went through during the crucifixion, no one was really very interested. It was the ultimate act of love on Their parts, but it has somehow lost its place of importance in the church. I was very shaken by this realization and felt moved to action. Thus the seed was planted for this book and the inspiration for the painting on the next page.

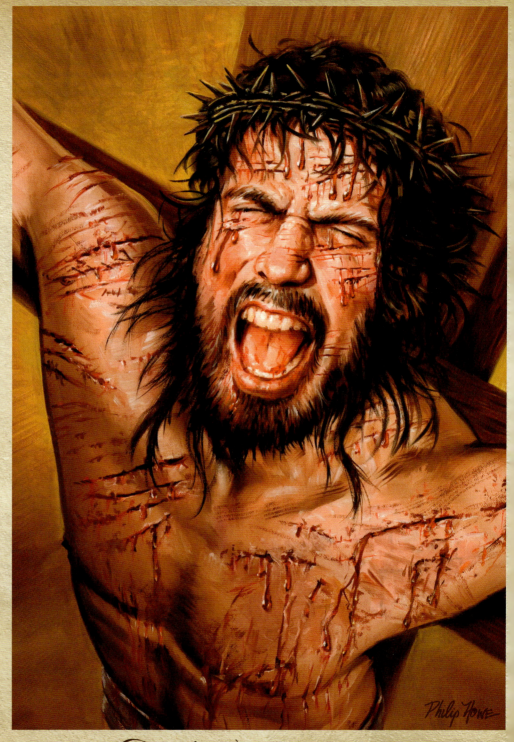

"Did We do this for nothing?"

My Personal One-on-One Encounter With The Lord

Also for Home Group Discussion

Has Satan stolen the message of the cross from me, so that Jesus Christ and Him crucified is no longer the most important thing in my life?
_____
_____
_____

Why did Satan steal the message of the cross?
_____
_____
_____

How did Satan steal it?
_____
_____

What has God shown me about how I'm going to get my stolen birthright back and enter His world of love and power?
_____
_____
_____
_____

Reflecting on the Art

- In what way does the painting that opens this chapter speak to me?
- Did the sketches have an impact on me? If so, how?
- As I look at the painting titled "Did We Do This For Nothing?", what is it saying to me?

_____
_____
_____

Opposite: Inspired by the painting *Pain of the Cross*, by Arthur Robins.

Jesus Took the Law Out of Our Way

CHAPTER 3

Jesus Took the Law Out of Our Way

How could Satan take something that is good and holy, the Law of Moses, and use it against us? He uses the principle of misapplication to cause misdirection. He takes the law, which was good in the Old Covenant, and misapplies it by placing it in the New Covenant. This misdirects us, out of the new and better covenant, back into the old.

I remember the day the Lord began to change this misdirection in my life. He spoke this to my heart, "For you and the church, the Law doesn't exist anymore." I was both shocked and offended. But this was the day that I came to understand a very important principle. The biggest stumbling block on the path of my spiritual journey would be Jesus Himself! Why? Because 1 Peter 2:8 says that Jesus is "a stone of stumbling and a rock of offense." The Gospels show time and time again how Jesus offended those He was teaching. That's because Jesus had a multifaceted personality. He was compassionate, full of wisdom, and many other things, but He was also a straight-shooter when He spoke, which offended many people. I have now come to know, that if I am not being challenged on a regular basis in my Christian walk, I am not going to get all that Jesus has for me.

So back to my offense. As I studied the scriptures, I found that even though I was challenged, what He said to me was true. There are several scriptures throughout the New Testament that back this up. Perhaps the most plain and simple, however, is Romans 10:4 (NIV), which says, "Christ is the end of the law so that there may be righteousness for everyone who believes."

Jesus brought the law to an end by fulfilling it. He was the only person who ever lived on earth but was without sin, so His sinless life fulfilled the law (1 Peter 2:21-24). Then when He died on the cross, He bore every sin and curse, and defeated every demon (Galatians 3:13, Colossians 2:15). As a result, He took the law that was against us out of our way, so we could become part of His body and return to our Father in heaven (Colossians 2:14, 1 Corinthians 12:27).

The written law that involves knowledge and works has been replaced with faith in Jesus that expresses itself through love (Galatians 5:6 NIV, paraphrased). Through a new covenant, and with grace and faith, He writes the law of love in our hearts. In Romans 13:10 Paul writes, "Love does no harm to a neighbor; therefore love is the fulfillment of the law." *But it is an internal law of love.* God gives us the ability to obey it because He's given us new hearts.

> THIS CHALLENGING TRUTH—THAT CHRIST IS THE END OF THE LAW FOR BELIEVERS—IS ACTUALLY ONE OF THE MOST COMFORTING TRUTHS IN SCRIPTURE.

This challenging truth—that Christ is the end of the law for believers—is actually one of the most comforting truths in Scripture. Let's look at some of the things the Bible tells us about the law to see just how scary the law can be—and how blessed we are that Jesus came and fulfilled it, to take it out of our way.

The number one truth about the law is that it can't get rid of sin; it can only expose it and increase it. Romans 5:20 says, *Moreover the law entered that the offense might abound. But where sin abounded, grace abounded much more.*

Let's take a real life situation for an example. Imagine a backcountry road with no stop signs, no traffic lights, one speed limit of fifty-five miles per hour, and there are hardly any police patrolling it. Here we see the presence of very little law. How many traffic tickets would a person get on that road? Few. However, if we take that same road and add the law—more signs, lights, different speed limits every quarter mile, and policemen all over the place—what happens? There would be more violations and more tickets. This is how the law increases sin.

Another troubling truth about the law is found in Romans 7:5, which states, *For when we were in the flesh, the sinful passions which were aroused by the law were at work in our members to bear fruit to death.* Our flesh is actually aroused by the law. This can be observed in any group of people, even toddlers.

Imagine putting a group of little children in a room with every toy imaginable. There are cookies, candy, television, videos—anything a child could want to keep him occupied for a long time. On the way out of the door, the adult in charge says, "You kids have a blast! But, now, I want to tell you one thing. See that drawer over there? Do not open that drawer. You can do anything you want in this room, but *do not* open that drawer."

What do you think would happen as soon as the adult was out of the room? There's no doubt about it—that law would arouse their passions, and they would go straight to that drawer and open it. If nothing had ever been said about the drawer, they would probably never think of it, but that's what the law does in our lives. It arouses our passion to want to sin.

It gets worse. Romans 3:10 tells us that no one can obey the law. "There is none righteous, no, not *one*." That scripture covers everybody… there is not one person who can obey the law…nobody is good. Even a super-duper, hotshot spiritual giant who could almost obey the entire law falls short because no one is righteous. And, James 2:10 says, "For whoever shall keep the whole law, and yet stumble in one point, he is guilty of all." That's terrible, or at least it would be if we were still under the law. It's a system everyone fails under.

I believe God gives us all of these verses in order to help us—to show us just how scary life can be under the law, so that we will want to run away from the law and run to the cross.

> GOD IS TRYING TO GET THIS MESSAGE ACROSS: THE LAW IS AGAINST US, BUT THE CROSS IS FOR US.

God is trying to get this message across: The law is against us, but the cross is for us. Let's look at Galatians 3:10: "For as many as are of the works of the law are under the curse; for it is written, 'Cursed is everyone who does not continue in all things which are written in the book of the law, to do them.'" Everybody under the law is cursed, because nobody can obey the law.

One day the Holy Spirit spoke to my heart and said, *Rick, the law is not your friend.* Consider this scenario: You're driving down the highway at night, listening to some music, really enjoying yourself. Maybe you're on a date with a special person, going out to dinner, and all of a sudden you see flashing lights in your rearview mirror. Is your first thought, "Oh, what a friendly officer. He probably sees that my gas cap is off, and he's just stopping me so he can assist me"? No. For most people, the first thought that would come to mind is "Oh no! I'm in trouble!" Even though policemen are supposed to be our friends, that's not how we typically think of them when we're getting pulled over, is it?

Jesus is our friend. Colossians 2:14 says, "[He has] wiped out the handwriting of requirements that was against us, which was contrary to us. And He has taken it out of the way, having nailed it to the cross." Something contrary to us—the law—is not our friend. It is against us. But the cross is for us.

If the law is against us, why do we love it so much? Think of all of the television shows and movies about the law, not to mention media coverage of court cases and other issues with the law. As a culture we are infatuated with the law. Why? The answer is that the law is about us—what we know, what we can do. Even Christians love the law because by it we can identify and measure, "This is what I know about God…. This is what I do for God…. I'm holy because…. I'm a Godly person…." It's all about us. That's the snare of the law.

> AS A CULTURE WE ARE INFATUATED BY THE LAW, BECAUSE IT'S ABOUT US—WHAT WE KNOW, WHAT WE CAN DO.

The cross is all about Jesus. Before the cross we are stripped bare. Our righteousness is as filthy rags. We are nothing. All we have at the cross is our need for a savior—and under the New Covenant, we have one. By grace we are saved through faith in Jesus, who puts the law of love in our hearts—not a set of outward rules to follow but a relationship, an inward life led by His Spirit. Jeremiah 31:33 puts it this way: "This is the covenant that I will make with the house of Israel after those days, says the

Lord: I will put My law in their minds, and write it on their hearts; and I will be their God, and they shall be My people."

There is another reason we love the law, and its source is very sinister. A seed has been planted by Satan in every human that causes us to lust after the law. To understand the huge and scary ramifications of this, we must go back to the Garden of Eden.

Based on Genesis 1:26-28, every human has a God-given birthright that says we are made in God's image and likeness to live in His presence, have dominion over the earth and Satan, and to be blessed.

> Then God said, "Let Us make man in Our image, according to Our likeness; let them have dominion over the fish of the sea, over the birds of the air, and over the cattle, over all the earth and over every creeping thing that creeps on the earth." So God created man in His own image; in the image of God He created him; male and female He created them. Then God blessed them, and God said to them, "Be fruitful and multiply; fill the earth and subdue it; have dominion over the fish of the sea, over the birds of the air, and over every living thing that moves on the earth."

When Satan tempted Adam and Eve to fall, he did it to steal our birthright. That's why from deep within our spiritual DNA comes what I call a *Divine Dissatisfaction*. We look at the state of our lives and the church and have an inner knowing that God intended for things to be much better. We cry from our hearts, "Where's the love?" and "Where's the power?" This Divine Dissatisfaction is not about grumbling; if it was, it wouldn't be divine. It's modeled by David in the Psalms, who cried out to God day and night to be delivered from his troubles, but praised God at the same time. The church seems full of two types of people: those who grumble and complain, wallowing in their troubles, and others who work at tolerating their troubles, trying to keep their spirits up by praising and thanking God. David was different. He had a Divine Dissatisfaction and praised God, both at the same time—that's one of the reasons he was the only person in the Bible described as a man after God's own heart.

So how did Satan steal our birthright? We gained some understanding in the last chapter when we discovered how he stole the message of the cross, but let's plunge in further. God told Adam and Eve not to eat of the tree of the knowledge of good and evil, and if they did they would die (Genesis 2:17). But Satan said, "You will not surely die. For God knows that in the day you eat of it your eyes will be opened, and you will be like God, knowing good and evil" (Genesis 3:4-5). Satan planted two seeds. "First, God is holding out on you; if He really loved you He would want you to be like Him—God isn't good! Second, who you are now is not good enough, you need to become something better—you are inferior!"

These seeds caused Eve to lust after the law. She looked at the tree, saw that it was good for food, pleasant to the eyes, and a tree desirable to make one wise (Genesis 3:6). She lusted for the knowledge of good and evil (the law), believing it would make her better—not inferior anymore—and give her the ability to take care of her own problems since she couldn't trust God. But guess what? It didn't work. She and Adam sinned, fell, and lost their birthright. They lost their face to face relationship with God, their rulership over the earth, and their world that was filled with blessings became infiltrated with curses. But deep inside, we remember what it was like before the Fall.

Satan's temptation produced the deadly sequence of a lie, a lust, and a loss. A lie that God is not good and I'm not good enough. A lust after knowledge and works to strive for success to gain self-esteem and take care of my own problems. The result was a loss of living in God's presence, with dominion over the earth along with abundant blessings.

I know this sequence very well. When I was told that my birth was an accident, I concluded that since I wasn't wanted, there must be something wrong with me. That was the lie that triggered my lust to strive for success. I'd show the world that I was very valuable; but eventually came the loss of my health, relationships, and my business. But as I died to self, God raised me from the ashes. He told me the truth, that I was wonderful. I replaced my striving with faith and reliance on Jesus, and I began to gain my God-given birthright back. What He did for me, He will do for you also.

Let's look at the New Testament to discover more about this sequence. Did you know there are three laws mentioned in the Bible? I didn't until it was revealed to me in the book of Romans, in chapter 7:21-25 and 8:2. It says there is the law of God (which is the law of Moses), the law of sin and death, and the law of the Spirit of life in Christ Jesus—three laws. With this in mind, let's look at Satan's deadly sequence and see how Jesus reversed it.

Romans 8:15 says we did not receive a spirit that makes us a slave again to fear. Satan's lie, that says God is not good, causes us to fear—we worry that God won't be there for us when we have problems. Along with fear, Satan also tells us we're inferior, that there's something wrong with us. That lying spirit creates a lust for the law, which is knowledge and works, to gain self-esteem and take care of our own problems. Instead of putting our faith in Jesus and entering His rest, we become toiling slaves! It gets worse. Romans 7:8-9 and 1 Corinthians 15:56 say that apart from the law, sin can't exist. The law literally powers sin and brings it to life. So the law we lust after brings sin to life. Finally, the Bible says sin causes death; in fact, it's called the law of sin and death. Just like the law of gravity causes an object to fall every time, sin brings demons, curses, and death every time.

But now for the good news. The law of the Spirit of life in Christ Jesus has set us free from the law of sin and death! This too involves a sequence. Romans 8:15-16 says we have received the Spirit of adoption by which we cry out "Abba, Father." In fact, God Himself bears witness with our spirits that we are His children. I'm not inferior, I'm the child of a good and wonderful God, made in His image and likeness. I don't have to strive to earn self-esteem, I'm content. I don't have to worry and work at taking care of my problems, He is there for me. In fact, Jesus defeated every sin, every demon, and every curse on the cross; I just need to put my faith in Him.

Romans 7:1-6 clearly states the law only has authority over me as long as I live. Once I die to self, by being baptized into Jesus' death, I get delivered from the law. No more law means no more sin. Romans 6:5-7, 14 says, *For if we have been united together in the likeness of His death, certainly we also shall be in the likeness of His resurrection, knowing this, that our old man was crucified with Him, that the body of sin might be done away with, that we should no longer be slaves of sin. For he who has died has been freed from sin...For sin shall not have dominion over you, for you are not under law but under grace.* The words *be done away with* in verse 6 mean *to be rendered inoperative.* Apart from the law, which is knowledge and works, the law of sin and death can't exist!

To really understand it, think of dandelions. If you just chop them down they'll always grow back and ruin your lawn. They must be taken out from the roots. The root of the dandelion takes up the lie from hell that says "God is not good and I'm not good enough." That lie fills the stem with a lust for the law, a desire to use our knowledge and works to gain self-esteem and solve our own problems. The law brings life to the flower, causing the law of sin and death to bloom. No root, no stem, no flower—that's the way to beat dandelions. No lie, no law, no sin—that's the way to beat the law of sin and death.

To summarize, here are the two sequences. One represents death, and the other life—here on earth and for all eternity.

Source of Sin, Satan's Dominion, and Curses

1. A LIE that produces a judgment that God is not good and I'm inferior.

2. A LUST for the law to use my knowledge and works to achieve success to gain self-esteem and solve my own problems.

3. A LOSS of my birthright, living in His presence, dominion over the earth, and blessings—because the law of knowledge and works brings the law of sin and death into existence.

Source of Righteousness, Man's Dominion, and Blessings

1. THE TRUTH that God is good and wonderful. I'm made in His image and likeness, so that makes me wonderful, not inferior in any way—I'm content with who I am.

2. FAITH in the fact that Jesus died on the cross to defeat every sin, demon, and curse, so I don't have to earn my own righteousness and solve these problems.

3. I GAIN BACK my birthright, my relationship with Him, my dominion on the earth, and my blessings. The law of the Spirit of life in Christ Jesus has set me free from the law of sin and death—it has become inoperative.

The truth that God is good and we're wonderful, and faith in Jesus' work on the cross, is our access door to the wonderful world of our birthright...our passageway from death to life!

Here are two final thoughts. First, how powerful is Satan's lie, the seed he plants in every human that God isn't good and we're inferior, to get us to lust after the law? We think of our struggle against Satan living in this fallen world as we deal with our own fallen flesh. But Adam and Eve bought into the devil's lie when they were not fallen and living in paradise in the very presence of God! That's a sobering and humbling truth. We humans are very susceptible to buying that lie and then judging both God and ourselves. And we humans love the law very much, even though it doesn't like us. That's why the Lord wants to get that lie out of us and get us out of the law, so He can put us back into His wonderful world full of love and power.

Second, individuals react to the lie that God isn't good and I'm inferior differently. I wanted to achieve great success to gain self-esteem. My wife, on the other hand, gained her self-esteem through service—she would do anything for anybody, and literally took on a slave mentality. Others think that if God is not good, and they're inferior, then what's the point of trying to achieve anything. This is where many self-destructive addictions enter in like drugs and alcoholism—or simply escapism, like watching lots and lots of movies, or playing video games all of the time. The three groups all seem different, but there's one thing that they all have in common: they're all lusting after and addicted to something. But, what my wife and I lusted after never brought us self-esteem, and what the other group lusts after never gets rid of their pain.

In closing, now that we've seen through Scripture the fear—and futility—of a life under the law, we must keep things in balance. First, the law was from God, making it good and spiritual. The problem is no one is good, so no one could obey the law. So second, God used the law like a governess, to watch over children until they were of age to receive their inheritance. Think of it as a placeholder until the new and better covenant would arrive. During that wait, the law pointed out the utter sinfulness of sin, and our desperate need for a savior. A salvation based on grace and faith, and not by works. Finally, the New Covenant replaces the written law by writing the law of love in our hearts—a New Covenant, a new heart, a new creation in Christ!

We now know that even though the law was good, it was against us. But the cross is for us. In fact, Romans 8:31-32 says God chose to give us all things through His Son: "What then shall we say to these things? If God is for us, who can be against us? He who did not spare His own Son, but delivered Him up for us all, how shall He not with Him also freely give us all things?" The Bible says, "God is for us." The proof that God is for us is that He gave His only Son to die on the cross for us, through that act freely giving us all things. This is the New Covenant, the new system under which we cannot fail because Jesus has done it all for us. He came, fulfilled the law, and then died in our place so that we can live in power and victory. The law, with its system of knowledge plus works, simply doesn't exist for us anymore. Our power does not come from knowledge or works. It flows freely from the cross of Christ. As the opening painting depicts, one greater than Moses is here! That's why our focus should not be on the old and inferior covenant, but instead, we should look to the new and superior one (Hebrews 3:1-3; 8:6-13).

Let's continue our spiritual journey and discover how to break out of the bondage that is the law, by experiencing a transformation, like a caterpillar into a butterfly.

> The law, with its system of knowledge plus works, simply doesn't exist for us anymore. Our power does not come from knowledge or works. It flows freely from the cross of Christ.

My Personal One-on-One Encounter With The Lord

Also for Home Group Discussion

How do I feel about the fact that the law cannot get rid of sin—it can only expose and increase it?
_____
_____

Do I realize that not one person, in and of themselves, is able to obey the whole law?
_____
_____

Have I discovered that if I stumble at just one point of the law, I am guilty of all of it?
_____
_____

For all of the reasons above, do I now believe that the law is against me, but the cross is for me?
_____
_____

How has the lie, the lust, and the loss played out in my life?
_____
_____

Reflecting on the Art

- In what way does the painting that opens this chapter speak to me?
- Did the sketch have an impact on me? If so, how?

_____
_____
_____

The Manifesto

Every human being has a God-given birthright to live in a world of relationship love and rulership power. It's a world of supernatural love, joy, and peace even in the midst of trials. And, there's supernatural power for victory over sin, Satan, and curses, to be blessed and fulfill our destiny to bless others.

A manifesto is a public declaration of intention by an important person or group. An example would be the Declaration of Independence for the United States. This is *the* manifesto, because the Lord is the most important person and group (Trinity) in the entire universe. This is His manifesto. This is the freedom we have through the cross of Jesus!

How would embracing this manifesto affect my life?
_____
_____

Do you have a Divine Dissatisfaction? Do you know deep in your heart there's got to be more to God than conventional Christianity is presenting, as you cry "Where's the love?" and "Where's the power?" Are you ready to get your God-given birthright back? If so, I strongly encourage you to read the following scriptures in sequence and ask the Holy Spirit to show you personally how Jesus took the law out of your way. Those who have done so say that it was a life-changing experience. Romans 3:10 – 8:17, Galatians 3:1 – 4:7, Colossians 2:4-23, Galatians 4:21 – 5:25, Galatians 6:12 – 16, Colossians 3:1 – 11, Romans 10:1 – 10, Hebrews 7:1 – 10:17

_____
_____
_____

Am I a Caterpillar Christian?

CHAPTER 4

Am I a Caterpillar Christian?

WHAT IS A CATERPILLAR CHRISTIAN? Let's explore a concept found in Philippians 3:10-11. In these verses we hear the cry of Paul's heart: "that I may know Him and the power of His resurrection, and the fellowship of His sufferings, being conformed to His death, if, by any means, I may attain to the resurrection from the dead."

If we break this down in the Greek, the word *fellowship* means "to partner." *Sufferings* is the word "passion," just like the *Passion of the Christ* or the "passion play." The phrase *to be conformed to His death* comes from two Greek words, *sum morphos*, *sum* meaning "union" and *morphos* being the same root as our English word, *metamorphosis*. In order to truly know Jesus and experience the power of His resurrection, we must undergo a metamorphosis. And that metamorphosis is like the transformation a caterpillar makes when it changes into a butterfly.

With that in mind, let's think about this image of a butterfly and the four stages of its life. It starts out as an egg, the egg hatches into a caterpillar, the caterpillar goes into a cocoon, and then in the last stage it emerges out of the cocoon as a beautiful butterfly. Those four stages are the same four stages we have in our Christian lives, only most Christians are stuck in stage two as Caterpillar Christians.

If we compare the first stage of a butterfly's life cycle to the Christian life, the egg represents being a born-again Christian. That egg didn't do anything to be born; it was just placed on a leaf. Being born again is not about what we do or earn, it's a free gift. Ephesians 2:8-9 says, "For by grace you have been saved through faith, and that not of yourselves; it is the gift of God, not of works, lest anyone should boast."

At this stage our focus is all on Jesus Christ and Him crucified. We recognize there's nothing we can do to get to heaven. We're humble and helpless, knowing we're sinners in need of a savior. When we believe that He personally died for us and receive His free gift of salvation, there's a tremendous sense of awe and new beginning, like a tiny baby coming into the world. It's great. And then comes stage two.

At the next stage, that egg pops, and out comes a caterpillar. Caterpillars are busy, busy creatures. They have so much to do—so many leaves to eat. We see them in trees just munching away on the foliage like they can't get enough. This is similar to many born-again Christians. A whole new world has opened up, and the born-again Christian cannot get enough of it.

Imagine five majestic trees, the most beautiful oak trees ever created in the world. They are tall, with strong branches that stretch far and wide, inviting children to swing on them, build tree houses, or play underneath their shade. Their leaves are lush and green, luxuriant. A caterpillar's dream. Imagine that the first tree represents the Word of God; the second tree, prayer; the third tree is praise and worship; the fourth tree, fellowship; and the fifth tree is ministry. Like a caterpillar, a new Christian just can't get enough of these five majestic trees. We love them all, so we go from tree to tree, just munching away on all of those delicious things they have to offer.

> UNLESS WE HANG FROM THE TREE, WE WILL NEVER BE RAISED FROM THE DEAD, TO LIVE IN NEW LIFE AS A BUTTERFLY.

But what does the caterpillar do after it has munched awhile? It goes on into stage three, and it spins a cocoon and hangs from the tree. It stops doing all of the activity and retreats from this big glorious world into its cocoon. As it hangs there on the tree, an observer might say it looks dead. There's no motion, no apparent life; it's brown and dead-looking. But guess what? That apparent death process was God's design for the caterpillar,

His way of transforming it into a new creation—a butterfly! Stage four means soaring on wings in the new life of a butterfly.

What do those stages represent for the born-again Christian? Well, unless we hang from the tree, sharing in His sufferings and having a transforming union with His death, we will never be raised from the dead to live in new life as a butterfly. And sadly, most Christians never become butterflies. Most of us are stuck in stage two, as Caterpillar Christians.

Stage two is necessary. God designed it for the caterpillar just like He designed it for us. The problem comes when a person stays in that stage too long. What would happen if a caterpillar just stayed in those trees feeding and never became a butterfly? What would it become? A big, ugly caterpillar. We're going to see why Satan wants to keep Christians stuck in stage two.

Let's take a look at the graph on the next page that describes the wisdom of the world. Think of sales and profits as the arrow going upward. Now, honestly and truly, if you owned a business, which one of these graphs would you choose? The one on the top or the one on the bottom? Of course, everyone would choose the one on the top. It's the way of Wall Street. It's brutal. They want it constant—every quarter, every year—increased sales, increased profits. That's all Wall Street cares about. You miss a blip and your stocks are going to go down. That's the wisdom of the world, the environment in which we live.

The church exists within this environment, and just like yeast in a lump of dough, that way of thinking has infiltrated and leavened the church. The wisdom of the world has essentially told the church, "If you continue to learn more about God and do more things for God, you will become a better Christian."

The result is that the church is full of very sincere Christians who are stuck as Caterpillar Christians, constantly wanting to learn more about God and do more things for Him. We see all of these books, teaching tapes, shows, seminars, and on and on, things that are good in and of themselves, but misdirected, they become like an addiction. Caterpillars Christians have to munch up more and more and more of this stuff because they believe the more they know, and the more they do, the better Christians they will be. It's the world's formula—knowledge and works—the wisdom of the world. Pretty soon, in all of this, the cross of Christ is forgotten.

Wisdom of the World

3. Big Ugly Caterpillar

2. Caterpillar

1. Egg

Wisdom of God

4. Butterfly

2. Caterpillar

3. Cocoon

1. Egg

World's Progress

God's Progress

Look at the graph with the caterpillar, though, on the previous page. It goes from the egg, up to the caterpillar, and then down into the cocoon to be still and die. Then it goes back up into the butterfly stage. It doesn't keep on munching and moving. This is God's wisdom.

We've discovered that Satan's strategy is to take something good, misapply it, and then misdirect it. But how do you deceive a sincere Christian? You can't dangle obvious sins in front of that person and expect him to fall. It's not going to work with one who has made a whole-hearted commitment to the Lord. The way to deceive a sincere Christian is to take something good, something that looks like God, and misapply it. Play on that person's good intention. Then misdirect him. The ultimate deception for the sincere Christian is a good intention. I know this from personal experience, because that's what happened to me. I brought my business success mentality into my Christian walk. I personally was going to be the very best Christian I could be; that was my good intention. The only problem was the "I." Notwithstanding my sincerity, I forgot that it was about Jesus, and not about me.

What happens if, with all of our good intentions about serving God, we get stuck as Caterpillar Christians? I believe there are five main results.

The first thing that happens is spiritual pride. 1 Corinthians 8:1 (NIV) says, "Knowledge puffs up, but love builds up." What does all of my continuing knowledge about God produce in me? Pride. I get puffed up. I start resting and relying on what I know about God and what I do for God, as opposed to what Jesus Christ did for me, and I get puffed up. I forget about my roots as a sinner, and all of a sudden I am self-righteous, and I get very, very puffed up.

That's very prevalent in the church. If we think about it, that's why we're not very good witnesses all of the time, because we're these puffed-up, self-righteous Christians. The poor sinner out there looks at us and says, "I can never relate to these people." Stuck in stage two as Caterpillar Christians, we get full of spiritual pride, and the world can't relate to us. God wants to save the world, and that's why he hates pride. It's one of the deadly sins.

The second thing that sets in is idolatry. Remember those five majestic trees? Those beautiful places where we as Caterpillar Christians hang out? They become more important than God Himself and actually

The Five Majestic Trees

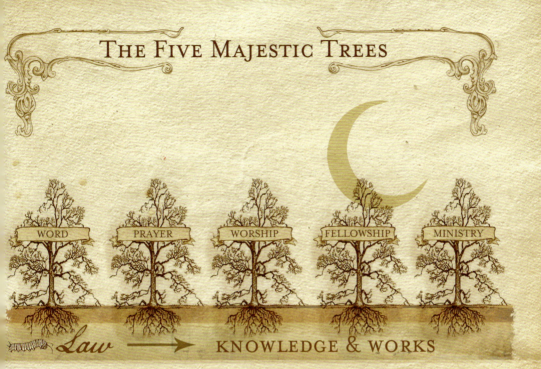

become idols. Even wonderful things from God (like the Bible, prayer, worship, fellowship, and ministry) can become idols if we make them more important than Jesus Christ crucified in our lives.

An example of how this can happen was told by a missionary friend of mine. He was traveling on a plane going to Africa when the Lord spoke to him and said, *You have a high place in your heart.*

He knew that a *high place* is an Old Testament term for idolatry—that the Israelites worshipped idols in the high places—and he was instantly pierced in his spirit and asked the Lord, "What is it?"

The Lord answered, *It's your ministry. Your ministry that I have called you to has now become more important than I am to you. No matter how great it is, no matter how many people get saved and no matter how many needy people get fed, never, ever, ever put ministry ahead of Me. Don't put anything ahead of Me, even if it is something from Me, because I'm God, and I'm jealous.*

Of course I am not writing against mission ministry or any of those things of God we see in the five majestic trees. I love the things of God and spend a lot of my time participating in them. But the key for me, just like for you, and just like for my missionary friend, is *priorities*. Jesus takes it a step further in Matthew 10:37-38, where He says (paraphrased), "Whether it's mothers, fathers, sisters, brothers, children, anything—don't put anything ahead of Me. Nothing is ahead of Me because I'm God."

Anything we put before the Lord is an idol. What is an idol? An idol is a false god. It's something you think is getting you to God but really isn't. In the case of the caterpillar, all of those lovely leaves we munch in the five majestic trees can become idols. As we see in the sketch, when this happens, those majestic trees shrivel up and become less effective. But when Jesus is in His rightful place of preeminence above those trees, and they are firmly anchored to the gospel of Christ crucified, they then flourish and become extremely effective.

> THE VERY THING I BELIEVED WOULD BRING ME CLOSER TO GOD, IS ACTUALLY CARRYING ME AWAY FROM HIM.

A third thing happens when we stay caterpillars too long. The more we know about God and the more we do for God, the less we need God. Isn't that strange? Why is that true? Because, if my holiness depends on my knowledge and works, then I can attain a self-righteousness apart from the cross. I come to believe that I don't need God, so the very thing I am striving to do, the very thing I believed would bring me closer to God, is actually carrying me away from Him. That's the misdirection.

Look at Luke 18:9-14, which says, *Also He spoke this parable to some who trusted in themselves that they were righteous, and despised others: "Two men went up to the temple to pray, one a Pharisee and the other a tax collector. The Pharisee stood and prayed thus with himself, 'God, I thank You that I am not like other men—extortioners, unjust, adulterers, or even as this tax collector. I fast twice a week; I give tithes of all that I possess.' And the tax collector, standing afar off, would not so much as raise his eyes to heaven, but beat his breast, saying, 'God, be merciful to me a sinner!' I tell you, this man went down to his house justified rather than the other; for everyone who exalts himself will be humbled, and he who humbles himself will be exalted."* The key phrase in this story is there in verse nine: they "trusted in themselves that they were righteous." Caterpillar Christians that are stuck in that phase become self-righteous. They begin to believe the lie that "the more I learn about God and the more things I do for God, the more it will help me become like God." Sounds familiar, doesn't it. We talked earlier about how Satan beguiled Eve in the garden. What did he say? "For God knows that in the day you eat of it your eyes will be opened, and you will be like God, knowing good and evil" (Genesis 3:5).

The knowledge of good and evil will make us like God, but here's an amazing truth the Holy Spirit shared with me: I don't want to be God. I want God to be me. There's a big difference. I don't want to be God; I want to be crucified with Christ, so that it's no longer I who live, but Christ who lives through me. I want God to be me, to flow through and work through me.

Knowledge and works is an attempt by man, no matter how sincere, to become God. The message of the cross is the opposite. It says, "I die, and God becomes me." There is a night and day difference between the two!

Remember in Applebee's restaurant, when Jesus and the Father were looking at each other, and they said, "Did We do this for nothing?" Galatians 2:20 says, "I have been crucified with Christ; it is no longer I who live, but Christ lives in me; and the life which I now live in the flesh I live by faith in the Son of God, who loved me and gave Himself for me." Look what comes next, in verse 21: "I do not set aside the grace of

God; for if righteousness comes through the law [knowledge and works], then Christ died in vain." The phrase "in vain" in the Greek means "for nothing." Without knowing it, the lifestyle of a stuck Caterpillar Christian says, "Jesus died for nothing."

If I, as a Christian, could attain self-righteousness, if I could advance my holiness by learning more about God and doing more things for God, if that's the end of my Christianity, then guess what? I head totally away from God, totally away from grace, and go completely in an opposite direction. I do not get closer to God; I get farther away from God. Unfortunately, the existing church produces a lot of Caterpillar Christians, because that's the environment we're in…but God is changing that. A well-known prophetic voice says that God spoke to him and his friends twenty years ago and said the cross is going to become popular again. I believe that's true—that it has to be true—because we're all headed in the wrong direction.

The fourth bad thing that happens to Caterpillar Christians is division. When what I know about God and what I do for God is different from what you know about God and do for God, there's an instant division. We start arguing about who is right and wrong.

> CATERPILLAR CHRISTIANS DON'T JUST EAT THE LEAVES OFF THOSE FIVE TREES, THEY EAT EACH OTHER.

A person focused on the cross doesn't do that. The message of the cross says, "Nobody is right. That's why Jesus died, because nobody is right; there is none righteous." Knowledge and works will always produce strife, but if we embrace the message of the cross, we can be in unity.

In Galatians 5:15 Paul warns, "If you bite and devour one another, beware lest you be consumed by one another!" That seems to fit perfectly with the image of the caterpillar. They are always eating leaves. Caterpillar Christians just take it one step farther. They don't just eat the leaves off those five trees, they eat each other. It's Christian cannibalism, and it happens all of the time. We bite and devour each other because all we know is eat, eat, eat, do, do, do, go, go, go, and when you get in my way, I'll eat you up. I'll trample you in the name of God, because I love God more than you love God. I'm going to eat you up and devour you. In this competitive environment, there is very little love, and sadly, that's the state of much of the church as we know it.

The fifth and final bad thing that happens to Caterpillar Christians, and thus to the church, is a lack of power. We talk a lot and do a lot, but when the trials of life hit us, we don't have much supernatural power to overcome them. Paul says in 1 Corinthians 4:20 (NIV), "The kingdom of God is not a matter of talk but of power."

At this point, if you are like me, you may be asking, "How could I have gone so long in this stage as a Caterpillar Christian? With all of my passion for God, how could this have happened?"

The first key to understanding why is that you are a target for evil. The temptation of knowledge and works is only designed for passionate Christians. A born-again Christian who has never made a wholehearted commitment to the Lord doesn't have this problem. Backslidden Christians don't have this problem because they're not on fire; they don't really care. The only people who suffer the fate of getting stuck as Caterpillar Christians are the most sincere, passionate Christians. Weird, isn't it? But, remember, the ultimate deception is a good intention.

Another key to understanding why this happens is understanding the state of the church. We are born into a church, just like we are born into a particular family. If you look at Nazi Germany as an example, most government supporters were typically not from dysfunctional families. They had fathers and mothers; many had good jobs; a lot of them believed in the Ten Commandments and were church-going people. However, if you were born into a Nazi family, what would you very likely turn into? A Nazi. Why? Because that's what you were born into. I'm not comparing the church to Nazis, it's just a way to make a point.

> **THIS DILUTED & POLLUTED GOSPEL—A WATERED DOWN AND WORLDLY VERSION—DOESN'T PRODUCE MUCH LOVE OR POWER!**

Likewise, as the art on the next page depicts, we are all born into a leavened church. It's one that has been infiltrated by the yeast of the Pharisees (see Matthew 16:6), which produces a divided heart. Our divided heart breaks God's heart because we don't honor His great sacrifice and

Our Leavened *and* Divided Heart

Soul

1. Wisdom Of World
   ↓
2. Knowledge & Works
   ↓
3. Law—Old Covenant
   ↓
4. Idols

Spirit

1. Wisdom Of God
   ↓
2. Christ Crucified
   ↓
3. Gospel—New Covenant
   ↓
4. Jesus Lord

share our affections between Him and idols. This diluted and polluted Gospel—a watered down and worldly version—doesn't produce much love or power! And sadly, that was the case with the Pharisees. They seemed to be spiritual but had little love and virtually no supernatural power.

Satan began infiltrating the church with the yeast of the Pharisees right after its inception in the first century. By the end of the fourth century, after Christianity had been legalized by the emperor Constantine, the process of taking on worldly characteristics was pretty much complete. Most of the love and power was lost, because the natural world cannot produce supernatural love and power. What happened at the fall of man was repeated: our love relationship with God and each other suffered dramatically, and our rulership power over sin, Satan, and curses was greatly diminished.

A leavened church idolizes knowledge and works, and because we were born into it, that's all we know. There seems to be no other pattern for Christians to follow, nothing else out there. But God in His mercy has given us a great example.

Let's look at the twelve apostles. Jesus went up a mountain and prayed and asked His Father before He chose them (Luke 6:12-13). He hand-picked these guys, and hung out with them twenty-four hours a day, seven days a week, for three years. You'd think that would change a person, to be in the physical presence of God for three years. But if we look at the character of the apostles before the cross, we see some interesting things.

First, they were very prideful. They said they'd never forsake Him, they'd die for Him, but in the garden they all fled. The second characteristic we see is that they were carnally minded rather than spiritually minded. They said things like, "He's come to restore Israel. He's come to throw off the Roman conquerors and restore the kingdom of David and Solomon." Their minds were on the earth and not the kingdom of heaven. The third thing we see in their lives is selfish ambition, as when the mother of Zebedee's sons James and John secretly asks Jesus for a favor: "Can my one son sit at your right hand, and my other son on your left?" (See Matthew 20:20-28.) When the other apostles heard about it, they were indignant, probably thinking, *Why didn't my mother get to Him first?* They were mad. It was a power thing. The fourth thing we see is they had little compassion. They tried to keep little children away from Jesus (Matthew 19:13) and even went so far as to ask Jesus if they should call down fire and brimstone from heaven on the Samaritans (Luke 9:54). And finally, they weren't in unity. They fought among themselves and criticized others who weren't in their group but were preaching Jesus (Mark 9:38-40). That's the character of the twelve apostles before the cross.

After the cross, though, we see a different story. Peter, the hotshot, was a broken man. Forevermore after the cross, when people tried to worship him, he told them, "Don't worship me, I'm just a man." (See Acts 3:1-16.) Second, they were heaven-minded. They became less interested in throwing off the Romans and more interested in building God's spiritual kingdom. They were beaten and battered, but they celebrated. There was nothing they wouldn't do for the cause of Christ, even when many of them were killed. They had great compassion for all of God's people, and when Paul was added, reached out to the Gentiles also. And there was no more selfish ambition; they were in unity. The Bible says "they were in one accord" (Acts 2:46). They sold things they had in order to share with those in need and met with humble hearts in their homes. Everything changed.

> THE TWELVE APOSTLES WERE PREY TO THE ULTIMATE DECEPTION. EVEN THEY WERE LIKE CATERPILLAR CHRISTIANS FOR A TIME.

By giving us this example, God in His mercy is saying, *Don't feel bad. The twelve apostles were even prey to the ultimate deception. Even they were like Caterpillar Christians for a time. That's what you were born into, and it can happen to the sincerest of Christians.* So God in His mercy constantly reminds both you and me that Jesus is the best, but beware the yeast of the Pharisees.

Caterpillar Facts: Here are a couple of other interesting facts about caterpillars and how they differ from butterflies. First of all, caterpillars destroy where they eat. They cannot live without destroying what brings them life. Isn't that wild? Compare that to the

Caterpillar Christian. The exact place where somebody is getting fed and nurtured—that's where he or she brings destruction. Many times Caterpillar Christians destroy the body.

Butterflies, on the other hand, do not destroy what they eat. They just land on the plant, suck out the nectar, and don't bother anything. In fact, not only does the butterfly not destroy the places where it feeds, it pollinates them. The butterfly helps the flowers to reproduce because it pollinates. It multiplies where it eats.

The second thing about caterpillars is that they cannot reproduce. The original blessing and command to "be fruitful and multiply" (Genesis 1:28) is lost on Caterpillar Christians, as well as the meaning of *Pentecost*, which is "harvest, or multiplication." We've all heard non-Christian people say, "Who would want to be like those Christians? They're a bunch of judgmental, holier-than-thou, no-fun people." Caterpillars don't multiply. It's a thing of nature. Only butterflies can reproduce.

Finally, caterpillars can't fly. They are earthbound, with a lot of feet on the ground. Butterflies are free-flying, having been transformed into heavenly creations.

Take a look at the piece of art on the following page, which tells a story. See the egg, representing the born-again Christian, and then the caterpillar, which is the Christian who has made a whole-hearted commitment and dealt with his/her known sins. Then comes the cocoon stage, and that represents the Christian who is dying to self and dealing with his/her hidden sins. A Caterpillar Christian never finds out their hidden sins; he/she is so busy going and doing and learning. Caterpillar Christians never go that deep. They stay out in the world where it seems bright and open. But the world of the cocoon is dark. It's enclosed, and it is messy. When God starts showing you the junk that's inside of you, the sin you are capable of, you may be surprised how ugly it is. I know, because that's what happened to me. The Bible says in Jeremiah 17:9 that "The heart is deceitful above all things, and desperately wicked; who can know it?" And then, in verse 10, it says, "I, the Lord, search the heart." When God does His work in you, you'll be like Peter: you'll find out what's really inside and be broken.

Caterpillar Christians are not asking God to search their hearts. They're so sure that they've arrived, that they've got it right. But after we

go into the cocoon and die with Christ, then we emerge into a beautiful butterfly. That's the stage where we get love, power, blessings, and destiny. So this is the image. You see the tree, and it shows the butterfly on that cross. I've got to hang on that tree in the cocoon in order to emerge as a victorious and beautiful butterfly whose life is now centered in the cross!

The other thing about this piece of art is the beauty of the butterfly. Think for a minute about Jesus and His return. The Bible says He's coming back for His bride, and the bride will be without spot or blemish (Ephesians 5:27). And Jesus Christ the bridegroom—He's the Lion of Judah, the Mighty Warrior, the Lily of the Valley, the Bright and Morning Star. When you envision Him coming for His bride, can you picture Him walking down the aisle with an ugly caterpillar? We want to be soaring, beautiful, and radiant like the butterfly. He died for us. We die to self for Him—that He may transform us.

Now we have laid the whole foundation: how the devil stole the message of the cross by using the wisdom of the world to empty the cross of its power—how it creates a leavened and blended church which is watered down and weakened—how this lust for the law in the church caused its members to lose their God-given birthright—and how that church then produces Caterpillar Christians. Now that we have this foundation, the question is, what are we going to do about it? The next stages of our spiritual journey are going to show what action we can take to begin this process—going from Caterpillar Christians to Birthright Butterflies! The first step is to get out of this "Wisdom of the World System" we've been living in.

Adam and Eve were the original Birthright Butterflies. They lived in a *non-how to* world—the Garden of Eden. There, it wasn't about learning and doing…it was just about living. Jesus, who is the second Adam, has made that world available to us again, today!

My Personal One-on-One Encounter With The Lord

Also for Home Group Discussion

Am I stuck in stage two of my Christian walk as a Caterpillar Christian? What would some of the signs be that I am stuck?

_____
_____
_____
_____

Do I understand that the ultimate deception is a good intention and that's why only sincere Christians have this problem? What are some of my past good intentions that have produced a bad result? What are my good intentions now?

_____
_____
_____
_____

Has my heart been leavened by the yeast of the Pharisees and become divided? What are some things that have infiltrated my heart, causing me to have a watered down and weakened version of the Gospel that has little power?

_____
_____
_____
_____

For pastors: Am I struggling with divisions or a church split? How might dealing with Caterpillar Christianity help these situations?

_____
_____
_____
_____

Do any of the following describe how you are feeling:

• Do you feel overwhelmed and burned out by your Christian walk? Has it become an endless stream of more things to learn and more things to do?

• Do you care deeply about the church but in your heart know that something just isn't right? When you look at the church do you ever wonder where the love and power are?

• Are you a faithful Christian who has had a relationship with the Lord for years, but your promised blessings never seem to come?

• Have you been praying for years to see and experience revival, but that too has yet to happen?

• Do you feel a call on your life for some form of ministry, to be in full-time fivefold ministry or some other form of ministry while keeping your current job, but that call is not yet a reality?

• When you do minister, is there little power?

_____
_____
_____

If so, take heart, you are one of the millions of sincere Christians stuck in the caterpillar stage who is now headed to the cross to become a butterfly!

 ## Reflecting on the Art

- In what way does the painting that opens this chapter speak to me?
- Did the sketches have an impact on me? If so, how?
- Can I now go back to the opening painting of chapter two and see myself in that picture?

_____
_____
_____

Religion, That's Me!

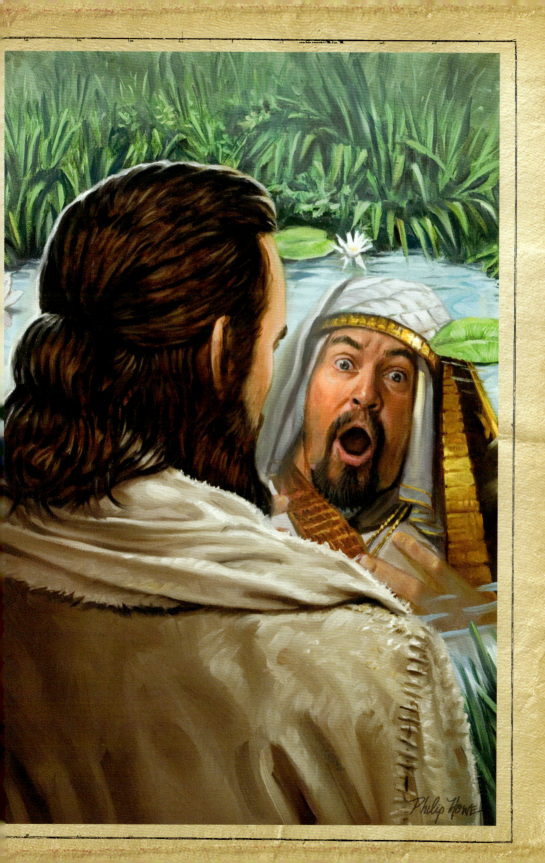

CHAPTER 5

Religion, That's Me!

Now that we understand how the church and our hearts have been leavened by the wisdom of the world, producing Caterpillar Christians, we're going to look at how to get out of this system. The way to do that is to look at religion and recognize, *That's me*. We all see religion in the other person, but it's time to look in the mirror and face the truth. Just like the guy looking into the pond in the opening painting, we may be more like Pharisees than we ever imagined. It's not about someone else this time, it's about me: I've got religion in *me*.

What is religion anyway? In this chapter we're going to discover the definition of religion, the result of religion, how religion started, and what the world of religion looks like (it's a very yucky world).

I believe a simple definition of religion is this: any attempt to become holy and have a relationship with God based on man's knowledge and works instead of the cross of Christ. Imagine a balance, and on one side is man's attempt to be holy, and on the other side is the cross of Christ. It's that simple. Once we understand that definition, we see that it includes all religions of the world, as well as any cult. Any belief system not based on Jesus Christ and Him crucified falls on the side of man's attempt to be holy. That side of the balance will always come up short.

It's easy to see how this definition of religion includes religions and cults outside of Christianity, but did you know that definition can also include us? Remember what we learned about the Caterpillar Christian, how in phase one, as an egg, we're born again; then in phase two we're becoming caterpillars—learning all of these wonderful things but getting stuck there, enamored with knowledge and works. The Caterpillar Christian *attempts to become holy and have a relationship with God based on his or her knowledge and works instead of the cross of Christ.*

> WHEN MY RELATIONSHIP WITH GOD IS BASED ON WHAT I KNOW ABOUT GOD AND WHAT I DO FOR GOD, WHAT JESUS CHRIST DID ON THE CROSS IS NOT RELEVANT ANYMORE.

We've all been there, haven't we? We all have religion, and, what is the result? It's very simple: man is exalted instead of God. When it's about what I know about God and what I do for God, it's not about what Jesus Christ did for me. It's about me. I'll say that again: When my relationship with God is based on what I know about God and what I do for God, *that's about me*; what Jesus Christ did on the cross is not relevant anymore.

Why is that such a nasty thing? Because, we learn in Romans 3:10 that no one is good, not one. Even our righteousness is as "filthy rags" (Isaiah 64:6). So when our relationship with God becomes about man, it becomes a filthy thing. We have a walk and talk that looks like we're elevating God, but the reality is we're elevating man. In reality, then, religion is the elevation of *man* in the *guise* of elevating God. The word *guise* means to dress up. It's a costume, or a semblance. Religion is a mask people wear in order to look spiritual and act spiritual, but the truth is, there is nothing spiritual about it.

Instead, it produces arrogance. We boast about whatever particular thing we're into—our group, our denomination, our church—and think it's the best. What are we really doing? We're boasting about men instead of the cross.

1 Corinthians 3:19-21 says, "For the wisdom of this world is foolishness with God. For it is written, 'He catches the wise in their own craftiness'; and again, 'The Lord knows the thoughts of the wise, that they are futile.' Therefore let no one boast in men. For all things are yours [in Christ]."

The Ultimate Deception is a Good Intention

A final thought on how religion elevates man. When a person was crucified during Roman times, his crime was posted at the top of his cross. What crime was posted on the top of Jesus' cross? —"This Is Jesus the King of the Jews" (Matthew 27:37). It's quite clear that the religious crowd had no interest in God being their King; to them it was a crime. Just as in the days when Israel cried out for a man to be their king instead of God and got Saul, so it was at the time of Christ, and so it is today with religion. It's really about men being kings, not Jesus.

We've defined religion, and we've examined its result, which is the elevation of man instead of God. Now we're going to look into its origin. Where did religion come from? It started in the Garden of Eden, at the Fall. God said, "You must not eat from the tree of the knowledge of good and evil" (Genesis 2:17 NIV). But the devil said, "In the day you eat of it… you will be like God" (Genesis 3:5). So man decided to eat of that tree. It all stemmed from a good intention, to be like God, but the reality is that human beings are never satisfied, so the thought of being *like* God became the desire to *be* God—to be sovereign.

The minute man fell, God said one of the curses is that you will toil. People began to have to work very hard to make a living. And what was the result of the Fall? Knowledge and works—religion. It all started in the garden.

But this is not just an Old Testament problem. In the New Testament, in 2 Corinthians 11:3, Paul writes, "But I fear, lest somehow, as the serpent deceived Eve by his craftiness, so your minds may be corrupted from the simplicity that is in Christ." Satan does the same thing today with Caterpillar Christians as he did with Adam and Eve in the Garden of Eden.

My wife always says, "God is very, very simple." Just as Paul said, there is a real simplicity, a real beauty, a real incredible attractiveness to Jesus Christ. And if you notice something about religion, it turns a lot of people off. It is not really simple or attractive. Religion repulses more people than it brings in. It stinks! But Jesus is described as the Rose of Sharon. He's beautiful. He carries the fragrance of God. People are very, very attracted to Jesus.

What is the world of religion like? It's a world that looks good but produces death. How do we know that? In Genesis 2:17 (NIV) God said, "You must not eat from the tree of the knowledge of good and evil, for when you eat of it you will surely die." But Genesis 3:6 says "So when the woman saw that the tree was good for food, that it was pleasant to the eyes, and a tree desirable to make one wise, she took of its fruit and ate. She also gave to her husband with her, and he ate." That's it. Religion looks good and seems desirable, but the only thing it can produce is death.

> RELIGION LOOKS GOOD AND SEEMS DESIRABLE, BUT THE ONLY THING IT CAN PRODUCE IS DEATH.

Remember the neat thing the Lord showed us about Caterpillar Christians? We said there are two important differences between a caterpillar and a butterfly: a caterpillar destroys where he lives, and caterpillars cannot procreate. Caterpillar Christians get sucked into religion, and all religion can do is produce death; it can't produce life!

We're going to paint a picture of a world of religion, and what it seems the Lord is trying to do with this picture is to make that world so smelly and stinky that we want to hold our noses and run the other way.

Imagine a world in which everything depended on a coin toss. Everything you did—the money you made, the house you lived in, the relationships you had—totally depended on you flipping a coin, and in this world the only winning toss was heads. Suppose, however, that the only coin you possessed had tails on both sides. How would it be to live in that world? That's the world of religion.

On one side of the coin is the Law of Moses, and on the other side are man-made rules. The Law of Moses is good, but it doesn't belong in the New Covenant. Picture a lawn mower, which was made for cutting a lawn. If the mower represents the law, and the lawn is the Old Covenant, then the lawn mower works great. But if the New Covenant is a flower garden, what happens if we take the lawn mower in there? It produces death. It doesn't belong there; a lawn mower wasn't made for a flower garden. Looked at this way, we can see that the law in the New Covenant doesn't work.

A perfect example of this is found in the life of a guy named Saul—Rabbi Saul. He was one of the best children of God—the elite when it came to God's chosen people. The Bible says that when it came to the law, he was flawless. Do you know what he did? He went about killing Christians. He was so good at the law that he killed God's children and basically opposed God. So back to the coin and the side that represents the Law of Moses. What happens when we flip that up? Tails, we lose.

What's on the other side of the coin? The other side of the coin is man-made rules. Ed Gungor, in his book *Religiously Transmitted Diseases*, describes these rules as "fence laws."

Gungor writes:
To ensure that a specific law of God was obeyed, the Pharisees believed they should make up rules that "fenced" people a step back from breaking the actual command. They thought of these "fence laws" as a first line of defense against disobedience. They reasoned that if a person would have to break the man-made fence laws before breaking one of God's real laws, it would be a deterrent and a protection for people. Noble enough. [1]

---

1 Ed Gungor, *Religiously Transmitted Diseases* (Nashville: Thomas Nelson, Inc., 2006): p. 53.

However, Gungor goes on to point out:

> Let's look at how fence laws are created. Parents who love their children build similar kinds of "fence laws" all the time. Take the rule "Don't get hit by a car." Good rule. If you think about this rule long enough—and you believe you must do everything possible to ensure it will be obeyed—you might be tempted to bundle another rule to it, to add a "fence" that could serve as the first line of defense so that the actual rule you are ultimately trying to obey doesn't get violated.
>
> One logical fence law to this would be "Don't play in the street." If you don't play in the street, a car won't hit you. That's reasonable.
>
> But pharisaic thinking goes way beyond reasonableness and gets much more restrictive. Pharisaic thinking would go something like this: The rule is, "Don't get hit by a car." We cannot allow anyone to be hit by a car...so, let's make sure that doesn't happen. Ah...let's make sure no one plays in the street—no street play will mean no one is hit by a car. Or better yet, it's probably best not to play outside at all, because then you won't happen into the street to get hit by a car.
>
> Or even better: Don't look out the windows of the house, lest you are tempted to think about going outside, which could lead into you wandering into the street to get hit by a car.
>
> Or perhaps best of all: Play and sleep in the closet so you aren't tempted to look outside a window at all—because you know where that can lead...
>
> The question becomes, at what point does the person we are trying to protect lose track of what the original law was all about? When she can't look out the window, or when she is kept in the closet? And that was the problem with the fence laws. They eventually overwhelmed the actual commands of God. Jesus said to the Pharisees, "You have a fine way of setting aside the commands of God in order to observe your own traditions!" (Mark 7:9).
>
> But, more than just distracting from God's law, these fence laws also became abusive. At what point does the legitimate desire to protect become a repressive system of abuse? Parents who make their kids live in closets need to go to jail. It doesn't matter if they started out loving, concerned, and protective. They end up

> **THAT'S JESUS' POINT ABOUT THE PHARISEES. THE FENCE LAWS BECAME WEIGHTS THAT CRIPPLED FAITH, NOT HELPED IT.**

controlling, manipulative, and repressive. That's Jesus' point about the Pharisees. The fence laws became weights that crippled faith, not helped it.[2]

Now that's a crazy story, right? We can't imagine a good-intentioned parent actually doing that to their child. But it happens all of the time in the church, across every denomination. There are tons of examples, but I'll just give three here.

THE BIBLE SAYS, "Do not get drunk" (Ephesians 5:18), so the church creates a fence law that says, "Do not drink."

THE BIBLE SAYS not to be sexually immoral, like in immoral dancing (1 Peter 4:3). The church's fence law is "Don't dance."

THE BIBLE SAYS not to look at immoral things (Ephesians 5:3; 1 John 2:16), so the church puts up a fence law that says, "Do not go to movies."

And the list goes on and on and on.

Guess what? This is news for all of us good-intentioned Christians. *God doesn't need our help.* God does not need our help to obey Him. James 5:12 says, "Let your 'Yes' be yes, and your 'No,' no," the thought being don't add anything to it. The same thought applies to fence laws. Our fence laws do nothing to help anybody obey God any better. They're all a complete illusion. They're the ultimate religious scam! They seem so good because here is my long list of do's and don'ts, and I get a star for each time I do well. But what about all of the times I don't? In a world of religion, we flip that side of the coin and it's tails. With man-made rules, we still lose.

Another aspect of this world of religion is that we don't become more holy, we become more carnal. Why is that? Religion is always an external focus; it is never, ever internal. That is the opposite of the kingdom of God. What God said when He picked out David as king was,

---

2 Gungor, pp. 54-55.

"Man looks at the outward appearance, but the Lord looks at the heart" (1 Samuel 16:7). He is not interested in how many stars we get for doing well nor in what we look like. He is interested in our hearts.

A very interesting scripture is Galatians 4:19. In this verse Paul calls the Galatians "my little children, for whom I labor in birth again until Christ is formed in you." The word *formed* as it's used here comes from the Greek *morpho* and refers to an internal reality. This speaks of a change in character, becoming conformed to the character of Christ in actuality, not merely in semblance. Religion is always the appearance of being holy, but the inside never matches up because it's all about the outside instead of the inside. Paul goes back to the subject of outward change versus inward change in Colossians 2:20-23:

> *Therefore, if you died with Christ from the basic principles of the world, why, as though living in the world, do you subject yourselves to regulations—"Do not touch, do not taste, do not handle," which all concern things which perish with the using—according to the commandments and doctrines of men? These things indeed have an appearance of wisdom in self-imposed religion, false humility, and neglect of the body, but are of no value against the indulgence of the flesh.*

The Amplified Bible states the end of verse 23 this way: *...they are of no value in checking the indulgence of the flesh (the lower nature). [Instead, they do not honor God but serve only to indulge the flesh.]*

Some leaders were telling the people "don't touch, don't handle, don't do any of these things." Paul says that these teachings are all about the external and appear to mortify or put to death the flesh, but in actuality they just indulge the flesh. Do you know why? This is a very sad thing, but when my Christian life is about what I know and what I do, then I get puffed up. In my heart I say, "Look at all of the things I know about God.... Look at all of the things I do for God. Look at all of the things I don't do: I don't go to movies; I don't dance; I don't drink. I don't do all of these things," and my flesh gets puffed up bigger and bigger and bigger. I believe that, in those times, God is saying *Who do you think you are? All righteousness comes through My Son*.

It's a very clever scam of the enemy to make us think that we're holy, that we're even mortifying our flesh, but all our being religious is really doing is puffing up our pride. Think of the Pharisees. Did all of those fence laws make them spiritual? No. They were highly religious, but the Bible says they loved money. They loved the most prominent seats. They were carnal! They were puffed up! Religion didn't bring them any closer to God, just like it won't draw us closer to Him.

It also didn't bring them any closer to other people. The word "Pharisee" in the Greek means "sect," or separatist. They had to "separate" from everybody else because they thought they were so holy. The saddest thing about this is that in all of their self-righteousness, they were separated from God. They missed out on Jesus. He was right in their midst, and they didn't recognize Him. And yet they thought they were the ultimate people of God. The Bible says that we are to be in the world but not of the world. We are to separate ourselves from the sins of the world but not be so aloof that we have no contact with the very people we are called to minister to. That's what Jesus did.

> IT'S A VERY CLEVER SCAM OF THE ENEMY TO MAKE US THINK THAT WE'RE HOLY, BUT ALL OUR BEING RELIGIOUS IS REALLY DOING IS INDULGING OUR FLESH.

Let's further explore this religious world where we are not close to God, and just like the Pharisees, we also don't get closer to other Christians. We get divided. When what I know about God and what I do for God is different than what you know about God and what you do for God, there's a split. That's the reality of the church today. Everybody's group knows different things and does different things, and therefore somebody has got to be wrong. And everybody thinks they're right. So we are all divided.

It's as old as time itself. Remember what happened right after the fall of man? Cain murdered Abel. Why? Over ways of serving God. Cain thought the good thing to do for God was produce crops. Abel thought the good thing to do for God (and he happened to be right) was to produce livestock. They were different, and Cain killed Abel. That's what religion does. It does not bring people together; it drives Christians apart. And every time it's very sincere people saying, "I'm better than you....

I'm holier than you.... That's why I can't hang out with you, because we're different." What if instead everybody was saying, "It's all about what Jesus Christ did on the cross"? We'd all be in unity, wouldn't we? We'd all have the same thing in common—Jesus—and He unifies.

What is this world of religion like?

ONE. It puts man on the throne, which is me, instead of God.

TWO. It makes me more carnal, not more spiritual.

THREE. It separates me from God.

FOUR. It brings division between people.

That's a pretty smelly picture, isn't it? God is saying, "Flee from religion." There's nothing good in it. It appears to be good; it appears to be valuable, but it isn't.

Jesus said, "You shall know the truth, and the truth shall make you free....If the Son makes you free, you shall be free indeed" (John 8:32, 36). Another scripture reads, "Where the Spirit of the Lord is, there is freedom" (2 Corinthians 3:17 NIV). Religion has nothing to do with freedom. It puts people in prison. I've done time in that prison, but the Lord in His mercy has gotten me out.

Let me share my religion prison story, when I had to admit, "Religion. That's Me." When I was an atheist and became born again, I really hated religion. I was very much against it, and I thought I was free of religion, but one day I found out otherwise. I was on my treadmill watching TV, and Marlo Thomas was being interviewed. Being a good charismatic Christian, I was a political conservative, and therefore against the liberal left. Marlo Thomas is a liberal and a feminist, and so the moment I saw her on TV, my knee-jerk reaction was, *Yuk. I don't like that Marlo Thomas.*

Well, I kept watching, and in the interview Ms. Thomas was talking about St. Jude's Hospital and how for fifty years they've been serving critically ill children. She's carrying on the legacy of her father, Danny

Thomas. And then she said, "We have never charged one dime for one child to ever be treated at St. Jude's and we have helped thousands of children that could otherwise never get help. I just want to keep this tradition going."

As I stood there on that treadmill, I could have melted and slunk underneath it. The still small voice of the Lord pierced my heart, and He said, *You hypocrite. You're over there judging her because of your religious beliefs, and she's doing something that is pleasing to me.* Like the Bible says, honor your father and mother, and in another place, help widows and orphans—which is true service to God. (See James 1:27.) The moral of this story is that *I had religion*, and I was judging another person because of our different political perspectives. For the first time, I looked in the mirror and admitted, Religion. That's me! It was painful to recognize, but it was the first step in getting free from that prison.

Another step came as I recognized my own reliance on man's knowledge and works. I've got a daughter, Mary, who was playing basketball. She was really struggling with having confidence. I would go over and over in my mind about how I was going to talk to her and help her out of the mess she was in. I just labored over it, thinking and figuring on how to best approach it. Then one day the Holy Spirit spoke to my heart and said, *Hey Rick, have you ever once, when thinking about how to help your daughter, brought up the cross of Christ?* I had to confess that I hadn't. Then He said, *That's religion.*

Ouch! Isn't that the definition of religion: any attempt by man through his knowledge and works to do something good, or do something holy apart from the cross of Christ? I was guilty. And I thought I was Mister Non-Religious. But it just isn't true. How many times, when we are concerned about a loved one, do we go over and over in our minds how to help the situation without ever bringing up the cross of Christ? This pretty much applies to everybody, so we all have religion.

Let's imagine a world without religion. What would that world be like? The original world created by God for Adam and Eve did not have

> I LOOKED IN THE MIRROR AND ADMITTED, RELIGION. THAT'S ME. IT WAS PAINFUL TO RECOGNIZE, BUT IT WAS THE FIRST STEP IN GETTING SET FREE.

religion in it. And what was that original world? The Garden of Eden. It was the polar opposite of the world of religion, and it was paradise. God was on the throne, not man. Adam and Eve were like little children—adults with childlike hearts. They were holy and without sin. What's more, they were sons and daughters of God who completely trusted in their Father for everything. They had a face-to-face relationship with God; there was no separation. On top of that, Adam and Eve were one—there was no division whatsoever between them. And as a final bonus, they had dominion over all of the earth. They even had dominion over the devil. The Bible says they had dominion over everything, including "reptiles, creeping reptiles." That included the snake, right? What a wonderful world!

But after the Fall we see a complete change. Mankind put themselves on God's throne and began to do as they pleased. They became carnal and sinful; they had fallen flesh with all of the curses that go with it. They lost their childlike relationship with their Father. They were separated from God, cast out of the garden. And there was division; the two brothers were divided, and one killed the other. And finally, who became prince of the world? Satan. He was the one behind it all—the one who introduced religion into the world. Think about it. Who needed religion to come into existence in order to gain power in the world? The devil. It's his deal, his system. It's a masquerade. It's something that appears to be God but isn't. The enemy's fingerprints are all over it.

> WHO NEEDED RELIGION TO COME INTO EXISTENCE IN ORDER TO GAIN POWER IN THE WORLD? THE DEVIL. IT'S HIS DEAL, HIS SYSTEM.

We learned that the wisdom of the world empties the cross of its power, and when the cross is emptied of its power, Satan regains power. When that happens, we lose our God-given birthright of dominion. Religion appears to make man holy—to elevate us spiritually by drawing us closer to God—but in reality it elevates Satan. That's why it's so clever: religion is this whole world that seems to be Godly but isn't. It's really all about man—and really all about Satan.

I want to close with something that was very offensive to me when I heard it. It's a very radical idea, and if I did not believe with all of my heart that it was from the Holy Spirit, I would not be able to accept it myself. I was sitting in a counseling session one day, and the Lord spoke these words to my heart: *There is a world that exists that you know very little about—you and other sincere Christians in the church. This world is called the kingdom of God. In this world is a blessing, "The Blessing," and it has nothing to do with what you do right or wrong.*

This stunned me. I said, "How can this be? It sounds like heresy!" Then the Lord helped me understand by showing me that the Garden of Eden was the kingdom of God. It was a place of blessing, as the Bible describes in Genesis. He saw that His creation was good, and He blessed it...and He blessed it...and He blessed it. Did that blessing have anything to do with Adam and Eve knowing the difference between right and wrong, and doing right or wrong? No, nothing. They didn't even know they were naked. Could a world like that exist? Not only could it exist, it did.

> THERE IS A WORLD THAT EXISTS THAT YOU KNOW VERY LITTLE ABOUT—IN THIS WORLD IS A BLESSING THAT HAS NOTHING TO DO WITH WHAT YOU DO RIGHT OR WRONG.

The second thing that the Lord helped me to understand was the concept of being born again. We all know that when we are born again, we enter the kingdom of God, and it has nothing to do with what we do right or wrong. If someone came up to us and said, "I want to accept Jesus as Lord, but I need to stop cussing and getting drunk first," what would we say? We would say, "No, it has nothing to do with what you're doing wrong. Just repent and accept Jesus as you are, and He will give you the power to change." If someone else came up and said, "I read the Bible every day, go to church three times a week, and give to the poor, so I don't need to accept Jesus as Lord to go to heaven," what would we say? We would say, "No, it doesn't matter how many things you're doing right and how good you are. The only way to heaven is through Jesus Christ." Why, then, are we so surprised that a world of blessing could exist for us which has nothing to do with what we do right or wrong? The answer the Lord gave me stunned me again: *It's because you've heard a watered down version of the Gospel for so long that when you hear the real thing, you think it's heresy.* Wow, that's scary, but the Garden of Eden and being born again prove that it's true.

It's worth saying again: as Christians, we have heard a watered down version of the Gospel for so long, that when we hear the real thing, we think it's heresy! No wonder we have so little love and power in the church—to *water down* means *to dilute and weaken*—meaning less love and power.

That beautiful world really exists, and guess what? *We're not in that world.* We know very little about it, because that world is about Jesus and what He did and not about what we're doing. *But we're headed toward it, as we discover more and more about the first part of the lost secret, which is making the cross of Christ the most important thing in our lives.*

We've seen the prison religion puts us in, and now in the next chapter we're going to take a wrecking ball to the very foundation of that prison. That foundation is the law, and once we knock it down, it will never be built back up in our lives again. We're going to replace the law with the gospel of grace and discover how to apply the power of the cross for victory in our everyday lives.

My Personal One-on-One Encounter With The Lord

Also for Home Group Discussion

Can I now admit that I have religion? What are some examples of religion in my life?
_____
_____

When someone that I love has a problem, do I go over and over in my mind of how to help them without including the cross of Christ? What are some examples?
_____
_____

Do I have human traditions and man made rules, fence laws, as part of my Christian walk? What are some of them?
_____
_____

What do I know about a world that exists called the Kingdom Of God, that has a blessing for me, but has nothing to do with what I do right or wrong?
_____
_____
_____

Reflecting on the Art

- In what way does the painting that opens this chapter speak to me?
- Did the sketch have an impact on me? If so, how?

_____
_____
_____

Judge Not

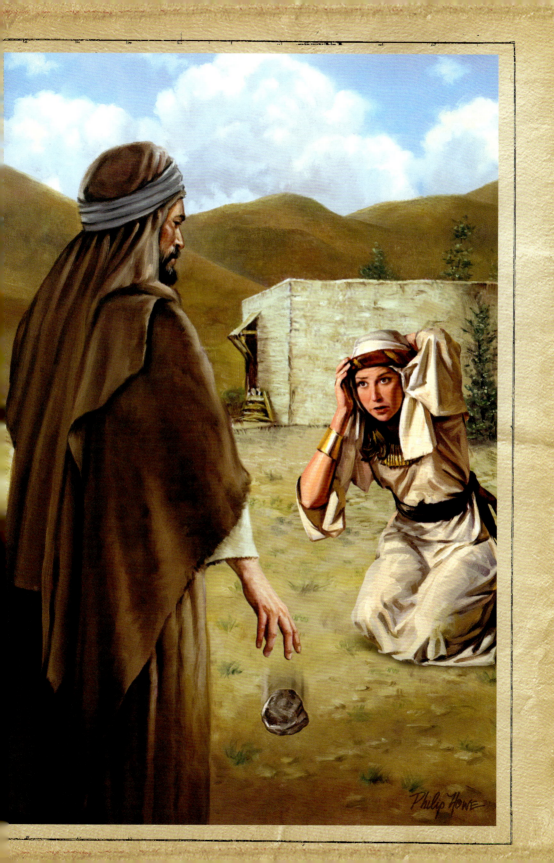

CHAPTER 6

Judge Not

AT EVERY TURN OF OUR SPIRITUAL JOURNEY, one thing always pops up: the law, which is based on knowledge and works. Whether it was me in second grade choosing knowledge and works to succeed, Satan using knowledge and works to steal the message of the cross, Jesus taking the law based on knowledge and works out of our way, Caterpillar Christians munching away on knowledge and works, or finally, religion based on what men know and do to be holy, the law has been there. Let's discover how to get rid of the law and replace it with the gospel of grace which is the cross of Christ.

1 Corinthians 15:56 says, "The sting of death is sin, and the strength of sin is the law." Phillips' translation states it this way: "It is the Law which gives sin its power." The word *power* there is from the Greek word *dunamis*, meaning "to be able or possible." And in Romans 4:15 it says—I'm paraphrasing slightly—that "apart from the law there is no sin." *So the law is the power of sin; it makes sin possible.*

Going one step further, we will now discover that judgment is what brings the law to life. Remember how Satan stole our birthright? He used a lie, so we would lust after the law, to bring sin to life. The lie that God wasn't good and we weren't good enough caused us to judge God and ourselves. A judgment set the whole sequence in motion. To understand, let's go back to the analogy of a lawnmower.

Your lawn is the world where the law belongs, and the lawnmower does a great job there; your lawn looks great. Your flower and vegetable garden represents the church, the New Covenant, where the law does not belong. Picture your garden in July or August. Your summer flowers are looking great. Your tomatoes and beans are strong and healthy and producing well. This garden is your pride and joy. Suddenly somebody comes, starts up the lawnmower, pushes it right into your garden, and begins mowing it down. What would you do? You'd be very upset, wouldn't you? Why? Because something good was misapplied, and it turned into something very bad.

Picture this lawnmower, and imagine that sin is the blade. That's what chopped all of your flowers and vegetables to pieces. What powered the blade? The engine, which is the law. But what started the engine? The pull-cord, which is judgment. Without the pull-cord, there would be no life in the engine. Judgment is the catalyst that brings the law to life, spinning the blade, and creating sin. So we must put judgment to death in our lives in order to get the law out of our life. Like everything else, it has to go to the cross. Then the law, which is the power of sin, will be gone and replaced with the power of the cross.

> So we must put judgment to death in our lives in order to get the law out of our life.

The word *judgment* in the Bible means "a decision for or against, to distinguish or decide mentally, the knowledge or the ability to distinguish good and evil or to decide what is right or wrong." The root word of *judgment* means "accusation, condemnation, damnation."

Let's take these words into Genesis three and consider how they played a part in the fall of man. The first thing the devil did was to offer a lying accusation. He told Eve, "God is holding out on you.... He doesn't really love you. The reason He doesn't want you to eat of that tree is because you're going to be like Him. And you need to be like Him because you're not good enough now—you're inferior." Satan started out with a lying accusation, which produced what in Adam and Eve? A *judgment against God and then themselves.* Going back to the analogy of the lawnmower, we see that Satan pulled the cord and produced a judgment.

Second, the Bible says that the fruit looked good for wisdom. Adam and Eve wanted to become like God, but what did they eat of? They ate from the tree of the knowledge of good and evil. To distinguish or decide mentally—the knowledge and ability to distinguish good and evil—it's judgment! They'd never even known judgment—it didn't exist in their lives—but first they judged God and themselves, and then they ate of the tree that put them into a lifestyle of judgment. *Judgment times two!* What happened after that? Damnation and condemnation and death. That's what judgment produces.

The first and only command that God gave to man in the Garden of Eden was "*Judge not.*" He created this whole universe, and He said, "There's only one thing you can't do. Don't judge. As long as you judge not, you'll have life with Me forever in paradise and have dominion over the entire world—our God-given birthright. Just don't do that one thing." It seems that if that was the only command God gave man in the beginning, it is extremely important. I believe it sums everything up: judge not.

> HE CREATED THIS WHOLE UNIVERSE, AND HE SAID, "THERE'S ONLY ONE THING YOU CAN'T DO. DON'T JUDGE."

The fall of man proves that judgment triggered the law. It powers it. And if you think about the law of the land, it proves that same point. If you break the law you will eventually stand before a judge. The judge decides whether you are good or evil, and if you are judged to be evil, then you are condemned. The legal system cannot exist without judges—no judges making judgments means no legal system and no law. Now we are on to something really big. *Judgment is really the root and source of all sin! And we know that the cross is the only source of righteousness.* If we compare the two side by side, judgment vs. the cross, they should be exactly opposite. Let's try it and see if it's true.

Let's first start with the cross. The essence of the cross, which is the essence of Christianity, is humility, faith and love. As New-Covenant Christians, we know that the first step to becoming righteous is humility. We must humble ourselves to be saved, as the Bible says in Ephesians 2:8-9: "For by grace you have been saved through faith…not of works, lest anyone should boast." Is it possible to be saved apart from humility?

I bet every born-again Christian, if he or she remembers back to their personal salvation experience—it doesn't matter how cocky we were, or where we were at the time; it doesn't matter how many people we scoffed at—at a certain point in time, we admitted, "I'm a sinner in need of a Savior." That's not cocky, is it? That's humble. "There's nothing I can do to get to heaven; I can't make it on my own. I need Jesus." That's humble, right? We first have to recognize that we are sinners in need of a Savior and then reach out in faith to receive Jesus' free gift. *It all starts with humility.*

But what is judgment? It is the opposite of humility. It is haughty. Have you ever seen the image used in some movies, in which a person is looking down his or her nose at another person? Or perhaps pointing a finger? What is that demonstrating? Judgment. *Just look at that riff-raff. I'm better than she is.* It's haughty—prideful—and we Christians do it all of the time. There is no humility in it. They are opposites.

What's the second aspect to being saved? Faith. Habakkuk 2:4 is a very famous scripture, and it says "Behold the proud, his soul is not upright in him; but the just shall live by his *faith*" (emphasis mine). And just as Christianity is associated with a humble person being saved by faith, *judgment is associated with being proud and having unbelief.* Think back to Adam and Eve. Everything was beautiful until they believed Satan's lie and judged God. They chose to stop believing that God was good *and instead believed that He was holding out on them. Their unbelief was the opposite of faith.* We now have two opposites, humility vs. pride and faith vs. unbelief. Only one more to go.

Another very famous scripture is John 3:16, which says, "For God so *loved* the world that He gave His only begotten Son, that whoever believes in Him should not perish but have everlasting life" (emphasis mine). The cross and Christianity are about love, but think about Adam and Eve. When they judged God and had unbelief, it hardened their hearts toward God, and their love for Him diminished. The same thing happens between people in relationships. The minute I judge you, I don't believe you're good anymore. Let's say we were the best buddies in the world. I thought you were great, and I talked you up to people. All of a sudden you do something I don't approve of, and I'm sitting in judgment over you. It doesn't even have to be a conscious thought, but internally I'm saying that I don't believe you're good anymore. That

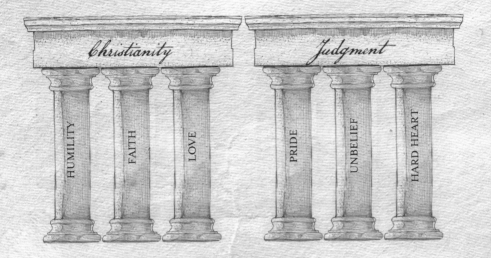

means my heart has hardened towards you and I no longer love you. *The final opposite is love vs. a hard heart.*

To put it all together, *humility, faith and love are the essence of the cross and Christianity. Pride, unbelief, and a hard heart are the essence of judgment. So Christianity and judgment are totally opposed to each other.* The sketch of the three pillars sums it all up.

If the only way to righteousness is an encounter with Jesus and His cross, based on humility, faith, and love, doesn't the opposite have to be true? The source of all sin is pride, unbelief, and hard unloving hearts, which is judgment. Replace judgment with the cross, and we are set free from sin.

Why do Christians judge so much? It's a weird thing. Judgment makes us feel holy. Think about it. Doesn't it make you feel holy and like you're serving God when you're judging everybody and everything? We think we're really arriving, but we're really taking a nosedive at nine thousand miles an hour to the pit of hell! It's a sly trick of the devil. I believe God would say of the Fall, "Little did Adam and Eve know that when they ate that fruit to supposedly become like Me, they were entering a lifestyle of judgment, which is death."

What are the fruits of a lifestyle of judgment? The first fruit of judgment is that *it separates us from God* as sons and daughters, and it turns us into slaves. Knowledge—works—toil. That's what happened to Adam and Eve.

They went from innocent children of God who had all of their needs met, into slavery after they ate of the tree of the knowledge of good and evil.

The second fruit of judgment is that *it separates us from our brothers and sisters in Christ*. When what I know about God and what I do for God, and what you know about God and do for God are different and I judge you for it, we can't have unity or fellowship. My judgment against you for being different will always produce division.

The third fruit of a lifestyle of judgment is *curses and death*. The Bible says in Galatians 3:10 that those who are under the law are under a curse. Why? *Judgment is what brings the law to life*, which then brings the law of sin and death into existence. The curses of famine, plague, and sword, that come from sin, produce death. That's what happened in Genesis chapter three, and that's what still happens today.

> JUST LIKE BREATHING, IT BECOMES INVOLUNTARY, AND WE JUDGE ALL OF THE TIME.

As I've grown in the area of recognizing judgment in myself, I've seen that it's like breathing. It can become so much a part of our lives that we don't even know we're doing it. Just like breathing, it becomes involuntary, and we judge all of the time. But the good news is that *God wants to set us free*, and we can begin to be set free right now. I believe there are three things He wants to say to our hearts:

ONE. Don't judge God.

TWO. Don't judge yourself.

THREE. Don't judge anyone else.

It's very simple. Don't judge God, because He is good all the time. Don't judge yourself. We'll either be too hard on ourselves or too easy, but we'll never get it right. We need to ask God to search us, and His judgments will be right. Don't judge others, because we have no right to judge anyone; everyone stands or falls to God alone. I believe God is saying, "If you stop judging Me, stop judging yourself, and stop judging each other, then the law will not exist in your life. Your

Christianity will no longer be anchored to the foundation of the law but to the foundation of My Son, Jesus Christ, and Him crucified." His foundation is based on humility, faith, and love, and judgment has nothing to do with those three things, does it? Judgment is basically the opposite of that foundation.

> IF YOU STOP JUDGING ME, STOP JUDGING YOURSELF, AND STOP JUDGING EACH OTHER, THEN THE LAW WILL NOT EXIST IN YOUR LIFE.

If we look to the person of Jesus to see what He said about judgment, we find a very, very bizarre truth. He was God, the Word become flesh, yet He did not have an opinion about anything. To paraphrase John 5:19 and John 8:28, Jesus said, "I only say what I hear My Father say, and I only do what I see My Father do. I don't have any opinions about anything." What Jesus was saying was that He didn't make judgments on His own. That's why He was also the only person who has ever been without sin. No judgment, no law, no sin. He fulfilled the law by not sinning, by not judging.

Let's consider 1 Peter 2:22-23, which reads, " '[He] committed no sin, nor was deceit found in His mouth'… when He was reviled, did not revile in return; when He suffered, He did not threaten, but committed Himself to Him who judges righteously." That passage is basically saying that Jesus didn't judge and pay somebody back. His attitude was, "You can do whatever you want to Me, but I will not judge you. I don't judge anything; I have no personal opinions about anything. That's why I don't have any sin."

It should probably be noted here that all Christians, and especially people in leadership positions, are sometimes called upon to make Godly *assessments*. Pastors, parents, all of us have to make Godly assessments or judgments. Jesus made them all of the time, but they always came through the Father. The key here is that Godly assessments don't involve pride, unbelief, or a hard heart towards a person. We're not trying to *be* God; we allow God to live His life in us, and His life is a life of humility, faith, and mercy.

Remember Adam and Eve in the garden? What were they trying to do? Become like God. That's what everyone wants to do. Like Cinderella's stepsisters, we're all pushing and shoving to fit our feet into God's shoes. Or to put it more comically, we're all scrambling to squeeze our own behinds onto God's throne of judgment. What was Adam and Eve's original sin? They said to themselves, "Let's eat this fruit to become like God." They were trying to force their two behinds onto the judgment seat of God, and now, following in their footsteps, there are six billion people on the earth striving for the same thing. We're all pushing and shoving, trying to cram ourselves onto that throne because, just like Adam and Eve, we think if we can judge between good and evil, we'll become like God. But you know what? God's watching all of this and saying, "You guys are going to all of this effort to sit in judgment over others because somehow you think that will make you like Me. But I have news for you. There is only one righteous judge—Me. And guess what? My heart is merciful." Want proof?

Psalm 136 says over and over that the Lord is good and His mercy endures forever. Look at the story of the prodigal son and the father who runs to embrace him. That father represents God the Father, who kisses and welcomes His wayward son back with great mercy. (See Luke 15:11-32.) What does James say? "Mercy triumphs over judgment" (James 2:13). If God's heart is mercy, and mercy triumphs over judgment, how could He be a God whose desire is to condemn and judge people? What did He say when He sent Jesus? John 3:17-18 out of the Amplified Bible says it best: "For God did not send the Son into the world in order to judge (to reject, to condemn, to pass sentence on) the world, but that the world might find salvation and be made safe and sound through Him. He who believes in Him [who clings to, trusts in, relies on Him] is not judged [he who trusts in Him never comes up for judgment; for him there is no rejection, no condemnation—he incurs no damnation]."

> IF GOD'S DESIRE WAS JUDGMENT, HE WOULD HAVE SAID, "SON, GO DOWN THERE AND TAKE CARE OF THOSE BAD HUMAN BEINGS THAT WE CREATED."

If God's desire was judgment, He would have said, "Son, go down there and take care of those bad human beings that we created." But He didn't say that, did He? He said, "Son, go down there and die for them and save them." If you start from the last supper and go to the crucifixion, you'll see Jesus had every opportunity to judge, starting with Judas. He could have exposed Judas and condemned him, but instead He washed his feet. In the garden, when He found the apostles sleeping, He could have said, "You're a bunch of losers. I'm done. I'm leaving before these guards come, and I'm going to find another group." But He didn't do it. The soldiers, the temple guards—Jesus could have defended Himself and even killed them for the mistake they were making. He didn't. He didn't judge the Pharisees, the chief priests and scribes, Pilate, the Roman soldiers, or the crowd that mocked and reviled Him. Instead, "[He] committed Himself to Him who judges righteously." It's simply not His desire to judge. We're all trying to become like God, and that's not what God is like.

I believe in the end—the final judgment day—our hearts and actions will judge themselves. We will choose not to be with God; it will be our decision. In the end it's going to be real obvious. I *decided* I didn't want God; *I* made the decision; *I* cut myself off from the Lord. That's how it's going to happen. As the scripture says, He's not willing that any should perish, but that all should come to Him. (See 2 Peter 3:9.) God wants everybody to be saved; His heart is mercy, not judgment.

What are we going to do? If we want to be separated from God and our brothers and sisters in Christ, lose our God-given birthright, and be cursed and die, we can choose a path of judgment. I don't want that path, do you? If we want to be united to God and become one with our brothers and sisters in Christ, regain our God-given birthright, receive power for blessings and be able to bless other people, then we will choose the gospel of Jesus Christ and Him crucified and truly draw close to God.

Is the Holy Spirit speaking to you as you read? Are you ready to remove the law as the foundation of your life by getting judgment out of your life? Are you ready to lay a better foundation for your life, made up of Christ crucified? If so, consider praying this prayer:

> *My Merciful Father,*
> *I realize I have drifted away from You—from my first love. In my effort to become holy, I have been beguiled by the enemy, and sucked into judgment.*

It felt good, Lord; it felt righteous. I thought it was the way to be close to You, but now I see that it isn't.

Lord, I don't want that stain on me—the stain of judgment—and I ask You now to wash me in the blood of Jesus. Forgive me, and cleanse me of all of that ugliness—pride, unbelief, and a hard heart—the sin that comes out of judgment. Bathe me in Your love. I'm destroying the foundation of the law in my life and asking You to build a new thing in its place. Replace this evil nature with Your nature—the nature of mercy—the nature of Your Son. Transform me into His image.

As I receive Your forgiveness, I ask that You would now plant my feet on the Rock. Anchor me into the humility, faith, and love of Your Son.

I'm coming back to You, Father, by coming back to my first love—Jesus! Thank You for running to embrace me. May I never be led away again.

In Jesus' name.

My Personal One-on-One Encounter With The Lord

Also for Home Group Discussion

How does the law power sin, literally making it possible for sin to exist (I Corinthians 15:56)?

_____
_____
_____
_____

Do I understand how judgment brings the law to life, like a lawnmower pull-cord brings its engine to life?

_____
_____
_____
_____

Is judging like breathing for me? Do I do it all the time without thinking of it? What are some examples of how I judge?

_____
_____
_____
_____

If the essence of our Christian walk is humility, faith, and love, what are the opposite fruits produced by judgment?

_____
_____
_____
_____

What did God reveal to me, personally, as I read and pondered this chapter?

_____
_____
_____
_____

Have I taken judgment to the foot of the cross to put it to death, so that I can stop judging God, myself, and others?

_____
_____
_____
_____

Reflecting on the Art

- In what way does the painting that opens this chapter speak to me?
- Did the sketch have an impact on me? If so, how?

_____
_____
_____
_____

Who's the Real Me?

CHAPTER 7

Who's the Real Me?

So far on our spiritual journey, we've discovered the wisdom of the world system we were in and have replaced the law with the gospel of grace. Now we can begin an inward journey, to find out "Who's the real me?"

We each have a God-given identity that is ours alone. It is not selfish to want to grasp hold of that identity because it is a gift from God, bought with the precious blood of His Son. The world, other people in our lives, even we ourselves, may try to impose another identity on us—but what is true is what God thinks about us. That is what defines our *true* self.

Part of the journey to God's world of love, power, blessings, and fulfilled destiny is a journey to the center of ourselves. We must find out once and for all who we really are. And to find out what my true identity is, I have to ask this question: *Who am I?* Not how I see myself, not how others see me, but how *God* sees me. Who is the real me?

There is a key scripture that speaks to this question, Proverbs 23:7. In the Amplified Bible it reads, "As [a man] thinks in his heart, so he is." In other words, how I act and what I do depends on who I think I am. And what I believe God

> HOW I ACT AND WHAT I DO DEPENDS ON WHO I THINK I AM.

wants to do with us on this journey is to open the eyes of our hearts. He wants us to think a different way. When I learn to think a different way, in the heart of who I am, then how I act and what I do will never be the same again.

There's a three-part truth to who we are. The first truth about the real me—and the real you—is that we are *wonderful*. We've always been wonderful. You were wonderful from the moment you were conceived. God says so! And, the second truth about who we are, is that we are *princes and princesses*—the moment we are born again we become sons and daughters of the King of kings! We all know that in a royal family, when the king dies, his heir becomes king or queen. Since our King died on the cross, the third truth is, we have the opportunity to become kings and queens.

When we can embrace these truths about ourselves, and start thinking differently, we will do things differently. Let's allow God to open the eyes of our hearts as we study them further.

That first statement, *I am wonderful,* sounds pretty audacious, doesn't it? It *is* a rather bold truth. A counselor friend, who shared this concept with me, tells a story about going to Germany to minister. He was getting ready to speak to a crowd of Germans who had never met him before. He walked up to the microphone, looked them in the eyes, and declared, "I want you to know something. I am wonderful." I am sure they were thinking, *What kind of egomaniac is this American?* But then he went on to tell them why.

In Genesis 1:27 it says, "So God created man in His own image; in the image of God He created him; male and female He created them." Then in Genesis 2:7 the Bible says, "The Lord God formed man of the dust of the ground, and breathed into his nostrils the breath of life; and man became a living being." This is confirmed in Job 33:4, which reads, "The Spirit of God has made me, and the breath of the Almighty gives me life." In the Hebrew the word *breath* means "Spirit."

This is what happened: God took a piece of Himself, who is the great I Am, and at the moment of conception of every human being, He put that piece of Himself inside of that fertilized egg. God is great, and at that moment we became wonderful because we became a God-carrier.

Did you know that a percentage of all healthy sperm and eggs that come together do not create a human being? There is no scientific

I Am Wonderful

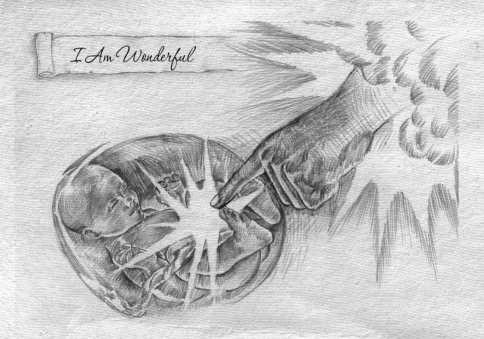

explanation for this phenomenon, but I believe the reason is that God did not decide to put a piece of Himself into that fertilized egg. Expounding on this thought, what do we call it when a woman becomes pregnant? She "conceives." The dictionary definition of *conceive* is "to become pregnant, to form an idea in the mind." Nobody is an accident—that's a lie from the pit of hell. God conceived us, thought about us in His mind, and planned for us to be here. We are "fearfully and wonderfully made" (Psalm 139:14). "His name [is] Wonderful" (Isaiah 9:6), and we are chips off the old block!

For more proof that we are all carriers of the breath of God, consider James 2:26. It says, "The body without the spirit is dead." When Jesus died on the cross, the Bible says, "He gave up His Spirit" (Matthew 27:50 NIV). We see there's a very clear spiritual truth that life begins when the Spirit

> LIFE IS CONNECTED TO THAT PIECE OF GOD THAT GOES INTO EVERY HUMAN BEING, AND THAT PIECE OF GOD IS THE PIECE OF US THAT IS WONDERFUL.

of God goes into a fertilized egg, and life ends when the Spirit of God leaves a body. This flesh is clay. Life is connected to that piece of God that goes into every human being, and that piece of God is the piece of us that is wonderful.

Let's consider the price of our redemption. We were purchased by the blood of Jesus Christ, right? That's the highest price the Father could ever pay, and He did it to save us. Would you pay a high price for something that wasn't valuable to you?

My wife Lu Ann had an experience that serves to illustrate this point. One day she lost her ring. It was a beautiful diamond ring, and it had special meaning for her because I had given it to her. When she realized it was gone, she thought she might have accidentally thrown it away with some paper. She began digging through the trash. That ring was so valuable to her that she dug through layer upon layer of stinky garbage to get to the bottom, where she found her ring. Do you know what she would have done if she hadn't found her ring in the trash can? She'd have torn through the entire house, and if she didn't find it there, she would have gone into the big garbage dumpsters head first. She would have done whatever it took to get back her ring.

> "I WILL SEND MY SON TO DIE FOR YOU TO GET YOU BACK, BECAUSE I'M NOT WHOLE WITHOUT YOU. THAT'S HOW VALUABLE YOU ARE."

If that ring was just costume jewelry, do you think Lu Ann would have gone to all of that trouble? Nobody goes to that much trouble to find something cheap or junky, and we can be sure that God would not have paid such a terrible price for us if we were not valuable to Him. When Father God took a piece of Himself, His Spirit, and put it in your mother's womb, it left a hole in Him that can never be filled again except by you. In the cross, it's as if He was saying, "I have to have you back, and I will send My Son to die for you to get you back because I'm not whole without you. That's how valuable you are."

It is hard for some of us to understand our value in God's eyes because we've always been taught that we are sinful wretches. And so we are. The song "Amazing Grace" says, "Amazing grace, how sweet the sound, that saved a wretch like me." But it is always important to remember that in Him who is the Truth, more than one truth can be in operation. While we are cringing paupers, in need of His saving grace, we are also wonderful because we have a piece of Him inside us. That's why He went to so much trouble to get us back.

Can you look in the mirror and say from your heart, "I am wonderful!"? Has He opened the eyes of your heart so that you can see yourself as He sees you? When the Lord allows you to see what He sees, you can truly look in the mirror and say that and mean it. Your life will never be the same!

It doesn't matter what opinion of yourself you had before; it doesn't matter what opinion anybody else had of you; the only opinion that matters is God's! You can look in the mirror, and you can say, "I'm wonderful." What's more, you can do that every day, because no matter what, it won't have changed. God never changes. I challenge you to start doing that today! This is the first aspect of getting your God-given birthright back—*replacing Satan's lie that you're inferior with God's truth that you are wonderful!*

Item two on the subject of identity is that *from the moment we are born again we are either a prince or a princess.* The minute I accept Jesus Christ as Lord and Savior of my life, I become a child of the Most High God, the King Immortal.

Doesn't every little girl dream about being a princess? Disney makes millions and millions of dollars perpetuating that dream. Cinderella, Snow White, the whole list of them, are all about a girl having Prince Charming come into her life and becoming a princess. To all of you little girls out there—and the ones who have grown up—God is saying, "I've got good news for you today. It's true! You are a princess! You don't have to daydream about it—you *are* a princess."

Doesn't every little boy want to be a prince? They want to ride a horse and go fight the enemy or slay the dragon. They want to grab that girl and put her on the back of the horse and ride off into the sunset. Boys want to be champions! God made us that way. And he wired us that way because *we are sons and daughters of a King.* That's the truth that makes us either a prince or a princess.

What do we have to do to earn that status? Nothing. This was illustrated to me one day as I sat in a café with my daughter. There was a little baby sitting on a table, and everybody was around the table staring at the baby. The parents, grandparents, and other relatives were cooing and smiling, focusing their complete attention on that baby. As I watched, it dawned on me that the baby was doing nothing to receive all of that love and attention. In fact, what that baby does is worse than nothing. She fills her diapers, spits up, screams—and she may do those things many times a day—but it doesn't matter. She is loved and cared for—their princess because she was born into that family.

> WHEN WE ARE BORN INTO GOD'S FAMILY, HE LOOKS AT US AND SAYS, "THERE'S MY BABY BOY! THERE'S MY BABY GIRL! MY LITTLE PRINCE! MY LITTLE PRINCESS!"

Did you know that's what happens to us when we are born into God's family? He looks at us and says, "There's my baby boy! There's my baby girl! My little prince! My little princess!" That's what He thinks about us, and I believe that's what He wants us to think about ourselves.

Challenge number two, then, is that whatever day it is, we need to look in the mirror and say, "I accepted you, Jesus, as Lord and Savior of my life. That means I'm a prince [or princess]." Believe it, and mean it, and you'll never act the same. You will never carry yourself the same way; you won't have the same posture; you won't have the same attitude; you won't have the same thoughts. We will not be the same people when we get that in our hearts. We are princes and princesses of the kingdom of heaven. This is the second aspect of getting your birthright back—*replacing being a slave under the law with being a son or daughter of God through faith in Jesus Christ.*

Now for the grand finale. Nobody can ever top God, right? We've learned that we're wonderful, and we're either a prince or a princess. But what happens to a prince or princess when the king or queen dies? What instantly happens? They become the king or queen. Our King died, so we have the opportunity to become a king or queen—but this will involve a process.

From the moment we were conceived, we have been wonderful, because we have a piece of God in us. At the moment we accept Jesus as Lord and Savior of our lives, we become a prince or princess. Becoming a king or queen involves a choice: we have to choose to die with Jesus and be raised a new creation. It's not automatic; it's a process.

Consider Romans 8:28. It says, "We know that all things work together for good to those who love God, to those who are the called according to His purpose. For whom He foreknew, He also predestined to be conformed to the image of His Son, that He might be the firstborn among many brethren."

As I shared, the word *conformed* in the Greek is actually two words, *sum morphos*, and it means, basically, a union that produces a new creation. (It's the same word behind the English word *metamorphosis* that we talked about in chapter four, describing when a caterpillar turns into a butterfly.) We have to undergo the process of transformation to be made a new creation, and the best place for that to happen is through trials.

There's a lot of debate about that, but the same word pops up in Philippians 3:10-11, where Paul says (to paraphrase), "I want to know Jesus, and I want to experience and share the power of His resurrection. I want to share in His sufferings, be conformed to Him in His death, so that some day I may attain to the resurrection from the dead, even while still in this body" (Amplified Bible). The word *conformed—sum morphos—*is there again, right after sharing in His sufferings. Guess what? There are going to be trials that involve suffering.

To become a king or a queen, let's not waste our trials. When you're going through a trial, ask the Lord to use it to transform you. When I went through my legal, financial, and health problems, I sure didn't enjoy them; but guess what, they have made me a far better minister today. Because of the pain that I went through, I can better understand the pain of people going through those same trials now. I can connect with them far better than ever before. Also, they

> TO BECOME A KING OR A QUEEN, LET'S NOT WASTE OUR TRIALS. WHEN YOU'RE GOING THROUGH A TRIAL, ASK THE LORD TO USE IT TO TRANSFORM YOU.

exposed a lot of my hidden junk, which I could then take to the cross. The Lord used the trials to build in me the character of Christ.

I didn't waste my trial, and you mustn't either. When trials come our way, we must remember that our ultimate destiny is to become kings and queens, but we must go through the cross—we need to experience *sum morphos*, a transforming union with our King—in order to be transformed into a butterfly.

Do you recognize the butterfly we've used throughout the book? It's a Monarch. According to the dictionary, a monarch is "a king, one holding preeminent position or power." It also says "a butterfly." This is where we start as an egg, are born again, and then turn into a caterpillar. What happens, as we said earlier, is that believers get stuck in the caterpillar phase; we never go into the cocoon and get transformed into a monarch—a king or a queen. But that can change today. This is the third aspect of getting your God-given birthright back—*dying to self to be transformed into a king or queen.*

It doesn't matter what building we're in, or what end of town; it doesn't matter what anybody thinks of us. God has ordained and proclaimed for every one of us to be a king or a queen—to take dominion on this earth and to be world changers. His Son, the King of kings, died so we as royal heirs could be transformed into kings and queens. He's going to bring us back to the positions we held in the Garden of Eden, where humans had rulership dominion as the king and queen of the entire earth. Satan came and deceived us, but we're going to get our dominion and birthright back. This book, *The Lost Secret*, is a part of that heavenly restoration. To get what was lost back, we need to continue our internal spiritual journey by leaving behind the life we know.

My Personal One-on-One Encounter With The Lord

Also for Home Group Discussion

Do I understand that how I act and what I do depends on who I think I am? What are some examples of how I'm living now that don't line up with how God sees me?
_____
_____

Do I believe that I am wonderful because God put a piece of Himself in me?
_____
_____

Do I believe that I'm a prince or princess because when I was born again I became the child of a King?
_____
_____

When a king dies, his children then become the king or queen. Do I believe that I have the opportunity to become a king or queen because my King, Jesus, died on the cross?
_____
_____

Reflecting on the Art

- In what way does the painting that opens this chapter speak to me?
- Did the sketch have an impact on me? If so, how?

_____
_____
_____

*Leave Behind
The Life You Know*

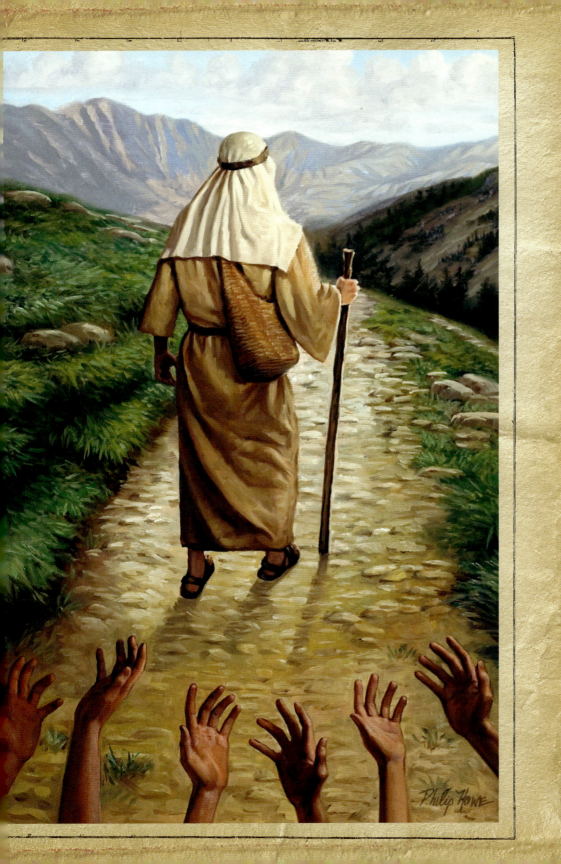

CHAPTER 8

Leave Behind The Life You Know

In the last chapter, we learned what's true and false about our identity. In Christ, the "real me" is wonderful, a prince or princess, and is destined to become a king or queen. That's the life we want—and the true life Jesus came to give us—but the "false me" still exists. That artificial person must be dealt with in order for us to embrace the new life we have in Jesus. The "false me" must be put to death on the cross in order to move on in resurrection life – a life full of love, power, and blessings – and a life of fulfilled destiny to bless others.

The way God is going to teach us how to do this is by using Abraham, a man God greatly blessed and used to greatly bless others. There was an article in *National Geographic* a while back about Abraham. In this article, the writer said, "Imagine a world saturated with ignorance and hatred, a lonely, brutish place without any hope of redemption. Now, picture a man—Abram, the Bible calls him—who hears a command from God: *Leave behind the life you know, and I will one day bless the entire world through you.* How this will happen, and why, is a mystery to this man, but he sets out."[1]

---

1 Tad Szulc, "Journey of Faith," *National Geographic* (December 2001): p. 90.

This concept, to leave behind the life you know, can be very scary. In fact, every time I teach this concept, I can tell by most people's reactions that they are scared. I'll admit it is terrifying to me! The fear of the unknown is one of the greatest human fears, but as we'll see through the example of Abraham, leaving behind the life you know can be a wonderful thing. Think about it, if we don't leave the world we're living in now, how can we ever enter God's world of love and power? Let's look at the life of Abraham within the context of the four stages of the Christian life—the four stages of the butterfly.

The Bible never describes Abram's initial encounter with God. He was living in Ur, in the land of the Chaldeans, which was full of idols. At some point, God spoke to him and said, *Guess what. See all of these idols that are here? They're nothing. I'm God.* When Abram realized that the idols of his homeland were not real and accepted the One True God, that was Abram's born-again experience. He entered the egg stage.

Then Genesis 12:1-3 (NIV) says,

> *The Lord had said to Abram, "Leave your country, your people and your father's household and go to the land I will show you. I will make you into a great nation and I will bless you; I will make your name great, and you will be a blessing. I will bless those who bless you, and whoever curses you I will curse; and all peoples on earth will be blessed through you."*

God spoke a birthright blessing over Abram, the one that had been lost by Adam and Eve in the Garden. The process of restoring our God-given birthright had begun—our relationship with God and our rulership over the earth—to be blessed and be a blessing. Jesus would finish the work on the cross.

The next stage, the caterpillar stage, would be when Abram went with his father from Ur to Haran. The Bible says, "Terah took his son Abram, his grandson Lot son of Haran, and his daughter-in-law Sarai, the wife of his son Abram, and together they set out from Ur of the Chaldeans to go to Canaan. But when they came to Haran, they settled there" (Genesis 11:31). They *set out* to go to Canaan, but instead of going to

Canaan, along the way they *settled*. That's much like the church today. We've settled for the Caterpillar Christian stage when God has so much more.

Abram's next step came when his father died. By obedience, he had to truly leave his father's house, people, and country and go to Canaan—Abram had to go into the cocoon stage. The next part of his life is when all of the transformation took place—and all of the scary things. Abram was transformed into Abraham. He went from being childless to becoming the father of many nations (Genesis 17:1-8). He went to Canaan, and Egypt; there was fighting and dividing land with Lot; and Sodom and Gomorrah; and then the ultimate test—Mount Moriah—where he was asked to sacrifice his one and only son Isaac. Did you know that Mt. Moriah is actually the same location as Calvary, where God's only son, Jesus, was sacrificed? And that *Moriah* means "place of clear vision"? That's what Abraham had to get to—the physical place of Calvary—the cross. That's where everything becomes clear. And when he was willing to sacrifice his only son for the sake of obedience to God, God said, *You've passed the test.* Abraham became a butterfly.

Would Abram, who was living in Ur, in the land of the Chaldeans, ever have been able to fulfill his destiny if he had remained in Ur? He would never have gone to the land of Canaan, the Promised Land, where the Lord said, "Every place on which the sole of your foot treads shall be yours" (Deuteronomy 11:24).

Would he ever have received his promised blessings? The Bible says he was a wealthy man in Canaan. That's also where his sons were born. Finally, would he ever have been the father of many nations and had the whole world blessed through him? If he had stayed in Ur, it wouldn't have happened, right?

> FOR ABRAHAM TO RECEIVE HIS PROMISED BLESSINGS, AND FULFILL HIS DESTINY TO BLESS OTHERS, HE HAD TO LEAVE BEHIND THE LIFE HE KNEW.

For Abraham to receive his God-given birthright—his promised love, power, blessings, and destiny—he had to leave behind the life he knew. Was it easy? No! Chaldea enjoyed a highly advanced civilization at the time, being in the midst of the region known as "the cradle of

civilization"—writing had been developed there fifteen centuries or more before Abraham's time—so it was a pretty good place to live. The book of Hebrews says that when he set out, *he did not know where he was going* (Hebrews 11:8). Abraham had to leave a place that was pretty good, a life that he knew, not even knowing where he was going. That was a big step, and that's what God is calling us to do. And by His grace, we will obey also. Just like Abraham, the father of our faith, we too will regain our birthright to be blessed and bless others.

I believe there's another really important point in those verses where God is telling him to leave. What did the Lord say? "I want you to leave your father's house, your people and your country." I think we can all really connect to this.

We've all been molded, influenced, and shaped by the environment we live in. The house where we grew up is our "father's house." The church we attended (or didn't) and the schools we went to—those things are our "people." And, of course, our country is our "country." I believe we are all, to some degree, prisoners of our past. We are all entangled by our past, maybe held back by it, controlled by our past in some way. We all understand who we are through the lens of our past, and I believe God is saying, *No. No more. That's not who you are; that's not the "real you." I've got better things for you.*

Let's imagine a prison and picture ourselves in that prison looking out of the bars. That person in the prison is the real you, the real me. Jesus Christ has come for a jailbreak, so we can leave behind the life we know, and enter God's world of love and power! Let's scope out this prison to figure out how the jailbreak will happen.

If we refer to the illustration, there are three windows for three rooms. The first one is our father's house—all of the things that have happened to us in the past with our family, in our home while we were growing up. The next window we look through is our religious upbringing and the schools we attended, which is our people. The third window is the United States (or whatever country we grew up in), and the culture of that room is the culture of the country.

Each room has four pieces of furniture in it that have dramatically influenced our lives and may have controlled us. The pieces of furniture are these: false teachings, wounds, good intentions, and the demons that are attached to those things, because they have become idols in our lives. I believe the Lord is saying, *I'm going to let you look inside and see those rooms—those pieces of furniture—and I'm going to let you understand what's really going on inside of you, and then I'm going to break you out.*

Let's talk about false teachings and think about a few examples. The first one is historical, and it is scary. Nazi Germany was full of "functional families," where people worked, took care of their kids, and even went to church. But in many of those families, the children were taught that they were the Aryan race and superior to others. Jews, blacks, and gypsies were compared to animals—lower than animals—and it was believed the "right thing" was to kill them. Of course this wasn't true—in fact it was grossly evil—but many children grew up not questioning it because it was a part of their family's culture. It was a false teaching that was accepted and passed down—with horrific consequences. That's the extreme of false teaching and the extreme of the damage it could cause, but how many other false teachings—none that dire, I hope—have we accepted simply because they are the beliefs of our family?

Consider this personal example. My wife, Lu Ann, had a great father, but she received a conflicting message from him. He told her something to the effect of, "Don't ever have a close relationship with anybody outside of the family. Never trust anyone outside of the family." She had a big family, a great childhood, wonderful relationships—but then she became a Christian. She was born again through the blood of Jesus into a second family, and guess what her biggest struggle was? Fellowship. Believers would try to include her and build friendships with her, but she could hardly do it. There was always some excuse as to why she couldn't enter into fellowship.

Do you know why she had trouble with fellowship? It was because of the false teaching she received in her father's house—it was an idol in her life. Therefore, to honor her father was pleasing to God, but to place his false teaching above the word of God was not. The Bible says not to forsake "the assembling

> THEREFORE, TO HONOR HER FATHER WAS PLEASING TO GOD, BUT TO PLACE HIS FALSE TEACHING ABOVE THE WORD OF GOD WAS NOT.

of ourselves together" (Hebrews 10:25) and to love your brothers and sisters, but Lu Ann would tell you there was an idol in her life competing with that truth, which was that false teaching. Until she got rid of that idol, fellowship was a real struggle in her life, and she was missing the blessing of other Godly relationships. We can see the dangers, both global and personal, of false teachings.

The next piece of furniture we need to examine is wounds. There was a guy in our small group one time, and I knew he had a lion's heart. He was a very gifted guy, but he never said a peep and never got involved in anything. We worked and worked and worked at drawing him out. Finally, one night he said, "I want to tell you something. When I was a kid, every time I said something, either my parents or my brothers and sisters would say, 'You're stupid; you're so stupid.' So now I don't talk."

Did God create him to be quiet? Or did his wounds make him quiet? I want to tell you something about the bondage of an idol, though. I can't count how many times we tried to set this guy free and he resisted. He would say, "You just want me to be like you," when in reality our heart was for his "real me" to be set free. That wound, the belief that he was stupid, went deep.

My daughter, Kristin, also knows something about wounds. She was a great athlete, but while playing high school basketball, she got trapped in a situation in which a coach really abused his authority. The words and actions of this coach deeply wounded Kristin and many of her friends. It was terrible. Kristin came to a point in which she said, "I will never pick up a basketball again in my life."

That's understandable, and we all do it, don't we? We set up this type of boundary to try to protect ourselves from getting hurt. But in the end, we have to consider God's will even over our own desire not to be hurt. What if God wanted Kristin to play basketball? What if he wanted her to play intramural basketball in college, to bump into a person she would witness to, who would get saved, who would then become the next Billy Graham? Without obedience none of those things would ever happen, right?

What Kristin had to decide was, who was lord of her life? Was it the coach and the wound? Or Jesus? If she bowed to the coach, vowing never to touch a basketball again because of what he did, then he was

> **WE CAN'T BE CONTROLLED BY OUR WOUNDS AND HAVE JESUS AS LORD OF OUR LIFE AT THE SAME TIME.**

in control of her life. That wound would be controlling her, keeping her enslaved. We can't be controlled by our wounds and have Jesus as Lord of our life at the same time.

Finally, probably the most dreaded obstacle of all is good intentions. There's only one problem with a good intention—there is no such thing. They do not exist, you know why? Romans 3:10 says, "There is none righteous, no, not one." And Romans goes on to say, "I know that in me (that is, in my flesh) nothing good dwells" (7:18), and Isaiah 64:6 says that all of our righteousness is like filthy rags. So there is no such thing as a truly "good" intention.

I believe one of the most toxic things in the world is a so-called good intention, and here's my toxic story. As a kid, I was a pretty good athlete, and my dad worked all of the time. He could never be there for me. All of the other kids seemed to have dads that went with them to little league, and to make a long story short, I had a lot of bad experiences. I got cut from teams and got really wounded—terribly hurt and wounded by athletics. Because of that, I made a promise to myself. I said, "When I get married and have kids, I am going to spend time with them. I'm going to help them develop their athletic abilities, and what happened to me will never happen to my kids." That was my good intention.

And you know what? I did it. I would be at meetings, or practicing for my own tournament water skiing, and I'd have to leave because I was going to coach little league, or soccer with my son Ricky. My friends would say things like, "Rick, you are such a model father! Man, you just lay down your life for your kids!" I liked that; it fed my image as a model Christian, but do you know what happened to every one of my kids in sports? Some good things, but many disappointments as well. My good intention to form a perfect sports world never worked out.

One day the Lord revealed to me what was underneath that good intention. He said, *You have judgments against your father. You hate your father. You have never forgiven him for hurting you by not helping you with sports. And do you know what My word says? It says, "Honor your father and your mother," the first commandment with a promise, so that it might go well with you. Have sports gone well with you?*

The answer, of course, was "No." And I came to see that the Lord didn't care about my good intentions. They were all based on the wrong motives. What God cares about is the heart—and whether His Son is King of our hearts. We're not good; He is. He came down to die for us and save us because we can't do it for ourselves. We can't be good enough. We can't impress enough people. We can't create the good life or ever be our true and best selves without Him. *There is no substitution for Jesus;* nothing else works but the cross. All of our good intentions fall to the ground at the foot of the cross. That's a good thing, because my good intentions hurt me; they hurt the people around me; and they hurt God. That's just as toxic as it gets—and it's so hard to recognize, because we think of our intentions as good things.

> I CAME TO SEE THAT THE LORD DIDN'T CARE ABOUT MY GOOD INTENTIONS. THEY WERE ALL BASED ON THE WRONG MOTIVES.

Are you beginning to feel like you live in this room? Is this your furniture? Let's look at that last piece—demons. Remember (from Deuteronomy 32:16-17 and 1 Corinthians 10:20-22) that attached to every idol is a demon. What is a false teaching, a wound, a good intention? They are all idols, because they are all competing with the Lordship of Jesus Christ.

This gets very sinister. Going back to the basics, when we accept Jesus into our lives we say that He is Lord of our life; but, we have hidden idols that compete with His Lordship. We say we're led by the Holy Spirit, but we have little demons attached to those idols who compete with the counsel of the Holy Spirit. They are familiar spirits, and they tell us lies, like, "You're just a quiet guy...." "There are other activities, you're not supposed to play basketball...." "You're not supposed to be in fellowship...." and on and on. Before we know it, they are intertwined with our personalities.

We've talked about Satan being the father of lies. In John 8, Jesus said that Satan is a murderer and a liar, and when he lies, he speaks his native tongue. When the devil and demons lie, they have no accent. Their lies can become so familiar we don't even second-guess them. We just take it as part of who we are—like my friend believing he's just a quiet guy—and actually the demons' lie becomes a part of who we are. That part is the false self, though. It's not our true identity, but, thanks be to God, the Truth can set us free.

Let's pause and look at the big picture of the "real me" vs. the "false me." Jesus says in John 14:6, "I am the way, the truth and the life. No one comes to the Father except through Me." Romans 8:14 says, "As many as are led by the Spirit of God, these are sons of God." The Lordship of Jesus and the leading of the Holy Spirit are the keys to sonship and daughterhood. *As long as we still have those idols competing with Jesus as Lord, and their demons competing with the Holy Spirit as counselor, we are not fully free as sons and daughters of the Father. Instead, during the times we are controlled by idols and demons, we are slaves!* The false me, which is a slave, gets no reward for its labor or a future inheritance—no blessings and no destiny. The real me, which is a son or daughter, gets both. That's why every Christian must ask him or herself, "Who's controlling me?" "Who's the real me?" Our promised blessings and God-given destiny to bless others depends on knowing the truth!

> "WHO'S THE REAL ME?" OUR PROMISED BLESSINGS AND GOD-GIVEN DESTINY TO BLESS OTHERS DEPENDS ON KNOWING THE TRUTH!

Think of it this way. When we are Caterpillar Christians, there's a world system from man that we are in—a system of knowledge and works—and we must get out of it. As we discovered in the opening chapters, we had no idea we were in it or that it was a bad system. But there's also a world system from man *in us*—hidden idols. We had no idea it was in us or that it was a bad system, but it must be taken out. There is, however, a right and wrong way to take this system out and leave our father's house, people, and country.

I Left the Wrong Way and it Doesn't Work!

Remember Abraham and the tale of how he left his father's house, his people, and his country? Well, I did that too, but the wrong way. I was angry with my father because he wasn't the kind of dad I wanted, so one day I simply moved out of his house. Before he even knew I had moved, we bumped into each other at a Burger King. I had a big confrontation with him and just blurted out all of my anger and hatred towards him. That's how I left my father's house. Not good.

I also did a very poor job of leaving my people. I was a devout Catholic, and I asked some questions of the brothers at my high school and priests at my church. When they couldn't answer my questions, I got fed up and upset with the church. I said, "This is a bunch of malarkey. God doesn't exist, and I'm going to become an atheist." That's how I left the church.

As for my country, I loved the United States of America and considered myself a big patriot. During the 1960s and the Vietnam War, however, I got very disillusioned with the U.S., and I said, "This is a sham. This is not a good country. I don't like the United States of America anymore."

I left behind the life I knew—my father's house—my people (the church)—and my country. I did it my way, and let me tell you, it didn't work out well!

> I LEFT BEHIND THE LIFE I KNEW—I DID IT MY WAY, AND LET ME TELL YOU, IT DIDN'T WORK OUT WELL!

If we look at the genealogy of Jesus Christ in Luke chapter 3, it starts with Jesus and it goes all the way back through His ancestors to Adam. Then—and this touches my heart—after Adam, it says "Adam, the son of God." Following this example, the Lord showed me that if we want to get out of slavery and fully become sons of God, we must go back through our ancestors. We cannot reject the mother and father He chose for us nor the entry-level religious experience He chose nor our country. If we do, we'll never get back to God.

As I went through this process, He opened my eyes to see things through the lens of grace. I realized that I actually had a father with many positive traits. He had character traits from God, and I got many of those traits from him. I now have honor and respect for my father and a good relationship with him. I see now that I came from my father, and if I reject him, I'm rejecting my own self.

I also looked at the Catholic church and realized similar things. You know what? Its history goes back a long ways. There were a lot of Godly people in the Catholic church in the past, as there are now. Catholics are pro-life and have great concern for the poor and needy. If I totally reject the Catholic church, I am rejecting the fruit God has produced in that church through history and the fruit He is producing now.

And finally, as I looked at my country, I accepted that even though it has many flaws, it's a wonderful country. Real God-fearing people came to found this country, and it was founded on Christian principles. There are a lot of positive things about the U.S. It's a place of freedom, a very generous nation, and it's the country God chose for me to be born in.

I was wrong in the way I left those three things—my father's house, my people, and my country—and if you've done that too, if you've left any of those things the wrong way, I'd encourage you to reassess them. We have to humble ourselves before the mighty hand of God and say, "You chose my parents, You chose how I would come to You, and this is the country You chose for my birth. I am the clay and You are the Potter. I trust You." After all, who are we as clay to wag our fingers at those things? When we do that, we're really wagging our fingers at the Potter, who is God! In my case, the Lord said, *Guess what. When you're done with your biggest protest, Cesar Suarez is still your father. You first heard about Me in the Catholic church. You're still a U.S. citizen. You can have a tantrum all you want, but it will never change those three things.* It's amazing.

I believe He wants to tenderize our hearts. We can't walk with Him with that kind of judgment, anger, or repulsiveness. We can't live in hatred of the sources of our life. It may feel like a high spiritual plain, but it's Death Valley. It's nowhere. That's what He taught me. Though this chapter is not primarily on forgiveness, we are to forgive our parents, our churches and schools, and our country. For all of the false teachings, wounds, and good intentions that came out of those things, we are to forgive them and say, "I forgive you just as I have been forgiven. I forgive you because you didn't know what you were doing." I release you. You don't owe me anything; your account is clear. My Source is God, and I'm going to put the ax to any bitter root that's been growing in me. At the foot of the cross, we forgive, we release, and the slate is clean. We have honor and respect and we have love for them.

Then guess what happens: now we can leave behind the life we know. My wife can leave behind the false teaching of her father and have fellowship with others. She can say, "I'm leaving that false teaching, but I'm not leaving my father." That's the difference. We can leave a false teaching or a wound without leaving the source of that false teaching or the source of that wound.

In leaving, we embrace. It's a mind-boggling concept, but remember, the Kingdom of God is about opposites: give to receive, be humble to be exalted. We leave by embracing. So we need to ask the Lord to search our hearts. Whatever's between us and our father's house, people, and country, let's deal with it. I would encourage everybody to do that. No matter how old we are, we can all still have issues. Time does not heal all wounds. I know an eighty-eight-year-old woman who, to this day, talks about her parents' deaths and being in an orphanage. That wound is as real to her today as it was then, but with Jesus it doesn't have to be. Look what Isaiah 53:3-4 says:

> He is despised and rejected by men,
> A Man of sorrows and acquainted with grief.
> And we hid, as it were, our faces from Him;
> He was despised, and we did not esteem Him.
> Surely He has borne our griefs
> And carried our sorrows;
> Yet we esteemed Him stricken,
> Smitten by God, and afflicted.

He bore the sorrows and pains of our wounds so we wouldn't have to. But how do we give them to Him? The key is the phrase *remission of our sins*. We need to both forgive the person who wounded us and remit their sin also—that is, give the pain, sorrow, and any damage caused by that sin to Jesus on the cross. Then not only are they released, but we are released also, so that wound does not affect and control us for the rest of our lives.

Getting rid of idols—and I can say this from experience—is very humbling, even breaking. We'll get into it a lot deeper in the next chapter, but I want to plant a little seed here. A humility seed. It's in Jeremiah 17:9-10, and it's God's way of helping us to see how badly we need Him. If we have any delusions that we can figure this out on our own—what our hidden idols are and what's really going on inside of us—we need this scripture. It says, "The heart is deceitful above all things, and desperately wicked; who can know it? I, the Lord, search the heart, I test the mind, even to give every man according to his ways, according to the fruit of his doings." If my heart is deceitful above all things, how in the world could I ever rely on my own heart, my own soul and mind, to figure out the truth? It's not going to happen. I will be deceived, and I will deceive myself.

I'll plant another seed. It says in Proverbs 28:26 (NIV) that "He who trusts in himself is a fool." And, Proverbs 3:5 says to trust in the Lord with all of our hearts and lean not on our own understanding. Why does the Lord tell us this? Because our minds and emotions can be tricked very easily.

Want proof? Consider how television works. I was in the television business, and I can tell you, everything in it is staged. It's all fake. But really, it's doubly fake. They take a fake staged scene, and then they have electrons that either fly through the air or through cables, and then they reconfigure them and they put them on a screen. That means what we see is really twice fake. Nevertheless, it can make us laugh and cry. It can make us angry or hate. It can make us scared. It can make us feel every emotion known to man—and it's all fake! Scary, isn't it?

The enemy's method is the same for the sincere Christian. His version of TV is our hidden idols with demons attached. He tricks us into feeling that what we're doing is a good thing—good ministry, good works, good parenting, good stewardship, good intentions. Yet all the while it's fake. We're operating with false motives, out of our false selves. Remember, an idol is a false god, something that appears to be good and God but isn't. So, as we say to the Lord, "Search me, and bring the *false me* into Your light," we must again apply the principle of embracing our past in order to leave it.

Embracing My Sins To Leave The Right Way

We've discussed that there is a right and wrong way to leave our father's house, people, and country. We must forgive, embrace, and respect them in order to leave the lifestyle of our *false me*. After we ask the Lord to search us, we will discover a second thing: our *false me* sinned and hurt the people around us who we love the most. What do we do about that?

When He shows us the sin and junk that was inside us that we were not aware of, and how it hurt Him, us, and the family and friends we love, we can't run and hide like Adam and Eve did. When they sinned, they covered themselves with fig leaves and hid behind the trees (Genesis 3:7-8). Spiritually speaking, we must stand naked and not try to defend ourselves. We must admit our sins to God and those people we have hurt. As we repent and ask for forgiveness, we confess that we desperately need God's grace that was poured out for us on the cross. What we are doing is fully embracing our past in order to leave it.

How can anyone of us do such a difficult thing? We can, when we come to know that we are wonderful—we're made in God's image and likeness because a piece of Him is in us—that we're a prince or a princess, because when we were born again we became the son or daughter of a King. We know who the *real me* is. We also know that the *false me* is forgiven by God. Romans 8:1 says there is no condemnation towards me because I am in Christ. In fact, all my sins have been remitted, meaning all of the judgment and punishment that I deserve has been taken by Jesus on the cross. In God's sight, which is the only view that matters, all of my sins have been removed. In fact, He says this: *For I shall be merciful to their unrighteousness, and their sins and their lawless deeds I will remember no more* (Hebrews 8:12 NIV).

Even though I understood who the *real me* was, and the *false me* was forgiven, for me, this was not an easy concept to carry out. For example, my *false me* was overly driven. I pushed myself and those around me very hard, and at times tried to control them, and this wounded them. But, I had also done many things with a pure heart that had blessed them. For some, all they remembered were the wounds, not the blessings. In their woundedness, they falsely accused me of things that went beyond my actual sins. This was very painful for me.

Here's how the Lord got me through. He spoke this question to my heart, "If it takes you being falsely accused of some things in order for those people you wounded to be set free by Me, will you do it?" When He asked this question, I realized that

> THE OPINIONS OF PEOPLE DIDN'T MATTER TO JESUS BECAUSE HE KNEW WHO HE WAS AND THAT THE FATHER LOVED HIM.

it was what Jesus did to save me! But His pain was far worse, because He was without sin. Not a single thing that He was accused of was true! That certainly put my little pity party in a whole new perspective. Philippians 2:7 says Jesus made Himself of no reputation; the opinions of people didn't matter to Him because He knew who He was and that the Father loved Him. Because of that, His only desire was to obey His Father and help people. When I fully embraced my past sins in front of these people, repented, and chose not to defend myself even against their false accusations, a funny thing happened—it actually improved my self-esteem! Through this toughest of tests, I came to the place where how I felt about myself was not connected to how others felt about me—whether they were right or wrong. It's a wonderful place of freedom!

This two-part big picture that we must embrace in order to leave behind the *life we know*, can be understood through the verses of this song:

> AT THE CROSS
> I know a place, a wonderful place
> Where accused and condemned
> Find mercy and grace
> Where the wrongs we have done
> And the wrongs done to us
> Were nailed there with Him
> There on the cross.[2]

First, no matter how many bad things happened to me from my father's house, people, and country I can now forgive, embrace, and respect them because it's all been taken care of at the cross. I leave the lifestyle of the *false me*, but I don't leave them. Second, I do the same with my *false me* sins that have hurt God, myself, and those around me. I can admit them, fully embrace my past, without defending myself, repent, and ask for forgiveness—because at the cross they're all gone. That's how to leave behind what's been done to us, and what we've done to others, the right way.

---

[2] Randy Butler, Terry Butler. Copyright © 1997 by Mercy/Vineyard Publishing. All rights reserved.

So we say to the life we knew, "Good riddance!" We're leaving that life behind—our father's house, our people, our country—and all of the associated baggage, which is the false teachings, the wounds, the good intentions, and the demons. We're going to the cross and dying to self. I know that sounds scary, but the good news is that, while the false self is being put to death, the real self—the real person—is being set free. We got brainwashed into thinking it's a bad thing to leave the old life behind, but it's a *good* thing. We will never enter the promised land to receive our inheritance, and fulfill our purpose and destiny, until we leave behind our false identity.

So let's go! Let's move out and claim our purpose, our destiny, our power, our peace—through the blood of Jesus. Remember, there's a right way (and a wrong way) to do it, so let's leave behind the life we know by first embracing it and then moving on in victory to a new life.

My Personal One-on-One Encounter With The Lord

Also for Home Group Discussion

Do I understand how much control my past has over me, that literally a false me was created by my father's house, people, and country? What are some examples of this in my own life?

_____
_____
_____
_____

Do I realize that these hidden idols in me, in the form of false teachings, wounds, and good intentions, compete with the Lordship of Jesus? As I say "Search me, O Lord", what hidden idols are beginning to surface?

_____
_____
_____
_____

Do I understand that the demons attached to these idols compete with the leading of the Holy Spirit? As these hidden idols began to surface, what lying familiar spirits were attached to them that were affecting my personality? (Example, a demon saying, "You're just a quiet guy.")

_____
_____
_____
_____

Do I truly believe that the wrongs I have done, and the wrongs done to me, were totally taken care of at the cross? If so, can I fully embrace both these things by bringing the *false me* to the cross, to leave that lifestyle behind? What is the Lord asking me to bring to the cross now?

_____
_____

Am I tired of being a prisoner of my past, and am I ready to be set free by leaving behind the life I know, so that I can receive my promised blessings and fulfill my God-given destiny?

_____
_____
_____
_____

Reflecting on the Art

- In what way does the painting that opens this chapter speak to me?
- Did the sketch have an impact on me? If so, how?

_____
_____
_____
_____

Vertical Beam of the Cross
Removing Hidden Idols

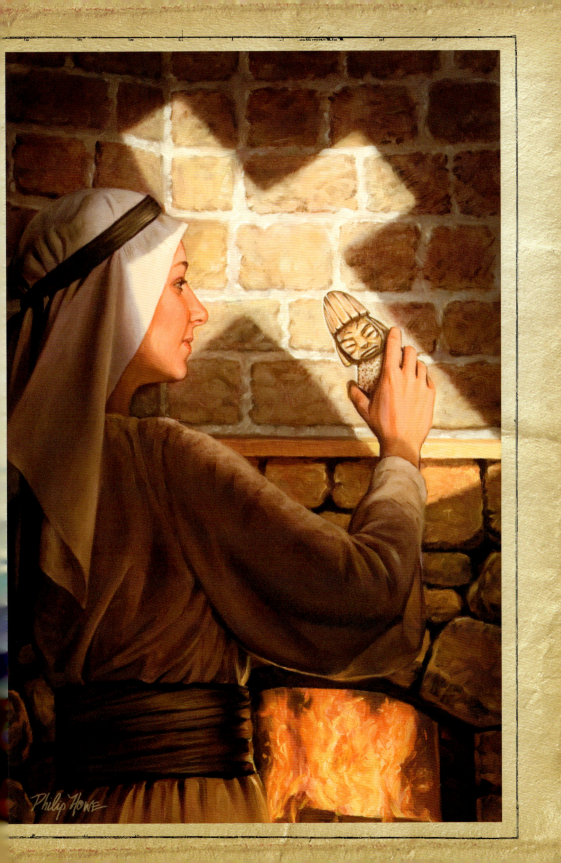

CHAPTER 9

Vertical Beam of the Cross
REMOVING HIDDEN IDOLS

Search me, O God, and know my heart;
Try me, and know my anxieties;
And see if there is any wicked way in me,
And lead me in the way everlasting.
Psalm 139:23-24

NOW THAT WE ARE LEAVING THE OLD LIFE BEHIND, we are ready to go to the cross—the first part of the lost secret. It's time to embrace the cross, and to do that, we're going to focus first on the vertical beam, the one that points upward and connects us to God. It's just between us and Him. Let's ask God to shine His searchlight on our hearts. Let's authorize Him to search us deeply, completely, to see if there are any hidden things we need to deal with and put behind us. We've talked about how to leave, and now we're going to talk about the things we're leaving, which are idols.

You know those verses above, from Psalm 139? It's a very interesting thing, but in Hebrew, the word *wicked* in that passage actually means "idols that cause pain." As we make those verses our prayer, let's allow the Lord to reveal to us any idols that are causing pain—to us, God, and the people around us—so we can remove them from our lives forever.

In Joshua 24, there are two kinds of idols that are identified, and they come from two different places. Joshua 24:14-15 says,

> *"Now therefore, fear the Lord, serve Him in sincerity and in truth, and put away the gods which your fathers served on the other side of the River and in Egypt. Serve the Lord! And if it seems evil to you to serve the Lord, choose for yourselves this day whom you will serve, whether the gods which your fathers served that were on the other side of the River, or the gods of the Amorites, in whose land you dwell. But as for me and my house, we will serve the Lord."*

There were two kinds of idols: idols from across the river and idols in the Promised Land.

We've discussed the idols of our father's house, our people, and our country—idols like those Abraham had to leave across the river. I think we all understand those. But what about the idols we've picked up in the Promised Land—the Caterpillar Christian idols?

You know, God says, "I am a jealous God; don't put anything ahead of Me" (Exodus 20:3-5, paraphrased)... This is what He taught me about Promised Land idols: There is a big difference between the things of God and God Himself. The things of God are the five majestic trees we caterpillars like to live in—the Word, prayer, praise and worship, fellowship in church meetings, and ministry. Those are all wonderful things from God, but they are not God. If we ever put one or more of those things ahead of God, guess what that is? Idolatry. An idol is a false god, because it is not God Himself.

> **THERE IS A BIG DIFFERENCE BETWEEN THE THINGS OF GOD AND GOD HIMSELF.**

I believe God is saying, "Let's keep first things first. The most important thing is not how much you learn about Me or do for Me. It's about Me and you." If there's one thing God wants us to get out of this, it's that *He doesn't want anything between us and Him*. Again, I'm not saying that the five majestic trees are bad. They are wonderful, but we can never place them above Him.

This can shake a lot of people up, but if we look at the different cultures in the church, we'll find lots of idols. In some places it's prayer. Prayer is the big thing—they are cutting-edge with prayer. Or worship. It's all about worship. They say, "You're going to be worshipping in heaven all of the time, so worship is the most important thing." Worship is big. Then there's fellowship and ministry—same thing. Many of the movements that have gone amuck, many of the churches we see out there today—they would swear on a polygraph machine that they don't have any idols in their culture. But they do. And God is a jealous God.

There is no more lucid example of this than the life of Abraham. Isaac, his son, was a gift that came from God. He was not God, but He was God's promised blessing—God's idea. Yet, in Abraham's final test on Mount Moriah, God was saying, "Here is the gift from Me, My promise that is totally Me. He is the most important thing in your life. Kill him, because I want to find out if you love Me more than anything."

The closest thing to God in Abraham's life was Isaac. He was the manifestation of God's promise. And yet, God wanted to see if Abraham was willing to give him up—even put him to death—to prove that God was first. That's a perfect picture of what we all must do at the cross. God is saying to each one of us, "What idols have you picked up, strange as this may sound, from Me?" What are the things you've picked up in the Promised Land, once you were born again?

> **WE'RE LOOKING AT EVERY ONE OF OUR IDOLS...ALL OF THEM.**

That's why this is a real shake-up message—because we're looking at every one of our idols. All of them, every one. Even the ones that look good. Maybe especially those! Remember, Satan takes something good, misapplies it, and then causes bad things to happen.

How good is the Word of God? Since my ministry call is being a teacher, I don't think the Bible is good, I believe it's great! What happens, though, when Satan tempts me or you to make the Word of God more important than God Himself or Jesus Christ crucified? He takes something good and misapplies it, puts it in a place that it doesn't belong—on the throne—and turns it into an idol.

You may be like me. When the Bible came up as a possible idol, my thought was: John 1:14 says that Jesus was the Word that became flesh, so my love for the Word is the same as loving Jesus Himself. But a thought came to me. When I go to heaven and meet Jesus, I won't be hugging a Bible with arms, legs, and a head attached, I'll be embracing a person! God who became man in a risen and glorified body! A living being with thoughts, feelings, and emotions. The person of Jesus is different than the Bible. Those of us who love the Word need to understand that. Then, the Word will be much more effective in our lives.

Think of a cannonball being the Word, and a cannon being Jesus. If we try and lift that cannonball and throw it, there won't be much effect. But if we shoot it from a cannon, we put a lot of force behind it. Jesus, who is the power of God, is the cannon force behind the Word. That's why Jesus said in Revelation 2:3-4, you "have labored for My name's sake and have not become weary. Nevertheless I have this against you, that you have left your first love." The message is this. We can put a lot of effort into the Word, but if we want it to be powerful and effective, we must keep Jesus as our first love.

Back to Abraham and Isaac. God never really wanted Abraham to get rid of Isaac, something from the Lord. He wanted Abraham to have both Him and Isaac, but to keep his priorities straight. So it is with us and the five majestic trees, including the Word. He wants us to have both, but with Him first! Then the Word, prayer, worship, fellowship, and ministry will be backed with much more power!

A closing thought on how much we love God Himself versus things from God. 1 Peter 2:6, says, "Behold, I lay in Zion a chief cornerstone, elect, precious, and he who believes on Him will by no means be put to shame."

What's my favorite thing? Is it Jesus?

The chief cornerstone is Jesus, and the word *elect* in the Greek means "favorite thing." If we were really honest with ourselves, would we say that one or more of the five majestic trees is our favorite thing in our Christian walk, or is it Jesus Christ and Him crucified? That's certainly something to pause, pray about, and consider.

If you're still struggling with the concept of God Himself vs. the things of God, remember, Jesus is a rock of offense. The biggest stumbling block on our spiritual journey will be Jesus Himself! Ask the Holy Spirit to show you whether this concept is wrong or if it's Jesus offending you—He will.

Moving on, let's take a closer look at idolatry. I know the Bible teaches that sin is sin, but we Christians are famous (or infamous) for harshly judging what we believe to be the "worst" sins, like homosexuality, but when it comes to gossip or gluttony—well, those go on at most any church potluck. We shrug them off as not really important. God says we're not supposed to do that. It's like a "white lie;" to Him there's no such thing. A lie's a lie, and sin is sin.

With that said, however, I do believe two seemingly conflicting truths can exist side by side in Him who is the Truth. The second truth I believe about sin is that *idolatry is the biggest and baddest sin*. Let's prove it by looking at three things in Scripture.

Number one is that idolatry was the first sin. Have you ever heard the saying, "You only have one chance to make a good first impression?" There's only one chance for something to be first, and guess what happened to be the very first sin? Idolatry. In Genesis 3:5, Satan told Eve, "For God knows that in the day you eat of it your eyes will be opened, and you will be like God." It was not enough to be God's child, she wanted to *be* God.

God said to Eve and He says to us, "I want you to be my child."

We say, "No, I want to be You." And He says, "No, you don't understand. I AM God."

Wanting to be God—judging right and wrong, being in control, being lord over our own lives—is idolatry. It was the first sin.

The second thing we will look at in the Scriptures is the Ten Commandments. Exodus 20:1-5 says,

> And God spoke all these words, saying: "I am the Lord your God, who brought you out of the land of Egypt, out of the house of bondage. You shall have no other gods before Me. You shall not make for yourselves a carved image—any likeness of anything that is in heaven above, or that

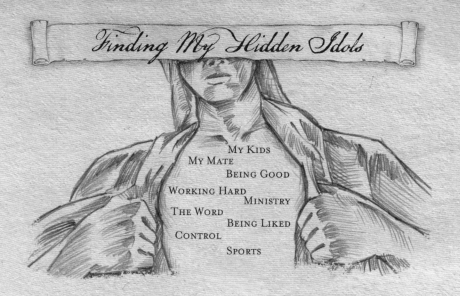

Finding My Hidden Idols

is in the earth beneath, or that is in the water under the earth; you shall not bow down to them nor serve them. For I, the Lord your God, am a jealous God."

Idolatry is the first commandment, though we tend to focus more on the other nine. *Gosh, I don't lie; I don't steal; I don't covet my neighbor's wife; I don't cheat; I don't kill. Look how good I am doing, Lord.*

And He says, *You've got big problems. You're full of idols, and that's the number one commandment. Don't put anything above Me. Not anything.*

> **IDOLATRY IS THE FIRST COMMANDMENT, THOUGH WE TEND TO FOCUS MORE ON THE OTHER NINE.**

Let's go on a hunt for idols. They can be in the strangest places! I'm going to tell you some of the idols we've seen in the church. One is the Godly spouse. We have husbands who say, "My wife is just so much more spiritual than me. She's the spiritual head of the house. If I want to check things out with God, I just go to my wife, because she's close to God."

That sounds great—sounds honoring. And many of these women *are* intensely Godly women. But when their husbands put them on a pedestal, they become idols. And God is saying, *I appreciate the fact that you have a spiritual wife. I'm crazy about her, too. But, guess what, I'm God. And I have called you to be the spiritual head of the house.*

What about work? I work. I'm a hard worker—have worked hard all my life. We're not to be lazy. It's a good thing to work hard, but work can get misapplied and misdirected, and then that good thing becomes an idol. It happens all the time.

Another one is kids. Parents love their kids so much they'll do anything for them. We're supposed to love our kids as gifts from God; we're supposed to bring them up to know Him and love Him. But they're not to be in *His* place. They need to learn from us that even they don't come before God.

These three things are all things we would never think could be idols, but they are, and the people that are in the bondage of idolatry have totally rationalized it. They are deceived, and they don't even know it. They're clueless. I know because I've been there!

Here's a little anecdote—a classic example of kids becoming idols. My wife and I were church hunting, and we said, "We're going to find a church for our kids. We're going to do research and find the church that has the best youth group for our kids, because we love our kids." Sounds pretty holy, huh!

We started out. We went from church to church to church, and our kids never got connected anywhere. We lived in a desert for seven years because it never worked! And, at the end of the complete folly of our good intention, do you know what the Lord said to us? *Can I ask you a question? Why didn't you ask Me where to go to church? I'm God. Don't you think maybe I know what the best place for your kids and your whole family is, better than you do? You never asked Me.*

So much for being parents of the year in the local newspaper. It's all a bunch of bunk. It was idolatry—that's all it was—and it never worked. Through our good intention to help our kids, we became lord of our own lives. This goes for every area of our lives: God is saying, *Why don't you ask Me? Am I Lord of your life? Or are you lord of your life?* Who is Lord?

For the slam dunk of why idolatry is our biggest and baddest sin, we'll go to Mark 12:28 (NIV). It's a straightforward question to Jesus: "Of all the commandments, which is the most important?" We've found out that idolatry was the first sin in the garden; it's the subject of the first commandment in the Ten Commandments; and now an expert in the Law asks Jesus, "Which is the most important commandment?"

Jesus didn't quote the first commandment. He quoted Deuteronomy 6:4-5: "'The most important one,' answered Jesus, 'is this: *Hear, O Israel, the Lord our God, the Lord is one. Love the Lord your God with all your heart and with all your soul and with all your mind and with all your strength*'" (Mark 12:29-30).

> IF SOMEONE WE LOVE DEEPLY HURTS US, IT CRUSHES OUR HEART. THAT'S A ROMANTIC TERM.

Can I love God with all my heart, soul, and strength if I have idols in my life? Or is there shared affection? Is there a *divided* heart, a shared heart, or a whole heart? All is *all*, isn't it? God said, "Don't have anything—no gods—none—besides Me. Love Me with *all* that you are." If I've got idols, that isn't loving Him with all of my heart, soul, and strength, is it? Part of my heart is bound to those idols. So here we have it three times in the Scripture. The biggest and baddest sin is idolatry.

We talked earlier about how in Psalm 139 the word *wicked* means "idols that cause pain?" How do idols cause pain? The first thing is that they hurt God very, very deeply. Ezekiel 6:9 says, "I was crushed by their adulterous heart which has departed from Me, and by their eyes which play the harlot after their idols." Isn't that a romantic term, that if someone we love deeply hurts us, it crushes our heart?

Think about if your mate was cheating on you. How would you feel? What if your mate said, "I love you ninety percent of the time, I really do, but ten percent of the time I've got to have something else going on the side. I've got this other relationship that I have to keep going." Husbands, could you handle that? Wives?

What if I told my wife, "Honey, I know you'll understand, because I do the lawn for you, I've provided for you, and I'm a good father. Here is my list of good things that I do for you, and I know you're going to understand when I keep a mistress on the side. It's only once every ten days that I go to her. You understand that, right?" Lu Ann would knock my block off, and rightly so. More than that, though, she'd be deeply wounded.

Why do we think the Lord feels any different? It bothers Him a lot. He didn't hold anything back from us; He gave His one and only Son for us. That's how much He loved us. He has nothing left—nothing better He could give. And yet we play the harlot. What did He do to deserve that? It's agonizingly painful to Him. Just as much as it would break our hearts, it breaks His.

The other pain that is caused by idolatry is the pain it causes us. Let's go to Psalm 115:3-7 to see how *we* get hurt. It says,

> But our God is in heaven;
> He does whatever He pleases.
> Their idols are silver and gold,
> The work of men's hands.
> They have mouths, but they do not speak;
> Eyes they have, but they do not see;
> They have ears, but they do not hear;
> Noses they have, but they do not smell;
> They have hands, but they do not handle;
> Feet they have, but they do not walk;
> Nor do they mutter through their throat.

This next part (vs. 8) astounds me:

> Those who make them are like them;
> So is everyone who trusts in them.

Those who have idols become like them.

Let's go to Matthew 13:14-15 and see if there's a connection between Psalm 115 and this other, very famous scripture. It says,

> And in them the prophecy of Isaiah is fulfilled, which says:
> "Hearing you will hear and shall not understand,
> And seeing you will see and not perceive;
> For the hearts of this people have grown dull.

> *Their ears are hard of hearing,*
> *And their eyes they have closed,*
> *Lest they should see with their eyes and hear with their ears,*
> *Lest they should understand with their hearts and turn,*
> *So that I should heal them."*

I believe that verse is describing Caterpillar Christians. We hear a lot of preaching and teaching. We see a lot when we read the Bible and Christian books. But we have become like our idols; our eyes have been closed, our ears are hard of hearing, and our hearts have become dull, so we never really change on the inside and turn and go in a different direction. In all of our doing, Caterpillar Christians never truly get transformed into new creations in Christ. It's called going through the motions.

> HOW DO IDOLS CAUSE US PAIN? THEY MAKE US DUMB AND NUMB, JUST LIKE THEM, AND BLOCK OUR ACCESS TO GOD'S POWER.

How do idols cause us pain? They make us dumb and numb, just like them, and block our access to God's healing power. Combining Psalm 115:3-7 and Matthew 13:14-15 helps answer our question *"Where's the power?"*

What can we do about these idols that cause God and us pain? Everybody is ready to do something about it, right? But what? Thanks be to God the answer is simple. Not easy, but simple. We must go to the cross. The first thing is humility. We admit to God that we don't even know what our idols are. It's impossible. Jeremiah 17:9-10 says,

> *The heart is deceitful above all things,*
> *And desperately wicked;*
> *Who can know it?*
> *I, the Lord, search the heart,*
> *I test the mind,*
> *Even to give every man according to his ways,*
> *According to the fruit of his doings.*

We understand that when we're born again, our spirit is brand new, but the heart—which also includes our soul (our mind, will, and emotions) has to be transformed through a longer process. We can't rely on it to find out what's really going on inside our lives.

That's why Proverbs 28:26 says, "He who trusts in his own heart is a fool." I'm a fool. You're a fool. Whenever we, as Christians have our little knee-jerk reactions about what is right and wrong in situations, we're fools. Something happens and we react: *I think that's good.... I think that's bad.... I think right now I'm being good.... I think right now I'm being bad.... That worship is out of order.... This is correct worship.... This is where I'm supposed to go to church.... This is where I'm not supposed to go....* The list goes on and on and on. How do I know? How do you know? Our hearts are deceitful above all and desperately wicked. Shall we then trust ourselves? No! The number one thing is to be humble. Say, "I don't know."

I'll use myself as an example on how we really don't know what's inside of us or what's causing our problems. I shared how I was at the end of my rope in 1993—in the pit of all pits. I had major health problems, family problems, legal problems, and I was going bankrupt. I was a Christian, serving God with all of my heart, but a Caterpillar Christian, and I cried out to the Lord. I said, "God! In one second You could heal me; You could solve all of my legal problems; You could solve my family problems; and you could give me a winning product for Fitness Quest. You could get me out of this! *Why won't You do it, God*? Why won't You do it?"

And (I'll never forget it) Father God spoke to my heart and said, *Son, let me show you your real problems. You have a hole in your heart. You have a cold spot in your heart. It's like the black holes in outer space, and no matter how much success you achieve, it gets all sucked in there. And it's never enough.*

He showed me that I had drive gone mad. You know how drive in our body causes our cells to reproduce—that's a healthy thing. But when it's out of control, it's called cancer. That's what I had. And that out-of-control drive was the source of all my problems. It made me sick, because I ran so hard and so fast that my body finally broke down. My drive to do good and my good intention with the Gut Buster safety cord started my legal problems. My attempt to do so many projects at the same time caused me to go broke. I was trying to do so many things at once that I wasn't doing anything justice, so none of the products became the next winner.

The Lord spoke to my heart and told me, *If I answered your request, in a very short period of time you'd be back in the same mess that you are in now. Your drive gone mad would make you sick again, bring other legal problems, and cause you to not have winning products.* Later on I came to realize the real reward of Him not answering my request. If he would have cut my trials short, I never would have been transformed and brought out of conventional Christianity. I never would have suffered loss in order to gain the greatest thing of all, Him!

During the course of these events, I was talking to a friend on the phone, and the Lord spoke these words to me: *You need spiritual surgery.* He gave me the scripture that says, "Create in me a clean heart, O God" (Psalm 51:10). You know what that word *create* means? It means "to cut." The Lord needed to cut my heart—to perform spiritual surgery in order to take out the junk that wasn't supposed to be there and put in what should be—to deal with my real problems. But I had to authorize Him to do it. It wasn't fun, and it got pretty ugly.

You know the story of David and Bathsheba? (See 2 Samuel 11:1-12:25.) When David walked out on his balcony and saw Bathsheba bathing, do you think in that moment he had any idea of what was in his own heart? Here's a man who loved God and whom God called to perform great and mighty deeds in Israel. He was called "a man after [God's] own heart" (1 Samuel 13:14; Acts 13:22). Do you think he knew his own heart? When he first saw Bathsheba, I don't think he had any idea there was adultery and murder in his heart, but they were there. Down deep, they were there all of the time.

I can tell you what, before my spiritual surgery, I could have passed any polygraph test. If anyone had asked me whether I had hidden idols in my heart—the nasty, filthy, stinking things that God had to remove—I'd have said flatly, "No."

"Do you have this?"
"No!"
"This?"
"No!"
"What about this?"
"No, no, no, no, *no!*"

I was totally unaware that any of the junk was in me, but guess what? It was there. God knew it, but I didn't.

This is very bizarre, but it's one of the most profound moments of my life, and of my spiritual surgery. I was at church, and I was down at the altar. I was worshipping God under the anointing of the Holy Spirit, and all of a sudden, from inside me, came every foul, vulgar word you could possibly imagine. They just came spewing out! It was so strange and shocking.

Later on, however, through Christian counseling, the Lord showed me that I was full of lies, pain and rejection. I was full of anger, hate and jealousy. I was full of every vile thing in the world, and I had no clue till that day at the altar when God revealed it to me. I had no idea. But the Father had put His hand on my shoulder and said, *Son, let Me show you what your real problems are.*

Son, let me show you what your real problems are.

Was it fun? No. Did it make me feel good about myself to find out all of that ugly stuff was in me? No. But you know the old saying, "Better out than in!" It's true for other things, but it's definitely true in spiritual surgery. *Better out than in.*

This is worth noting. All of us to some degree suffered rejection and lack of perfect nurturing as children. Since we're all different, we reacted in different ways. I strived for success. My wife, on the other hand, got into the slavery of service. Her striving was to be the perfect daughter, mother, and homemaker. Others see themselves in less than favorable light. They actually underachieve and live below the level of their God-given gifts and calling. No matter how we react, we all need spiritual surgery.

At the end of the chapter I'm going to include a prayer—and it's an individual decision whether a person wants to pray it—to authorize God to give us spiritual surgery. First, though, I want to share what I believe is wisdom: do not do it alone. Ask the Holy Spirit if you need to get a counselor, and I'll just say this about a Christian counselor: he or she has to be cross-based, and repentance and forgiveness-based. If they're not into that, then don't go to that counselor. Or do it with a small group of people. (I will share principles on how to form a home support group in chapter fifteen.)

In closing let's talk about those demons that are attached to idols. Remember, idols are man-made gods—gods of this world—and Satan is prince of this world. The devil's demons have a legal right to be attached to them. In fact, picture these idols as a beautiful beach. The demons set up lounge chairs, umbrellas, take out their drinks, and are really enjoying themselves.

The Lord showed me this about spiritual warfare, and how to break up their little beach party. He said, *If you want to write a one hundred page book on spiritual warfare, write ninety-nine pages about going to the cross and dying to self, and making Jesus totally Lord of your life and being led by the Holy Spirit. Then you can spend the last page on whatever else you want.* Why? Because if a person dies to self, gets rid of their idols, makes Jesus Lord of all his or her life, and is led by the Spirit, then the party's over for Satan. "*It is no longer I who live, but Christ lives in me*" (Galatians 2:20).

Picture yourself walking up to this beach; however, it's no longer you, but Jesus in you. Do you think those demons will just sit there casually sipping their drinks? The "warfare" happens like this: The demons see Jesus, and they're gone. There's no discussion, nothing to talk about, it's over. Jesus is the mighty King of glory. He's a mighty warrior, and demons can't live in His presence. They have to get out of there. *The devil will wrestle with us in our flesh, but he can't touch Jesus.* James 4:7 summarizes spiritual warfare: "Therefore submit to God. Resist the devil and he will flee from you."

This process of embracing the vertical beam of the cross and saying, "Search me, O Lord, and show me my hidden idols," all happens in the cocoon. The cocoon is a messy place, but it's worth it! It's worth it so the real me can emerge, a wonderful prince or princess becoming a king or queen—a Birthright Butterfly. It's worth it to stop causing God, myself, and the people around me pain. It's worth it to have the power of the cross released to receive my promised blessings. It's worth it to receive the power I need to fulfill my destiny to bless others.

The false me, controlled by idols and demons, can never experience these things. Just like in the art at the beginning of the chapter, these idols must be exposed by the bright light of the cross of Jesus Christ. No matter how hard it seems, God says it will be worth it!

We've embraced the vertical beam of the cross...now it's time to explore the horizontal beam.

My Personal One-on-One Encounter With The Lord

ALSO FOR HOME GROUP DISCUSSION

Do I understand that idols are false gods, something that appears to be good and God but isn't? What might some of my idols be?

_____
_____

Have I discovered that idols come from two places: across the river which is my father's house, people, and country, but also from the Promised Land, which are the five majestic trees?

_____
_____

When I ask myself, "What's my favorite thing?" am I honest enough to admit that one or more of the five majestic trees have taken the place of Jesus Christ and Him crucified? If the answer is yes, which of these five trees have become idols in my life?

_____
_____

Why is idolatry the #1 sin?

_____
_____

When I choose idols, what am I actually doing to God's heart? What painful experience, in human relations, does the Bible compare idolatry to?

_____
_____

Does the prayer on the next page express the deepest desire of your heart? If so, use it as a guide as you ask the Lord to search you.

_____
_____

Spiritual Surgery Prayer

Search me, O God, and know my heart; try me, and know my anxieties; see if there is any wicked way in me (idols that cause pain); and lead me in the way of everlasting. Create in me a pure heart and put a new, steadfast spirit within me. I trust You, Lord, like I would a surgeon, to open me up and expose my hidden idols so I can take them to the cross. I do not want shared lordship any longer between You, Jesus, and idols. I choose this day to make You Lord over every area of my life. I invite You now to be Lord of my entire heart, which is both my emotions and thinking, Lord of my body and my behavior, Lord of my tongue and the things that I say, Lord of my will and all of my decisions, Lord of my sexuality, Lord of my time, my home, my family, my work, my money and my possessions, and all of my relationships with others. I also ask You to expose any demons attached to those idols that are competing with the Holy Spirit as counselor. I will then command them to flee in the name of Jesus and through the power of His blood. From this day forward, I only want to receive counsel from Your Holy Spirit. Thank You, Jesus, that Your blood was shed that I might be free.

Amen

 ## Reflecting on the Art

- In what way does the painting that opens this chapter speak to me?
- Did the sketches have an impact on me? If so, how?

_____
_____
_____
_____
_____

Horizontal Beam of the Cross
Dealing With Offenses

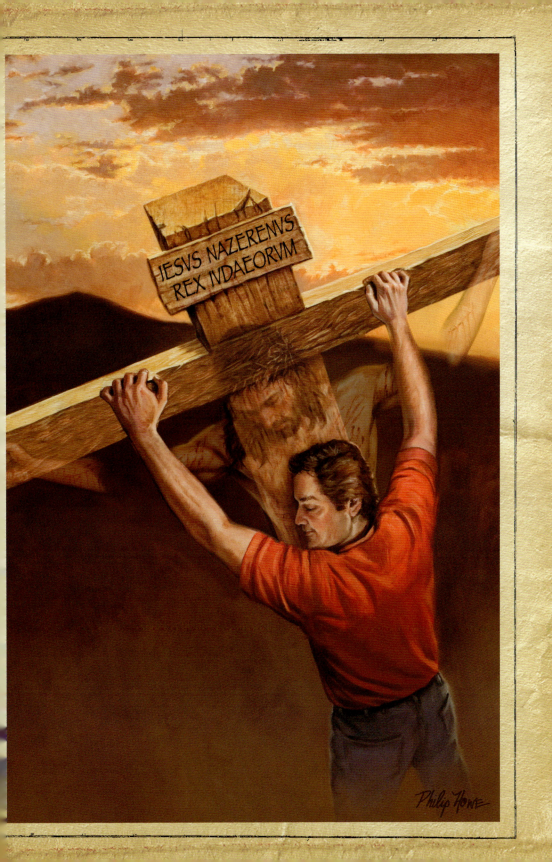

CHAPTER 10

Horizontal Beam of the Cross
DEALING WITH OFFENSES

IF WE'RE HONEST, the lost secret of the cross is not an easy one to embrace. It's a scary thing to do. But I believe at this point in the book the Lord is reaching out to calm your fears. He sees the big picture, and He wants to instill in your heart—once and for all—that the cross is *for* you, not against you.

You can stand before that cross, and no matter what you're going through, you can reach out and take hold of it. You can grab hold of that cross and hang on for dear life. When the going gets tough, if you are grabbing onto the cross you will never be blown away; you will never be destroyed.

I've been there. I know. Now the cross is my anchor. It's my lifeline in an unpredictable sea. No longer am I tossed about like a person without any hope. The winds may come, and lightening may strike all around me. Worldly success may blow in and out. But with my head resting on the chest of Jesus—just like the apostle John at the last supper—I'm secure. I know that Jesus Christ in me cannot be overcome.

What does Jesus promise when we grab hold of that cross? First and foremost, He transforms us into His image and likeness; we become new creations in Christ. He then reconciles us as sons and daughters to His Father, who becomes *our* Father. Next, He reconciles us to ourselves—no more false me versus real me—we see ourselves as wonderful princes and princesses becoming kings and queens. Finally,

He reconciles us to each other as brothers and sisters in Christ, and we will never be alone—*never*. We won't have to fight battles alone; we will always have fellowship. Whatever separation there was between us and God, us and ourselves, and our brothers and sisters in Christ, that separation is gone. In this supernatural world of love we also have joy and peace, even in the midst of our battles.

After that, He promises to release power. Victory over sin, victory over demons, victory over the curses in our lives—complete victory is ours in the cross, because Jesus won the victory for us there. He bore every sin and curse, and He stripped the principalities of their power and made an open display of them all on the cross (Colossians 2:15).

We don't have to walk slumped down as failures. We're going to have power to walk in victory, the power to receive our promised blessings, and fulfill our destiny to carry out our call to bless others. What is more, I believe we will do it with signs and wonders following. God is not playing games; this is the real deal. But we have to use the cross as our handholds.

What are we holding onto when we grab the cross? We're holding onto the horizontal beam of the cross. We've talked about the vertical beam, right? It symbolizes our relationship directly between us and the Lord.

But guess what? A cross is not a cross without a horizontal beam. It's just a big "I." That's all it is. It has to be crossed! What is the horizontal beam? It's *people*. And what the Lord is showing us is that if we want to find out where our hearts truly are toward Him—vertically—then we need to check out where we are horizontally. That's the part we leave out in the church, and that's the *second part of the lost secret...real Christian community!* In chapter fifteen we will discuss how being in home group relationships, connected by the cross, releases God's love and power. But for now, let's focus on how our relationships with each other are an indicator of the health of our relationship with God.

> TO REALLY KNOW HOW WELL OUR VERTICAL RELATIONSHIP WITH GOD IS GOING, WE MUST CHECK OUT OUR HORIZONTAL RELATIONSHIPS WITH PEOPLE.

What's the very first thing we do to check out a person's physical heart? We go to the doctor's office and take their pulse, right? If we want to find out what's going on with our hearts, with regards to the Lord, the pulse is this: How are we loving one another? Simply stated, to really know how well our vertical relationship with God is going, we must check out our horizontal relationships with people.

In Scripture, Jesus was very clear about how we are to love. He says in John 13:34-35, "A new commandment I give to you, that you love one another; as I have loved you, that you also love one another. By this all will know that you are My disciples, if you have love for one another."

The old commandment was, "Love your neighbor as yourself" (Leviticus 19:18). That's not good enough. Do you know why? Because apart from Christ, we don't really love ourselves. The new command is to love one another *as He* loves. That's the new standard—the gold standard.

Jesus puts it all together in John 14:15 when He says, "If you love Me, keep My commandments." What He is saying is, if you truly love Me vertically, you will keep My commands. And My horizontal command is to love one another as I have loved you. That's a pretty tall order, but by God's grace we can do it.

Let's explore this horizontal beam a little bit. A lot of Christians (and I was one of them, and to what degree I still am I don't know, but my prayer is to daily put the old man to death at the cross) say that they really love God, and their proof—their résumé—is what they do with the big five. Remember the five majestic trees? We say, "My proof that I love God is that I am into the Word all of the time, I pray a lot, and I praise a lot (lots of thanksgiving, praise and worship); I go to church services on Sunday morning and Sunday night and Wednesday; I go to conferences, seminars, and camp meetings; and I do a lot of ministry projects. That proves that I love God, right?"

Admit it. We've all been there, haven't we? We've measured ourselves and other people—at least to some degree, some of the time—by looking at how we did on the big five. But there's one hitch. There was another group of people when Jesus walked the earth called the Pharisees. They *said* they loved God more than anyone else. They knew more *about God* than anybody else, and they did more things *for God* than anybody else, but it's interesting. This all worked as long as God was invisible.

1 John 4:20-21 says this: "If someone"—and that someone could be me, or you, or the Pharisees we're talking about—"says, 'I love God,'

and hates his brother, he is a liar; for he who does not love his brother whom he has seen, how can he love God whom he has not seen? And this commandment we have from Him [Jesus]: that he who loves God must love his brother also."

It all worked in the fake little world the Pharisees were living in. They were able to deceive themselves and others into believing they were holy; it worked great as long as God was invisible. But when Emmanuel came—"God with us" (Matthew 1:23)—they killed Him. *They killed Him!*

Now fast forward two thousand years. Is God with us as Emmanuel today, visibly? Yes He is. You know why? Because the Bible says everyone is made in God's image and likeness—all human beings have a piece of the Father in them. And those human beings who have accepted Jesus as Lord and Savior of their lives take another step. We have Jesus Christ and the Holy Spirit living inside of us—we're the temple of the living God. Therefore we aren't in any different boat than the Pharisees are. God is visibly here for all of us, and here's the question: How are we treating Him?

> GOD IS VISIBLY HERE FOR ALL OF US, AND HERE'S THE QUESTION: HOW ARE WE TREATING HIM?

He's right here, as you read this book. He's in our marriages and with our children. He's in the church and all around us, in the people we know. He's right here in visible form. And I believe He is saying, "Don't tell Me how much you love Me just based on your vertical relationship. Show Me how much you love Me based on your horizontal relationship, and then you will get *all* of the cross." That takes it to a little different dimension—to a little different place. It brings much more reality to our relationship with God, and it separates the fakers and actors from the real deal.

Do you think it's an accident that He warned, "Be on your guard against the yeast of the Pharisees" (Matthew 16:6 NIV)? His meaning was to beware of hypocrisy. You know what the meaning of the Greek word for hypocrisy (*hypokrisis*) is? "To act or be an actor." Some of us are great actors—we're acting a good part. But, as a TV host during my childhood, Captain Penny, said, "You can fool some of the people all of the time, and all of the people some of the time, but you can't fool Mom." We can't fool God! He sees through the act every time. The church may go through the motions, but we can't act with God. His standard is, "How are you loving one another?" And He sees our *hearts*.

Remember when we talked about the leavened and blended church, and how when you blend something, you water it down or dilute it? It becomes weakened. And that's what Caterpillar Christians are living in—a leavened and blended church, watered down by the wisdom of the world. To connect that concept with what we're addressing here, what kind of Christians would a weakened church produce? Weakened church = weak Christians = weak relationships. And when the going gets tough, relationships fall apart because they are weak. Just like a tree without strong roots, a storm can blow it down. We need to change our weak relationships into strong, deep ones.

One way we do that is to be each other's mirror. Did you ever try putting on make-up or shaving without a mirror? Try it sometime. I can't see my own face without a mirror, so I will never see all of my blind spots without you as my mirror. This is a very important concept when it comes to the horizontal beam of the cross. We will never deal with all of the junk inside of us just by vertically saying, "Search me, Lord." We need each other. We need to bump into each other and interact with each other for all of our blind spots to be exposed. John Donne said, "No man is an island," and no woman is either. We need each other desperately in order to deal with our blind spots. That's why the second part of the lost secret of Christian community is so important.

> **WE NEED EACH OTHER DESPERATELY IN ORDER TO DEAL WITH OUR BLIND SPOTS.**

But I don't just need you for my blind spots. I also need you when I'm down. We're on this journey together, and I need your help along the way. We've got to be vitally linked to each other to be linked to Him. Like sap flowing through the branches that are attached to the vine, we can't function without each other. And cutting off ourselves from one another eventually cuts us off from life—from Him who *is* our Life. There are a million reasons to get unlinked—a whole bunch of reasons, like wounds and distasteful experiences—but God is saying, "No. Hold on. Hold on to that horizontal beam."

Let's go back to being mirrors for each other. There is a whole list of scriptures that say this in one way or another. Proverbs 27 (NIV) contains just a few: "Better is open rebuke than hidden love" (verse 5); "Wounds from a friend can be trusted, but an enemy multiplies kisses" (verse 6); "Perfume and incense bring joy to the heart, and the pleasantness of one's friend springs from his earnest counsel" (verse 9); and "As iron sharpens iron, so one man sharpens another" (verse 17). God is saying, "You have friends there for a reason, to rebuke you when you need rebuked, to give you a blow when you need a blow." Right? We just can't make it without our friends.

That leads us to the concept of accountability. I know there has been a ton of abuse in this area, and people are scared to death of it because they don't understand it. But we have a choice to make whether or not we're going to be connected to—and accountable to—other Christians. It's a choice. If I make that choice, I'm coming to you to say, "This is my destiny; this is what God called me to do or change; this is what God told me to work on. I am asking you to hold me accountable for that. I'm asking you to cover my back, where my blind spots are. I'm asking you to be there, to discipline me and rebuke me when I need it."

You're not butting into my life or trying to manipulate or control me. You're not telling me what to do. I'm asking you to do this. As it says in Ephesians 5:21 (NIV), "Submit to one another," I am choosing to submit myself to you. To be vulnerable to you. You can't help me unless I open up myself to you, so for the sake of safety, I'm choosing to be accountable.

It's really this simple. I come to you and say "Here are the areas of my flesh that I'm working on to put to death on the cross. And here's my God-given purpose and destiny that I'm walking out. If there's anything that you see that I don't, please let me know."

Do you know why God wants us to enter into these accountability relationships? Because He loves us. There's an aspect of God's love that never flows directly, or vertically, from God to us, because He chooses to use a vessel. Those vessels are people. We will never be totally transformed or fully fulfill our destiny without the help of other believers. A cross is not a cross without the horizontal beam.

A CROSS IS NOT A CROSS WITHOUT THE HORIZONTAL BEAM.

We see that we need each other for accountability, for support, for blind spots. Another big reason we need each other—and this one is not quite so obvious or pleasant—is for hurts. Sometimes there are hurts that greatly help us.

Remember the movie *Snow White and the Seven Dwarfs*? Remember all of those little guys, how they would go to work down in the mines? And what was down there? Cartload after cartload of precious gems. There were diamonds, rubies, emeralds—every little kid watching the movie wanted to get into one of those carts and go down to dig.

Did you know that place exists outside of Disney's fantasy world? It is the most precious mine that could ever be tapped for our spiritual growth. Do you know what it is? Rejection. The times we've been hurt. That's where the diamonds are.

In Isaiah 53:3 the Bible says that He was "despised and rejected by men." If we apply the kingdom principle of loss turning into gain, we can see why our hurts greatly help us. Rejection takes us into the cocoon of loss, but what we gain through the experience is identification with Jesus. It's a cross experience. By partaking of His sufferings, and being conformed to His death—our *sum morphos* transforming union into Birthright Butterflies—*we gain God Himself*. And I'll say this again: We only get so much of the jewels with the vertical beam of the cross. We will never hit the mother load until we visit our rejections—the offenses in our lives—and put them under the Lordship of Jesus Christ. When that happens to you personally, you'll be blown away at the riches. I have been.

Why do we run from it? The reason is flat out proof of how shallow and carnal we are as Caterpillar Christians: fight or flight. When an offense occurs, we handle it like we live in the animal kingdom. When there is a confrontation, animals either have fight or flight. There is no middle ground; they never try to reconcile. And in all honesty, that's the same as the church much of the time. We say we're different, and we say that we're spiritual and not carnal. But most of the time, I'm either going to get together with you to straighten you out, and we're going to get into a fight, or we're done. I don't care how long I've known you. I don't care about the depth of my relationship with you. I don't care about anything else. I'll never talk to you again in my life—and we're super-spiritual Christians?

Are we? We're not. We're more like members of the animal kingdom. They do that. And the last time I checked, there's not one animal that is born again; they don't exist. But there are lots of born-again Christians who fight like cats and dogs because we're not quite as spiritual as we think we are. We're on a big high horse.

That's a sobering segue into the Lordship of Jesus over our offenses. What did Jesus say? "Not everyone who says to Me, 'Lord, Lord,' shall enter the kingdom of heaven." There will be people who plead with Him, "But, Lord, we did mighty things in your name…we've cast out demons…" And He will say, "That's all great, but are you doing the will of My Father?" (Matthew 7:21-23, paraphrased).

Let's look at offenses and see what Jesus said about them. He said four basic things about how to deal with an offense with a brother or sister. This means that we each have a decision to make…will Jesus be Lord over the offenses in our life? The first is, "Be humble." In Matthew 7:3-5 Jesus asks "Why do you look at the speck in your brother's eye, but do not consider the plank in your own eye? Or how can you say to your brother, 'Let me remove the speck from your eye'; and look, a plank is in your own eye? Hypocrite! First remove the plank from your own eye, and then you will see clearly to remove the speck from your brother's eye."

We've learned that Jesus is the wisdom of God, so let's explore the wisdom of His words. First, Jeremiah 17:9 says, "The heart is deceitful above all things, and desperately wicked; who can know it?" Second, the Bible says that Satan is the accuser of the brethren (Revelation 12:10). Jesus is warning us that when we get offended we may be dealing with a double deception. The problem may be with me, but the devil is saying it's the other person's fault. The plank is in my eye, and the little speck is in theirs. Radical concept, huh?

What Jesus is saying is that when I'm offended the first thing that I should think is that it is probably my fault. Jonathan Edwards, the great revivalist, understood this when he said: "I am most suspicious of my own heart."

I've observed first hand in my Christian walk that Jesus' words are true. First, many times when a person gets offended, it is not because someone did something wrong to him or her, it's because someone told that person the truth and, in so doing, bumped into a hidden idol—a false teaching, a wound, or a good intention. When this happens, watch out; usually the relationship is over.

The second thing Jesus said is that when the truth is told, a choice is made. Do I focus on myself, or blame the other person? Satan, the accuser, always jumps in and says, "You're innocent. It's the other person's fault."

The fact that our heart is deceitful and Satan is a lying accuser of the brethren says that many times—not always—it's about us, not the other person. Therefore when we are offended, humility cries out, "Stop. Search me, O Lord. Is the problem with me? Is the voice I'm hearing from You, Lord, or is it Satan the accuser?"

In this process it might be good to stop right here and consider all of the people who have offended us. Say, "Lord, I'm going to back track and I want to know what part of the offense was me?" This revelation is more precious than gold or silver. We will find out more about ourselves, learn more about the character of Jesus, and become more like Him through this activity than you could ever imagine. "Show me, Lord; search me. Where is my fault?" After you do this, you should seek the Lord about going back to the person to reconcile with them. That's number one—humility.

The second thing Jesus said is that He wants us to love unconditionally. "A new command I give you, to love one another as I have loved you." If I start with the assumption that it's probably my fault—which it may be, at least to some degree—and God says no, it's totally the other person's fault—I'm still to love that person. Jesus says, "You have heard that it was said, 'You shall love your neighbor and hate your enemy.' But I say to you, love your enemies" (Matthew 5:43-44). Even if it's totally the other person's fault, it's still about me! He wants *us* to love *them* unconditionally, like the Father does.

> **EVEN IF IT'S TOTALLY THE OTHER PERSON'S FAULT, IT'S STILL ABOUT ME!**

This is a reality I never understood until the Lord showed me the truth of how He loves. In fact, it so impacted me that I made it the Dedication of this book. (Since this is the "unbook", it appears at the end.) It says, "This book is dedicated to Jesus Christ and Him crucified, who allowed us to torture and murder Him in order to save us."

He allowed me to torture and kill Him, in order to save me. And He commands me to love that way. What on earth does that mean? Here's the question He put in my heart: *If you were across from a person at a table, and you had a gun, a .44 Magnum, and you knew that person was going to burn in hell for the rest of eternity unless he killed you, would you give him the gun? If it was the only way for him to be saved, would you do it? Would you give him the gun and say, "Go ahead, point it at my head, and shoot me"?*

That's what Jesus did. The Bible says no man took His life from Him; He laid it down. Would we allow somebody to kill us in order to save them? That's what it means to lay down your life for a friend. That's what it means, according to Jesus, to love.

Therefore, in an offense, even if it's totally not my fault, I must choose to love you unconditionally. Maybe, for a period of time, He will even require me to let you hurt me in order to save you. (However, if you are in a truly verbal or physically abusive situation, and it's not getting better, you should go to your pastor or a counselor to seek advice; they may tell you to leave that situation for a time.) An offense is always about *me* in the sense that He requires *me* to be humble, and *me* to love. I am responsible for my sins, and guess what? If I don't love others the way Jesus loved me, then that's a sin.

He said, "A new commandment I give to you, that you love one another; as I have loved you" (John 13:34), and, "Greater love has no one than this, than to lay down one's life for his friends" (John 15:13). If I do not obey His commands, I am sinning. It's always about me. Either I was the one in the wrong in the first place, or partly wrong, or I am totally innocent and still obligated by my Lord and Savior to love you as He loves you. Wild, isn't it?

The question is, how many Christians—born again, Spirit-filled, Green Beret Christians—are Christ-like? We all say we do, but who among us can keep His commands? Who could ever love as He loves—enough to allow someone to kill us in order to save them? And yet that is exactly what He commands us to do. He says, "If you love Me, you will keep My commandments" (John 14:15 NASB).

I've got bad news for everybody, including myself: it ain't happening! It is totally impossible to love others as Jesus loves. Do you think I'm going to hand you a .44 Magnum and have you kill me in order to save your hide? Not in a million years. I'd shoot you before I'd let myself be shot. Who's kidding whom? I could be a Bible school graduate and go to one thousand camp meetings, but when it comes to the moment of truth, I won't let you shoot me. I can't love as Jesus loves. It's totally impossible!

So the Holy Spirit has used the whole .44 Magnum story to make a point: living a Christian life is impossible! That's the message of the cross in a nutshell. Jesus is saying, "Give up! You have to die, and I've got to live through you in order for you to love as I love, because you can't do it." Anything else is a joke; it's just a big rouse. It's a bunch of people play acting; it's not Christianity. Why? Because we can't do it. *Without the cross and death to self, the Christian life is impossible.* That's it in a nutshell.

The words of Jesus on dealing with offenses are, first, *Be humble,* and second, *Love like I love,* which is impossible without going to the cross. What is third? *Have faith, and pray for the person who offends you.*

> **WITHOUT THE CROSS AND DEATH TO SELF, THE CHRISTIAN LIFE IS IMPOSSIBLE. THAT'S IT IN A NUTSHELL.**

Matthew 5:44-45 says, "Pray for those who spitefully use you and persecute you, that you may be sons of your Father in heaven." Don't try to change the person, but pray for him or her. Leave the work up to God. By faith, view the situation as part of a process in which God wants to change you and bless you, and through which He is also working in that person's life. You may never see the result you desire, but it is still a privilege and an act of obedience to pray. And you may see a miracle! Stay open. Leave the results to God and be at peace.

Love them unconditionally, pray for them, and then you know what I would add? We need to pray also for ourselves. I have to say, "Lord, help me to die, because I don't have the ability to do that. I'm going to rely on You to help both me and the other person."

There does come a time—and this is item four—when we need to *share the truth in love.* Only after numbers one through three have been done, and only after the Holy Spirit has released us, should we go to the person one-on-one with the purpose of gaining them back.

Matthew 18:15 (NIV) says, "If your brother sins against you, go and show him his fault, just between the two of you. If he listens to you, you have won your brother over." It goes on to say what we should do if he doesn't listen, which is to take two or three witnesses, and then finally to bring him before the church.

Have you ever seen this done effectively? If so, you're very lucky. Matthew 18 contains the red words of Jesus. He's the Lord of everybody, and church members all say they've accepted Jesus as Lord and Savior of their lives, yet I have never, ever, even once seen this entire process in a church confrontation. It's one of those deleted sections of the Bible. It is treated as though it doesn't exist, and we wonder why the church isn't working so hot. We're not following the words of Jesus!

Did you ever hear the saying "Making a mountain out of a molehill?" If you're ever asked to mediate an offense between two believers, here's a way to shrink the "offense mountain" down to size. Have each one of them write out this four part list:

ONE. What was my role in the offense; where was I at fault?

TWO. What are the Godly character traits of the other person?

THREE. How has God used the other person to bless me?

FOUR. What was their sin—offense—against me?

You will be amazed that after they read 1 through 3, the offense listed in 4 won't look so big anymore—the mountain will have shrunk to a molehill. You can also choose to do this on your own if someone's offended you.

We've seen how we all need each other for fellowship and addressing our blind spots. We've also seen how our hurts can be used by God to greatly benefit us and actually move us along from the Caterpillar Christian stage into that of the Birthright Butterfly. Offenses are valuable because of the jewels that can come out of them—the humility, the love, and the faith. Such deep treasures cannot be mined from any other place or situation. The horizontal beam forms the whole cross. We're going to die, and it's going to hurt, but we're going to be raised as new creations, with Jesus living His life in us. It's the whole enchilada!

In closing, I would like to share another time at lunch with my friend Steve, a time when the Lord taught us a profound truth. Steve

Forgiveness Forms the Cross In Me

A TRULY WHOLE PERSON

had been a full-time pastor who was happily married. Suddenly, he experienced a divorce, and shortly thereafter, he left the ministry. He went through a dark time in his life, when, as he put it, he was dancing with the devil on Saturday night. He repented of his sinful lifestyle and knew that the Lord had forgiven him.

However, one day he was led by the Holy Spirit to look in the mirror and say, "I forgive you Steve." He then realized God had forgiven him but he had never forgiven himself. He then felt an internal release to forgive others. Before that lunch, I had never thought about forgiving myself. My focus had just been on the Lord forgiving me.

The Lord gave us an image at the lunch table which was put in a sketch on the previous page. It was God handing an olive branch to me and forgiving me, then me handing the olive branch to myself and forgiving myself, and finally me in turn handing the olive branch to someone else, to forgive them. This complete three-part process of forgiveness forms the cross in me. Me forgiving myself is the centerpiece, the missing link between God forgiving me and me forgiving you. Only then can I become a whole and complete person.

The Lord went on to explain how forgiveness was the taproot of the cross. The taproot of a tree is the deepest, most important root for the life of a tree. Forgiveness is the taproot of the cross because it has a voice that says it's not about me, it's about what Jesus does for me when I sin and for others when they sin against me. So don't just accept forgiveness from the Lord. Go the whole way, and don't beat yourself up for your sins, because it's not about you. After you've forgiven yourself, do the same to others. Don't beat them up—let them off the hook—because it's not about them either! When we truly understand that it's not about me, or you, the process of dying to self and being transformed can flourish. Reconciliation as sons and daughters of the Father, and brothers and sisters in Christ, will follow. The power of the cross will then emerge out of this oneness, like a mighty oak shooting skyward!

We are now well into our spiritual journey, and have discovered both parts of the lost secret—making Christ crucified the most important thing in our lives and experiencing real Christian community. We're on our way to getting our God-given birthright back and entering a

Forgiveness is the Taproot of the Cross

POWER

RECONCILIATION

TRANSFORMATION

FORGIVENESS

wonderful, two-dimensional world. It's a place of supernatural love, joy, and peace even in the midst of trials, and access to God's power to be blessed and fulfill our destiny to bless others. We've discovered that we were Caterpillar Christians in a wisdom of the world system of knowledge and works, and the way to get out was admitting "Religion, That's Me" and living by "Judge Not." We also discovered who the real me is, a wonderful prince or princess becoming a king or a queen—a Birthright Butterfly. Unfortunately, though, the real me was a prisoner of my past because of the worldly system of hidden idols that was inside me. That's why we had to leave behind the life we knew by embracing the cross. As we read the next chapter, we will understand why it is so important to do so.

My Personal One-on-One Encounter With The Lord

Also for Home Group Discussion

Do I now understand that the cross is for me and not against me? How does this now make me feel?

_____
_____
_____
_____

What is the proof of how much I love the Lord? Hint: This is the horizontal beam of the cross.

_____
_____
_____
_____

The other aspect of the horizontal beam is that no one can do it alone, which is the second part of the lost secret. We all need support and have blind spots that only others can see. Do I reach out to other Christians for help? Am I an input-oriented Christian, and do I choose to make myself accountable to other trusted Christians?

_____
_____
_____
_____

How do I deal with offenses? What offenses in my life might God use to take me into the cocoon where He can transform me, and teach me more about how Jesus loves?

_____
_____
_____
_____

The New Covenant standard is to love one another as Jesus loved us. Who does Jesus want to love through me right now?

_____
_____
_____
_____

Am I now putting offenses, when they come, under the following four-part Lordship of Jesus Christ?

HUMILITY—Ask the Lord to show me what my role was in the offense, and what involvement Satan may have had in falsely accusing the other person?

LOVE—Forgive the person the way that Jesus forgives me, and love the person the way that Jesus loves me.

FAITH—Pray for the person that God will show them their problem and help them to change.

SHARE THE TRUTH IN LOVE—After you have done the above, and are released by the Holy Spirit, go to the person one-on-one to gain them back. If that doesn't work, bring two witnesses. And, if that still doesn't bring reconciliation, bring it to the church.

REFLECTING ON THE ART

- In what way does the painting that opens this chapter speak to me?
- Did the sketches have an impact on me? If so, how?

_____
_____
_____

The Great Custody Battle
Father God vs. Satan

CHAPTER 11

The Great Custody Battle
Father God vs. Satan

We've seen that even though embracing the vertical and horizontal beams of the cross is not easy, both are necessary to our growth and development as children of God. In this chapter, we're going to explore another reason for embracing the cross. It is absolutely essential because there is a joint custody battle going on, and the stakes are very high.

Picture for a moment a court proceeding involving a divorce, and a judge is deciding the fate of a little girl. One side of the courtroom is light and life, and the other side is darkness and death. It's a long, drawn-out process, and everyone is waiting on pins and needles to find out what will happen. Finally the judge is finished deliberating, and he sits down in his seat. He delivers this ruling: "I'm going to award joint custody. The child will go with one parent one week and the other for the next, and we will alternate every week."

He slams the gavel down, and that's the order of the court. As the people begin to leave, you see a dark figure approach the child and take her by the hand. Wrapping his sharp, ugly claws around her, Satan whispers in a sinister voice, "You're mine for this week."

That's a pretty chilling image, isn't it? Is that possible? Could it be possible for a child of God?

Let's consider John 8:42-44. "Jesus said to them, 'If God were your Father, you would love Me, for I proceeded forth and came from

God; nor have I come of Myself, but He sent Me…[but] you are of your father the devil, and the desires of your father you want to do.'"

If Jesus had been speaking to the Pharisees, or other Jews who didn't believe in Him, this passage would not pose a custody problem. However, if we go back up to verse thirty-one, we find out whom Jesus was addressing. "Then Jesus said to those Jews who believed in Him." *Who believed in Him.* This speech wasn't addressed to the people who didn't believe in Jesus; it was addressed to those who did! All of a sudden that creates a problem, doesn't it?

Let's look at another scripture, 1 John 3:10—which, incidentally, is an epistle written to born-again believers. "In this the children of God and the children of the devil are manifest: Whoever does not practice righteousness is not of God, nor is he who does not love his brother."

What John is saying is that when we choose to sin and not love our brother, *in those times the devil is our father*. That's to us Christians. Ouch.

Remember earlier in the book where I referred to Jesus as a stumbling block along this journey? Well, here is another place where that happens. This is a very offensive scripture, isn't it? It's offensive because we tend to believe that as born-again Christians the devil could never be in a custody battle over us. We're God's children. The truth is, however, that even though Satan can never have full custody, he still fights for partial custody. There is a great custody battle going on.

> WHAT JESUS DID ON THE CROSS ISSUES A DIFFERENT VERDICT, AND THAT VERDICT GUARANTEES THAT THERE IS NO JOINT CUSTODY.

Now the *good* news is this: Jesus won the battle on the cross. What Jesus did on the cross issues a different verdict, and that verdict guarantees that there is no joint custody. We are in our Father's house for all the days of our life, and we sit at our Father's table. Satan has no custody whatsoever.

Why is that incredibly important? Because the Scripture says, in Numbers 26:55, that "the land shall be divided by lot; they shall inherit according to the names of the tribes of their fathers." What this is saying is that our inheritance depends entirely on who our father is. That shouldn't surprise anyone—it's the same for earthly fathers.

Another reason the verdict won on the cross is very important has to do with destiny. Many psychologists agree by saying that when it comes to kids, we get nurture from our mother but our destiny is from our father. What have we said over and over again in this book? The power of the cross is going to get us two things: our promised blessings and fulfillment of our God-given destiny, with signs and wonders following, right?

What we're learning is that *our promised blessings, our inheritance, and our destiny are connected to who our father is*. And, *if our father some of the time is Satan, we're not going to receive all of our promised blessings, nor will we totally fulfill our destiny*. It's really just a simple concept.

So how could a sincere Christian ever have Satan as a part-time father? One word: *deception*. It's deception, because no child of God would ever voluntarily choose to have Satan as their father.

On the subject of deception, we're going to keep reading in John 8, where Jesus was talking to the Jews who were believers in Him. He said, "If you abide in My Word, you are My disciples indeed. And you shall know the truth, and the truth shall make you free." Their reply to this was, "We are Abraham's descendants, and have never been in bondage to anyone. How can you say, 'You will be made free'?" (John 8:31-33).

Can you imagine such a silly statement on the part of those believing Jews? First, Abraham's descendants were in Egypt as slaves to Pharaoh for hundreds of years. They were brought out of slavery. (That's why they celebrate Passover every year, to remember being brought out.) After being delivered from slavery in Egypt, they didn't obey God's laws and were taken captive to Babylon under Nebuchadnezzar, and they were slaves again for seventy years.

And what was the case during Jesus' time? Israel was occupied by Rome. They were slaves right then, at the moment of their conversation with Jesus. They sat there bold-faced, and said, "We've never been in bondage to anyone. We're not slaves to anyone." Why? They were under the delusion that because they were seeds of Abraham, God's chosen people—because they were good—they weren't slaves. They just couldn't imagine it being true.

Could that happen to us? Could we say, "I'm a born-again Christian; I go to church; I have Bible studies; I watch Christian TV and listen to Christian radio; and there is no way I could ever, ever be a slave.

There is no way I could be under joint custody in Satan's house." It's the same thing—deception.

They were God's chosen people who believed in Jesus. But Jesus said, "Satan is your father." Are we God's chosen people, seeds of Abraham? Galatians 3:29 says, "If you are Christ's, then you are Abraham's seed, and heirs according to the promise." Romans 11:17-24 says, to paraphrase, "The Jews are the olive tree, but you Gentiles have been grafted in through Christ."

Are we God's chosen people? Yes. Do we believe in Jesus? Yes. Then could Jesus' words apply to us? Yes. How could a sincere Christian be deceived by Satan and allow him to become his father?

Let's keep going in John 8:34-36. "Jesus answered them, 'Most assuredly, I say to you, whoever commits sin is a slave of sin. And a slave does not abide in the house forever, but a son abides forever. Therefore if the Son makes you free, you shall be free indeed.'" Simply put, *sin produces slavery*. Slaves were not in the father's house, but they lived in quarters outside the house. The Bible says that if you sin as a child of God, as one of God's chosen people, then that puts you under joint custody of the devil. How could that happen to us?

Well, the ultimate deception is a good intention. Hidden sin. When born-again Christians have good intentions—things that seem good but aren't—that's how the devil gets us. We learned that in the earlier chapters. He is never going to boldly come up to us, like a kidnapper, and grab hold of us and drag us away. He's never going to get us to go to his house that way, because we'd recognize him. We'd tell him to scram in the name of Jesus. No, he's much more subtle. He's going to *deceive us with good intentions*.

What did we learn earlier? There are two systems of good intentions. There's the good intention system that we're in, which is knowledge and works. In this system we believe that somehow, if we learn more about God and do more things for God, we'll get closer to God. That's the law, which happens to be the wisdom of the world. Satan uses the lie that God isn't good and we're inferior to make us lust after the law, to take care of our own problems and earn self-esteem. In so doing, he sucks us into the world's system.

The other system of good intentions is the system that is in us. We get this system from the hidden idols of our father's house, our people and country, wounds, false teachings, and the good intentions those things produce. These man-made idols are the world's system in us. We are in a world system, and a world system is in us. Satan is prince of this world, so is joint custody possible?

Proverbs 6:27 (NIV) says, "Can a man scoop fire into his lap without his clothes being burned?" In our minds we're saying, *Well, because I am a born-again Christian, I'm able to have the world's system in me and operate in the world's system.* But it doesn't work that way. Satan is prince of the world. The whole world is under his control, so if by our good intentions we get duped into having these world systems as part of our lives, that gives him access to our lives. We give him the right to mess with us when we get deceived with good intentions.

Let's refer to the heart diagram on the next page to understand that this really is a fatherhood issue. Do you see Jesus as Lord versus idols? The Bible says no one comes to the Father except through the Son (John 14:6). If Jesus brings us to the Father, who would idols bring us to? Satan!

In an earlier chapter, we learned very specifically from Deuteronomy and also from the New Testament that demons are attached to idols. Romans 8:14 says, "As many as are led by the Spirit of God, these are the sons of God." If those who are led by the Spirit of God are the children of God, doesn't the opposite have to be true? If we're led by demons, doesn't that make us children of the devil? If one is true, then the other has to be.

> **IF THOSE WHO ARE LED BY THE SPIRIT OF GOD ARE THE CHILDREN OF GOD, DOESN'T THE OPPOSITE HAVE TO BE TRUE?**

Please hear what I am saying. First, a Christian cannot be possessed by demons, but we can be influenced by them. Second, a born-again Christian is a child of God, but we can get duped into joint custody. We can be deceived and sucked into living in Satan's house for whole seasons. God is saying, "I want you in My house all of the time!"

The last scripture we're going to look at on this subject is Romans 8:7: "The carnal mind is enmity against God; for it is not subject to the law of God, nor indeed can be." The word *carnal* here is *sarx* in the Greek. *Sarx* stands for animal *and* human—the flesh world. Our carnal and

worldly mind is under the authority of the prince of this world. Again, our carnal mind can be duped into joint custody.

We talked about this earlier, but it's worth visiting again. When animals have a confrontation, there are only two things that ever happen, right? Fight or flight. If a raccoon gets into your garbage can and your dog comes out, they're not going to have a heart-to-heart conversation about it, are they? There's not one recorded instance in history where a dog and raccoon have sat down and said, "You know, why don't we just talk about this?" The dog says, "You're hungry, and I like to eat garbage too, and I'm sure that you were very, very tempted, but this is my master's garbage can, so could you just put the lid back on and kind of head out of here and just not let it happen again?" Has that ever happened? Ever?

There's only one of two things that happen one thousand percent of the time in the animal world. They either get into a fight, or there is flight. Why? Because they're animals. They're carnal—*sarx* in the Greek. They're of this world, where Satan is prince.

What about when there are offenses in the church? The vast majority of the time, what happens between Christians when there is an offense? Fight or flight—it's true. Normally it starts out with a fight, and then after the fight, there's flight. There's division.

The children of the heavenly Father who live in God's house don't do that, though. They reconcile. They go to the foot of the cross and say, "Hey, whatever you did, Jesus took care of it, so let's go to the foot of the cross and have forgiveness, and let's reconcile with each other."

Does this give us a little inkling that maybe there are times in Christians' lives that they're doing a little joint custody time in Satan's house? Because guess what—Satan does not reconcile, ever. That's just not his cup of tea. So like it or not, when we don't make Jesus Lord over our offenses, we're victims of joint custody. We are that little child being led away by Satan.

> **WHAT IS SCARIER? LEAVING BEHIND THE LIFE WE KNOW OR HAVING SATAN AS A JOINT-CUSTODY PARENT?**

This brings us back to the concept of leaving behind the life we know. Remember that *National Geographic* article with Abraham? Remember how scary it seemed to think about leaving behind all we are used to, all that is familiar? What is scarier? Leaving behind the life we know to follow Jesus and go to the cross, or having Satan as a joint-custody parent? The Lord is giving us a choice.

The key is the heart. *The human heart is a very scary place. It takes a lot of courage to go in.* It does, doesn't it? Our hearts, our own hearts, are very scary places, especially if we've been reading our own press clippings about what good Christians we are. To really go in and say, "Holy Spirit, show me what's inside of me"—well, it's a scary thing. It's a messy thing. *It's a cocoon thing.*

Did you know a cocoon is a very messy place? So is the cross. It's very, very scary, but I believe what God is saying is, "The fear of the Lord is the beginning of wisdom" (Psalm 111:10). He scared me with the fear of the Lord by letting me imagine being that little child whom Satan takes by the hand. I had to bow before God and pray, *Oh, my God, if I have a choice, I will go to this fearful place of the cross, because at least there I know that I have a High Priest who understands my infirmities. I've got a God that's sensitive. At the cross I've got Somebody who loves me.*

> I WILL GO TO THIS FEARFUL PLACE OF THE CROSS BECAUSE AT THE CROSS I'VE GOT SOMEBODY WHO LOVES ME.

King David, the man the Bible describes as the man after God's own heart, cried out to the Lord in a similar way. When he really messed things up, God gave him the choice of who would punish him, the hand of God or the hand of men. Do you know what David said? "God, You punish me. I trust Your mercies, and I'll put my life in Your hands, but don't put me in the hands of men" (2 Samuel 24:14, paraphrased).

Do you know what God is saying to us right now? "Trust *Me*. Don't keep holding on to your own life; don't trust yourself more than you trust Me. Truly give your heart to Me."

Let's make this our prayer: *Lord, it's scary, but search me. I know that no matter what You find You're still going to tell me that You love me. No matter what You find—it's all been taken care of by Jesus Christ on the cross. There is nothing that can separate me from Your love and from the love of Christ, so I would much rather choose to fall into Your hands and for You to put my false person to death than for the devil to have joint custody over me.*

He's motivating us to get out of Satan's house and get into His house—the heavenly Father's house. And I'll say this again, as offensive as it sounds, *this is for born-again Christians*. This is not about the unsaved. This is saying that born-again Christians can be deceived. *The ultimate deception is a good intention, and we can be deceived into joint custody*.

We're going to close now with an interesting story. There's a high school near where I live called Massillon Washington High. It's very famous for football. In fact, there was a national documentary done about it, and *Sports Illustrated* had a big article when Massillon and their rival, McKinley High School, played their one-hundredth anniversary football game. Their weight room has a quote on the wall that caught my attention. It was by Chris Spielman, who had played football at Massillon and went on to become an All-American in college and an All Pro in the NFL. The quote says, "Train at a level where your opponents are unable or unwilling to go." The clear message is, do this and you will win.

> TRAIN AT A LEVEL WHERE YOUR OPPONENTS ARE UNABLE OR UNWILLING TO GO.

Who is our opponent? Did you know that Satan's name means accuser, but it also means "adversary"? So, Satan is our opponent. Where is he unwilling to go versus where is he able and willing to go? If we can find that out and go there ourselves, we can win, right?

Satan is comfortable with *the wisdom of the world*. In the wisdom of the world's system of knowledge and works…he loves it there. We start out great as a born-again Christian. Then we become a Caterpillar Christian, and we're learning and growing. But we get stuck. We get totally enamored with the system of knowledge and works—doing more for God, and judging good and evil—we get into that.

Is Satan willing and able to go there? You bet. Guess what? He's the one who tempted people to go there in the first place. Remember, the Bible says Eve was beguiled by the serpent in the garden to eat of the tree of the knowledge of good and evil. He's all for it, he's very willing and able, and he encourages many millions of Christians to go there. Applying the quote from the weight room, the system of knowledge and works is like lifting little five-pound dumbbells. We may think we can really beat Satan by constantly learning and doing more, but he's already got us beat.

The second place is *hidden idols*. They are man-made gods in us—gods from our earthly father's house, our people, and our country—gods that came from the world we grew up in. Guess what? Satan says, "I'm prince of this world. I am legally prince. The entire world is under my dominion. I am glad to go there!" He is more than willing and able. He runs this system, so he's very happy to compete on that playing field.

Now fasten your seat belts. This is the third place, and it was very offensive to me, and could be to you also. Where else is Satan willing and able to go? *The five majestic trees*—those five things of God—the Word, prayer, worship, fellowship, and ministry. Do we need proof?

Think about when Jesus was tempted in the desert. Was the Word off-limits for Satan? No, he quoted it. What about prayer? Prayer is talking to God, isn't it? Check out Job 1:6-12. It says Satan presented himself to God and talked to Him. So prayer isn't off limits for Satan either. How about praise and worship? He was in charge of it before he fell from heaven (Isaiah 14:11-15). He knows a lot about it. And we all know he gets right in the middle of fellowship and ministry. How many times have you heard pastors and believers share how they sensed spiritual warfare going on during a church service or a time of ministry? *Satan is more than able, and more than willing, to compete within the arena of the five majestic trees.*

Does that mean we can't use those against him? No. Jesus spoke the Word back to Satan; He prayed; He worshipped; He sought fellowship; He cast out demons during His ministry. Please don't over-react to what I'm saying, but we mustn't under-react either. Don't ever think Satan is unable or unwilling to go to the five things of God in order to deceive us, because he can. That doesn't mean we abandon them or that we quit using them against him. Understand, though, that we don't *honor* the enemy but we *respect* our enemy. There's a big difference. We'd better understand how he operates if we want to beat him.

> ARE YOU READY FOR THE GOOD NEWS? YOU WILL NEVER FIND SATAN AT THE CROSS.

Are you ready for the good news? Where is the devil unable and unwilling to go? Where can you be guaranteed not to find him? *You will never find Satan at the cross.* He's unable and unwilling to go there. He doesn't want any part of it!

First, *Satan can't embrace the vertical beam of the cross.* He cannot stand in the light; he's a liar and the father of lies, and he will never, ever, *ever* go and stand in the light of the Holy Spirit and ask to be searched. He cannot go there. He's a creature of darkness. It's completely impossible.

Second, *Satan also can never embrace the horizontal beam of the cross.* He cannot deal with offenses. He can never say that, never do that, because he's a murderer. He can never forgive, and he can never love.

The third place *Satan cannot go is the place of humility*. He can never go to the foot of the cross and lay down his pride. Satan cannot go there, you know why? Because he's arrogant. He can never, ever humble himself, because he is the most arrogant creature in the entire universe. He wanted to be God, remember?

Finally, *he can never go to the cross because he was totally defeated there*. When Jesus said, "It is finished," it meant "Satan you are finished." He'd rather forget it ever happened.

God has given us a secret. We do lots of spiritual exercises that don't do us much good when it comes to real spiritual training, but if we will go to the cross we are going where our opponent is unable and unwilling to go. We die, Jesus takes our place, and then *Jesus fights Satan for us, and that's where the victory is.*

Now we're at a place he can't go! Sayonara, joint custody. I'm not living in Satan's house anymore, and there is no way he can keep me there because I'm at a place he can never go. Jesus has taken us to His Father's house through the power of the cross.

My Personal One-on-One Encounter With The Lord

Also for Home Group Discussion

Do I now understand that it is possible for a sincere Christian to spend time in Satan's house with joint custody? How much time am I spending there?

_____
_____
_____
_____

The ultimate deception is a good intention. Is it clear to me now that Satan lures sincere Christians to his house through the deception of good intentions? Are more of my good intentions being revealed to me?

_____
_____
_____
_____

Has the very scary thought of living in Satan's house part-time helped me to overcome my fear of "Leaving Behind the Life I Know"?

_____
_____
_____
_____

What does it mean for me, personally, to train at a level my opponent is unwilling and unable to go?

_____
_____
_____
_____

Am I ready to get my God-given birthright back, to live in a world of love, joy, peace, and power in my Father's house?

―――――――――――――――――――――――――
―――――――――――――――――――――――――
―――――――――――――――――――――――――
―――――――――――――――――――――――――

Reflecting on the Art

- In what way does the painting that opens this chapter speak to me?
- Did the sketch have an impact on me? If so, how?

The Author's Journey
CROSS ENCOUNTERS

CHAPTER 12

The Author's Journey
Cross Encounters

I RECENTLY BUMPED INTO an old high school friend of mine who reminded me of an encounter we had back in 1972. We'd both been drafted for the Vietnam War and were on a bus ride to get our physical examinations.

"You know, I will never forget that bus ride," he told me. "I've told tons of people about it, especially after all of the success that you achieved."

I'd totally forgotten about that ride until he reminded me of it, and the story he told shook me to my core.

He said, "I got on the bus and sat down next to you. You were reading Adolf Hitler's autobiography, *Mein Kampf*. As you read it, you turned to me and told me you were going to be a millionaire."

I had forgotten all about that darkest side of my depraved past when I was an atheist, when I had actually admired Adolf Hitler! Back then my highest aspiration was to be president of the United States. I had read everything I could find about Hitler and how he rose to power. My plan was to become a multi-millionaire through marketing and get the money to finance a campaign. I wanted to follow in Hitler's footsteps, using marketing propaganda to get into office, and become a very, very powerful man. I believe now that there were many layers to that ambition, rooted in the lie that I was inferior, with an overwhelming drive to prove myself worthy to the world. Regardless of all of the reasons, however, admiring Adolf Hitler was evil. I was truly depraved, with no boundaries, and no way to fence evil in.

After my friend reminded me of that story, I was very emotional for two days. (By the way, neither of us went to Vietnam; his number 96 never got called, and I had a 4F classification for bad vision.) I thought about what Jesus did on the cross—how far he went to save a person as far gone as I was. During those two days, the Holy Spirit spoke to my heart, and He said, *Rick, there were millions and millions of other people that also admired Adolf Hitler in the nineteen-thirties and forties...God-fearing, church-going Germans. They were very regular people.*

Strangely enough, if you read and talk to the GIs, they say that out of every country they entered in Europe, whether it was England, France, Belgium, the one most like the United States was Germany. The highways, the houses—everything reminded them of home. These people were no different than you or me, but, they idolized Adolf Hitler, and as a result, six million Jews—God's chosen people—were murdered. What's more, millions and millions of other people were killed by church-going, God-fearing people who followed Adolf Hitler.

So what was the purpose of the bus ride story my friend reminded me of? It helped me to understand how depraved human beings can be, and how depraved I was. The Lord then connected that truth to a series of visions and experiences He had given me about the cross. And anytime the Lord shares something with us, it's so we can eventually share what we've learned with others. There were lessons and teachings in these visions, which I'm now sharing with others.

> I BELIEVE THE GOD WHO IS THE SAME YESTERDAY, TODAY, AND FOREVER STILL GIVES HIS PEOPLE PROPHETIC VISIONS.

I realize there may be readers who are unfamiliar with or even skeptical of visions. Clearly, people had visions all throughout the Bible, and I believe the God who is the same yesterday, today, and forever still gives His people prophetic visions. Peter, in his great sermon in Acts 2, preached that dreams and visions are signs of the last days and the out-pouring of the Holy Spirit. Because I believe we are in the last days and experiencing a fresh out-pouring of the Holy Spirit, I believe these visions are becoming more and more common. They are a part of God's plan to accomplish His will among us today. There are two kinds of Biblical visions: open visions and mental images. Mine were mental images but with the feeling of actually being there.

Before I share some of my "Cross Encounters" through the visions He gave me, I want to say that I don't claim to have experienced even one-millionth of what Jesus went through on the cross. I could never comprehend all of His agony. But He has given me a little sliver—just a tiny glimpse—and I believe He wants me to share it. I'm certainly not up on any pedestal. I'm simply a messenger of the cross, who is on a spiritual journey like everyone else. As I share these visions, you will see that I too was a Caterpillar Christian who had to go into the cocoon of the cross. I might add that my transformation into a Birthright Butterfly is still a work in progress.

The first vision was given in the spring of 1993. My pastor's wife was very ill; she had shingles, which in middle age is a very painful condition. That was when I was in a deep pit in my own life, but I went over to lay hands on her and pray. As I did, I got a vision of the feet of Jesus. There were spikes through His feet, and the blood was running down the cross. It was actually following the grain of the wood, which was very distinct. The blood would flow down the grain of the wood and then drop to the ground. After I prayed, she quickly thereafter was healed.

A second vision connected with the first one. In it I saw the cross firmly planted in a mound of dirt here on the earth. In a third vision I was at the foot of the cross and looking up. There was a very distinct sign over Jesus' head, and I know it was in Latin and Greek and Aramaic, but for some reason I was able to read it. It said, "Jesus, the King of the Jews." As I stood at the foot of the cross looking up at that sign, the Holy Spirit said, *I want you to look up the word* king *in the Greek and Hebrew.*

I obeyed, and do you know what the most basic derivative for the word *king* is? *Foot.* The idea of *king* is that His foot rules. He puts it on the neck of His enemies; all things are at His feet. The concept of a foot indicates a king, and the lesson is that there's victory at the foot of the cross. When we're at the foot of the cross, we are at the foot of the King of all Kings. He's the Lord of all Lords, and there is victory and power under His rule. And His kingship flows from the foot of the cross.

I believe the lesson of these three visions is this: Jesus truly came down from heaven to the earth; His cross was firmly planted in this earth; His blood flowed down and touched the ground; then total victory over every sin, demon, and curse was won. At the foot of the cross, the King of all Kings and the Lord of all Lords has total dominion and rule. As the painting opening this chapter depicts, it may not be easy to get there, but if by God's grace I can get to the foot of the cross, the devil can't get me! At the foot of the cross, all the wrongs that we have done, and all the wrongs done to us, are totally taken care of. At the foot of the cross, we have trained at a level where our opponent was unable and unwilling to go. We are seated with Christ high above all principalities and powers. Our God-given birthright of power and dominion over Satan is restored.

> AT THE FOOT OF THE CROSS, THE KING OF ALL KINGS AND THE LORD OF ALL LORDS HAS TOTAL DOMINION AND RULE.

With this lesson in mind, how important is the cross? In the spring of 1994, when I was in the midst of losing my company, Fitness Quest, I had another vision of the cross, which I believe answers this question. I was in my office, and I was totally alone. I went to the window and was looking out at the warehouse, the new one-hundred-thousand-square-foot facility, and I had a totally supernatural experience. There was a speck of dust on the window, and like a special effect in a movie, my eyes zoomed into it. It was as if everything else surrounding me disappeared. All of the focus was on that one speck of dust. Then the Holy Spirit said, *I want you to understand something. Everything that has ever happened in the entire universe and everything that ever will happen can be totally distilled down to one thing: Jesus Christ on the cross. All things were created by Him, for Him, and through Him—God is reconciling everything back to Himself. It can all be understood by Him on the cross. His resurrection was never the question; the Father would have never left Him in the grave. The question was, would He endure and stay on the cross? Jesus had to make a choice.*

The obvious lesson there is the preeminence of the crucifixion and resurrection of Jesus—that one thing is the most important thing. It is absolutely preeminent over everything in the entire universe, which is stated clearly in Colossians 1:15 – 20. There is a second lesson, however, and it is this: Jesus had a free will; He had to make a choice and say, "Not my will, but your will be done Father." I had never really understood that before. *So just as He made a choice based on His love for His Father and us, we have to do the same.* We also have a free will. Will we choose to make the cross preeminent in our lives and embrace it, to die to self because of our love for God and the hurting and dying world He wants us to minister to?

> SO JUST AS HE MADE A CHOICE BASED ON HIS LOVE FOR HIS FATHER AND US, WE HAVE TO DO THE SAME.

Many years later, after this experience in my office, I read two separate articles in National Geographic magazine. On the cover of the one issue were these words, "Search For The God Particle." The article was about this mystery: According to the "Big Bang Theory" for the start of the universe, the equal amounts of matter and antimatter created should have annihilated each other, leaving a largely empty universe. But the universe if full of millions of galaxies, it's not empty. Scientists think the reason is this: They know about particles called atoms—made up of electrons, protons, neutrons, quarks, and gluons. But they believe there has to be an invisible particle that brought mass and matter into existence—it's called the *God particle*.[1]

The second article was on the Hubble telescope, and it revealed another mystery. The movement of distant galaxies and supernovas suggest that there must be an invisible force in space. In fact, when scientists tried to mathematically calculate it, they came up with a number that was infinitely bigger than all the known matter and energy in the entire universe. This calculation really had them scratching their heads.[2]

These two articles posed two questions: "Why is there anything?" and "What force fills the emptiness of space?" The answer to both questions is Jesus. John 1:3 says, "All things were made through Him, and without Him nothing was made that was made." Colossians 1:17 in the Amplified Bible says, "And He Himself existed before all things, and

---

1 Joel Achenbach, "The God Particle," *National Geographic* (March 2008): pp. 90-105.

2 Timothy Ferris, "Raising Heaven: Hubble Telescope," *National Geographic* (November 2007): pp. 140-153.

in Him all things consist (cohere, and are held together)." Jesus is the invisible God particle the scientists are looking for, the One who brought all matter into existence. And, He is the infinitely powerful invisible force that fills the universe and holds it all together.

After reading these articles and meditating on these scriptures, I now better understand the "speck of dust on my window" experience. Everything in the entire universe really can be distilled down into one thing—Jesus Christ on the cross. This thought then came to me:

Grasping The Power Of The Cross

When you take the preeminent being of the entire universe—Jesus—the one and only entity that contains the fullness of the Godhead—through whom all things that exist were made and are held together—and that being volunteers to step down from His place of preeminence to be beaten and destroyed—only to be raised from the dead—then there is nothing left to do—it's all been taken care of—for everybody—for everything—for all time. It is finished.

When He who is all and all, lays it all down, all is taken care of. That's how powerful and complete the work of the cross was. Did Paul understand something that we don't, when he said, "But what things were gain to me, these I have counted loss for Christ. Yet indeed I also count all things loss for the excellence of the knowledge of Christ Jesus my Lord, for whom I have suffered the loss of all things, and count them as rubbish, that I may gain Christ" (Philippians 3:7-8)? Do we truly understand that when we get Jesus, we gain everything?

Another vision, one that was quite disturbing, correlates with Isaiah 50:6. I never even knew that this scripture existed before I had this vision, but it says, "I gave My back to those who struck Me, and My cheeks to those who plucked out the beard; I did not hide My face from shame and spitting."

In this vision there was a crowd of people who absolutely hated Jesus' guts. In most instances the Bible says that He passed through the crowds who wanted to kill Him or stone Him, but during His time of the cross, He went towards the crowd. He gave Himself to the crowd, and it was real. He gave His back to be flogged, and He gave His cheek. In the

vision I saw, the people actually took their fingers and pulled His beard out of His face, and Jesus gave Himself to that. I wept.

As I was in this vision, the Holy Spirit showed me that humans react with fight or flight when we are hated. We either beat up the person who hates us, or we run away from them. But Jesus actually went toward the hatred in order to once and for all dissolve it. He went into it in order to get victory over it—that's what the scripture in Isaiah means. *Only this kind of love can bring victory over offenses and hate in the church and the world — and this love can only come from one place—Jesus! He allowed people to torture and murder Him in order to save them from their hatred.*

I'm going to share three other experiences from the Lord in a sequence, and there's a lesson here. One day before my trials started, I was just a happy-go-lucky Caterpillar Christian. I was standing in my study, and I picked up a book called *Jesus is for Jews*. I had received it from the ministry *Jews For Jesus*. When I opened the book, the scripture I saw was from Jeremiah 29, and it said, "You will seek Me and find Me, when you search for Me with all your heart" (vs. 13).

It's never happened to me before or since, but that scripture literally knocked me down into a chair. It physically knocked me down. And I heard the Holy Spirit say, *I am God. I am the Most High God who is the possessor of heaven and earth—that's who I Am. And if you seek Me with all your heart, you can have Me as your personal possession.*

To help me understand, the Holy Spirit explained it to me in very human terms. You've seen how ladies sometimes collect Lladros—those figurines that are very valuable—and they put them in a cabinet to display. Or what about men and their prized guns? A man with a very expensive Remington shotgun might put it in a case with a lock. Those are possessions that are very valuable too. The Lord showed me that we as Christians can have Him literally as our personal possession in the same way. I had always known our bodies were His temple, but to take it to the next level, to say that I as a mere human could have God Himself as my personal possession, was amazing and exciting to me! Little did I know what He was actually talking about, and how He would make His point later in my life.

> THAT I, AS A MERE HUMAN, COULD HAVE GOD HIMSELF AS MY PERSONAL POSSESSION, WAS AMAZING AND EXCITING TO ME!

Fast forward, then, into the desperation years—to the midst of my big trials. It was 1997 or 1998. We were at a prayer meeting, and a friend of mine came up to me and said, "God told me to come and pray for you."

I said it was okay, and then he said, "The Lord has a love for you that is unbelievable. He told me to pray for you, and you're going to get this love."

I'll be honest with you; I was thinking he was a little off, but I was desperate for God's love. What did I have to lose?

As my friend laid hands on me, I immediately fell on the floor—and this sounds stupid, but it happened. I started swimming like a salmon. I felt like I was a salmon going upstream, back to the place where I was conceived, back to where I came from. I had the sensation that I had to get to God. I just had to get back to God, and as I was swimming, the Holy Spirit spoke to me: *I'm going to give you a love that doesn't care. I'm going to give you a death love. I'm going to give you a martyr's love.* I had never heard of love described that way before, "a love that doesn't care."

When I got up, my friend said, "It isn't over yet. In the weeks to come, you're going to have other encounters with the Lord God. God is not finished."

A couple of weeks later, I was in bed with my wife in our big mansion. Our bedroom had a twenty-four foot ceiling, and our bed looked like something out of a Cleopatra movie. It was a fifteen-foot-tall poster bed with curtains draped all around it. Lu Ann got out of bed and went downstairs, and I was just lying there, not thinking about anything or doing anything spiritual. I looked up and sensed the power of God was coming through the ceiling. It literally came down through the ceiling, and like a half-moon stainless steel knife, it went straight through my body.

> I HAD NEVER HEARD OF LOVE DESCRIBED THAT WAY BEFORE, "A LOVE THAT DOESN'T CARE."

The Holy Spirit said, *I want you to go listen to Celine Dion's love theme song from the movie* Titanic, *"My Heart Will Go On."* It made no sense to me; it wasn't praise or worship music, but I obeyed.

I got up, went down into the weight room, and I put that song on the huge Infinity speakers we had in there. I sat down on a weight machine and listened. For what seemed like hours, I played that song over and over again, hearing the lyrics,

> Near, far, wherever you are
> I believe that the heart does go on
> Once more you open the door
> And you're here in my heart
> And my heart will go on and on.
> Love can touch us one time
> And last for a lifetime
> And never let go till we're one.[3]

---

3 Celine Dion, "My Heart Will Go On," from album *Let's Talk About Love* by James Horner, Will Jennings. Famous Music Corporation (ASCAP)/Blue Sky Rider Songs (administered by Irving Music, Inc.), 1997.

As I listened to that song, it was like there was an insane love coming at me. God's insane love would come toward me, as if He was saying, *I have to have you*. And then an insane love would come out of me, back towards Him saying, *I have to have You*. Back and forth, back and forth, as I kept pushing the replay button for I don't know how long. I was beginning to better understand "a love that doesn't care."

Two weeks later I felt led to do it again. I went back down to the weight room, and this time it was different. I put the song on, and I don't know for how long it was, maybe ten seconds, He brought me back to the Father's bosom. In that brief encounter, I was back in His bosom, my true home before I was in my mother's womb. Then He brought me back here. As soon as I got back, I was so lonely; I missed my true home with the Father so much. It was the loneliest feeling I had ever experienced in my entire life! I was in China one time on business where I was away from my family and really missed them, but this was a thousand times more intense.

I was so lonely I thought I was losing my mind. I knew if I sat there any longer, I would, so I tried to watch TV, but the minute my mind would stray from what was on TV, this unspeakable loneliness would come over me again. Finally I got through it, and there was a voice inside that said, *I've got to get back, no matter what. I've got to get back. That is my home*—it's where the salmon was trying to swim back to—it's where I originated. I have to get back to that place. No matter what it takes, even if it means that half-moon-shaped stainless steel knife going through my body. I now understood "a love that doesn't care," a death love—a martyr's love.

> **I'VE GOT TO GET BACK, NO MATTER WHAT. THAT'S MY HOME.**

So how do I get God as my personal possession now and make sure I get back to Him for all eternity? I didn't know yet, but I was about to find out—by learning what it meant to choose to die—to die to self.

I was at a Christian counseling session, and I was going through a lot of trouble; there was a lot of junk coming to the surface in my life. These counselors decided to pray for me. When they did, there was the third supernatural event. I instantly entered a scene, just as real as real can be, and I was in front of a firing squad. The soldiers were in a line, with their rifles pointed at me, and a big executioner was getting ready to put a black hood over my head.

I had the sense that God was going to give the command to shoot me. I was terrified. I felt it was really going to happen, that I was going to die. I was waiting for a big, booming voice from heaven to say, "Fire!" and I started screaming out—literally screaming at the top of my lungs in front of these counselors—"I don't want to die! I don't want to die! I don't want to die!"

I was in a cold sweat. It was very real, and as I was screaming, I was waiting at any point for His voice to say "Fire!" And then there was this silence, and out of that silence came a sweet, soft voice, and I knew it was Jesus. He said, *I died for you*. That's all He said, with no pressure whatsoever. The sense was, an all-powerful God wasn't in heaven commanding me to die for Him, but an all-powerful God did choose to die for me. Based on that truth, He wasn't commanding that I die; He was giving me a choice and gently encouraging me by reminding me that He made that same choice for me first. He was helping me to understand that holding on to my life wasn't as important as I was making it out to be. He was helping me to understand "a love that doesn't care."

If we connect those three encounters, I believe the Lord is saying, *You know what? You genuinely have the chance to possess Me for real as your personal possession. I made the decision to have a love that doesn't care when I died for you on the cross. Will you make the decision to have a love that doesn't care and embrace the cross to die to self for Me? Because when that happens, you will get Me now and get back to Me for all eternity.*

Jesus said to me, *Rick, I have a love that doesn't care. I did not care about My own self; I died for you.*

And now I can say, *Jesus, I have a love that doesn't care. I don't care about my own self. I will die to self for You.*

The Lord showed me that when this duet is sung, nobody can interfere. There's not a person on the face of the earth, and there's not a demon in hell, including Satan himself, that can ever mess with that kind of love. When we have this kind of love between God, us, and each other, the Lord will fill us with power.

In a nutshell, that's what I'm trying to explain as best as I can in this book. *This is what Christianity is about, and it's not conventional. It's not the norm. It's the lost secret.*

What lessons have I learned on my spiritual journey? The very first thing that I learned, as I was weeping and reading the Bible right after I got saved, was this: I really liked everything about Jesus; He was truly the best thing that ever happened in my life. I also learned: Beware the yeast of the Pharisees, and how getting infatuated with knowledge and works as a Caterpillar Christian could rob me of my relationship with my best friend. Little did I know, that these two concepts I received as a baby Christian would turn into the two towering pillars of my faith.

Jesus is the best, but beware the yeast of the Pharisees.

The next thing that I discovered is that very sincere Caterpillar Christians like I was do not have God figured out. If I didn't even know what was inside of me, how could I ever presume to have God all figured out? So the whole idea that I was a super-spiritual, Green Beret Christian and had it all figured out was a joke. The idea that anyone attains that is just not true. I learned that. The good news is that He has me figured out. He knows what I need, and that's good enough for me.

Early in this book, I showed these two graphs, representing the world's progress and God's progress. I learned those graphs are true. I was convinced that in order to grow spiritually, my life needed to look like the first graph. But in reality, I was just growing into a big ugly caterpillar. I am genuinely convinced now, that God has a plan for on-fire Christians to fail, just like the original twelve apostles. That place was their encounter with the cross, their failure replaced by Jesus' success! I believe that the only way we ever really "get it"—meaning, get Him, and understand what Christianity is about—is to fail. I am convinced of that.

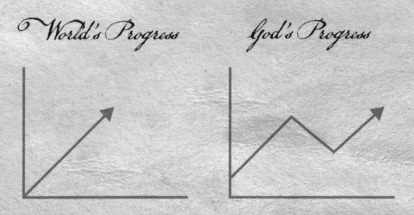

Further, I am convinced that the reason for this planned failure is love. God wants us to know that love truly is what matters—a supernatural three-dimensional love. First, we can never understand how much God loves us until we find out how rotten we are on the inside. Why is that? Because of what Jesus said: "If you only love people who are nice to you, what credit is that to you? Even tax collectors and sinners do that" (Matthew 5:46, paraphrased).

If how much God loves me is based on how good I am—how I perform—then that's not really love. *Anybody can love like that*. But when you find out the junk that's inside, and God says, *I still love you, no matter what*, then you begin to understand the deep unconditional love of the Lord. I would argue that conventional Christianity never goes there. Caterpillar Christians only understand performance-oriented love, not failure love.

The second dimension of this love is that we can never truly love ourselves unless we fail. Do you know why? Well, as a very success-oriented person, I loved myself and valued myself as long as I was successful. But when I failed at everything and was a worm in my own eyes, the love of Jesus freed me to love myself regardless of performance. He showed me that He loves me, I'm wonderful, I'm a prince because I'm born again, and I'm on my way to becoming a king. Those things don't change with my performance. They are eternal truths, and if I choose to embrace those eternal truths, I am free to love myself. No strings of performance attached.

The third dimension is that we can never really love God or others unless we fail. Remember the sinful woman that burst into the Pharisee's house and anointed Jesus' feet with expensive oil? (See Luke 7:36-50.) She washed His feet with her hair. It caused a huge scandal among the Pharisees. They said, "If He was a prophet, He'd know what manner of woman was doing that." Do you know what Jesus said? "The one who is forgiven much loves much. The one who is forgiven little loves little. You will never have the capacity to love Me big, or love others big, until you have failed and been forgiven." To sum up my love lessons, *I learned that failure was worth it to better*

> YOU WILL NEVER HAVE THE CAPACITY TO LOVE ME BIG, OR LOVE OTHERS BIG, UNTIL YOU HAVE FAILED AND BEEN FORGIVEN.

understand how much God loves me, to finally love myself apart from success, and to gain a greater capacity to love God and others. Oh yes—it was all worth it—because great loss can produce great gain.

I also want to share that God is faithful. Once the trial has produced the needed transformation, the Lord then blesses. My chronic fatigue syndrome is gone and my health is getting better and better. The legal problems were all resolved. Miraculously, I did not lose all of our finances, and my family still maintained a wonderful lifestyle. The riches I did lose were replaced with something far more valuable—rich relationships. My relationship with God, myself, my wife and children, Christians and friends, far exceeds what I had before. And I believe more supernatural love, joy, and peace is coming, along with more power to receive my promised blessings and fulfill my destiny to bless others.

If somebody asked me what my perspective is twenty-one years into my unconventional Christianity journey, I'd have to honestly say that the cross has been the worst thing and the best thing that has ever happened to me, both at the same time. It was everything I feared—like Job—and everything I needed. God's lavish grace, which I didn't deserve, His severe mercy when I needed disciplined, and this multidimensional love—these are the treasures I found at the foot of the cross. Jesus is all. And that is all that matters.

My summary of all my *Cross Encounters* is this: It's not about learning more about God and doing more things for God—it's about Jesus. And because of what He did for me on the cross, I can get God as my personal possession. When I get Him, I get everything—love, power, and my promised blessings. I can then fulfill my destiny to bless others by giving Him away. When my mission here on earth is accomplished, I'll go back to Him. Get God, give God, get back to God—pretty simple, huh?

My Personal One-on-One Encounter With The Lord

Also for Home Group Discussion

What specific vision or insights in this chapter has the Lord used to help me understand the cross of Jesus better?
_____
_____
_____
_____

Based on the depth of the depravity humans are capable of, do I appreciate everything Jesus had to go through to rescue and save us?
_____
_____
_____
_____

Do I truly believe that when His cross was planted in the earth and His blood touched the ground, that victory over every sin, demon, and curse on this earth was won?
_____
_____
_____
_____

We were all in the Father's bosom before we were placed in our mother's womb. Is the cry of my heart now, *I've got to get back*?
_____
_____
_____
_____

Do I now realize how failure helps us understand how much God loves us apart from performance, to love ourselves apart from performance, and greatly increase our capacity to love the Lord and one another?

_____
_____
_____

Conversation Starter

We have now discovered that the fullness of the Trinity is in Jesus, everything was created through Him, and He fills and holds the whole universe together. He volunteered to be beaten and destroyed, only to be raised again. Is this truth that He who was all, laid it all down, to take care of all things, worth focusing on and understanding? What would happen if this would become a big topic of conversation for many Christians?

_____
_____
_____

Reflecting on the Art

- In what way does the painting that opens this chapter speak to me?
- Did the sketches have an impact on me? If so, how?

_____
_____
_____
_____

Satan's Field of Slaughter

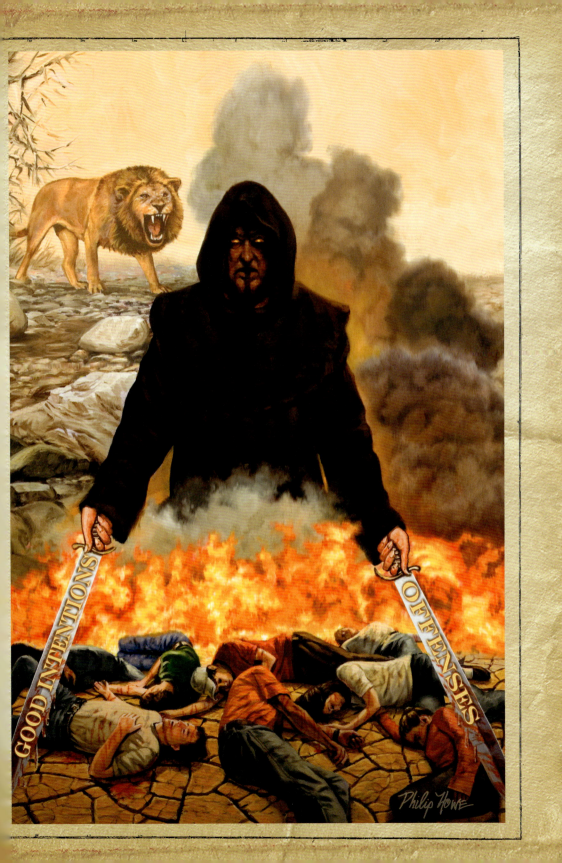

CHAPTER 13

Satan's Field of Slaughter

Picture in your mind a supernatural battlefield. Strangely, to our natural eye, this battlefield looks like a very prim and proper place. It's full of very good people who seem to be doing all the right things. In fact, the focus of all these people is God, because the battlefield is the church!

But let's put on a pair of supernatural goggles like the night vision goggles worn by soldiers. Instantly a whole different scene comes into view. It's Satan's field of slaughter, the painting that opens this chapter. The carnage is horrible—the devil is wreaking great havoc in the church. His weapons of choice are good intentions and offenses, and they are really working. The fallen Christians in the scene have no idea they are being slaughtered. They never had a chance.

So it is today in the church. Jesus won the battle on the cross, but Satan is winning the battle now, because he is deceiving well-intentioned Christians. But help is on the way. Jesus, who is the Lion of the Tribe of Judah, is coming on the scene in the painting. What's the first thing Jesus must bring to this field of slaughter to change the tide of the battle? *Truth*, to dispel the deception. Jesus is the light of the world, and He is the way, the truth, and the life. So let's shed the light and truth of Jesus on Satan's swords.

The two swords are "Good Intentions" and "Offenses." Interestingly, two of the devil's names are, Lucifer and Satan—umm, could there be a connection? Lucifer means light, so literally Satan is an angel of light. His most effective tactic is to dress something up that is evil and make it look good—a masquerade! Let's break down his good intentions and see how this works.

We've learned that Caterpillar Christians get sucked into the wisdom of the world system of knowledge and works, which is the law. Learning more and more about God and doing lots of works for Him appears good, doesn't it? But let's penetrate the masquerade and go to the source of this system—the fall of man in the Garden of Eden. Eating of the tree of the knowledge of good and evil to become like God was not good. It was a sin. It was based on the lie that God wasn't good and we weren't good enough. It was man's attempt to take care of our own problems and gain self-esteem. In addition, the law and the Old Covenant have no place in the New Covenant. So much for being good. Remember, there is no such thing as a good intention, and the ultimate deception is a good intention.

One last thought on good intentions: Can something that caused a problem in the first place ever be used to get rid of that problem? The knowledge of good and evil caused man to start sinning, so how could it ever be used to stop sin? The truth is this: using the law to stop sin is like pouring gasoline on a fire. Remember Romans 5:20 (NIV): "The law was added so that the trespass might increase."

How about the good intention system in us of hidden idols? Idols are false gods—things that appear to be good and God, but aren't. No matter how Godly these idols from our father's house, people, and country seem, we must remember that they are from man. Man's system is a fallen world system, under Satan's control. There is no good thing in our flesh, and even our righteousness is as filthy rags (Isaiah 64:6). Also, whose idea was idolatry in the first place—someone or something trying to take the place of God? It was Satan's idea to try and overthrow God and become a false god. Are we starting to get the idea that all these good intentions we get sucked into have their source in Satan? It's true! Lucifer, the angel of light, is the master at deceiving sincere Christians. My wife and I have come up with this saying to guard against being deceived with good intentions: "Is this a good idea or a God idea?"

How about the devil's second sword, "offenses"? A world full of good intentions based on knowledge and works is the perfect breeding ground for offenses. Why? When what I know about God and do for Him is different than what you know and do, there's going to be an offense. But it doesn't stop there, because the devil's second name is "Satan." The name *Satan* means accuser of the brethren, and boy, does he! He's really good at it; Jesus said he is the father of lies, and when he lies, he speaks his native tongue and has no accent. When he lies to me about you, making all kinds of accusations against you, most of the time I buy it hook, line, and sinker and get offended. I'm reeled in like some unsuspecting fish.

Where there are offenses and accusations, relationships end, sometimes in a very dramatic fashion. Let's look at the story of Cain and Abel. Cain got offended, never dealt with it as God suggested, and he murdered his own innocent brother. So Satan was there from the very beginning. He swung his sword of good intentions by tempting Adam and Eve to eat from the tree of the knowledge of good and evil. He swung his sword of offenses when Cain murdered Abel. One...two. The swords were swung in the book of Genesis, and Satan's been swinging them ever since on poor, unsuspecting human beings.

> ONE...TWO. THE SWORDS WERE SWUNG IN THE BOOK OF GENESIS, AND SATAN'S BEEN SWINGING THEM EVER SINCE.

As believers we need to wake up! We must realize there is a real war going on, a power struggle. To help us understand, think of this principle of physics: nature abhors a vacuum. For example, if a jet is flying at 40,000 ft. and a window breaks, all the air will rush out of the cabin to fill the "thin-air vacuum" outside of the plane. There is a similar principle in the spiritual realm: power abhors a vacuum. When there are areas of our life that are not under the Lordship of Jesus, idols rush in to fill the vacuum. Where the Holy Spirit is not our counselor, demons rush in to fill the vacuum. When we are not in our Father's house, Satan rushes in to grab our hand and take us to his house for joint custody. It's as real as an airplane window blowing out, but we are just not aware of it.

What we have just described is a heart that has been leavened and divided by the yeast of the Pharisees, which is knowledge and works. A heart with a watered down and weakened version of the Gospel. Weakened and war make for a bad combination. With this in mind, what I'm about to share, I say with great sorrow. I have known sincere believers, who were very passionate with the five majestic trees. They were full of God's word, prayed continually, praised and thanked God even during trials, went to church twice on Sunday and Wednesday night, and ministered to those in need. This is what the church taught, and was all they knew. This system worked well as long as there were no major problems. But when a serious health, financial, or marriage problem arose, the power for victory wasn't there. In fact, some of these dear believers died, went broke, and got divorced.

I'm not saying believers won't experience problems, that loss can't turn into great gain, or that sometimes the Lord calls those who love Him home at an early age. My business went broke and I lost it, but that turned into great gain for me. Isaiah 57:1 says, "The righteous perishes, and no man takes it to heart; merciful men are taken away, while no one considers that the righteous is taken away from evil." But what I do believe is this, when Jesus died on the cross and was raised from the dead, He defeated every demon and curse. In fact, here are His direct words to us: "I saw Satan fall like lightening from heaven. Behold, I give you the authority to trample on serpents and scorpions, and over all the power of the enemy, and nothing shall by any means hurt you" (Luke 10:18-19). Deep within our spiritual DNA, we know that this was the way it was meant to be. We are to have power and dominion over Satan, not vice versa. So when we see a believer who is standing on the Word, praising God, and seeking prayer during their trial die, go broke, or get divorced, a Divine Dissatisfaction arises in us. This is why millions of Christians are asking God, "Where's the power?"

I believe there is a simple answer. When Jesus Christ crucified is in His rightful place of preeminence above the five majestic trees and those trees are firmly anchored in the Gospel, we will have power. When that's not the case, we won't. And that is not the case today in most western churches. That's why finding the lost secret of the cross and community is so important. To illustrate, let's show the contrast between two different worlds, that of a Caterpillar Christian without the lost secret, and a Birthright Butterfly with the lost secret.

A Caterpillar Christian's World

1. **Knowledge**: Learn more and more about God. (Genesis 2:17; Romans 5:20)

2. **Works**: Do more and more for God. (Galatians 3:11-12; Ephesians 2:8-9)

3. **Little Transformation**: Appears to be very spiritual, but actually very shallow. Low level of dying to self to be transformed into a new creation in Christ. (Colossians 2:21-23)

4. **Little Love**: Divisions, splits, bite and devour each other. (Galatians 5:15)

5. **Little Power**: Lots of talk but few miracles. (1 Corinthians 4:20)

A Birthright Butterfly's World

1. **The Cross**: The most important thing in my Christian walk is the crucifixion and resurrection of Christ and Jesus being my first love. (Colossians 1:15-20; Revelation 2:4)

2. **Community**: We gather together in homes with believers who have a passion for the cross, in trusting and caring relationships. (Acts 2:42-47; Acts 4:32-35; Acts 20:20)

3. **Transformation**: We are transparent with God and each other, in order to die to self and be transformed into new creations in Christ. (Romans 6:3-4; 2 Corinthians 5:17)

4. **Reconciliation**: As new creations, we are reconciled to the Father as sons and daughters, and to each other as brothers and sisters in Christ. We enter His relationship world of supernatural love, joy, and peace, even in the midst of trials. (Romans 8:15-16; John 13:34; 2 Corinthians 5:18-20)

5. **Power**: In this world of love, we are fused together as one and God fills us with His supernatural power. We enter His rulership world of victory over sin, Satan, and curses to be blessed and fulfill our destiny to bless others. (John 17:20-23; Acts 1:4-8; Acts 2:1-4)

Now we have the answer to our two big questions, "Where's the love?" and "Where's the power?" We have little power because we have little love. We have little love because we have little transformation into new creations in Christ. Why? Because learning more about God and doing more things for God doesn't change our inner man much. But making Christ crucified the most important thing in our lives and being in transparent and trusting relationships with other believers who share that passion brings huge change!

I call the five-part Birthright Butterfly world "The Lost Secret Sequence." Think of the sequence like a five-pronged key that opens a treasure chest. Inside this treasure chest is God Himself! When we get God, we get love, joy, and peace even in the midst of trials. And we get power for victory over sins, Satan, and curses, to be blessed and be a blessing. Our lost birthright world of love relationships and rulership power has been found!

The Lost Secret Sequence

1. THE CROSS
2. COMMUNITY
3. TRANSFORMATION
4. RECONCILIATION
5. POWER

Since *The Lost Secret Sequence* represents the core message of this book, let's explore it further. First comes the cross. The crucifixion and resurrection of Jesus is how Christianity began—without it our faith would not exist. To this day, it represents the very essence of Christianity. That's why Christ crucified must be the most important thing for all believers and Jesus must be our first love. This truth is clearly confirmed in the following scripture:

> *He is the image of the invisible God, the firstborn over all creation. For by Him all things were created that are in heaven and that are on earth, visible and invisible, whether thrones or dominions or principalities or powers. All things were created through Him and for Him. And He is before all things, and in Him all things consist. And He is the head of the body, the church, who is the beginning, the firstborn from the dead, that in all things He may have the preeminence. For it pleased the Father that in Him all the fullness should dwell, and by Him to reconcile all things to Himself, by Him, whether things on earth or things in heaven, having made peace through the blood of His cross (Colossians 1:15-20).*

But somehow the most important thing in Christianity is no longer the most important thing in the church. That somehow has a name—Satan! He stole the message of the cross and has been running for dear life ever since. He knows once he gets caught, and we get the message of Christ Crucified back, it's over for him!

Second comes Christian community. It's what we all long for, to be in real caring and trusting relationships. Right after Jesus ascended to heaven, we see this deep human need of love being fulfilled in the book of Acts. They met in homes, got to know each other, built trust, and were there for each other in times of need. This continued for hundreds of years. But shortly after the emperor Constantine legalized Christianity in 313 AD another change occurred. He began to build church buildings, and Caterpillar Christianity emerged. Soon, well-intentioned believers would brush shoulders every Sunday as they walked in and out of church. The sweet and intimate home fellowships they had enjoyed became a thing of the past. I'm not advocating shutting down all the church buildings. What I am saying is we all need to make Jesus Christ crucified preeminent and have home fellowship with believers who share this passion (we will explore home fellowships further in chapter fifteen).

> TRANSFORMATION IS THE KEY ELEMENT TO ENTERING GOD'S WORLD OF LOVE AND POWER.

Christians who embrace the lost secret of the cross and community go on to experience number three, transformation—the key element to entering God's world of love and power. With a passion for the cross and trust in each other, we are able to be transparent with God and one another. We allow the Lord to shine His light inside of us, so we can die to self and be transformed into new creations in Christ—it's no longer I who live but Christ who lives in me (Galatians 2:20). Remember, I don't want to be God, I want God to be me! Adam and Eve tried to turn the Garden of Eden into a *how to* world of knowledge and works to become like God, and it didn't work. Transformation is not about learning how to do something, it's about dying to self so that God can do things through us.

Now comes the good part, number four, which is reconciliation. We are reunited with the Father as sons and daughters and each other as brothers and sisters in Christ. We go beyond just human caring to a world of supernatural love, joy, and peace—even in the midst of life's trials.

Number five is the grand finale…power! God's chosen method to release power in the natural world is through fusion—the thermonuclear explosion of a hydrogen bomb, which is the power of the stars. So it is in the supernatural world. The book of Acts says that when they were gathered together in one accord (fusion), the Holy Spirit came and filled them with power. It's the power for victory over sins, demons, and curses. It's the power that Satan fears!

A simple summary of The Lost Secret Sequence is this: What's missing in conventional Christianity is the cross and community. Together they transform us into new creations in Christ—a metamorphosis from Caterpillar Christians into Birthright Butterflies. Then the cry of our heart is answered, as we enter the lost world of God's love and power.

That's the world I want to live in, don't you? In this world, the truth that Satan isn't as big as we make him out to be will be understood. We will agree with Isaiah 14:16-17 which, talking about Lucifer, says, "Those who see you will gaze at you, and consider you, saying: 'Is this the man who made the earth tremble, who shook kingdoms, who made the world as a wilderness and destroyed its cities, who did not open the house of his prisoners?'" Satan, compared to God and Jesus in us, is very, very small. The biggest thing that gives him power is the fact he is *the great deceiver*.

Here's a final motivation for all of us to take those two swords out of Satan's hands and live in a world of power and dominion over the devil. The seed to write this book was planted at a restaurant, with a vision of

Jesus and God the Father looking at one another, saying, "Did We do this for nothing?" They were both very sad. Their hearts were broken. Now let's play out some real-life scenarios involving good intentions and offenses and see how we could break God's heart and not even be aware of it.

Here's one scenario. What if, even if my commitment is very sincere, my relationship with God and my Christianity develops into one based on how much I know and how much I do. What is that saying? "I can attain a righteousness based on knowledge and works, and I don't need You anymore. I'm this generator, and I'm cranking up my own righteousness." We don't think about it, but Jesus and the Father are real, live beings in heaven who hear and feel what we are saying. They are trying to tell us, "You're off on your little trip here, learning, learning, doing, doing, learning, learning, doing, doing; and what you're really saying without knowing it is, 'You died for nothing.'"

Scenario number two is represented by one of the deadliest things that a Christian can ever say: "That's just the way I am." A decision comes up in our life, and the Bible says, "For waging war you need...many advisers" (Proverbs 24:6), and, "In a multitude of counselors there is safety" (Proverbs 11:14), but we say, "I'm just not an input-oriented person!" The Bible says, "Give generously" (Psalm 37:21; Romans 12:8), and, "If you sow abundantly, you will reap abundantly" (Luke 6:38; 2 Corinthians 9:6, both paraphrased), but we say, "I'm just not a big giver." The Bible says, "Don't put your light under a bushel basket" (Matthew 5:15, paraphrased), and to live this out, the Holy Spirit prompts us to share something with a person, but we say, "I'm just a quiet person." The list goes on, and on, and on. The most famous—or infamous—words of every Christian are, "That's just the way I am."

THE MOST FAMOUS—OR INFAMOUS—WORDS OF EVERY CHRISTIAN ARE, "THAT'S JUST THE WAY I AM."

No one ever thinks, when we're saying those 'innocent' little words, that we're really saying Jesus died for nothing. However, when I accept the "false me"—my personality based on hidden idols and the demons attached—I'm really telling the Lord exactly that, "You died for nothing," and it hurts Jesus and the Father a lot.

The last scenario is when I'm offended by a brother or sister I love and I end that relationship. Do you know what I'm saying without knowing it? "Lord, what You did on the cross was not enough to cover this problem. In this situation You died for nothing." We don't know we're saying that; no one would knowingly say that. We all super-spiritualize breaking off relationships with people, but the reality of the fact is that when we do that, we are saying, "You died for nothing."

As I said before, there are some physically and mentally abusive situations that the Lord will tell us to get out of. But I can tell you, from personal observation, there are many Christians who claim they are in unbearable, abusive situations when that is not the truth. The reality is this, many times their idols were getting bumped into and they were being offended by Jesus, who is a rock of offense; but the devil and their emotions convinced them otherwise—it's always easier for us to blame someone else than to look inside and deal with our own junk.

Thank goodness, God is gracious, compassionate, and full of mercy. When He passed before Moses, He said, "The Lord, the Lord, the compassionate and gracious God, slow to anger, abounding in love and faithfulness" (Exodus 34:6). Thank the Lord He understands we are dust. The church never intended to get into the wisdom of the world system, right? No Christian ever intended on getting stuck in the caterpillar stage. Nobody ever wanted to get into idols, right? No one plans to end relationships with people they love. But, guess what? The *good news* is this. God understands that. He's speaking to our hearts, and what He's saying is, "Look, I have mercy on you. I understand you've been duped, deceived, and ripped off."

The Bible says that if we know the truth, the truth will set us free, and those whom the Son has set free are free indeed (John 8:32, 36). Jesus said, "The thief does not come except to steal, and to kill, and to destroy. I have come that they may have life, and that they may have it more abundantly" (John 10:10). That's the purposes of this book, to get the truth out, so we can live an abundant life. It gives us all the opportunity to make a choice—to embrace the cross and take those two swords out of Satan's hands. To say, "Search me, Lord, and expose all of my good intentions." To cry out, "You've forgiven me of my sins; how can I not forgive those who have offended me?"

We can embrace the vertical beam of the cross and remove the sword of good intentions by saying this simple prayer:

Father God and Jesus, I am so sorry I broke Your heart with my good intentions. I thought I was getting closer to You with all of my knowledge and works, but in reality I was getting farther away. And worst of all, without knowing it, my path of self-righteousness was saying You died for nothing. My false me being in control also hurt You. All the times I said "That's just the way I am," thinking it was a good thing, even though it went against Your Word. Again, without knowing it, I said You died for nothing. You didn't die for nothing—You died for me! And I accept all that You did on the cross for me and trade in all my good intentions for the only goodness that is real—the righteousness I have by putting my faith in You Jesus.

Are we now ready to embrace the horizontal beam of the cross and take the sword of offense out of his hand? We can, by saying this prayer,

Lord, I forgive the person (people) who offended me just as I have been forgiven by You when I have sinned and hurt people. I release them; their slate is clean. They don't owe me anything, because You alone are my source for everything. I remit the effect of their sin on me. I give all the pain, sorrow, anger, and hate to You on the cross so I don't have to carry any of the junk. I take the ax to any bitterness that is trying to take root in me; by the blood of Jesus, I cut it off and remove it. I repent for any judgments I had against that person and ask You to forgive me. And finally, I pray that You will help that person to see the error of their ways and how they are hurting people. I also pray that You either have them return to me or have me go to them to share the truth in love so that our relationship can be restored.

When we pray this prayer, we are putting a big smile on Father God's face. Remember, we are made in His image and likeness. Think about what it would be like if you were a parent and your children were offended and decided never to see each other again. Wouldn't that break your heart? But wouldn't you be overjoyed if instead they prayed this prayer and were reconciled? It's the same for our heavenly Father.

Did you pray these prayers? Were you sincere? If so, gaze at the closing painting for a while. Picture yourself as part of that scene, with the Lion of the Tribe of Judah victorious. Your smile will grow just as big as your heavenly Father's!

My Personal One-on-One Encounter With The Lord

Also for Home Group Discussion

How are the devil's two swords, "good intentions" and "offenses," connected to two of his names, Lucifer and Satan?

_____
_____
_____
_____
_____

Why has Satan so intensely swung these swords since the Garden of Eden? What does he have to gain or lose?

_____
_____
_____
_____
_____

Do I understand the physics principle that nature abhors a vacuum? What does that mean when applied to spiritual things?

_____
_____
_____
_____
_____

What's most important to me: is it learning more about God and doing more things for God—*or*—is it Christ crucified and real relationships in Christian community? What's my identity: is it knowledge and works, which produce achievements—*or*—is it dying to self and being transformed into a new creation in Christ, a wonderful prince or princess becoming a king or queen?

_____
_____
_____
_____

How, through my thinking and actions, have I unknowingly said to Jesus and the Father, "You died for nothing"? What are some of the examples of this in my life?

_____
_____
_____

What is the Lord showing me about how to make the lost secret of the cross and community part of my life, to be transformed into a Birthright Butterfly? Am I ready?

_____
_____
_____

Suggestion: Do you want to have power and dominion over Satan instead of vice versa? If you haven't read the scriptures at the end of the chapter three One-on-One Encounter, I would really encourage you to do so. Everyone who has, reports that it's been a life-changing experience.

Reflecting on the Art

- In what way does the painting that opens this chapter speak to me?
- Did the sketch have an impact on me? If so, how?
- Can I now picture myself in this chapter's final painting titled *Triumph of the Lion of the Tribe of Judah?*

_____
_____
_____

A New Covenant
A New Heart—A New World

CHAPTER 14

A New Covenant
A New Heart—A New World

How would you like to get the heart of the Lion of the Tribe of Judah, who is standing victorious over Satan? We can! In fact, it's our God-given birthright to have dominion over the devil. God wants to give us that new heart, and the way He's going to do this is through a New Covenant. Through His Old Testament prophets Jeremiah and Ezekiel, the Lord spoke about a new and better covenant that He was going to bring to us. It's an incredible covenant because it was cut with the blood of His one and only Son.

As we've already talked about in this book, we often look at ourselves and the church and have to ask, "Where's the love? Where's the power?" If we're asking those two questions, then we're obviously not fully receiving everything that He has provided for us in the New Covenant, are we? I believe the Lord wants us to know how we can fully enter into this wonderful New Covenant—the new world of love, blessings, and fulfilled destiny that the lost secret opens up to us. The first part of the lost secret is that we *make Jesus Christ and Him crucified preeminent* in our lives. The logic of this is that if God the Father established the covenant through the crucifixion and resurrection of His Son, then any diminishing of that from its place of preeminence will weaken what we're going to receive out of that covenant. Sometimes we make things too complicated, but it really is that simple. As we load other things on top, and put them ahead of what—and Who—created the covenant in the first place, then we're diminishing the covenant. That's the first and simplest truth as to why we're not experiencing the fullness of the New Covenant. The number one secret to God's power has been lost.

To get a better understanding of the covenant and its promised blessings, we're going to address three questions. The first is, *What is a covenant?* We take for granted that we understand what a covenant is, but when we really study the meaning, there's more to it than most of us probably realize. The second question is, *Why is the New Covenant different and better than the Old Covenant?* And third, *How do we literally get this New Covenant inside of us—into our hearts?*

Let's dig right in. What is a covenant? The biggest mistake most of us make is to think of a covenant as merely an oath. We say, "I'm going to enter into a covenant with you. I'm going to give you my word, and we're going to make a pledge to do something." That's a very, very weak definition of what a covenant is; it's not God's idea of covenant. The first thing we need to understand is, God's idea is that a covenant governs relationships. It's all about relationships.

Genesis 15 sets up a covenant between Abraham and God. When we look at the actual word usage in that chapter, making the covenant meant "to cut." God *cut* a covenant with Abraham. Did you ever hear the term "cut a deal"? It came from here—from the word covenant. It means, in Hebrew, "to enter into a compact, a confederacy, an alliance, a league, made by passing between two pieces of flesh." It's a very visual concept.

How important is this covenant we're entering into? We're going to take an animal and cut it in half to symbolize two people. There will be blood shed—you can't give anything higher than life, can you? When that blood is shed, we're saying that those two halves are entering a league. They're going to enter an alliance, and they will walk together as one. That's way beyond a typical oath. Think of NATO, the North Atlantic Treaty Organization. That's a covenant, or an alliance. And what that commitment means is that if someone attacks one member of NATO, it is as if that someone has attacked all of the members. We will fight to the death to defend any country in NATO. That's what the word *covenant* means.

There are a couple of other root words in the Scriptures related to *covenant* that bear noting. In Genesis 1:1, when it says, "God created the heavens and the earth," the word *created* is a derivative of *covenant*. It literally means "to create by cutting." The idea is the same as when we cut down trees; we select and choose certain trees, in order to use the wood to create and form something else. It's a formative process.

The other root word for covenant is similar because it means "to select." But it also means "to feed, give meat, and render clear and manifest."

I never knew this before, but if we take all of those Hebrew words for covenant, and put them together, God is sending this message to us: *I want to make it clear to you that I have chosen you to enter into an alliance with Me, so I can feed you and bless you. I cut this covenant with you by the body and blood of My one and only Son, so that you and I, and your brothers and sisters in Christ, can be one. Will you let Me cut you in half, to divide the false you from the real you so that this false fleshly you can be put to death on the cross of My Son and you can be raised a new creation? Then you can enter into this New Covenant with Me, and I will fill you with all of My love and power so you can receive your promised blessings and be used by Me to bless others.*

> I WANT TO MAKE IT CLEAR TO YOU THAT I HAVE CHOSEN YOU TO ENTER INTO AN ALLIANCE WITH ME, SO I CAN FEED YOU AND BLESS YOU.

That is what those words associated with *covenant* mean. It gives the concept a whole different feeling, doesn't it? It's a very, very powerful message the Father is giving us—way beyond just giving us an oath or making a pledge. Now that we've learned what a covenant really is, there's a very simple truth we have to acknowledge if we're going to be joined together with a holy God. He cannot join together with a fleshly me, no matter how much He wants us to be joined. It is impossible. No matter how much we try to learn the difference between right and wrong, and no matter how hard we strive to do what is right, that will never put our flesh to death, and God can never join in union with our flesh. Therefore, apart from the cross, no one can fully enter into the New Covenant.

We make things very complicated, but it's really very simple. Holy God, sinful flesh. He says, "I cut a covenant with My Son so your flesh can be put to death. You can be raised a new creation, holy in the image and likeness of My Son, so that you and I can be one." That's the deal.

We've learned, though, that we have strayed. We start out at the cross when we're born again. We start out making a wholehearted commitment and dealing with our known sins, but then we get off on a tangent of trying to learn more and do more, and our flesh says, "Thank you very much, but I'm still alive and well." We wind up wondering, *Where's the love, and where's the power?* It's where it's always been, in the cross. Knowledge and works will never put our flesh to death.

That takes us right on into the answer to question number two: *How is the New Covenant different and better than the Old Covenant?* The Old Covenant was about man's works—my knowledge of right and wrong and what I do right. Guess what the New Covenant is about? What Jesus did on the cross! It's not about *my* works. Do you see the fork in the road? It comes up immediately; the Old Covenant goes one way, and the new takes off in a different direction.

What was the Old Covenant about? It was external, visual, and temporary. It had a temple; it had sacrifices; it had feasts. It had very visible, tangible elements; but the Bible clearly states in the New Testament that it is now obsolete. Hebrews 8:13 in the Amplified Bible says, "When God speaks of a new [covenant or agreement], He makes the first one obsolete (out of use). And what is obsolete (out of use and annulled because of age) is ripe for disappearance and to be dispensed with altogether." It was there as a placeholder—temporary.

What is the New Covenant? It's internal—we are the temple; it happens inside of us. It's invisible, and it is eternal. The New Covenant is a totally different thing, isn't it? It's a night-and-day difference. We're starting to understand how much better the new is than the old, but this is the jackpot of it all: relationships. Remember, a covenant is something that governs relationships.

Under the Old Covenant, if a person sinned it affected his relationship with his brothers and sisters, and with God, right? Very clearly, in Leviticus 20, the Bible lists certain sins that, if committed, would cause the person to be cut off from the assembly or even put to death. In this way, under the Old Covenant, my sin would dictate my relationships with others and with God. Guess what the New Covenant says? *Nothing we can ever do will sever our relationship with God or with each other because of the cross.* What do you think is a better way to govern relationships between people, and between people and God? Since I need lots of mercy, I'd pick the New Covenant every time. We all would, wouldn't we?

Why do you think Satan tries so hard to get us back to the Old Covenant? Because under the Old Covenant, relationships can end, can't they? And everybody has seen this happen—either to themselves or someone else: I'm learning a lot of things about God; I'm doing a lot of things for God, and all of a sudden something bad happens in my life. *Hey, what's up? There must be a problem with You, God, so I'm going to end my relationship with You.* Right? It happens all of the time.

> SINCE I NEED LOTS OF MERCY, I'D PICK THE NEW COVENANT EVERY TIME.

Or maybe I'm in a relationship with you. I'm doing a lot of things for you, bending over backwards for you, and all of a sudden you do something inappropriate and nasty to me. Whoo! I'm going to end my relationship with you! It happens every day in the church. Why? Because we're not fully in the New Covenant.

That sort of severance in relationships is not a New Covenant activity. It's Old Covenant thinking. We paint it, spruce it up, and make it look holy. We actually think we have the right to sever from each other or terminate our relationships with God, but we don't. Not under the New Covenant.

The New Covenant says that nothing can separate us from the love of Christ—not nakedness, famine, peril, principality, or anything else (Romans 8:35-39). And *nothing* can sever our relationship with God the Father and the Holy Spirit, or with our brothers and sisters in Christ. That's why Satan wants so desperately to get us back into the Old Covenant of religion and super-spirituality, because under that covenant we can end relationships. Also, he knows what we've already discovered in this journey: There is power in relationships. When we fuse with God and with one another, we get power. Who is adversely affected by that power? The devil. This stuff is not rocket science; it's all very simple. God is now removing the scales off of our eyes so we can understand.

Now let's answer the third question: *How do we get this New Covenant into us—into our hearts?* When you read the scriptures from Jeremiah and Ezekiel about the coming New Covenant (they are listed in the one-on-one encounter at the end of the chapter), five distinct aspects of this covenant emerge. It's these five things the Lord wants to put into us to give us a new heart.

Do you know what the word *new* means? "A fresh new heart, cheerful and full of glad news." Sounds like the good news of the gospel to me! So let's imagine ourselves in the cocoon, and God taking a lump of coal, which represents our Old Covenant heart, and with great pressure and heat turning it into a raw diamond. He then cuts five beautiful facets into that diamond, and when He's done, He's going to step back and say, "I've created an absolute masterpiece."

When you read these Scriptures from Jeremiah and Ezekiel, there's a common thread through all of them: idolatry and harlotry. The number one sin—or flaw—we see is that man creates gods and wants to take over for God. That's the bad news. That's what has to be cut out. The good news is that through the cross of Christ, He can remove those idols and transform our divided heart into one heart. Jeremiah 32:39 says He's going to give us "one heart and one way." There will be no more affections divided between God and idols. Remember what we learned about having a divided heart—that we make Jesus our Lord, but we have hidden idols that vie with Him for control? We believe the Holy Spirit is our Counselor, but the demons that are attached to the hidden idols are always whispering in our ears. We believe God is our Father, but then Satan gets us into a joint custody battle, because he wants to be our father. We are divided—we have a divided heart—but the first beautiful facet is *one heart*.

Now comes the second facet. We learned in Psalm 115:4-8 that those who have idols become like them. What are idols made of? Stone. And stone is dull and stupid; it can't see, hear, or think. To make this point more clear, let's look at the story of the loaves and fishes in Matthew 15:29-16:12. Jesus has just performed the miracle of the loaves and fishes and fed the five thousand people. He gets on the boat with His apostles, and He says to the apostles, "Beware the yeast of the Pharisees." The apostles, who seem very dumb at this point, look at one another and ask, "Gee, did we forget the bread?"

And Jesus answers (paraphrased), "How dull are you? Don't you remember? Didn't you see with your eyes and hear with your ears when I multiplied the loaves and fishes?" They didn't because they had hard hearts. It was before the cross. Jesus had spoken earlier about this concept in Matthew 13:13-15. He said, "Isaiah prophesied, 'You see with your eyes but you don't see. You hear with your ears but you don't hear. You perceive with your heart, but you don't understand, lest you would turn and I would heal you.'"

Idolatry causes even whole-hearted disciples of Christ to have hard, dull hearts. Even the simplest things—perhaps especially those simplest things—we don't get. But He promises to give us a heart of flesh, soft and compassionate, and quick to understand (Ezekiel 11:18-21). I like that. It's a great exchange. I'm getting rid of my hard, dumb, stupid heart, and He's replacing it with a soft, moist *heart that can receive and be filled*. If we picture this master jeweler, He's cut the second facet.

The third facet is that He wants to put the reverential fear of God in our hearts so we will worship Him alone (Jeremiah 32:38-40). And this is worth saying again: God is jealous. He's telling us, "Don't put the things of man ahead of Me, the world system of knowledge and works or the idols from your father's house, people, or country. Don't even put the things of God ahead of Me. I'm going to put such a reverential fear in you that you will never even put My Word ahead of Me. You won't put worship ahead of Me; You won't put ministry ahead of Me. You will have reverential fear of Me." It's a worshipful, reverential fear because we know He's recreating and changing our hearts. We're at a place where we say, "I wouldn't think of putting anything above You. You are worth it."

That's a pretty powerful place to be, isn't it? It's a place of ongoing worship. Our hearts are always worshipping God, all of the time, and as we go through life, there's nothing we'll put ahead of God. Nothing is enticing enough for us to put it ahead of God—we worship Him and Him alone. It's the same place that Abraham was on Mt. Moriah, which, as we know, is Calvary—the place of clear vision. He didn't put his one and only son ahead of God, and that's why God said, "Now I know that you fear Me." Abraham had *reverential fear*. That's the third facet.

The fourth facet is that the Lord said He's going to put *His law and His Word into our hearts* (See Jeremiah 31:33). In the Old Covenant, the finger of God chiseled His law into stone; in the New Covenant, the finger of God chisels it onto our hearts. Like a master jeweler, He takes that diamond and He carves *love* into it. Romans 13:8-10 says that all the law and the prophets are summarized by one thing: love. Jesus reminds us to "love the Lord your God with all your heart, with all your soul, and with all your mind," then adds, "You shall love your neighbor as yourself," and states that "On these two commandments hang all the Law and the Prophets" (Matthew 22:37-40). In addition, He gives us a new commandment, "As I have loved you…you also love one another" (John 13:34). He removes the external commands of the law to love, and then He writes the law of love into our hearts.

> LIKE A MASTER JEWELER, HE TAKES THAT DIAMOND AND HE CARVES LOVE INTO IT.

What does the cut of a diamond determine? How light is let in and how it goes out. As the Lord is carving these facets into your heart, picture it opening up to receive more of His light. It begins to shimmer and blaze like fire, and with every beat, every vibration, your heart is saying, "I love you, Lord, with all of my heart, all my soul, all of my strength. And, I love my brothers the way You love them. I'll never judge them; I'll never shun them; I will lay down my life for them as You laid down Your life for Me." As that spiritual heart beats inside of us, resonating with that message all of the time, it lets in more and more light. And we glow—we become radiant—and let more of His love out.

The fifth facet we also find in Jeremiah 31, this time in verse 34: we're going to *know God*. The word *know* here means "to know by experience." It's a marital word, as when we know one another intimately in marriage and become joined as one flesh.

What would happen if we knew—by experience—the Lord? Where would our level of faith go? We would *know* that God is light—that God is love—that God is one—and that God is Spirit and power (1 John 1:5; 1 John 4:16; Deuteronomy 6:4; John 4:24).

If something comes up—a need, a temptation—you know what? God isn't a theory anymore or a concept, but we possess Him inside of us and know Him by experience. We *know* He is light, which means that the words He speaks are true. We *know* that He is love and that He loves us. We *know* that He is one—the Father, Son and Holy Spirit are one—and we are one

with Him. And that out of oneness, His power is released and nothing is impossible for Him. He has the power to back up His word to me and His love for me. Our faith becomes internalized and organic because we know God and God lives inside of us.

    Now I know that everybody is scared—we're always scared about going to the cross—and it is a scary thing to say, "Cut me in half." But imagine if we allowed God to do that, and allowed the master jeweler to fashion that beautiful, five-faceted diamond gem inside of us; would our lives ever be the same? It's a whole new world, isn't it? That's why it's called the *New Covenant*. It's not the old world of the Old Covenant. It's not about this world at all; it's about a new world that the cross opens up to us.

    I encourage everyone to go deeper into this in the one-on-one encounter by reading the Jeremiah and Ezekiel scriptures, but right now let's just summarize them. There was an *abomination*. That's the word that is used. That abomination was playing the harlot with idols, by both the leaders and the flock alike. This abomination provoked God to anger, and when we do it today, it separates us from Him just like in the Old Testament. It brings us into captivity, curses, destruction and death. That's what happened to the Israelites, and it's happening to the church today.

When we choose to make Jesus Christ and Him crucified preeminent, we fully enter the New Covenant—cut with the body and blood of Jesus Himself. It brings God joy; He's not angry. He totally unites us with Himself and brings us blessings and life. That's our choice—it's life or death.

I believe God is wooing us back to Him, and I believe that at this point in the book He is saying, *Why don't you ask Me to enter into the fullness of this New Covenant relationship? All you have to do is ask. I stand ready to answer.*

Remember what was said earlier in the chapter, the message God gave about the New Covenant? Go back and read it. And then let's tell the Lord, "I want that!" He's interested in us; He's gone to a lot of trouble for us. He's ready to give us everything in the New Covenant—everything Jesus won for us on that cross. We've been seeking; we've been asking; we've been knocking—but on all of the wrong doors. And the Lord is saying, *Now that you understand what a covenant is, and how much different and better the New Covenant is—now that you see how I want to fashion your heart in these five ways, like a perfect diamond—ask Me. I will give it to you.*

If that is your heart's desire, you can use the following prayer as a guide to enter into this New Covenant with the Lord.

> Father,
>
> I want You to cleanse me of the filth of my harlotry. I want You to purge me of all of my idolatry—my good intentions. I want You to cleanse me of that. I want You to give me one heart. I don't want a divided heart anymore. I want my heart to be totally and completely consumed with You. I want You to take out my heart of stone, my dull, hard, and stubborn heart, and replace it with a soft heart that's compassionate and quick to understand. I want You to put the reverential fear of God inside me, which is the beginning of wisdom, and I want You to write Your Word—Your law—on my heart. That law is love. Last but not least, I want to know You. I want to get You and possess You. I ask You to give me more of Yourself. Fill me with Your light so that I can shine forever like a diamond in Your hand.
>
> I am Yours, my Beloved. All of me. And now I receive You as mine—completely.
>
>   Amen.

My Personal One-on-One Encounter With The Lord

Also for Home Group Discussion

What is the difference between a covenant and a mere oath?
_____
_____
_____
_____

As I read again of the Father's desire for me to experience all the riches of His covenant, do I long to be in covenant with Him?

I want to make it clear to you that I have chosen you to enter into an alliance with Me, so I can feed you and bless you. I cut this covenant with you by the body and blood of My one and only Son, so that you and I, and your brothers and sisters in Christ, can be one. Will you let Me cut you in half, to search you, so your carnal nature can be put to death on the cross of My Son, and you can be raised a new creation? Then you can enter into this New Covenant with Me, and I will fill you with all of My love and power so you can receive your promised blessings and be used by Me to bless others.

_____
_____
_____
_____

No one can experience this beautiful covenant with the Father without the cross. Am I now motivated more than ever to embrace the cross which is for me and not against me? What things may still be holding me back?
_____
_____
_____
_____

Do I understand the difference between the Old Covenant, which was external, visible, and temporary, and the New Covenant, which is internal, invisible, and eternal? Which one do I choose for my life?

_____
_____
_____

Can I visualize my heart being transformed from a lump of coal into a flawless, fiery diamond because of what Jesus did for me on the cross?

_____
_____
_____

Take the time to read these scriptures from Jeremiah and Ezekiel and see for yourself the five facets of the New Covenant that God, as a Master Jeweler, wants to carve in our hearts: Jeremiah 31:31-34; Jeremiah 32:27-44; Ezekiel 11:18-21; Ezekiel 18:1-32; Ezekiel 36:17-38

_____
_____
_____

Reflecting on the Art

- In what way does the painting that opens this chapter speak to me?
- Did the sketch have an impact on me? If so, how?

_____
_____
_____

Love and Power in a Home Group

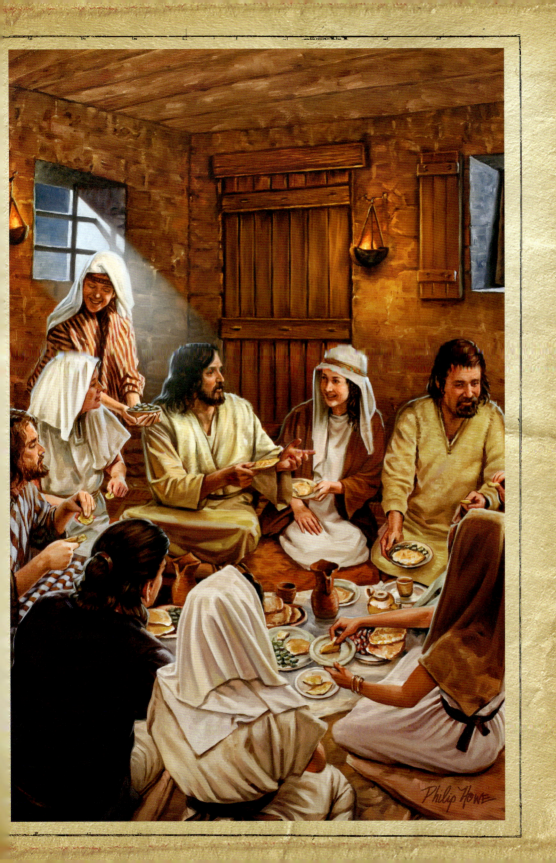

CHAPTER 15

Love and Power in a Home Group

NO ONE CAN GO ON THIS SPIRITUAL JOURNEY ALONE. The experience is meant to be shared. Just as the original release of power came to a hundred and twenty people in the Upper Room, so it will be now. We need to be with others, persons whom God will place in our lives, in order to go through this process of transformation. Based on Scripture, I believe the ideal situation is a home support group.

Let's start by asking the question, "What was truly new in the New Covenant?" The word new in the Greek means *novel* or *fresh,* i.e. *unused.* Would the five majestic trees fit this definition? The Word, prayer, worship, fellowship, gatherings, and ministry all existed in the Old Covenant. They all moved forward into the New Covenant with some changes and additions. What two things, though, never existed in the Old Covenant? The crucifixion and resurrection of Jesus, and God's people meeting in homes. The church puts a lot of emphasis on the majestic trees, which is needed. But the core of Christianity, which was introduced in the book of Acts, is all but forgotten. The cross and community, the secret to unlocking God's power, have been lost!

We've spent a lot of time on the first part of the lost secret, the message of the cross. Let's take a closer look at the second part—believers with a passion for the cross meeting in homes.

There's something different about a home. A home is where people live, eat, and raise children. It's a place to rest, a place of family. A home is different than a building. Previous to the New Covenant, God's people went to the temple and synagogues, but they had never met in homes until the New Covenant. The concept of believers bonding together in small home groups started in the New Covenant church.

If anybody questions the importance of being together in a very tightly knit small group, the simplest way to prove it is this: before anything existed in the whole universe, there was a Trinity. That was the original small group. God the Father, God the Son, and God the Holy Spirit were working together as one. If the Lord ever intended for us to be loners—to be alone and on our own—there never would have been a Trinity. If God Himself chose not to go it alone, how much more should we sit up and take notice and realize that we've got to be in close relationships in order to experience transformation, reconciliation, and receive supernatural power? We all need these close relationships in order to fully experience The Lost Secret Sequence, to restore what's been missing in conventional Christianity.

The Lost Secret Sequence

1. THE CROSS
2. COMMUNITY
3. TRANSFORMATION
4. RECONCILIATION
5. POWER

The second part of the lost secret, *community*, is what really creates momentum in this sequence, propelling us forward on our spiritual journey. Within Christian community we can encourage one another to enter the cocoon to be transformed into Birthright Butterflies. We then enter a world of supernatural love, joy, and peace even in the midst of life's storms. Once we are fused together as one, God fills us with supernatural power. A world of victory over sin, Satan, and curses, to be blessed and fulfill our destiny to bless others awaits.

Since Christian community plays such an important role to entering this world, we're going to look at what works, when we get together as Christians, and what doesn't work. We're not doing this to judge anyone or knock anything. The reason we're doing this is because, again, when we look at ourselves and the church, we have to ask, "Where's the love, and where's the power?" If what we're doing now was working to produce a lot of love and power, we wouldn't have to figure out anything different, right? So we're simply asking, "What do we need to do differently?"

Let's look at the first thing. Does going in and out of a church building on Sunday picture a visual image of brushing shoulders with fellow Christians—does that produce enormous amounts of supernatural love and power in the church? It hasn't. I'm not advising ministers to shut down their churches. In fact, Acts 2:46 states that early believers went to the temple and met in homes. But to me it's obvious that we need more than just meeting in church services.

I know some people may say, "What about home Bible studies or home cell groups?" There's a lot of that in the church, right? But do we see that producing supernatural love and supernatural power? No. Why?

There must be a difference in the way we gather together and how they gathered together in the church of Acts. They had supernatural love. The Bible says that all the believers held everything in common, selling their possessions and distributing the proceeds according to each others' needs (Acts 2:44-45). Is there a lot of that happening in the church today? They also had supernatural power. The Bible also says that when they laid hands on the sick, people recovered. We don't see a lot of that happening, either. It's pretty clear they had something we don't. What was it?

There are three scriptures that tell us—three right in a row, in fact. And that's not an accident; God is trying to show us something. In Acts 1:14, the Bible says, "These all continued *with one accord* in prayer and supplication, with the women and Mary the mother of Jesus, and with His brothers" (emphasis added). That's before Pentecost.

Then, in Acts 2:1, it says "When the Day of Pentecost had fully come, they were all *with one accord* in one place" (emphasis added). Finally, in Acts

2:46, it says, "So continuing daily *with one accord* in the temple, and breaking bread from house to house, they ate their food with gladness and simplicity of heart" (emphasis added). The Bible uses the phrase *with one accord* in each of those verses. Do you know what *one accord* means in the Greek? "Unanimous passion." And what did these people have a unanimous passion for? Jesus Christ and Him crucified and raised from the dead.

> WHAT DID THESE PEOPLE HAVE A UNANIMOUS PASSION FOR? JESUS CHRIST CRUCIFIED AND RAISED FROM THE DEAD.

A good way to illustrate this is if we think back to the 9/11 terrorist attacks. Before 9/11 the U.S. was a very divided country, but when an event far bigger than everybody in this country happened, it brought America together, didn't it? It brought the U.S. into unity. In the weeks and months after 9/11, there was nothing more important than that event. Many attempts had been made before 9/11 to unify the country. They involved people getting together to discuss areas of common ground, and projects and programs to bring about unity. They rarely work, but a 9/11-type event does bring unity. What happens, though, when the memory of the event fades? The unity soon disappears. But the cross was a 9/11 with a second phase. The people who were brought together in unity then died to self and were transformed into new creations. These people then cared more about others than their own selves and were able to stay in unity. That's the difference between man's attempts versus God's success at unity.

That's the way it was with the believers in Acts. When Jesus was crucified, it totally devastated them. Then when He was raised from the dead, all of their petty differences fell aside. Everything else in their life took second place—the most important thing in their lives was Jesus Christ and Him crucified and raised from the dead. They had a *unanimous passion*. Then, as they were transformed into new creations, they were able to sustain and even strengthen that unity. That's the first difference between our home gatherings and the church of Acts. The cross was the center of everything for them, but for us it's not. I'm not criticizing cell groups or Bible studies. They're good, and I'm not saying to stop having them. But is the unanimous passion for the cross of Christ the most important and unifying aspect of these home gatherings? Even home churches need to ask themselves this question.

The second difference between those earlier believers and us is *humility*. They were broken. The apostles left all and actually lived with God in the flesh 24/7 for three years. That's a very high spiritual experience. Then, however, because of the cross, their hidden inner problems were exposed. They got knocked off their spiritual high horse, right? These were people, like Peter, who said they'd never deny Him, but they did deny Him. People who doubted He was really who He said, or that He would really rise again. When they encountered the cross, they were humbled—given a reality check of what was really going on inside of them—transformed.

These people were not only unanimously passionate about Jesus but broken as well. There's not enough of that in the church today. In the church today—and I know because I was one of them—there are many people who think they are super-spiritual. We think we're something that we're not. We're not humble.

So what was the church of Acts like? The cross was preeminent, they gathered together in homes, they were humbled and transformed, they had supernatural love to sell and share possessions, and they were filled with the power of the Holy Spirit. Guess what? They had the Lost Secret Sequence and were living in the world of Birthright Butterflies. I believe God is saying that He wants to start forming groups that have that flavor, that texture, that make-up that the church of Acts had. Then we'll start seeing a lot of love and power—the world that was lost will be found.

Here's a concept for small home groups that I believe the Lord wants us to consider:

> *God is gathering together small groups of Christians in homes. No man will be the head of these groups; Jesus will be their only head. Their primary focus will be Jesus—His cross and resurrection. These*

> WHEN THEY ENCOUNTERED THE CROSS, THEY WERE HUMBLED—GIVEN A REALITY CHECK OF WHAT WAS REALLY GOING ON INSIDE OF THEM—TRANSFORMED.

groups will allow the Holy Spirit to show them the truth about the junk inside of them—the hidden idols that are competing with the Lordship of Jesus and controlling them. These will be safe places, cocoons where believers will be in trusting and transparent relationships. As these small groups of Christians interact within these cocoons, the glorious process of transformation will take place—dying to the false self and all of its good intentions, to be raised as new creations in Christ—the real me set free. They will become one with God, one with themselves, and one with each other, to be filled with power! Then they will emerge as Birthright Butterflies, to live a life of being blessed and fulfilling their destiny to bless others. The power of God Himself will emanate out of these groups, to multiply and expand His Kingdom.

There are several principles we can glean from this concept in order to understand it better. The first is that *God is gathering*. It is *He* who is gathering together small groups of Christians.

If we read Luke 6:12-13, we see that before Jesus picked the original twelve apostles, He went up onto a mountain and prayed all night. *Then* He chose the twelve. Who put that original group of twelve apostles together? It was God the Father through Jesus. They didn't choose who they would be with, God did! That's the principle.

> WE PICK SITUATIONS WE'RE COMFORTABLE WITH, BUT GOD PICKS SITUATIONS THAT WILL CHALLENGE US, TO TRANSFORM US.

As Christians, do we pick our church? Do we pick the people we have fellowship with? Or does God? I'm afraid we do. We shop for churches like we shop for cars. *This church has a great facility. I like this style of worship and preaching. It's so comfortable!* We do the same thing with Bible study groups. We pick the people we are comfortable with, but what God is saying to us is, "Why don't you try letting Me pick the people you're supposed to be with? Maybe you'll have more love and power." We pick situations we're comfortable with, but God picks situations that will challenge us, to transform us. It's a very subtle point but a big one. God is gathering small groups of Christians. Don't rush out after you've read this book and form your group. Instead, pray and ask God to form the group. He might surprise you.

The second principle from the concept is that *Jesus will be the only head of the group*. He was the head of the twelve apostles, and He should be the head of every group. This doesn't mean that there will be no human leader; God always works through leadership. These home groups have to have leaders, but the most important quality of a leader is whether he or she promotes the Lordship of Jesus Christ. Is there a passion for Jesus to be Lord of everyone's life? Paul said in 1 Corinthians 2:2, "For I determined not to know anything among you except Jesus Christ and Him crucified." Paul was not promoting his own leadership; He was promoting the Lordship of Jesus Christ. That's the job of a true leader. That's the criterion! If a person is leading from any other platform, well, he or she shouldn't be leading the group. It's a very simple test.

The third principle is *trust*. There has to be trust in a home group, because the bottom line is, eventually you've got to get to the point where you open up and spill your guts out to each other. If you don't open up and do that, then all of the junk just stays inside. However, trust doesn't happen overnight. It's going to take some time to build it in real relationships. We have to take time going out apart from our home groups, having dinner, doing recreation—whatever we can to develop relationships so we can actually trust each other. Without trust we'll never really open up with each other, and that's one of the most important things about being in a home group. Remember, being transparent is a key to transformation. Trust takes time. Transformation takes time. A ram-it-through project and program mentality doesn't work in this home group world.

Are you starting to see the difference between the world God has for us and the kind of experiences we're used to?

The fourth principle is that once trust has been built, we *choose to become accountable* to one another. We all have blind spots that we can't see without others helping us. Stand in front of a mirror and try to see the back of your head. Can you see it? Is there any way humanly possible for you to see the back of your head? Not without another mirror, or a couple of mirrors. That's what the people in a home group become to each other. We are mirrors, and as the group progresses and trust deepens, we start saying to each other, "I am seeking your input. I need your prayer. I'm choosing to be accountable to you."

That doesn't normally happen in a Bible study. Bible studies are generally about studying the Bible, which is great, but a whole new dynamic is introduced when people submit to one another in love and become accountable. It's not about controlling anyone else; it's a choice made by a free will. We say to one another, "I'm learning the Trinity principle. God didn't do it alone; I can't make it alone. I need you."

The fifth principle is that it all has to be *led by the Spirit* of God. Nothing is happening, nothing that matters, without the Holy Spirit. The way this works is that as we gather together, we open in prayer and totally submit ourselves and our time to Him. *Holy Spirit, take over whatever agenda I had; I'm laying it down. Whatever You want to accomplish, do it.* The leader of the group can't have the desire to be in control; instead he must promote the Lordship of Jesus and allow the Holy Spirit to be in control.

That's my prayer for this book as well. It's in the form of a map for a spiritual journey, and maps are good. The one-on-one encounters at the ends of each chapter are good, and they are designed for home group discussions. But the Holy Spirit has to be free to be in control of the journey. Each group is different, every person is different, and God knows what we all need. A home group—or this book studied in a home group setting—will never work as a formula. We have to get out of the way and let the Holy Spirit lead. I can't tell you how many times, as the leader of our group, the Holy Spirit had me drop my planned agenda for the evening. And every time that happened, our fellowship was rich and wonderful.

> A HOME GROUP WILL NEVER WORK AS A FORMULA. THE HOLY SPIRIT HAS TO BE IN CONTROL OF THE JOURNEY.

When we put these principles into place and let God be God, people together will be transformed into new creations in Christ. We will be reconciled with our true selves, with God, with each other, and we will become one. Then, through that oneness, God is going to release power—the power of the Holy Spirit.

To elaborate a little bit more on becoming one, here's a concept called The Greatest of the Greatest: Three Ways. The scripture that the concept is based on is 1 Corinthians 13, the very famous "love chapter." Paul writes a lot of things about love, then, at the end he says that there are three, faith, hope, and love. "But the greatest of these is love." And in John 15:13, Jesus says, "Greater love has no one than this, that he lay down his life for his friends." What those verses together are saying is this: Love is the greatest thing, and the *greatest love you can ever have is to lay down your life* for somebody—the greatest of the greatest.

What if we applied the "greatest of the greatest" three ways in a small group of Christians? Number one, we'd say, "Lord, I want to lay down my life for You. I'm going to let You split me open. I'm going to let You put the false me to death—I don't want any more idols controlling me. I want intimacy and oneness with You, for real." The first thing is that we love the Lord enough to lay down our lives to become one with Him.

The second thing is, if we have a mate, we say, "I want to lay down my life for you. I want to be one with you in the truest, most intimate sense." That's not just *phileo* love, which is brotherly love, and it's not just *eros*, which is sexual union. I'm talking about *agape* love, which is how God loves us. It's an all-consuming love. This is the love that says, "I'm laying down my life for you to become one with you."

The third way we'd apply this love in a group is to lay down our lives for the people in the group in order to become one with them—in order to have unity.

What would happen in a home group, if through the power of the cross people were actually living this out? It's very, very interesting. Do you know what a nuclear bomb explosion is? It's a chain reaction, a series of events, not just a single event. As that chain reaction begins and then gains momentum, it releases incredible power.

Using that as our analogy, the chain reaction would go like this. I become one with myself first. No more false me versus the real me; I am one. The next part of the chain reaction is that I become one with God… and one with my mate…and then I become one with the fellow members of my group…and that chain reaction produces power even stronger than a hydrogen bomb explosion: *the power of God*! How?

Remember earlier in the book where we asked, "Who is the real me?" We said that at the moment of conception, God takes a piece of Himself, puts it in the fertilized egg in the womb, and that's how people come into existence. Did you ever think that when God takes a piece of Himself out, that He's splitting? He splits off a little piece of Himself and puts it in you and me.

As this chain reaction occurs, do you know what God is doing? (This is cool.) He's putting Himself back together again. What do you think would happen if the God who created the whole universe, who had split off little pieces of Himself in order to create billions and billions of people, started to fuse Himself back together again? How much power would be released? That's power, right? He's taking all of the pieces, male and female, and He's fusing Himself back together. This sequence is visually depicted in the sketch on the previous page.

I believe that means God is reconciling the world back to Himself, and it's no accident. In Colossians 1:19-20, it says, "For it pleased the Father that in Him all the fullness should dwell, and by Him [Jesus] to reconcile all things to Himself, by Him, whether things on earth or things in heaven, having made peace through the blood of His cross." God's purpose in Jesus Christ is to reconcile all things back to Himself—to put Himself back together again. And then we are in Jesus, so "in Him we live and move and have our being" (Acts 17:28).

God fusing Himself back together again to produce power is an amazing concept. The whole idea is that the power of God Himself will emanate out of these home groups. It won't be about projects and programs, but God Himself touching people through people. That's a whole different paradigm than what exists, isn't it? Let's think about just how important it is—this *becoming one*.

Jesus opened up His public ministry with the Sermon on the Mount. He closed His ministry with His teaching at the Last Supper. But do you know the last words that Jesus said before He went to suffer and die? He said,

> *I do not pray for these alone, but also for those who will believe in Me through their word; that they may all be one, as You, Father, are in Me, and I in You; that they may also be one in Us, that the world may*

believe that You sent Me. And the glory which You gave Me I have given them, that they may be one just as We are One...that they may be made perfect in one, and that the world may know that You have sent Me, and have loved them as You have loved Me (John 17:20-23).

Jesus says it again and again, "Make them one the way We are One." Watch out world! Watch out when that happens, because through the lost secret of the cross and community, there is now a way for people to become one with their true selves, with God, and with each other. The simple setting of a home group is the best place for this to happen. The book of Acts shows us that.

This is kind of interesting. Do you think science could be used to prove this concept of power through oneness? There's always a big battle going on between science and the church, right? I'm going to explain further the science behind a nuclear explosion to prove this simple concept of home groups and people gathering together in one accord, bringing about the release of enormous power.

The most powerful force in the entire universe is a thermonuclear explosion. It's the power of the stars and the sun. Do you know where that power comes from? *Fusion.* It comes from little hydrogen atoms coming together as one, and it is the most powerful force in the universe. That's a scientific fact.

There's another nuclear reaction, also very powerful, called *fission.* Fission was used in the original nuclear bomb, and the way it works is that you take the element uranium and split its atoms. By splitting uranium atoms, you cause a great amount of energy to be released.

But *fusion*— fusing things together—is actually much more powerful than fission. When you take hydrogen atoms and fuse them together, you get a much bigger explosion than the original nuclear bomb. They say it's *three to four times more powerful* –that the amount of mass transformed into energy is that much greater in a fusion reaction than by fission.

> JESUS SAYS IT AGAIN AND AGAIN, "MAKE THEM ONE THE WAY WE ARE ONE." WATCH OUT WORLD! WATCH OUT WHEN THAT HAPPENS.

More transformation occurs in fusion than fission, and that's one of our key words: *transformation*. We've learned that transformation leads to reconciliation, which releases power.

This is where the science gets really amazing. Scientific fact: Uranium is the heaviest thing. Uranium's atomic mass is 238; it's the heaviest substance on the face of the earth. Guess what hydrogen's atomic mass is? 1. It's the lightest thing in the universe, even lighter than helium. The least is actually the greatest—has the greatest potential for power.

If we look at the system of knowledge and works, it's heavy, right? *This is what I know; this is what I do.* Jesus said to the Pharisees [paraphrased from Luke 11:46], "You load them down with burdens, but you won't lift one finger." Sounds heavy, doesn't it?

What did Jesus offer? "Take My yoke upon you and learn from Me...for My yoke is easy and *My burden is light*" (Matthew 11:29-30, emphasis added). Do you know what being saved by "grace though faith" is? Total reliance on God—it's light. It's not about me, it's about Jesus.

> GUESS WHAT FUSION IS? IT'S TWO PEOPLE HOLDING HANDS LOOKING AT THE CROSS. IT'S NOT ABOUT ME OR YOU, IT'S ABOUT JESUS. WE'RE IN UNITY.

What does knowledge and works produce? When what I know about God and what I do for God is different than what you know about God and what you do for God, we get into a fight. What do we do? We split—we undergo fission. It causes a lot of energy to be released, because two very heavy people who think they are super-spiritual get into a fight and go separate ways.

Guess what fusion is? It's two people holding hands looking at the cross. It's not about me, or you, but it's about Jesus. We're in unity, because what we have in common is what *He* did, not what either of us knows or does. And that fusion will generate a lot more power than the fission of bickering over who's right or wrong.

Here's a final scientific comparison that illustrates another parallel with God's plan for home groups. There was an article in *National Geographic*, October 2001, and it was called *The Power of Light*. This is a true story. There is a project called the National Ignition Facility, or NIF, and it's being built in California. It's costing 3.2 billion dollars to fund it. There's a group of scientists working on this concept, and they have a very simple theory. They have a little pellet, smaller than a tootsie roll, and it's filled with gas. The pellet is inside a huge ball that weighs one million pounds, and that ball is full of lasers. The theory goes that if they can concentrate enough light from those lasers on that little pellet, they will create a miniature star. An NIF project physicist has proposed that "NIF will produce more power in a one-nanosecond laser pulse than all the power generated in the rest of the world at that moment."[1] What he's saying is that, if they can get enough light on the little tootsie roll canister full of gas to create nuclear fusion through the power of light, then they will create a miniature star. And that will generate more power in a nanosecond than has been created across the entire world at that same moment.

You know what I believe God is saying to us today? I believe He's saying that He wants to generate this power in small home groups. He wants to release His power in thousands and thousands of groups around the world. And how is He going to do it? He's going to put a small group of people in a little tube. You know what a tootsie roll tube looks like? A cocoon. It's a tight place, and He's going to bombard it with light. The light is Jesus—the vertical beam of the cross where we are transformed as we say, *Search me, O Lord,* to become one with ourselves and the Lord. The horizontal beam is where we become one with each other. So underneath all of that light—Jesus who is the Light of the World—we're going to be transformed into new creations in Christ so we can be fused together, and in this process God is going to fuse Himself back together. That will release enormous power!

If you think it can't happen, check out the Upper Room. There were 120 people there, most of whom were not even named. After they were transformed by their experience with Jesus—His death and resurrection—they were in one accord. Then the Holy Spirit came down with power and created a miniature star there in Jerusalem. And you know what? It changed the entire world! What's more, He's going to do it again.

Here's the question: Are we serious? Do we believe it? These people spent 3.2 million bucks at the NIF; that's how much they believe

---

1 Joel Achenbach, "Power of Light," *National Geographic* (October 2001): p. 10.

it. They believe it's possible to create miniature stars. God is saying, "I don't just *believe* it's possible, I *know* it is! I know by experience. I've already done it in the church of Acts."

God gave me a very interesting warfare concept for my own life that connects to this NIF project. He said to my heart, *You're a warrior like Joshua and David, and I've called you to fight.* I thought that was cool—and a little bit daunting. But then He said, *I'm going to give you a secret to getting the power you need for victory in battle. You need to be* simple *and* little. I didn't really understand what that meant.

> THEY BELIEVE IT'S POSSIBLE TO CREATE MINIATURE STARS. GOD IS SAYING, "I DON'T JUST BELIEVE IT'S POSSIBLE, I KNOW IT IS! I'VE ALREADY DONE IT IN THE CHURCH OF ACTS."

It took years, but when I finally studied what it meant to be *simple*, I discovered that the Biblical meaning is "unmixed." No more mix between the wisdom of the world—the knowledge and works system I was in—and the worldly system of hidden idols that was in me. No. He wants me unmixed, and He wants me to be pure.

You know what *little* means? "To become *less* and come to the *end of yourself*"—to be a person who has died to self. So a person who's simple and little is pure and light and easily fused—easily becomes one with God and his or her brothers and sisters in Christ—and out of that oneness will come power for victory in battle. Let's connect that with what the article on the NIF project went on to say:

> Here we come to one facet of the miracle of light. It has no volume. And photons have no charge, so in the process of being concentrated into a very small space [the tootsie roll size capsule], they don't repulse each other as negatively charged electrons do. (NIF will fit 4×10^{24} photons into the target capsule.) "They don't bother one another."[2]

What does the word *little* mean? To come to the end of yourself, to have no volume. What does the word *simple* mean? Unmixed, no more

---

2 Achenbach, p. 10.

negative charge from the worldly systems. A person who becomes simple and little through the cross becomes like light: They can come together in one accord in the cocoon of a home group and not bother each other. Then God's supernatural nuclear fusion can occur. Ephesians 5:8 says, "For you were once darkness, but now you are light in the Lord. Walk as children of light." And 1 Thessalonians 5:5: "You are all sons of light and sons of the day. We are not of the night nor of darkness." The miracle of light happened at Pentecost, through the cross and the Holy Spirit; those 120 people were transformed into children of light who were in one accord. The power of the Holy Spirit came and the rest, as they say, is history. But history is about to repeat itself in an even greater way during these end times.

This is all very heady stuff—miniature stars in homes, wow! But we need a reality check before we embark on God's NIF project. Here are three pieces of wisdom. First, *offenses* will come in your group. Cocoons are safe places, but they are not a perfect little world; they are a messy place too. When these offenses come, you will have a choice: bring them under the four-part Lordship of Jesus as described in chapter 9 or handle them on your own. If you bring them to Jesus, the dealing with offenses will accelerate the transformation process and make your group stronger. If you don't bring them to Jesus, they could rip your group apart. God's NIF project is not a joke; it represents a serious Kingdom advancement that will bring serious opposition from the devil, who happens to be the accuser of the brethren, the master at causing offenses. So know ahead of time, offenses will come to your group! But ultimately that's what makes the cocoon a truly safe place—taking care of all offenses at the cross.

The second thing is *control*. Sincere group members with good intentions will be tempted to control the leader. What's more, sincere leaders with good intentions will be tempted to control the group. Therefore everyone must remember that no man is head of the group. Jesus is, and the Holy Spirit is in control. If this control issue rises up and causes offenses, you again must make a choice to submit it to the four-part Lordship of Jesus to resolve it. If you do, dealing with control will speed up your transformation process of dying to self and the group will become stronger. If you don't, control could rip the group apart.

Finally, with the power will come *persecution*. Jesus said in Matthew 10:24-25 that no student is above his teacher, and if they called Jesus

Beelzebub, how much more you or I. You may not be welcomed with open arms by your family, friends, or the church. Look what happened to the apostles in the book of Acts: They were beaten by the authorities, but they rejoiced and considered it an honor to suffer for Jesus' namesake. When we face these trials in our groups, we must have the same attitude.

    To summarize, remember the painting Satan's Field of Slaughter, with his two swords? He will come at your group with offenses and the good intention of control, but take heart, Jesus has defeated him at the cross. And when you start experiencing persecution, rejoice, because that's a sign that you have and are spreading the real, full-strength gospel.

    Speaking of real, you may be wondering how these home support groups work in real life. After three years, here's what we have to report from our group. One of the biggest things is a sense of family. Many of us have experienced splits within our natural families. As humans, we all have a strong need to be part of a family. God promised in Psalm 68:5-6 to place orphans in families, and He has with us. We may not be a family based on natural blood, but the blood of Jesus has turned us into a family that is just as real. Maybe better.

    How about trials? One night, the Holy Spirit showed us that a strong attack of the enemy was coming and we needed to *circle the wagons*. We did and the attack came—health, marriages, finances, you name it. But because we circled the wagons and didn't try to fight alone, we achieved victory over every attack. We talked about it after, and we were all convinced that the home group concept was a key to making it through.

    Next comes answered prayer. When Jesus Christ crucified is the most important thing in your life, your prayers have power. Why? Because Jesus is the power of God! And when you really know someone and care for them, your prayers go to a higher level. The other factor was group members weren't just asking for prayer; they sought advice also. And it really worked. One couple who had been living together got married. (That may not sound real churchy, but it's the real world and God used the group to make things right). Another had a calling to buy houses, fix them up and then sell them. After many failed attempts, the first house happened! One member lost his job and the Lord placed him in a new and better one. We now have a prayer and praise journal.

We all list things to lift up in prayer, and when the Lord answers, we move it to the praise side and add another one.

Should we be surprised? God's ways really do work.

In closing let's consider this. We are all familiar with the book of Genesis in the Bible. It means the beginning, the creation of something. Did you know there is a *Genesis part two* in the Bible? It's chapter two in the book of Acts. It's the beginning and the creation of the New Covenant church. What does it say? 120 people with a unanimous passion for Jesus and the cross were gathered in an upper room. The Holy Spirit fell and filled them all with power. The sound was so loud that people in the streets heard it and came to see what was going on. Peter shared with them, and 3,000 people accepted Jesus as Lord and Savior that day. And those people who now, too, had a unanimous passion for Jesus then began to break bread and fellowship in their homes. From the Upper Room to living rooms, the cross and community would multiply again and again and again!

> FROM THE UPPER ROOM TO LIVING ROOMS, THE CROSS AND COMMUNITY WOULD MULTIPLY AGAIN AND AGAIN AND AGAIN!

The start—the beginning—the creation—of Christianity involved these two things, the cross and community. They are still the core of our faith today. This is the lost secret that will truly transform us into new creations, so we can enter God's world of supernatural love and power. This world is available to us right now, just as it was to them! *For the promise is to you and to your children, and to all who are afar off* (Acts 2:39). Our cry to God of "Where's the love?" and "Where's the power?" has been answered. The only thing left is our decision. I pray that many worldwide will make it.

My Personal One-on-One Encounter With The Lord

Also for Home Group Discussion

As a believer, do I long for real relationships with my brothers and sisters in Christ, to be part of Christian community? Why do I feel this way?

_____
_____
_____

Do I understand that the crucifixion and resurrection of Jesus, and believers meeting in homes are the two new things in the New Covenant? Are these two things, which make up the lost secret, missing in my life?

_____
_____
_____

Would I trust God enough to pray and ask Him to place me in a home group, or use me to form one? How important is being in one accord (fusion) to receiving God's power?

_____
_____
_____

Have I discovered that a home group is different than a Bible study or church cell group? Do I understand that even a home church, without the preeminence of Jesus Christ and Him crucified, is different than the home group concept shared in this chapter?

_____
_____
_____

Do I realize that home groups are not perfect little worlds, and that cocoons are messy places? Will we choose to take our offenses and the good intentions of control to the cross, to truly make our home groups a safe place?

Questions From The Lost Secret Sequence

1. THE CROSS: Is the most important thing in my Christian walk the crucifixion and resurrection of Christ and Jesus being my first love?

2. COMMUNITY: Do I gather together in homes with believers who have a passion for the cross, in trusting and caring relationships?

3. TRANSFORMATION: Am I transparent with God and my group members, so I can die to self and be transformed into a new creation in Christ?

4. RECONCILIATION: To what degree have I been reconciled to the Father as a son or daughter, and to other group members as brothers and sisters in Christ? How much supernatural love, joy, and peace am I experiencing even in the midst of my trials?

5. POWER: How much supernatural power am I experiencing for victory over sins, Satan, and curses, to be blessed and fulfill my destiny to bless others?

Reflecting on the Art

- In what way does the painting that opens this chapter speak to me?
- Did the sketch have an impact on me? If so, how?

Christianity Reduced to Its Simplest Form

CHAPTER 16

Christianity Reduced to Its Simplest Form

So far our spiritual journey has been about us making the cross the most important thing in our lives and gathering together with believers in homes who share this same passion. That's the micro-view. Now we're going to switch gears and take a macro-view. Let's look at the bigger picture of the church today and how to get the worldwide revival that we all desperately need.

There is a scientific principle—*simplicity*—which says that if you can understand things at their simplest, most basic level, you can do amazing things. Chemists understand this. Once they discovered the basic periodic table of the elements, they've been able to do combinations and accomplish incredible things in chemistry.

Medical professionals understand it. Once they broke the genetic code and began to understand the DNA double helix, a whole new world opened up to medical science.

And physicists understand it. When they unlocked the secret of the atom and understood things at an atomic level, they were able to release and harness nuclear power. Sometimes this knowledge has been used for destruction and sometimes for good, but that's the principle of simplicity.

What if *we* could reduce Christianity to its simplest form? What could the church—the body of believers—do with that? We're going to ask two questions: "Who is God?" and "What's His plan to save mankind?" It doesn't get any simpler than that.

A good place to start is by scripturally exploring who God is. A first scripture to examine is 1 John 1:5, which says that *God is light.* A neat thing here is that it doesn't say God *gives* light; it says He *is* light. So literally, if you could go inside of Him, you would see that He is made up of light. He is a body; He is a being of light. His supernatural molecules are light.

The second scripture we can look at is 1 John 4:16, which says that *God is love*. Again, we've got to take note of this: it doesn't say that God merely *loves*; it says He *is* love. If you went up to Him and stuck your arm inside of Him, it would be like sticking your arm inside a river of liquid love. He *is* love. Your arm would just be in this amazing environment of love. That's who He is, through and through—love.

The next scripture we can check out is Deuteronomy 6:4, where the Bible says that *God is one*. The amazing thing is that there are three divine persons—the Father, the Son, and the Holy Spirit—and somehow these three separate divine persons are one. They are actually distinct *and* one in the same being. That is a supernatural quality. Only God can do that.

The final verse to examine here is John 4:24, where it says *God is Spirit*. When the Bible says *God is Spirit*, it's saying *God is power*. He's not limited to the natural power of this world...He has supernatural power.

> **LET'S LOOK AT THE LOGIC OF THIS SEQUENCE—THERE'S AN INCREDIBLE PICTURE THAT COMES OUT OF IT: LIGHT, LOVE, ONENESS, POWER. "THAT'S WHO GOD IS!"**

Let's look at the logic of this sequence—there's an incredible picture that comes out of it: light, love, oneness, power. First, without light, it's impossible to have love. If there are accusations, lies, or any other darkness between people, there is no way to have love. There's *no way to love each other when we're in darkness*—it's just all confusion. Misinformation rules and reigns, and it destroys any possibility for people to love one another.

The second principle that emerges from this logic is that *without love it's impossible to be one*. Why is that? Because we've got to love each other unconditionally to be one. Everybody is going to make mistakes; everybody is going to blow it. If our oneness depends on perfect performance, no one will ever be in unity, because no one is perfect. We must deeply love in order to stick it out through the hard times. We have to have *agape*—unconditional love—to be one.

The third principle is, *without oneness there is no power.* Whether we like it or not, and whether we agree with it or not, God has chosen a way to release power in the universe. That way is fusion. It's the power of the stars, the power of the sun. When He fuses hydrogen together, it makes a thermonuclear explosion, and that is the greatest power in the entire universe. So the third principle of oneness produces the fourth principle of power. When we put all four together, we get this sequence: He's light—to produce love—that produces oneness—that produces power. That's who God is.

Now let's explore the second big question: *What is God's plan to save mankind?* He instituted that plan two thousand years ago, again with four parts. Number one was *God with us*—Emmanuel. That's Christmas. The book of John is very clear. It says Jesus was *the light of the world.* So, when God came down to be with us, He was the light of the world, and the very first thing that Jesus did was what? Teach. Even when He was a young boy in the temple, He taught. And they couldn't imagine where He got His teachings. Here's an interesting fact: in church history, the earliest major feast or celebration day was actually Epiphany, on January 6, not Christmas. It was the day marking the arrival of the Wise Men. Epiphany means a *flash of light*, and it celebrated the coming of the Light into the world.

What's the next thing in God's plan? *He died for us and was raised from the dead.* That's Easter. And John 3:16 says what? *God so loved the world that He sent His only begotten Son to die for us.* Then, in John 15:13, He said, "Greater love has no one than this, than to lay down one's life for his friends." God's second act was to die for us, because He loved us that much.

The next thing God did was to *make us one*. His group of followers who were arguing, contentious, and debating who was the greatest—all of a sudden the division was gone. The Bible says "they were all with one accord in one place" (Acts 2:1). Why? Through the power of the cross, they were made one. Just as God was one—Father, Son, and Holy Spirit—they became one with Him and with each other.

What was the fourth thing that happened? *God filled them* on Pentecost—as He fills us. The Holy Spirit came down when they were in unity and filled them. What did Jesus distinctly say? He said, "Tarry in the city of Jerusalem until you are endued with power from on high" (Luke 24:49). What were they filled with? *Power.*

God's plan to save mankind involved light, love, oneness, and power. *So who God is and His plan to save mankind are one and the same.* That's a very simple yet profound truth. What is more, once that truth has been opened up for us, I don't believe we'll ever read the Bible the same again. We're going to see that sequence—its truth—repeated over and over again in the Bible.

> SO WHO GOD IS AND HIS PLAN TO SAVE MANKIND ARE ONE AND THE SAME.

We said earlier that if you could take the simplest elements and understand them, then you could do amazing things. What is the amazing thing that all sincere Christians are looking for, praying for, and crying out for? We want revival to come to the earth, right? I believe what the Lord is saying to us today is that, "I have explained Christianity in its simplest form, which is who I am and what My plan is to save mankind. I did it to give you insights on how to get this amazing thing that you have been seeking without very much success, which is revival."

Remember, the theme of the chapter is *simplicity*. What if the Holy Spirit is saying, "I know how interested you are in revival, so why don't you look at how the original one happened two thousand years ago?"

If we think of it from a consumer point of view, everybody wants the original. There's an original formula, an original recipe, and nobody wants the imitation version, right? So the Holy Spirit is saying, "Why don't you guys check out how the original revival happened?"

What if we take the four elements and make it simpler yet? Let's reduce the four into three by looking at *kyros* time (*kyros* being a Greek word for time). It's different than *chronos,* which is a stretch of time. *Kyros* is a specific time, like the day you were born or the day you got married.

Here is how we can simplify those four elements by using *kyros*.

Two thousand years ago there was a three-part, *kyros*-time, sovereign move of God to bring revival to the earth. Number one was God with us—Emmanuel. That's Christmas. Number two was God dying for us and being raised from the dead. That's Easter. Now let's

God with us

God dies for us
to make us one

God fills us

combine Easter with the third thing, which was when everyone was brought together in one accord through the cross. Number three is Pentecost, and they were filled with the Holy Spirit. Do you know what the word *Pentecost* means? That time in the Jewish calendar was the customary feast of the harvest, and what happened immediately after the third sovereign move of God occurred? Three-thousand people were brought into the church. *That's* a big harvest in one day!

If we look at the sketch, we notice a few things. The cross is the centerpiece of the three elements. That's because Jesus is the Capstone, the Chief Cornerstone. He's to be preeminent. Do you think the centerpiece of these three elements would have something to do with revival coming? Or do you think it would be possible to skip over the centerpiece and still get revival?

> I KNOW HOW INTERESTED YOU ARE IN REVIVAL, SO WHY DON'T YOU LOOK AT HOW THE ORIGINAL ONE HAPPENED TWO THOUSAND YEARS AGO?

The answer's pretty obvious. You're never going to be able to skip over the centerpiece. Somehow, though, the most important thing in Christianity that can bring revival is no longer the most important thing in the church. That's a big clue God has given us as to why we're not having revival.

Did you know that several years ago, Bill Bright, founder of Campus Crusade for Christ, mobilized 100,000 people to fast and pray for revival in the United States? He was led by the Holy Spirit, and God told him the U.S. desperately needs revival. It wasn't a regular thing. It was a forty-day fast, and many of the people actually just drank water for those forty days. What if God's answer to that fast was totally unlikely—and stunningly simple? What if the answer was not God sending down revival from heaven, but God sending down instead an explanation of how the original revival happened. What if He said, "Make Jesus Christ and Him crucified preeminent in the church. As a result, have believers with that passion gather together in homes—to be transformed into new creations in Christ and become one. Then I will send the Holy Spirit from heaven with power for revival." That's not what we'd expect, is it? But God is the God of the unexpected, isn't He?

So let's think about that. If we're waiting for a second visitation from heaven to come to bring revival to the earth, we may be waiting a long time. The second step for the Lord to bring revival into the earth is not a visitation from Heaven; it is a decision and a choice based on an event, the crucifixion and resurrection of His Son. It's wild isn't it? But study the original.

In the original revival two thousand years ago, there was a visitation, God with us. There was a second event, God died for us, and people had to decide at the time whether they accepted it or not. The ones that did became one, and then the next visitation came: they were filled with the Holy Spirit and with power. So this is a clarion call to the church: *If you want revival, understand how the first one happened!*

Did you ever hear the saying, *I've got good news and bad news for you?* I believe God is saying that the bad news is this: He's not going to fall from heaven in the next step and magically bring revival onto the earth. That's the bad news. The good news, however, is this: *We no longer have to wait—the lost secret has been found.* We can make the decision right now to make Jesus Christ and Him crucified preeminent again, to get together with small groups of believers who share that passion, to be transformed into new creations in Christ, and become one. Then guess what? We'll be gathered together in one accord and praying, just like Jesus told the original small group of 120 disciples to do. Then the second visitation will come. The Holy Spirit will fall on us with power, and it will be a much greater power than the church knows now, because the cross will once again be preeminent and believers will be in one accord. And with that power will come revival. That's pretty good news, isn't it? We don't have to wait anymore; we can take action now.

Let's look at what God started with 120 people in the Upper Room—the church of Acts. In light of what the early church *didn't* have, how do you think they accomplished what they did and produced such great fruit? They did not have the Bible as we know it; the New Testament wasn't even written yet, and the Old Testament was still on scrolls. People did not have the individual Bibles we have today and most would not for many centuries. They didn't have study Bibles, they didn't have a *Strong's Concordance*—none of that.

What is more, once they got kicked out of the temple and dispersed, they had no big public buildings, no specialized facilities or meeting rooms. They certainly had no sound systems, books, tapes, CDs, DVDs, radio, or television, right? They didn't have choirs or orchestras or worship teams. They had none of that stuff. Yet how well did they spread the gospel and bring about revival, even without all of those things? A lot better than we do.

> **WE ARE SPIRITUALLY SOPHISTICATED, BUT THEY WERE SPIRITUALLY ADVANCED.**

Why? There are two important concepts we need to explore: *advanced* versus *sophisticated*. There's a big difference between being spiritually sophisticated and being spiritually advanced. We are very spiritually sophisticated, but they were spiritually advanced.

During this teaching my wife said, "You know what? We Christians today think we're very powerful because we look at our buildings and our facilities and all of the resources we have. We look at all of that sophistication, and we genuinely think we're very powerful and advanced. But the reality is that when a real problem comes, where is the love? Where's the power?"

When an offense comes, or somebody bumps into somebody else, are we loving, or do we split? When somebody is in need of a healing, do we lay hands on the sick and see them recover? Not too often. We appear to be powerful because we are mixing up spiritual sophistication with being spiritually advanced. However, God says, "I'm not interested in how sophisticated you are. I told you to become like little children." He wants us to *keep it simple!*

This real-life story illustrates it better than anything. There was a missionary in India named Hillary Harrison. There are relatively few Christians in India; they are persecuted, and the women especially are treated poorly.

There was a particular Christian woman whose husband had died, and she had no protection. She was persecuted unmercifully in her village. People threw rocks in her windows and egged her. She was looked down on because of her sex and hated because of her faith, and she had nobody to defend her.

One day the missionary, Hillary, went to the lady and asked, "What scriptures are you hanging onto, to help you deal with this horrible persecution you're going through?"

The woman looked at Hillary very sincerely and answered, "Hillary, I just want you to know that I don't have a scripture because, first of all, I don't have a Bible. Second, if I did have a Bible, it wouldn't matter because I can't read. Who I *do* have is Jesus Christ." That is all she had, and He was more than enough.

> THAT LADY WAS AS ADVANCED AS THEY COME. SHE WAS A SPIRITUAL GIANT. AND DO YOU KNOW WHY? SHE HAD JESUS!

Now I'm not knocking the Bible; I'm a Bible teacher. But the principle is this: we can be very spiritually sophisticated and not be spiritually advanced. That lady was, in my view, as advanced as they come. She was a spiritual giant. And do you know why? She had Jesus!

There's a guy in Scripture who also illustrates this point very well. His name was Saul—Rabbi Saul. Here's his sophistication résumé, found in Philippians 3: "Circumcised the eighth day, of the stock of Israel, of the tribe of Benjamin, a Hebrew of the Hebrews; concerning the law, a Pharisee; concerning zeal, persecuting the church; concerning the righteousness which is in the law, blameless" (vss. 5-6).

What did sophisticated Saul find out?

> But what things were gain to me, these I have counted loss for Christ. Yet indeed I also count all things loss for the excellence of the knowledge of Christ Jesus my Lord, for whom I have suffered the loss of all things, and count them as rubbish, that I may gain Christ and be found in Him, not having my own righteousness, which is from the law, but that which is through faith in Christ, the righteousness which is from God by faith; that I may know Him and the power of His resurrection, and the fellowship of His sufferings, being conformed to His death, if, by any means, I may attain to the resurrection from the dead (vss. 7-11).

He goes on to say in verse 15, "Therefore let us, as many as are mature, have this mind; and if in anything you think otherwise, God will reveal even this to you."

What is Paul saying? It's an oxymoron, isn't it? Whoever is mature in the faith, have this mind: to take all of your sophistication and throw it out the window. In verse 8 he tells us whatever we thought was gain and great to count them as rubbish, which in the Greek literally means dung—to look at all of our so-called sophistication as cow manure. Then, knowing this, to trade it all in—*for the sake of knowing Christ.* And here's a pretty wild fact: the Hebrew word for *idol* actually meant dung ball! So all of our sophistication, our knowledge and works, our good intentions, and our idols, actually had the worth of a dung ball compared to knowing Christ!

Paul happened to write a huge portion of the New Testament. He was a major force for getting a lot of the Gentile world saved at that time. It's safe to say, then, that he's a person we'd want to emulate, right? You know what Paul said? "I resolved to know nothing while I was with you except Jesus Christ and him crucified" (1 Corinthians 2:2 NIV). Saul was spiritually sophisticated, but Paul was spiritually advanced. There's a big difference. Paul also said one more thing we need to take note of. In his world there was a lot of competition going on. People were claiming to be super-apostles, saying this and that, and he responded to them in a very blunt way: "The kingdom of God is *not a matter of talk* but of power" (I Corinthians 4:20 NIV, emphasis added). That wouldn't apply to the church today, would it? Ouch.

This could be another ouchy one. Back to what my wife said about thinking we're powerful because of our buildings. Look at the Old Covenant. God's people in the Old Covenant were very intrigued with buildings. Not just the Pharisees, but even Jesus' own disciples. They said, "Jesus, look at this temple! Look!" You know what His response was? "A time is coming when not one stone is going to be left on another stone" (Matthew 24:1-2, paraphrased).

In the New Covenant, it's not about buildings anymore, is it? *God doesn't inhabit a temple; He inhabits people.* Caterpillar Christians, if we're honest, are very interested in buildings and facilities, and projects and programs to carry out ministry. We're very addicted to that. Right?

> PEOPLE AREN'T INTERESTED IN WHAT I KNOW ABOUT GOD, OR THE PROJECTS AND PROGRAMS I'M DOING FOR GOD. THEY WANT GOD HIMSELF, BECAUSE THEY DESPERATELY NEED HIS LOVE AND POWER.

Butterfly Christians have a different focus. Their focus is *getting God, and giving God* to other people. The focus is people, not buildings. God is far more interested in people than He is in buildings, and He can be far more effective in spreading His kingdom through people than through buildings. Why is that? Because *people need other people.* There is no substitute. Computers will never replace people, robots will never replace people, and machines will never replace people. People who are in trouble need other people to come up beside them, look at them, touch them, and love them. That's the way God's supernatural power transfers between us.

But think of a truly needy person who has a health problem, a financial issue, a marriage problem, etc. That person isn't interested in what I know about God or my pet projects and programs. They desperately need God Himself. If I'm not really carrying a lot of God with me, I can't really help them, can I?

With that thought in mind, let's refer back to our spiritual journey map. At the end of the map there is a treasure chest at the foot of the cross—think of it as the vault that we've been talking about, that the combination in the Lost Secret Sequence opens up. Here's what's in that treasure chest. It's not worldly blessings. It's not what you think it might be. *It's God Himself.* The promised land for God's chosen people is no longer a place. It's a person, and that person is God Himself. The cross is our way to get to this promised land. Jesus is saying, "I actually died for you, not just to tear the veil of the Holy of holies, not just to give you access to God, but to actually give you the opportunity to have God as your personal possession, your personal treasure." *That's* the ultimate power of the cross. But think about it, when we get God we get everything—love relationships and rulership power. It's like borrowing money versus owning the bank. Which is better? Now when we go to minister to a person in need, we have a lot to give them. Like the apostle Peter, who said, "Silver and gold I do not have, but what I do have I give you: In the name of Jesus Christ of Nazareth, rise up and walk" (Acts 3:6). And that, my friends, is a different ministry paradigm than what we're used to—get God then give God.

> THE PROMISED LAND FOR GOD'S CHOSEN PEOPLE IS NO LONGER A PLACE. IT'S A PERSON, AND THAT PERSON IS GOD HIMSELF.

Let's close with a final thought on this restoration-revolution God is bringing about. Picture a puzzle that God is putting together. Let's start with the five majestic trees. He's brought the Word back to a very high level. Intercessory prayer has dramatically increased. Praise and worship are far more enthusiastic. There are many types of gatherings and fellowships now available. And now ministry has been expanded to include the prophetic and other gifts of the Spirit. How about the fivefold ministry that existed in the original church? Ephesians 4:11-12 says, "And He Himself gave some to be apostles, some prophets, some evangelists, and some pastors and teachers, for the equipping of the saints for the work of ministry, for the edifying of the body of Christ." It's not just pastors and evangelists anymore; the offices of teacher, prophetic, and apostolic are now being restored. But the Lord has saved the best for last. The last piece to be

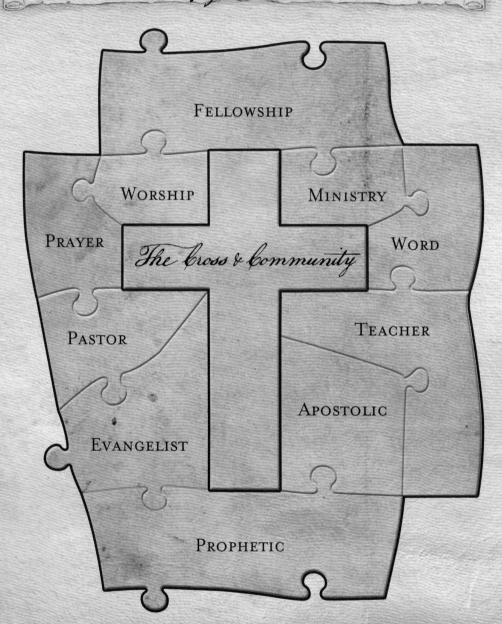

restored is the centerpiece, the cross and community. When that happens, watch out! Incredible power will flow into the five majestic trees and the fivefold ministry. Why? Because Jesus Christ crucified is the power of God, and God's chosen method to release power is through fusion. It's a double dose of power!!

When this happens, the end time revival will actually surpass the first one in the church of Acts. The Scripture says that the latter rain will be greater than the former (Joel 2:23-29). It has to be because the Gospel must be preached to the four corners of the earth, and the church must be without spot or blemish for the return of Christ. That's a greater revival than in the church of Acts, and we get to be part of it—if we choose to make Jesus Christ crucified preeminent and share that passion in a home group, to be transformed, reconciled, and filled with power!

So there we have it, Christianity reduced to its simplest form. *Who God is, and His plan to save mankind, are one in the same.*

ONE. God, who is light, came down to be the light of the world—we celebrate that as Christmas.

TWO. God, who is love and one, died for us on the cross to make us one with Him and each other—we celebrate that as Easter.

THREE. God, who is Spirit, which means power, filled the 120 people who were in one accord with the Holy Spirit and power—we celebrate this as Pentecost.

To close this chapter, let's look at a simple history of man. God created Adam and Eve and gave them a birthright—to have a face to face relationship with Him in love, joy, and peace, and to have rulership over the world and Satan in order to be blessed and be a blessing. At the Fall, that birthright of relationship and rulership was lost, stolen through a deception of the devil. The process of restoring our God-given birthright was begun with Abraham. It was completed by Christ on the cross, who was then raised from the dead. But by the end of the fourth century, Satan had stolen our birthright again. The time has now come for every human being to get their God-given birthright back, once and for all!

Do you want *your* God-given birthright back? If your answer is yes, you can join God's cross and community restoration revolution today.

My Personal One-on-One Encounter With The Lord

ALSO FOR HOME GROUP DISCUSSION

Do I understand the four parts of who God is? Do I understand His four-part plan to save mankind? Do I now see that who God is and His plan to save us are one and the same?

_____
_____
_____

Can I now simplify the four to three? What is the simple message of Christmas? Easter? Pentecost?

_____
_____
_____

Have I been praying for and seeking revival? Do I now realize it will involve a choice based on an event, joining with other believers to make the crucifixion and resurrection of Jesus Christ the most important thing in our lives?

_____
_____
_____

What is the difference between being spiritually sophisticated and being spiritually advanced? Based on this, do I see what the church of Acts had that we don't have today? What are some of the ways that I may be spiritually sophisticated?

_____
_____
_____

Have I come to the end of the map, now knowing that inside the treasure chest is God Himself? Do I realize that when I get God, I get everything? Is my new ministry paradigm this: Get God, Give God?

Am I ready to join God's end-time restoration revolution involving the cross and community? What might my first few steps be to join this restoration revolution?

Reflecting on the Art

- In what way does the painting that opens this chapter speak to me?
- Did the sketches have an impact on me? If so, how?

What Will Happen When God Restores the Cross and Community?

Close

What Will Happen When God Restores the Cross and Community?

In the days of King Josiah, Hilkiah the high priest found the Book of the Law among some rubbish in the temple. A long-lost treasure had now been found! When it was brought before the king, he tore his clothes and assembled all of the priests and the people. He ordered the book to be read, and afterward the king and all of the people repented and renewed their covenant with the Lord. Then they cleansed the temple and the entire land of idols (2 Kings 22 and 23).

So it is with us today—or can be—as we uncover the meaning of the riddle on the map: "Lost and Found to Be Unbound…Up Then Down to Get My Crown." Something very old and very valuable that was lost for 1,600 years, has now been found—the lost secret of the cross and community. When we make Jesus Christ and Him crucified preeminent in our lives and gather in homes with other believers who share this passion, we fully embrace the New Covenant again and are unbound. Then, as Caterpillar Christians, we go down into the cocoon to be cleansed of our idols and transformed into beautiful monarch butterflies—kings and queens who get our crowns.

This transformation takes place as we experience the Lost Secret Sequence. Think of this sequence as a five-pronged key that unlocks a treasure chest that's filled with God Himself and His world of love, power, blessings, and fulfilled destiny.

The Lost Secret Sequence

1. **THE CROSS:** The most important thing in my Christian walk is the crucifixion and resurrection of Christ and Jesus being my first love.

2. **COMMUNITY:** We gather together in homes with believers who have a passion for the cross, in trusting and caring relationships.

3. **TRANSFORMATION:** We are transparent with God and each other, in order to die to self and be transformed into new creations in Christ.

4. **RECONCILIATION:** As new creations, we are reconciled to the Father as sons and daughters, and to each other as brothers and sisters in Christ. We enter His relationship world of supernatural love, joy, and peace, even in the midst of trials.

5. **POWER:** In this world of love, we are fused together as one and God fills us with His supernatural power. We enter His rulership world of victory over sin, Satan, and curses to be blessed and fulfill our destiny to bless others.

What's been missing in conventional Christianity has now been restored—the cross, community, and the transformation they bring about. Now the cry of our hearts for God's love and power has been answered. This sequence isn't a how to formula; it's a Holy Spirit-led process that is personalized and different for every individual and group. The Lost Secret Sequence is for every church, every minister, and every believer—in fact it is for every person on the face of the earth! It's low tech, with no need for facilities or finances, so this world of supernatural love and power is available to everyone. This sequence is one of three major concepts shared in this book. The second big concept is this:

CATERPILLAR CHRISTIANS MUST DIE TO SELF

Christianity is not about doing; it's about dying and being raised a new creation in Christ. If it was about doing, Jesus would have been born into a royal family. He would have been sent to the best schools and then headed up various positions in the kingdom for further training. He would have ruled as a king for a long time and instituted many huge projects and programs. Instead, He was born to a lowly family. He lived a nondescript life and worked as a carpenter until age thirty. His public ministry lasted for just three years. Then His true mission occurred. He died for our sins and was raised from the dead. Caterpillar Christians who are very much into doing must come to realize this truth and begin to focus on dying to self. The third major concept is this:

No One Can Make this Journey Alone

We all need to die to self, but we can't do it alone. In a small home group, we help each other with our blind spots. We support each other through our trials. Together we are transformed into new creations in Christ. The lost secret of the cross and community has been found!

I believe God's decision to restore the cross and community represents a restoration revolution that will reform the church and bring revival to the whole world. Do you want to be part of it? Jesus' hand on the cover of the book is sending a universal message, inviting everyone to make that choice. To the born-again believer, it's saying, "Stop! I love you. Return to Me as your first love." To the minister it's saying, "Stop! I love you. Remember what's the most important thing for you and those I've called you to minister to." To the person who is not born again, it's saying, "Stop! I love you. Come and get to know Me."

> GOD'S DECISION TO RESTORE THE CROSS AND COMMUNITY REPRESENTS A RESTORATION REVOLUTION THAT WILL REFORM THE CHURCH AND BRING REVIVAL TO THE WHOLE WORLD.

If you've never accepted Jesus into your life, you can get to know Him right now by simply saying from your heart, *I need You, Jesus. I believe You personally died for me on the cross and were raised from the dead. My name is written on Your hand. I'm sorry for my sins. Forgive me, and come and enter my heart. I make You both Lord and Savior of my life.*

Now we can all look at this last painting, entitled "First Love," and see ourselves in it. At the foot of the cross, with Jesus as our first love, there is rest. The lie that God is not good and we're not good enough is gone. It's replaced by the truth that God is good and we're wonderful. The lust for the law, to use knowledge and works to take care of our own problems and succeed to gain self-esteem, is gone. It's replaced by faith in Jesus and what He did on the cross. The law of the Spirit of life in Christ Jesus has set us free from the law of sin and death. A river of life now fills us with supernatural love, joy, peace, and power. Now we can all say, "Jesus, You did not die for nothing!"

One final thought. Sixteen hundred years is a long time for the two core keys of Christianity to have been lost. That represents a lot of momentum for entrenched human traditions, so it's going to take lots and lots of God's grace and mercy for this restoration revolution to happen. Fittingly, the book started with a parable of grace and will close with a prayer for grace. If the Lord has put a fire in your gut for the lost secret to be restored, join with me in prayer. Let's pray like Daniel did during Israel's captivity in Babylon (Daniel 9:1-19). His heart-felt cry was heard, and I believe ours will be also.

> *O Lord, we have sinned. We have left You, Jesus, as our first love. The great sacrifice of Your cross is no longer the most important thing in our lives. We don't gather in homes in loving, trusting, and caring relationships. We got caught up with the wisdom of the world and have become enamored with knowledge and works. We harbor many hidden idols that vie for our affections and compete with Your Lordship. We fight with each other and easily end relationships. We know that all of this breaks Your heart. We are sorry. Forgive us.*
>
> *O Lord, we need another kyros-time sovereign move of Your grace in our generation. We know this is the only way that this restoration revolution will happen. Open our eyes to the cross and community. Enable us to be transparent, to be transformed. Then pour Your supernatural love and power into us so we can spread the sweet fragrance of Jesus to a lost and dying world. It's not because of our righteousness that we ask this but because of Your great grace and mercy. O Lord, hear! O Lord, forgive! O Lord, listen and act! Do not delay for Your own sake, my God, for Your church and Your people are called by Your name, and the whole world is waiting for You!*

Let the journey continue...

About the Author:

Rick Suarez was the son of a blue-collar worker who achieved great business success at a very young age. As a wealthy atheist, by God's grace, he experienced a dramatic conversion to Christianity. Because of his wealth and wild lifestyle, he struggled to make a wholehearted commitment to the Lord. Through God's strength, he finally dedicated his life totally to the Lord. Then something unusual happened. Instead of his life getting better and being blessed, things got worse! He went through a long period of very fiery trials and suffered great loss. God used this time to show him the junk that was still inside of him (hidden sins and idols he knew nothing about). The conventional Christianity he knew and lived came to an end, being replaced by a Christian walk with the cross and community as his primary focus. He was transformed by this experience, as were other members of their home group. Rick is the founder of Fresh Start Ministries. His passion now is to share the freedom, intimacy, and blessings that are available to all through the cross and community. He has been married to his wife Lu Ann for 32 years. They have four children, a son-in-law, a daughter-in-law, and a grandson.

How To Obtain Art And Receive More Teachings:

The painting below and some of the art in this book are available as posters, or as prints that are suitable for framing. There are also other life-changing teachings by Rick Suarez that are available. To learn more about the art, teachings, or having Rick speak to your church or organization, use the contact information below.

Contact information:

Web: www.lostsecret.org

Email: info@lostsecret.org

Mailing address: The Lost Secret
P.O. Box 35217
Canton, Ohio 44735

Continue Your Journey On Our Website

www.lostsecret.org

- Share your thoughts on *The Lost Secret* and see what others are saying
- Read the author's blog
- Communicate with the author at rick@lostsecret.org
- Go inside other home groups around the country and the world
- Get a behind the scenes look on how the book was created
- Order additional copies of *The Lost Secret* at bulk purchase discounts

Sharing The Secret

Many people who have been touched and transformed by *The Lost Secret* give it to family and friends. It makes a wonderful gift because it's a beautiful art-filled book that also contains a life-changing message. Others use it for ministry in churches, youth groups, counseling sessions, battered homes, and prisons. Bulk discounts are available for purchases of five books or more. This book has been self-published by a small ministry, so your help in getting this message out would be greatly appreciated. Here are a few ideas: You could talk about the book on your e-mail lists or other places that you interact with people on the Internet. We suggest not making it an advertisement, but just to simply share how the book has touched and transformed you. If you have a website or a blog, consider sharing how the book impacted you. Don't give away the lost secret, but recommend that they read it and then give them the link www.lostsecret.org. If you own a business, consider putting the book on your counter for resale. We offer wholesale prices for retail sales.

Acknowledgments:

Please don't give me credit for this book; it truly was the Lord's doing. I didn't even know these concepts and principles existed until the Lord shared them with me. The Holy Spirit worked through an entire creative team to produce this book and even gave "downloads" for art ideas through family members of the team. In doing so, the Lord modeled a powerful principle for us: it really is Him making things happen through a body of believers. So know that it was the Lord touching you as you were reading this book, not me.

I thank my wife, Lu Ann, for standing by my side during my twenty-one year experience of nonconventional Christianity, which I neither understood nor handled very well at times. I thank my children for doing the same: Ricky, Kristin, Elisha, and Mary. I thank our home group: Wayne, Kay, Shawn, Lisa, Steve, Janet, and Aaron, who for three years listened, interacted, and prayed as the book was being taught. A very special thanks to my dear brother in the Lord, Julius Toth, God's businessman who sponsored the first printing of this book.

I also want to thank the entire creative team for their passion for this project: Jason Rovenstine, the creative director who connected me to many members of the team; Gwen Faulkenberry, who worked with me on the rewrites and became a true sister in the Lord in the process; Philip Howe, an established artist who did many of the oil paintings; Lisa Wood, an up-and-coming artist who also did oil paintings; Richard Carbajal, an established illustrator who did all of the sketches; Janice Manuel, who did the final edit.

And a special thanks to you, for getting to know my best friend better...Jesus.

Creative Team Contact Information:

Here is the contact information for the members of the creative team that I mentioned in the Acknowledgments on the previous page:

Jason Rovenstine — *email:* info@roverhaus.com

Gwen Faulkenberry — *email:* gfaulkenberry@hotmail.com

Philip Howe — *web:* www.philiphowe.com
email: philip.howe@verizon.net

Lisa Wood — *web:* www.lisajacksonwood.com

Richard Carbajal — from Deborah Wolfe LTD, *web:* www.illustrationonline.com

Janice Manuel — *email:* manuel1941@aol.com

Dedication:

TO JESUS CHRIST AND HIM CRUCIFIED,
WHO ALLOWED US TO TORTURE AND MURDER HIM,
IN ORDER TO SAVE US.

PRAYER:

For I resolved to know nothing (to be acquainted with nothing, to make a display of the knowledge of nothing, and to be conscious of nothing) among you except Jesus Christ (the Messiah) and Him crucified. And my language and my message were not set forth in persuasive (enticing and plausible) words of wisdom, but they were in demonstration of the [Holy] Spirit and power [a proof by the Spirit and power of God, operating on me and stirring in the minds of my hearers the most holy emotions and thus persuading them], so that your faith might not rest in the wisdom of men (human philosophy), but in the power of God

1 Corinthians 2:2, 4–5
Amplified Bible

Notes:

Notes: